W9-BSD-774

To Mike Case
with very best regards
Marvin L. Brown, Jr.

LOUIS VEUILLOT

French Ultramontane Catholic

Journalist and Layman,

1813-1883

MARVIN L. BROWN, JR.

MOORE PUBLISHING COMPANY
Durham, North Carolina 27705

Library of Congress Catalog Card Number: 77-82882
ISBN: 0-87716-070-8

In memory of

JOHN WILLIAM BUSH, S.J.
Ph.D., Professor of History
1917-1976

to
James Michael Case
1-31-78
from
his
Mom and Dad

(Bibliothèque Nationale)

Louis Veuillot

CONTENTS

PREFACE

Louis Veuillot was a leading militant in post-Revolutionary Catholic Christendom. He was a unique figure in the literary and religious world, impossible exactly to categorize. It is even difficult to choose just the right adjectives for him. "Papist" has too early and too English a connotation, while "papalist" is too recent and not sufficiently militant. "Clerical", in the sense of describing people with his general political interests, a word not much more than a century old with this meaning, still has something of the formal ecclesiastical implication about it, even when used this way. "Ultramontane" is an old word, but certainly that is what he was. Veuillot may be thought of as a prime example of nineteenth-century ultramontane "clericalism," in Gambetta's, or Bismarck's sense.

Most treatments of him tend to reflect the generally unsympathetic attitudes of contemporary historians toward the movement he symbolized, though some quite the reverse. Veuillot was the symbol of the rise of lay influence in the Catholic church, the rise of the lay Catholic press, together with the press in general, and the spirit of nineteenth-century nationalism, tempered by Catholicism. As such his career in literature and journalism had significance.

I am entirely of American protestant background, detached from many of the currents that have prejudiced the views of Frenchmen and various communicants in the Roman Catholic church with regard to differing attitudes toward Veuillot. I also do not share any doctrinaire protestant preconceptions. Any attitudes I may seem to have about him have been developed as a result of studying his career and the times in which he lived.

Many people have aided me in my efforts to study Louis Veuillot. Professor Lynn M. Case has influenced all my ideas about European history. Professor Ernest Labrousse first guided me to the Archives of the Préfecture of Police in Paris. Madame Jeanne Harburger, the administrator of these archives, was most helpful. I got various ideas guiding my study from Professor Guillaume de Bertier de Sauvigny of the Institut Catholique de Paris, Monsignor Joseph N. Moody, formerly of The Catholic University of America, the late Father John W. Bush, S.J., and the staffs of various archives and libraries, including Father Irénée Noye of the Bibliothèque de la Compagnie de Saint Sulpice in Paris. I thank Madame Anne Grüner (née Schlumberger) for permission to consult the Fonds Guizot in the Archives nationales. I am indebted to the American Philosophical Society for aid in doing my research. My wife, Elizabeth W. Brown, rendered great aid to me in the preparation of the manuscript.

Marvin L. Brown, Jr.

Raleigh, North Carolina
1 February 1977

INTRODUCTION

Louis Veuillot was a striking personality, even for the nineteenth century, when vivid characters were no rarity. In the controversies with which he filled his life he dealt daringly with many of the great questions of modern times. In fact, he was engaged in head-on conflict with some of the most characteristic forces of the modern age. In a manner of speaking he was trying to overcome the effects of the Enlightenment and the French Revolution – by the use of paper and ink. Into the fray he brought an inborn talent. He was a master of the French language who, although mostly self-taught, could muster words and information in such a formidable array as to intimidate leading intellectual spokesmen, while at the same time rousing troublesome enthusiasm in such unexpected quarters as among poor peasants, conservative priests, or overlooked gentlefolk. He did not try to resolve problems or deal with other schools of thought. Compromise was abhorrent to him. He had a simple view of authority, of right and wrong, and he addressed himself to the mission of striking down post-Revolutionary ideologies and forces, even within the Catholic church, in what he believed to be the cause of God, Catholic Christendom, and the supreme authority of its authorized leader, the pope. Toward these ends he worked as a journalist, man of letters, and, when necessary, raiser of funds. "Obey! This is the word which dominated and recapitulated the entire life of Louis Veuillot."[1] The funeral oration of the Abbé Paul Bruchesi for Louis Veuillot included some most descriptive phrases. According to this oration, Veuillot "liked to call himself sergeant of Jesus Christ."[2] If the forces of Christianity may be likened to an army, which it is appropriate to do when the militant Veuillot is being considered, sergeant is exactly the position he filled. He was no recruiting sergeant, however, but a campaigner who tried to close up the distracted Catholic ranks in marching order. He tried to keep the fidelity of the rank and file directed to the rightful commander-in-chief, the pope, especially when subordinate commanders seemed to be straying in other directions. He tirelessly barked a sharp and regular cadence of march.

Any historian dealing with topics in nineteenth-century France is apt to have to mention Louis Veuillot, since Veuillot managed to involve himself in most national issues for four decades. However, in general treatments of nineteenth-century France, Veuillot is most often dismissed in a stereotyped way, and generally with unexamined hostility. This hostility was given impetus by the master and pioneer historian of the Third Republic, Gabriel Hanotaux, who, while allowing that Veuillot was an "exquisite writer," branded him a "violent Christian", who "distributed holy water as though it were vitriol and handled the crucifix like a club."[3] Ultramontanism, or the enhancement of papal authority, which had been a liberal movement in the first half of the century, came to be almost personified by Louis Veuillot, and all of its enemies subsequently, whether liberal Catholics of the post-1850 period, protestants, or secularists, have managed to follow the sort of interpretation that Hanotaux helped establish. Louis's brother, Eugène Veuillot, and Eugène's son, François Veuillot, brought forth a remarkable and overwhelming four-volume biography that of course puts him in the most flattering possible light, but aside from this family production a large part of the French and English historical literature which in any way deals with Veuillot gives only adverse, if incidental, judgments of the man who was spokesman for so many great causes, "Catholic before all," and a founder of nineteenth-century clericalism. The not unsympathetic contemporary historian, Jacques Chastenet, does little to revise the stereotype of Veuillot, "Veuillot the ultramontane journalist with the illuminated soul, the tormented spirit, the corrosive ink, Veuillot dear in the presbyteries and incomprehensible to the *parlementaires*."[4] The broad English historian, C.S. Phillips, who does not hesitate to put himself into the shoes of a historical figure, probably has more insight into Veuillot than do most twentieth-century French and American modernists in the profession. "The fanaticism of Veuillot's views and the unbridled virulence of his invective must not blind us to his good qualities.... He had loved those he fought – *surtout Montalembert*. He contrived to be supremely offensive: but it is doubtful if he realized how offensive he was. He was one of those people who say the most abominable things to or about an opponent, and then are genuinely surprised and even hurt that he should resent them.... It must be added that if he was virulent and aggressive, his adversaries were often the same. The complaints of the anticlericals concerning his 'want of charity' strike one as somewhat Pecksniffian; and as for the Liberal Catholics – if they received many hard knocks, they did their best to provoke them.... In fact, of the two sides, it is even possible to hold that Veuillot comes out the better."[5] This view, first published in 1936, has not prevailed generally, and twentieth-century liberal historians have perpetuated an antipathy distilled from the anguished cries of nineteenth-century liberal men of action. Veuillot is held up as an ogre still today to students who read textbooks. One leading American scholar says: "His only regret about the Reformation, someone remarked, was that John Huss had not been burned sooner, and Luther not at all. He crusaded vindictively against the republicans, all of whom he considered to be antisocial and fomenters of disorder. The idea of social reform was to him a dangerous delusion."[6] The "someone" who made the remark was young Louis Veuillot himself, provoked to this sarcasm by specific offensive attacks on the Catholic Church by its enemies. He was not vindictive. He immediately forgot the past, as the case of Msgr. Freppel, an opponent who reversed his stand, shows. Veuillot was a champion of social Catholicism, as his relations with Msgr. Mermillod, De Mun, and La Tour du Pin abundantly testify, and he could be a republican, at least as long as the Second Republic had appeal to Catholics. Another highly regarded and usually thorough author tells students that Veuillot's "violent and vulgar attacks on unbelievers and Frenchmen of other faiths, among which he included liberal Catholicism, were read in *L'Univers* and repeated in pulpits all over France by a clergy whose education in public affairs was rarely equal to its moral fervor."[7] Veuillot was of course a man of the people and ever close to them. Vulgar? Certainly not in the sense of the word ordinarily understood by students today. He was a fighter, he was a peasant, but he generally observed linguistic proprieties. It is hard to say how the idea of the "vulgarity" of Veuillot got started. Popes, bishops, and priests do not encourage vulgarity in the Anglo-Saxon derogatory sense of the word. His columns were highly moral in tone. However, as Philip Spencer said, his language was "as direct as a punch on the nose."[8] Henry de Pène, the aristocratic counselor of the Comte de Chambord, once reproached him for what he thought was crudity. Veuillot came back at this man whom "chance of birth" had favored: "Gentleman de Pène, I rose from a barrelmaker, and you, from whom did you descend?"[9] On the other hand, Louis Madelin, writing at the time of Veuillot's centennial in 1913 about letters Veuillot had addressed to Madame Volnys, said: "One discovers in these letters a very singular mixture of native *vulgarité* and quite profound culture, of mystical devotion and quite bitter irony, of touching tenderness and vigorous energy, of hardness and of goodness. Yes, there is a bit of all these in such letters as these – and it is Veuillot."[10] Veuillot's columns in *L'Univers* were not written in the same tender tone as his letters, but even so his rousing columns ought not to be dismissed with the simple Anglo-Saxon word "vulgar." If he was crude, so also were most of the liberals and democrats of his day.

No doubt many of Veuillot's detractors would have liked the indoctrination of the clergy in public affairs made equal to their moral fervor. But Veuillot did not put his faith in public policy, did not place it before private moral fervor in importance, and he did indeed furnish ultramontane orthodoxy of the militant sort with talking points that served as the basis for sermons all over the land. Not surprisingly, therefore, Veuillot often is seen in bad light by liberals of the twentieth century, however learned, because undeniably he presented an obstacle to the rise of secular liberalism.

"Plebeian" would be a good way to summarize Veuillot's background and approach to life.[11] He was *autodidacte*, a Catholic Maccabbee, and according to the great critic Jules Lemaître one of the six greatest users of prose of the century.[12] Conversely, the secularist Edmond Schérer could hardly say enough against him. Frenchmen often use the concept of being *déclassé;* thus Veuillot became in Schérer's terminology as *inquisiteur déclassé.* "Make way for the insulter! Here are the Saturnalia of Catholicism," Schérer declared.[13] Veuillot, although himself a man of the people, did not think the people were gods. He knew what peasants and workers were like, he wanted to save them from themselves and from each other as well as from the tyranny of every kind, and he made no bones about it. Those with a secular faith in the common man as savior of himself must perforce have regarded Veuillot as unfaithful to his class and the Revolution, hence: *déclassé.*

Veuillot always denied he was a romantic. Certainly he was against the disorder present or implied in much of nineteenth-century romanticism. Yet, at least according to family tradition, Veuillot as a boy like to imagine that his Burgundian ancestors had been among the crusaders who set out for the Holy Land. In any case it would be hard to find anyone among the nobles of France, Belcastel, Charette, and their fellows, a more dogged antagonist of the Revolution than Veuillot. The historiography of the French Revolution has been very diverse, but as yet the purely anti-Revolutionary field remains limited. The battle of the books has been carried on largely between those historians who have bourgeois-constitutional sympathies and those sympathetic to the far left. Small wonder that today, long after the eventual general acceptance of certain phases of the French Revolution, most historians assume Louis Veuillot was out of step with his own times in opposing them. Veuillot had some refreshing ideas about the Revolution, but they were too far out of sympathy with it to be acceptable, or even tolerable to doctrinaire secularists.

Veuillot in his day, however, was a forward-thinking man. He saw that the press could be a "more sincere organ of public sentiment" than the parliamentary tribune."[14] The rise of the press in the nineteenth-century and its relation to public opinion was one of the features of the age. Veuillot's role in developing this phenomenon was even greater than that of most of his secular-press counterparts. Also in the church, as a layman, he was challenging through his influence upon his readership the authority of the episcopacy. Many of the episcopacy recognized the changing times in the importance of the press, and these bishops approved or disapproved his stands according to what those stands were. But the whole feature of lay influence through an independent press in the Catholic church was new. Veuillot was a founder of the political grouping which came to be called "clericalism," a term not altogether palatable to ecclesiastics because of the essentially lay influence which was behind it. Clericalism's influence went beyond royalism in base of power. Sometimes associated with it, and sometimes not, it transcended the royalist parties toward the end of Veuillot's life. "Clericalism, there's the enemy!" cried the great republican Gambetta in 1877 (quoting Peyrat). He might almost as well have cried: "Look out for Veuillot and his likes, and don't worry too much about the divided House of Bourbon." Today, in a world long accustomed to republican disestablishment of the church, how can we see a man like Veuillot as a power, or anything other than a wrong-headed opponent of the eventually victorious secular tradition? Perhaps only by judging him by his own standards.

The teachings of Paul of Tarsus and others to the effect that perfect freedom is to be found in slavery to Christ evidently is not universally construed by religious liberals of today to mean prime and sole devotion to the Catholic church. In fact, Veuillot's lively devotion to papal power has been assumed by a large part of those consciously liberal to be the antithesis of the right scheme of things. If Veuillot was anything, he was a believer in papal Catholicism. He was a believer in the miracle at Lourdes and in all accepted miracles. He believed because he wanted to believe, not because of reasoning about any given event. He was a mature adult when he decided to accept the church, to serve it, and to accept with his heart all it believed. Edmond Schérer is quoted as saying that if Veuillot had been told that Jonah had swallowed the whale, he would have believed it![15] Such was the exaggerated nature of the slurs on Veuillot.

The Catholic church, even after 1870, was not monolithic. Liberal Catholicism received a great setback at that time, but it was not dead. By the twentieth century insistent new waves of liberalism appeared in it. Despite superficial personal similarities which exist between Pius IX and the popular John XXIII, Pius IX has not been regarded as a hero by twentieth-century liberal Catholics. In making their complaints, Veuillot has been a convenient figure, along with Cardinal Antonelli, on whom to put the onus for affairs that went against the liberal Catholics. Admittedly the matter is beyond documentation, but Veuillot has probably served as a lightning rod for criticism of the pontificate of Pius IX.

It must be recognized that Veuillot was directly associated with social Catholicism and with La Tour du Pin, and in a way he prepared the ground for Drumont and Maurras.[16] When Philip Spencer flatly says that Veuillot would have rejected them,[17] that is presuming he had lived into another generation, which he did not. Veuillot did indeed support authoritarianism as personified by Louis Napoleon, but he rejected him as soon as the "strong man" abandoned the Catholic church. As long as the papacy had taken no stand with regard to the *Action française,* Veuillot might have been favorable to it, had he lived to see it. However, as the pope rejected it eventually, presumably Veuillot would have too. Veuillot looked on Jews more as individuals of a different religion than as a race. The new anti-Semitism, which he never experienced, could hardly have swept him along, therefore, despite the many harsh things he had to say about the descendants of Caiaphus, who condemned Christ. Despite the submission of Veuillot to the papacy and the papacy alone, Veuillot's at times anti-democratic and anti-liberal attitudes make him seem to some, although this is quite illogical, to foreshadow twentieth-century totalitarianism. Hence, he is sensed to be an evil man, as well as an archaic one. Veuillot's reputation today suffers we might say from events in which he never took part. He was not in the mainstream of the eventually victorious liberal-democratic-secular tradition. He was not even a mild-mannered, concession-making opponent. He persisted in wanting to win.

Perhaps his worst sin in the eyes of most of those who write history was that he sometimes sounded anti-intellectual, despite his own wide-ranging thought, and intellectual interests. Some of his principal lines of thought were never fully worked out. He planned a study bearing the title *Jésus Législateur* [18] but he never finished it. He formulated ideas about an *Idéal d'un chef des Français*, but it never was finished.[19] His religion was not unexamined faith, but a faith whose nature he spelled out very carefully for himself. "Religion is the recognition of faith itself, the science of life, the art of attaining the goal of life, the fullness of life."[20] He defined in his private papers in what ways religion must be an act of faith.[21] He thought a great deal about esthetic matters and their relationship to religion and life. He had sensitive taste in French literature. Despite many disputes with individuals in the *Académie,* he was a sympathizer with its purpose, finding it *bien inventée*[22] However, he was a violent opponent of the university monopoly and the *universitaires.* He was capable of tripping them up and even of criticizing on occasion the Latin used by them, but here he put himself in a camp not readily pardoned by intellectuals of the eventually triumphant tradition. Their enmity was passed on to followers. To have been anti-university, therefore, is now equivalent to having been anti-intellectual. Veuillot wrote penetrating analyses of works of Guizot and many of the big names of the day, but he said the wrong things. He did not share the opinion of the future doctrinaires. Accordingly, he is generally at least ignored.

Veuillot's "great silence" or retirement because of bad health began at just the time when Jules Ferry was coming into power. He could see the signs of the final separation of church and state at various stages, but his objection to the subordination of the church to the state, in what he regarded as Russian style, had been voiced throughout all his career. However, what he idealized was the "ancient union of spiritual and temporal powers,"[23] and he dreamed of a France asserting herself once more as eldest daughter of the church. He mourned the passing of Christendom. At various times, on the eve of the Crimean War, for example, he had some reason for optimism, but in general he saw the church fighting only a defensive battle. The subsequent almost total victory of the partisans of separation of church and state in the West has made of Veuillot an advocate of a lost cause, or a cause at least for the age submerged. Majorities appear to confirm the rectitude of the causes they support. Thus Veuillot, whatever the merits of his cause, must therefore have been wrong. In the eyes of a substantial school, he is so considered.

Veuillot and *L'Univers* have been called many things. Msgr. Parisis called *L'Univers* "a great Catholic institution."[24] The importance of Veuillot is rather well explained simply by such a judgment. Veuillot detested as a libel against church Molière's creation of the character Tartuffe, but he himself was labeled by opponents a "rare Tartuffe."[25] Commenting on Veuillot's irony, Msgr. Dreux-Brézé called him a "Christian Voltaire,"[26] an epithet picked up recently in the form of "Pius IX's Voltaire."[27] At the time of his death many eulogistic phrases were used about him, but the colorful insults have had a greater lasting impact. These labels reflected the personal animosity of various opponents toward Veuillot, and when labels become identified with a man, objectivity becomes ever more difficult.

Veuillot never hid the errors of *L'Univers*, and himself. He admitted to "too much bitterness" and to "too much initiative in questions which are specially in the domaine of the church," although he thought in many matters he had "legitimate indignation."[28] He did not do much, if anything, about correcting either of these faults, even after the pope found too little charity in his camp, but certainly he was willing to admit his shortcomings as well as attack others for their own. The very fact of admission of fault, however, along with general frankness about his own feelings has also tended to work against his reputation. Like anyone else, he had both his assets and his liabilities. Emmanuel Gauthier has made an interesting attempt to group and list them. In what he calls "qualities of heart" he lists virility, firmness of ideas, obedience, resignation, courage, and disinterestedness. For "intellectual qualities" he cites sincerity, honesty, independence, prudence, generosity, simplicity, and love of work, among others. He saw delicacy, conviviality, nobleness, goodness, joviality, and charity (despite the pope's one-time observation) among Veuillot's personal traits. For "inner virtues" he saw faith, hope, humility, piety, and love of the church. For faults he saw gluttony, uneven disposition, exaggerated sensibilities, presumption, intolerance, violence, narrowness, bitterness, and pessimism.[29] While the negative list is the shorter, it is nevertheless imposing.

Schérer asked: "Have you heard these savage cries? Have you seen this frenetic? . . . Has our civilization with all its vices ever produced anything as frightful as this writer in whose heart religion has become an ulcer which has gnawed one after another of these sacred traits of humanity?"[30] But Sainte-Beuve, who had also been attacked by Veuillot, looked further. He had met Veuillot. He spoke of his "affectionate, almost caressing," tone of voice. He declared "it is impossible to have met him and to have talked with him without having recognized in this much-detested ogre, and one who has done everything he could to be just that, a man well endowed with civil and social qualities."[31] The view of Schérer, of course, is the more catchy. In an undated private piece, probably written late in his life, Veuillot wrote: "God having created us to love him, and God loving us himself, only wins us over by love."[32] Veuillot must have loved his fellow man; his actions show it. He cared about others so much that he became extremely angry when what he believed were false ideas destroyed what he believed to be the true relationship of man and God. His anger is what has been selected by historians to be recalled. However, he cared very deeply about his fellow man. Whether he or his opponents chose the right beliefs is a matter of faith and of judgment.

CHAPTER I

BACKGROUND AND EARLY YEARS

The Gatinais is an ancient country situated between the valleys of the Loire, the Seine, and the Yonne. The land is flat, and the clayey nature of the soil is such that rainwater stands in ribbons along its plowed fields. The area has long produced grain and cattle, but honey and blossoms for saffron, have been a more characteristic part of Gatinais life. Pithiviers, a center for handling grain and flour, is the main town in the Gatinais. A few miles to the east and about fifty miles south of Paris is Boynes, a small market town of perhaps as much as one thousand people in the early nineteenth century. Wine was, of course, produced in this town, and for it barrels and barrelmakers were needed. In 1811 an itinerant workman, François Veuillot, who knew nothing but his trade of making and repairing barrels and tubs, and whose only possessions were his tools, arrived in Boynes. He espied a lass working and singing in the window of a humble dwelling covered with honeysuckle.[1] Before long they were married, and of this union Louis François-Victor Veuillot was born on October 11, 1813.

Louis Veuillot's paternal grandfather, Brice Veuillot, had been a miller, born at Noyers in Burgundy (Yonne).[2] His mill was entailed in some way to a monastery, and with the coming of the Revolution was confiscated as ecclesiastical property, to the ruination of the family. After the death of Brice Veuillot only the efforts of one of the older daughters saved his numerous orphans from starvation. Two of the older brothers were in the disastrous Russian campaign of 1812-1813. A story was preserved in the Veuillot family that the two settled for a time on the Berezina River on the way back, the younger eventually leaving but later returning to seek his brother. The still younger children of Brice Veuillot, including François, father of Louis, did not even learn how to read, in that era of the Revolution which promised to be making all men equal.[3] Under these circumstances François not surprisingly knew nothing but his trade, having to fend for himself at an early age. Nevertheless he was reputed to be of pleasant disposition and hard-working.[4]

Louis Veuillot's maternal grandfather, Jacques Adam, desirous of avoiding a career as wheelwright, served for a time in the Gardes Françaises, returned to Boynes shortly before the Revolution, and, marrying, fell under the domination of his wife, Marianne Bourassin.[5] Although his grandfather Jacques was alive during Louis's boyhood in Boynes, his strong-willed grandmother may well have been the member of the family with the most important influence on Louis, at least in retrospect. In 1793 some "sans-culottes" from Pithiviers had headed for Boynes with the purpose of knocking down the big crucifix on the edge of Boynes. The family story has it that Jacques Adam and other men of the village absented themselves, but that Marianne, followed by other women, armed herself with a large axe and declared she would finish off anyone who touched the cross, which she then carried off to security.[6] Throughout his life Louis Veuillot treated women with respect! Just possibly his grandmother's heroism was the basis of his attitude that women were worthy allies. And certainly many adversaries must have felt his pen as threatening as her axe.

Boynes had a sturdy gothic church with a square to its right-front which may or may not have been paved with stone at the time of Louis's boyhood. The square tower at its front entrance, however, had no bell,[7] probably because the bell had been melted for cannon during the recent wars. For five years Louis was the only child of his parents, whose laborious life he shared. Plucking blossoms for saffron, however, was something the tiny boy hated. To demonstrate his feelings he declared he would throw himself into a nearby well rather than continue plucking and forthwith started running toward the well. His robust mother overtook him, fearing that it would be consistent with his character to carry out his intention. But rather than discussing the merits of blossom-picking as opposed to throwing oneself in a well, or punishing him in some other way, she held him by his feet over the well, allowing natural fear to have its salubrious effect.[8] Undoubtedly his upbringing was very rough, but folk-wisdom accompanied it.

Despite difficulties the Veuillot family must have had more success than usual during the first five years of Louis' life. Somehow the family had gotten ahead by several hundred francs, with the mother's needle undoubtedly having contributed to these savings. They had bought a small dwelling of their own, but unfortunately they were soon obliged to resell it. The details of their troubles are hopelessly lost, but somehow their savings were in the hands of the principal businessman of the area, a wholesale merchant of wines and saffron, who apparently went bankrupt. The blow was heavy, especially for Marguerite-Marianne, who was proud by disposition. Moreover, at this time, a second son, Eugène, was born. At the instance of Marguerite-Marianne, François decided to move elsewhere, to flee humiliation and to seek better opportunities.[9]

François got a position in Bercy, a town on the right bank of the Seine to the east of Paris, which was not yet incorporated into Paris, but which was an important depot in the city's wine trade. He became the principal workman for an entrepreneur who had a number of warehouses he let out to wholesalers. As barrelmaker and custodian François received three francs, fifty centimes a day, plus bread, wine, and lodging.[10] The baby Eugène was taken to Bercy, but Louis was left behind with his maternal grandparents in Boynes.[11] He got along apparently as well as might have been expected. He broke his left arm, but it was set well enough so that he never complained of any trouble with it. He recovered from smallpox, but was badly marked by it. Of all this his parents heard little because of their difficulty in written communication.[12] However, in the home of Jacques Adam, Louis had primers and a few other books, including *Les Quatre fils Aymon,* the *Almanach de Mathieu Lansberg*, and some isolated volumes of the novels of La Calprenède. He was able to read all these at an early age, and particularly enjoyed *Les Quatre fils Aymon*. If there was any evil in these it was over his head at such a young age, in the later judgment of his brother.[13] The principal book in the home of Jacques Adam, however, was the Bible, though it would be impossible to say whether that was read by Louis very much.

After he reached the age of ten the parents took Louis off the hands of his grandparents. When his Aunt Rosalie, who kept a yardgoods shop in Beaumont, set out for Paris in a covered cart (*carriole*) to get supplies for her business, Louis had a way to go to his parents. The trip took three or four days, with frequent stops besides spending nights in inns. This must have been an exciting trip for the young boy, who anticipated seeing his baby brother, his parents, and the great city, but according to the account of Eugène he feared what would be said about his smallpox. And to be sure, his mother did not recognize him with his blue cotton bonnet and his pocked face. But after this unhappy initial reaction there was the expected affectionate return,[14] and many years later Louis romanticized his pleasure in seeing his baby brother for the first time since the cradle, in one of his books.[15]

At Boynes Louis had had the benefit of a school where he had learned reading, writing, and arithmetic. Though the boy could have been apprenticed at this point, his mother had higher hopes for him and he was sent instead to the *école mutuelle* at Bercy, part of the university system that had been established during the days of Napoleon. Although he had had to work in the fields at Boynes, his life there had been far more pleasant and unregulated than it became at Bercy. He found it painful to see his father jump up at the first stroke of the bell,[16] and his lifelong tendency to praise the existence of peasants over that of city people may be traced to his experiences as a ten-year-old. He also disliked the kind of people with whom they lived in Bercy, and obviously had a low regard for the school and his master. The master had his pupils read the trashy novels of Paul de Kock, Lamothe-Langon, and other superficial writers, which he called *productions charmantes*.[17] Looking backward later Louis Veuillot sarcastically called his *école mutuelle* "religious," because the master liked holidays, and suspended school on the days of very minor saints – but for the purpose of indulging his weakness, drunkenness, rather than for church attendance. From this person Louis had his catechism. Thus prepared, "pushed to the Holy Table by ignorant hands,"[18] it is small wonder that his first communion made little impression on him. Fortunately, the master of the school had an assistant, who, although not a very remarkable teacher, recognized the exceptional talents of this pupil. He gave him a little instruction beyond what was required for the primary level in history and grammar, and introduced him to Latin.[19] But Louis's instruction at Boynes and Bercy was so haphazard that he may be regarded as self-educated.

The impetus for Louis's first communion must have come from his mother. The church had not recovered from the Revolution, and great inroads had been made on the connection to it of the middle class and workingmen of Bercy. Louis Veuillot described his father as "fundamentally Christian," but thoroughly ignorant of the church. His mother, who worked hard both with the needle and in raising the family, seems to have confined her attendance to great feasts. However, some of her own mother's devotion remained, and she sent her children to mass on Sundays and encouraged the saying of prayers. The indifferences that turned to hatred of the church in so many households of Bercy and like places did not creep into the Veuillot home.[20]

Despite the fact Louis was under no illusions about the wine-depot district of Bercy, he looked back on it in later years with some fondness, particularly as he contrasted its earlier days with the way it had become after tighter national administrative centralization and the incorporation of Bercy into Paris in 1860. He recalled roads lined with trees where railroads later came, and children picking violets in places later paved. There had once been terraces, even at the *école mutuelle*, and grassy yards. Excursions on foot to the Bois de Vincennes had been part of the existence.[21] Tremendous events had made their effect in Paris, but daily life was much slower to change in nearby Bercy. There workingmen had a life much more like the eighteenth century than that of the era just dawning. The old corporative spirit still existed, and trade-union organization and the concept of striking had not yet become general. The era of Louis Philippe was to bring far more change to people like François Veuillot than had the years of the Revolution, at least according to the tradition of the Veuillot family,[22] but in the 1820's life was still not yet much influenced by the characteristics of capitalistic industrialization. A measure of freedom such as Louis experienced could yet be had in Bercy, and the nearly complete lack of central supervision of the school masters at least permitted a situation of salutary neglect that he later contrasted favorably with the strict surveillance of his aunt that followed.[23] And with it all he found time to read, the obsession of his life.

By the time Louis was thirteen the Veuillot family had four childern. Élise, the youngest, was born in 1825; Annette was sixteen months older. Expenses were heavy. In the spring of 1827 it appeared that Louis' education was over. It had cost seven francs a month to send him to the *école mutuelle*, "two days of cursed work to pay for the lessons of corruption which I received from my comrades, and from a master who was drunk three-quarters of the time."[24] His father was not well and, Louis realized, he had been killing himself with work, thirteen hours a day in the winter and fourteen a day in summer (presumably with time off to eat).[25] Obviously Louis would now have to work. His father thought he should become a watchmaker, cabinetmaker, mason, or shoemaker, but his mother objected. She would have preferred that he be a tailor or *épicier*, to which, in turn, his father objected with scorn. Then the ambitious mother wondered why the bookish boy could not become a lawyer. The father did not know what the term *jurisconsulte* meant. When the mother tried to explain that a *jurisconsulte* was a sort of super-notary, the father could not imagine such a climb for their son. Napoleon went from corporal to emperor, the mother asserted. The father rejoined that he could well imagine, and fear, that Louis might become a corporal, but *jurisconsulte*, never.[26] The mother's thinking, however, prevailed.

Through Louis' father's employer, M. Brisson, the family heard of a lawyer who was seeking a clerk. Louis had a fine handwriting and was a good speller, although but thirteen. Not only would the seven francs a month be saved, but in addition the little clerk would earn twenty.[27] The opportunity seemed great and was accepted. It was even better than it seemed. The lawyer was Fortuné Delavigne, brother of Casimir Delavigne, the dramatist and poet, then at the height of his career.[28] Fortuné Delavigne's study was at 19, Quai Malaquais, Faubourg St.

Germain, just next to the École des Beaux Arts.[29] Along with politics, literature and the theater were preoccupations of Parisian lawyers of the day, and no better situation in which to explore these preoccupations could be found than the office of Delavigne. His other brother, Germain, was also much involved with the theater, and at his office Scribe and other luminaries were frequently seen.[30] For intellectual development that meshed with the practical tutelage of men important in the changing climate of Paris, Louis could not have found a better position.

At first Louis tried to live at home and walk to work, but to do this he had to walk five or six kilometers each way, which was impractical, not to say exhausting. An Aunt Annette, sister of his father, who had married a candlemaker, was living on the Rue Saint-Martin, which was not as far from his work. She has been described as the rich member of the family, but apparently any money she had was obtained through stinginess. What the young clerk was given for a "room" must have been little more than a closet, while his bed of straps inadequately covered, and "chair" stuffed with straw, hardly constituted furniture. Of course a pump in the court was all he had in which to wash. But these discomforts were slight in comparison with his relationship with the aunt who was supposed to look out for him. She required him in return for his room to help with the production of candles! The smell of the tallow invaded everything, but it was the crossness of his aunt that brought him to the limit.[31] No matter how attractive his position as clerk to M. Delavigne was to him, Louis wanted to change his existence. He applied on his own initiative to the Archbishop of Paris for admission, and without gratuity, to a seminary. No answer was ever received from Msgr. de Quélen, the Archbishop.[32] Had Louis Veuillot been admitted, it would be interesting to speculate what his ecclesiastical career would have been. To have entered a seminary at the age of thirteen would have meant that his formative experiences would have been very different. However his application at this time indicated only a desire to escape from the unpleasant aunt and the smell of tallow. Louis Veuillot in writing about his youth went out of his way to record all his important inclinations and associations with the Catholic church, and this episode recounted by his brother Eugène is not given much emphasis, though we are told it was not the only time he ever thought of entering the church.[33] The fact he did not persist in his application perhaps shows it was not serious. Even while he was reacting against his lodgings, he was rapidly acquiring the literary tastes and interests which would dominate his attention for a decade.

His living arrangements soon were changed without so radical a move as his going into a seminary. An old tailor from Boynes also lived in Paris. Louis' mother also had disliked the aunt, and now it was arranged for him to move to the residence of the tailor, named Renard. Here he not only did not have to contend with things incidental to the candle trade and the stinginess of his aunt, but also had much more liberty of action.[34] This move was more significant in the early teenager's attainment of manhood than the first. Louis apparently had much more time to read, and in the better circumstances in which he now found himself the steady drain on the strength of his eyes was well underway. M. Renard helped him some with the repair of his clothes,[35] the sad condition of which undoubtedly presented an obstacle in his activities. In a room with a mansard window through which the sun shone the young clerk was now happily and independently situated.

Within a short time Louis was advanced to the position of second clerk, with a salary of one-hundred francs a month,[36] about as much as his father had earned while ruining his health with heavy labor. Nevertheless, the ends of the months were very hard for him. In order to eat at these times he had to do other work. This work was the menial but picturesque function of loading sand from the bottom of the Seine into little flat barges.[37] He was obviously embarrassed to have to be so engaged, proof being that he feared a certain blonde woman whom he fancied might learn of this job, before he was eventually able to give it up.[38] Indeed, the rising clerk gave at least one sign of being a dandy by engaging a black man who was the servant of someone in the building to shine his shoes for two francs a month. Regrettably, he did not have enough money to pay for the services rendered, and the man, whom Louis called "Friday" (though he himself was hardly a Robinson Crusoe!), was unpaid for some time. When Friday's master departed, he took his servant with him, and thus the debt was never discharged. Louis was troubled by his failure to pay his debt, and, much later, when contributing to a Catholic *œuvre* in Africa he declared, "I am paying Friday!"[39] Although Friday would not have agreed, at least Louis had not forgotten him.

Louis made progress rapidly in his work as a legal clerk. His mother's dreams seemed to be coming true. But early in his legal apprenticeship he began to feel more strongly the allurements of literature and journalism. Right in the law offices of Fortuné Delavigne these allurements were working. There was not only the obvious influence of Casimir Delavigne but also that of many other literary figures who were seen by the clerks as they drew up legal documents. The clerks themselves were young men of literary promise who spurred the interests of each other. Several of them achieved literary success. Jules de Wailly composed comedies, and Natalis de Wailly became a member of the *Académie des Inscriptions et Belles-Lettres.* Damas-Hinard wrote increasingly serious pieces and studies, eventually becoming *secrétaire des commandements* to the Empress Eugénie. Auguste Barbier was early recognized as a first-rate poet, and in due course elected to the Academy. But the clerk who was of the greatest influence on Louis was Gustave Olivier. Although perhaps ten years older than Louis, and from a more fortunate background, Olivier became a close friend to the younger clerk from the start. His literary interests were very broad. Just as at a later date he stimulated Louis Veuillot's interest and feelings for the church, at this earlier time he introduced him to political journalism.[40] A well-known figure who made his personality felt in the law offices of Delavigne was Émile Perrin. Perrin was a painter, a critic of art, director of the Opéra Comique, and eventually of the Opéra itself, beside being elected municipal councilor of Paris.[41] And near to the law offices was the study of Henri de Latouche, a journalist of literary merit who wrote for *Le Figaro.* Latouche befriended and encouraged the young clerk. His was the first direct aid from someone already well established. In Latouche's study Veuillot saw many important persons of the literary press, including Alphonse Royer, Léon Gozlan, Michel Masson, Raymond Brucker, Nestor Roqueplan, Félix Pyat, and Jules Sandeau. Of these Raymond Brucker became a friend and associate, and later like himself became a militant Catholic. In Latouche's study he also saw George Sand.[42] The stimulation derived from seeing such people near to his place of work must have been great, but the influence of Latouche went further.

Like most other young people of the age, Louis Veuillot was much impressed by Victor Hugo. But as his literary sensitivity developed he was steered by Latouche away from Hugo and the romantic style. (Although Veuillot liked to think of himself as classical in style and taste, some imprint of Lamartine, Hugo, and the whole movement remained fixed on him, nonetheless.) In turning Veuillot from Hugo, Henri de Latouche led him to the less powerful but extremely witty style of the popular journalist, Jules Janin, whose articles appeared in *Le Figaro.*[43] Janin became the principal model for the young writer. But perhaps of most importance was the fact that it was Latouche who in 1831 was to aid the young clerk in publishing his first piece. Having recommended it be short, Latouche found it unnecessary to make any changes, and a short article about an affair of the day appeared in *Le Figaro*! Thus Louis first tasted the proud feeling of seeing his words in print.[44]

The young clerk seems to have derived his pleasure more and more from literature. Not just at the office but also on his free hours he indulged in its pursuit. He liked to hear authors like Victor Cousin lecture, and he liked to discuss literary matters with his friends, especially Gustave Olivier. It was not surprising he began writing himself. The earliest of his literary efforts are to be found in an exchange of letters with a friend named Émilien, wherein they discuss the merits and defects of each other's poetry.[45] At eighteen, he had already become serious in his interests and sensitive to the use of words.

During the years 1827 through 1831 the life of Louis Veuillot had been radically altered. From the humble situation of son of an artisan in Bercy he had reached while still a child the fringes of Parisian professional and intellectual circles. In general the transition seems to have been comparatively smooth. He became absorbed in his new ways without turning against his background and without his origins apparently having presented him with too many difficulties. He liked the artistic excitement of Paris, and together with the other clerks was captivated by the actress Léontine Fay. A police agent writing a sketch of him in 1875 said that he changed from his clumsy manners and sloppy dress in this period, took boxing and fencing lessons, and "followed a life of more irregularities."[46] There is, however, no real evidence to support this conclusion. His friends were, with the exception of Gustave Olivier, for the most part very worldly, but apparently their morals were better than those of the young people in Bercy. By hindsight at a later date he deplored the empty secular approach of the Parisian world in which he had lived at the general time of the Revolution of 1830, but his days were interesting and at the time satisfying.

The great event of his young days was the July Revolution of Louis Philippe. In due course as an ultramontane Catholic, he came to hate the bourgeois régime of the July Monarchy, but when the coup occurred he approved of it. Charles X had said mass *en blanc*,[47] and in any case was out of step with progress. How could a boy of less than seventeen see features of the Orleans Monarchy that had not yet fully revealed themselves? The Revolution was exciting, but its events were quite incidental to him and not something with which he was associated directly. Among the violent characters he met on the streets in those days was an old man who showed him a likeness of Napoleon tattooed on his chest.[48] Even at the most exciting hour of the Revolution of 1830 Louis probably realized that ghosts of greater events still hovered in the background. Looking back later Louis Veuillot would recoil against the sacking of the *Archévêché* and the desecration of Saint Germain L'Auxerrois in early 1831[49], which occurred without apparently distressing the régime, but there is no evidence that at the time he had any great reaction. He was absorbed with his work, and even more, the literary and cultural influences to which he was most receptive.

The main immediate effect on Louis of the Revolution of 1830 was that some of the other clerks, such as Auguste Barbier, who now had other opportunities, left the offices of Fortuné Delavigne. Soon he himself had an opportunity which he could not refuse. In September, 1831, when he was not yet eighteen, he was offered a post with a journal in Rouen, *L'Écho de la Seine Inférieure*, which shortly afterward became *L'Écho de Rouen*.[50] This opportunity had not exactly fallen out of the blue sky. His older friend, Gustave Olivier, who had successively engaged in Scandanavian studies, Chinese studies, poetry, archaeology, and the law, had gone to this northern city and become a political editor. He needed a colleague, and he knew the talents of Louis Veuillot. Young Louis promptly accepted and set off for Rouen to begin a period of five years of provincial journalism. This step was a big one. He turned his back on law, not because of any dislike for law, but because of his love for letters, and particularly because of the involvement of journalism in affairs of the day. In Louis' life this first plunge into journalism in 1831 was a decision of great importance, comparable only to his decision to become a practicing Christian in 1838, and his assumption of his life work, editorship of *L'Univers*, in 1842.

Rouen was an ancient town of increasing industrial importance. It had great churches, but it also had the marks of the nineteenth century. It was a cultural center. In its theaters Rouen hissed plays that were successful in Paris,[51] and as particularly the cultural articles and theatrical reviews were to be written by Louis, he was going to have a broad and tricky field to cover. *L'Écho de la Seine Inférieure* had been launched by the supporters of the new régime. It represented the party of resistance, or the *doctrinaires*, the conservatives who supported the July Monarchy. Its political orientation did not trouble the young man at the time. By his own confession he could have even more easily joined the party of movement. There certainly was little attention to the Christian God among these people. Their god was Public Order. "Not having enough brains or heart to defend themselves," they turned to journalists like himself and paid well for it. According to Louis Veuillot, he already had a higher salary than a bishop![52] What a change from being poor son of a barrelmaker! The position of the church in this city, where once Joan of Arc had been burned at the stake, did not apparently make a notable impression on the young journalist.

There was a wide range of plays and musical productions to review. Beside classical plays, the works of Scribe, Ancelot, and many other contemporaries, including Casimir Delavigne, were staged in Rouen. Actors and actresses, well-known and local, good and bad, walked the stage. The music of Weber, Meyerbeer, and Hoffmann was introduced to Rouen at this period. For a critic yet in his teens the challenge was great. Nevertheless, the young ex-lawyer's clerk was quite undaunted. He had been much to the theater in Paris and now had no inhibitions about plunging in and describing actors and plays with the most sweeping terms. "Ventilation" was what he said the audience needed after one bit of acting.[53] Restraint never characterized his critiques, and as might have been expected, such reviews did not pass unchallenged. A group of partisans of one actress who had come in for bad treatment from Veuillot's pen were on the point of beating him up right in the theater until a certain local strongman for undetermined reasons intervened in his behalf. However, the same actress had a husband, handsome but vain, whom Veuillot had also ridiculed. The result of this indiscretion was a challenge to his first of three duels which he fought in this year. The duel was described only in terse terms in the 20 February 1831 number of *L'Écho de Rouen*, but Louis' brother Eugène recounts the episode in some detail in his *Vie*. The duel was fought with pistols, and neither party hit the other, but the actor's ball passed through the brim of Louis' hat. "The young critic did not become more gentle on actors,"[54] however, his brother tells us.

This encounter was not his only one at Rouen. Although preoccupied with artistic and literary matters, he was, of course, part of the régime's journalistic front, which was assaulted both from the left and from the right. A favorite vehicle of attack in those days was the personal caricature, often highly obscene. The mayor of Rouen came in for such treatment at the hands of the republicans who published the *Journal de Rouen*, and Louis Veuillot sprang to his defense in such a way that "son cher confrère" of the *Journal* took offense, and a duel was arranged. Theoretically the republican had the right to choose the weapon, and would have named sabres, but Veuillot knew nothing of their use, and pistols again were brought to the field of honor. Olivier accompanied Veuillot to the contest. According to Eugène's tale, Louis refused to fire first, since it was his weapon that was to bring about satisfaction. This time it was his redingote that was penetrated. Though the young editor was unharmed, he too missed his target. Some of his friends gave him a "redingote de combat" by way of consolation.[55]

During his days in Rouen Louis worked hard. He had friends, including Émile Perrin, with whom he had been associated when he worked for Fortuné Delavigne, and the worker-poet Libreton, but he took out little time for pleasure.[56] Whatever his indiscretions in the field of artistic criticism were, he strove for success as a journalist. He had a model, the journalist for *Le Figaro* whom Henri de Latouche had held up for him in Paris as a stylist superior to Victor Hugo – Jules Janin. Editorials were often signed by the initials of the writer, and "J.J." had made a great impression on Louis Veuillot. Louis rather inanely signed most of his nonpolitical pieces in this era "V.V."

Late in 1832 a new opportunity presented itself to Louis, now barely nineteen – that of becoming editor-in-chief, with a free hand, of a similar journal in the much smaller southern town of Périgueux. He could not refuse it. On 2 December he arrived in Périgueux, the former capital of Périgord in Gascony, to take over the editorship of the *Mémorial de la Dordogne*, the ministerial sheet, which was contending with the republican organ, *L'Écho de Vésone,* and that of the legitimists, the *Gazette de Périgord.*[57] The town and the surrounding area were charming and quite different from Rouen. Périgueux was a town of not so many thousands of people and largely untouched by modern technology and industry. It had much of the charm of the South, and the people seemed to enjoy living, though far out of touch with the center of things. Périgueux had second-century Roman ruins, an eleventh-century cathedral, Saint-Front, irregular streets and buildings, and was famous for truffles. In the sixteenth century it had been in the hands of the Huguenots, and in the nineteenth century still certainly was not very Catholic, though religious indifference chiefly characterized the outlook.

The dominant personality of the town was Marshal Bugeaud, the organizer and eventual conqueror of Algeria, who was a significant leader among the conservative Orleanists. Louis Veuillot had seen him in Paris, and now to have an interview with the formidable soldier was the high point of his initiation into the life of Périgueux. The gruff warrior first asked him what his age was, and observed that twenty-five would have suited him better than nineteen, to which the newly arrived replied that he preferred nineteen. Bugeaud then asked him to sit down and write a page *on* Odilon Barrot, a supporter of the Revolution of 1830 who had promptly become its critic. Veuillot dashed off a page *against* Odilon Barrot, to the great satisfaction of Bugeaud.[58] Thus the young editor not only launched himself successfully in Périgueux, but began one of his own most important personal associations.

Within relatively few years much of the modern age was to come to Périgueux, but in the 1830's there was neither railroad, nor telegraph. Once a day the post arrived from Paris with news that was three days old. The *Mémorial de la Dordogne* appeared only twice a week, except when parliament was in session, when it appeared three times.[59] Under circumstances like these the editor of the newspaper had as much opportunity to engage in polemics to his own taste, as he had little in the way of news to report. The opportunities for digesting reports of happenings and for leaving the personal stamp of the editor on the journalist were great. In the growth of the editor, the sojourn in Perigueux was of fundamental importance.

Involvement in politics in defense of the régime occupied much of young Veuillot's attention and tended to delay his development in certain other directions, notably the religious. He paid only one call on the Bishop of Périgord, Msgr. de Lostanges, because the latter had been an emigré and was suspected of being a "Carlist," or supporter of the exiled Charles X. Moreover, his only long-term friend who was a devoted Christian, Gustave Olivier, was now far away, and even less able to influence him than he had been at Rouen. Only after some time in Périgueux did Veuillot meet a rural curé, the Abbé Guines, whom he was to meet again much later after the curé had become a Capucin monk under the name of Père Ambroise.[60] But there was little Christian influence in the society of Périgueux, where worldly existence was so pleasantly adjusted. Apparently only the women furnished any regular core of church-goers, and even their attendance may have been partly occasioned by a desire to take part in the virtual parade they put on for the men, who would arrive outside the cathedral after mass to watch the woman coming out in high toilette.[61]

One of the key figures in his life in Périgueux was the préfet, M. Romieu. This official was a very different sort of man from Marshal Bugeaud, but also not without influence on Veuillot. Romieu's family had been supporters of the Empire, and up to the Revolution of 1830, Romieu had been a very worldly and perhaps dissipated fellow, dabbling in journalism and becoming a real connoisseur of the stage. With the establishment of the July Monarchy he had been appointed préfet, first in Quimperlé, and in 1834 in Périgueux.[62] Contact with Romieu was, of course, fundamental for the fulfillment of Veuillot's function as editor. The worldly-wise Romieu had highly developed literary taste, and no doubt much of Louis Veuillot's literary sophistication can be traced to his influence. Indeed, Veuillot neglected his literary work not at all during this period. When at Périgueux a sheet called *Montaigne* was established by Albert de Calvimont, Louis contributed various pieces, including poetry, to it. This he did under pseudonyms, once calling himself "Alice Herpin," and another time "Vicomte Donatien de Vaise."[63] But despite his stormy political life, classicism as the ideal of the writer clearly emerged victorious over romanticism in this period for Veuillot.[64]

Louis's adventures in Périgueux included at least one more duel. An exchange of polemics between the *Mémorial* and the republican *L'Écho de Vésone* resulted in offense being taken by the republican editor, and pistols were chosen. Louis had become a good shot by this time, but his opponent fired first. Fortunately, for a second time (according to Eugène) only his redingote was punctured with no harm to its wearer. Louis took careful aim, but his pistol did not go off. Although offered, in accordance with the code, a second try, Louis ended this venture onto the field of honor with a bit of sarcasm to the effect that his opponent's relatives might be getting nervous.[65] With all due regard for twentieth-century aversion for the code duello, one must remember that it was differently regarded in the 1830's. Young Veuillot had thrice demonstrated that he was ready to face the fire of an enemy, and if his brother's accounts be correct, he may have established some sort of record for being grazed in three consecutive duels.

In 1836 Gustave Olivier came again into the life of Louis Veuillot.[66] He wrote him a letter saying that he had become a Christian and that he had a confessor and took communion. Louis, worrying whether some malady had befallen Gustave, showed the letter to Romieu, who observed that indeed he must be crazy! The immediate result of the resumption of relations between Louis and Gustave, was that Gustave brought Louis back to Paris in 1836. Guizot, whose ministry had first fallen in February of 1836, when back in power decided to establish a militant journal in Paris to be called *La Charte de 1830*. This journal was to have aggressive editors, and to find such editors a search was undertaken. The versatile Gustave had connections in the Bureau de la Presse, and he indicated to them that Louis would be a good choice. When invited, Louis asked his experienced friend the préfet what to do, and the latter without hesitation unselfishly recommended that he depart for Paris immediately.[67] Another important turning point in his life had been reached when he left the charming provincial town of Périgueux and his friends there, including a young lady in whom he was interested, for the manifold opportunities in Paris which Romieu could not conscientiously advise him to let slip by.

As he traveled, in late 1836, from Périgueux to Paris by diligence coach, he had mixed feelings. Despite some melancholy at leaving gentle Périgueux, he was carried onward with excitement toward what Paris might hold for him. "I was twenty-three, no longer poor nor timid, and on the way, amid the dreams of a traveler, ambition came to me. I will be sincere: I entered Paris with ideas of conquest, completely

Louis went to have dinner with Gustave. His feelings seemed to have been sharpened by the atmosphere of that time of year when the grotesque masks of the joy-seekers seemed perhaps symbolic of the life about him. At this point Gustave made a startling proposal: to leave it all for some time; to go to Italy, yes, even Sicily, Greece, Malta, Egypt, Constantinople, Palestine, and perhaps Persia.[85] Evidently Gustave did not dwell on Rome. All this travel would certainly be the medicine Louis needed. Madness it seemed to Louis, but he had come to be so completely tired of his life. Why not? Why not even for a year? What was there to prevent these two young (Gustave was however considerably older than Louis) bachelors from setting out on this breath-taking journey which Gustave was proposing? Gustave was financially better prepared than Louis, so Louis naturally thought about finances. Also, there was his family. He bestirred himself immediately on their behalf, and did not leave until their wants were provided for during his projected absence.[86] He needed money himself. Turning to the director of the journal that employed him, he was wisely advised to seek aid from the ministers of the interior and public instruction on the grounds of a study project which might be of interest to them! The subject was to be a study of schools and welfare establishments in Italy.[87] Apparently nothing much was expected, and the stipend he received amounted to a reward to a young journalist the ministry wanted to keep on their side. Thus fortified he left for Italy – for Rome – and what Louis called, with some poetic license, his baptism.[88]

CHAPTER II

VEUILLOT'S CONVERSION TO CATHOLICISM

Louis Veuillot is remembered for his association with the Declaration of Papal Infallibility and his journalistic quarrels with liberals, Gallicans, and some of the most important bishops. He is likewise important for his role in the growth of journalism, specifically the lay Catholic press. But so far as he himself was concerned, the great event of his life was his conversion to Catholicism during Holy Week of 1838. Such an event poses a special problem for the historian because the "happening" is in the heart and mind of the person in question, offering less that is objective to study than most other events. Practically speaking we must rely on what Louis Veuillot himself says, though his brother's account was undoubtedly influenced by his observations of his brother as well as by what Louis wrote and said. To a degree all of his subsequent writings were influenced by his change in heart, and a number of his books, including the early *Les Pèlerinages de Suisse, Agnès de Lauvens, Le Saint Rosaire médité*, and *Pierre Saintive,* reflect his conversion. But *Rome et Lorette* tells the story intimately.

Rome et Lorette is an extraordinary book. It was not his first, but his third book, appearing about three years after his return from Rome, in 1841. In it he attempts to tell the reader the story of his inner struggles and of his great discovery of the Christian God, "this hope of all times, inexhaustible richness, this infallible aid." In this discovery is the "treasure of the poor, equality, order, fortune, joy." No *Charte* will ever give these things.[1] He would like to separate himself from his experiences for the benefit of the reader, but how to do this? Of necessity the book is highly personal, telling of his impulses, wishes, reserves, and doubts. But with the aid of three friends, Holy-Week atmosphere in Rome, and the intercession of a Jesuit priest he sees the light and enters into a new life. Letters which he wrote on this trip also are revealing as to his psychological changes, and give concrete evidence of his travels,[2] but *Rome et Lorette* is the principal and most interesting account. His own brother points out that properly speaking it is not really an autobiography of this part of his life, since it is an account of spiritual experience, and that in getting at the greater truth of his brother's feeling some of the information is not exactly correct.[3]

Within a week of their decision Louis and Gustave were off on their travels. In a day when there were as yet no French railroads, they headed for Marseilles. Although this part of the trip has no real significance in the life of Louis Veuillot, it is interesting that the man who was to write so much about himself has left no record at all, long as such a trip was, and through country he had never visited. His brother simply says only that they traveled almost without stopping.[4] At Marseilles they took ship for Civitavecchia, which they reached after several days of sailing. Louis was no sailor. Admitting that there had only been a light wind for eighteen hours, he wrote his brother, "I thought I would vomit my *orteils*,"[5] From Eugène's few words the ship could have been a steamer, but the voyage was no smoother for the voyagers.

Louis says he had bitter thoughts on leaving France. "This land of France is given over to folly. One does not know what to do with it anymore, what to love, what to believe, what to respect." At twenty-four he had no God, no king, no *dame*, and not even a country. "*La patrie* is a bazaar where everyone sells his cheatings at auction." His resentment of the *chevaliers d'industrie* was specific when he wrote these words in *Rome et Lorette*, but it was more the general void and the way it was being filled that he lamented.[6] Allowing for a number of things, particularly his evangelistic efforts at the time of writing this book about his religious experiences, it is certain that the young man was disturbed and ready for a change of some kind.

On March 15 his ship put into Civitavecchia. The papal customs officials checked his baggage – for "bad books." He had read thousands of books that would not have passed the test, and only a handful which would have. Whatever may have transpired between him and the official, he did some thinking. Well he might have. Liberty, at least of a sort, was to remain an important part of his scheme of life even after his passionate espousal of ultramontane Catholicism. On reflection he concluded that the pope governed neither "badly nor feebly" in taking measures to prevent the wrong sorts of ideas from being brought into his lands.[7] But although he did not develop the theme, the question was raised in his mind: how does one reconcile highly individualistic and original writing with the acceptance of absolute doctrine?

The weather was good. It had been cold and cheerless when he left France, but on reaching Italy things seemed different. "L'Italie est bien belle!" he declared to his brother after walking in its sun.[8] Good companions were awaiting in Rome also, and they went to Rome the evening of the first day they were in Italy. Adolphe and Élisabeth Féburier were the friends. Louis and Gustave had known Adolphe, a man of means and good social position, for some time, but Élisabeth, whom he had married since they last had seen him, they did not know. However, their close friendship and high regard for Adolphe were such that they were sure they would like Élisabeth.[9]

Louis Veuillot did. "Young and charming, and of a solid piety" was the way he described her a few days after meeting her and before he had reoriented his life.[10] In 1875 he said that three friends had brought him to the Church, including Gustave and Adolphe, but that this "pure and timid young woman whom I saw praying in the churches and who said nothing to me," was the one who principally convinced him.[11] Whatever may be said against Louis Veuillot in respect to his personal relationships, his regard for and relations with various women seem to have been on the highest plane, and he seems to have identified them with his ideals. When he went on this trip he still had a certain young woman of Périgueux on his mind. She must have been a good example of the countryside there, charming but without religion or depth. In any case, after knowing Mme Féburier and becoming himself a practicing Christian, he found it easy to forget this girl, who had without doubt already forgotten him.[12]

The first night in Rome, the four, who were all lodged in the same place, went on a foot tour of the forum and the area about it. Adolphe, an old habitué of Rome, and Gustave did most of the talking, and both had a lot to say about the popes, saints, and martyrs of the past. Louis Veuillot timidly (his word – it is hard to imagine him not at least holding his own in any conversation) said what he could about Horatius and Scipio. On this tour Louis was "guided" by the statue of Marcus Aurelius to the Church of the Ara Coeli. The Host is always exposed in some church in Rome, for twenty-four-hour periods, and at this time it was the turn of this church. His friends entered naturally enough, and there he saw a thousand lighted candles and all kinds of people kneeling and praying. He was scarcely less astonished at seeing all these strange things in Rome than his Gallic ancestors were, he wrote. His friends prayed, and not wishing to be left standing, he too knelt. He thought of his sisters whom he had left in France, and he prayed too. This, he said, was his first prayer. After leaving the church they went through the forum and the Arch of Titus on their way back home. Louis already was overwhelmed with these impressions.

He did not stay long in Rome. In four days' time all four of them departed for Naples, Vesuvius, Sorrento, Capri, Pompeii, and Herculaneum. Nevertheless, after four whole days in Rome Louis, with youthful enthusiasm was speaking in sweeping terms about life in Rome. He could not refrain from trying to share his discoveries and his plans for further travel, even beyond Italy, with his brother back in Périgueux (where he now edited the *Mémorial de la Dordogne*), and with his other friends there, to whom he shortly wrote from Naples. He found the living in Rome cheap. For thirty francs each the four had rented a "vast" apartment, covered from one end to the other with rugs, with a terrace outside and orange trees. The view, the air, the sun were wonderful. The food was comparable to the quarters. For fifty francs a month one could live like a prince. He told his brother that the time he was spending in Rome he would use to learn Italian, which would be so useful on his travels in the Levant. Also, he would study Roman history.[13] From many of his writings it is obvious that he must have applied himself to both, and his letters even before his conversion contain a surprising number of Italian words. But even before he left Rome for his Neapolitan tour he visited St. Peter's, where his friends confessed. He was overwhelmed with the architecture and decoration of St. Peter's, but the central point that it was all built over the bones of the man to whom it was said: "Tu es Petrus" made the greatest impression on him. All this and the communion of his friends proved a powerful combination. That very evening he prayed with them. He had his difficulties, and excused himself for them, but the three, especially Élisabeth, were already leading him into a new practice.[14]

Not only was he witnessing practicing Christians, he was also having discussions with them. Adolphe was a model of discretion, and Gustave apparently also. In Paris Gustave must have made Louis uneasy, especially with words to the effect that the kind of modifications in dogma demanded by Luther, Calvin, and others could not be accorded to him, Louis, either.[15] In Rome Louis was outnumbered three-to-one. Not only was one of the three especially persuasive by her whole example, the excitement of Rome itself was also a factor. As though all this were not enough, Louis was introduced to a venerable Jesuit, Father Roshaven, with whom he conversed shortly after his first exposure to Roman Christianity.[16] So, while Louis may have spoken to his brother and friends in Périgueux with his usual dash about his travels, present and projected, his mind was now becoming strongly reoriented.

In some ways, however, Louis was still the same. He wrote a lengthy letter to seven old friends of Périgueux, including his brother, which was published in *La Mémorial de la Dordogne*. He told this group of intelligent stay-at-homes, including officials and professors, all about Naples, Ischia, Capri, and the other beauties of the Tyrrhenian Coast. He was not shaving at this time, and described his new whiskers. He was going not to "see-Naples-and-die," but to return and tell all his old friends about it – and despite his preoccupations of the moment, he clearly had not forgotten the life of Périgueux. His principal pooh-pooh was for Vesuvius, which he erroneously declared to be dead, despite what all the Neapolitans would have him believe. A note which sounded like the later polemicist crept in when he said about the English: "... the ruins, the monuments, the flowers, the great paintings speak a language which everyone understands, excepting, of course, the English. My friends, the world would be beautiful if there were no Englishmen!"[17]

Despite the broadening experience of his travels, he wrote little about Italy south of Rome. In *Rome et Lorette* it is practically passed over. All that part of the trip was but an interlude in the real spiritual happenings to him. His friends wanted to come back to Rome for Holy Week, and so they did. There, aided by Father Roshaven, he was formally converted on Good Friday.[18] Hitherto he had been disposed to want to adjourn a decision about unconditional surrender to the church. Consideration of reservations remained a factor down until this time. He had his last discussions with his friends during Holy Week, and obviously they used the right kind of tact to allow the growing inclination within Louis' heart to mature. The reading aloud of some sermons of Bourdaloue by his friends, especially *Sur le retardement de la pénitence,* disposed him for the final step.[19] As a group they went to the headquarters of the Jesuit order in Rome to the sombre halls of the structure called the *Gesù.* Father Roshaven did the rest.[20] Louis Veuillot confessed. What he confessed only Father Roshaven ever knew, despite a section Veuillot wrote in *Rome et Lorette* called "Peccavi." Whether he was very specific about violations of the Law, or whether the emphasis was on his previous misconceptions of individual will and liberty, is a matter of confessional secret. Most likely he confessed fundamental attitudes. Indeed, his "confession" was acceptance of Catholic belief. Having confessed, he took communion on Good Friday in Santa Maria Maggiore,[21] thus beginning a new phase in his life. True, the full impact of his "baptism" may have been felt by Louis only after he resumed his travels, as his brother indicates,[22] and not until 12 June did he write his brother of his confession and that the Italy which Eugène had told him to study had made him a Catholic.[23]

Shortly after passing this turning point in his life Louis Veuillot resumed his travels, but not without a papal audience. With his friends he was presented to Gregory XVI sometime shortly after Easter. It is hard to think of Louis Veuillot and a pope – when that pope was not Pius IX – but Louis Veuillot became a militant Catholic eight years before the elevation of Pius IX. Led by a Jesuit priest, Father Vaure, Louis and his friends were brought before a "tall and vigorous old man,"[24] the pope himself. Gregory had been born in 1765, and in 1831 he had become pope. Now seventy-three years old, he seemed to the new convert to radiate benevolence. On his knees before the Holy

Father, together with his friends, he kissed the shoe of the pope. Gregory exchanged a few words with Veuillot and his friends, and his particular advice to Veuillot was to read the lives of the saints. Veuillot had not sought to meet important prelates or other notables in Rome, and as a result the papal image must have made an impression of a unique sort. In view of his later career and position, there was something significant about his not dealing with others of the hierarchy. The pope was Peter, and all the prelates were to obey him. Certainly this line of thought was well fixed in Louis Veuillot's mind from this point, long before Pius IX mounted the papal throne.[25]

Although Louis was converted in Rome, it was Italy as a whole that made an impression on him as he traveled and watched his friends.[26] He set out again on his tour of Italy not long after Holy Week and worked his way to the north. His letters show that he was in Tuscany in early May, and that by early June he had reached Venice. He tells about the places he visited in *Rome et Lorette*, but as Eugène points out, these accounts were no careful itinerary. *Rome et Lorette* ranked among his most popular writings, but the latter part of it was hastily assembled. He began it only in 1839, and it was not published until 1841. In many ways it is impressionistic, a description of his religious feelings as the full force of his acceptance of Roman Catholicism took hold of him. He mixed description of his travels south of Rome with those to the north, and his section or chapter headings varied between his newly formed religious thoughts and the places he visited. Two places loomed especially important to him on this *voyage renovateur*, Venice and Loretto, to which Father Roshaven had directed him. But while he was captivated by Venice,[27] Loretto became the highest point after Rome. Among the many unkind things that have been said of Veuillot and his faith was the observation that he was ready to believe that which was not worthy of belief, if such belief were required of him.[28] In the era when renewed impulses toward the veneration of the Virgin Mary were eventually capped by adoption of the Doctrine of the Immaculate Conception in 1854, much attention was fixed on a house in which the Virgin was said to have lived. The tradition was that this house had been miraculously transported in the thirteenth century to the Adriatic coast and then more recently to the town of Loretto, not far from Ancona. To the skeptical this account seemed particularly difficult to accept. Yet the discussion Veuillot gave of the matter was a remarkable example of salvaging the inspiring aspect of the story of the house's translation by angels on the wing by explaining the spiritual significance of the story.[29] In a way he was more sophisticated than the scoffers, and certainly he wrote about the question with literary skill.

During the last part of his travels in Italy Veuillot was alone. His friend Gustave Olivier who had ambitious plans for travel in the Near East, ran out of money and returned to Paris. The two parted at Ancona. It is interesting to note that a regiment of French troops were still in Ancona, who had been sent there in 1832 when uprisings had seemed possible. These men, who were recalled later in the year, were anticipating the role of the garrison that was to be in Rome, with only a short break, between 1849 and 1870. It is not known what impression this situation may have made on Louis Veuillot. The young writer now was on his own, spiritually. Olivier's influence had had as much effect as was possible and was now to recede. Gustave's change in plans caused some consternation for Louis,[30] but going alone at this point was best for the development of his independent thinking. Doubtlessly he could have profited by traveling to the Holy Land, Egypt, Constantinople, and so on, but for the full force of his sojourn in Italy it was probably best that his travels were terminated by his peaceful and meditative period in Switzerland. Féburier was ready to be his banker for the ambitious original schemes, but he did not accept the offer of this generous and well-to-do friend.[31] Amusingly, however, Louis did run short of money before his return to Paris and wrote to none other than Gustave Olivier not much later than a month after Gustave had left him appealing for the sending *tout de suite* of 150 francs so that he would be able to return to Paris![32] He must have been very low indeed in cash at hand to have felt such urgency, because his daily expenses in Switzerland were very small.

Not until 28 June 1838 had Veuillot reached Switzerland. Except for special incidents it is remarkable how little he tells of the details of his travels. Also quite striking is the way in which he brings out in his letters and his later writings the history and the special characteristics of places that tie in with his ideas. He saw things very subjectively. After reading guidebooks and historical accounts of great events he seemed to be seeing the immediate aftermath of all these past events as he would enter the various towns on his travels. No doubt such imaginative perception has more meaning both to travelers and to readers than the objective approach. His eye took in things that were associated with events of the Middle Ages and of the Reformation. The accounts that he later sold by the tens of thousands were vivid. They were amplified by the descriptions of the buildings and objects which were seen by his eyes, but much of the fire of his descriptions came from his feelings, which resulted from a curious blend of religious fervor and geographic and historical information. Thus attuned, through towns of northern Italy he made his way to the "Protestant Rome," Geneva.

Veuillot's impression of Geneva was conditioned by his passion for Rome. Popular songs about coming back to Rome are flat compared to Veuillot's words *Non, je ne te quitterai pas sans te saluer de la voix et du cœur, ville immortelle ou mon âme a tant vécu*![33] No such words did he have for Geneva. The weather on his arrival was fine, but what was going on in this perverse city, in which was standing a bronze statue to Jean-Jacques Rousseau? A fête in honor of the philosophe was in progress! What a contrast to the observance of Corpus-Christi Day that he had just seen in Ancona! What a heretical people! That such things were to be encountered in the city of Calvin, however, surprised him not at all.[34] His first impressions of Geneva appear to have lasted throughout his life. After all, the world is full of contrasts, and only by contrasting things can their qualities really be differentiated.

From Geneva Veuillot went on to Lausanne, which he confessed was "smiling, pretty, and as picturesque as any city or countryside in the world." The Bishop of Lausanne and of Geneva had been obliged by the protestants at an earlier date to take up residence in Freiburg, and since that time, in Veuillot's estimation, Lausanne had a great church, and even a religion, but had no God.[35] Nevertheless, he found much of interest in Lausanne. One of the legends about Lausanne gave him occasion to demonstrate what might be regarded as a "modern" attitude toward traditions on the fringe of the church. The story was that Pilate had been condemned to wander the earth in constant torment, the earth itself having refused to permit him to be buried in it. Charlemagne, according to the legend, had ordered that he be banished for some reason to Lausanne, but of course he was not wanted there. At length he had gone to the greatest height overlooking the lake beneath the city and fallen into the waters, from which ever afterwards once a year he emerged in the dress of a magistrate, bringing death to anyone who might be so unfortunate as to see him. Stoutly Veuillot maintained that this sort of tale persisted in spite of the church, and that superstition should never be associated with the church.[36] But although he had already become so defensive about the church that he felt he should say something about matters like this, he obviously enjoyed recounting the romantic tale.

He traveled extensively in Switzerland, visiting Basle, Interlaken, Zurich, Neufchâtel, Einsiedln, the cantons of Schwyz, Uri, and Unterwalden, and a variety of other places in which he found various kinds of significance. In general he derived inspiration from those scenes associated with Catholicism, and uniformly reacted against the modern secularism to be observed where Calvinism had prevailed. He did not hesitate to use a guide in purely German-speaking areas, and when he went as a pilgrim on foot to Notre Dame-des-Ermites he was led by a young seminarian whom he described as *déprotestantisé.*[37] The use of such a word speaks loudly about the religious conflict of the area, particularly as his eye saw its sharpness and significance. He had never been in a protestant land before, though his own had been severely de-Catholicized, and after his own recent religious experiences in Rome there must have seemed to him something dramatic about being with a *déprotestantisé* seminarian in a Catholic shrine with protestant strongholds all about!

Much of July Veuillot spent at Freiburg in a Jesuit establishment. This retreat was an important part of his trip. Here, as elsewhere on his travels, he read about the lives of the saints as the pope had told him to do.[38] The countryside was a great change from Paris. Had Gustave Olivier not been a religious person, he might have counseled Louis from the first to take a trip to some retreat in Switzerland, and this he might have done with great profit to his nerves. At last he was having a peaceful change of air in a land were cowbells and cheesemakers were never far away.[39] But he thought intensely during this period about his new direction in life and what he should do in order to follow it. The director of the Jesuit community was a Father Geoffroy, and he had great influence on Veuillot as he sought to decide what to do.

Louis Veuillot had observed his friend Gustave Olivier. He had led him to Rome and his Christian reorientation, but he had returned to Paris and to journalism. Louis was sick of journalism and dreaded going back to the very life from which he had recently run away. But what else was he to do? He worried about his family, about both helping his parents and providing for his sisters. Nevertheless, he felt ready to go into the church. He dressed himself according to the rule of St. Ignatius, and asked Father Geoffroy what he should do next. If he did not actually go into the church, he asked, would Father Geoffroy tell him whether he should marry. Clearly he seemed ready to change his life radically if he were so directed. Father Geoffroy must have been a practical man. Let us suppose that Louis Veuillot had gone into the church. Would he have been less combative? Would he have avoided bringing down the wrath of many on the Catholic church? Would he have shown the Christian gentleness that any clergyman should be expected to show at all times? Perhaps. But then it is also very possible that as monk or priest he would have wielded the pen in much the same way as he did as layman. Father Geoffroy gave him the wise advice to go back to Paris to his family.[40] According to Eugène, Father Geoffroy knew Louis better than Louis knew himself.[41] and Louis was eager to accept his advice. Father Geoffroy gave no specific advice about what Louis should do by way of a career after his return, not did he give him explicit advice about marrying. Deep down in his heart Louis must have wanted to go back to the excitement of Paris, even while directing his life to a new purpose. Perhaps Louis Veuillot might be expected to have radically changed his personal ways, like Vicomte, later Father, Foucauld,[42] but pronounced personalities like Louis Veuillot's are much more apt to keep their characteristics, even when working for new ends, after religious conversion. Whether Louis was relieved or not with Father Geoffroy's advice, after having promised he would follow it, there is no way of knowing. But if Veuillot had a confirmation of his intense religious dedication while at Freiburg, he was also reconfirmed there as a layman.

Veuillot's letters from Switzerland, like those he wrote from Italy, were a curious mélange of religious intensity and interests which, although very natural, were on quite another plane. Just before leaving Italy he had written a very nondisturbing letter to his parents, telling calmly of his new outlook, and speaking in a very simple way about his whole trip.[43] His letters from Switzerland, at least those that have survived, were solely to Gustave Olivier and his brother. These letters are full of concern for his family. Much of this was directed to Gustave, who, unlike the brother, who was in Périgueux, was in Paris where he could do something for the Veuillots and talk to them. But Louis had not forgotten the vicissitudes of provincial journalism. He had advice for Eugène, such as telling him to turn to Bugeaud if he needed money. And he enjoyed talking about his experiences. He wanted Gustave to know what a long hike did to one's legs, how hungry he felt when he could find only a few wild berries on the way, and the peculiar ways of Swiss laundresses.[44] He observed many moving and curious things about the religious life of Switzerland, but the new man still saw some of the things the unconverted man had been wont to notice. *Les anglais* were already regular tourists in Switzerland, and his wit spent no little time in finding the right words to ridicule what he regarded as their attitudes of superiority masking empty superficiality.[45] Despite the change of heart, he was still the same man. French politics, which had been the preoccupation of his early years in journalism, and which remained important to him in his subsequent years as a Christian writer, seemed to have receded into the background of his mind as he traveled through Italy and Switzerland, but bitterness concerning it still characterized his outlook. One curious thing he observed in Switzerland brought out this attitude. Near Vevey lived the family of Naundorff, a member of which was one of the many individuals who clamed to be Louis XVII. Veuillot fully acquainted himself with the remarkable story this man put forth and recounted it at length in the first book he was ever to write.[46] The fact that some old servants recognized Naundorff as Louis-Charles, Duc de Normandie, the Dauphin, was indeed noteworthy, as well as the way in which the princes of France pointedly ignored him. Because his existence was a challenge to the legitimacy of the restored dynasty of France, Naundorff had received attention both in France and in Europe as a whole. His case obviously interested Louis Veuillot as a curiosity. Nevertheless, Veuillot declared: "Whether he be Naundorff or Louis XVII, I scarcely care. One pretender more or less to the throne of France is nothing to us. If Naundorff has his partisans, I do not have the desire to destroy their convictions. I say only that falsehood is king of this world, and that never has its dominion been better established. It treats us despotically. It stops at nothing, and we all suffer."[47] In speaking thus Veuillot was not really commenting on the claims of this unusual pretender. He was not attacking one or both of the dynasties under which he had lived. He was criticizing the whole world of the post-Revolutionary period in which the Christian church was being submerged by various secular forces that had come to the fore. The new militant Christian had at first insisted he was not going back into journalism, but this observation, written shortly after his return from Switzerland, certainly indicated that he was again ready to wield the pen.

Louis Veuillot returned to Paris in early August and took up his lodging on thy Rue de Lille. His sisters had been living in a pension which he did not like, and he made other arrangements for them.[48] So far as family matters were concerned he was glad to be back in Paris. Immediately he set himself about the writing of *Pèlerinages de Suisse*, but just as immediately he contacted old friends to tell them of his new outlook. He wrote to some, but many were right there in Paris. Their reactions were varied. His best friends were not themselves practicing Catholics, but they were disposed to be sympathetic. These included Émile Lafon, Eloi Mallac, Émile Perrin, Lemachois, and Debon. Louis's conversion made an impression on them, and, particularly in the case of Lafon, his enthusiasm influenced them in the direction of the Catholic church. Other friends, not so close, like Toussenel, listened with interest, but also tried to induce Veuillot to look on life as they did. Toussenel, listened with interest, but also tried to induce Veuillot to look on life as they did. Toussenel was inclined toward phalansterianism. Henri de Latouche listened unsympathetically. Worse than the response of this despairing soul was the mocking humor of Louis' old friend Romieu, the préfet in Périgueux. Although much later Romieu changed, and indicated he himself wanted to die a Christian, Veuillot broke with him after their correspondence in 1838.[49]

He wrote to various old friends in Périgueux, including Albert de Calvimont, who was already oriented in the direction of the church, and Armand d'Hautefort, to whom he announced: "My life has become very humble and modest; I have completely renounced the journals." In the same vein he declared: "The main burden which has been lifted from my heart is ambition."[50] He also wrote in similar tone to other people, including several women acquaintances. One woman had said to his family that she thought his conversion would be damaging to his future. He wrote to her that he was indeed a Catholic and that he was happy. Love and fear of God transcended all.[51] From the start he was not shy about discussing his faith. He also wrote the mother of the girl whom he had thought about marrying in Périgueux. Apparently he must have found this lady more intelligent than her daughter. But for a young man to write such a person about the need to suffer in order to have a better chance of salvation was most unusual to say the least.[52]

Of course Louis wrote a great deal to his brother. While still in Italy he said: "I do not ask that you become converted, although naturally I desire it very much, because, having committed fewer sins, you will have less to suffer; but I ask you to think some time about what I am saying to you; to give some attention and study to these ideas; to read the Gospels. . . ." He told him that the Christian seeks perfection.[53] His pressures brought results. Eugène promptly set about emulating the brother he had always admired, and in due course because an important figure in the movement led by Louis Veuillot. If Eugène had written all the books and editorials he eventually produced during his life, without Louis ever having lived, he would have been a notable figure.[54] But of course it is highly unlikely he would ever have done any of these things if he had not been following the lead of Louis. Eugène's son François was also not without importance in French clerical circles, and François' son Pierre became archbishop of Paris in 1966. Had the career of Louis Veuillot ended before he had done much more than launch Eugène on his course, it would not have been without significance.

Louis also wrote to his new friends in the clergy. To the father superior of the seminary in Freiburg he described the Catholic movement in Paris. He made it sound like a vital movement. He told of his plans, especially the writing of his first book, *Les Pèlerinages de Suisse.*[55] To Father Roshaven, who had brought him to the altar rail, he said: "I am now very happy being a Christian here, and quite tranquil although in the middle of Paris. Having had the good fortune of reforming my heart, I have been able to reform my life, something I had often tried in vain to do, and I feel happier each day in the absence of all that I had previously thought would make me happy." Most strikingly he declared, "Ambition is the principal trash (*fumier* was his word) which the Good Lord has taken off my heart."[56]

It was natural enough for him, a born extrovert, to be writing letters and communicating with his friends about his new-found religion, but his immediate and concerted efforts in the writing of his frist book were a stronger testimony to the intensity of his feelings. He had a number of projects in mind, and he devoted much thought to them before they took shape, but nevertheless *Les Pèlerinages des Suisse* came into being with a minimum of delay. Between his return to Paris in early August and the start of October he wrote a book of not far from 250 pages. He signed the introduction on 15 October, the Day of St. Theresa, thus beginning his custom of referring always to the church calendar. Apparently the public was ready for such a book, since a new publishing house, Canuet,[57] had it on the market by February, and this unknown young author, who had turned twenty-five just before finishing the book became an instant success.[58] It would be hard to ascertain how many copies were sold, but by 1844, when he sold the rights to another house in order to be able to provide as much as he could for the *dot* for his sister Annette's marriage, four editions had been made. The second house eventually sold nearly two hundred thousand copies of *Rome et Lorette*, and while *Les Pèlerinages de Suisse* may not have been quite so notable a success for them, it too was very popular.[59] Few writers of any kind of literature have started with more enthusiastic initial reception – and Louis Veuillot continued at this pace of popularity through much of his career. In no way should one minimize the great importance of his role of leadership as editor-in-chief of *L'Univers* but with good reason Louis Veuillot called himself not editor but writer, *écrivain,* on his passports. No matter how important he became as editor, the editor did not overshadow the author.

The book can be described, but it has to be read for one to understand how it could have had the appeal it had. It is arbitrarily broken into four books, and has the effect of an anecdotal travel book. The author takes the reader from place to place in Switzerland, which he allows is well enough known as a country. But as he goes he gives short sketches of the parts of history he wishes to bring forth as background for the religious struggle that looms as so fundamental to him. He had a touch in his tale-telling that is masterful. The author is in dead earnest, but at the same time he selects to recount happenings which either arouse the emotions or otherwise amuse. Louis Veuillot regarded himself as a writer in the classical style.[60] Much of his study of Latin came as an adult, and the political and religious attitudes of many of the romantic authors offended him. But the way in which he looked with religious enthusiasm back on the medieval period and excited the emotions of the reader in so doing surely suggests the romantic approach. At any rate, he had a large and excited audience which would have been the envy of many a romantic author.

The most striking lines in *Les Pèlerinages de Suisse* occur in the fourth book in a section entitled, *Du droit des gens en matière de religion*, in which the convert of a few months discusses heresy. "Pestilence, war, and famine are reparable, and of short duration, but heresy has its effects for centuries, and, even worse, destroys souls forever." It is the duty of princes to punish crimes, especially heresy, but various princes have been remiss in their duty. "God will judge these princes, and we hope he will show them mercy. (Alas! We hope that one day He will pardon all, even Luther, even Judas, eternally accursed!) But it is the duty of history to say that they carried out their mission badly, that they were perifidious or negligent leaders. They allowed the greatest social crime to be committed of which man is capable. It would be better to tolerate in the bosom of a nation poisoners and murderers, better to bring war, pestilence, and famine than to let heresy enter." Despite what seemed altogether clear to Louis Veuillot, intelligent people, including Catholics, complained that the Catholic church was responsible for blood having been shed about heresy, and that the church had caused the death of John Huss. "For my part," declared Veuillot, "I will frankly and clearly say, before explaining my whole thought: If anything is to be regretted in all this, it is that John Huss was not burned sooner, and that Luther was not likewise burned." The heresy of Huss made three hundred thousand men perish, and that of Luther, according to Veuillot, millions, with his victims continuing to the present.[61] Veuillot continued his argument powerfully, but these opening lines attracted great attention, and followed him through his life.

Various writers of a totally different outlook, such as Émile de Girardin in *La Presse* and Adolphe Géroult in *La République,* took him to task for his words. Curiously many of these attacks occurred long after the appearance of *Les Pèlerinages de Suisse* in February of 1839. Perhaps the most important lay figure to attack Louis Veuillot on this point was that son of an English protestant minister, William Gladstone.

From Veuillot's point of view the criticism of Msgr. Sibour, Archbishop of Paris, which was brought forth in 1851, was of especially great importance as his troubles of that era with the episcopacy developed.[62] Veuillot could scarcely have been more irritating to his bishop when in 1851 he not only refused to disavow these words which, he said, were being attacked by "red philanthropists," but, ever conscious of the best use of the French language, declared: "Literarily this phrase concerning John Huss could be better turned, but since I have the good fortune not to be among those who make much over their language, I will in no way disown it. I stand by it since it is rejected, and I am not insensible to the pleasure of finding myself faithful to my opinions. That which I wrote in 1838 I still think."[63] What a rejoinder for a Catholic layman to fling at his own bishop! But these words had come by then to be as well known as any that he was ever to write, and to renounce them would have been tantamount to renouncing his whole general stance. These words which he had written as summer turned to fall in 1838 expressed the intensity of his partisanship in the religious struggle he saw in Switzerland. And before very many years the days of the Sonderbund, in the mid-forties, showed that some of the intensity of the sixteenth century still existed in this land thought by many to be so peaceful. Louis Veuillot felt all the charm of Switzerland, but he looked upon it as a zone of combat, with heresy as the root of the warfare.

During 1839 he continued to write books inspired by his recent experiences, but he wrote at a slower rate now than he had when writing *Les Pèlerinages de Suisse*. He wrote his first novel and published his first poetry. The novel was a short one, and its form was essentially that of a collection of letters and journals of the characters he invented. *Pierre Saintive* (Saint-Yves) was a highly moral story, influenced by Veuillot's personal experiences, but not autobiographical. The two main characters in it were Saintive and Sourzac, who may be regarded as Veuillot before and after his conversion. The atmosphere of the society in which these people were moving was that of Périgueux. Saintive (the young Marquis de Saint-Yves in disguise) is given good guidance by his friend Sourzac, and he turns from the worldly Mlle Sylvie d'Adronne, without, however, marrying the pious Thérèse Lacroix, as might have been expected by the usual audiences of novels. But there was at this time a great demand for decent novels, especially of the sort that young girls might read without blushing, and when the publishing house of Olivier Fulgence brought the book out in May of 1840, it found an instant audience. It went through many editions, both of this publishing house and its successor, Mame, in 1845. The total number of copies was not quite so many as *Les Pèlerinages de Suisse*, but it is surprising how successful the young author was in turning from the kind of writing he had just done to the popular novel. Years later, in the summer of 1861, while visiting a high-born friend of a later period in his life, the Marquise de Champagné, he reread this novel. The thoughts at the heart of the story were still so close to his feelings that he tells us he shed tears. Nevertheless, some of the style did not please him at this later reading.[64] But a man who can move even himself, a fifth of a century later, obviously had the power to move those readers who were looking for a fresh type of religiously oriented story.

During this same general period soon after his conversion, he wrote a collection of prayers and poems called *Le Saint Rosaire médité.* Divided into five joyous, five sad, and five glorious mysteries, and ostensibly for devotional use, this work carried the formal approbation of Denis Affre, the Archbishop (elect) of Paris. Pious though it was intended to be, its principal merit was literary, and many of the devout who opened it may have felt that the concentration of the author was on the literary effects more than the religious content. Nevertheless his brother believed, even years later when Louis quarreled with Montalembert and Lacordaire, that the words he wrote in 1839-1840 were in his heart: "O, all you whom I have offended, pardon me, I repent! All you who have hated me, I pray for you, I feel that I love you; pray for me!"[65]

Louis Veuillot was able to write this type of literature in an easy frame of mind, indifferent to its eventual success, because of the financial security he came to have from an assured political appointment that required very little effort. He was no longer attracted, as we have seen, by the press in general. *L'Ami de la Religion* left him cold. *La Gazette* and *La Quotidienne* were more legitimist than Catholic, and he did not want to get into political journalism again. He had debts in 1838 amounting to 5000 francs, but a way to pay these now opened in the following manner.[66] A custom of the day was the practice of important political figures having the power to appoint young men as their attachés with practically no duties. A steady salary would go to these men, although their patrons might need them only on occasion. Guizot, the minister of the interior who dominated the cabinet through the 1830's had long recognized the talents of Louis Veuillot. As time went on the interests of this important protestant and those of the fiery new Catholic happened to coincide, especially in the matter of free schools, each fearing that his religion would be overwhelmed by secularism. Guizot had appreciated the strength of Veuillot's pen in Périgueux and wished to keep it at his service. He offered Veuillot the post of *rédacteur expéditionnaire* in the ministry of the interior, and Louis Veuillot accepted this post in April of 1839, drawing a salary of 2,400 francs. At the end of the year 1839 he was made *sous-chef du 3e bureau du secrétariat général*, with a raise to 2,700 francs.[67] Later, in January, 1841 he was transferred to the post of *sous-chef du bureau des monuments historiques*, which remained his official position until the end of 1844, when he gave up the post.

One might criticize Veuillot for drawing a generous salary for practically no work, except for the fact that giving this type of post was common accepted practice in the French government at the time. Technically, the big advantage of the kind of appointment he received was that the office-holder did not have to sign the *feuille de présence* which other functionaries had to sign in order to draw their pay.[68] It would be hard to discover what Veuillot thought about the post. Late in life, at a time when he was inclined to speak of the sacrifices he had made, he spoke of opportunities he had had for advancement in the government.[69] That he really had renounced the political ambitions he had had when coming to Paris from the provinces there can be little doubt. He now had his great purpose, and that was to devote himself as a militant lay literary man to fighting what he conceived to be the battle of the church against secular and heretical forces. He greatly admired the Jesuits. Perhaps he shared the feeling which enemies of the Jesuits have maintained characterized them: that if the end be right, one ought not to have overly many scruples about the means. The ironic point about the salary he was receiving in return for practically no service was that this benefit came from the patronage of an outstanding protestant leader! One of the curious threads in Veuillot's life is the longstanding and friendly relations he had with Guizot, the beginning of whose active religious life as a protestant was also in 1838.[70] In any case the pen of Veuillot was something no statesman would wish directed against himself, and, moreover, the future coincidental interests of Veuillot and Guizot proved to be real.

Veuillot's life had much sadness in it, and one of the first sad events was the death of his father. Despite his devotion to his own career, he was very much a family man, and already he had been worried about providing for the members of his family. His father had had a hard life. Although he had once been a strong man, a fever, at first neglected, carried him off after a few days, and he died on 15 March 1839. For the heavy work he had done he had received only a fraction of the pay Louis shortly began to collect for his honorary post. The son and father were probably as close in affection as two such very different men could be, but understanding by the father for the son could not have been very great. The father's way of addressing the son as "Veuillot" would suggest something rather blunt about him.[71] The son, when converted, tried to talk to his father about becoming a practicing Catholic, but the attempt only troubled the simple older man, who, despite the lack of church affiliation, never had become antichurch in his attitude. He adjourned his son's attempts until, on his deathbed, he did see a priest

Louis had brought. According to Louis, he confessed and received extreme unction.[72] While Louis was in Italy he had been touched by a death in Foligno, and when he later wrote *Rome et Lorette* he was no doubt influenced in its description by the death of his own father.[73] His mother, forty-eight in 1839, subsequently remarried. She lived until 1863. He maintained filial attitudes toward her, but Louis Veuillot had felt an especially significant bond with his father. Although he never expressed any resentment against the upper classes, and seems even to have gravitated to Catholic representatives of the old families, he never forgot his humble peasant origins and that he was himself a man of the people. Some of the bluntness of the people always remained with him. His response to Henri de Pène in which he contrasted their origins was significant.[74] It had been impressed upon Louis Veuillot that Christian life finds meaning in death, and though there is no way to show that his desire to rescue ignorant humble people from the robot march of secularism was closely related in his mind with the image of his overworked father, already lying on his deathbed in his first bond with the church, the death of his father probably was an intangible influence in his life.

CHAPTER III

THE CATHOLIC JOURNALIST AND THE JULY MONARCHY

One of the phenomena of the nineteenth century indeed was the blossoming of journalism. As journals representing the whole spectrum of opinion in France sprang up during the July Monarchy, naturally enough among them a Catholic press came into being.[1] In the vanguard of the movement already opened by the *Mémorial catholique* was the paper founded by the priest Félicité Lamennais, *L'Avenir*, which, during its brief existence, between its founding in 1830 after the Revolution of 1830 and its suspension in 1831, certainly lived up to its name, both with regard to social questions and to independence from the hierarchy.[2] Lamennais may be regarded as the most notable influence in nineteenth-century French Catholicism, but he was ahead of his time in several matters and apparently believed that a Catholic paper could go independently on its own way without necessarily reflecting the desires of the hierarchy. Although some of his ideas were actually to be proclaimed a half century later by Leo XIII, because of disputes over them, he became estranged from the church. Nevertheless, he was a Catholic pioneer both in social matters and in pointing the way for a lay Catholic press.

The saintly Gregory XVI was not fully apprized of the division of French Catholics between the traditional Gallicans and the new brand of ultramontanism, supporters of centralized power for the papacy, a split which became apparent when *L'Avenir* was attacked by the Gallican episcopacy. Lamennais, at the suggestion of the renowned preacher Lacordaire, and with the adhesion of Comte Charles de Montalembert, set off for Rome in 1831 in the company of these two eventual pillars of liberal Catholicism with the purpose of gaining papal support. The pope, however, not only gave no encouragement to them but issued the encyclical *Mirari vos* the next year, which not only ended *L'Avenir* but began the estrangement of Lamennais. For a decade thereafter the Catholic press was to be relatively unexciting.

With the demise of *L'Avenir* the Catholic press largely consisted of a Gallican and royal-oriented journal, *L'Ami de la Religion*, and a sheet largely read by priests, the *Journal des villes et campagnes*. For those who wanted to assert the new ultramontanism and to concentrate on religious issues there was little here either for the priest or for the layman. The prime mover behind the establishment in 1833 of *L'Univers religieux, politique, scientifique et littéraire* was E.-J. Bailly, who had already attempted to achieve his purpose with the *Tribune Catholique*, which had failed. The first number of *L'Univers* appeared on 3 November 1833, bearing the devise, *Unité dans les choses certaines, liberté dans les douteuses, charité, vérité, impartialité dans toutes*. For most of the first decade of its existence this motto was suitable enough, but after the domination of Louis Veuillot began, those *choses certaines* tended to eclipse some of the other words. The journal was aimed "as much to people of the world, to thinking youth and men of good faith of all opinions, as to members of the French and foreign Catholic clergy." This little sheet of 27cm X 37cm and three columns a page had for its editor a priest, Father Migne, who designated himself "founder-director." He had been born in the Orleanais and served as a curé in the Gatinais, the country from which Louis Veuillot came.[4] The Abbé Migne was an abrupt and cross person with a violent temper. On one occasion when departing from his office late at night he heard two vulgar individuals yell "couac, couac!" at him. He promptly worked them over with an umbrella to show them that priests were people with whom liberties should not be taken.[5] His disposition was not pleasing to Bailly, Montalembert, or Melchior Du Lac, another clergyman, who was the mainstay of the regular force of *L'Univers*. Consequently Father Migne remained in direction of the journal barely three years. Nevertheless, his activity was of the greatest importance in stimulating the development of the Catholic press.

That *L'Univers* intended to be a major force in the future was suggested by the principal article in its first number which was a piece written by the Abbé Gerbet, an able follower of Lamennais, entitled "La Toussaint. – Vision." The article was apocalyptical in style and content. In it appeared Saint Denis, Saint Germain l'Auxerrois, and Sainte Geneviève. At the end came the announcement that France, born Christian, would become Christian again.[6] Obviously something new in the way of programs had been added to French journalism. Despite the startling nature of the journal's début, it did not venture significantly into politics during its early years. "Catholic before all," it was essentially friendly with regard to the régime. Its editors, collaborators, and special contributers (who included Frédéric Ozanam), were writers of a high order, and it attracted considerable attention. Its regular subscribers, however, were very few in number, and finances constituted its major problem. With this new journal Louis Veuillot became associated by degrees not long after his conversion.

Curiously, the first connection of Louis Veuillot with *L'Univers* was not as a result of a religious issue. Veuillot had already come to know and like *L'Univers* when he read in its columns an article hostile to Marshal Bugeaud. This article in *L'Univers* was hardly of a political nature at all, since Bugeaud seemed to be an open target for many journals in France. The subject of this particular attack was a duel of the Marshal's in which he had killed a deputy in the Bois du Boulogne. Although Veuillot and Bugeaud were very different kinds of men, and the Marshal certainly was not religious, Veuillot had come to admire the great soldier and administrator. He understood the circumstances in which the Marshal had killed a republican. He himself had fought duels, and, to be sure, was thought by some to have an inclination toward dueling. Also, he was under the influence of Guizot and the ministry. Accordingly he wrote a letter to the journal. He put the matter on Christian grounds, affirming without any reticence at the start that both the journal and he himself were Christians, and that in this spirit they would not want to see an injustice done to a great man, who by unhappy circumstances had become involved in this catastrophic duel.[7] While the seeking of the Christian ground had a touch of the Veuillot line, the article might well have been written by any of a large number of administration supporters, or by some other personal friend of Bugeaud. The significance of this letter lay simply in the fact that hitherto Veuillot had not been known to *L'Univers* or its readers, and now the ice was broken.

After nearly seven months he wrote his first article for *L'Univers* as a contributor. A particularly important convent in Paris was the Couvent des Oiseaux, which for many years had educated girls, including many from the best social circles. Shortly after his return from Rome and Switzerland Veuillot had visited the convent and had talked with the mother superior, who was much interested in his determination to fight the good fight for the Catholic church. The Reverend Mother Sophie, a notable figure at the convent since 1819, encouraged him to take his sisters from the pensions where they lived and to send them to the Couvent des Oiseaux.[8] He became much interested in the convent and the work that was taking place at it. At length a new chapel was completed on 27 May 1839, the dedication of which he described in an article dated 16 June. This article was published by *L'Univers* and marked the beginning of his literary collaboration. In addition to showing considerable knowledge about architecture and commenting on the importance of this sort of educational establishment, he also took the occasion to describe briefly some of the work of his friend Lafon, the painter. The publication of this article marked the beginning of his important association with the Abbé Dreux-Brézé, then a vicar-general of the archbishop of Paris and later bishop of Moulins.[9] The piece was significant, therefore, for reasons beyond any literary merit demonstrated, as his debut before the audience which would be his for four decades.

In 1839 the first volume of Amédée Gabourd's lengthy *Histoire de France* appeared and it was reviewed on 4 December by Louis Veuillot as his next contribution. Gabourd had been a republican editor in Grenoble, and very much an enemy of the "parti-prêtre," when he suddenly had had a change in heart, becoming a supporter of what soon would be known as clericalism, and of the monarchy. His work greatly pleased Veuillot, who showed special zeal in reviewing it. Veuillot was anything but a scientific historian, but history fascinated him. It was something to be used to support his theory that Christianity was the foundation of civilization; the work of Gabourd did just this. Although the Calvinist Sismondi had with ill-will called France a "monarchy formed by bishops," Veuillot invoked the same idea "with a more inspired heart."[10] The whole idea that French civilization and French history were inextricably bound up with the church greatly appealed to Veuillot, and this theme, already developing in his thinking, seems to have been developed by the stimulation of the work by Gabourd. References to Clovis and his successors were to characterize the editorials of the future editor-in-chief, and into this sort of writing he plunged with gusto in the Gabourd review article. He even liked the paper on which the book was printed!

Not until the start of 1840 did Louis Veuillot publish anything else in *L'Univers*, but by that time he had plenty of interesting material for its readers. An intriguing subject in French history is the origin and growth of the *parti catholique*.[11] The party is rather elusive as to origins, and throughout its existence, which was, roughly speaking, from the mid-part of the July Monarchy until early in the Second Empire, it had to struggle from being overwhelmed by the legitimists and their heavy emphasis on what soon came to be called clericalism. In a way these people who were "Catholic before all" did not exactly make up a "parti-prêtre," the term in common usage in the 1840's, because the composition of the group was heavily lay, and with a lay orientation. In Paris the more intellectual and artistic of these Catholic laymen met in what almost amounted to salons. These meetings were not dominated by the auspices of prominent ladies, or anyone else in particular, but neither were they clubs in the more usual sense of the word. Catholics gathered at different places to talk. Political action was not the purpose of these meetings, and the political outlooks of the people who attended them were widely different. All the participants, however, shared a common Catholic Christian religious bond, and with this as the basis of their union people of differing interests and backgrounds disseminated their ideas in a sympathetic atmosphere. What Louis Veuillot heard here, and what he was prompted to say, became the basis for a series of articles in *L'Univers* called "Propos divers" that appeared from February through June of 1840, and which was again revived in the second half of 1842.[12]

For the most part the people who attended these Catholic assemblages for discussion were not particularly well known, though many of them had solid accomplishments and knowledge about some matter of interest. Among the better known attenders were Henry and Charles de Riancey, Amédée Gabourd, Edmond de Cazalès, and Eugène Boré. Édouard Dumont, a good Catholic although a professor in the university, was one of the group, and there were others in strictly intellectual posts. The clergy was not unrepresented, and even the somewhat retiring Melchior Du Lac attended at times. In such company "the militant ultramontane school, which sought to disengage itself from the political parties, strengthened itself."[13] Many of the people had special areas in which they had traveled, or about which they had studied, and the ferment of discussion was as active as any established salon could hope to achieve. As reported in "Propos divers" the subjects discussed ranged over a wide field of literature, the theater, history, belief, social questions, charity, education, art, the need for an Institut Catholique. Almost anything that might in any way be relevant to Christianity was fair picking, and the relationship of these broad subjects was frequently not associated in so many words to the fundamental purpose of the assemblages. What made it all have special interest to the readers of *L'Univers* was the way in which the articles Louis Veuillot wrote under the heading "Propos divers" seemed to sound like the actual conversations at those gatherings. Complete with quotation marks words were coming from the mouths of people whose identity might easily be guessed. Apparently he did not cause any tendency toward reticence on the part of the other discussants, and "Propos divers" not only was a big success but also a good example of a felicitous way of keeping inspired conversation lively even after reduced to black and white.

At this very time Louis Veuillot developed a large correspondence as *Les Pèlerinages de Suisse* was giving him an international reputation. Some of the people with whom he began to correspond in 1840, were the Abbé Morisseau, Canon of Tours, and Baron Prosper Guerrier de Dumast, a literary man who helped him in the preparation of some of his early works. The most interesting and significant of his exchanges of letters, however, was with Comte O'Mahony. This intransigeant legitimist, albeit fundamentally Catholic, was a good example of the royalism which threatened to engulf the Catholic movement. At an early date Louis Veuillot's inclination towards traditional monarchy can be seen, but, "Catholic before all," he was willing to accept any of a wide variety of governments if only Catholicism were truly the basis. To suggest that he was "liberal," even in this respect, would be to go counter to the prevailing interpretations of Louis Veuillot, but perhaps "liberal" is as good a word as "opportunistic," which would probably be more acceptable to most interpreters of nineteenth-century French Catholicism. In any case, while protestant journals in Switzerland ignored the appearance of *Les Pèlerinages de Suisse*, Comte O'Mahony, director of the *Invariable* of Freiburg, wrote two articles praising the work.[14] He also got in touch by mail with its author. Apparently knowing something of Veuillot's earlier and current associations, he begged him to free himself from all the liberals about him and to stand "au pied d'une crois fleurdelysée."[15] The all-out legitimist, with his preference for a certain type of cross, thus presented Veuillot with something of a challenge. On April 14, 1840 he answered the Comte O'Mahony:

> Alas, yes, I was liberal, I was doctrinaire, I could not tell you all I have been. But now I would not be able to say all that I am not. The only thing that is certain is that I wish I had a bit of talent and of force to demolish all these horrible institutions of our epoque, the press, parliament, colleges, primary schools, etc. . . . All this is pride and organized revolt. . . . . I am simply a monarchist, and I do not place any name on the throne. I pray God to call a Christian prince there, but I do not know the name of that prince. . . . No truly, Monsieur le Comte, there is no man in the world I would wish to see King of France in the times in which we live. I profoundly respect the family that has fallen; that is not putting it strongly enough, I love it, but not in the way you love it. I am not of the birth to feel for it the affection which appears to me so touching and so honorable in hearts such as yours. I am not able to have this legitimist faith which animates you, and I do not know if it is a misfortune. . . . I have fear of this sad debris of the nobility which is represented by the *Gazette*, the *Quotidienne*, and some of the other journals. . . . How they have lost religious and political sense!
>
> Let us throw ourselves at the foot of the cross, let us pray to God for justice and for France. And if God places on the arms of this

> simple cross the flowers of the lilies, certainly my hand will not put them down, and I will never cease to pray for this. But let God decide. For me the simple cross suffices, and lest the fleurs-de-lys should mislead thirty million souls, I would say to you, let us forget the fleurs-de-lys. Long live the cross![16]

This general position, as dramatically stated to Comte O'Mahony, remained the stand of Louis Veuillot throughout most of his career, though after his disillusionment with Napoleon III he warmed increasingly to the legitimist cause, especially as the pretender himself, the Comte de Chambord, ever more appeared to be "Catholic before all."

Not all of Veuillot's writing in the spring of 1840 was on the same plane as his letter to O'Mahony. One piece grew out of his sociability and was in a considerable measure about himself. He thought of marriage at several times in his life, and as was to be the case again in 1842, his friends tried to arrange for a suitable marriage. Somewhere in the era when Louis was attending the Catholic assemblages which inspired his *Propos divers* he met a good-looking young lady, who, despite her aristocratic-sounding name of De la Valette, was essentially of a bourgeois Catholic background. The Abbé Joseph Varin, his confessor, the Abbé Aulanier, one of the habitués of the Catholic assemblages, another priest, the Abbé Boulanger, Olivier, Féburier and his wife, and apparently others pushed him toward domesticity. Louis must have had inclinations toward marriage, but, as has been the case with many others, recalled in time that marriage also brings problems. The young lady's family had strong doubts about the marriage of their daughter to a literary man, with all the economic uncertainties which that career entailed, especially since he had two sisters who were in his effective charge. Without any unpleasantness the project of Louis' marriage was abandoned, the young lady married his friend Lafon in about a year, and all might have gone unheeded by any except for the fact that Louis felt impelled to write a very short "novel" about the episode.[17]

L'Épouse Imaginaire was written by May 1840 and promptly appeared in a new publication, *Nouveau Correspondant*, and then again in 1844, and finally in a bigger collection called *Historiettes et Fantaisies*, in 1850. In the latter year, but speaking of 1840, he wrote that he was tired of hearing about liberty, equality, fraternity, and the various rights of man, and that he was writing a little book in which Christian charity was the point.[18] In this case the charity involved in the "story" was that the "hero" found a good excuse for not going through with the planned marriage, thus sparing the young lady many trying things attendant on marriage. Indeed, Veuillot starts the tale with the maxim of Saint Francis de Sales to the effect that if the custom were to practice marriage before entering into it, few people would take the step![19] What is interesting about the story is that the description of the "hero" (who was supposed to be living in 1735) is practically a sketch of himself.

> This vigorous body supports a head which might be a bit less voluminous without being out of proportion. . . . The eyes are black and rather small, sometimes very lively; the eyebrows well placed, perhaps a bit heavy; the chin is good enough, but unfortunately I am beginning to have two, and withal a pale brownish color. It is true that I certainly am not good-looking. . . . If I stir myself into conversation, my expression sparkles; with those whom I like my smile is tender and good; and with everyone my air is frank. . . .
>
> I am sad, I am gay; a mere nothing makes me burst into laughter or brings tears, and often, really at my age, I weep still at nothing. I am very quick to make a decision, and very irresolute. . . . Timid, I have often dared much; lazy, I have often dared much; heedless, I have not conducted myself without wisdom. I am *one*. . .in the manner of two armies engaged in a single battle. I have some faults from which I take an air of virtue, like those furious cowards who, as they fear, lose all feeling for danger. For example, I reconcile a lively enough natural taste for the comforts of life with a persistence truly stoical in the face of privations.[20]

So the twenty-six-year-old Veuillot described his fictional self. He forgot to mention that his face was pock-marked, as his brother pointed out, to which he replied that he did not want the reader to be forced to recognize him in spite of the pseudonym.[21] He probably also realized that such pockmarks would not have been reconciled with the romantic role by many readers. The description, however, must have been a good one, because his new friend Dumast wrote to him, distressed about what seemed to be a sad bit of autobiography. Veuillot responded: "Reassure yourself, moreover, about that which you call the sad reality of the *Épouse Imaginaire*. There is nothing real in any of it except the circumstance in the air and the portrait I made of myself, and even that is a bit flattering. This adventure has left nothing in my heart, and I scarcely remember it."[22]

While he might write about a love affair as an "adventure" in 1840, the year 1841 brought him as close to a real adventure as he ever got, and, of course, he romanticized it to the full – a mission to Algeria with no less a figure than Marshal Bugeaud, complete with exposure to combat conditions in the desert. After the seizure of Algiers on 5 July 1830 French operations in Algeria had slowly pacified resisting forces. From 1837 to 1839 something like peace reigned. Then a fierce wave of resistance flared up under the leadership of Abd-el-Kader, and the French forces had their hands full. Marshal Valée, who had distinguished himself as a soldier as late as 1837, was governor, but he was now old, and Bugeaud was designated to go to Algeria in 1840 as his replacement. In due course during the forties the pacification of Algeria was completed, and although frustrated in some respects, Bugeaud began a system of colonizing Algeria for France. It was at the start of this mission that Louis Veuillot was remembered by the Marshal and Guizot.

The Marshal needed a secretary, because his mission was governmental as much as military. He had been well satisfied by Veuillot as an editor in Périgueux, where as a civilian he had shown traits that might well have appealed to the Marshal. Whether Bugeaud first thought of asking Veuillot to join him, or whether Veuillot was suggested by Guizot, or even someone else, cannot be absolutely answered though Bugeaud might well have had the idea. In any case it was not long before Guizot began to persuade him. Unquestionably the reason Louis Veuillot felt he had some obligation to go was the salary he had been drawing as Guizot's "attaché." Veuillot admired Bugeaud, but the well-known arbitrary ways of the soldier were such as to make the young literary man hesitant to accept the position. Of course, going to Algeria at the start of 1841 had some other obvious drawbacks. But Guizot, to whom Veuillot was much indebted, was persuasive and pointed out that if he accepted he would be going as an envoy of the dominant minister of the interior and that he would be preparing reports for him. Put this way, the offer was such as to attract Veuillot.[23] He accepted and turned to putting his affairs in such order as to permit him to be away for what might be a very long time.

While making arrangements occupied some of his attention, the biggest problem at hand was finishing *Rome et Lorette*. He had previously put it aside for other projects but now was determined to complete it before leaving. The latter part was obviously done in great haste, yet he felt he could not delay its publication any longer. Bugeaud was named governor of Algeria on 29 December 1840, and on 24 January 1841 Veuillot wrote to his new friend Dumast that the book was finished. "Never have I suffered more. . .during this infanticide committed against my ideas."[24] But at last he had told the story of his conversion. The book was really not ready for the press, and it was left

Veuillot after the revictualing of Medeah, apparently because he respected Veuillot's fidelity to his own religion.[49] At one time the two engaged in ostentatious competition in religious devotion, Ben-Kaddour reciting verses of the Koran while Ave Marias, Pater Nosters, and Credos were being intoned by Veuillot, with a Jew, a protestant, and "two renegade Frenchmen" present at the demonstration! The two exchanged compliments, the Moslem declaring that he would pray to Jesus Christ that the two might be able to enter Heaven together.[50] Another Moslem who supported the French was a coulougli (son of a Turk and a Moorish woman), Sed-Ahmed-Ben-Bou-Gandoura. With this individual Louis Veuillot had a conversation one night lasting until two in the morning. Although Gandoura was steadfast in his own faith, he observed to Louis Veuillot that things would go better with the French in Algeria if they were all practicing Christians. Veuillot went out of his way to deny that this remark was a compliment, but in fact it was exactly the remark he wanted in support of his scheme of things. He was much impressed with Gandoura. "I have found in this young coulougli an excellent soul, right-thinking, with thinking that is naturally religious, and a predisposition to receive the truth which I have rarely encountered in Paris among the *scholars*. Islam is but a Christian heresy, there are many points of contact, . . .and M. Laurence [director of Algerian affairs] is a *sot*."[51] Clearly Veuillot felt himself to be more of a kindred spirit to devoted Moslems than to secular Frenchmen. Early in his Algerian sojourn he was impressed with Moslem piety,[52] and this feeling did not pass away.

With regard to the mission and purpose of the French in Algeria, he had very mixed feelings, as his book, *Les Français en Algérie*, showed when it appeared four years later. He presented in this work, which was not a military, administrative, political, or learned work, but simply a literary piece revealing his feeling about the whole situation, two totally different worlds, the French and the Arab, in sharp contrast with each other.[53] He saw great possibilities, but so far as actual colonization or any moral results he saw little. The letters he wrote in 1840 were full of feeling about Catholic services in Algiers,[54] and about the role of Bugeaud,[55] but he also showed despair. On May 1 he wrote his brother that "it would be better to *abandon Africa* if we were able to do so."[56] A few days later he observed to a friend, "Believe me, we will get nothing out of Africa unless we convert it."[57] However, he saw the French government at great pains to impress the Algerians with the idea that propagation of Christianity was the last thing they wanted to do. While he greatly admired Bugeaud as a soldier, he despaired at his lack of religion.[58] About the only evidence he saw of Christianity being carried with the army was an Alsatian chaplain named Gstalter.[59] Although Abd-el-Kader was fighting a holy war, the French were not.

Louis Veuillot's mission in Algeria was not only to serve as a secretary to Bugeaud, but also to write reports to Guizot.[60] These were long, as he told Leclerc at the time,[61] and in them he dwelt on his essential theme that it was all in vain if the Christian ideal were not brought to Algeria.[62] He did not soft-pedal the material problems, seeing the transport system far beneath what it had been in the spring of 1840 when there had been six times as many mules in Algeria for the French army as there were in the spring of 1841.[63] He saw many other problems impeding both the conquest and the colonization, but at the heart of matters he saw the religious question. To the protestant Guizot he quoted Psalm 126: "Nisi Dominus aedificaverit domum, in vanum laboraverunt qui aefidicant eam."[64] Just what impression Veuillot made would be impossible to say, but at least in the realm of political expediency Guizot later showed that he did not agree with Veuillot's recommendations as to religion.[65]

During his stay in Algeria he wrote nothing for publication in the press or elsewhere. However, busy though he was, he found time for something like his usual correspondence. While some letters went to people like Gustave Olivier, Émile Lafon, and others, it was heavily directed to Eugène and to Edmond Leclerc, the latter having just been at work getting *Rome et Lorette* ready for the press. Apparently Veuillot had no quibbling with his editors, after having simply surrendered the manuscript into their hands as he departed for Algeria. *Rome et Lorette* was reviewed May 16 in *L'Univers*, with the reviewer doing little more than quote from the introduction of the book, which he called a "novel." Curiously the review did not mention Veuillot's name, designating him only as "author of *Pèlerinages en* (instead of *de*) *Suisse*. Veuillot had a lot to say about literature and the press in his letters to Leclerc and Eugène. It was obvious where his heart was, and of course he had plans about his own writing. Although *Les Français en Algérie* came in due course to be the principal fruit of the Algerian era, he was first preoccupied with another project. With great enthusiasm he told Eugène about the Christian novel, *Frère Christophe*, he was going to write. It was going to be a spectacular mélange of impressive things and people brought together to dramatize his Christian purpose,[66] but somehow it never got beyond the planning stage.

How long Veuillot was intended to stay in Algeria, how long he himself expected to remain, why he returned, how well satisfied either Bugeaud or Guizot was with his mission, and indeed, all the reasons why he was sent in the first place are questions which cannot be very satisfactorily answered. After staying barely four months he wrote Leclerc with some enthusiasm telling him not to bother to write him in Algeria anymore.[67] Then, about three weeks later he wrote his brother that Bugeaud, who had been away, told him he needed him and asked him to stay a few days longer.[68] In fact, he remained through August giving little indication as to the length of his stay or the reasons for it. One can only conjecture about his relations with Marshal Bugeaud and whether the old soldier really had much need of the Catholic literary man. Just why the imaginative Guizot would have sent a special observer also is a question. The following spring there was talk of Guizot's sending him back to Algeria,[69] but that time nothing came of it. Veuillot had continued to receive a good stipend from the government for doing practically nothing. Such a subsidy, of course, would tend at least to protect the government from his pen. The possibility of sending him on missions might be further persuasion against his attacking too many policies of the cabinet. Consideration of the motives Guizot may have had is pure speculation, but it seems safe to say that at least indirectly the key minister in the Soult cabinet must have influenced the career of Veuillot at this period, possibly even as to the length of his stay in Algeria.

By mid-September of 1841 Veuillot was back in Paris. For several months his career was still uncertain as to its exact direction. In some ways his existence seemed much the same as it had been before his departure for Algeria. He attended the meetings of the Catholic circles. His literary activity was intensified but clearly was a continuation of the same kind of work. As the education of his sisters drew to a close his concern about their welfare was increased, if anything. His cultural interests and activities in the years immediately following his return declined proportionately with his other preoccupations, but it was in this era that he came to know Georges Bizet and to take an interest in music as it related to the church.[70] The same pressure on the young man to marry continued, much of the pressure coming from the Abbé Aulanier, supported by Father Varin,[71] but Lacordaire, the inspiring preacher, whose lectures and sermons enthralled Veuillot at this time, solemnly counseled him to remain celebate in order to devote himself the more completely to the cause.[72]

During the years 1841-1843 after his return from Algeria, Veuillot lived at several addresses, including 38, rue Vaneau, 41, rue Madame in the former Hôtel Clermont-Tonnère, chez M. Bailly, who was key man in the practical affairs of *L'Univers,* and after that 21, rue de Babylone. Although these moves were all in the vicinity of 10, rue des Saints-Perès, offices of *L'Univers*, in what is now the Seventh Arrondissement, this moving was unlike the pattern he afterwards established by living approximately three decades at 40, rue du Bac.

The great decision Louis Veuillot had yet to make was the decision to break with the government and to give full-time collaboration to *L'Univers.* Throughout his life he spent a great deal of time in writing books about his politico-religious scheme of things, and this activity may have been the dearest thing to his heart. As his brother Eugène, in his foreword to the first volume of his life of Louis Veuillot, says, "He loved literature more than journalism."[73] On his passports Louis was always identified as an "écrivain," as has been noted. The very fact that his literary production would be undiminished by long hours in the editorial office of the journal with which he was to become identified would prove this point. But at the journal his literary career could be made to dovetail with his efforts as editor. Despite the fact that he was practically free from time-consuming duties with the ministry, the kind of assaults he was going to want to launch against the government could not be reconciled with drawing a good stipend from it. Besides not being free in this sense, Louis Veuillot was also aware that Guizot might decide that he needed him for another mission to Algeria. For some time, from his return from Algeria until into 1843, Veuillot tried to have his cake and eat it, and he gave his full-time and paid collaboration to *L'Univers* before finally burning his bridges with the government. But eventually the choice had to be made.

One of the more interesting of Veuillot's personal connections was this nearly lifelong association with Guizot.[74] On his return from Algeria his relations with Guizot were very friendly indeed. The young literary man dined with the key statesman of France and brought trinkets to his children, which according to his correspondence they joyfully received.[75] He prepared a 48-page mémoire for the foreign ministry during the fall of 1841,[76] and, even though he was civilian, he fancied that he had just written a letter of advice to Bugeaud that would make the marshal take notice.[77] Apparently Guizot was very favorably disposed toward Veuillot, and would like to have pushed him ahead as a servant of the ministry like Veuillot's friend, Mallac. While the implication was that Veuillot would be able to have free time in general, he would have to make another trip to Algeria. Bugeaud had indicated to Veuillot that he would like to have him do this again, but, though the full story here is lacking,[78] Veuillot obviously did not want to become more involved with the ministry, particularly if it meant another trip to Algeria. He was receiving 500 francs a month as it was, and Guizot, speaking of how good the economy was, said that 1200 or 1500 would go to him rather than only 1000 as Veuillot suggested.[79]

Certainly this was an opportunity with great possibilities in politics. He realized that and never forgot it, for writing late in his life he still spoke of the "sacrifice" he had made in putting aside this opportunity. However, it was an entirely necessary sacrifice. Meanwhile he held onto his stipend as long as he could. Income from his early publications began to come in and his debts could be paid, and in mid-1842 he claimed he did not need more than 250 francs a month,[81] but it was not until early 1843 that Louis Veuillot gave his resignation to the ministry of the interior, giving up his 500 francs a month, well after he had become de facto editor-in-chief of *L'Univers*. Thereafter his course was clear. As he had written his brother while still in Algeria, "I would rather work twelve hours a day for nothing than devote six hours a week to an easy function with lots of money and the croix d'honneur which would tie me down."[82]

The activity which beckoned to Veuillot was Catholic journalism. Despite the thousands of hours he would sit at a desk in his editorial office, he enjoyed his kind of freedom in this activity. Of course an editor could go on trips in the fulfillment of his function, but freedom from any responsibility to secular authority was what he sought, and in fighting the battles of the Catholic church as he saw them he would find perfect freedom. In the complex picture of the emergence of the Catholic press at this time there was of course opportunity other than with *L'Univers*. *Le Correspondant*, for example, sought Veuillot's collaboration in 1842, and one of his early novels, *L'Honnête Femme*, began appearing in this bimonthly literary journal in 1843.[83] But his future was to be with the daily-except-Monday Parisian journal, *L'Univers*.

From 1839 until July, 1842 his collaboration had been irregular and at all events strictly voluntary.[84] However, even before he began his regular paid relationship with the journal, as early as 13 April 1842 a police report referred to Louis Veuillot as a "secretary in the Ministry of the Interior and the most enthusiastic editor of the journal *L'Univers*."[84] His articles entitled *Propos divers* that had appeared in *L'Univers* from February until mid-June of 1840 had attracted a good deal of attention, as had his *Esquisses du Temps présents*,[86] which appeared in early 1842. These later articles pointed to his subsequent book, *Libres Penseurs*. Although these items were unsigned, *Rome et Lorette* and *Pèlerinages de Suisse* were already so well known that many recognized his writings in *L'Univers* as by the same author. In the period of the July Monarchy articles in the press were unsigned, and it is not at all safe to guess at their authorship solely on the basis of style. At the time when Veuillot became a regular member of the staff he was relatively more outstanding as a writer, in comparison with the other staff members, than he was in his later days, when there were numerous other editors of the highest calibre. In 1842 the only other first-rate editor was Melchior Du Lac, who might well himself have become the leading light and shaper of *L'Univers* instead of Louis Veuillot.

Du Lac had been with *L'Univers* practically from its beginning, and in the words of François Veuillot was "the best editor of *L'Univers*" in 1842. Louis Veuillot himself called du Lac "mon maître."[87] Du Lac, however, wished to become a Benedictine and in a few years entered the Abbey of Solesmes (where Dom Guéranger revived the Roman rite in France) leaving, it seemed, *L'Univers* to Louis Veuillot. However, although he remained at the Abbey until 1848, for family reasons, he was never able to devote himself fully to the way of life he preferred, and he continued to collaborate with Veuillot despite having taken vows.[88] At the time Veuillot began his full-time collaboration at *L'Univers*, he pointed out to his brother that Eugène Taconet (a manufacturer of military equipment) was the owner, that the good M. (often called "Père") E.J. Bailly was the titular editor-in-chief, but that Du Lac was "unique." He and Du Lac did all.[89] His 200 francs a month certainly did not suggest much importance,[90] but then the journal was very small. Louis Veuillot is generally said to have become the real editor-in-chief during 1842, and it has even been suggested that he issued a species of "manifesto" on 4 December 1842.[91] However, Louis Veuillot wrote in March of 1843 that Du Lac "enters the Benedictines this week, and therefore I am obliged to replace him as principal editor." He spoke of the absolute necessity of taking over this burden, and called it an *ennui inimaginable*, but also he realized the battles that were to be fought both against the government and against the legitimists.[92] One may speculate that had Du Lac not been moved to take the vows, perhaps *L'Univers* would have been identified primarily with him rather than with Louis Veuillot, and that the latter would have been able to give freer rein to his literary activites while serving as only one of the editors of the rousing Catholic vehicle of polemics.

With the withdrawal of Melchior Du Lac, Veuillot inherited the full burden of the battles his "dear and excellent friend"[93] had begun. Already a struggle with the ministry over education had begun, but even more fundamental was the contest between the "Catholics-before-all" and the legitimists, who would subordinate the cause of the church to that of the restoration of legitimate monarchy. The legitimists would have liked to combine *L'Univers* with *L'Union catholique*, which was essentially a legitimist sheet. Pressure to do this had existed for some time and was the result of the closing of ranks of different varieties of Catholics which took place in the latter half of the reign of Louis

Philippe. Catholic reaction against the Revolution, and against secularly oriented organs of both dynasties after the Revolution, of course, was anterior to the 1840's,[93] but by 1840 a very distinguishable Catholic party had been formed. In the eyes of "Catholics-before-all," like Louis Veuillot and Melchior Du Lac, the most immediate threat to their purpose was the smothering effects of the legitimists. True, the legitimists were Catholics too, but first of all they were dynastic, and such men as Veuillot and Du Lac would not be patronized by anyone. Queen Amélie and her sister, Princess Adélaide, albeit of the Orleans dynasty, were religiously speaking akin to the legitimists. When during the summer of 1840 Balzac accused *L'Univers* of being *un journal ami du Château,* secretly supported by two women [the queen and her sister], this point enraged Louis Veuillot more than the fact that the great novelist called *L'Univers illisible, inconnu, ennuyeux.* He responded in an article in *L'Univers* of 2 and 3 September 1840 in a violent counterattack.[94] It was clear that Balzac had struck near to a sensitive spot, not that the journal was being influenced by the queen, but because legitimists on its staff were increasing their influence. The principal individual concerned was Alexandre de Saint-Chéron, a staunch Catholic but a man who throughout his life was particularly associated with the cause of Henry V. From 17 June until 2 September 1840 Louis Veuillot had interrupted his contributions to *L'Univers* on account of this same Saint-Chéron's influence, and only on the occasion of this provocation by Balzac did he cease sulking in his tent and return to the battle.[95] It was not that Louis Veuillot really was not a legitimist throughout most of his life, particulary identifying himself that way in his later years, but he became so only because that party was the most Catholic, and when Henri V revealed himself as more a Catholic than a king, Louis Veuillot became ever more the legitimist.[96] But in 1840 for Catholicism to be overshadowed by legitimacy seemed the most immediate danger.

The fusion of *L'Union catholique* and *L'Univers*, as first envisaged by leading clerical-legitimist figures in Paris, in 1842 and 1843, would have subordinated the latter to the former. Du Lac, while remaining a legitimist in political principle, was adamant against such a fate for *L'Univers.*[97] Veuillot was exactly like-minded. Du Lac was now on the point of entering the Benedictine order, but Veuillot was just becoming free to engage in politics. He went to Lille to get support in later 1842, and in January of 1843, he visited Nancy. He met with important laymen and bishops. One of the key personalities whom he approached was Lacordaire.[98] These missions were successful. Although some concessions of a nominal sort were made to the legitimists in the interest of Catholic unity, the victory was for the "Catholics-before-all." On 31 January 1843 the fusion of the two journals was announced, but the masthead had *L'Univers* on top, and under it in much smaller letters was *L'Union catholique*. Du Lac and Saint-Chéron were co-editors, and Taconet and Bailly shared the functions of director and administrator without any rigid distinction. Du Lac, of course, was to depart for Solesmes very shortly after these arrangements were made. Even before Du Lac left, however, he and Veuillot contrived to manage things completely themselves. They decided what articles were published, and the surveillance committee was unable to check them.[99] When Du Lac left and Louis replaced him, Louis alone dominated the journal, but for a few months this domination was tenuous. To a friend he wrote: "Taconet is, so to speak, at my feet; you know the situation, you see what I can do. But if I am absent *L'Union* is mistress, subject to some move of Saint-Chéron, and *L'Univers* is lost."[100] Veuillot's grip tightened very quickly, and the legitimist elements began to be eased out, without any sharp rupture. *L'Univers* had gained financial support, gotten more readers, and had not sacrificed its independence, despite the committee which gave it nominal surveillance. Veuillot now had a salary of 4000 francs a year,[101] but he still felt that he was making something of a sacrifice when he said to a friend that he had given himself to *L'Univers, corps et biens*, and having to deal with a staff that had grown with people he did not want and which now lacked Du Lac.[102] However, things were now in his hands. "I am editor-in-chief in such a way that Taconet absolutely belongs to me, that nothing can go against my will, that I can do anything against the will of the other."[103] Veuillot was well aware that this situation would not go on forever, and he was actually trying to prevent the immediate separation of the two elements thus coalesced in *L'Univers*, because there were advantages for the "Catholics-before-all" as long as the fusion lasted. He was undoubtedly closely pinned to his office while it lasted. He had won a victory, but in consolidating it in 1843 he had little time for matters outside of journalistic battles.

The years 1841 and 1842 had constituted a particularly busy period of writing for Louis Veuillot. *L'Univers* was only one of the journals to which he contributed. He helped revive *Le Correspondant* and also wrote a variety of pieces for lesser Catholic organs.[104] A certain amount of his attention was devoted to revisions and new editions of works already published. His brother Eugène at this period was editor-in-chief of the *Journal de Maine-et-Loire*, and Louis' correspondence regarding his brother's affairs was very extensive. During the fall of 1841 he was working on a second edition of *Rome et*

Lorette, and apparently he had differences of opinion with his friend Dumast about punctuation, the latter being much more rigid than Veuillot about traditional rules.[105] Veuillot had debts to pay, but by the spring of 1842 it was obvious that his work, notably *Rome et Lorette*, was going to be very profitable.[106] Indeed, it even came to be translated into German. The success of his books was part of the reason his position with the ministry became less important to him.

In addition to his articles, revisions, plans for *Les Français en Algérie*, and other projects, Louis Veuillot was largely preoccupied from the time of his return from Algeria until well into 1842 with a strange literary work, strange, that is to say, for a man of the world who had just returned from association with Bugeaud and others of his sort. This book appeared under the title *Agnès de Lauvens, ou Memoires de Sœur Saint-Louis, contenant divers souvenirs de son éducation et de sa vie dans le monde*, which purported to be the letters and memoirs of a young woman who had entered a convent to be educated and then to join the order. It was obvious that the education of a young woman was a matter of importance to him. True enough, to him the instruction itself was secondary, and just what kind of mathematics or grammar was not important, but education in the full sense of the word and the development of the young lady's mind along Christian lines was a particularly serious matter,[107] whether she was to be a mother of a family or a nun. The book must have been a challenge for the roughly schooled Louis to write, imagining what it was like for a young lady to arrive at a convent, to continue to have connections with the world, to have her trials, but finally to decide to take the veil and give herself to the church. He must have searched his mind very closely. Even the title was not easy. For months he called the book *Sub tuum* (from *Sub tuum praesidium confugimus, Sancta Dei Genitrix*), and not until the end of May, 1842, after he had been working on it for nearly a year, did he change the title to *Mémoires de la Sœur Saint-Louis*,[108] which in turn was reduced to a subtitle after the name of the central figure, *Agnès de Lauvens*. Some of the letters and memoirs show much sensitivity, but a poem, "The Violet," particularly reflected the spirit he captured, and sounded like something a girl might write. This poem in childlike form describes the many flowers on a hill boasting of their differing beauty, until the Holy Virgin descends on the hill to pick the one that has said nothing:

> Or, sur cette colline,
> Que le ciel, que le ciel illumine,
> Or, sur cette colline,
> La Vierge descendit;

Et de sa main divine,
Que le ciel, que le ciel illumine,
Et de sa main divine
Sous l'herbe elle cueillit

La fleur que l'on devine,
Que le ciel, que le ciel illumine,
La fleur que l'on devine,
Et qui n'avait rien dit.[109]

Such writing, if nothing else, showed the ability of the author to project himself into the feelings of someone quite different from himself and to write for a sensitive audience. His friend Gustave Olivier, whose publishing house was called Olivier Fulgence, brought it out in mid-1842. Louis anticipated considerable sale, but probably nothing like the eventual figure. By early in the twentieth century it had gone through 29 editions, totaling 174,000 copies.[110] In order to keep up the pretence that he only collected the material, it did not appear under the author's name. To his friend, the Abbé Morisseau, he said it was a work of "no consequence." However, he guaranteed its orthodoxy and added, "Perhaps it will be pleasing in the convents. I very much hope that it will be of service to all women educated in these holy houses."[111]

No doubt this hope was genuine, since of course Louis Veuillot had personal reasons for interest in young women at this time because of his two sisters whom he was having educated. Their mother had remarried and lived in the rough section of Bercy where she ran an inn for the bargers who brought wine to Paris. His sisters were his concern. During and after his sojourn in Algeria, while they were at the Couvent des Oiseaux, whose mother-superior he held in the highest esteem, he must have regarded that institution as their salvation, and there can be no doubt that it is reflected in *Agnès de Lauvens*. Sometime after his return his sisters joined him, and by the fall of 1843 they were all living together in a five-room apartment at 21, rue de Babylone. Apparently their existence was quite simple, the girls performing household chores. The elder by sixteen months, Annette, was clever with a needle and did the mending, but the function of Élise was much more significant – she wrote the letters that her brother dictated to her.[112] Her work as a secretary lasted through Louis's life, and she was a major aid to him, including during his long stay in Rome in 1869-1870. Throughout his life his eyes gave him a great deal of trouble, apparently as a result of smallpox. The trouble seems to have resulted from impaired lacrymal ducts or glands. At any rate he complained to his brother about their bad condition at this period,[113] and the aid that Élise must have been to him as he returned home, tired from his early struggles to keep *L'Univers* in hand, no doubt was something not to be underestimated. Annette was to be suitably married in due course, and it was a gratification for Louis Veuillot that his publications were successful. "Alleluia," he wrote his brother, "Annette's dot is amassed!"[114] In some ways Louis was very perceptive about young women, but possibly he was not perceptive in others. Nearly a year earlier he had noted that Annette was not looking well and was getting thinner. Perhaps even at that period it was easier to marry off a thin girl than a fat one. Élise's eyes were "like an angel's," but she had the "shoulders of a mason" while "attaining maternal proportions,"[115] Eugène was informed. If Louis himself was not married, these young ladies, concern for whose education had influenced his literary production, were important among the reasons.

As Louis Veuillot took charge of *L'Univers* in 1843 in his thirtieth year of life, the question arises as to what thinkers had guided him in the formation of his ideology. A distinguished historian said of him: "Thoroughly cultivated though self-taught, he was no intellectual and remained down to earth."[116] The statement that a man wholly engaged in a battle of ideas was no intellectual might serve as the basis for a good debate, but Veuillot was highly doctrinaire and in no way a systematic student of ideas for their own sake. He was not sympathetic to the development of an idea if it did not lead in a direction which he believed correct. As he was self-taught he had a great store of information of his own choosing, and he chose what would be of value to him in establishing and supporting his own beliefs. Not only was he able to muster a staggering amount of information at times, he could string it together in a clear, forceful way. His polemical exposition could run away from many regarded as intellectuals. A fact might be successfully challenged, or even a step in the logical development of his argument, but by the time this had been done the indefatigable Louis Veuillot might have written several more articles. Doctrinaire he was, but how many intellectuals of his or later periods are not likewise doctrinaire, even when sincere in their own cause of liberalism? In his own way he believed in the necessity of harmony between liberty and religion, though no "liberties" might he permit to be taken with ultramontane Catholicism and the orthodoxy of the church, as interpreted by the pope.

As he was self-taught, orthodoxy was self-imposed. He had not gotten it at home, much less picked it up in Bercy. He had found his great cause in Rome and violently clutched at it and the Roman orthodoxy that went with it, in reaction against the shallowness of the world in which he had been living. No thinkers had done any subtle persuading to cause him to take this stand. But once he had set his face in the direction he chose he found able justifiers. He read the works of Bossuet and Fénelon, De Maistre and Bonald. Particularly the latter two, the Catholic giants of the nineteenth century, gave him ammunition for his writings. His own brother Eugène, however, casually admitted that he had never disquieted himself as to whether they were always in exact accord.[117] In this respect he was not the cool intellectual who enjoys subtleties without particularly caring what the major concerns are all about. De Maistre and Bonald had furnished Catholicism with great works, and he was determined to use them, no doubt deliberately avoiding anything obscure that might seem to diminish the strength of the front. He knew and admired Lacordaire, though he did not personally care for him. The Catholic historian Gabourd wrote the kind of work he could use without hesitation, and even Montalembert had had some influence on him. The most significant figure in Catholic circles in the nineteenth century was Lamennais, but, influenced by Du Lac, Veuillot rejected him. However, at least indirectly, Lamennais must also have had much influence on the young polemist.

In some ways the parallel between Félicité de Lamennais and Veuillot is striking, though in other ways they were very different. Lamennais was of noble extraction and thirty-one years older than Veuillot. He was born at St. Malô in Brittany and had Celtic blood. After having been a freethinker for many years, he joined his brother in the clergy in 1816, hearing a voice at his first mass saying, "I am calling you to carry my cross – just my cross, you must remember that."[118] The next year he wrote his *Essay on Indifference*, which had an extraordinary and new basis for belief. He was tremendously concerned about society, particularly the ashes of it which he saw in the aftermath of the French Revolution, and he saw hope for it only in the church. His concept of the role of the church was anything but vague. Without the pope its power would be gone. For the bishops, at least as viewed in their episcopal offices, he had contempt. His line was little different from that enunciated by De Maistre in *Du Pape*, but La Mennais (as his name originally was written) wrote first and is the real father of this revived medieval line of thought.[119] One might expect La Mennais to have been a restoration supporter. For a while he was, but by 1828 he gave it up as hopelessly Gallican, and thus well before the Revolution of 1830 he had founded the really startling journal, *L'Avenir*, which combined liberalism with ultramontanism. Brief as was its existence, no journal in nineteenth century French history had greater significance.[120] Inevitably, however, it was in trouble both with the episcopacy and with conservative elements not long after its beginning. It had some very outstanding contributors, in addition to La Mennais, including Lacordaire and Montalembert, the latter specializing in foreign affairs.[121]

Also associated with *L'Avenir* was Charles de Coux, who later was to be made co-editor of *L'Univers* with Veuillot, in 1844 when the still reasonably united Catholic party tried to keep the latter in check. Coux was not a very significant figure himself, but his association with both *L'Avenir* and *L'Univers* can hardly be overlooked when considering the possible extent of influence of La Mennais and his journal on Veuillot.

The Gallican clergy was determined to stop the leaven of La Mennais. The rising Abbé Dupanloup, perhaps the most able of Veuillot's later enemies, encouraged Cardinal de Rohan, Archbishop of Besancon, to condemn *L'Avenir*. Monsignor d'Astros, Bishop of Toulouse, and Monsignor Clausel de Montals, Bishop of Chartres, did the same. By the autumn of 1831 La Mennais and *L'Avenir* were in difficult straits, but it was nevertheless with no little confidence that La Mennais decided to appeal to the aged Gregory XVI, and together with Lacordaire and Montalembert went to Rome. There they found that there was no place in the pope's view of the world for revolution, and their defiance of the bishops and the existing order was not approved by him, despite La Mennais's advocacy of a supreme role for the papacy. The mission failed. Montalembert and Lacordaire accepted the decision of the pope, but not La Mennais, who never reconciled himself to it and left the church forever. He even altered his name at this point to Lamennais.[122] The irony of the situation lies in the fact that by the late nineteenth century his general scheme of things, including his radical social concepts, was accepted by the church. Because of his defiance of the pope, who was supposed to stand at the pinnacle of world order, Lamennais was rejected by Louis Veuillot by the time the latter had joined the church. However, Lamennais's combination of liberty and Catholicism, his defiance of the bishops, his general ultramontane scheme, and his fiery journalism were such that one can only suggest that Lamennais, up to his failure to obey the pope, was the model for Louis Veuillot. Veuillot had the understanding and support of Gregory XVI's successor, Pius IX, throughout most of his career. When Pius IX censured him, he responded with contrition. When Leo XIII subsequently showed himself to be differently disposed than Pius IX had been, Veuillot suffered pain, but he accepted the ultimate decisions of the pope. He was really more consistent than Lamennais, who presumed himself practically alone to be correct. But surely Veuillot, at the early stages of his leadership of *L'Univers,* must have been much influenced by his journalistic precursor, Lamennais.

When Louis Veuillot found himself guiding *L'Univers* without the collaboration of Du Lac or any one else, he was free for the first time to take up whatever cudgels he might choose. Working for re-establishment of Catholicism as the ultimate authority, and the papacy as the controlling force of that, journalistic combat was obviously the course on which *L'Univers* would go. The exact direction in which to point his guns Veuillot would now choose. As it turned out public instruction was to be the first great battleground. The decision was not surprising, although *L'Univers* of this era showed many other interests, including ones that might have become major preoccupations. When *L'Univers* and *L'Union catholique* were merged, attacks were launched on the merger by the legitimist *Quotidienne* and the *Gazette de France. L'Univers* in an editorial no doubt penned by Veuillot emphasized the religious background of both the merged journals.[123] Nevertheless a press war with the legitimists and Gallicans might have become the big preoccupation, despite the Catholic unity forces which were represented in the merger. General sniping at the régime of Louis Philippe might have become the business of the day. One editorial alone in early 1843 attacked corruption, prostitution, the prison system, the need for credit institutions, and the gaps in French production.[124] In one general assault on the régime, *L'Univers* said that beside the official world "there is another France, silent but active, to which belong good works, serious studies, and the austerity of prayer and devotion; vulgar notice still ignores this one. It is patient in oblivion. It accepts the present humiliation as just expiation for past wrongs; but it trusts an infallible word."[125] Veuillot suggested the awakening of this silent majority. Foreign oppression of Catholics was a likely issue, and surely one that would have had Montalembert's support. *L'Univers* in 1843 gave support to Irish agitation;[126] the position of the Catholics in Russia was much lamented;[127] Spanish Carlism was championed.[128] The restoration of glass windows at Chartres[129] and the state of vandalism in France[130] were topics not entirely neglected in favor of larger issues. The suggestion of the formation of *réunions des ouvriers catholiques* in early 1843 was nothing less than prophetic.[131] In short, *L'Univers* showed a disposition to dissipate its energies. Doubtlessly its readers would have been bored if it had not taken a very broad view – after all its name was *L'Univers*. But its favorite topic of the forties, and at many other times during its existence, was public instruction and the domination of instruction by the secular state to the exclusion of Catholic teaching.

Louis Veuillot had himself had very little formal schooling, and, as a person who had taught himself much more thoroughly than most others who are instructed by the best systems, it is almost a wonder that he cared so much about the system of education in France. The political issue that public instruction became, of course, put it in a very prominent position from any point of view, yet it was remarkable that this man, said not to be an intellectual, took up the cause of free education against the smothering effects of a universal system. The battle threw him into contact with important allies and enemies and intensified all of his feelings and beliefs.

Napoleon had established the university system by decrees in 1806 and 1808. There was a clause in the decree of 1808 (article 38) which provided that the Catholic church, at least as re-established by Napoleon, was at the basis of the total system of higher education called in France the university.[132] The constitution of 1830 granted freedom of instruction (article 69).[133] As pressures from the university system developed during the 1840's, the line that Veuillot and the Catholics came to follow was that either one or the other course should be observed by the government. Herein they had some logic. In 1833 Guizot, the minister of education at that time, had brought about a fundamental law that had greatly extended the school system. That law had required every commune to have a primary school. Guizot, the protestant, had seen to it that religious instruction was part of the curriculum, and despite the skepticism of the parliament a desire to utilize religion for the preservation of the public order had carried the day. However, it was not at the primary level that trouble developed, but at the higher level. The university system had come to be staffed almost entirely by religious skeptics and secularists, and from it men like Michelet and Quinet attacked the Catholic church in a devastating way. But what especially hurt the Catholics was that the way the secondary system was controlled was such as to block the preparation of candidates for the seminaries.[134] The monopoly of the university in the field of education, which had been extended even during the reign of Charles X in 1828, was such as to choke the free development of education for the priesthood and to stifle Catholicism. Guizot, the key man in the ministry during the forties, never wanted this situation, but he was unable to restrain the moves of those who wanted to press on against the Catholics. Villemain was minister of public instruction in this period, and it was against him that Veuillot fired his opening shots.

Villemain was a literary man and a historian of no mean ability who since early in his life had been a skeptic. He was appointed minister of public instruction in 1836, and for the better part of a decade thereafter had projects for reform of the university in the offing. The campaign was particularly intense between 1841 and 1844.[135] In late 1842 Veuillot opened fire on a variety of enemies of Christianity,[136] and during 1843 the university itself and its champions of the liberal press came in for very concerted attack from *L'Univers*. The Catholic press in general joined the attack, but none of the other journals in a way that compared with the campaign of *L'Univers*. Although *L'Ami de la Religion* and *le Correspondant* both warmed up somewhat by the end of 1843,[137] *L'Univers* carried the brunt. A good many bishops joined in raising their voices publicly in 1843, albeit generally with tact. Three, Msgr. Clausel de Montals (Chartres), Msgr. d'Astros (Toulouse), and Msgr. Devie (Belley), were in the fray very early.[138] Many of the bishops had been appointed by Louis Philippe, and hence were inclined to be *politique*. As Veuillot assaulted Villemain, Cousin, Quinet, Michelet, and the whole liberal establishment that was endeavoring further to weaken the Catholic church, he had to fight off the counterattacks of *Le Journal des Débats, Le Constitutionnel, Le Siècle, La Revue des Deux Mondes, Le Courrier de Paris*, and others, while other Catholic journals grew timid and bishops, including Msgr. Affre, Archbishop of Paris, tried to restrain the press from turning on the government in the name of the church.[139] Veuillot was accused by Ozanam of "not trying to convert unbelievers but to rouse the passions of believers,"[140] but at this stage rallying the faithful was no small chore.

The menaces of the university system constituted the key danger to Catholicism in this era in the eyes of not only Veuillot but a large part of the politically active Catholics. This rally against the eclectic philosophy of Victor Cousin, who stood at the head of the university and whose ideas were also those of Louis Philippe, was the clinching factor in making a Catholic Party in France.[141] The political enemies of the Catholic church, notably Michelet and Quinet, attempted to divide Catholics in different ways, especially by aiming attacks at the Jesuits, tactics which increased in the mid-forties. *L'Univers*, however, in an editorial probably written by Veuillot, in mid-1843 insisted that in attacking the Jesuits these men of the university meant simply to attack all Catholics.[142] Pressures on the church certainly were brought to bear,[143] and the ranks of the Catholics closed in response to these pressures. In the fall of 1843 *L'Univers* was the key organ in effecting this unity. It published letters such as that of Cardinal Bonald,

Archbishop of Lyon, protesting against policies of the university system. Veuillot made such publications not entirely on his own but in accord with members of the clergy, notably Msgr. Parisis, Bishop of Langres.[144] Already he was encountering resistance from many bishops who resented that a layman was being so forward in clerical matters,[145] but Parisis and Salinis, Bishop of Auch were among those giving encouragement to the embattled editor.

As the attack of Villemain developed, the counterattack of Veuillot and the Catholics grew in intensity. An editorial of *L'Univers* on 8 September was particulary violent, and accordingly was reported by the Préfet of the Seine to the régime.[146] The most notable piece from the pen of Veuillot at this time, however, was his letter to M. Villemain, minister of public instruction about public teaching.[147] This "letter" was very long and did not appear in *L'Univers*, as one might have expected, but was put out as a separate tract. There had already been declarations of war on the part of other Catholics. The Abbé Desgarets had published a piece, *Le monopole universitaire destructeur de la religion et des lois*, which had caused a split in episcopal ranks as to whether the stand should be supported or not, with the Archbishop of Paris, Msgr. Affre, definitely not allowing himself to be associated with it. However, Veuillot's letter to M. Villemain was probably the most significant Catholic manifesto that a battle would be fought on that field. He freely used some obvious words; it was no mere battle, but a *war* that was going to be fought. A real polemic resulted. The government had complained that a Catholic journal had calumniated it; Veuillot proudly retorted that the journal so-accused was *L'Univers*. He fully developed the theme that freedom of instruction was granted by the Charter and that Catholics had every political and religious right to challenge the monopoly of the university. Surely distinctions can be made between the approach and line of "the gentle" (Heine's designation) Michelet and that of the more trenchant Quinet, but Veuillot's letter to M. Villemain furnishes a good example of Veuillot's technique, deliberate association of men representing the same general cause. He attacked "MM. Michelet et Quinet" together for the way they tried to divide the Catholics on the score of "Jesuitism." In this era Veuillot wrote very strongly on many issues, such as on the question of the profanation of the Sabbath that the government permitted,[148] but nothing was as strong as his letter to the minister of public instruction. It was a wonder that proceedings were not brought against him at this point.

The effects of Veuillot's stand on key men in France were significant, and their actions were sometimes strikingly different; notably the reactions of Guizot and Montalembert offer a great contrast. On many occasions, both earlier and later, Guizot had taken a stand for religious liberty, freedom of education, and the rights of the individual. Guizot believed that education was a greater thing than instruction, and that state instruction should not invade the rights of individuals and families, particularly in the realm of education as it affected religious affairs. He believed that the Charter granted religious liberty, and that the individual had rights as well as the state.[149] Guizot's concern about protestants in France obliged him by principle to feel the same concern for Catholics being overwhelmed by the state, and throughout the lives of the two men this coincidence of realization of the need for religious liberty was perhaps the principal bond between Guizot and Veuillot. However, Guizot was in the estimation of Veuillot one of those *espirts vraiment politiques*, and at the time of the battle of the mid-forties Guizot was the key minister in the cabinet of Soult, and it was therefore this régime that was being attacked. Guizot, of course would like to have chained up the attacks of Michelet and Quinet, and he would have much preferred it had Villemain's project for the further invasion of Catholic preserves never been put forth. However, such things were reality, and as a *politique* he wished to temporize and remain in power. Veuillot was aware that Guizot was not in the assault, and he assumed that Guizot must have been pained by some of the advocates of the university.[150] "Guizot," he said, "has had clearer vision [than Villemain], and has not dared say all that he has foreseen."[151] He gave him credit for being on a higher plane than the leaders of the university cause,[152] but did not overlook his silence and careful politics. Guizot, of course, could not endorse the stands of Veuillot and remain in his commanding position, and Veuillot's broadsides at the government were aimed at the cabinet Guizot dominated, whether he liked all its policies or not. The mid-forties, therefore, constituted the period of the greatest rift between this pair, whose generally amicable relations offer one of the remarkable features of the careers of both.

The battle over the university monopoly, on the other hand, threw Veuillot and Montalembert into the closest relations these two great but very different Catholics ever enjoyed. Comte Charles de Montalembert was of the highest social caste. His bearing vacillated, at times being arrogant and proud. Although various persons of noble background were on good terms with Veuillot throughout his life, particularly in his later days, the chances of intimate relations between him and the Comte would seem to have been most unlikely. Nevertheless, Montalembert forced himself on Veuillot in 1844, presuming apparently that Veuillot would be glad to have his friendship and support, and that, of course, it would be altogether fitting for himself, Montalembert, to tell the journalist what stands he should take on key matters. A great historian of the French Catholic church has taken Veuillot to task for keeping Montalembert at his distance during the forties. Although Montalembert came to address Veuillot as "my dear friend," Veuillot always addressed Montalembert as "Monsieur le Comte."[153] It seems only fair to say that Veuillot was not only trying to be correct in his response to Montalembert, but that he showed a certain wisdom thereby, because if he had responded with the same intimate terms Montalembert employed, particularly after their relationship cooled, the fiery nobleman might well have resented what he might have interpreted as forwardness on the part of the peasant-clerk-journalist.

While at the Madiera Islands, where his wife was trying to recuperate from an illness, Montalembert wrote Veuillot a notable letter, avowing the closeness of his support, but also giving the editor advice and warning about a matter on which Veuillot had already proved himself and with regard to which Veuillot was more consistent than Montalembert. The Comte felicitated him about the letter to Villemain, which he judged to be "admirable" which "transported me with sympathy and enthusiasm for you." But having gushed for a few lines on that matter, he took Veuillot to task for a reply the latter had made to the *Journal des Débats*. The *Journal des Débats* had printed an attack on the legitimists, following a legitimist rally at Belgrave Square in London, held to show their support of the Comte de Chambord. Montalembert said that "in spite of profound aversion for democracy," he wanted to have nothing to do with the legitimists, because they would compromise Catholicism with dynasticism. Any such union would destroy everthing that had been done for Catholicism from the time of De Maistre to Lacordaire. Indeed, Veuillot, according to Montalembert, had been guilty of *maladresse* in the reply – a term which Montalembert excused himself for having so frankly used. Not only did Montalembert, the nobleman, critic of legitimacy, say all this, but he further advised Veuillot to make *L'Univers* more laïc. Finally he assured Veuillot that he had obtained the sanction of Taconet, owner of *L'Univers*, for the ideas which he had just so frankly expressed.[154] Although Montalembert was thoroughly dominated by his passion for the Catholic church, and no doubt was enthusiastic in his backing and advice for Veuillot, and invited him and others of the editorial board of *L'Univers* to his home very soon afterwards (the two men within a short time of each other moved to 40 and 44, rue du Bac, where both lived many years, during a good part of which time they had no relations at all),[155] such a tone was hardly the one to please a man who wanted to be his own master. In purely personal matters, as between the two, Veuillot's tone seems much more tactful and appropriate than Montalembert's.

In the first months of 1844 an episode of great importance for Louis Veuillot occurred. It drove all Catholics closer together, but it also put Veuillot in prison for a month and left a deep impression on him. A priest named Abbé Combalot, a former supporter of Lamennais, an enthusiastic, sincere, vigorous opponent of the campaign that had been launched by the university against the Catholic schools, issued a brochure which the government chose not to overlook. There was nothing politic about the Abbé Combalot, and he stated plainly the sort of things that could scarcely be overlooked. Louis's brother was hard pressed to say anything very positive about the Abbé Combalot as an asset to the cause, and described him as "decorative," and without saying that he actually *was* naive, declared that he looked that way.[156] In any case, he was judged to have defamed and injured the university and to have sought to trouble the public order by arousing hate against the government. The act of the Abbé Combalot that brought these charges was his publishing of the brochure, *Mémoire sur la guerre faite à l'Église et à la société par le monopole universitaire*. Combalot was extreme in his attack on officials of the university as he reacted against the prospect of the Villemain project and other invasions of the university in the realm of Catholicism, and in general his rashness was recognized as such in Catholic circles. Certainly the nature of his attack had not received the sanction of Msgr. Affre.[158] In December of 1843 he had put proofs of his brochure into the hands of Louis Veuillot, who advised him to tone it down, and especially to be careful about anything that might apply to the king and the archbishop. Combalot, however, was not happy about this caution (which coming from Veuillot should have seemed impressive), and his reply was that the publication of these ideas might serve to revitalize the church in its deadly struggle. The only thing that Veuillot did for the Abbé Combalot was to sell copies of his brochure at the offices of *L'Univers*, and to announce by a very few words in the issue of 2 January that the piece was on sale. Five days later all copies in the hands of *L'Univers* were seized by the government, and basis for legal proceedings against the editor-in-chief and the *gérant* of the journal was established.[159]

Whatever the merits of the case against Combalot might have been, Catholics had little alternative now but to come to his defense. *L'Ami de la Religion* and *Le Correspondant* did so with caution, but *L'Univers* took up his cause with passion and without reservation. The case was followed closely,[160] and the pages of *L'Univers* were the vehicle for expression of protests by the episcopacy.[161] News that otherwise might have been given more space received only short mention. Studied reversals of usual concepts featured some of the editorials. For example, *L'Univers* (no doubt Veuillot) maintained in an editorial that the "liberals" were not "liberal,"[162] and the question was raised as to whether the "liberal" government would be dominated by the "tyrannical hatred of old liberalism."[163] Allowing for the usual warnings about playing with terms and throwing back charges to the other side, there was much strength seen in these arguments. Added to whatever valid or effective arguments Louis Veuillot and the rest of the editorial staff of *L'Univers* could muster at this time (and the group was greatly strengthened by the addition of Eugène Veuillot who joined *L'Univers* in February, 1844), were those of numerous bishops who at this juncture joined the assault in the pages of the lay journal, despite misgivings that the episcopacy as a whole had for this arm of Catholicism. Some of them, the Archbishop of Lyons together with the Bishops of Autun, Langres, Saint-Claude, Grenoble, and Dijon, aimed general arguments at the Ministry of Justice and Religion[164] about the growing monopoly of secular education, while others, including the Archbishop of Bourges and the Bishops of Clermont, Saint-Flour, and Puy, addressed their appeal to the king and council.[165] The outcry was broad and strong, but Veuillot's voice was conspicuous, even in such company.

Once the case of the Abbé Combalot was brought to the court room, there was little hope. He was defended by Henri de Riancey, who himself had written a work entitled *Histoire critique et législative de l'instruction publique et de la liberté d'enseignement.*[166] In view of the antagonism between legitimists and the Catholic party at this time, it is interesting to note that Riancey was later particularly to be identified with the legitimists. Significantly for the fate of Combalot (and later Louis Veuillot), this was his first case! Although Veuillot wrote that Riancey was to be congratulated for his efforts, Veuillot was more specific about the fact he was a mere twenty-eight years old and was "pious as an angel."[167] Piety of the defense counsel is of little avail to the defendant, and Combalot was convicted on 6 March, receiving a fortnight of imprisonment and 4000 francs fine for defamation of a public administrator.[168] There is evidence that Louis Philippe desired to cushion this imprisonment as much as possible with considerate treatment for the cleric, and of course, collections were made among the Catholics to pay the fine, but shortly after his release in April Combalot added fuel to the very flames the king was trying to smother.

Louis Philippe invited Combalot to his palace, to which Combalot, in the company of the politique Bishop of Arras, went. When the king, in a light vein, asked Combalot for his opinion about the university monopoly, Combalot answered by censuring in the strongest tones this favored institution of Louis Philippe. Ever careful in his bearing, the king must have been wounded, and may well have determined to carry on the battle as a result. The government was next aiming at Louis Veuillot.[169]

Of course the sale of Combalot's brochure was a convenient pretext for the governmental proceedings, and if this were not enough, the editorials in *L'Univers* would themselves have served the purpose. However, Louis Veuillot wrote a special tract of his own on the case of the Abbé Combalot, *Liberté d'enseignement: Procès de M. l'abbé Combalot*, of which 20,000 copies were printed.[170] On 21 April *L'Univers* was notified action would be brought against its editor-in-chief and *gérant* in the court of assizes of the Seine.[171] On announcing the sentence of Combalot, Veuillot had said "our turn will come,"[172] and he certainly was right. Although Barrier, the *gérant* was defended by another young lawyer, Veuillot's case was argued by the same pious young legitimist, Riancey, with only the Combalot defense behind him. By 12 May he could write as a martyr to lay and ecclesiastical friends that he had been condemned to a month's imprisonment and 3000 francs fine.[173] The trial that took place on 11 May had lasted over three hours, and during its course Riancey resorted to pleading the "incessant persecutions of the government against religion," but apparently the prosecutor satisfied the jury with his case. "Perfect calm reigned constantly throughout the debates,"[174] and Veuillot went off to prison with a request to the préfet for solitary confinement and for his books.[175] On the day after his condemnation he explained to a lay friend that *L'Univers* did not have the money to pay his or Barrier's fine (also 3000), and that a subscription should be launched. "Vive Jésus!" he closed this letter.[176] He entered prison at 5 p.m. on 11 June, expressed satisfaction with his room (for which he had to pay), thanked the police agent, and confided he now had the opportunity to finish a book (non-political) which hitherto he had been unable to do.[177] While in prison his letters were on the same general lines as usual,[178] and although he claimed this incarceration made him give up a trip on the Rhine, his stay seems to have been without unpleasant incident. Normally he was not very careful to indicate the place from which he wrote his letters, but all his letters from the Conciergerie are carefully so indicated. He felt personally persecuted by the government for his religion, and he never forgot this episode. His extremist tendencies certainly were intensified by it.

Before and during his imprisonment various important Catholics who later opposed him seemed close to him, including the future Archbishop of Paris, Darboy, who was then in a much lower situation in Langres. Darboy wrote a very strong letter giving his benediction, and saying that the cause of the clergy and Veuillot's cause were the same.[179] A quarter of a century later, as Archbishop of Paris at the time of the Vatican Council of 1869-1870, Darboy, the martyr of the Commune, represented Gallicanism, and was far apart from Veuillot. In 1844, however, the young cleric warmly espoused the cause of the thirty-year-old journalist convicted of *délit de presse*. Veuillot for his part wrote many clerics at this time, and one of these whom he thanked for their marks of support for him was the Abbé Dupanloup, canon of Saint-Sulpice, later to be Archbishop of Orleans, and his greatest opponent within episcopal ranks. To Dupanloup Veuillot wrote:

> It is a great blessing that God puts me here, because I had need of a little rest, and here I am, granted my wish in prison, finding liberty of the spirit. . . . Pray the Sovereign Master to continue proofs of mercy, in order that I may go out of here more incorrigible than I entered, more decided to serve Him without coldness, without calculation, in the sole purpose of deserving Heaven.[180]

Among the expressions of solidarity from Catholics with whom Veuillot later parted ways, none were more striking than those of Montalembert. In February 1844 Montalembert addressed Veuillot "my dear and valiant warrior."[181] No doubt Veuillot was impressed with the salutation, and certainly he must have noticed the word "warrior." Montalembert practically alone in the Chamber of Peers was fighting the battle of Christianity. There he declared: "We are the sons of the crusaders; we will not retreat from the sons of Voltaire."[182] No doubt Veuillot would like to have thought up that phrase himself. At any rate it won him at the time even more to Montalembert, and he must have recalled such expressions many times while in the Conciergerie. He left prison on 9 July.[183] Not long after his release he wrote the nobleman a letter. Pathetically he spoke of his eyes as "a second prison," and he confined his message to personal matters, especially his gratitude to Montalembert for introducing him to the examples of Saint Elizabeth, Saint Anselm, and Saint Bernard. He expressed the hope the ill Madame de Montalembert might pray for him to Saint Elizabeth. He said nothing about tactics of the Catholic party. Montalembert wrote "extremely affected" on this letter.[184] Had these two men been able to stand together in the next decades, the force of their cause would have been far greater in the political field, but the nature of the two men and their ideas ruled out such a possibility.

The fight that had sent Veuillot to prison had essentially concerned the Villemain bill for education. It came to a head at the time of Veuillot's imprisonment, but the results were hardly decisive, and the battle shifted to another field. The bill had been put before the Chamber of Peers in April, and was furiously debated until late May. Montalembert had left the Madeira Islands in order to lead the Catholic resistance. Louis Veuillot had missed only one of these sessions, the one on 11 May when he had been obliged to appear before the court of assizes of the Seine for his own trial.[185] The régime did everything it could to gain a clear victory, but many of the peers, for one reason or another, voted against this pet project. Practically the entire chamber was present in late May for the vote, and the cabinet did carry the day with an 85 to 51 division.[186] However, in such a matter, where the government, backed by the secular press, including *Le Siècle, Le Constitutionnel,* and *Journal des Débats*, on a question about which the king himself strongly backed Victor Cousin and the whole tradition of secular education, the victory was unimpressive. Whether a real victory would be won if the bill were passed by the deputies and applied as law already seemed questionable. Some points dear to the university would be won, but Catholic opposition to the entire régime might make such a law too costly. The bill of course went to the chamber of deputies, and its sponsor there was none other than Adolphe Thiers, who put it forward with vigor at first. But as the Catholic attack mounted, at the very time of Veuillot's conviction and imprisonment, the ardor of the government languished. Some of the men most devoted to secular tradition were of the opinion that the measure did not go far enough. Others questioned the expediency of the bill under existing circumstances. In any case adjournment and vacation lay ahead, and the matter never came to a vote. The pressure on Villemain became too great and he suffered a nervous breakdown, which gave Guizot opportunity of retiring the bill.[187] The project was really of the greatest importance, for of the opposition to it was formed the short-lived Catholic party, but as the focal point of a fundamental struggle it had an unspectacular end.

The secularists and the Catholics shifted the area of their antagonism to an area where it was easier to let the former have the satisfaction of a victory. Michelet, Quinet, and the whole of the secular press had already turned their guns again on the Jesuits, in an effort, by now obvious, to divide Catholics, particularly with regard to a religious order which had been controversial in the past. *L'Univers* staunchly defended the Jesuits as obedient members of the church, and in no way to be singled out in the Michelet-Quinet fashion,[188] but men like Dupin and Isambert continued the theme in parliament. The Bishop of Châlons in a letter to *L'Univers* declared anew that these attacks on the Jesuits were in fact simply attacks on the Catholics as a whole, and that they were so intended by the secularists.[189] These tactics were common and affected different levels of the battle. Not only were Jesuits singled out in the secular press to be simultaneously a way of attacking Catholics as a whole and also of dividing their ranks, but also the Jesuits were attacked in other literature outside of the editorial columns. Eugène Sue's *Juif errant* was the leading book in the category of the broadside on the Jesuits, of course itself being attacked by *L'Univers.*[190] But this kind of assault became the government's substitute for the troublesome matter of the Villemain education project. The cabinet decided to have a victory over the Jesuits rather than to continue to probe the scholastic hornet's nest, and by the end of the year 1844 Comte Rossi was sent to Rome to persuade Pope Gregory XVI to allow the dissolution of Jesuit establishments in France in exchange for letting Louis Philippe back down on the broader attack on the position of the Catholics in France. Matters did not proceed very rapidly, and it was not until halfway through 1845 that the affair was finished.[191] Louis Philippe was able to say "the Pope has pulled a thorn from my foot."[192] The Jesuit fathers individually did not have to leave France, but their organizations were checked. Again the government won a victory of a sort, but in some ways it seemed more like the end of a round in a fight yet to be decided.

The editor-in-chief of *L'Univers* had been imprisoned, and Catholics, although united in opposition, were divided as to tactics against the secularists in the government and in the university. The provocations were growing, even though the Villemain bill was being laid aside in the second half of 1844. *L'Univers* fulminated when the préfet of Corrèze closed a convent in Tulle in August, and chose this occasion to recall that Voltaire had said, "All great men have been intolerant, and it is necessary so to be."[193] *L'Univers* pointed out the following day that Thiers declared, "The state is the enemy of religion," and that Quinet had pronounced, "The Catholics are the schismatics, the heretics of this era."[194] Even the punctuation of the *Journal des Débats* aroused the dander of *L'Univers*, which found that thirty-seven exclamation marks had been used in one of its editorials attacking Montalembert![195] The chance of the fiery editor's being sent back to prison and the journal's getting into much greater trouble was considerable. The influence of

L'Univers, which had approximately quadrupled its circulation during the first half of the decade, to over 5000, was great, far greater than the circulation, which was still only a fraction of the *Journal des Débats* or *Le Siècle*, would indicate. Many parish priests subscribed to *L'Univers*, and not only was it passed around widely among laymen and clergy, it was incorporated also into countless sermons and gave the basis of argumentation for many of the less articulate clergy. The caution of politic bishops caused many pastoral letters to be rather thin with replies to militant secularists. Louis Veuillot filled the vacuum. He was well aware of what he was doing.[196] Many priests were very open in their acknowledgments to him of their gratitude. All this being the case, prominent Catholics deemed it wise to try to regulate the Catholic press as a whole, particularly *L'Univers*, and to try to coordinate the different elements of the Catholic party.

On 22 October 1844 *L'Univers* appeared with brand new and cleaner-looking type. This change was symbolic of other change. At this general time five great figures in the Catholic movement formed a committee which was to control the policies of *L'Univers*. The formation of this committee came about not through the actions of a regular political organization, which the Catholic party was not, nor through the initiative of the hierarchy, a large part of which had serious reservations about the lay press. These five men, representing different currents among the Catholic activists, decided among themselves that regulation of *L'Univers* was desirable for their common cause, and they persuaded the owner of *L'Univers* Taconet, that he should submit to this surveillance. The big five, who were to restrain *L'Univers* and Louis Veuillot until after the Revolution of 1848 and deepening divisions among the Catholics of that era, were the Comte de Montalembert, the great preacher Lacordaire, the rising churchman Dupanloup, the Jesuit scholar Ravignan, and the ex-universitaire Lenormant. Louis Veuillot, was demoted to adjunct-editor, and the Comte de Coux, one of Lamennais' associates in the days of *L'Avenir,* was made editor-in-chief.[197] Restraint seemed to be the order of the day, at the editorial offices of *L'Univers*.

Elsewhere other Catholic lay forces which could influence the journal were taking shape. One of these was the *Comité pour la défense de la liberté religieuse*. This group was another organization of which the indefatigable Montalembert was president and the rising Henry de Riancey was secretary.[198] Both Veuillot and Taconet were members of this commitee, and it illustrated the fact that there actually was a general desire for concerted effort, which Veuillot shared to a degree. As Eugène Veuillot later put it, "*L'Univers* was an independent force, in all respects disciplined and capable of discipline."[199] That the committee of five which was to supervise *L'Univers* would work in harmony was more than one could expect, and Louis Veuillot no doubt realized this situation from the beginning. Only Montalembert had aided *L'Univers* previously,[200] a fact that may have troubled Veuillot as much as anything else. Individualist that he was in his own way, he could subordinate himself to a cause, at least to the general Catholic cause, but it was painful to give up the recently earned title of editor-in-chief. In one letter to a friend, a letter he asked his friend to burn (which was not done), he says people have accused him of pride in the matter. Obviously he must have thought of abandoning the whole undertaking, but he remained, "not daring to abandon poor Taconet, nor my poor *galère.*"[201] The same Taconet must have encouraged Veuillot. To Montalembert himself Veuillot wrote:

> M. Taconet, perfectly in agreement with me about the direction of the journal, desired to keep me, in spite of all the opposition, at a post where I have only stayed to the present because of scruples of conscience. In his place I would do the same, and I praise him for this firmness. But you are our chief, and just as I believe myself to have the duty to disobey you sometimes, I recognize your right to put me aside. You have but to say the word. My resignation is in your hands.[202]

Veuillot's biggest hope to be able to run things for the most part in the way that he saw fit lay in the different ideas that the five had. Divide and rule must have been the principle that held out hope. De Coux, who had been an editor with Lamennais, and who had social position, gave *L'Univers* a respectable and much less controversial front, but he simply was not the sort of man who shaped things. Veuillot saw through him at once. Montalembert and Dupanloup were the politically active forces with which to reckon. Even if Taconet were to allow the committee to go in a direction he and Veuillot did not approve, which Veuillot thought was doubtful, he was sure those two would disagree. Should Montalembert win in a struggle with Dupanloup, he would be imprudent, but if Dupanloup should carry the day, he would "be vacillating and feeble."[203] The others, of course, complicated the picture and added other divisions that could permit *L'Univers* to continue pretty much as it had been going under Veuillot. This situation became clear to Veuillot while he was speculating about whether to remain at his post. Lacordaire was politically democratic, at least to a degree. Montalembert was described by Veuillot as politically "dynastique avec beaucoup d'absences." The Abbés Dupanloup and Ravignan he lumped at this era as legitimists, and Lenormant, despite sacrifices he made for his Catholic beliefs, Veuillot described as politically *doctrinaire et guizotin.*[204] How to be an editor, even adjunct-editor, under such people? Only by profiting from their divisions seems to have been the answer. In the next few years the influence of Veuillot was little diminished, and while *L'Univers* may have been more careful about its polemics than it would have been without the committee of five, Veuillot's calculations at the beginning of 1845 seem to have been proven essentially correct.

Louis Veuillot never forgot his imprisonment,[205] and one of the periods of greatest outward stress during his life was this year 1844. Yet troubles in any one aspect of his existence never seemed to bother him too greatly as he turned his attention to other things. It has been observed that he could heap invective on an opponent and be doing so as an assault against a public figure without the feeling that the private person was also being struck.[206] He could say the strongest things about a man, as though there were a public side of the person separate from the intimate being, and then meet the person socially and individually as though this were someone else. Whatever the explanation may be, the furious battle in which he participated in 1844 apparently did not ruffle his private feelings very deeply. His literary activities were not hurt by the religious-political battles. In fact, his month in the Conciergerie, once imposed, was, as he said, at least partially welcomed by him as a respite from the preoccupations that had slowed his preferred activities as *écrivain.* The case of Villemain's breakdown may be contrasted with the way Veuillot stood up under pressure. Villemain, too, was a literary figure of ability, but he did not have the resiliancy to play the game of attacks and counterattacks. Villemain apparently went completely mad, according to an account Eugène accepted, fancying inanimate objects to be Jesuits pursuing him, and even flinging himself, during one of his hallucinations, out of a window which, happily for him, was on the *rez de chaussée.* Eventually he recovered, although much changed, and continued his literary career. But in later life he had a Jesuit for his confessor, after returning to the faith, and supported the temporal power of the pope.[207] Whereas Villemain had gone to pieces in a most spectacular way before being able to return to writing, Veuillot's efforts were hardly interrupted.

In the period 1844-1845 at least three major projects resulted, each one of which made an impact. One of his leading novels was *L'Honnête Femme*, which had already appeared in the form of a *feuilleton* in *Le Correspondant*. However, Veuillot wanted to revise it in response to criticisms he believed well founded. The story essentially dealt with two worlds, the Christian and the non-Christian, and hence was strongly moralistic. However, it had considerable literary appeal as a reflection of life in Périgord, specifically Périgueux called "Chignac" in the book. It had many of the same sort of traits that Flaubert's *Madame Bovary* was to show with regard to realism. When published in 1857 Saint-Beuve, often sympathetic with Veuillot, said the book *copied* the life of the region described.[208] Veuillot had his story to tell of a provincial woman and the forces of the two worlds, but he was fixing on a literary tintype with great care the life that was the background for his tale. Quite likely he was glad to be able to date his preface, "la Conciergerie de Paris, 6 July 1844."[209] He also brought together a collection of miscellaneous writings, including *L'Épouse Imaginaire*, and put them between one cover, called *Les Nattes*. This volume, which appeared in 1844, was later further reworked and supplemented, reappearing in 1862 as *Historiettes et Fantaisies*. Also, during this era, he worked on his considerably delayed *Les Français en Algérie,* which was published in 1845. Any one of these volumes would have required a literary man of a different stamp a long period of time to prepare. Louis Veuillot, whose eyes were particularly a problem then, was nonetheless able to put them all in publishable form, while carrying on his battles with the secular press, struggling with other forces in the ranks of the Catholics, and weathering a term in prison. As though all these preoccupations were not enough, the matchmakers were still at their work and succeeded in bringing about his marriage in 1845!

At several periods in his life he had thought about marrying, and particularly since his return to Paris from his provincial journalistic career his friends had attempted to arrange a marriage. As a man so fanatically devoted to his cause it would seem almost inappropriate for him to marry, and in a way one might have expected such an enthusiast to give himself entirely to the cause in celibacy. Yet it really was entirely fitting that he took a bride and had a decade of harmonious domesticity, since Louis Veuillot was so much the incarnation of the layman. He was far from insensitive to the allures of the ladies, and the life of a bourgeois of Paris was most appealing to him. At no time did the cares of marriage distract him from his cause, and some of his most important efforts and battles took place at the very time when several tragedies took from him his wife and three of his daughters. Marriage was certainly not a prison for him, and even prison had not prevented him from his projects. He spoke of himself as "married to *L'Univers*" on one occasion, and called himself "the illegitimate spouse of the muse" on another,[210] but he was a model husband, almost spectacularly so. If one were looking for a good example of the fortunate arranged marriage, Louis Veuillot's would serve very well.

According to his brother, Reverend Fathers Aulanier and Varin were at the heart of the conspiracy to get him married, being joined by his old friend Émile Lafon, and the couple whose Catholic domesticity had been so persuasive to him in Rome, the Féburiers.[211] Moreover, the power of suggestion was also at work in the matter of the marriage of his sister. Fortunately for Louis Veuillot, Élise never married, serving as his lifelong aide, but in the spring of 1845 their sister Annette was married to Stanislas Desquers, a solid young man whom Louis had come to know in Périgueux, and whose later career as a Catholic printer gave him a bond with Veuillot.[212] This marriage was apparently a catalyst for Louis's own marriage which took place 30 July 1845.

The bride was a very proper Catholic young woman of petit-bourgeois background named Mathilde Murcier. Her parents had a small baking establishment in Versailles, and could hardly have furnished a dot of any size, but there was a well-to-do grandmother. The girl was twenty-one, not badly educated, not bad looking, and was thoroughly unassuming, but by the usual concepts governing marriage arrangement needed a dot of 40,000 francs. This sum her grandmother at first promised. The grandmother was thoroughly in the mercantile caste, and as she came to know Louis Veuillot turned against him; he in turn found her not to his liking either. The grandmother accordingly made known not only her disapproval, but the withdrawal of the 40,000. Veuillot had debts of several thousand francs at the time of his conversion, and was not in much better shape in 1845. He would have been even worse off had a subscription for his fine and costs of imprisonment not been taken. It was his controversial journalism and its attendant problems that turned the grandmother against him. Veuillot, not without some distress, was willing to accept what seemed to be the inevitable end of the matter when part of the contract could not be kept, but an interview with an even more distressed M. Murcier caused him to follow an unconventional course. The father pointed out that everyone had expected the marriage. The *linge* was already marked "Veuillot." The dressmakers were at their job. In short, his daughter would be torn to pieces if everything fell apart at this point. Mathilde had seemed an acceptable bride to Veuillot, but her name had not pleased him. He could easily enough have let matters drop with the withdrawal of the 40,000 francs. But at this point he began to feel compassion for the poor young woman. He assured M. Murcier that he did not want anything from the grandmother, much less her excuses; that he would marry the girl in any case. At this turn of affairs they headed for Versailles. Veuillot wrote that had their train not been on time he might have done some reflecting, but this train departed punctually on the Rive Gauche line, and he was shortly afterward face to face with Mathilde. Her relieved and grateful look did the rest. Veuillot's pock-marked face must have looked good at least that once – to a young girl who dreaded facing the couturières! The marriage took place shortly after this episode, and it had a happy development; the maternal grandmother who had not liked the prospective groom delivered the dot after all![213]

The man of 32 and the bride of 21 were married by Father de Ravignan at the end of July. Marshal Bugeaud, of whom Veuillot wrote: "His sword was a frontier, his name a flag."[214] was among those congratulating him. The tough old general told him frankly he had not cared for some of the articles he had seen in *L'Univers religieux* and he was happier speaking of his marriage. "Adieu, my dear Veuillot; be happy in your new estate, and always recall that I am strongly interested in you in spite of your extraordinary ideas, which I hope your wife will make disappear."[215] His wife gave him a new dimension in life, but she did not fulfill the wishes of Marshal Bugeaud. Veuillot became even more outspoken in the ultramontane cause, after becoming a family man. Certainly one cannot say demure Mathilde Murcier restrained her husband in any way or impeded his career.

The bride and groom eventually went on a honeymoon of over a month's duration in Savoy and Switzerland, but they could not leave for nearly a month after their marriage. The pressure of affairs at *L'Univers* made Veuillot feel bound to his post even at a time like this, and he might not have set off even when he did had the Bishop of Annecy, Msgr. Rendu, not asked him to come.[216] It was at this time that the announcement of De Coux's appointment was made. The trip must have had its delights, but the one letter he wrote to brother Eugène, who, practically speaking, was the business manager of the journal at this time, hardly sounded idyllic. He explained that Mathilde had "un certain malaise," and that as for himself he had a "gros rhume," but one that was not so bad that he could not smoke. He mentioned that Saint Francis de Sales and Sainte Jeanne de Chantal were buried at Annecy, but the most extraordinary line in the letter was: "The *présence* and the condition of Mathilde had changed all my plans."(!)[217] This letter of mid-September certainly indicates that Louis Veuillot could turn on and turn off his moods. One of the most famous passages he ever wrote was the opening part of *Ça et là, Du mariage et de Chamounix*, written sometime after 1852 and published in 1860. The charm of this description lay in the way in which he blended reality and religious ideas. Simple human existence reaches a high plane amid happy circumstances in the beautiful Chamounix Valley, according to the way Veuillot describes it. The conversation of "Marianne" and "Sylvestre" is, of course, that of himself and his bride.[218] Jules Lemaître much admired the *souplesse incroyable* and the *extrême diversité de ton et d'accent*.[219] Fourteen years later Louis Veuillot, speaking of the felicitous expressions he used of his bride, declared he had not exaggerated.[220] Certainly he did put some graceful religious lines into the mouth of the bourgeois girl of Versailles, who is made to utter poetry in the presence of a priest at an appropriately religious juncture:

> C'est la madone du village!
> Encor un peu de chemin,
> Bientôt tu verras son image:
> Courage, bon pèlerin![221]

Even this priest, "l'Abbé Théodore," was a real person, the Abbé Moigno, a literary man himself,[222] and the whole area from Annecy to Geneva was real enough. But Veuillot took an actual relationship, a well-known vacation area, and typical Catholic attitudes, blending them into a first-rate literary piece, the kind a special clientele would like to read. Thus, even his honeymoon was not wasted time for his readers.

Throughout his life, particularly in later years, Veuillot had many intelligent ladies among his friends, and few men have valued intelligent women any higher. He was a good middle-class husband to Mathilde, but she was never exactly in his world of ideas. Even on his honeymoon he wrote to the prior of Solesmes, Dom Guéranger: "My wife is very Christian, obedient, and unliterary, not so unlettered, however, that she does not know and love with all possible respect the children of Saint Benedict, and that she does not read *L'Auxiliaire*" (by which he meant that she did not keep up with the literary world).[223] Actually he customarily spoke very chivalrously of his wife, and made such statements as that not Henri V but Mathilde was his sovereign.[224] Whether he would have been happy with an intellectual wife (such as Juliette de Robersart, for whom he showed great interest at a later date) is questionable. Donoso Cortés, for whose ideas Veuillot had the highest esteem, thought Mathilde a model of demureness and piety,[225] and this judgment alone must have been a great satisfaction to Louis Veuillot. In any case the next few years were very difficult ones for him, and he certainly benefited from having no reason for asserting himself at home where he was thoroughly master, and where his wife answered the description of an ideal wife of the traditional sort that must have pleased him.

A glance at his *Œuvres complètes* shows that he did not write very many articles or letters between the summer of 1845 and the spring of 1846. This period was certainly one of the most quiet periods of his life before the period between 1860 and 1867. He worked on plans for writing, probably writing all of *Corbin et d'Aubecourt* (which appeared in the 10 July-10 August 1846 numbers of *Le Correspondant*). The articles which he did write for *L'Univers* showed that much work had gone into them. His discussion of the persecutors of the Jesuits in various countries including England was almost overwhelming in the mass of precise information he brought forth.[226] His treatment of the Russian persecutions of the Poles dipped into a good deal of history for the buttressing of his arguments.[227] His linking of Voltaire to the same topic, in such a way as to show the man of the Enlightenment as an enemy of the French at the same time that he encouraged Catherine in her projects against Poland, was done with care and skill.[228] Clearly he was taking his time with what he did write. But Louis Veuillot was as nearly on the sidelines in this era as he ever would be while he still had his health and was not being forcibly restrained by the régime.

On 12 August 1845 the announcement appeared in *L'Univers* that the Comte Charles de Coux, former professor of political economy at the Catholic University of Louvain, had become editor-in-chief, with Louis Veuillot the *Rédacteur en chef adjoint*. It has been suggested that Louis Veuillot laughed when penning the title.[229] However, by October there were genuine signs that De Coux was something more than a respectable front for the *enfant terrible* of Catholic journalism. Writing early in October to his close personal friend Dumast, Louis Veuillot noted: "M. de Coux has very seriously taken the reins of the journal. Bit by bit I have shed my personality for him, I have withdrawn, I have disappeared, I have buried myself. It is ever an easy thing, and I have had as much satisfaction and convenience as I desired. If it pleases God, I will see the desired moment and appear no more; I will be of the journal behind M. de Coux; at home I will be behind my wife, who does not love the world; at the publishing house I will be anonymous. That is my dream; I have desired nothing but the victory of God, as I want silence and oblivion at present."[230]

At least for a little while Veuillot gave indications of being satisfied with the work of De Coux. Near the end of the year 1845 he said to his confidant Dumast: "M. de Coux has written some excellent articles which you will recognize without any difficulty, articles which I never would have been able to write, *et ne m'allége pas d'un fétu.*" However, he complained of "unbearable boredom" in having to keep quiet, and that his style of polemic was the foundation of the true *L'Univers.*[231] He defended De Coux against charges De Coux was not treating him well, calling him *le meilleur homme du monde*.[232] In mid-1846 he referred to De Coux in a letter to his naval officer friend, Commandant de Maisonneuve, as "the excellent M. de Coux, whom you have seen at my house."[233] However superficial Veuillot's inclination to be charitable toward De Coux at this time may have been, there was indeed in his attitude a tendency toward solidarity at a time when the ranks of the Catholics suffered from some serious internal splits.

By the spring of 1846 the existence of a new journal, *L'Alliance*, attacks made in Rome against *L'Univers*, and the personalities of several men, particularly Montalembert, complicated matters for Veuillot and for *L'Univers*. The ambassador of the King of the French in Rome, Comte Rossi, who was an adventurer of a sort, spread criticism against *L'Univers* at the Holy See. Despite the efforts of Rossi to get the postal inspectors of the States of the Church to ban *L'Univers* from the pontifical mails, only a few numbers were thus prohibited, and both Gregory XVI and his secretary of state, Cardinal Lambruschini, were generally well disposed toward *L'Univers*.[234] In this situation Montalembert wrote a mémoire for the papal government, in general defending the freedom of *L'Univers* and pointing out the unwisdom of suppressing it on any ground. Actually, the Comte de Montalembert was hardly in any special favor at the Holy See, partly because of his criticisms of the papacy for not doing more to aid Poland against Russian persecutions and partly because of his liberalism.[235] But Montalembert was never reluctant to tell anyone what was right, including the government of the Holy Father. There was nothing sneaky about his approach, so far as *L'Univers* was concerned, as he let the journal know what his recommendations were. However, his mémoire included such lines as "no one knows better than I the many faults of *L'Univers*!" He continued to the effect that it would nevertheless be a pity if it went out of existence, because, who else would be fighting the ultramontane battle? If *L'Univers* were suppressed, the dozen or so provincial papers which took their cue from it would also disappear. If the Papal States banned the paper, the régime in Paris would use this move as an excuse to suppress it, to the general loss of the whole Catholic movement.[236] Ultramontanism, indeed, was often associated with liberalism in that era. This frank mémoire not only displeased Lambruschini, but also Gregory XVI himself, who said to Montalembert's brother-in-law, Comte de Mérode, "Your brother-in-law Montalembert is a great orator, full of fire, his pen is excellent; he speaks truly very well, but he speaks too much."[237] Montalembert was irritating not only at the Holy See, but at the offices of *L'Univers*.

For a moment it appeared as though the death of Gregory XVI on 1 June 1846 might bring harmony between Montalembert and Louis Veuillot. Even this occasion, however, gave rise to new differences. The first writing that Veuillot did after the passing of the pope, a brief eulogy, contained a statement about the pope's courage in protesting against the Russian persecution of the Poles.[238] Certainly this line did not please Montalembert. However, Veuillot's next article dealt with the conclave and the intrigues of Rossi, with incidental barrages at the editor of *Siècle.*[239] This discussion was more to Montalembert's liking, but after a brief mention of his pleasure over Veuillot's attack, he brought up the matter of the new journal, *L'Alliance*. For some time the favor that Msgr. Parisis, Bishop of Langres, and Montalembert had shown for it seemed to blend with plans that were being pushed for Taconet to sell out to it. Presumably there were some well-to-do Catholics behind it whose generosity would make the transaction possible. Taconet, harried by a variety of pressures, understandably gave consideration to some sort of deal. As matter of fact, however, the matter was only in a discussion stage. The men connected with *L'Alliance* were not of the calibre of those who ran *L'Univers*, and the forces behind *L'Alliance* were partly in the camp of the legitimists. At any rate, the whole suggestion disturbed Montalembert, and he said a number of very rash things to Veuillot. Speaking in a way that he may have partly intended as flattery for Veuillot, Montalembert referred to the "inadequacy of *L'Univers* under the scepter of M. de Coux." He also chided Taconet for being *reduced* to treat with the proprietors of *L'Alliance.*[240] What particularly bothered Veuillot was Montalembert's presumption that he, Veuillot, could do anything about it all as *adjunct* editor, especially since Montalembert suggested that there must have been some personal gain for him in the deal. Veuillot stoutly defended De Coux,[241] and his spirited answer on 4 July 1846 about his own role certainly put the future relations of the two men in jeopardy.[242]

After this episode, good fortune for the Catholic party in the elections of 1846 may have helped set the stage for more personal trouble between the two, involving the papacy's reaction to the French Catholics. Montalembert remained practically the only clear representative of the Catholic forces in the parliament, but the Catholic party, instead of contesting seats, had gained commitments from a very considerable number of politicians to support its projects.[243] With this victory in mid-summer, Canon Dupanloup went to Rome with projects of his own about the future of education in France. By this time the death of Gregory XVI had occurred, and a new pope, had been chosen,

Giovanni Maria Mastai-Ferretti. He was a different man from Gregory XVI, and it was possible that he might have been turned against Louis Veuillot and *L'Univers* from the very beginning of his pontificate. It was not Dupanloup's fault that he was not, because he made known at the Holy See a letter which Montalembert wrote to a friend in Rome. By this time the idea had been suggested to Montalembert that he should be controlling *L'Univers* himself. Writing to his friend, the Abbé Hiron, Montalembert accused Veuillot and Taconet of "a great crime" in not turning Taconet's paper over to him. Only a little earlier in the year Montalembert had been pointing out the virtues of *L'Univers*, but by summer he had apparently forgotten them. *L'Univers* had become "the shame of Catholicism."[244] Louis Veuillot, of course, was not long in hearing of this description.

Veuillot fired back at Montalembert in a way that made any permanent reconciliation practically impossible. "M. Taconet and I, but especially I, according to you, have refused out of *pride* to submit to the direction of important men in the Catholic party." At great length Veuillot refuted and defended "Taconet et moi" against these charges. He said he was not surprised that Dupanloup had been slandering him, but he made it clear he was shocked at what Montalembert had been saying about him. He was a man of pride – he wanted to know what he had done that Montalembert was taking vengeance in this way.[245] De Coux joined Veuillot in coming back at Montalembert, particularly in resenting the statement that the direction of *L'Univers* was *occulte*.[246] Veuillot poured out his heart to Du Lac, then at Solesmes, over these charges.[247]

Montalembert, of course, came back at Veuillot. Maintaining that he did not take Veuillot's reproaches personally, and that he was only directing his criticisms at *L'Univers*, he nevertheless attacked Veuillot, Taconet, and Du Lac afresh. He said that it was "criminal" of Taconet to consider selling *L'Univers* to the group of Catholics behind *L'Alliance*. He referred to the "hardness and bitterness" of Veuillot's reproaches, and the "violence" with which he made them. He claimed that Du Lac had told him that he acted like a *thief*, and that other "subordinates" at the offices of *L'Univers* had treated him in such a way that he was not going to come back there again! Eugène Veuillot maintained that this charge was unjust, but at the same time admitted that Montalembert had been coldly received, and that his picture on the wall had been turned around! One interesting revelation in Montalembert's rejoinder to Veuillot was his claim that the idea of the committee to control *L'Univers* had been Lacordaire's, not Montalembert's. Lacordaire may indeed have voiced the proposal first, but he showed little interest in the functioning of the committee after it was formed. The mutual lack of rapport between him and Dupanloup may also have accounted for the fact that neither of them played any really active role. In any case it is curious that Montalembert pointed out that the function of supervising *L'Univers* had not been proposed by himself.[248] After a time Montalembert and Veuillot were to stand together again, but a return to anything like their former closeness was henceforth impossible.

Pius IX, however, was not influenced against Veuillot by this controversy. The very first piece Veuillot wrote about the new pope showed some insight. The protestant and secular press, notably the *Semeur* and *Siècle*, had been criticizing the papacy in such a way that the new Catholic journal, *L'Alliance*, was prompted to answer by saying that the new pontiff "would have knowledge of the new times." Without quibbling with *L'Alliance*, which Veuillot protested he respected, he said Pius IX would be a pope for these "new times" in the same way that the apostles and Christians of all ages are of their times when they renounce the world for God. He discussed the terrible changes of the last century, but he suggested what might be the outlook of the new pope. Admitting he did not know what Pius IX might have read, he suggested that De Maistre's *Du Pape* had appeared in 1819, a time when the Abbé Mastaï was forming his ideas, and that this new assertion of Catholic absolutism was very likely to be at the basis of his thought.[249] The article was confident of the leadership of the new Vicar of Christ, and although Veuillot did have some unpublicized fears that he expressed the next year to Du Lac about the possibility of the new pope's appointing new and questionable cardinals,[250] his faith in Pius IX was deep. He staked everything on him in any case, and in so doing was very fortunate in his calculations. The ideas of Pius IX could not have turned out to be more to his liking, particularly after 1848, and in pinning his hopes to Pius IX he also chose the pope whose reign was the longest of any in history.

In the period 1846-1848 Pius IX followed somewhat different policies in the papal states from those to be developed during the succeeding thirty years. The significance of his pontificate was not yet clear, and different groups of Catholics had different hopes about his effect upon the future. The Italian statesman, priest, and political philosopher, Vincenzo Gioberti, hoped that Pius IX, as a liberal pontiff, would make a good rallying point for Italian nationalists. Many, both within and outside of Italy hoped that Gioberti's ideas were being espoused by the pope, and many others believed that in any event this liberal line of thought would prevail. But in the same period great concern about the Jesuits, both by their supporters and by their opponents within Catholic ranks, complicated the picture, especially as a result of the recent measures taken against them by France, Bavaria, and other states, and the persecution of them in Switzerland. Not surprisingly these considerations produced yet more division among the French Catholics, and the staff of *L'Univers* was further divided.

This general situation especially caused a split between De Coux and Louis Veuillot, who had only recently been driven together by the impetuosity of Montalembert. The regular correspondent for *L'Univers* in Rome, the Abbé Chéruel, who had been inspired by the ideas of Giobertian liberalism, wrote enthusiastic letters about the new direction in which he believed the papacy was heading. He believed Pius IX and his secretary of state, Cardinal Gizzi, were definitely embarked on a new course, and that the nuncio in Paris, Msgr. Fornari, and the Jesuits would be obstacles to this papal progressivism. De Coux, who had once been on the board of *L'Avenir* and had been an enthusiastic supporter of Lamennais, was sympathetic with this position.[251] Louis Veuillot, however, was not. He was staunchly a supporter of the Jesuits, and he feared that the liberals in Italy were trying to sweep Pius IX along on their course of political action. Despite De Coux's position as editor-in-chief many of the editorials written by Veuillot during mid-1847 reflect opposition to Giobertian liberalism.[252] The staff of *L'Univers* suffered from this division. Unfortunately for Veuillot, Du Lac, at the Abbey of Solesmes, had not yet taken up again his regular duties with *L'Univers*, but as correspondent especially for matters concerning the question of liturgy, then much in the limelight, he did exercise his influence as strongly as he could from a distance in support of Veuillot. Barrier and Coquille were behind him also, as were Bailly and Albéric de Blanche. Of course Eugène was too. The Riancey brothers, Henri and Charles, who remained with *L'Univers* until the Revolution of 1848, also inclined towards him. Jules Gondon, the specialist for Great Britain, an important function at that era because of the Irish question, was neutral, as was Auguste Avond, who was concerned with parliamentary matters. But although none of these men opposed Veuillot, Taconet's role as owner was unclear. He was under the influence of the liberal Abbé Hiron, despite the fact that his bourgeois nature made him hesitant about any precipitateness in political action, but whatever he thought, he did not offer much check to Veuillot's editorial line,[253] thus leaving De Coux in a nearly isolated position.

As the Catholics became more divided in the late forties, the movement for replacing the twenty-one different liturgies used in the eighty-one dioceses of France made matters more complicated, sharpening the growing ultramontane-versus-Gallican issue, and involving laymen in a matter which would seem to have been initially the preserve of the clergy. The center of the movement was the Abbey of Solesmes, where Dom Guéranger worked for the replacement of these French liturgies, especially the one of Paris (which was used in thirty-four of the dioceses, as opposed to only twenty-four that used the Roman liturgy), with the Roman liturgy.[254] Until 1848 Melchior Du Lac was there, corresponding copiously in 1847 with Veuillot, and writing the material that appeared in *L'Univers* on this subject. The idea of such a unifying influence as a common liturgy appealed strongly to Veuillot, who threw himself enthusiastically behind the movement. By this time his correspondence with the episcopacy had become quite extensive. He was writing to various bishops about such matters as education,[255] problems concerning the refusal of burial to non-Catholics in Catholic cemeteries,[256] and even such matters as reported visions of the Holy Virgin.[257] Only Msgr. Parisis, Bishop of Langres, and possibly Msgr. Gousset, Archbishop of Reims, gave him any encouragement in the matter of the Roman liturgy.[258] However, *L'Univers* persisted in support of the movement for the Roman liturgy, which indeed was eventually uniformly adopted throughout France.

Education and the conflict between the Catholics and the university-supporting regime continued to be burning questions through the reign of Louis Philippe, developing ever more complexity. Canon Dupanloup, playing the role of the *politique* in 1846-1847, had a project for education that was something of a compromise. Rossi had been working for an entente between church and state in France, and the force of someone like Dupanloup could have made a great deal of difference. Veuillot turned thoroughly against him in this era, and on Christmas Day of 1846 wrote to Du Lac of his "duplicity."[259] Already another prelate not an adversary of some of the policy of *L'Univers* had criticized Veuillot for violence and inappropriateness of language. Veuillot had gone to some length to defend himself, admitting however that "indiscretions are inseparable from the existence of a journal." He said, "There is an inconvenience of publicity which has to be excused in view of its advantages."[260] In the matter of Dupanloup's activity, particularly a brochure of his entitled *De la liberté de l'enseignement. État de la question*, Veuillot really opened fire despite the recent warning.[261] Montalembert did not care for Dupanloup's project, but he nonetheless defended Dupanloup, and something of a rapprochement took place between the two at this point.[262] Msgr. Parisis tried to effect a general conciliation, but he was not successful. Veuillot resented

Dupanloup's haughty attitude along with his compromising politics.[263] Again Montalembert contributed much to the divisions, and on the occasion of a banquet honoring O'Connell he refused to sit at the same table as the editors of *L'Univers*, for which Henri de Riancey chided him.[264] Veuillot for his part resented both Montalembert and Dupanloup, and declared to Du Lac, "I will demolish Dupanloup and humble Montalembert."[265] Such was the unity of the Catholics.

At this juncture Villemain's successor as minister of public instruction, Salvandy, a person whom Veuillot regarded as essentially well-meaning though misguided, presented a bill to the deputies that embodied some of the ideas of Dupanloup's project. Veuillot classed it along with Villemain's scheme. The measure had the same fate, at least, as Villemain's bill. It was hotly debated both in parliament and in the press, with *L'Univers* exchanging salvos with the *Journal des Débats, le National*, and *le Constitutionnel.* Distinguished figures like the Duc de Broglie and Dupanloup served as targets of Veuillot's attacks.[266] But despite the lively tempo of the campaign, there never was a decision on the bill before the Revolution of 1848 buried the issue.

The educational question of 1847 not only intensified difficulties between Veuillot and other Catholic leaders, but also further alienated Guizot from Veuillot. In *L'Univers* Veuillot wrote that in backing the "absolutism" of this new university scheme Guizot "appears to us to have forgotten his liberalism of 1837 and his wisdom of 1846."[267] However, another matter which tended to cloud relations between Guizot and Veuillot gave Montalembert and Veuillot something on which they could again stand shoulder to shoulder. This situation was the affair of the Sonderbund in Switzerland.

Twentieth-century Switzerland presents an aspect of peacefulness that belies its history, including that of the nineteenth century. The federal government of that time was confronted by a group of cantons desiring more local power, and the situation became inflamed as a result of long standing Catholic-protestant antagonism. Governmental questions already were serious when in 1844 the Catholic canton of Lucerne recalled the Jesuits, who had been expelled by the central government. By 1845 a league of seven states, Lucerne, Fribourg, Uri, Unterwalden, Valais, Schwyz, and Zug was formed to resist what may be described as liberal, protestant, and federal pressure. In 1847 actual fighting broke out, and a considerable crisis existed in Europe. Especially during the fall of 1847 Veuillot was greatly concerned about the fate of the Swiss Catholics. He wrote to the commander of the league, or Sonderbund, General Kalbermaten, expressing his high esteem and hopes,[268] but since the liberal-central forces greatly outnumbered the Catholics, he realized that their only hope was for the intervention of outside forces. Such forces could only come as a result of the policy of either Metternich or Guizot.[269] The issue was soon decided in the fighting in Switzerland, particularly at Gislikon in November of 1847, before any outside force had an opportunity for intervention. In fact, Guizot wrote in his own memoirs that French intervention in behalf of the Sonderbund would have brought dangers hardly commensurate with the gains that might have been made for religious freedom for the Catholics there.[270] Veuillot appreciated Guizot's high regard for the pope and for Catholicism, and counted Guizot as the most perceptive of protestants, as well as the most highly placed,[271] but to him the sacrifice of religious liberty in Switzerland, compounded as it was with victory for the anti-Jesuits, was a defeat of the first rank, further embittering him against the régime of the July Monarchy.

After watching the forces of the Sonderbund going down to defeat, Veuillot resented attacks on the Jesuits in his own country, attacks which he believed really directed against Catholicism, although labeled anti-Jesuit because of the supposed suspicion about this order in the public mind. The question of the Jesuits further split the ranks of the Catholic party after the Revolution of 1848 but in late 1847 had already driven the wedge between De Coux and Veuillot. Various journals referred to *L'Univers* as "the journal of the Jesuits." Veuillot explained to De Coux why he felt these tactics were used, and declared that their journal would be just that in so far as Jesuitism represented Catholicism as a whole. In any case, the pope would see what was behind the attacks on the Jesuits, Louis Veuillot believed.[272] Since De Coux had great doubts both about the Jesuits and about the Sonderbund,[273] the journal could hardly have been expected to continue much longer with such divided leadership. The Revolution decided the issue, it would seem, but the return of Du Lac to Paris and to active participation in the affairs of *L'Univers*, which coincided with the Revolution, might well have been enough alone.

In private life Louis Veuillot seems to have had a placid period of happiness in these years. At first he and his bride lived in rather tight quarters at 21, rue de Babylone, with Eugène and Élise. Eugène and Élise, both of whom worked as closely with Louis as only a brother and a sister could, moved out during the early part of 1846 leaving the newlyweds alone at last.[274] By late spring Marie was born.[275] By this time they had moved to the address where Veuillot lived until the last decade of his life, 44, rue du Bac, on the third *étage* of a *magnifique hôtel,* with a court and a garden. He described it to Du Lac as "the strangest in the world, simple and primitive, but, all considered, commodious, airy, spacious. It has the loft of a palace. No bourgeois would want it, and Mathilde, who is a bit bourgeois, made a bit of a grimace at these magnificent mansards. Eugène claims that it suits me because I am peasant and grand seigneur."[276] The most extraordinary feature of the apartment was that it looked into the garden of the apartment at 40, rue du Bac where Montalembert resided for much of his life. The two could talk to each other without leaving their own quarters.[277] Here, through estrangement and through reconciliation the Catholic party's leader and its editor resided in the closest physical proximity for many years.

At 44, rue du Bac Veuillot's second daughter, Agnès (who was to have been Pierre had she been a boy) was born in 1847.[278] In general things went well with his family in the period before the Revolution of 1848. He had some illnesses of Mathilde's and of the children's to write about,[279] but no hint of the tragic developments that were to come. In August of 1846 Louis Veuillot went to visit Msgr. Rendu, Bishop of Annecy, without taking his wife, whom he left with her parents in Versailles. It was rather unusual that a man should be going alone to the scene of his honeymoon only a year after his marriage, and be writing his bride about it all,[280] but apparently Veuillot saw nothing odd about it. His private existence seems to have been altogether happy at this time. At times he visited the salons of the Comtesse de Gontaut and of Madame Swetchine,[281] but these circles seem to have been very unimportant to him and not altogether to his taste. In short, his private life was well adjusted and satisfactory. Lamentations about his eyes and other health problems were then at a minimum. Not being the titular editor-in-chief may even have agreed with him. He got full credit for his ultramontane stands and successfully forced his journal into a pro-Jesuit stamp without having to bear the final responsibilities for getting out the journal. A showdown was developing in the offices of *L'Univers*, however, and even before the coming of the February 1848 Revolution, some changes seemed to be lying ahead for him. The overthrow of Louis Philippe and the advent of the Second Republic insured that there would be a new era in his life.

CHAPTER IV

THE REVOLUTION OF 1848 AND LOUIS NAPOLEON

As in 1830, the regime in France in 1848 had lost much of its support and also had many adversaries. City workingmen were much more prominent among the opponents of the government in 1848 than had been the case in 1830. Nevertheless pressure again from disenfranchised middle-class people precipitated the Revolution of 1848, as in 1830. Through 1847 the peculiar method of protest was the banquet movement, the practical answer to the government's prohibition on political rallies. As this movement grew, and as Louis Philippe's key minister, Guizot, became the special target of protest with his "enrichissez-vous" attitude towards those who did not pay high enough taxes to qualify for the electorate, Veuillot and *L'Univers* gave little heed. *L'Univers* was concentrating heavily on strictly Catholic concerns rather than those of secular politics. In fact, Guizot's relative sympathy for the Sonderbund caused Veuillot to deal with him gently in this period. On the eve of the Revolution of 1848 Veuillot's view of that "most enlightened" of French protestants, who had declared that "the papacy is today both the supreme element in progress and the supreme guarantee of order in all human societies,"[1] was somewhat detached:

> Our sentiments for Guizot are known. They are neither those of love nor of confidence. We admire his talents; we do not believe in his character, and we expect nothing from him. He was able to do a great deal for order and for liberty. God has admirably endowed him for defending them. He has been in a position to do immense good for healthy doctrines which alone could restore and save the country. . . .What has come from all this? Some great speeches, but nothing else. He has betrayed his talent, his integrity, and his friends, and his destiny.[2]

After Guizot fell and fled to England, Veuillot resumed his friendly personal correspondence with him, once more proving the point that he made a great distinction between the public and private aspects of a personage.[3] Although Veuillot had in no way given aid and encouragement to the opposition, he had certainly held no special brief for Guizot.

On the very day before events began to take place in Paris leading to the downfall of the July Monarchy, Veuillot well summed up the ironic situation:

> Nothing could be more bizarre and at the same time more sad than the situation in which the government and the opposition find themselves today. They have thrown themselves into a labyrinth of ridiculous embarrassments; but these embarrassments are capable of and are almost certainly on the point of leading to complications of a most alarming kind for the country.[4]

He could well forsee that great trouble was ahead, and although political reporting and prognostication was not an important feature of *L'Univers* he had his finger on the national pulse throughout 1848 as well as anyone.

On 22 February 1848 a great "National Banquet" was scheduled to take place in Paris, to protest in behalf of political liberalization. The prohibition of this rally set a chain of events into motion, which culminated in rioting on the 23rd and an invasion of the Tuileries and the parliament on the 24th. Guizot resigned on 23 February, but this step was taken too late to save the monarchy, and the royal family fled shortly afterward. Security measures failed altogether. The intimidated legislators set up a provisional council with Lamartine as foreign minister and Ledru-Rollin as minister of the interior, while much more radical men, including Louis Blanc, installed themselves as rivals in the Hôtel de Ville. At the same time these big events were taking shape, a showdown was shaping up at the offices of *L'Univers* where the Revolution of 1848 overlapped with the crisis of leadership of the journal.

The issues that had to be decided included the question of whether *L'Univers* was to support the Jesuits, and the matter of editorial control – whether De Coux was to continue, or whether Veuillot was to have charge. The question of the Jesuits became ever sharper when the Comte de Messey was sent to Rome by De Coux in the fall of 1847 as correspondent for *L'Univers.* Veuillot endeavored to maintain good personal relations with both these men, although just as much as he was devoted to the Jesuits these two were disposed against them. He wrote an admirable note to Messey explaining that the Jesuits were not a monolithic bloc with regard to matters of the day,[5] and one to De Coux reiterating that they had been made scapegoats for those who deceptively avoided directly attacking Catholicism itself.[6] Lacordaire made the problem more difficult still. Veuillot felt the blows on the Sonderbund and the Jesuits in Lucerne almost personally,[7] but Lacordaire reacted against both of these, declaring to Montalembert after the Revolution broke out: "You are finished, your Sonderbund campaign, your passion for the Jesuits; your entente with retrogrades condemns you to disappear; you can not be a force, and you will be an embarrassment. I do not want to undertake anything with you."[8] Losing the support of the great Dominican preacher, who now became a supporter of the republic, and a journalistic rival serving with *L'Ère nouvelle*, was a considerable blow, but this loss was more than compensated for by fortunate developments.

Melchior du Lac, who had been writing for *L'Univers*, mostly about the campaign for the Roman liturgy, from the Abbey of Solesmes, now returned to take a more active part. His family was in need of support, and with some reluctance he left his post at Solesmes to accept the position of *précepteur* in Paris, *largement retributée*. Taconet hoped he would now feel free to resume his old functions at *L'Univers*. He asked him if he would come back even though De Coux was there and Lacordaire was behind him. Du Lac replied that if Veuillot stayed, he would; if not, not.[9] The choice between De Coux and Veuillot had been shaping up for some time. Since a letter of Veuillot to De Coux of 8 November 1847,[10] it was apparent that their deep differences about both Gioberti and the Jesuits might mean that he would have to resign. By 14 February 1848 the breaking point had nearly been reached. Veuillot wrote Du Lac, "I can say to you that the week will not end without M. de Coux retiring, or I will retire myself. This poor M. de Coux is completely a Giobertist. There is nothing more to be done."[11] Louis Veuillot had almost exactly expressed the situation.

On 21 February 1848 a quarrel over an article from the correspondent in Rome brought the festering situation to a head. Louis Veuillot was not at the offices of the journal at the moment, and when De Coux attempted to insert this piece attacking the Jesuits, Eugène, who was at the time in charge of the composition of the journal, refused to take it. Without any further exchange, according to Eugène, De Coux let him have his way.[12] The real decision was made at that point. De Coux was not seen again after 25 February. He left for Versailles, and his resignation was announced in *L'Univers* on 3 March. This announcement said it was as of 14 February that De Coux resigned. In a sense this date determined his resignation because both editors told Taconet that day that they no longer could cooperate. However, 25 February would have been more accurate.[13] At the same time the Riancey brothers, who got along smoothly enough at the offices of *L'Univers* resigned. Taconet had found their legitimist attitudes irritating, but the Veuillot brothers do not seem to have had any difficulties with them. The addition of Du Lac again was a great event so far as Louis Veuillot was concerned. Du Lac soon turned down even the light duties he had been offered in Paris as *précepteur,* and he was free by the start of March to devote himself full time to editorial work. Veuillot, who referred to Du Lac as "mon frère et mon maître," wanted to share the title of editor-in-chief with him, but Du Lac refused.[14] For many years Du Lac was to be a key factor in the direction of *L'Univers*, ever remaining in the background, but writing many of the strongest editorials. It would be impossible to say just what the difference would have been had he not joined forces with Louis Veuillot, but because he had taken religious orders and apparently preferred to take a back seat, *L'Univers* has always been identified with Veuillot. However, in the actual functioning of the journal and in the force of much of its columns the hand of Du Lac must be seen.

With all these changes occurring in the staff of *L'Univers*, it is a wonder that the ownership, and the real nature of the journal, did not change as the Revolution of 1848 dawned. The move to combine *L'Univers* with *L'Alliance* had collapsed, but no less a figure than Canon Dupanloup was trying at the turn of the year 1847-48 to establish another new Catholic journal, and to that purpose absorb *L'Univers*. Perhaps for this reason he was deliberately trying to stand on a good footing with Louis Veuillot,[15] with whom he had recently clashed over educational policy. In mid-January Veuillot responded to overtures of Dupanloup, writing that he had forgotten everything, declaring what a pleasure it was to press his hand.[16] Taconet, however, apparently must have wanted to avoid the royalist Dupanloup, and in any case he continued to steer his own course. Taconet was described by Veuillot as "prolétaire et laïc," and no doubt part of the reason both Louis Veuillot and *L'Univers* avoided an encumbering alliance with the royalists must have been the influence of Taconet.

Particularly dramatic was the reconciliation with Montalembert. The latter's strong language about *L'Univers* in Rome should have been enough to produce a permanent split. However, the leader of the Catholic party could not be shunned by Veuillot, and the coincidence of interest of the two over the Sonderbund and the position of the Jesuits brought them together again, at least for a time. By late 1847 the two were corresponding again over Swiss affairs, discussing Eugène's trip to Switzerland in support of the resisters.[17] It took the fall of the monarchy to bring the two men together face to face again. The night of 24 February, after mobs had broken into the Tuileries, a religious journal had no small problem in determining just what should be said in its editorial columns. The now decimated staff was engaged in an emotional discussion about it. At this juncture Montalembert walked in; Louis and he seized hands, and the nobleman declared there were no more peers of France, that he was nothing, and that he had come to work for Veuillot. The two sat down at the editorial table, and Veuillot wrote out an editorial that was suggestive of a manifesto by the Catholic party:

> The dynasty of July has succumbed. The battle was decided before the end of the third day. The Revolution is consummated, and it is one of the most astonishing in history.
>
> All is carried off by the storm, new men are appearing on the scene. God accomplishes his work through all means.
>
> He proceeds toward his ends by ways the world does not know.
>
> Today as yesterday, nothing is possible but by liberty, today as yesterday religion is the only base possible for society: religion is that which prevents liberty from corrupting itself.
>
> It is in Jesus Christ that men are brothers, it is in Jesus Christ that they are free.
>
> Sincere liberty can save all.
>
> The new government has great duties for France, for all of human society. We wish her the power to fulfill these. All governments have in themselves the capacity of asserting themselves: it is enough for them to love justice and to serve liberty freely.[18]

When he had written these lines he handed them to Montalembert, who read them and declared: "It's good, – very good! I am with you."[19] With not only Du Lac but also Montalembert now at his side, Veuillot was able to plunge ahead with little restraint as the events of 1848 transpired.

The Revolution itself was a strange spectacle. Obviously the national guard, the police agents, and the army were not used effectively or determinedly. The régime gave up without much of a struggle. The composition of the mobs was not clear. There were constitutional reformers and extreme radicals, bourgeosie and workingmen mixed together. What would happen at various turns was also not at all clear. Unlike 1830 there was no reaction against the church. Indeed, the alienation between the church and the July Monarchy worked in favor of the safety of the church.[20] Liberalism and ultramontanism were still associated, in a way that was to disappear before long. The mobs were ready to cry out: "Long live Jesus Christ! Long live religion." On breaking into the Tuileries the mob seized a great crucifix, which was carried without profanation from the palace to the Church of Saint Roch under the escort of students of the École Polytechnique and members of the national guard.[21] The time seemed ripe for men like Cabet and Buchez, and these socialist-Christians did have their fling before the spring was over.

At heart Louis Veuillot retained much of the peasant throughout his life, but bourgeois characteristics were very much there, and they showed up clearly as the Revolution took place. Paris did not seem a very good place for a family, and he sent his wife and infant daughters off on the 24th to Mathilde's strong-minded grandmother who dwelt in the Saint-Martin quarter of Versailles. He wrote Mathilde immediately and touchingly that although he had slept well, he had done so not without the sad experience of walking through the nursery and dressing room and finding there no children or wife. He expressed hope for the future, especially for the church, which he hoped would be free, and if this were to be the case, "Providence will have given us a great gift by this clap of thunder, and there will be no better republican than I."[22] However, his republicanism was conditional on the church's receiving good treatment, and despite the optimism he expressed to his wife it was obvious he feared the mobs and disorder. At some point Louis Veuillot, together with his brother Eugène, joined the national guard, and on 27 February he went on duty with a unit in Paris – of course still finding time to write for *L'Univers*! He checked in with his unit at eleven thirty at night after buying a uniform, attending mass at Notre Dame-des-Victoires (the soldiers' church in Paris), doing his editorial work, and dining with Eugène. He had become bored with the evenings he had been spending alone, and although fatigued by all his extra activity, he now felt a new kind of satisfaction. "I feel truly content," he wrote Mathilde, "in having fulfilled what I regard at this moment the most important duty of an honest man." He felt the spirit within the national guard to be reassuring, but he only hoped that the mob would not be able to take law into its hands. "Beside the communists, who dream of and desire pillage, there are forty thousand *malfaiteurs* in Paris, armed to the teeth, and no police."[23] Here the bourgeois citizen, as well as the Catholic journalist, was speaking. A number of the appellations given Louis Veuillot during his life and later suggest the soldier. The role of bourgeois soldier in the national guard at this time of disorder certainly was an appropriate role for a man of his disposition.

Despite his fear of the mob and willingness to check it, Louis Veuillot sounded a thoroughly republican note in the editorial columns of *L'Univers* in the days after the February Revolution. Following the line of the short editorial written on 24 February with Montalembert's approval, he composed two much longer sequels on the theme of adhesion to the new republic. In these he looked forward hopefully to the new freedom he wanted for the Catholic church. The monarchy had fallen because of its defects, but perhaps the republic would take the shackles from Catholic education, the existence of the religious orders, and the other functioning of the church, as in "the grand and glorious republic of the United States."[24] He saw the republic saving society from anarchy, and this republic would have to be for liberty, equality, and fraternity.[25] However, his optimistic attitudes did not last long. In fact, privately he had had his doubts from the beginning. When his papers were collected later for the publication of his *Mélanges,* he inserted a letter written to "a friend" on 24 February, which revealed more exactly his true feelings. Louis Veuillot added a footnote to the publication of this letter: "I had not been able on the evening of 24 February to say in the journal all of my thoughts about the events of the day." In this "letter," if that is what it was in fact, he sounds much more like a newspaper reporter on the spot than he normally did in his editorials. He describes with some distress the manifestations of the mob, and how the cries of "à bas Guizot" sounded much like the same cries, "à bas Polignac," he had heard when a boy. He had noted the procession of the mob from the Tuileries to Saint-Roch and was relieved at the respect shown to the Christian church, but nevertheless appalled at the invasion of the Tuileries. He was standing in the crowd of spectators outside, and talking with a stylishly dressed man (*un monsieur très comme il faut*) with gold-rimmed spectacles, who found the scene "picturesque" as Frenchment were seeking "reform." Veuillot replied: "Monsieur, what you see signifies something else again. All this means that nothing guarantees any longer your property or your life, and that one is able right now to take your glasses. You will have reform, and probably also the Convention." So Veuillot wrote in his "letter to a friend " attacking the rampaging "imbeciles." With bitterness he noted that the socialist-Christian Buchez commanded the company of the national guard which entered the palace to send the king on his way, after Émile de Girardin had advised him to abdicate. In disgust Veuillot lumped Lamartine with Girardin and Crémieux, and with them included the Duc de Montpensier, who had been in such a hurry to get out of the palace that he forgot to look for his wife before leading the royal exodus. And on the way from the scene he saw the inevitable *filles publiques* on the Rue de Saint-Honore, singing revolutionary songs, one of whom tutoyed him with the title of *citoyen*. He did not "correct" her, because "it is necessary to respect an equal."[26] Perhaps indeed he did write this letter on 24 February 1848, but whether written then or later, it is interesting to note how bourgeois disgust was its key theme, while hope that the freedom which might come from the republic might benefit the church was the point emphasized in *L'Univers*. Of course, he could not have attacked the mob editorially at that point without being in real danger from it or from the sort of government that might well have followed.

Writing nine years later, Veuillot said:

> France has but two ways of existing: it is either as a Christian monarchy or as a pashadom. A hereditary king governs it according to the laws of Christ, or a horde of janissaries imposes by force the code of its frenzies.

At the time of the Revolution, however, Veuillot denied that *L'Univers* was favoring Henri V, which the brand-new paper of Lamennais "and his acolytes" accused *L'Univers* of doing.[28] Whatever sentiments Veuillot had concerning the monarchy at this time, he revealed only his passion for the church, and certainly he was "Catholic before all" in his editorials.

During the spring of 1848 Montalembert wrote along the same lines as Veuillot. He too was "Catholic before all," seeking primarily freedom for the church as the great salvation of the situation, and invoking as did Veuillot the example of the United States.[29] When Montalembert attacked the newly founded *L'Ère nouvelle*,[30] he particularly strengthened the hand of Veuillot among Catholics, who in that new era were not sure about the road that so-called liberalism was offering. Soon Veuillot saw more blows being struck against the Catholics, particularly the further measures taken in Lyons, not long after the Revolution, against the favorite target of the liberals, the Jesuits.[31] The main drift of his editorials was for freedom from this sort of attack. To his friend, Comte Gustave de La Tour, who shortly afterward was elected to the new constituent assembly, and who remained one of his closest confidants, he spoke of the anti-Christian "sect" as "illiberal," despite all its attempts to appropriate the term "liberal."[32] But anti-Christian "liberalism" was not the most serious danger that he saw: that danger was "communism." He told Msgr. Rendu of Annecy that France was on her way to communism, probably to be followed by military dictatorship.[33] He continued to repeat the term throughout the spring, saying to his friend Dumast, "the mad logic of this revolution is communism"[34] The spirit of enthusiasm for the republic which his first editorials reflected was ever more outweighed by fear of what might be in store for a France hopeful of freedom but perhaps destined for catastrophe instead.

One challenge for Veuillot's forces was of course the appearance on 14 April of *L'Ère nouvelle*, the Christian-democratic journal. Its editors and supporters were a formidable group. Lacordaire himself was the titular editor, though he did not stay with the enterprise long. De Coux, who likewise did not remain long with the radical publication, was nevertheless with it at its inception. Frédéric Ozanam, a professor at the Sorbonne, noted historian, and organizer of the Society of St. Vincent de Paul, was also one of the staff. The principal figure in the operation of the journal, however, was the able and radical professor of theological dogma, the Abbé Mater. Basic to the strength of this group was the support of Msgr. Affre, Archbishop of Paris.[35] In the tragic "June Days" Msgr. Affre died a martyr's death at the barricades,[36] and the death of this liberal archbishop, together with the general reaction that had set in by that time, took the pressure off the conservative Catholics and largely destroyed the basis for a successful development of the Christian-democratic movement, but at least for a time before its demise in 1849 it appeared as though *L'Ère nouvelle* might have the kind of destiny some had previously hoped for Lamennais' *L'Avenir*, and also might make the successful challenge that the cautious *L'Ami de la Religion* and the intellectual *Correspondant* never were able to give to *L'Univers*.

Veuillot saw dangers arising not only to France but to Europe as a whole stemming from the revolution begun in France.[37] He bitterly resented the *fêtes nationales* that were taking place all over France with the planting of liberty trees. He resented the cults of Franklin, Washington, Voltaire, Goethe, and Robespierre, and he noted that the celebration of Easter was being pushed aside.[38] He saw all sorts of danger to the country; he had once held a government post; why not stand for election to the constituent assembly that was arranged for in early March and finally held on 23 April? He considered the idea. From at least four different districts in the Loiret, Pas-de-Calais, Brittany, and Avignon suggestions had come that he should run. To the Abbé Boucheny in Orleans he gave a lengthy explanation, pointing out particularly his role in the Catholic cause as editor of *L'Univers*, but he also added a bit about himself and his political outlook:

> For two years I do not believe a day has passed that I have not written something in favor of religion and liberty which, in my opinion, in France defend and maintain each other. On the other hand I am not a *conservative* in the old sense of the word, it is true,

> but I am a great friend of order. I am not a legitimist, but I am a great defender of property. Child of poorer people by birth, worker (since I live by my work), bourgeois by my relations, expectant proprietor, I hold by the strongest bonds, by bonds of blood, by those of the heart, by those of interest, to all social classes. By personal experience I know something of all the troubles which disturb these times.[39]

It is quite likely that Veuillot had the makings of a popular politician, and, at a time when universal manhood suffrage was being introduced, he might very well have been able successfully to appeal to many groups. But he had the judgment to realize that "as editor-in-chief of a journal I have a part in the action and in the responsibilities that is more than satisfying."[40] For this reason he held aloof from such allures in 1848 as at other times.

Both Montalembert and Lacordaire, however, ran for seats and were elected in due course, and their candidacies were strongly supported in *L'Univers*. Particularly in a program which was published in *L'Univers* on 6 April, Montalembert sounded much like Veuillot: he was a republican if the republic, like the United States, would guarantee the liberty of religion.[41] As for Veuillot, the thing that especially irritated him about the elections was the delay in holding them, and the day on which they were to be held. He declared to his readers that the provisional government was a dictatorship, and that it ought not to continue ruling any longer than could be avoided. And when the elections to the national assembly were delayed from 9 April to 23 April, he was furious. But what particularly vexed him was the fact that the latter date was not only Sunday (as was 9 April), but Easter.[42] He called on Catholics to answer the call of duty both at church and at the polls. Throughout this period, despite the presence of spectacular radicals like Louis Blanc and Proudhon, he was obsessed with the minister of the interior, Ledru-Rollin. But the blame for this shift in electoral dates the minister shared with someone else – George Sand – who Veuillot believed had given him the idea.[43]

Veuillot's bitterness about the situation during the election was great. He told a priest with whom he was corresponding that with Ledru-Rollin leading the government the country could easily slip into civil war and communism. Not only that, the country really did not deserve any better.[44] While expressing his desire to see Montalembert elected, he said that Lacordaire also could play a big role in shaping things.[45] But at last his relations with Montalembert seemed completely repaired. The latter corresponded warmly with Veuillot during the spring of 1848, even inviting him, by mail, to dine with him.[46] How unlike the previous year!

The election resulted in a conservative victory.[47] In a situation like that it was not surprising to see the influence of Thiers rising again. Parliamentarianism under the leadership of a "party of order" seemed to be very much on the ascendancy despite the continuing presence of Blanqui, Louis Blanc, Marrast, Flocon, Buchez, Cabet, and various other radical leaders. Veuillot was now on the alert for other dangers. He took his stand for liberty, at least for the church, and he feared that the liberal parliamentarians were not for liberty in his sense of the word, but were in the general tradition of the previous régime. Publicly he declared that "France, in her passion for order, sacrificed liberty."[48] In the situation resulting from the elections Veuillot feared that some of the leading Catholics, notably Montalembert, might be taken in by the party of order. In his private diary he noted that while Guizot had fled to England, where he was getting along well, Thiers was on the other hand getting on well in the new national assembly. "Montalembert has been very content with Thiers," he wrote, "perhaps too much so. He has a certain inclination towards parliamentarianism. He has said that Thiers is very agreeable in his attitude and in his speeches. He laughingly added that events have given him a shade of melancholy which go well with his kind of good-looks."[49] Montalembert had always been disposed toward aristocratic parliamentarianism, and now something of a significant difference between him and Veuillot was developing again.

While Louis Veuillot professed to sympathize with the combination of liberty and order that the large majority of the new assembly seemed to represent, he was obviously distrustful of whether the assembly would really be able to bring about this fusion. The first session of the assembly, 4 May 1848, he sarcastically noted was little other than a long cry of *vive la république!*[50] His suspicions remained divided. Men like Marrast, Louis Blanc, and Flocon he feared, but were Thiers, Odilon Barrot, and Dupin "our saviours," he asked?[51] Surely there was plenty of reason for fear with regard to domestic tranquility at this point. On 15 May complete disorder again reigned in Paris, with mobs parading through the streets and invading the assembly.[52] Soon some kind of showdown between the moderates and the radicals seemed inevitable. Although Veuillot was much disturbed about the manifestations, his descriptions of the events themselves suggest, along with his writing of late February, that he had much of the pure journalist in him.[53] Illiterate signs, cries of agitators, behavior of inept national guard leaders, and other picturesque bits, pithily strung together, reveal Veuillot as a lively reporter, interested in the scene for itself whatever his political sympathies were.

Although one did not have to be prophetic to foresee the coming of the "June Days," Veuillot did not devote particularly much attention to the social and economic causes of that catastrophe. On the contrary, some of his more characteristic preoccupations stood out in May and June of 1848. While he showed his full contempt for the proceedings that brought about the formal banishment of the House of Orleans, he more particularly blasted at the minister of justice, the arch-freemason and secularist, Crémieux. Crémieux had introduced a project for establishment of divorce in France, but his proposal was laughed at to the point where Crémieux himself was forced to smile. According to Veuillot, a minister who relied on the advice of the author of *Lélia* (George Sand) was poorly advised.[54]

Perhaps the most interesting subject about which Veuillot wrote in June of 1848 was the matter of whether Louis Napoleon Bonaparte should be expelled, or whether he indeed should take his seat in the national assembly. Veuillot had followed with interest the connecting of the name of Napoleon with some of the manifestations of the cult of the state.[55] At the meeting of the national assembly Prince Napoleon (son of Jérôme) spoke.[56] Albeit brilliant, naughty Prince Napoleon was only second in line for the Napoleonic succession, and he was neither practical nor sufficiently consistent to be pretender in any case. His cousin Louis Napoleon Bonaparte, however, had all the makings of a pretender.[57] No one had bothered to try to block the validity of the election of Prince Napoleon, but a considerable flurry ensued over the triple election of Louis Napoleon. Cries of *Vive Louis Napoléon*! fascinated Louis Veuillot,[58] and the proposition by none other than Lamartine himself to block the certification of his election provided all the elements of a rich editorial. Veuillot was intrigued with the matter as such, and he took sides from the start. He had opposed the formal banning of the Orleans family, and he opposed the invalidation of Louis Napoleon. "To declare him a pretender was almost to force him to be one," was the wise observation of the journalist. Lamartine's demand that Napoleon he excluded *by acclamation* struck Veuillot as profoundly unwise. In any case, whatever Napoleon's role as a pretender might be, he had the rights of a citizen, and he should be allowed to take his seat without attack, in the opinion of Veuillot.[59] The stand which Veuillot took proved to be the expedient position, because without difficulty Louis Napoleon was able to claim his seat, and the support that Veuillot gave the future president and emperor gave Veuillot and *L'Univers* an advantage which at least might be exploited as events developed.

While *L'Univers* continued to feud both with the secularist *Le*

National over the powers of the episcopacy,[60] and with the liberal Catholic *L'Ère nouvelle* over the powers of the papacy,[61] the dangers of radical democrats like Buchez and the new minister of commerce, Flocon, again received much of its attention.[62] Veuillot's fears seemed well substantiated by the events of 15 May.[63] *L'Univers* of the next day spoke of "terrible scenes" as the assembly was invaded by radical mobs.[64] The stage was being set for further violence that would lead to strong reaction. Lacordaire resigned as a deputy shortly after these events,[65] Montalembert, however, seemed ready to deal with the forces that were now making themselves felt in France. "The republic," he said to the voters of Doubs, "should and will be democratic. One cannot conceive of its being otherwise. Democracy is the only vital force of modern politics. . . . The working classes have acquired the prime position in all political thinking, of all good citizens."[66] Veuillot, however, without any apparent lack of solidarity with the head of the Catholic party, appeared more concerned about the dangers to the body politic offered by the violence of workingmen, than with any practical measures to make concessions to them. The national workshops, which were essentially projects for giving work, and some low pay, to the unemployed, had reached great proportions by June. The cost to the republic was very great, and the immediate benefits were not very obvious. Not surprisingly the conservatives moved to cut off the funds that were being poured into these activities. A proposal by the Comte de Falloux accomplished this purpose.[67] Almost immediately barricades were thrown up, and the worst violence that Paris had ever experienced broke out from the 23rd of June through the 26th.

L'Univers had recently attacked *Le National* for declaring that while "Communism is an impossible dream, socialism is a positive doctrine."[68] Whatever the workers thought they were, whether dream or doctrine, Paris was in a state of seige for three days, and thousands of people were killed. While the conservative republican General Cavaignac commanded the forces that finally crushed the bloody revolution, *L'Univers* managed to get out a number on 25 June even though the area where it was published was not cleared until 3 p.m.[69] One of the leaders of the *gardes mobiles* was killed near the printery, and his assassins were taken and shot directly.[70] Louis Veuillot himself, and his brother Eugène, were in the national guard and participated in the measures of restoring peace. They were in the same legion, but not the same battalion, and were on duty for two days. Louis was at a post at the Tuileries.[71] Just what he did during this service seems to be lost, but he observed at first hand the general dangers, and the condition of those who had been in the struggle. His post was near a statue called

Vindex, and before long his pamphlet, *L'Esclave Vindex* which was a notable dialogue about revolutionary doctrines, appeared.[72] Even the most extraordinary and unpleasant of his personal experiences seemed never to be wasted so far as exploitation for literary purposes was concerned.

Denis Affre, Archbishop of Paris, had not been Veuillot's idea of an ideal prelate, his liberal and Gallican tendencies not being in line with Veuillot's ultramontane and more authoritarian views. But now Affre went to the barricades in an effort to bring peace. It was there that he was fatally shot and heroically managed to express the hope that he would be the last victim, even while being carried off from the terrible scene.[73] *L'Univers* reported his final heroism and loftiness with appropriate sentiments.[74] But with the death of the archbishop the strength of the alliance between democracy and the church also passed away. As an ally of the church, following the June Days democracy really seemed discredited. This situation, of course, was important for Louis Veuillot and the Catholic press in general.

There had been similarities in the editorial stands of all the Catholic organs during the days immediately after the February Revolution, when caution seemed in order, and when the newly founded republic and the church appeared on a honeymoon,[75] although differences began to develop promptly. *L'Ami de la Religion* had now been purchased by friends of Msgr. Dupanloup, who may well have wished he could also have controlled *L'Univers*,[76] but no rift developed between the two journals or between Veuillot and Dupanloup during the period immediately after the June Days. Once established, *L'Ère nouvelle* had advocated the political alliance of Christianity and democracy in a most immoderate way, and from the resulting battle *L'Univers*, with the aid of Montalembert and general circumstances, emerged the victor during the fall of 1848. *L'Univers* had initially hailed the republic, and in opposing the excesses of radical republicans during the spring had not taken a negative stand toward the plight of the working classes. However, the attitude of *L'Univers* was that from the Christian point of view it was not by devices of the state that the welfare of all would be achieved, but by the establishment of Christian principles and practices. While *L'Ami de la religion, Le Correspondant*, and the rest of the Catholic press followed a cautious line with regard to the government's role in the solution of the social question, *L'Ère nouvelle*, now without Lacordaire and largely under the influence of Maret, pursued the Christian-democratic alliance line strongly, even after the June Days.

During the summer of 1848 *L'Univers* kept its guns trained in the direction of the clear-cut socialists, complaining of their concept of assistance to the working classes and advocating the measures of the Catholic orders would follow to do the same.[77] *L'Ère nouvelle*, however, kept its emphasis on the social-democratic line, and Veuillot and *L'Univers* found themselves in a feud with this rival Catholic sheet. Fortunately for *L'Unvers*, Montalembert was totally out of sympathy with the radical direction of *L'Ère nouvelle*. The bond between Veuillot and Montalembert still seemed solid, and Veuillot almost seemed to yield the initiative to the leader of the Catholic party in this era. Montalembert had trouble making himself heard in the assembly while the radicals shouted and gestured, an unfair situation which provided ammunition for the continuing struggle against the university forces who were now joined by the social democrats.[78] But Montalembert's pen was as great a weapon as his tongue, and in October of 1848 he wrote two letters for *L'Ami de la religion* in which he attacked the social activism of *L'Ère nouvelle*.[79] Veuillot followed these blasts with a continuing assault in the columns of *L'Univers*, attacking the socialism espoused by *L'Ère nouvelle*.[80]

Most of the episcopacy opposed *L'Ère nouvelle*, but not the newly chosen Msgr. Sibour, Archbishop of Paris, who carried on some of Msgr. Affre's liberal ideas. Sibour invited the editors of the different Catholic journals of Paris (which included the Abbé Migne's *La Voix de la vérité*) to dinner with him in November in order to effect a reconciliation.[81] Veuillot soon got into very serious difficulties with the archbishop, but one must certainly say of the archbishop that he made an effort to conciliate the lay wing of the Catholic press before these troubles developed. However, no reconciliation was effected. Veuillot told Montalembert that he had lost all patience with *L'Ère nouvelle*.[82] *L'Ère nouvelle* managed to carry on until into 1849, but in fact it was finished not long after its auspicious start. It mushroomed from April through June, reaching a circulation of approximately 20,000, but collapsed rapidly after the crushing of the June revolution. By early 1849 it had sunk to not much over 2,000.[83] *L'Univers*, on the other hand, burgeoned greatly in this same period. In July Veuillot boasted to a friend that the journal he edited was publishing 7,650 (citing to the nearest 50 certainly shows that there was something almost intimate about it!), and that if they sold it on the streets (which they did not) it would go as high as 20,000.[84] Within another month he reported to Dumast, "Things go very well with *L'Univers*. We have reached 9,000, and we will be at 10,000 in two months, if we still exist."[85] Veuillot had his triumphs, but the growth of *L'Univers* in this period, particularly since it was standing only for Catholicism-before-all and not backing any political party, was surely one of his biggest.

Beside the immediate question of Christianity and its relationship with democracy, and whether democracy ought to be socialistic, *L'Univers* also dealt with the whole field of problems facing Catholicism in 1848. Meanwhile the star of Louis Napoleon Bonaparte was rising. Sometimes Veuillot had troubles of an unforeseen sort. For example, despite the assaults of the journal on Proudhon,[86] Msgr. Clausel de Montals, Bishop of Chartres, attacked Louis Veuillot for being ready to open the columns of *L'Univers* to Proudhon! It seems that the matter of a debate had arisen, and through others, including Montalembert, the idea of allowing the celebrated revolutionary to publish his ideas in *L'Univers* was under discussion. The aged bishop became indignant about the matter, and Veuillot had to write with all the tact of which he was capable, explaining that Proudhon was not going to be able to use his usual invective, and that his case was going to look very feeble when pulled apart by the editors of *L'Univers*. The debate would be of value to the Catholic cause, and the readers of the journal were not going to be exposed to Proudhon's language. After the affair took this direction, Proudhon naturally did not want any part of it.[87] Having to explain such matters to such a formidable bishop surely did not make the burdens of the lay religious editor any simpler.

Despite revolutions, reorganization of the direction of the journal, duty with the national guard, some travel, less than perfect health, family concerns including Mathilde's expectancy of a third child, and what may be described as a complex of preoccupations, Veuillot found time to write, proofread, and publish more of his own work above and beyond what appeared in *L'Univers*. The principal item was a book entitled *Libres penseurs*, which made its appearance in the fall of 1848. He had actually been at work on this book some time before the Revolution of February and had had to put it aside at that time. This volume of some three hundred pages was a sketch-book with eight major parts divided into disparate sections.[88] The first part was about literary men, followed bv parts dealing with journals and journalists, women authors, *les honorables préopinants,* "Tartuffes," persecutors, and the public – to which an eighth book or part, was added, "people who do not think at all." The sections within these parts stand on their own, and the subject matter could have been subdivided in other ways, no doubt. The whole work was a brilliant reflection of the seamy side of political, social, and literary life in the age of Louis Philippe, showing the foibles of a variety of the free-thinkers of the age. The church is in the background, to provide emphasis on the shallowness of those deliberately standing clear of it. Some of the tales recounted in the collection are three lines long, and could have been used almost anywhere in Veuillot's writing. Others are more substantial. Except that the term *histoirette* was reserved to be used in another book of Veuillot's, this word would have been most descriptive of the kind of piece that characterized *Libres Penseurs.* A good many made-up names are used in these tales, and some readers have attempted to see in these names an overall key to the work. There was no key, however, and the representative fictitious characters were simply given names by Veuillot.[89] Despite the general purpose of attacking free-thinkers, the writing is reminiscent of his earlier pre-conversion literary efforts. Although French authors of course are the principal frame of reference, English authors, and even English words, crop up with some frequency. Veuillot's trademark in much of his writing was to pull no punches with regard to specific persons, and to be sure, George Sand, Balzac, Eugène Sue, Thiers, and other obvious figures are brought forth to illustrate Veuillot's points, but *Libres Penseurs* has more of the oblique and more anonymity in it than was quite typical of the man. Veuillot must have written it more for intellectuals than for the audience he had gained with some of his novels, and obviously he was pleased with Montalembert's high praise of the book. He also noted that his own Mathilde had not read it, nor would she, on the pretext that she had too much washing to do![90]

In the same period Veuillot worked on and planned other items that were in due course grouped in a collection called *Dialogues socialistes,* which appeared in his collected works in the same volume with *Libres Penseurs.* Particularly significant among the pieces making up the *Dialogues socialistes* was *L'Esclave Vindex.* This item was a true dialogue, the conversation between two figures, Spartacus, representing the bourgeoisie, and Vindex, representing the extreme revolutionary of the mid-nineteenth century. The dialogue was inspired by the statue of Vindex at the point in central Paris where Veuillot took his post during the June Days. This literary device was very curious in that he was using two different kinds of enemies of his ideal order, as enemies of each other, to bring out the things he disliked about each one in their discussions.[91] *L'Esclave Vindex* first appeared in early 1849 by itself. Much longer and much more complicated, with more than two dozen characters, was *Le Lendemain de la victoire. Le Lendemain de la victoire* was very simply an anti-socialist book painting various socialist and revolutionary types in dark colors. The book had a curious dedication, made on 15 November 1849 (Saint Eugène's Day) – to his brother, who is identified only as the author of *L'Histoire des guerres de la Vendée,* which had been published in 1847. Both books were about struggles, although the two struggles, and books, were different in nature. Already, however, Louis was giving recognition to his brother Eugène, who has been nevertheless constantly overlooked in the shadow of the older brother. It would indeed be interesting to speculate what might have been Eugène's career without Louis, or what Louis' problems might have been without Eugène, or Du Lac.

In the second half of 1848 the great internal preoccupation in France concerned the rise of Louis Napoleon Bonaparte. The attention of Louis Veuillot naturally turned to this phenomenon.[93] The inheritor of the Napoleonic tradition was a careful politician, playing his cards carefully at a difficult time. Reaction was in the air, but that situation might equally have pointed toward a legitimist restoration or some other form of conservative solution. In fact, Napoleon was hard-pressed to appeal to the elements of order and the Catholics. Much of the duel between *L'Ère nouvelle* and *L'Univers* in the fall of 1848 was fought over the choice of presidential candidates for the Catholic voter. *L'Univers* certainly was the more astute and logical, though the very nature of *L'Ère nouvelle*, with its emphasis on republicanism, limited its choice, whereas *L'Univers* could decide on a Catholicism-before-all basis.

Of the various candidates, two emerged as the real contenders. Despite the lingering attractions of Lamartine's name, these two were General Cavaignac and Louis Napoleon Bonaparte. *L'Ère nouvelle* quickly took a clear stand, and for that came under sharp fire from *L'Univers*.[94] Violence in Rome, which included the assassination of Rossi, who had become the prime minister of the government of the Papal States, of course intensified Veuillot's concern about the position of the church, but cold logic was to be the basis of any stand of *L'Univers*. Veuillot was under no illusions about Bonaparte, the nephew of the man who "restored the altars,"[95] and despite the Napoleonic appeal as a guarantee of order, Veuillot could see the dangers of despotism a Bonaparte could bring as much as the dangers of the sort of "liberty" which could come with Cavaignac.[96] The question boiled down rather simply: to vote for Cavaignac was to vote for a man known to be in the camp of the secularists, who at best would do nothing for the church, whereas to vote for Napoleon was to vote for an unknown, who might or might not be good for the cause of Catholicism, but at least was not known to be hostile.[97]

While the constitution was being determined in the late summer and fall of 1848, Veuillot was sceptical of the problem-solving powers of the national assembly, his general position being that apart from Christ there was no solving of problems, whatever determination the secularists might show. When the instrument was completed his hopes were no greater, though with many independent powers reserved for the president, it was obvious that the choice of the man for this office would make a great deal of difference to Catholics, as well as to everyone else.[98] *L'Univers* was divided in its councils, and the Veuillot brothers were slow in pronouncing themselves for anyone. Louis noted that while Montalembert and his colleagues at the journal, Coquille and Barrier, were for Bonaparte, on the other hand Roux, Taconet, and Cazalès supported Cavaignac. All he would say in late November was that he and Eugène did not like Cavaignac.[99] To the argument of the Bonapartist press that the great Napoleon had restored the church, Veuillot could only recall that Napoleon had also established the university monopoly and that Louis Napoleon was determined to imitate his illustrious uncle in every way.[100] Not until nearly time for the election did Veuillot allow himself to be convinced that it was advisable to support Bonaparte, despite the strength of his opposition to the reasoning of *L'Ère nouvelle*.

It was the situation in Rome that precipitated Veuillot's backing of Napoleon. As political matters deteriorated in Rome, the question of intervention by the powers of Europe came to the fore,[101] despite the confused conditions that existed in Europe as a whole. Napoleon played his cards very carefully. When Rossi was assassinated and papal government became impossible, the French government addressed itself to the question of intervention in Rome. There was little sentiment for this course in the national assembly, and Napoleon, cautiously, determined to disassociate himself from it. However, it seemed safe enough to the régime, and to Napoleon, to offer asylum to the pope, in accordance with the tradition of the country with regard to refugees of mark from other lands. Although *L'Univers* would have preferred much more positive action, it was already aware that Napoleon was promising to protect the family, and freedom of worship and of education.[102] Hearing the words of the nuncio, and of Montalembert, Napoleon was quick to see that he could gain the support of the Catholics in December if only he would go somewhat further in his stand on the pope.[103] Hereupon he wrote a letter to the editor of *L'Univers*, dated 2 December – a fortuitous date in many ways for the Bonapartes – which was inserted on the third, that showed considerable political acumen. He explained his position in opposing the sending of a French relief expedition to Civitavecchia in support of the liberty and *authority* of the pope as dangerous to the *sacred interests* that were to be protected.[104] While being cautious, he gave the appearance of saying all the right things. Perhaps what may have been more convincing to Veuillot was the fact that Napoleon specifically disavowed the revolutionary activities against temporal sovereignty by the Prince of Canino, eldest son of Lucien Bonaparte.[105] In any case, except for the element that clung to the Catholic-democratic line of *L'Ère nouvelle*, Catholics joined the great mass of the electors in December.

Voting returns were given in *L'Univers* between 13-20 December, and from the beginning there could be no doubt as to the outcome. The "republican phase" of the Second Republic was surely over.[106] Louis Napoleon Bonaparte was elected by nearly five and one-half million, receiving more than four million votes more than Cavaignac. Lamartine and the other candidates received an insultingly small sliver of the votes. The Napoleonic star had risen again, and Veuillot hoped that it would turn out to be favorable for the Catholic church, but he was still as doubtful as he had been prior to the election. While the vote was being counted he observed to a friend that everyone was crying "Vive L'Empereur!" "Vive Jesus!" was what he persisted in crying, however.[107] Bonapartists had been trying hard to convince him of their leader's religious sentiments, notably Madame Cornu, wife of the painter and daughter of one of Queen Hortense's chamber ladies,[108] but he remained sceptical. Jules Favre's observation that Napoleon was the only person who could save the republic seems to have made a certain impression on Veuillot, but he derived no comfort from Napoleon's inauguration. No doubt Veuillot would have preferred to see some republican parallel to a coronation in Reims, but Bonaparte took a simple oath at the tribune, which was "not exactly the altar of truth."[109] For better or for worse Louis Napoleon Bonaparte was now president of the Second Republic, and despite his doubts Veuillot hoped for a better situation for the Catholic church than had been the case under Louis Philippe.

While matters went well for the Catholic party in France until mid-1849, for Veuillot there were many worries over the well-being of his family. Mathilde gave birth late in the winter to a third daughter, Gertrude, whose arrival he happily announced [110] though no doubt he would have liked to have a little Pierre. Unfortunately, Marie, the eldest, was sick for a long time that spring, and Mathilde was "toujours au lit."[111] She was slow to recover from the delivery, and along with her little Agnès was also described as "souffrante." Veuillot was asking for prayers for his sick family and for himself.[112] In due course they all recovered, at least for the time, and though Veuillot normally had a good deal to say to his friends about his own health, the spring of 1849 did not give him much opportunity for lamentations of this sort.

The spring of 1849 was a happy period for the leaders of the Catholic party. Veuillot and Montalembert were about as close as they ever had been. Albeit in a light vein, Veuillot said to Montalembert that he was his "liegeman,"[113] and when writing tracts for the elections of that spring, he said to Montalembert that they were "proof of his obedience."[114] He threw himself with special vigor into the elections of that spring, but was unusually willing to do so along the precise lines indicated by Montalembert, who prescribed a definite format for pamphlets to be used. Veuillot wrote two such pamphlets, entitled *Noir et Rouge* supposedly a letter directed by the people of Beaumont in the Gatinais to Félix Pyat, and *Le Fond des Cœurs.*[115] Montalembert had already expressed his pleasure with articles Veuillot had written about the elections,[116] but the way he filled the bill with these two pamphlets brought special praise.[117] With Dupanloup Veuillot's relations were still good. He sent Dupanloup, still an abbé, though about to become Archbishop of Orleans, a copy of his *L'Esclave Vindex* with warm expressions of regard.[118] The disagreements they were to have over educational policies were still in the future.

The most interesting of Veuillot's personal relationships in this era was his renewed friendship with Guizot. When Veuillot's *Libres Penseurs* was published a leading attacker was the editor-in-chief of *Liberté de Penser*, a free-thinking journal of the university supporters. This journal called Veuillot an "ex-pensionnaire de fonds secrets," referring to the pension he had received when he had enjoyed the favor of Guizot. Veuillot was quick to retort that he had turned from this kind of support when the government sponsored policies toward the church and education which he could not accept,[119] but at the very same time it was clear he had retained a certain warmth in his heart for Guizot. Guizot had taken his fall with dignity and had gone to England where he had busied himself with literary and historical studies.[120] Under these circumstances Veuillot could only remember the reasons he had admired Guizot.

Early in 1849 Guizot's *Democratie en France* appeared, which he predicted would meet with the approval of Montalembert and Veuillot. On hearing this piece of information Veuillot observed, "M. Guizot has great talents, and I have always thought better of him than of his politics. I expect to see him do quite differently from M. Thiers."[121] Already he had sent him his recent works with a cordial letter,[122] and articles in *L'Univers* about *Democratie en France* were warm toward Guizot. *L'Univers* denied it had been Guizot's "enemy," only his "adversary" on given matters. His attacks on "democratic idolatry" brought the support of *L'Univers*, which asserted that now that his successors had been seen, his role was much more excusable.[123] The correspondence of the two continued with further exchange of publications and compliments.[124] By late spring Veuillot was warmly supporting the candidacy of Guizot, who was seeking election to the parliament from Calvados. Veuillot did not think that Guizot had much chance,[125] but he poured forth to him his ideas about the dangers of universal suffrage.[126] Had Guizot indeed been successful in his candidacy, it would have been interesting to see just what would have come of their rewarmed friendship. As he lost they continued to exchange friendly letters and to find common grounds. Particularly on the score of the need for Christians to cooperate Veuillot wished to cultivate the greatest bond possible between the two different sorts of Christians who feared the secularists in France. When Veuillot said "it is certain that all Christians should understand each other,"[127] he surely was not expressing his ultimate goal, but the desire, of ultramontane Catholics and of French protestants alike, for a front against the rationalists and secularists. Recognition of the common danger goes far to explain how these two men could look sympathetically on each other under the existing conditions.

While Veuillot was cultivating his relationship with Dupanloup, Montalembert, and Guizot, another remarkable figure came into his life. This was Juan Donoso Cortés, Marquis de Valdegamas, who occupied the post of Spanish ambassador to Berlin. Donoso Cortés, whose earlier thinking had been in the same general stream as Victor Cousin's eclecticism, had steadily evolved toward a defense of traditionalism during the 1840's, becoming a major intellectual in the traditionalist vein. He became deeply religious in 1847 at the time of the death of his brother. He supported the early liberal direction of Pius IX's pontificate. However, the Revolutions of 1848 intensified the reactionary quality of his thinking, and it was just at this point in his development that he became a friend of Veuillot's. Veuillot certainly was not unique in this respect, since Montalembert and even Louis Napoleon also became friendly with him. Nevertheless, he must have made a far greater impression on Veuillot, who throughout his life was influenced by Donoso Cortés, although he outlived him by thirty years. Donoso Cortés eventually became ambassador to France in 1851, a post he held until his death in 1853. His major ideas were developed in his *Ensay sobre el catolicismo, el liberalismo, y el socialismo* (1851), which was directed against various trends of the modern age. Hoping for a restoration of Christendom, he wanted to see the revival of a concert of Europe which he would like to have seen Louis Napoleon form. Although Veuillot was only beginning at this time to fall under Donoso Cortés' sway, the start of this friendship was one of the most important things in this period of his life.[128]

In this same era Veuillot also suffered a personal loss when during the cholera epidemic that afflicted Europe, Marshal Bugeaud died. Just at the dawn of a new fight between the Catholic church and the university, and also on the eve of a brief revolutionary uprising as the new parliament was assembling in Paris, Bugeaud contracted cholera and died almost immediately on 10 June 1849. The marshal had kept his full vigor up to this point, thus figuratively dying with his boots on. Veuillot's differences with the marshal, beginning in 1832, had been largely owing to the marshal's indifference to religion, but for reasons of admiration and sentiment, and because Bugeaud certainly was a man of honor, Veuillot had always had affection for him. However, late in life there were signs of at least a formal acceptance of Catholicism by Bugeaud which pleased Veuillot. His death was much lamented in the columns of *L'Univers*, where Veuillot also regretted Bugeaud's electoral defeat, and developed the theme of Bugeaud's conversion. Bugeaud was presented as a family man dying a Christian death.[130] No doubt Veuillot had long desired to see his old friend the marshal dramatically embrace the true faith, and he made the most of such signs as there had been of this wished-for conversion.

Polemical exchanges characterized the whole career of Veuillot, but the relative solidarity of leading Catholics in the spring of 1849 saw *L'Univers* in harmonious relations with the rest of the Catholic press. At the expense of *L'Ère nouvelle* it had gained a great victory. *L'Univers* definitely had won in its quarrel with *L'Ère nouvelle*. The latter in the end took the position that a really good law on education could not be made. While there may have been some truth in this position, it was hardly consistent from either the university or the Catholic point of view.[131] *L'Univers* exploited the extreme advocacy by *L'Ère nouvelle* of the "alliance of the Church with modern society,"[132] an advocacy which had been popular in early 1848, but which by the spring of 1849 worked completely to the advantage of *L'Univers*. With the new political direction in France clearly reactionary, *L'Ère nouvelle*'s defense of the right of people to revolt played into the hands of Veuillot and *L'Univers*, though the arguments of the latter were not unqualified.[133] By early April the original editors of *L'Ère nouvelle* stepped aside, the journal announcing that it was going to become conciliatory and devoted to religion as such.[134] Maret had lost, and the day of *L'Ère nouvelle* was nearly over.

Veuillot's polemical battles were not only with Catholics of the left, however. The *Journal des Débats* he viewed as a particularly dangerous enemy of the pope, working to establish a bourgeois government in Rome that would be free of the papal government.[135] In addition to the *Journal des Débats* Veuillot clashed with a new and significant sheet, *L'Ordre*, which represented the reactionary spirit that sought order, even by use of the church but which constantly attacked what it called clerical power, the clerical party, clerical ambition, stupidity, tyranny, and so on. The editor of *L'Ordre* was the former editor of *Le Siècle,* Chambolle, who had ambitions himself for taking advantage of the spirit of the times in forming a party of order.[136] In taking this position he naturally brought upon himself an attack by the principal militant of the Catholic party.

The collapse of papal government and the establishment of a Roman republic by Garibaldi and Mazzini had forced the pope to go into exile. By 1849 Europe as a whole had turned the tide against revolution, albeit it with many compromises, and it was only natural that the powers would seek to remedy the situation in Rome. Just how the Papal States would be restored and what power would enforce the change, was discussed increasingly during the spring of 1849.[137] It is most likely Austria would have acted as the policeman as in the days of the Holy Alliance, had not Napoleon seen the advantages of his assuming this role. Cardinal Antonelli, in the name of the pope, appealed to the powers for aid in restoring temporal power, and of course *L'Univers* reacted in the most positive way.[138] France sent an expeditionary force under General Oudinot, whose progress was closely reported by *L'Univers* during May, June, and July. Oudinot had his share of troubles, and Napoleon even wrote him a letter in May saying he was sorry about his situation.[139] At length Garibaldi and his several thousand men were driven from Rome, and the way was prepared for the return of the pope, although curiously the pope took his time about returning. At any rate, a new Charlemagne could have been in the making with Napoleon having reestablished Pius IX.

Louis Veuillot wrote upon this occasion consistently with his previously taken general stands, and generally in harmony with his position many years in the future in 1860-61, when he would passionately espouse the cause of the Papal States as they finally collapsed. Perhaps the very success of the 1849 expedition took the edge off his concern in 1849, but it seems fair to say there was a difference between the militancy of *L'Univers* in 1849 and its militancy in 1860. In 1849 editorials were still unsigned, but even if one assumed the strongest of these articles to be Veuillot's, the comparison can still be made. It is interesting to note that to Dumast Veuillot wrote in May of 1849 "affairs of Rome are in the hands of Du Lac."[140] It is perfectly true that Veuillot deferred in many matters to the man he called "his master," and it was indeed his policy to leave ecclesiastical matters generally to Du Lac. However, the military situation of Rome in the spring of 1849 was hardly what might be considered under the heading of "ecclesiastical" matters. Perhaps it may be suggested that Veuillot's personal devotion to Pius IX in 1849 was not yet what it was to become by 1860, and that the pope himself had not yet taken some of the positions he was to assume after his return to Rome following this expulsion. Somehow, what might be regarded as the "crusade of 1849" just does not seem to have dominated the attention of Louis Veuillot in quite the way one might expect.

On 13 June 1849, as French troops put the final touches on crushing the Roman Republic, Ledru-Rollin attempted to embarrass the French government by organizing a demonstration in France. Although he could see that his demonstration would be a failure and attempted to call it off, events matured anyway. Despite the fact that no violence was perpetrated by the radicals in Paris, seven were killed as several thousand were being dispersed. In Lyons, however, the radicals did take the initiative, and quite a few casualties on both sides were inflicted there before order was restored.[141] The cause and the methods of the revolutionaries in this *petite journée de Juin* of course were decried by Veuillot. One of the results was the exile of Ledru-Rollin, who was nevertheless not forgotten in the ensuing years by the Catholic editor. These days of turmoil gave Veuillot an opportunity for further eulogy of Marshal Bugeaud, contrasting him with the leaders of the unsuccessful revolt.[142]

In the year 1849 the beginning of the struggle over the Falloux Law of 1850 saw Veuillot's attention drawn again, and in a very great concentration, on the question of education. He had fought with passion during the days of Villemain, but, after the formation of the Second Republic, the atmosphere now seemed more auspicious for a Catholic victory. The events that ensued did have considerable importance for French education, but as ever, education, or public instruction, was treated as a football for conflicting ideologies. Veuillot proved to be one of the most spectacular antagonists on the field. Unfortunately for him, however, his team became divided in their tactics, and when the game was over no one was quite sure who had won. But at least Veuillot had given the ball some hard kicks in the direction he desired.

It was in late spring, when the constitution had been shaped and elections had brought a legislative assembly to Paris, that educational matters came to the fore. Under the chairmanship of the Vicomte de Falloux a commission was established to investigate the whole subject.[143] Falloux was considered a good Catholic, but his outlook on life was characterized more by his devotion to legitimism in a practical way. The role of Falloux was important in the renewed struggle, but perhaps the principal figure behind the whole question was Thiers. Thiers was responsible for the choice of Falloux by President Bonaparte for the ministry of education, from which Falloux resigned before the work of the Commission was finished. Thiers was also responsible for pressing Falloux to accept the post, at least so Veuillot believed.[144] In any case the results of this project did much to split the ranks of the Catholics, although the matter of the schools in France was fixed for three decades by its acceptance.

The issue over the bill proposed by Falloux became a preoccupation for Louis Veuillot for the better part of a year, and he never forgot this issue the rest of his life. It would be difficult to find another example of a self-taught man who spent so much time and energy over any debate on the organization of education. In fact, the issue went to the roots of the public and religious life of France. Fundamentally it was a question of whether Christian or secular precepts were to govern life. In a period after a revolution there was also the question of whether or not the secular government, quite apart from the religion of its leaders, should make use of the church in the cause of order. Obviously compromises were going to be made, and on both sides of the line there was question as to how far to go. One debate that has arisen among scholarly interpreters of this era is the matter of just what was the issue. Was it a matter of the state and the church, or was it more specifically the university and the church?[145] Also the question arises as to whether or not it actually was such a simple matter as liberal support for the Falloux law and conservative opposition.[146] To a degree, of course, any attempt to generalize about such a complicated problem may lead to over-simplification, but Louis Veuillot himself may have given the best answer when he attacked *l'état enseignant*,[147] a phrase that is a bit broader than "university monopoly" or simply "the state." The question was raised whether the church ought not to be sufficiently *politique* to arrange a reasonably satisfactory *concordat* with a state now turning to it as the party of order looked for positive safeguards against revolution. As Catholic ranks split, or were split, further than they had been as a result of the revolutionary events of 1848, the question arose as to who was to blame for Catholic disunity. Shortly after the parliamentary struggle, Falloux published an account of the split, laying the blame on *L'Univers*,[148] which Veuillot eventually answered in 1856 with his *Le Parti catholique*, in which he traced the role of many groups, such as the radicals in 1848, but put the blame especially on compromisers within Catholic ranks, while maintaining that he obeyed the stand of the papacy in 1850 in himself accepting the law once enacted.[149]

Thiers, Cousin, and the group that had given its character to the parliamentary liberalism of Louis Philippe were afraid of radicalism. This element of substantial liberals turned to the church for aid in a way that would have been almost beyond imagining earlier in the 1840's. One of the principal ways in which the services of the church were to be enlisted was to be in the field of education, and Falloux seemed to be the man for the ministerial post. He had been very careful in his political stands in the early days of the Second Republic, and Veuillot thought that he was more concerned with making himself known than with becoming involved in knotty issues. He noted that friends of Falloux dwelt on the role he had played in supporting inoffensive reforms of the postal system.[150] Although he was not destined to remain minister of education very long, his ministry was successful quite apart from his introducing the law that was to remain the basis of the French educational system for three decades, until the days of Jules Ferry. The portfolio he held combined both public instruction and religion, a circumstance significantly underlining the fact that the question of their interrelationship was at the root of the problem he had to face. Apart from the school question Falloux was adjudged able by Veuillot, particularly for his astute proposals for the occupants of ecclesiastical sees.[151] Indeed, among the clerics he named were Dupanloup, who became Archbishop of Orleans shortly before the formulation of the bill for education, and the Abbé Salinis, a person particularly admired by Veuillot, who was named Bishop of Amiens at this time before later becoming Archbishop of Auch. When Veuillot trained his guns on Falloux, he knew he was taking aim at a big man.

Falloux established at the outset of his ministry extraparliamentary commissions for elementary and secondary education, which were promptly fused into a single group. This commission was very carefully chosen in such a way as to represent all groups, "but with an exquisite choice to assure a majority for the sort of conciliation desired by the minister," in the words of Veuillot.[152] While the twenty-four members included such people as Victor Cousin, who now followed a line not dissimilar to that of Thiers with regard to the Catholic church, the Catholics were indeed well and ably represented by Dupanloup, Montalembert, Henry de Riancey, and Laurentie, editor of *L'Union*. Veuillot noted that the Bishop of Langres, Msgr. Parisis, and Charles Lenormant, editor of *L'Univers*'s rival, *Le Correspondant*, might well have been included,[153] and, of course, Veuillot himself was passed over in the selection of the commission. It is significant that the liberal *Le Correspondant* made common cause with *L'Univers* when the issue of the Falloux Law was joined.[154]

Practical compromise was the spirit of the dominant figures on the commission, and Falloux and Thiers, who presided when Falloux was not present, made this spirit prevail. There was fear of revolution on the part of those identified with the party of order, and even the philosophically inclined among them now were ready to make concessions to the church. The Catholics, on the other hand, including Montalembert, were not prepared to make the sort of stand they had made in 1844 to demand liberty of instruction. The spirit of their group had become somewhat *politique*. The result was agreement upon a project that accepted the principle that university degrees were necessary qualifications for teaching in any kind of school, and that university examinations alone would determine these. The university would inspect all education, and particularly in the matter of books its approval was necessary.[155] As the project was developed there would be much latitude for the Catholics in the establishment of primary schools, and of primary education religious instruction would be an established part. The Catholics had much satisfaction with regard to primary schools, but not so much with regard to secondary education, where university qualification greatly limited their possibilities. By June 1849 the general nature of the law had been formulated, and it was in such form that it might be presented to the parliament for public debate. It was at this point that Veuillot became involved in the matter.

During the spring of 1849 Veuillot had been watching as well as he could what was transpiring, but definitely from the outside. On June 1 he wrote that since Falloux had become minister he had only seen him twice.[156] He spoke highly of Dupanloup well into the spring,[157] and as late as June signed himself "Votre tout devoué" to Montalembert.[158] Then suddenly Montalembert and he again became "enemy brothers" over the Falloux Law.[159] By August Veuillot wrote to Msgr. Rendu, Bishop of Annecy, "I am *désolé,* especially about the attitude of Montalembert. M. de Falloux has surprised me less; I had never counted on him. Although a Christian full of fervor, he has never been exactly one of us, that which we call Catholic before all." Ambition and compromise characterized him, said Veuillot. The same for the new Archbishop of Orleans. Falloux had gotten credit in the eyes of many for the reestablishment of the pope, but according to Veuillot the president himself was the man who deserved credit for this act. "I did not rely on Falloux," said Veuillot, "but I did on Montalembert." Sadly, in Veuillot's view, he had yielded before two main influences – Dupanloup and Thiers, especially Thiers.[160]

Falloux may have foreseen that Veuillot would cause trouble, because in June, before the bill was presented to the parliament, he called on

Veuillot to try to gain his support. He used all the arguments he could muster to try to persuade Veuillot that the law was the best that could be obtained under the circumstances, and that while the goal of real liberty of education was not to be had, the Catholics would have many gains as a result of the changing attitudes of leading political figures. Veuillot was in no way persuaded, however, and only agreed to one request: that he should not attack the law until it was formally brought to the parliament.[161] The two had different outlooks on life: Veuillot did not think it unreasonable to talk about the kind of society Saint Louis symbolized; the Vicomte de Falloux did.

The attack that Veuillot launched on the project naturally was resented by Falloux. He claimed in his memoirs and in a brochure that Veuillot had attacked it as soon as it appeared,[162] which was not technically the case, since Veuillot waited until it was presented to the parliament for debate. Falloux also claimed that Veuillot had attacked with vehemence. Eventually Veuillot may be said to have done so, but against this charge Louis Veuillot defended himself in his *Parti catholique* by saying that Falloux was confusing *L'Univers* with *Le Correspondant*. It was Lenormant, not himself, who was initially vehement, according to Veuillot.[163] In any case it is refreshing to note this good example of the liberal and reactionary wings of the Catholic press joining hands in a common cause and not feuding with each other.

The Falloux bill presented a major test for the relationship of the new Catholic lay press with the episcopacy.[164] An important part of the Catholic movement, the power to sway public opinion, being newly in the hands of laymen, the reaction of the episcopacy was therefore to be a significant development during the crisis. The press was of course not unified, yet the only important paper that supported the project was *L'Ami de la religion,* the director of which was none other than Dupanloup.[165] It is interesting to see Lenormant of *Le Correspondant* attacking the project for the same reasons as Veuillot did: the requirement for university diplomas for teachers in church schools, the right to judge candidates, and the right to supervise the choice of books.[166] Other Catholic and legitimist papers were not as outspoken in their opposition, some of them trimming their sails considerably as the end of the debate approached. The major quarreling took place between Dupanloup's *L'Ami de la religion* on the one hand and *L'Univers* and *Le Correspondant* on the other.

Late in June Veuillot wrote to a friend that the Falloux bill was not good at all, and "we are about to combat it," and by June 29 he had launched his campaign. His tone was sarcastic from the beginning, and he made it a key point that the university system was not liberal. He wanted liberty. It has been said that Veuillot wanted liberty when his opponents were in power, but that he did not care whether they had liberty if his forces were dominant.[168] At this time he believed the same forces which had dominated during the days of Louis Philippe still held the upper hand, and he wanted liberty. He scorned the idea that it was necessary to accept the measure that was being presented, because it was desirable to settle the whole affair. "Without doubt it is urgent to be done with the matter; but with the monopoly, and not with liberty! It is urgent to vanquish, but not to come to terms." Against the fatal influence of the university he invoked the names of Guizot, Marshal Bugeaud, and even Thiers,[169] though he cited none of his exact words, and, of course, he realized that Thiers was at present a key force in the university forces. At the root of the problem, as Veuillot saw it, was the *esprit politique* that pervaded the commission that drew up the project. He quoted his new idol, Donoso Cortés, to the effect that Catholic civilization was good without a mixture of evil, and that the *civilisation philosophique* was evil without an admixture of good. Therefore, any kind of transaction, any so-called *concordat* between these elements was impossible.[170] In an editorial early in the struggle Veuillot said that the partisans of the bill criticized him for "ideas too absolute and not enough of the *esprit politique*." This was no reproach, he said, but a *grand éloge.*[171]

Veuillot talked in general terms a great deal in assaulting the Falloux bill, but much that he brought out was also remarkably precise. In his analysis of article 56, which provided that any Frenchman of the age of 25 could found a secondary school, he listed an imposing group of conditions, and he noted that only associations, according to article 22, could establish primary schools. He believed that associations, and in particular congregations, should have the right to form secondary schools, that rights for certain groups should not be rendered impossible, and that certifications by the university should be abolished. Who cares where you studied, he demanded; what is important is what do you know? The *petits seminaires* should be places where professors could found colleges, and the *congrégations* should have the right also to found colleges. Interestingly, despite the events of 1848, he cited the clauses of the Charter of 1830 about liberty of education.[172] Full liberty of instruction was his position.

While Veuillot picked away at the legal side of the bill, attacking aspects of the administration contemplated as well as the primary and secondary schools envisaged,[173] he gave free rein to the more general side of his attack. He especially turned on the deputy Bac for his advocacy of the "sovereignty of reason."[174] Present society, he said, was built on sand, and it was crumbling. The system of education was smothering everyone, and the only answer was freedom of education. His historical precedent was the demand of liberty by the church in the days of Constantine.[175] Curiously, at the time he was thus stressing liberty of education, he expressed fear concerning the desire of Grévy for freedom of the press such as was being practiced in America. America and France were different, said Veuillot, and with the existing danger of revolution in France he preferred the system of warnings and control that the French regime maintained over the press.[176]

The role of the bishops in the matter of the Falloux project was, of course, not only important, but significant with regard to the rise of the lay press.[177] From the start the episcopacy generally had reservations with regard to the bill. However, *L'Univers* began to publish letters of various bishops, which had been written against the Villemain law of 1844, as a case against the Falloux bill.[178] Since they had opposed the law of 1844, they were thus supposed to be opponents of the new bill. Their hands were being forced, they were being maneuvered into taking positions of opposition in the new situation.[179] No doubt many of the bishops, whatever their feelings and beliefs may have been, resented the role of the press, especially in the hands of laymen, which did not hesitate to take the initiative. Many of them avoided outspoken criticism of the projected law and took the position of criticizing given points and hoping for revisions. However, an interesting count shows that only three of twenty-six bishops writing to Falloux, Dupanloup, and Montalembert approved the project, while eighteen had reservations.[180] On the other hand a number of bishops reacted against Veuillot's stands,[181] and important figures like Msgr. Parisis stood aside. In the seizing of the initiative for the lay religious press, Veuillot no doubt incurred much episcopal displeasure, which may have been most inexpedient both for his cause and for himself.

Naturally Veuillot engaged in clashes with secular papers like *Le National* in this struggle,[182] but his most important battle was with *L'Ami de la religion*. The latter tried to maintain that the bill sustained liberty of instruction, but Veuillot could not see how it did. Both what the bill did not say regarding liberty of instruction, and what it *did* say made *L'Ami de la religion's* case insupportable in Veuillot's eyes.[183] Although "quelques écrivains" had written the articles in *L'Ami de la religion*, Veuillot saw in them the hand, or at least the inspiration of Dupanloup, whom he alternately called "M. Dupanloup," "M. L'Abbé Dupanloup," "Msgr. l'évêque d'Orléans," but most often "M. l'évêque nommé d'Orléans."[184] Veuillot not only resented the arguments insisting on the excellence of the law, but also resented the charge about the "rashness of those who by blind and basically senseless fury" were threatening the bill.[185] Finally when opponents of the law were accused of a "légèreté railleuse," Veuillot struck back directly and with force.[186] In 1848 he had had the advantage of good relations with the rising Abbé Dupanloup. Now he had a serious enemy in the same person just elevated to an important see, where he indeed claimed Louis Veuillot, born in Boynes in the Archbishopric of Orleans, as his dioscesan.[187]

Most of the bishops were moderate, as might have been expected, both in their stands and in their words about the issue, but the old Bishop of Chartres, Clausel de Montals, was not among those. He had his doubts about laymen's roles, and he was something of a problem for Louis Veuillot at other times. However, in the matter of the Falloux bill he was very clearly on the same side. As early as 16 July 1849 he published a letter in *L'Univers*, attacking both this bill for education, and communism and socialism, in the same sweep.[188] The lay religious press was something to be taken advantage of, at least in this affair. Before the struggle was over he had written many more letters, attacking the university as a great enemy of the church.[189] Lenormant and Clausel de Montals made interesting co-belligerents for Louis Veuillot.

Veuillot may be credited with realizing that attention ought to be given to higher education. On 14 July 1849 *L'Univers* reported hearing that a commission would be established for a measure affecting higher education, to which the answer of Veuillot was that, with all the revolutionary and socialist dangers in the world, such a move would be to the good; theological instruction especially should be re-established.[190] Whether his heart was really in that position, however, is questionable. Just one week later he praised the system under the ancien régime, and reiterated his opinion that the Revolution and subsequent developments had brought France to its present state.[191] On 1 September *L'Univers* declared: "The creation of free and *independent universities* is in effect the only means of assuring full and real liberty of instruction. As long as this situation does not exist, people will vainly exhaust themselves in ingenuous combinations where there will be no free instruction, nor Christian instruction, and where one will have under one form or another nothing but the university of the state and the state instructor. Moreover, the state is only able to teach what it believes, and it believes everything, this is to say, it does not believe anything."[192] Thus Veuillot attacked Cousin's eclecticism in its implications for education at all levels. As matters transpired the Falloux project was restricted to primary and secondary education, but the self-educated man from the Loiret was willing to fight the battle at all levels.

Few laws in all of French history rank with the Falloux Law of 15 March 1850, but one of the first-fallen in the battle for its passage was Count Armand de Falloux, who resigned late in October 1849 because of the generally difficult nature of his position. Many big figures remained in the ranks of the party of order, now supported by Montalembert and Dupanloup, and Marie-Louis Esquirou de Parieu was promptly named to succeed Falloux as minister of instruction and of cults. However, the resignation of Falloux showed the strength of the opponents of the project, who included, of course, Voltaireans who would not compromise any more than Veuillot's adherents would. Veuillot seemed to take new hope at this resignation that the Catholics might be able to avoid compromise with the party of order and the university. He hoped that the party of order would fear new discord, and that the majority might decide it best to withdraw this particular bill. Then perhaps, he believed, liberty for Catholic education would have a chance.[194] No such development took place, but only the sponsor of the bill he so disliked was forced to resign, nearly five months before its eventual passage.

At a time when the ranks of the Catholic party were split into those who resented the kind of compromise Dupanloup and Montalembert were making and those who supported them, it is interesting to see Veuillot reassert his old admiration for Guizot. While flattering him by saying that he was one of the few people in those times who were listened to, and that God had blessed the savant Guizot, he declared to him that "it is certain that all Christians should come to an accord."[195] He was sounding an ecumenical note to a protestant leader, who also feared the university system, in the hopes of bolstering his quest for freedom in education.

While Veuillot's relations with the protestant former minister were pleasant enough, his relations with key Catholics, in the fall of 1849, were very bad. Montalembert was quibbling with him in print as early as July,[196] and within a short time Montalembert was thoroughly angered at Veuillot and *L'Univers*, among others.[197] Throughout the whole matter of the Falloux bill Montalembert had had to take a back seat. Dupanloup was the most significant of the Catholics in the project, not surprisingly, because of his academic leadership, but Thiers stood out among the political figures. Quite apart from the issues and the fate of Catholic education, Montalembert would have been in a tantalizing position. The break between Montalembert and Veuillot was described by the latter as "imminent" in late July,[198] and very shortly afterward Veuillot was being called names by the big three. Veuillot's polemic was described as an "indignity" by Montalembert, an "impiety" by Dupanloup, and as "une étourderie et une sottise" by Falloux. Veuillot, nonetheless felt that they, not he, were being abandoned by the great majority of Catholics. "I will have bitter regrets, but not the least remorse, because I will have saved the flag, and around the flag of the party that they accuse me of ruining. . . ."[199] But bitter as the split was, Veuillot wrote in late October of 1849: "Although I have not seen Montalembert for a long time, I am sure there is no enmity between us."[200] Perhaps there was not; Veuillot certainly seems to have been able to attack the public man and to treat the private man socially in a completely different way. Montalembert, for his part, was impetuous, and had other irritations that could have distracted him from the full force of Veuillot's criticism. However, the Catholic party, which had really developed, especially in the era of 1844, as a force against state monopoly of education, had just about come apart at the seams in the fall of 1849 and had little reason for further existence. A case can be made that Falloux had wanted it to break up some time before this crisis, and that Dupanloup politically was legitimist rather than Catholic. Montalembert, on the other hand, was sad at the rupture of the group of which he had been the leader up to this point. Perhaps Dupanloup and Falloux "congratulated themselves to see it disappear."[201]

Veuillot's relations with Falloux had never been close, and even before Falloux became minister, Veuillot felt, Falloux had been "cold" towards him.[202] His relations with Dupanloup as a rising abbé had been good. This situation, however, was now changed. The stands the two took were enough to force a rupture, but in addition an impetuous Jesuit, Father Combalot, who was to cause still more trouble later on, precipitated an awkward situation for Veuillot. As a result of the heated differences Montalembert, Falloux, and Dupanloup believed they had been denounced to the pope at the instigation of Louis Veuillot. Actually, there is no evidence that the pope was a factor of any direct sort in these French Catholic troubles, nor was the nuncio, Msgr. Fornari, in any way involved. Nevertheless, it was rather natural that suspicions might have been aroused. Father Combalot, described by Eugène Veuillot as "this excellent priest, the best man in the world, and also one of the most enterprising, as well as one of the most naïf," became incensed at Dupanloup, the compromising policy, and those who supported this approach. He particularly turned his wrath on Father Ravignan, the priest who had married Louis and Mathilde, and proposed to denounce him to the general of the Jesuit order. Veuillot tried to dissuade him, but Father Combalot, while respecting what he termed Veuillot's "scruples," wrote to the head of the order, denouncing

Ravignan, whom he associated with Dupanloup."[203] This episode was at the foundation of the rumor that there had been denunciations to Rome by Veuillot. These rumors added to the misunderstandings within the Catholic party and to the intensity of Veuillot's difficulties within it.

Not until 14 January 1850 did parliamentary debate actually begin on the Falloux project. Comte de Beugnot formally reported the measure, which the parliamentary committee of fifteen, including Parisis and Montalembert, had prepared. The parliamentary debate was sharp, and *L'Univers* followed it avidly. Veuillot questioned the sincerity of the supporters of the university who professed to fear for its existence, of Thiers, and of Montalembert.[204] One remarkable part of the compromising, was that, led by Thiers, arrangements were made to permit the Jesuits to open schools, which provision was voted by the parliament, 450-128,[205] a greater majority than the Falloux law itself was accorded. Montalembert, who called the measure a "concordat" and an "œuvre sacrée," was particularly bitter in the debates, particularly with regard to the criticism paced by *L'Univers*, and it was at this point that he claimed he had been denounced to Rome.[206] Veuillot took sharp issue with this accusation, maintaining that the friends of the measure had sought to present it to the pope in such a way as to gain papal approbation. Certainly the bishops were interested in the position of the pope in any case, and a memorandum was prepared by the Archbishop of Reims and signed by a number of prelates and sent to the pope. Veuillot complained that Dupanloup intimated that the signatories were favorable to the project, whereas in fact most of the bishops signing the document were doing so only with reservations put forward by Parisis.[207]

One of Veuillot's most interesting points in the assault on the measure was a parable from an anonymous bishop, who might have been Clausel de Montals. The anonymous prelate was quoted as saying there were enough good things in the bill to win many people over to it. But alarmed by the weaknesses he said: "This marriage of the episcopacy and the university bodes no good: the wife will want to carry the scepter and to beat her husband with it." But while he was attacking the bill in such picturesque ways, Veuillot resented Montalembert's claim that he was presenting the supporters of it as "either imbeciles or traitors." Up until the time Rome should speak any Catholic had the right to defend his own opinion, he declared.[208] Such was Veuillot's theory, but this theory did not prevent him from very strong language with regard to the bill, though he did not actually use the words "imbecile" or "traitor" in his columns.

The measure was more favorable to the Catholics after parliamentary modification than it had been as drafted by the extra-parliamentary commission, but it was still a compromise. As such it was voted into law on 15 March 1850 by a vote of 399 to 237. According to Eugène Veuillot, this vote demonstrated strong sentiment for liberty of instruction,[209] which, despite the *politique* spirit of many of the legislators, it did to a degree. Needless to say, the vote did not please Louis Veuillot, who had hoped that the whole bill would be thrown out, and that a measure which would allow Catholic schools, completely free from university surveillance, to be established would take its place. The "doctrine of transaction" had prevailed,[210] and many of the Catholic party had followed Montalembert rather than Veuillot, though the latter must have found satisfaction in the abstention of Parisis. Although Eugène used the word *améliorer* to describe what the parliamentry commission had done to the original proposal,[211] Louis professed to see none of this when he wrote of the passage of the Falloux Law:

> The law on instruction is voted. We have fought it without cease, with all the vigor we could bring to bear, and with perseverance equal to our conviction. We wanted to bring about its rejection because we thought it bad; we were not able even to ameliorate it. It comes from the vote full of obscurities, with all the inconveniences, all the dangers we have indicated. It has created for the church a difficult and dangerous situation; it has consolidated the university; it has retarded, perhaps for a long time, the day of liberty, of which we believed for a moment we were finally greeting the dawn.[212]

Bad as the law seemed to Veuillot, it was better than the status quo, though he even feared that the status quo might possibly seem better someday. He shifted the burden of responsibility to the bishops. "The bishops are the guardians of Christian consciences. The law will be for us what it will be for them."[213] In due course papal reaction took the pressure off the bishops, and the pope accepted the "imperfect liberty" the new law afforded.[214] There was not much Veuillot could do after the pope took this position, and his position thence forward was that of accepting the law, though its imperfections he did not fail to continue to point out. Attacks by Falloux caused him eventually in 1856 to publish his *Histoire du parti catholique*, which was a defense of his position. Old wounds never really healed.

By the time of the passage of the Falloux Law one may question whether the Catholic party had any reason for existence, particularly as *l'Ami de la religion* and *L'Univers* were still feuding about points in the law.[215] Nevertheless, there was a temporary reconciliation between

Veuillot and Montalembert that gave the appearance of hope for renewed life for the Catholic party. Eugène described a scene not long after the passage of the Falloux Law, when Montalembert, hat on the back of his head, monocle in his eye, and cigar in his mouth, walked again into the offices of *L'Univers* as though nothing had ever happened.[216] He was welcomed by everyone, and a reconciliation between the two antagonists, whom Beugnot called the "cossacks of the Christian army" because they appeared to him to be riding in the front,[217] seemed to have taken place. For a time there did indeed seem to be hope for a reunited Catholic-before-all force. Beyond the compromises made to what Veuillot regarded as the materialistic party of order headed by Thiers, he still could envisage the revival of the shattered group. He wrote Msgr. Rendu: "I believe that in sum, after this *bagarre*, the Catholic party will endure, and even that Montalembert will remain its chief, only warned, and this is necessary, that his authority is not absolute."[218] Surely his authority was not absolutely restored, if it had ever been such, and although one of Veuillot's most exalted representations of Montalembert came when Montalembert was contrasted with Victor Hugo as the two opposed each other over electoral changes in 1850,[219] the reconciliation was only temporary. In due course Montalembert broke with Louis Napoleon, not long after the coup d'état of December 1851, following which period he and Veuillot were never reconciled.

Despite the way the issue of the Falloux Law dominated Veuillot's attention in late 1849 and early 1850, other matters were not neglected. Under the inspiration of his new friend, Donoso Cortés, Spanish ambassador to Berlin, he wrote a remarkable piece that was published in *L'Univers* about Prussia and Russia. In the form of a letter written from Berlin to a friend in Paris, Louis Veuillot described the constitutionalism and socialism he saw developing in Prussia under Frederick William IV, a monarch whose talents, but not his judgment, he admired. Following the general thesis of Donoso Cortés, he saw an overconfident monarch destroy the bureaucratic and aristocratic Prussian system, and a revolutionary state arising. Such a state would no longer be able to cover Western Europe from the march of Russia, which as Prussia declined would tartarize the West.[220] Well-written, this exposition of the dangers of revolution and of Russia was one of the less original of Veuillot's themes, being taken directly from the ideas of his new Spanish inspiration. Nevertheless, such writings show the diversity of Veuillot's concerns when, in November of 1849, he was very much preoccupied with the struggle over public instruction. The same may be said of a series of articles that appeared in *L'Univers*, beginning 1

January 1850, on *le Siècle de Voltaire*.[221] This series had little connection with his principal preoccupation, yet is remarkable for the passion that went into it, as he connected or in some way associated many of the people and things he disliked with Voltaire. Although the second half of the nineteenth century was beginning the eighteenth century was hardly over because of the ideology of Voltaire which was still prevailing. Veuillot's valid challenge of strict chronology was heavily based on prevailing literature. But of his great criterion he said: "Literature, properly speaking, is not *de bon place* in France. It is the daughter of protestantism; it has pagan affinities: skepticism, raillery, and lewdness are its principal characteristics. It is enough to name its founders, Villon, Rabelais, Marot, Desperriers, Brantôme, Marguerite de Navarre, Montaigne, Amyot himself, although a bishop. Of its unfortunate and impure origin, it has always felt the effects! Conquered for a moment by Christian genius, which gave it Balzac, Pascal, Corneille, Racine, Bossuet, Fénelon, Bourdaloue, it soon resumed its course. The impious and unclean flow of sap, which even in the time of this great glory and of these great men was able to produce La Fontaine and Molière, became after them the torrent which is called Voltaire, and which has left nothing standing. The protection accorded to literature by persons of high rank was almost entirely for the profit of its worst instincts."[222] Thus Veuillot spoke of French literature as being epitomized by Voltaire Men like Rousseau he fitted into an appropriate place in the Voltairean scheme.[223] Henceforth all history seemed to have been the Age of Voltaire, and "Bonaparte closely resembled Frederick of Prussia." Even such a figure as Proudhon, whose voice crying "anarchy" he tried to capture in print, was a logical follower of Voltaire. The whole question confronting man would seem to be the choice between Christ and Voltaire.[224]

Along with the gloomy picture of French literature Veuillot could present in one series of articles, he was also disposed to draw lessons from other quarters, even from a rather surprising source, Guizot's *Discours sur l'histoire de la révolution d'Angleterre*, which was just at this time appearing. Veuillot, who presented Guizot in different ways at different times, held him up as an exalted but mistaken man at this period. "M. Guizot is neither a fatalist nor a materialist; a truly religious spirit, because he is *vraiment élevé,* he seeks for and studies the hand of Providence, the great Personage in all human history."[225] Just as he had asked what a century really was when he talked of Voltaire he now asked what a revolution was, a theme he was to use again. Just as the French Revolution had begun long before 1789, so he saw in Guizot's writings that the English Revolution had begun under Henry VIII, who was like France's Voltaire. However, he took Guizot to task for avoiding some obvious conclusions, for avoiding judgments on the establishment of protestantism. England after the conquest had become an "isle of saints," thanks to the monks, according to Veuillot,[226] but all this was destroyed by the work of Henry VIII, his agents and successors. "Protestantism has destroyed human society. We would be astonished if M. Guizot himself did not believe it."[227] Nevertheless Guizot held up two protestant countries, as the countries that were the most Christian in the world in his view, England and Holland. Brushing Holland aside Guizot pursued his theme for England, bringing forth the bitterest of Veuillot's sarcasm. No need to change anything in the *credo*, so long as the words "I do not believe in the Catholic church" are left.[228] The whole example of England he developed in article after article in *L'Univers* during the spring of 1850,[229] exploiting to the full the prejudices of many Frenchmen with regard to English ways and institutions, developing traditional French Catholic concepts against this backdrop. Although he pointed out that it was necessary to have a degree from Oxford or Cambridge in order to enter the public service, he said nothing else about education in this long series except for this reference to "Anglican certificates."[230] At the end of his work Guizot wrote: "The revolutionary spirit is fatal to the powers it raises up." Veuillot concluded that protestantism and revolution were synonymous, and that England in the long run would be brought down by it. When pagans of Byzantium asked of a Christian what his carpenter was doing for Julian the Apostate, the Christian replied He was building him a coffin.[231] This story Veuillot thought was appropriate for Catholicism and England. Thus the writings of Guizot, whom he really did admire in a special way, loomed as important subject matter for argument and for moralizing, even at a time when Catholics in France were having to accept the passage of the Falloux Law.

Actually the greatest threat to the Second Republic and to President Louis Napoleon Bonaparte came not from the revolutionary left, but from the royalists. In fact, had the royalists only been united, Louis Napoleon would have had little chance of becoming emperor. However, deep ideological differences split the Orleanists, the "usurpers," from the legitimists, supporters of the Comte de Chambord.[232] For a generation, from the events of 1848 through 1873, practical politicians of the different rightist groups stirred around, seeking some formula that would bring about a "fusion" of the two branches of the royal family. Notable among these figures were Falloux and Dupanloup.[233] But none of them ever succeeded, the main reason being that the legitimist pretender, the Comte de Chambord, would not consider any kind of transaction, in regard to bringing about a "fusion," which would be significantly compromising to the principle of legitimacy which he represented.[234] There were two periods, however, when hopes of such a fusion were high. These were 1850-51 and 1873, and on both occasions Louis Veuillot was much absorbed with the problem.

Before the first of these crises in royalism came to a head, Veuillot wrote a letter to the Comte de Chambord:

> December 1849
>
> Monseigneur,
>
> It is the duty of every Frenchman who believes that he has ever expressed a thought at all serious to put it under the eyes of the man for whom Providence seems to have reserved the glory of finally re-establishing France on the eternal bases of the social order.
>
> I have always believed in the monarchy, never so much as under the republic. But the monarchy itself will never be anything except with religion, by religion, for religion. God, by whom alone we are capable of having liberty, is the first master to be obeyed. Such is the thought which inspired in me the work which I have the honor to present to Your Highness [*Le lendemain de la victoire*]. This thought, in my conviction, should be that of the man for whom the world has need. It will gain for him the disinterested devotion of whoever will truly love God and France.
>
> Your Highness will deign to receive the homage of my profound respect.[235]

The pretender answered Veuillot on 20 February from Venice, apparently pleased with the sentiments the editor of *L'Univers* had expressed. To be sure, the Catholic-before-all stand he had taken ten years earlier, had been hardly what the legitimist pretender wanted to hear, but Veuillot's recent letter had a royalist ring to it. The apparent essence of Chambord's reply was that the two now had the same outlook. However, as Eugene Veuillot pointed out, what Chambord really said to Veuillot was: "I rejoice to hear that you recognize the impossibility of separating the church from my cause." This was not exactly the view expressed by Veuillot.[236] However, the peasant from the Loiret and the head of the House of Bourbon did have similar outlooks, and Veuillot was not inclined to split hairs with the pretender to the detriment of either's cause. In the month of June, on the basis of information from an old friend, the provincial journalist Mallac, who had become a staunch legitimist, Veuillot wrote two long articles about the fusion question, putting them in the form of letters from London.[237] The essential theme that he struck was that a proper reconciliation of the princes of the royal line was needed. Unfortunately he said, this reconciliation was impossible, despite the wishes of the princes of Orleans, because the Duchesse d'Orleans and certain others, notably Thiers, kept bringing up the bourgeois constitutionalism that Chambord could not accept. It was because of the intrigues of Thiers, that establishment of Catholicism as the dominant force to accompany the monarchy was being prevented. National will was what Thiers stressed; but what was this will, asked Veuillot?[238] Veuillot remained *catholique avant tout*, but in 1850 his preference for royalism certainly was apparent as Thiers stressed constitutionalism to the Princes of Orleans.

A major political question during the first part of 1850 was that of the requirements for suffrage. The constitution provided that only a short residence was necessary before a man could establish himself as a resident of an electoral district and avail himself of the universal suffrage privilege. Generally, conservative elements desired to amend this provision, to safeguard against revolutionary forces. An episode that gave rise to this movement was the election of Eugène Sue in the Department of the Seine. By 1 May 1850 *L'Univers* reported that this radical (and enemy of Veuillot) had over 128,000 votes, while his opponent of the party of order had just under 120,000.[239] The author of *The Wandering Jew* was to be a deputy. Veuillot was distressed and intensified his editorial stand on behalf of the requirement for three years' residence. Actually Veuillot did not believe a measure like this would prove to have much efficacy,[240] but Montalembert did believe in it, and he defended his belief staunchly and ably, exciting Veuillot to the admiration which led to his remarkable contrasting of Montalembert with Victor Hugo.[241] The three-year law governing residency for voting did pass, and Veuillot was for the moment in step with French domestic politics and reconciled with Montalembert.

Politics in the broad sweep of European events intrigued Veuillot from time to time. At the end of 1849, when he traveled to the capital of Belgium, ostensibly to meet various Belgian Catholics, he was able to meet Prince Metternich, who had taken refuge in Belgium after the revolution of 1848. Veuillot was "charmed" with Metternich and told Eugène that on meeting him he had plunged into a conversation that lasted two and one-half hours.[242] He wrote not only to Eugène about this visit, but also to his wife and Foisset.[243] To the latter, about two and one-half weeks later, he boasted that he had seen Metternich four times in eight days, and that the shortest of their talks had lasted three hours.[244] He must have been very eager to hear and talk to this man who had dominated Europe for a generation, for he was careful not only to carry a letter of introduction from Guizot, but also to present himself in company with Comte Théodore de Bussières, who had long been friendly with Metternich.[245] Despite a few proud and satisfied references to this meeting in his letters to those close to him, however, Veuillot said nothing about the meeting publicly for ten years. Obviously, his conversations with the prince were not useful to him in a newsworthy way at the moment. His satisfaction in the meeting was in hearing the views of a great man, and in contrasting them with the ideas of Donoso Cortés. Veuillot has frequently been dismissed as merely anti-intellectual. In the sense that he did not think along the lines of the *universitaires*, and that he was not interested in intellectual pursuits as an exercise for their own sake, this designation has some meaning. However his interest in and analysis of Metternich's discourses show a Veuillot much fascinated with political and social thought.

Metternich at this time was seventy-five years old, but straight, still very alert, and obviously eager to express ideas. Veuillot had written many articles maligning Metternich and his system, but, fortunately, in those days editors did not generally sign their pieces, and so when they met Metternich did not have to regard him immediately as a personal detractor, although this consideration was in the mind of Bussières at their introduction.[246] One of the first things that Metternich discussed was his unusual view of the French. Mankind, he said was divided into people of yesterday and people of tomorrow, but the French people somehow were people of now. Veuillot protested that some French people looked ahead further than the two or three years Metternich suggested, and from this strange beginning of the conversation they went on to Napoleon, the pope, and problems of the nineteenth century. Important among these problems was Poland, and incidental to the matter of Polish nationalism, Metternich explained to Veuillot, Metternich had incurred the rancor of Montalembert for not allowing him to travel in parts of Poland. Metternich and Veuillot had at least had the same experience of irritating Montalembert, though the number of such persons was legion. While discussing Poland, for which Metternich professed to have admiration, the exiled great man said that it was *Polonisme* that he detested. *Polonisme* was a "detestable spirit, a spirit of agitation impiety and iniquity."[247] Following up his attack on this special "ism," he turned on the rest, nationalism, liberalism, optimism, pessimism, nihilism, Gallicanism, protestantism, and even Catholicism and royalism. To speak in the same vein as Metternich, Veuillot threw in "Josephism," to which Metternich warmly agreed. But although Veuillot was much in sympathy, he added a note in the publication of his works which showed that Donoso Cortés' conviction, that Catholicism did not belong in this category with the other "isms," was his own. "Ism" here was only a usage and the twist that the suffix usually gives to a noun had none of its usual flavor in regard to his religion.[248] No doubt, however, he was in complete agreement with the former Austrian foreign minister when the latter came back to his "isms" in deploring the menances to Germany coming from "Teutonism" and "Prussianism," which he linked with Jacobinism and protestantism. Metternich deplored the activities of the Jews in the German world, where he saw them taking first place among revolutionaries, writers, bankers, publicists, and philosophers. Veuillot, on the other hand, saw no menance in France from Jews as such. He admitted their important place in the world of commerce but aside from that he replied: "In the mass of unbelievers the effect of the Jews is not at all noticeable."[249] Thus they ranged widely over many ideas and specifics.

No doubt Veuillot was fascinated with the opportunity to talk with so important a man, particularly since the statesman said he had long subscribed to *L'Univers* under a pseudonym, and had read the journal with much satisfaction, except of course with regard to Austria. He added, however, that although he had in the past wanted to explain some matters to Veuillot, now unfortunately he no longer had need for so doing.[250] Although Veuillot found Metternich a witty and remarkable man, he nevertheless did not admire his system, nor did he admire his fundamental nature. For want of a more precise way of putting it, Veuillot said that to him, after exploring the mind of Metternich, and hearing him say many things that had wisdom, prudence, and finesse, the effect was the same as though he had read "an excellent book on ethics by a protestant."[251] The fact that his letter of introduction was from Guizot would seem appropriate, if this assessment were a good one!

It was no protestant, however, who presented Veuillot with his greatest challenge in 1850. Not many months after the passage of the Falloux Law the Archbishop of Paris condemned *L'Univers*, and Veuillot found he had to appeal to the highest authority in order even to adjourn for a little while the struggle with his own bishop into which he was drawn as a result of both conflicting principles and the peculiar situation of the lay religious press in mid-nineteenth-century France.

Not long after the tragic death of Msgr. Affre the régime of General Cavaignac had brought about the elevation of Msgr. Marie Dominique Sibour, Bishop of Digne, to the Archbishopric of Paris. At that time the move had seemed to be auspicious for *L'Univers*. Msgr. Sibour, an intelligent man, had long been acquainted with Melchior Du Lac. Msgr. Sibour, whose cousin had been on the extra-parliamentary commission

Falloux had established, gave the appearance of being an ultramontane.[252] As a matter of fact, the terms "ultramontane" and "Gallican," which came to be such important labels and subjects for dispute, were only beginning in this era to take the definitions that applied later on in the period of the Vatican Council. Hitherto, men like Sibour and Montalembert had thought of themselves as ultramontanes in their struggle for their French church against temporal power. In their eyes the pope was not everything, but as the head of the whole world church a force to which appeals might be made in the struggle for liberal Catholic purposes against French national forces using the church for their own ends.[253] During the pontificate of Pius IX the term "ultramontane" became more and more authoritarian in its meaning, and more synonymous with the concept held by Louis Veuillot. Not surprisingly, Sibour, who was thoroughly a liberal Catholic, ceased to talk about being an ultramontane within a short time.

The new Archbishop of Paris, despite his liberalism, was very conscious of the powers and prerogatives of his position. The authority of his archbishopric loomed big to him, and he regarded his post as the most important among the episcopal sees of France. Logically enough, as he came to see the challenge to the episcopacy that the new lay press was offering, he tried to do something about it. When he came to Paris his attitude was at first that of accepting *L'Univers*, of adopting it, so to speak. Du Lac and Veuillot, according to Eugène, were wary of him, and from the start did not take his effusions of friendship at their face value.[254] He seemed to be conciliatory during the days of 1848-1849, as exemplified by his attempt to bring *L'Univers* and *L'Ère nouvelle* together on the occasion of the dinner in November 1848,[255] but some time after this he either turned against *L'Univers* and Louis Veuillot, or despaired of conciliation between the factions of Catholic activists and decided to choose between them instead. His choice, of course, did not fall upon *L'Univers*.

L'Ère nouvelle faded during 1849, but by the start of 1850 another Catholic journal, the *Moniteur catholique*, began publication in Paris. The archbishop decided to make this journal his special organ, and at another dinner the Archbishop, in an awkward fashion, explained that the conciliatory *Moniteur catholique* would set the tone of Catholic journalism in the future instead of the combative *L'Univers*. The discourse of the archbishop was interrupted by Louis Veuillot, albeit with allusion to a story from the Gospels: "Good enough, Monseigneur, I understand the situation. The *Montieur catholique* will be Mary and take care of the drawing room, while *L'Univers* will be Martha and perform the heavy work (*fera le gros service*)." As though this interjection were not enough affront to the archbishop, the redoubtable Abbé Combalot cried out in his *superb* (Eugène's word) voice, "Bravo!"[256] The *Moniteur catholique* was a thorough failure, and lasted only six months, but the archbishop took other measures against *L'Univers* that would have been enough to destroy a journal any less sturdy.

Unraveling the background issues which caused Msgr. Sibour to turn against Veuillot is not a simple matter. The revival in 1849 of provincial councils of bishops was a source of enhancement of episcopal power, which could counterbalance the strength of the papal authority. Veuillot's exalted view of Rome inevitably was in conflict with any such challenge from local bishops. But many of the polemics in *L'Univers* which annoyed Sibour came in response to attacks on Catholics in the secular press. *L'Ordre,* directed by Chambolle, and *Le National* especially provoked response by *L'Univers* in the late spring of 1850. Ridicule of Catholics by unbelievers, particularly in the matter of miracles, brought strong responses. Veuillot quoted the Bible at length, discussed various theological ideas, and generally reproved and lectured the secular journals.[257] He got into deep water when talking about Bossuet, the Inquisition, Ozanam, and various aspects of miracles. Undoubtedly he went very far for a layman in matters about which there are differences among learned ecclesiastics. Also by his manner of responding to attacks by the worldly, he was inviting more attacks. That he was presuming to do what the hierarchy might be expected to claim as its own prerogative, is evident. Yet the situation of the mid-nineteenth century in the world of the press was such that lay Catholic journalists were in a natural position to answer the assaults by the secular press. Veuillot was to some degree in a position to speak for the hierarchy in an arena where the bishops could hardly be expected to speak for themselves. In so doing, although he was usurping their prerogative, he was saying many things that many of the bishops were glad someone would say. Archbishop Sibour, however, did not share the mixed feelings typical in other members of the hierarchy. On the contrary, he was exasperated, and in late August 1850 he struck the first of several blows against Louis Veuillot.

As the Gallican-Ultramontane issue sharpened, and as a showdown between Veuillot and the archbishop approached, Veuillot's reputation in Rome markedly improved. He began to pay more attention to *L'Univers*'s correspondent in Rome, who now was the Abbé Bernier. The Abbé's stipend was raised to 1000 francs a year, to alleviate the holy poverty a priest was supposed to bear. Veuillot obviously thought the role of Bernier would be of much importance, particularly since he erroneously feared that Msgr. Parisis, who ultimately proved to be his greatest supporter, was not favorably disposed toward him.[258] According to Eugène, Louis had not previously prepared his position in Rome, but he felt sure of the support of the nuncio, Msgr. Fornari[259] In addition to the nuncio, two "ambassadors" performed valuable services for *L'Univers* in Rome: Bernier, and Eugène, who made a trip there in the late summer of 1850.

Until the Abbé Bernier, together with another French cleric, had an audience with the pope on 22 July, the pontiff apparently knew little about *L'Univers*. As their conversation turned to the Sonderbund, the pope warmed to Bernier and the journal he represented. Twice he asked for the name of the editor, apparently having believed up to that moment that *L'Univers* was a Jesuit paper. The pope did not understand when he began the audience that Bernier was Veuillot's correspondent in Rome and when he did he declared: "Oh, then, we must give him a medal."[260] Bernier was obliged to comply with the wish of Pius IX, but the episode brought out a trait of Veuillot's character that was consistent with his whole personality: he disliked decorations. In theory he had nothing against the formal recognition of services, but he disliked the arbitrary way in which they tended to be dispensed in his era.[261] It is interesting, however, that despite the cynicism he himself felt for formal decorations, several times he aided in obtaining them for other people who desired them.[262]

The Abbé Bernier had thus already opened the door in Rome when Eugène arrived not long afterward. Eugène had been sent by his brother to Turin with the cross of the late Msgr. Affre which had been on his chest when he was killed at the barricades, to be given to Msgr. Fransoni, Archbishop of Turin, another stalwart, who had been fined and imprisoned by the Piedmontese government for his protestation of the rights of the church. Having accomplished this mission, he went on to Rome, where he had audiences, first with Cardinal Antonelli, secretary of state, and then with the pope, on 17 August 1850. Antonelli had been thought not to be favorable to *L'Univers*, but Eugène quickly discovered the opposite to be the case. Antonelli informed Eugène of Fornari's recommendations of *L'Univers*, but quite for himself the cardinal declared: "We know *L'Univers* by the services it renders to the church, and we here know about the beautiful mission with which you are charged." After speaking a while of Eugène's trip to Turin, he came back to *L'Univers*, exclaiming: "It is the only journal His Holiness wants to read."[263]

In the evening Eugène was presented to the pope, with whom he talked about the problems of Catholics in France. During the course of

(Alsatia)

Eugène Veuillot

the conversation Pius IX said: "I know *L'Univers*. I approve its works. It is the French journal you will find here." However, the pope continued, he had seen an article in it that had been directed against the authority of the president of France, which did not please him. Eugène gave him assurances that any regime which the pope accepted would be supported by *L'Univers*. The pope was pleased. *L'Univers* now appeared to be on the best footing in Rome.[264] The satisfaction Louis Veuillot felt as a result of Eugène's report was great.[265] Veuillot had looked forward to the visit of his brother to Rome almost as though he were going himself, and had instructed the Abbé Bernier to take him to the places that had meant so much to him at the time of his own visit and conversion. He especially wanted Eugène to be taken to the tomb of Saint Peter, to the Ara Coeli, the first church he had visited in Rome, to the Gesù, especially the spot where Father Roshaven had lived, and to Santa Maria Maggiore, where he had first taken communion as a practicing Christian.[266] He was also interested in the fact that Lafon was with Eugène for a while in Rome.[267] Just as he was exulting over this happy situation, Msgr. Sibour issued an *avertissement* on 31 August, warning that *L'Univers* was following a course that he condemned.

The archbishop did not choose an opportune time to condemn Veuillot. Had he done so a year earlier, he might have done so much more effectively. But now, with the battle over the Falloux Law at an end, practically all Catholics, including Louis Veuillot, had closed ranks, at the pope's behest, in the nominal acceptance of the arrangement as the best that could be had at the time. The refusal of the conservative and Gallican Bishop of Chartres to recognize the compromise clouded Veuillot's relations with the venerable prelate, and ended in Veuillot's presuming to instruct the old bishop about the advisability of following Rome,[268] but on the whole the situation was favorable for the journalist. Because of the growing strength of ultramontanism, toward which many of the conservative prelates were turning, a reaction against the religious radicalism of 1848-1849 developed. The appeal of *L'Univers* among the upper clergy grew stronger. Moreover, the function of a religious lay press seemed more to be accepted than it had been some years earlier, and less something to be questioned when difficulties with a bishop developed. Furthermore, *L'Univers* exuded a fervor that roused enthusiasm in its readers. When Louis Veuillot was trying to recruit Léon Aubineau for the staff in June 1850, he pointed out the obvious social and economic advantages that his journal and the city of Paris had to offer in comparison with any post in the provinces, but he underlined as his main appeal: "*L'Univers* est un mission."[269] This sense of mission attached to the rising tide of ultramontanism made

Veuillot's position more powerful than Msgr. Sibour realized.

The *mandement* and *avertissement* of the archbishop were based on a decree of the recent council of bishops that had met in Paris, a decree dealing with journalists who treated ecclesiastical matters. The *avertissement* included initial recognition of *L'Univers* merits: "One will easily understand our sadness. The journal *L'Univers* has rendered great services to the church. It is in the thick of the journalistic fray that able writers, full of courage, have joined in the defense of religion. It was for a long time a useful auxiliary because of its devotion, before becoming a dangerous friend by its imprudences and digressions."[270] *L'Univers* was criticized by the archbishop for many things, including lack of loyalty with regard to the matter of education; imprudence with regard to utterances about the Inquisition; lack of charity and proper knowledge in its polemics with the secular press about the question of miracles; unfairness in presuming to describe certain Catholics as "Gallicans"; and lack of respect for the authority of the archbishop, particularly in the matter of its attacks on the *Dictionnaire universel d'histoire et de géographie* by Bouillet, a volume which bore the imprimatur of the archbishop, but which Veuillot had condemned. The archbishop threatened excommunication if the editors of *L'Univers* did not return "in the ways of charity, humility, obedience, and respect."[271] "God forbid," answered Veuillot, "that we enter into a public contest against our archbishop! We know how to give an example of the respect that we have always recommended for episcopal authority, preferring a thousand times to sacrifice any right of ours rather than to risk offending it." Promising submission, Veuillot, however, served notice of appeal to the pope. *L'Univers* was not to be transformed into a purely political paper.[272] Thus the issue was joined between the Parisian lay journal that would like to speak universally for Catholics, and the Archbishop of Paris who would like to have been at least *primus inter pares* among the French prelates.

Veuillot wrote to Msgr. Parisis, Bishop of Langres, that he wept when reading the warning.[273] Quite likely Veuillot did, at least in a figurative way, even though his most handicapping physical disorder was that his lacrymal ducts did not readily provide the needed moisture to his much over-worked eyes. To his wife, whose poor health at this point required her and the children to stay with her family in Versailles, Veuillot wrote: "If the pope also condemns us, then we should bless the Lord, who seeing us in error, will have taken the care to warn us and draw us from it."[274] But in addition to these manifestations of piety, Veuillot stirred around in all of his usual vigor. His work, correspondence, and attention, not only to *L'Univers* but to the *Bibliothèque nouvelle*, a huge series of books written for Catholics, the edition of which he was directing, went on with little interruption. He assessed his position carefully, sought all the support he could get, and generally girded for a struggle with what must have seemed to many an overwhelmingly powerful adversary, and one with whom he should not have been preparing to struggle in the first place. Although Veuillot had no intention of giving in, he did indeed prepare to accept defeat should the papacy not back him. However, on this score he was well covered.

The archbishop, of course, had many advantages. In the first place, as he was the archbishop, he had reason to think that his episcopal authority could not be challenged by a layman without the episcopacy's presenting a fairly solid phalanx with him against the assault. Moreover, on the matter of the defense of the Rimini miracles, which were questioned by many scholarly Catholics, Veuillot had taken an immoderate stand.[275] Reportedly the eyes of the Virgin Mary in a picture in a chapel in this small town in Lombardy blinked, causing a stir with Austrian officers hanging their decorations on the wall. Chambolle, editor-in-chief of *L'Ordre*, provoked Veuillot into the strongest defense, just as he did with regard to attacks on the institution of the Inquisition. Immediately after the archbishop's warning the secular press took up the cause of the archbishop, but while praising the archbishop, the secular press continued its blasts against miracles, the Inquisition, and other matters, causing Veuillot to despair for the church.[276] In an age when liberalism and materialism were on the rise, it would certainly seem as though such public support would have made the archbishop's position beyond assault, although even the temporary blessings of these secularists may have hurt Sibour very much in the eyes of other bishops. Veuillot resented the fact that liberal Catholics, including those who had been associated with *L'Ère nouvelle* and the *Moniteur Catholique* rallied to Sibour, but he particularly resented the time that Sibour was spending with Chambolle, whom Veuillot thought the archbishop was trying to convert.[277] This example, incidently, would be a good one for illustrating that Veuillot was not interested in converting opponents of Catholicism, and that winning sceptics to the faith was not a prime interest of his. Apparently he thought conversion should be sudden and complete, as his had seemed to be. In any case, Sibour appeared to be well prepared to force a recalcitrant lay Catholic editor into submission.

A disadvantage that worried Veuillot at the time was the circumstance that his staff at *L'Univers* was not in good shape. Eugène, who as a matter of fact was doing Louis much more good in Rome than he could have in Paris, was nevertheless away. Coquille was at Auxerre.

Gondon, whose reports from London were important, was never really one of the group and was abroad as well. Du Lac was not well, and only barely able to play with the scissors. Barrier, he said, never could do anything. Only Roux was available to work with him, as Aubineau had not yet joined the force.[278] But to balance his problems Veuillot had surprising advantages. Not only was he able to say with truth to another lay editor that the pope was favorable to *L'Univers*, but also he was able to declare: "The nuncio is completely with us. We do nothing without consulting him, and he approves of our sentiments which we bring to him as to a confessor."[279] Cardinal Antonelli also pronounced *L'Univers* "une bonne œuvre bien faite."[280] The Abbé Bernier was a good representative in Rome, and he and Veuillot were in close communication Veuillot considered going to Rome himself, but had he done so *L'Univers* could hardly have continued to function in his absence. Perhaps he simply felt he ought not to leave, despite advice from many to do so, or perhaps the effort of making the trip did not appeal to him. To Bernier he wrote "...that which I fear above all in this affair would be to succeed by mere adroitness." If defeated, he said he would not complain, but simply repeat the words of the pope, "Death is a gain for us." However, he still appeared far from such a point in his journalistic career. Actually Eugène was a far better person than himself to be in Rome. Louis noted that he himself did not speak Italian (though it is interesting to see how many Italian phrases he used in his writings, and to remember how well he arranged affairs during his trips to Rome), and that he was personally unsuited for negotiations,[281] which was no doubt true.

The support that came to Veuillot during this crisis was widespread. A letter from Tours said that everywhere in that area people were "vigorously in favor" of *L'Univers*, not only the conservative Archbishop Pie.[282] From Brittany he was told: "You and your journal have been the subject of conversation everywhere, even after the arrival of the deputies who have made the pilgrimage to Wiesbaden [to pay homage to the Comte de Chambord]."[283] However, it was not only from the grassroots of Catholic areas of France that support came. Donoso Cortés, now the Spanish ambassador to Berlin, wrote several letters of encouragement and advice during September. He told Veuillot how sorry he was about the action of Sibour, and gave him what he most needed, some words of caution. No doubt the pope did favor the line of *L'Univers*, the Spanish diplomat and thinker said, but his position was very delicate. The pope could not lightly allow the authority of the archbishop to be undermined. "I believe strongly that he will not condemn you, but I believe that he will not humiliate the archbishop.

He will not condemn you because you are in the right; he will not humiliate the archbishop, because he has authority."[284] Donoso Cortés proved to be correct in reading the mind of the pope and it was well for Louis Veuillot that he realized his victory could not be complete in the interests of the church.

In one complaint Veuillot recognized that the archbishop was correct, although he accused him generally of inexactitudes in the *avertissement*. The *Dictionnaire* of Bouillet had initially received the imprimatur of Sibour, but after a time had been placed on the *Index*. Veuillot had attacked this work with vigor, after he had spoken only with the secretary of the archbishop, and not with Sibour himself. He admitted he had erred in this respect. However, he saw reason to criticize the way that the book was revised to make it acceptable to the censors. The work was revised by the Abbé Delacouture, whom he described as "very Gallican,"[285] and in the process of getting the work removed from the *Index*, 1500 francs were given to the examiner.[286] It may have been inappropriate for him to question the propriety of a fee for work the examiner may have performed, but Veuillot was appropriately interested in the literary aspects of his dispute with the archbishop.

Throughout the quarrel the nuncio remained on the side of Veuillot. Support by Msgr. Fornari was very important in further disposing the pope and Cardinal Antonelli to the cause of *L'Univers*, particularly after Eugène Veuillot left Rome, arriving back in Paris in late September.[287] Louis was able to write of the nuncio's support, after returning from one of several interviews with him, in these terms: "I have just seen the nuncio, who always shows much interest in us, and who takes our affair to heart even more than we ourselves. Considering the blow which has struck us as especially directed against Roman doctrines, he desires that some of the bishops known for their clear and energetic support of the Holy See make known that they are thinking about the future consequences the acts of the Archbishop of Paris will have, if the journal succumbs."[288] Many French bishops early made clear their backing of Louis Veuillot, including the Bishops of Beauvais, Moulins, Langres, Lyon, Poitiers, Rouen, Amiens, and Rennes. Dupanloup, at this time Archbishop of Orleans and owner of *L'Ami de la Religion*, not surprisingly did not.[289] Old Msgr. Clausel de Montals, Bishop of Chartres, despite his other differences with Sibour, backed him in this matter.[290] After all, as Veuillot expressed it, "*L'Univers* will remain what it is: a machine of war against Gallicanism."[291] The disapproval of Montalembert during the affair saddened Veuillot. Throughout his life he always seemed to care particularly what Montalembert thought, and was so often disappointed. "Montalembert is the only friend of yesterday who has abandoned us."[291]

But of all the important figures who took one stand or another, or who played any significant role, Msgr. Parisis, Bishop of Langres, was the most conspicuous, coming boldly to the side of Veuillot and giving him support which Veuillot had not fully expected. Early in the affair he went to the heart of the trouble, and wrote directly to Sibour: "Yes, it is true, he whips editors severely, cruelly. Apostles of falsehood and calumny, he delivers their ignorance to ridicule, their audacity to indignation, their baseness to public shame, but who would dare to say they did not deserve it, those who for so long have availed themselves of these same weapons against all that is most holy and inviolable?" While admitting the problem posed to episcopal authority, the Bishop of Langres pointed out that "*L'Univers* does not confine itself to proclaiming Christian truth; it combats error."[292] Mid-nineteenth century Europe was subjected to many new doctrines which the church regarded as fallacious, and here was a bishop praising a layman for taking the initiative in denouncing them. Veuillot corresponded with Parisis extensively during September, and the role of Parisis in effecting arrangements favorable to Veuillot was a crucial one.

The efforts of some of Veuillot's other supporters were not always helpful. For example, Taconet made *démarches* with the Archbishop of Rouen which must have been undiplomatic. At any rate, Veuillot described them as "untimely and indiscreet" to Parisis.[293] The Archbishop of Rouen then wrote to Veuillot: "For ten years you have defended the Catholic principle in your writings. It would be fine and edifying for you now to demonstrate in your deeds the proper Christian application." He suggested he drop his appeal to Rome and go to his *premier pasteur*, sparing the pope the painful problem which he had laid before him.[294] Veuillot did not feel called upon by conscience to show himself self-effacing at this point, and he explained to Parisis that he did not think he could "regret" having made the appeal, which was one of the points desired by Sibour.[295]

Msgr. of Rouen was not alone in trying to get Veuillot to make a gesture of submission to the Archbishop of Paris. The venerable Archbishop of Reims, Msgr. Gousset, accompanied by the Bishop of Amiens, came to Paris on behalf of Louis Veuillot. They visited Sibour and did what they could to soothe his feelings. However, they did not succeed in their effort to persuade Veuillot to write a letter to his bishop along lines similar to those advised by the Archbishop of Rouen.[296] Perhaps the source of Veuillot's obstinacy was the fact that he heard indications of the most definite support from Rome. After the affair came to a head he wrote Parisis in October: "The news that we have received from Rome has not ceased to be excellent for us. I have read a letter of the secretary of state that the *mandement* was censurable in substance and in form."[297]

Even in September Veuillot must already have felt that his support in Rome was sure. At the end of September two "plenipotentiaries" of Msgr. Sibour, the Abbé Sibour, cousin of the archbishop, who recently to the distress of Veuillot had been appointed curé of the Church of Saint Thomas Aquinas, Veuillot's own parish, and the Abbé Bautain, came to negotiate with Veuillot. They asked him to acknowledge the wisdom of Sibour's *avertissement*, but this he would not do. The Abbé Sibour was conciliatory, but the Abbé Bautain was not particularly so.[298] Nevertheless, the meeting helped bring about a temporary peace. On 3 October Louis Veuillot, Du Lac, Eugène Veuillot, Roux-Lavergne, Gondon, Coquille, Taconet, and Barrier signed a letter to the archbishop, which was published on 5 October in *L'Univers*. They announced, "Our intention has always been to avoid raising questions which would appear inopportune." They also gave indications they would "moderate our language." In effect they said they were giving up their appeal. The archbishop for his part answered in a letter that was printed on the same page: "The homage which you render to episcopal authority fills my soul with consolation, because of the honor rendered to religion and to the church. But this homage is also the accomplishment of a duty for you." He stated that while the pope was indeed head of the church, he, Sibour, was the head of the Diocese of Paris. The letter also expressed the archbishop's wish that Veuillot and two collaborators come to see him.[299] The issue was far from settled, but the published exchange enabled the archbishop to uphold his authority publicly.

Veuillot, Eugène, and Du Lac immediately went to see the archbishop. The results were not happy; in fact, Veuillot described them as "sad." In a very involved way the archbishop upheld his original arguments about the lay press. He insinuated that the journal should support the French government, and that it should leave ecclesiastical matters to the hierarchy. Veuillot observed that the archbishop spoke like a man with a fever. How he [Veuillot] wished to kiss the feet of Pius IX! In any case, he said his own conscience was clear.[300] To the general public, however, Veuillot's letter had given the appearance that he was no longer defying his archbishop. Many people congratulated him, including Donoso Cortés, the Archbishop of Rouen, and Msgr. Guibert, Bishop of Viviers, later Archbishop of Paris, on making his peace with Sibour.[301] No longer could he be accused of defiance. Meanwhile, support for Louis Veuillot continued to grow. Sibour had been told by people like Msgr. Dreux-Brézé, Bishop of Moulins, "at least let us not destroy our defenders and our friends."[302] Veuillot received many kinds of manifestations of this support, ranging from anonymous letters, to personal resubscriptions to *L'Univers* by prelates, such as the Bishop of Nevers.[303] Despite the show of episcopal authority made by the archbishop Veuillot must have felt very reassured.

By the middle of October Veuillot was able to feel that he had won the round, despite the submission he appeared publicly to have made to Msgr. Sibour, when he was informed of the views Antonelli had expressed to the nuncio.[304] Other sources also clearly indicated that the pope had given his support to Veuillot.[305] He felt sufficiently sure of himself to write to Sibour, practically telling his own archbhisop of the pope's support for his editorial policy. He allowed that it had been "practically inevitable" that a work, such as *L'Univers*, would have its faults and thus get into trouble, but he pointed out the number of prelates coming in at least as mediators in the dispute. He made it clear that he wanted to give ostensible satisfaction to Sibour's ecclesiastical authority, but he did not hesitate to make it clear he had papal backing:

> Our sentiments, known in Rome, have not been blamed. To this day we have received nothing but words of encouragement, and we have had no question in this recent affair as to what conclusion to draw. For this purpose Msgr. the Cardinal Fornari has transmitted to us from the Sovereign Pope the most precious testimony of satisfaction. Each editor of the journal has received a gold medal, and even today I have been sent a letter of Cardinal Antonelli, dated 17 October, which expressly renews the benevolent things my brother had the fortune of hearing from the very mouth of Pius IX some days before the *avertissement* of Msgr. de Paris was published.[306]

Veuillot rubbed in the full import of papal support in a way that told Sibour he, not the archbishop, was in the right. He never did promise the archbishop that *L'Univers* would avoid discussion of the miracle at Rimini, or give up its defense of the Inquisition; later he explained to the nuncio that *L'Univers* found it impossible to make such a promise.[307] Moreover, Veuillot had the additional satisfaction of seeing Bouillet's *Dictionnaire* go back on the *Index*. On the whole, despite the submissive letter published on 5 October, Veuillot won the round. The archbishop had to derive what solace he could from having published his letter of assertion of authority in *L'Univers* and wait for a better occasion to try to break the lay editor who dared to intervene in affairs that many thought were more properly those of the hierarchy.

The next clash was not very long in coming. By the next spring the venerable Bishop of Chartres, Msgr. Clausel de Montals, pressed Veuillot for the use of *L'Univers* in publishing a *mandement* that was politically conservative and contrary to the line sponsored by Sibour in Paris. Again Veuillot was in an awkward situation, not primarily of his own making. Clausel de Montals had warmed to *L'Univers* during the struggle over the Falloux Law, despite his expressed Gallicanism. When Veuillot and *L'Univers* took the stand of enduring the law for such merits as it had, in order to be in line with the papal position, the venerable (he was eighty-two years old) prelate had turned from them. After Veuillot ignored a brochure of the Bishop of Chartres aimed at Dom Guéranger, their relations had certainly not improved. However, early in 1851 both had their guns trained on the "reds," with Clausel de Montals particularly concerned over Michelet's attacks on the Jesuits and glorification of the Revolution.[309] The Archbishop of Paris had shown a leftist direction in his pastoral letters, and Clausel de Montals was determined to speak in another tone Had the two prelates simply published their *mandements* in their own dioceses, the problem would not have been great. However, the influence of the Archbishop of Paris, especially as Sibour wielded it, was broad, and what he had to say was carried in the press all over France, the secular press lately joining in aiding his publicity. The only Catholic journal that had a broad circulation was *L'Univers*. On the ground that he needed publication in it in order that his voice, and that of other bishops, not be stifled, Clausel de Montals appealed to Louis Veuillot.

Veuillot gave a great deal of thought to the ticklish matter. Well he might have, because he had just received the following letter from Sibour:

> Demogogy, checked in civil society, has invaded the bosom of the church by means of a part of the press called Catholic. Demagogy in the church is presbyterianism and laicism, seeking to substitute themselves for the episcopacy in the instruction and government of souls.
>
> Under the mask of greater devotion to the Holy See, it attacks first the authority of the episcopacy, while awaiting the hour to attack the Holy See itself.

Sibour said he wanted to sweep away this mask, and in particular wanted public condemnation of *L'Univers* for misuse of the terms "Gallican" and "ultramontane."[310] Under other conditions, it might not have seemed rash to allow another bishop, whose views on Gallicanism were similar to Sibour's, to express himself in the columns of *L'Univers*. However, with Sibour already so angry at *L'Univers*, and with Clausel de Montals challenging Sibour in all of France in this fashion, Veuillot was running a real risk. He realized this risk, and on hearing Clausel de Montals' request he promptly turned to the Archbishop of Reims, Cardinal Gousset, for counsel. It does indeed seem remarkable that this son of a peasant, without any wealth or social standing, the editor of a journal that had scarcely 10,000 paid subscribers, was conferring with the highest level of the prelates, including the nuncio, and engaging in their differences in the sharpest of terms. Herein, of course, lies the significance of the career of Louis Veuillot. In March of 1851 he was about as deeply involved in church policy as it was possible to be.

Veuillot fully explained his problem to Cardinal Gousset, and Gousset apparently gave him every encouragement to let the aged Clausel de Montals have the use of his forum. The whole discussion must have been communicated to Cardinal Fornari, since an unpublished memorandum to him exists in the Veuillot papers, but there is no positive evidence that the nuncio encouraged him. However, it is unlikely that Veuillot would have proceeded without the nuncio's tacit approval. Gousset liked what Clausel de Montals said in his *mandement* that Veuillot had been asked to publish. He said the church would gain by its publication, since the aged prelate was combatting what he called the errors of Sibour. Sibour had called the Bishop of Chartres an erratic old man, and Veuillot further emphasized Sibour's threat of excommunication. Veuillot's memorandum for Cardinal Fornari contains the lines: "It's my calling to face peril, as long as the church may gain something."[311]

Thus fortified, Veuillot went ahead and published Clausel de Montals' letter to his diocesans of 12 March 1851. Replete with quotations from Bossuet, this letter attacked a *mandement* of Sibour's dated 15 January 1851, which clearly was radical in tone.[312] Sibour replied immediately in a letter published in *L'Univers* the next day, March 19, saying that he would refer this action by Clausel de Montals to the next provincial council of bishops.[313] The struggle had flared again. Apparently this threat did not trouble Msgr. Clausel de Montals, who still mildly told Veuillot that he wanted to avoid quarrels.[314] He further told him not to worry about excommunication. As for Sibour, Msgr. of Chartres said: "This poor archbishop is a mystery. He has a good heart, he is full of faith, and he is full of intelligence, and at the same time he is deluded about a very essential point."[315] The threat however was serious, and Msgr. Rendu of Annecy advised Veuillot to talk with the nuncio before taking any action.[316]

At the general time that Sibour reacted against Veuillot for publishing Clausel de Montals' *mandement*, Cardinal Fornari, recently elevated to that rank, was relieved as papal nuncio by Msgr. Garibaldi. This new situation had both an advantage and a disadvantage. Cardinal Fornari returned to Rome, where he was able to speak a strong word for Veuillot, but Veuillot's position in Paris was weakened by the loss of a strong friend. In early April Veuillot wrote Fornari: "In Paris, as ever, something unfortunate is being prepared for *L'Univers*. People are speaking of an interdiction in the diocese. What is certain is that we will not be left in peace.[317] Veuillot communicated regularly with the Abbé Bernier, and the latter was in touch with Cardinal Fornari. The Bishop of Chartres came to Paris and saw Veuillot, but the result was hardly reassuring. "It is too bad that this great courage [of the Bishop of Chartres] was not given to a firmer intellect and one more enlightened in true doctrines," wrote Veuillot to Bernier.[318] Meanwhile, many bishops made clear their support for Veuillot in this matter, but the new nuncio did not fill the place of Fornari. Msgr. Garibaldi, to the distress of Veuillot, moved among the salon society of Paris, from which he gained the impression that the main thing that Frenchmen desired was peace.[319] However, papal support was not only real, it was also apparent again shortly. By late April Msgr. Gignoux, Bishop of Beauvais, wrote to Veuillot about the backing he had from Pius IX,[320] and Bernier made clear to him how things stood in Rome.[321] The Archbishop of Paris, despite the high authority of his episcopal see, was simply out of harmony with papal attitudes and the growing ultramontanism in France. Veuillot's publication of Clausel de Montals' criticisms within his own diocese must have been infuriating, but the offense was not enough for him to be able to strike a major blow at the lay Catholic journal, since the attitude of many of the other prelates was not unfavorable to Clausel de Montals. For the time being Sibour simply had to call off the attack. Without any statement of principles being resolved, an apparent reconciliation was arranged between the two bishops by an exchange of letters.[322]

Yet another round of trouble between Veuillot and Sibour began a few months later in the fall of 1851. This new situation was similar to that of the previous year, and the archbishop again reprimanded Veuillot for his lack of charity towards some of the secular journalists. In 1850 Veuillot had been chastised largely for his attacks on Chambolle and *L'Ordre*, while in 1851 Sibour reacted against Veuillot largely because of what he had to say about Émile de Girardin and *La Presse*. Girardin was a radical figure, who had once been arrested by order of Cavaignac, in 1848, for disorders he was thought to be fomenting. Unlimited liberty was his theme, and he made the church a particular target of his tirades in *La Presse*. To him the church appeared to be the enemy of humanity.

There was nothing gentle about Girardin's reputation. He had killed Armand Carrel, director of *Le National,* in a duel growing out of their editorial battles. In the late summer and early fall of 1851 Veuillot turned his attention more and more on Girardin. His attacks were rich.[323] He accused him not only of misrepresenting general Catholic positions, but of misusing the words of prelates and of Montalembert to support his ideas on unlimited liberty.[324] On the personal side also Veuillot went very far: "M. de Girardin has no talent at all. As a thinker he is nothing. Never has an idea entered, nor ever will one enter, the head of the man who has boasted of having an idea each day. He does not have an idea because he has a fevered mind. Inspirations from a theorizer can not pass for ideas." On and on Veuillot went about the man in a most personal way.[325] Not surprisingly he was reprimanded, but the reprimand grew out of past relations as much as from the polemics that were appearing and were part of the general clash in views that existed between the archbishop and the lay Catholic editor.

On the eve of Veuillot's renewed troubles with Msgr. Sibour, none other than Msgr. Clausel de Montals turned against him, with somewhat different, though overlapping criticisms. The combination of attacks by the Bishop of Chartres and his own archbishop put Veuillot again very much on the defensive. Msgr. of Chartres at least wrote his criticisms in a very private way: "I write to you alone and for you alone. I saw a word in your journal four or five days ago that horrified me, and which is truly revolting " The idea in question was that the royal family had been beheaded as a result of Gallicanism. This judgment was deemed an "atrocious insult" directed at the clergy. The royalist Gallican bishop continued his blast at Veuillot's "extravagances," labeling them "true madness." He accused Veuillot of confounding Gallicanism with Arianism, protestantism, and other error. He insisted on the religious orthodoxy of the Gallicans before the Revolution. "You inject disorder and trouble into the church by the divisions which result from these despotic opinions which you seek to impose on young clergymen." Theology, he maintained, was an exact science requiring long study. "You have some general truths which you defend with force, but you ignore an infinity of truths."[326] Clausel de Montals was a political reactionary, and Sibour a liberal, but their attacks coincided in some key respects, and the dressing down Veuillot received from the former must have unsteadied him for the renewed pressure from Sibour.

On Monday, 29 September 1851, Msgr. Sibour summoned Veuillot to meet him at the seminary at Saint-Sulpice, where the archbishop delivered to him a lecture on their differences. Sibour, although he had a gentle manner, was a difficult man with whom to agree, however. For example, during the struggle with the university while he was Bishop of Digne he had resented members of the lower clergy publicly displaying their support of him. In his view public display of support was improper, because, naturally, the lower clergy would be assumed to be in support of him. To allow them to manifest this support implied that the lower clergy had the right to approve, or perhaps to disapprove. This behavior he labeled "presbyterianism."[327] Veuillot on the other hand simply could not desist from expressing himself. The "liberal" archbishop could not stand such assertions of individual attitudes, particularly from presumptuous laymen.

Of course, the archbishop did most of the talking. He told Veuillot about the gentleness and moderation of Saint Augustine, which was no doubt an appropriate subject. Before long, however, he turned to specifics, and notably Émile de Girardin, the dueller and avowed anti-clerical advocate of unlimited liberty. While Veuillot certainly had not been moderate toward Girardin, he had shown some care recently in his troubles with Sibour. The redoubtable Abbé Combalot had turned on his archbishop again, and Sibour, supported by Dupanloup, had suspended his powers. No doubt Combalot was an embarrassment to Veuillot in a tactical way. Veuillot wrote to Combalot in early September telling him that he should make amends to the two prelates.[328] But while he might advise the stormy priest to make excuses to his bishop, he himself found difficulty in accepting the prelate's line. Sibour pointed out the great influence he thought Girardin had with certain elements. Apparently Sibour must have hoped to convert Girardin. At any rate, he felt it was inexpedient as well as un-Christian to attack him in the manner that Veuillot was employing. Sibour foresaw the rising of popular elements, which, as a result of this sort of attack, would themselves turn on the church in due course. All this must be avoided.

The pressure of the archbishop was such that Veuillot promised him he would end the polemics against Girardin but he said that he had already decided on this course anyway. The archbishop wanted even more: he wanted Veuillot to promise that he would publicly express his regrets to Girardin about the past. Veuillot refused, even though the archbishop tried to give him the precise words that he should use. Sibour told Veuillot that he had the faults of Lamennais (he said nothing of the latter's virtues), in a comparison that was applicable from the point of view both of journalism and of personal stubbornness. He reminded Veuillot that the church was often harder on its children than on its enemies. It is certain that Sibour was in contact with Girardin and that part of the secular press that was at this time exalting the prelate's side in his quarrel with Veuillot. He was, of course, implying excommunication and the threat of forbidding the reading of *L'Univers*. Of all the uncomfortable interviews Veuillot ever had, this one with Msgr. Sibour must have been one of the most trying.[329]

Having conceded nothing more than the promise to give up his attacks on the anti-church editor, Veuillot headed for the offices of *L'Univers* late in the evening. *L'Univers* was then a morning paper, and Veuillot, as was his custom, picked up a copy of an evening paper, *L'Avènement,* a radical journal inspired by Girardin and *La Presse*. In it he saw a very accurate account of the interview he had just had with Msgr. Sibour! Obviously the account had been leaked into the hands of the Girardin circle by permission of the archbishop. Veuillot was horrified. His own spiritual governor revealing his words to those with whom he fancied himself at war! Within a short time he wrote to Sibour:

> When I had the honor of talking with you at the seminary Monday, I thought then of ending all polemics with *La Presse*. I was strongly inclined in this matter after having listened to you, by the desire of being agreeable to Your Grandeur. I counted without my adversary. I did not see that he would dare to accuse me of material dishonesty. I can stand many injuries, but I cannot permit any doubt about my honesty. I therefore must reply. This I do containing my indignation as much as possible.
>
> Monday evening, some hours after the interview with which you honored me, I had the surprise and chagrin of reading a sort of resume in *L'avenement*, a journal inspired by M. de Girardin. There was announced in it a new *avertissement* against *L'Univers*, and the motives are in part those Your Grandeur gave me to understand. It was not I, Monseigneur, who revealed these details. I have no relation with the people who put out *L'Avènement* and other journals of that sort.[330]

Few Catholic lay leaders would conceive of writing to their bishop in such a tone, but Veuillot was already in poor standing with the bishop and he believed he had much support from other prelates. Many bishops, including those who had reservations about the lay Catholic press, were glad to see a man with such a broad popular following making war on defamers of the church, even though in the process he was undermining episcopal authority. In view of recent demonstrations of papal satisfaction with the work of *L'Univers*, Veuillot's position was indeed a special one. But Sibour's Gallicanism was newly assumed and actually not well known, and he probably did not suffer much embarrassment for this reason. His leadership in promoting regional councils of bishops had probably brought him sympathy from some of the hierarchy, despite his evident desire to dominate among the prelates of France. Ironically Sibour's strong espousal of the introduction of the Roman liturgy had probably detracted from his support as much as anything. Probably he did not see any reason why he would not be able to deal with the rising tide of ultramontane lay influence as personified by Veuillot. In fact, however, although he had forced Veuillot into deep thought about the utlility of the lay Catholic press, the lay editor came out of this meditation "like a man who was enlightened from all sides and who sets out again with a firm step, convinced as to the first route he had taken."[331] Veuillot's battle with the archbishop might have gone further at this point, but Sibour was not yet ready to carry on with it. Meanwhile the coup d'état of 1851 was shaping up, distracting Veuillot as well as Sibour.

While Louis Veuillot was in trouble with members of the episcopacy, Sibour, Clausel de Montals, and Dupanloup, his difficulties with Montalembert were also continuing. These difficulties were partly ecclesiastical and partly political. They were the same difficulties generally tending to divide the remains of the Catholic party. The split between Montalembert and Veuillot had remained very sharp from the time of the enactment of the Falloux Law. "Some very important people, who are angry at us for not having changed our course as they have," were trying to undermine the position of *L'Univers* in Rome in May 1850, according to Veuillot,[332] and it is obvious that by this insinuation Veuillot was referring to Montalembert. Veuillot feared that *L'Univers* was being pictured as stirring up the people against the bishops and setting itself in revolt against the pope over the education law. Montalembert and Msgr. Parisis were corresponding about the dangers of the lay press, and causing Veuillot to worry.[333] In the fall of 1850 when Montalembert visited Rome the observation from one of Veuillot's correspondents was that "he has not come here to aid you."[334] This observation was probably quite astute, because at the time Veuillot was staggering from the first *avertissement* Sibour issued against him.

By early 1851 there was seeming reconciliation, but it was not solid. In mid-February Veuillot wrote to Vicomte Gustave de La Tour of his "great pleasure" in dining with Montalembert.[335] At the same time Montalembert wrote to the same Gustave de La Tour that he had twice seen Veuillot again at the home of a common friend.[336] A copy of the letter from Montalembert to La Tour, along with copies of other such letters, is to be found among the Veuillot papers. One cannot be sure when these letters reached Louis Veuillot or why La Tour told Veuillot what Montalembert said of him. Presumably, however, La Tour must have sent these letters to Veuillot at the time to disabuse him as to any illusions he might have been under about a reconciliation or the reliability of Montalembert. La Tour had said to Montalembert that *L'Univers* was the only way to reach Catholics, to which remark Montalembert retorted: "I cannot suppose that God has delivered at this point the government of souls within the bosom of the church to journalists." La Tour apparently could not resist informing Veuillot of these sentiments, so that Veuillot would not rely on Montalembert's sincerity. Eugène Veuillot concludes one should not assume that Montalembert was insincere, but only that he was mercurial. While Montalembert had great mastery of his tongue as an orator, he suffered from "epistolary intemperance," and alone in his room with a pen could not be relied on not to write things he would never have said on the tribune.[337] In any case it is true that Montalembert was not prepared for a genuine reconciliation with Veuillot. Montalembert's letter of February 19 says: "We talked for a long time, and very amicably about the present situation, without making any allusion to the past. But, alas, there is no way of counting on him – his current attitude and that of his journal are excellent, but how to explain this sudden change and this contrast with all that he said six months ago? And will he not recommence in six months to tell us that outside of the Bourbons and anarchy there is nothing?"[338] Indeed, although both men were Catholics beyond all else, French politics became their principal bone of contention in the period 1851-1852.

The Second Republic had been in a shaky position from the start, and by 1851 its days seemed numbered. Had the royalists been united, a restoration could have been effected, but the legitimists and the Orleanists by nature could not be united, at least so long as the Comte de Chambord's strict principles prevailed.[339] Both Veuillot and Montalembert saw merit in the régime of Louis Napoleon, but while Montalembert looked to the man, Veuillot contented himself with the institution of the presidency as it was in Napoleon's hands. With regard to monarchy, Montalembert had no time for the legitimists, while Veuillot, albeit seeing their follies, favored their general principles. Thus while both Montalembert and Veuillot remained Catholic-before-all, they managed to keep sharp differences of opinion as to the best political solution in 1851.

Veuillot wrote a series of editorials from the fall of 1850 to the spring of 1851, discussing current politics from the Catholic point of view.[340] Thiers warned early in 1851 that the republicans and the royalists would have to stand together, or the empire of Napoleon would be established. Veuillot also could appreciate the situation that was developing. In September 1850 he made clear his preference for the principles of the Comte de Chambord without expressly favoring the legitimist party:

> M. le Comte de Chambord represents the monarchical principle; he alone represents it. There is his strength; it is immense. If he accepted the sophism of sovereignty of the people, if he did not deny it absolutely, all distinction would be in vain; if he abdicates his principle, he is, like the Princes of Orleans and M. Bonaparte, no more than a courtesan of the revolution, a candidate for the presidency, distinguished from the others only by having less chance and appearing less sincere."[341]

If God has not condemned the Bourbons, Veuillot maintained, nothing can ruin the cause of the Comte de Chambord. However, he thought the legitimist party was a most inexpedient group. He concluded that the time was simply not right for the restoration of the governmental principle and form of monarchy, even though it ultimately would be most suitable for the Catholic church. Nevertheless, over the next few months many people got the impression that *L'Univers* and Veuillot were actively legitimist. Montalembert in 1851 spoke of Veuillot's *fugue legitimiste* of the summer of 1850,[342] and Veuillot himself had to comment on the inevitable disappointment of provincial legitimist journals which professed to have believed in his backing, though he would not admit that he had deserted their cause in favor of the "rising sun" of Napoleon.[343] In fact, during 1850-1851 Veuillot tried to make it quite clear what he thought of the legitimist party, as opposed to Chambord and his principles, and he also expressed his dark view of the Orleanists,[344] whose leaders were pressing for fusion with the elder branch. He saw simply no practicality in the monarchist movement at this time. Like his old friend Romieu he saw a red spectre looming for 1852.[345] It became ever clearer to him that Louis Napoleon offered the one immediate answer to this threat.

In August of 1850 Louis Napoleon went on an extensive trip through France on which he was often met with cries of *Vive L'Empereur*! Veuillot followed reports of this triumphal tour with much interest,[346] but was far from being on the bandwagon. However, as the term of the president wore on he supported the cause of constitutional revision,[347] which would give Napoleon a chance to be the preserver of order, at least for the near future. Montalembert wrote Gustave de La Tour that he thought Veuillot was inconsistent in his line, and was causing divisions among Catholics by his editorials during the summer of 1851,[348] but he nevertheless found himself in a position shortly thereafter where he too had to support the cause of the president. Montalembert who had difficulty in keeping personalities out of his thinking, felt it was Veuillot who, by "unworthy polemic against me," had started the split in the Catholic party. He resented first Veuillot's sympathy for the legitimists, and then his seizing the initiative in support of Napoleon. "It is *L'Univers* which is the real and principal cause of trouble." He felt isolated, without the legitimists and without *L'Univers*. He criticized the vehemence of *L'Univers'* attack on the candidacy of the Prince of Joinville, and he resented the things Veuillot had to say about the bourgeoisie. Ever a *parlementaire*, he declared that if France were to be saved it would be because of noble spirits among the bourgeoisie.[349]

The coup d'état should have surprised no one. The president's term was to expire in mid-1852, and in the summer of 1851 plans were laid for a Napoleonic coup. This bold action was originally scheduled for September 1851, if not earlier,[350] and dramatically took place on the anniversary of coronation of Napoleon I and of Austerlitz. Montalembert clearly saw it coming, and wrote La Tour: "It is a matter of preventing the president from doing anything imprudent, and when he becomes the conqueror from abusing his victory." While still criticizing the line of *L'Univers*, he thought he was assured of Veuillot's support.[351] Montalembert, as head of the Catholic party, expected some important position to be offered him at this point, and he was of course right in thinking that Veuillot would back him. Louis Veuillot, who had sized up the general situation at least as well as Montalembert, was surprised nevertheless by the timing of events as they transpired. When the coup took place he was out of Paris on a trip in the provinces. However, the course he followed after the coup was steadier than that of Montalembert, and subsequently for the better part of a decade, he accommodated himself and *L'Univers* to the authority of Louis Napoleon Bonaparte. Taking into account the nature of the president-to-become-emperor, Louis Veuillot felt for some years that he had something constant with regard to which he might map the course of the Catholics-before-all.

CHAPTER V

ACCOMMODATION TO NAPOLEON

Through most of the authoritarian period of Napoleon as president for ten years and as Emperor of the French, Louis Veuillot was able to maintain satisfactory relations with the government and to assert the interests of the Catholics-before-all. While the influence of Veuillot and *L'Univers* was at its greatest point in the period of the Ecumenical Council of 1869-1870, at least in Catholic circles, certainly it was on a relatively high level until the sacrifice of Catholic support in 1858 by Napoleon. The assertion of power by Napoleon in 1851 therefore was one of the significant turns of events in Veuillot's career.

The fact that Veuillot was not in Paris when the governmental notices went up on 2 December 1851 permitted several circumstances illustrative of the situation of *L'Univers* to be particularly clear. The roles of Montalembert and Eugène Veuillot in the guidance of *L'Univers* were pointed up by the events of the first week after the coup, but the decisive force that Louis himself exerted became abundantly obvious. When Eugène, still active in the national guard at that time, was alerted on 2 December to what was taking place, he showed that there were certain rules of behavior already prescribed for him by his brother. He did not want to take any stand until so directed. At first it did not appear in Paris as though there was going to be any resistance to the coup, and he observed first hand, like a reporter-on-the spot, events of the day. The resisters in the National Assembly went from the Palais Bourbon to the *mairie* of the old tenth arrondissement to protest. Berryer gave a harangue to a "crowd" of scarcely 250 people in the street, an assemblage that the eyewitness Eugène described as more curious than anything else. Troops sent by the new dictatorship arrived and dispersed the meeting of the deputies, with due respect to Berryer and the rest according to Eugène, and escorted them to the barracks on the Quai d'Orsay.[1] Thus the coup started in a way that seemed certain to succeed. Eugène did not have to get out a number of *L'Univers* until the morning of 3 December, and, besides trying to get a good view of events himself, he wanted to ascertain Montalembert's views while waiting for the return of Louis. Eugène met Montalembert on the street at the very time the deputies were being taken off, and he later recounted that, as best he could remember, Montalembert was "more amused than indignant" while witnessing the scene.[2] In the judgment of Eugène, Montalembert had had considerable faith in Louis Napoleon as a rallying point for Catholics, at least for the time, but, in contrast with Eugène's brother Louis, Montalembert had had more faith in the man than in the presidency. Louis, he says, was more inclined to see a safeguard for public order in a strengthened presidency.[3] In view of Louis' much greater interest in the principles of legitimacy, this state of the two men's opinions, if Eugène was correct, seems a bit strange.

The *Moniteur* the next day indicated that Montalembert, recognized by all as political leader of the Catholics, would be appointed to a consultative commission by the newly decreed "president-for-ten-years" or dictator. In order to see what the party leader would do, with Louis still not back, Eugène hastened to meet Montalembert. Montalembert showed mixed feelings. Fundamentally he was prepared to accept the coup as a solution to the threats against the public order, and against Catholics, appearing from the left. But Montalembert already did not care for some of the measures that Napoleon had taken, and he indicated to Eugène that, finding himself nominated for this commission without being first sounded, he was not sure whether to accept or not.[4] Obviously this question was important to the Catholic party, and for him to obtain the advice of Louis Veuillot among others was a matter of importance.

Louis returned as soon as he could, consulted with Montalembert, and also publicly committed *L'Univers* to the support of the prince-president. The editorial dated 4 December, and appearing 5 December, came at a critical time. On 2 December events had seemed completely to favor the painless takeover of Napoleon, but on the third and fourth news of increasing resistance in Paris spread to the provinces, and in twenty or so departments the issue of events seemed questionable. For several days the grip of the president in his new authoritarian role was seriously challenged. The course followed by any important group was vital to the determination of events, and the Catholics-before-all were an important group. Against these circumstances Louis Veuillot penned some strong lines against socialist revolutions. The thrust was pragmatic, certainly not primarily Bonapartist or for the choosing of Louis Napoleon for his own sake, but for the support of a stable régime that would provide the kind of order he believed the Catholic church needed. In central France in a department he thought was "suffering from the gangrene of socialism," he said the coup was welcomed as "a necessity long anticipated." In this matter "there is nothing to choose, no recriminations to be made, nothing to be debated. The government must be supported. Its cause is that of the social order." While he wrote, the resistance to the government grew, and by the fourth of December for several days there seemed some question as to whether Napoleon were going to be able to maintain himself. The readers of *L'Univers* were told: "The President of the Republic is your general; do not separate yourselves from him; do not desert him. If you do not triumph with him, you will be conquered with him, and irreparably conquered." Veuillot ended this editorial invoking the Deity to save France.[5]

Veuillot, during the days of the coup, does not seem to have brought out his uniform as in June of 1848, although he still was in the Fourth Company of the Seventeenth Battalion of the National Guard under a Captain Rousseau, as he pointed out later with some pride to Mme Édouard Thayer (sister-in-law of the postal chief of Napoleon).[6] However, his militant support in rallying Catholic sentiment behind the prince-president was no small factor in events as they developed. In addition to his editorials his counsels to Montalembert were significant. Montalembert had previously prepared himself to support Napoleon when the coup occurred, but once Napoleon had suspended the constitution and had taken measures against the parliamentary opposition, Montalembert seemed to have second thoughts. As chief of the Catholic party he received plenty of advice, but one of the main people advising him was Veuillot, who advised active support. The principal matter on Montalembert's mind was the offer by Napoleon of a post on the consultative commission which he had immediately set up, and to which he had appointed various key men but without first discussing their appointments with them. Montalembert's temptation was to reject this position, without however taking a stand of opposition to Napoleon. The general advice he received was to accept the position and avoid showing any reluctance to follow the lead of Napoleon. Archbishop Parisis, Cardinal Gousset, the papal nuncio, Donoso Cortés, Amadée Thayer, Gustave de La Tour, and many others advocated this postion.[7] Of course men like Falloux and Berryer, royalists but parliamentarians, did not think he should accept the post. Montalembert apparently was very sensitive to the criticisms of this latter group, and his reluctance had been influenced by the personal consideration of not liking to undergo this particular kind of criticism. Falloux put the blame for Montalembert's taking the post on Veuillot, when he wrote his *Mémoires d'un royaliste*, an attack that Eugène hotly disputed.[8] There really seems to be no special reason why Eugène would have denied this assertion if it had been true, and his insistence that Louis gave no stronger advice than anyone else to Montalembert about the consultative commission seems to have the ring of truth. Throughout his life Eugène was practically an *alter ego* to his brother, but at no time were they any closer than in 1851. Moreover, relations between Falloux and Louis Veuillot were good in 1851, and the extraordinary circumstance was that Eugène Veuillot and Falloux lived in the same building on the rue du Bac. Therefore Eugène particularly resented Falloux's implication that Louis Veuillot alone was the special force pushing Montalembert into initial cooperation with Napoleon.[9] Eugène reacted by nicknaming him *Falloux Fallax,*[10] or liar.

Montalembert, thus, decided to act in accordance with the advice generally given by the key Catholics (despite the opposition of Sibour and Dupanloup), and he went to the prince-president to accept the appointment. At this interview Napoleon made the curiously frank observation, with regard to his future relationship with universal suffrage: "I want to be baptized, but I do not want to spend my life in water."[11] Now for a few weeks Montalembert was in close accord with Veuillot, giving his editorial policies what must have been the closest support he ever showed. He wrote an editorial himself, dated 12 December, pointing out the broad consultation he had had for his endorsement of the coup. He said that the act of 2 December had forestalled "all the revolutionaries, all the socialists, all the bandits of France and of Europe." All groups should resign themselves to this new leadership, which had guaranteed liberty of education, reestablished the pope by French arms, and given back to the church various attributes it had lost. "I do not see (outside of Napoleon) anything but the gaping abyss of triumphant socialism. My choice is made. I am for authority against revolt . . ., for *possible* liberty of good against *certain* liberty of evil . . . and in doing this I consider myself now, as always, to be acting on the side of Catholicism against the Revolution."[12]

Louis Veuillot's appeal of 4 December, and the reinforcement which Montalembert's article gave it, constituted only the beginning of the press campaign in *Univers*. The piece Veuillot wrote on 8 December not only asserted that the die had been cast, but acclaimed the support of "the most eminent defender of the Catholic cause [Montalembert]."[13] The lines he published dated 19 December, just before the plebiscite of 20 December, continued to have a desperate tone "The second of December is the most antirevolutionary date we have had in the last sixty years of our history. The spirit of sedition, in all its forms, experienced that day its most humiliating defeat . . . . Property has no longer pillage as its perspective, the family dishonor and destruction, religion martyrdom . . . . The bases of human society are no longer put in question . . . Public blasphemy has ceased . . . For our part, before

God and man, with hand upon heart, as Frenchmen and Catholics, we say: "Yes, a hundred times yes."[14]

The plebiscite proved to be a great victory for Napoleon, for he received seven and one-half million votes of endorsement. He had polled only slightly in excess of five and one-half million in the presidential election of 1848. However, it must be remembered that the 1848 election had been a free election with several respectable contenders, while this plebiscite, held after the opponents of the new régime were already in custody, was a yes-or-no vote, the names of the voters recorded with their votes. Nevertheless, it was a remarkable feat of getting out a large vote on relatively short notice. Veuillot continued his exultant tone in discussing the results, and spoke as though France had really been spared imminent anarchy and revolution.[15] The Catholics, the legitimists, and the liberals were the groups that, editorially speaking, were the subject of his concentration after the plebiscite. Louis Veuillot no doubt sincerely feared revolution as he remembered it from 1848, but whether the situation in the later part of 1851 warranted the extreme concern he expressed in December of 1851 is very questionable. In some ways he was a very practical man, but at this time he was so convinced by his own preconceptions that he no doubt read a good deal of this sharp contest between Napoleonic order and socialist revolution into what was actually a much less clearly defined situation. As to the Catholics, the legitimists, and the liberals, he was somewhat more analytical. When the new régime began clamping down on the opposition press, he had a field-day in discussing the downfall of liberalism. He took the opportunity of coming again to the defense of De Maistre and others who had formerly suffered at the hands of the *Journal des Débats*. He ridiculed those who were "part Christian, part heretic, part royalists, and part revolutionary." However, as a prophet he was a gloomy one, maintaining that Catholicism, which was the negation of liberalism, was not destined to be liberalism's conqueror. Socialism was destined to carry out that mission. "The world will be socialist or Christian; it will not be liberal."[16] Veuillot was warning the liberals they would not make the final round of the world championship, but would be eliminated in the semi-finals by the socialists with whom the Christians – he shifted the designation of the other finalists from "Catholics" – would battle for the ultimate victory.

As for the Catholics and the legitimists, concerning them he had plenty of overlapping complications with which to reckon. A good many of the bishops were royalists, but for the most part they rallied to the support of Louis Napoleon, who, after all, had recently done them a number of good deeds for which they were surely grateful. Msgr. Pie,

Bishop of Poitiers, who like Msgrs. Parisis and Salinis would continue a strong supporter of Louis Veuillot over a long period of time, indicated his own backing of the new order in a personal letter to Veuillot. He also spoke of the support of the aged Archbishop of Chartres, but in both cases he said they could not overlook the rights of Henry V. Force and right were to be distinguished.[17] On the same point a Father Dugas of Lyon wrote Veuillot that the position *L'Univers* had taken in support of Napoleon was wrong, or would be believed so by many in Lyon. "Droit de la force" may work for a time, but "force du droit" is the only way to preserve justice, authority, and the hierarchy of the church.[18]

In general, throughout his life, Veuillot received his greatest support from the parish priests many of whom looked to him for leadership, but was often in trouble with powerful bishops. The situation was somewhat the reverse in 1851. Some of the bishops, as for instance, Pie, made clear their reservations about the coup, but Veuillot had no confrontations with either Sibour or any of the others over Napoleon. After all, the bishops served under Napoleon in their official capacities. Father Dugas, however, was not the only parish priest who undertook to criticize Veuillot. The Abbé Demiau, Curé of La Callière (Vendée), wrote Veuillot that "*L'Univers* is without principle and injurious to religion." This blast from the heartland of both legitimacy and Catholicism was written by a priest who had been sent *L'Univers* in place of *L'Opinion publique*, a legitimist publication, which had been suppressed by Napoleon's régime. By arrangement of the two journals, *L'Univers* was to be substituted for a continuation of the suppressed journal's paid subscriptions. When Louis Veuillot answered this letter personally he told the disgruntled priest that although he had every right to refuse the substituted journal, it was remarkable that he could comment on material that he claimed he had never read. Veuillot told him to complain to the former editor of *Opinion publique* if he did not like *L'Univers*, and meanwhile Veuillot let him know, his manners and sense of justice were hardly those befitting a priest.[19] Veuillot could be blunt with the clergy and would not necessarily overlook anything in an effort to keep their favor. Actually *L'Univers* and Veuillot gained considerable popularity among the former subscribers of *Opinion publique*. This journal had been a royalist sheet with subscriptions of 4,000. Adding that number of readers to those already subscribing to *L'Univers*, not counting multiple-number subscriptions, brought the total number of subscribers to 13,000.[20] Considering the fact that many more people read the journal than subscribed to it, and that it was the basis of much of the rural Catholic propaganda and influenced many a sermon, the journal could be said to have attained considerable influence, though still only a fraction of the size that *La Presse* had reached in paid subscriptions.

The particular press deal, by which *L'Univers* was picked as a suitable substitute for a legitimist journal, illustrates that relations with the legitimists were not bad on the whole. In an article written 16 January 1852 for *L'Univers*, Veuillot not only defended the new constitution promulgated by Louis Napoleon, but, rather pointedly for the legitimists, declared: "It is Catholicism that has saved France, it is Catholicism which will regenerate it and save it through liberty of the church."[21] Various legitimist organs, notably the *Gazette de Lyon*, attacked *L'Univers* for its support of Napoleon, and Veuillot was obviously hurt and stung by their stand. He made an effort to parry these various charges, and also to try to keep the friendships he thought he had among the legitimists as he penned a piece entitled "Nouveaux conseils aux legitimistes."[22] In his personal correspondence he did the same thing. He made a gallant effort to convince Alexandre de Saint-Albin, editor of *L'Union de l'Ouest*, the legitimist journal of Angers, that he and Saint-Albin simply had different tactics for attaining the same end. However, he went so far as to say to Saint-Albin: "Even with the legitimate king, the legitimist party would do no better today than Louis Napoleon, perhaps it would not even do as well, and it would have no more chance of survival." Moreover, the very stability that Henry V would promise would have the double effect of lulling us to sleep and rousing our enemies, said Veuillot.[23]

The highest-ranking legitimist who corresponded with Veuillot at this turn of events was the Comte de Damas, counselor to the Comte de Chambord. In his fine hand Damas wrote to Veuillot on 14 December, telling him that he had long subscribed to *L'Univers*, and that he had particularly liked those articles which had born his signature. However, he took exception to Veuillot's recent claim that Louis Napoleon was chief of the party of order. According to Damas, Napoleon really based his position on the revolution, and only when he attacks revolution will he be chief of the party of order.[24] This great legitimist did not succeed in swaying Veuillot, though Veuillot publicly used the curious expression about their relationship: "Moi plébéien sans amertume, vous, patricien sans vaine excuse." Damas did not understand just what Veuillot meant by the phrases, and he let him know of his wonderment.[25] Veuillot certainly was not bitter about his own humble origins, and he saw nothing hollow about Damas' position. The lack of complete understanding between these two men illustrates the differences in viewpoint between the Catholics-before-all and the legitimists. They were natural political allies, but they were not of the same mind, especially as to the coup.

On more than one occasion during his career, as has been noted, Louis Veuillot considered, at least momentarily, going into politics. The era of the coup was not one of these occasions. It would have been very interesting if Montalembert had been joined by Veuillot in the Corps législatif! Perhaps for a brief time they might have been notable as a legislative pair. Early in 1852, when certain liberals from the university who had taken exile in Belgium spoke slurringly of "Montalembert and his company," Veuillot proudly retorted: "We are of that company."[26] At least during December and January of the new era he and Montalembert were working in close harmony. Early in 1852 Montalembert was elected to the Academy, which election Veuillot hailed as significant in the "de-Voltaireization" of that august body.[27] The "enemy brothers,"[28] as Veuillot and Montalembert have been called, were friendly brothers at this juncture. Montalembert was in due course elected to the Corps législatif and Veuillot's name was strongly mentioned in this connection. Gustave de La Tour wrote him that the Bishop of Quimper would favor his candidacy, though there would, of course, be some opposition to him as an "ultramontaine theocrat."[28] Moreover, according to Eugène, Magne, minister of finance, let his brother know that the government would support him if he decided to be a candidate. Veuillot gave the matter consideration, but was not seriously tempted and declined the opportunity.[29] He might well have won a seat had he run, especially if he had run in the North, but such a position would have distracted him from *L'Univers*, and by 1852 the journal had become part of him. In early 1853 La Tour published an article saying that several members of the clergy of the arrondissement of Loudéac, in Brittany, wanted Veuillot as a candidate, and that political figures like Cuverville had asked him to be one. According to La Tour, Veuillot was touched, but refused.[30]

Veuillot conceivably might have been appointed to a high post in the Napoleonic regime. Napoleon would have been glad to buy his pen and to have his support. Veuillot had no liberal, democratic, or aristocratic scruples to prevent him from accepting a post. His old friend Romieu, former préfet of Dordogne, did become one of the familiar figures in the Tuileries. He could refer also to two of Napoleon's ministers, Magne and Saint-Arnaud (finances and war) as "my friends." He declared: "They have good intentions and wise views. They are of a totally different type from those we have tried before. They are unbelievers who detest incredulity, *viveurs*, but not Voltaireans, and intelligent enough to realize that the church should govern itself."[31] A letter of Albéric de Blanche-Raffin erroneously claimed that Veuillot had had an interview with Napoleon, who offered him a post in the council of state at 25,000 francs. According to this account, Veuillot refused in order "to keep the independence of my pen and my conscience." Napoleon then supposedly pointed out to him that if, while keeping his independence he should displease him the journal would be suppressed, asking what would then remain for him. Veuillot was supposed to have answered, "My faith, my conscience, and my five children." Eugène corrects any doubts about the interview, which definitely did not take place, by explaining that Montalembert had indeed received such an offer for Veuillot, and that Veuillot had refused Montalembert's attempt to get Veuillot to enter the council of state for the Catholic party.[32] Veuillot certainly did rightly, for many reasons, not to accept the opportunity; he could not have played a subordinate role such as this any better than Montalembert.

Veuillot seemed at first to be off to a good year in 1852. The journal was growing, if only as a result of the suppression of other journals. Although he was in no governmental position, highly placed friends were in a position to be receptive to the needs of Catholics as he would define them. The state of things politically in France was orderly, and the foreign policy of the Napoleonic regime appeared to be satisfactory. The year, 1852, however, in fact was to be a terrible one for Veuillot. He became involved in a dreadful struggle with the Archbishops of Paris and Orleans, largely over the question of the use of the classics in Catholic education, complicated as usual by the whole matter of what role a lay journalist might deservedly play in ecclesiastical matters. His wife and one of his daughters died. And he broke with Montalembert, again during the year. Despite these events his day-to-day activities continued little differently from any other year, a circumstance demonstrating his dedication to duty.

Veuillot had already had differences with Montalembert, but not long after the consolidation of the coup they parted ways permanently. Until the spring of 1852 Veuillot had always regarded Montalembert as chief of the Catholic party, but at this point he had completely pegged *L'Univers* and himself to Napoleon, thinking that Montalembert too had solidly endorsed the new order. Montalembert, however, was fundamentally parliamentarian, and he resented the arbitrary measures of the prince-president. It may be hard on Montalembert to call him vacillating, but a political leader can hardly remain as such after giving strong support to a group and then breaking with them for no very apparent new reason. That, however, is exactly what Montalembert did. In the spring of 1852 he withdrew from all functions in the government and became an open enemy, much to his own suffering.[33] Although not in the Corps législatif, Veuillot now became the effective leader of the Catholics-before-all. The Catholic party of the 1840's was at an end. Montalembert became ever more the critic on the sidelines, sniping largely at Veuillot. In due course he penned *Des intérêts catholiques au dix-neuvième siècle,* a brochure which was published in September. In it he said terrible things about Veuillot, accusing him of baseness, of recanting with regard to previous stands, and of "capital error." He spoke of "adventurers of the pen" and "advocates of perpetual dictatorship."[34] Veuillot replied to Montalembert at length, trying to sound faithful to his old leader, but rejecting Montalembert's attacks on the new system and his pleas for liberty. He had a good many clever retorts in his editorials of early November,[35] but in the opinion of Eugène, Louis' "gentle and terrible irony" – that "Montalembert *s'ennuie*" – was the most telling.[36] Veuillot seems ever afterward to have been mildly haunted by the political ghost of Montalembert, and he never appears to have written him off. At Montalembert's death in 1870 Veuillot expressed concern about his soul.[37] But henceforth Veuillot had no "chief" to whom to look, unless one regards that place as eventually filled by the Comte de Chambord.

During the height of the affair of the classics, the struggle over the nature of Catholic education, an affair which might well have seen the downfall of Louis Veuillot and even his excommunication, had it not been for the intervention of the pope himself, Veuillot lost his fifth daughter. She was only six months old and does not seem to have been ill for long. In July his wife was at Vitry-sur-Seine, with the children and without other adults in the family, when little Thérèse, godchild of Donoso Cortés[38] (who himself died that year), needed a doctor. An unknown doctor was procured, and Louis Veuillot seems to have believed that his medicine may have killed her. He never was able to find this doctor. "Perhaps this man has killed my daughter for five francs" was a line appearing in his intimate notes. The sister-in-law of his old friend Mallac was the only person able to be with Mathilde at the time, and her presence was the only consolation throughout the ordeal.[39]

Mathilde herself had never been in very good health. She had been spared hardship in some ways, and had spent quite a bit of time with the Murciers in Versailles (Louis had been and remained on good terms with his in-laws) and elsewhere, but she must have had a difficult life in general. He often referred to her in his letters as though her lot were not easy. When Thérèse died Mathilde was expecting her sixth child, Madeleine, who was born 19 November 1852. Peritonitis set in for

(Alsatia)

Mathilde Veuillot with Marie and Agnès

Mathilde, and she died a week later. Louis Veuillot was grief-stricken. The two were not on the same intellectual plane, and just how much they talked of his career is doubtful: his letters to her are affectionate, but he does not seem very often to express himself about ideas in the way he did to other women correspondents, such as the Comtesse de Montsaulnin, Madame Testas, or Madame Thayer. Still there is no doubt she was an ideal wife in his eyes, and he visualised in her the suffering Christian. He had thought a great deal about his children, and now they had no mother. He was able to write to the Bishop of Beauvais, Msgr. Gignoux, that his sister Élise would be able to take her place about as well as a mother could be replaced,[40] but there is no doubt his life was greatly saddened. Many people wrote their condolences to him, including Guizot, whom Veuillot promptly summoned by personal letter to the funeral.[41] The funeral was held at the Church of Saint Thomas Aquinas, which was Veuillot's parish throughout his days as editor of *L'Univers*, and would later be the church of his own funeral. Montalembert, despite the polemic over *Des intérêts catholiques*, wrote Veuillot twice, and the second letter was primarily to forward a letter from the Comtesse.[42] These letters, and their answers, which contained a good many affectionate words, marked no reconciliation between the two with regard to their stands on the questions of the day. "I would be consoled, if I were able to be," Veuillot wrote Montalembert.[43] And he wrote the same words to his friend Cuverville, telling him how consoling it was to hear from Montalembert.[44] Louis Veuillot was not one to keep his mourning – or much of anything else – to himself, but his many lamentations about "my poor Mathilde" were heartfelt, and even his assertion that "my sister throws herself" completely into my needs, and into my cares; she is about to bring up five little girls who have lost their mother, the eldest of whom is not seven,"[45] was no exaggeration.

The most important episode of the period 1852-53 in Veuillot's public life was the "affair of the classics." It may be that by hindsight it can be overrated. Many other matters made great demands on Veuillot's attention, such as the continued struggle of the Swiss Catholics, the persecutions of the Polish Catholics by the tsarist régime, and the progress of socialism in the world.[46] But the "affair of the classics" was significant from several points of view and involved Veuillot squarely with the hierarchy. The Catholics of France were further divided by it, and the spectacle of a lay editor without much formal education presuming to challenge scholarly bishops, and to gain the support of the pope, brought the question sharply into relief.[47]

At first, in the early part of 1852, Louis was well satisfied with the way the Napoleonic regime was proceeding with respect to education. Montalembert wrote La Tour that "prudent silence disguises his much too strong sympathies" for the program.[48] Veuillot, however, soon proved himself less than prudent and he wrote to Sibour advocating the policies of the government, and excusing himself for not sooner publishing certain letters Sibour wanted published in *L'Univers.*[49] He was in fact probably adding more fuel to the flames that were about to flare up.

The Abbé Gaume, vicar-general of Nevers, a very sincere catechist who was alarmed at extraneous elements that had slipped into Christian education, about this time published a book, *Le Ver rongeur des sociétés modernes*, which singled out the classics as the chief competitor of the writings of the Christian fathers and as a danger in general to Christian morals.[50] Veuillot had seen preliminary studies written by the Abbé Gaume along the same lines, and as early as September 1851 had anticipated the struggle that was to erupt. He could easily foresee the stand that *L'Ami de la Religion* and *Le Correspondant* would take, and notably what the stand of the Archbishop of Orleans, Msgr. Dupanloup, would be.[51] Perhaps it is surprising that the quarrel held off as long as it did. *L'Ami* and *Le Correspondant* had been feuding with *L'Univers* about miracles for some time before 1852, but here was a non-political issue that offered real promise to Veuillot, Lenormant, Dupanloup, and others. Gaume's book appeared under the auspices of the Cardinal Archbishop of Reims, Gousset, who became also a senator in 1852. Consequently, to oppose the strong support that Dupanloup would muster against Veuillot within a short time, Veuillot had some strong backing from the beginning.

After the appearance of *Le Ver rongeur des Sociétés modernes* Dupanloup sprang into action. Dupanloup's background was very mysterious. He was the illegitimate son of a peasant girl and some very high-born figure, about whose identity there has been interesting speculation.[52] In the futherance of his obvious talents he must have had some help from the paternal side, because he was given excellent assignments amazingly early in his career. He was the means of bringing Talleyrand back into the bosom of the church before the latter's death, and had at one time been the teacher of girls of the highest social circles in Paris. Now associated with the best training given the scholars of the church, he represented the leading element in Catholic education. He favored the classics. Msgr. Dupanloup took a stand that might perhaps be desctibed as liberal, from the standpoint of the church, and he voiced his views officially in a letter to the professors of the *petits seminaires* of his diocese. Louis Veuillot took it upon himself to oppose such a man.

Veuillot's own formal education had certainly been meager. However, he had studied languages, including Latin, and, at least with regard to those subjects he felt concerned him, he had read a great deal. He never would have allowed himself to be called a rationalist, but within limits he was quite analytical, and produced rational arguments in defending his positions. Never one to hang back at any rate, he did not hesitate to attack the instructions given by Dupanloup, in his capacity as bishop, to teachers under his jurisdiction. Dupanloup prescribed the study of Virgil, Cicero, Ovid, and other leading classical writers. Veuillot thought the basis of his decision was slight. The principal basis cited by Dupanloup, according to Veuillot, was a passage from Saint Basil, which, Veuillot reasoned, did not cancel the contrary opinions of Augustine, Jerome, and John Chrysostom. Moreover, Veuillot maintained, in pagan days it was necessary to study paganism in order for it to refute itself. Also, in the days of the martyrs, whose personal example canceled the deleterious effects upon morals of pagan literature, there was no great amount of Christian literature available and pagan literature was therefore of value for the acquiring of learning. Veuillot scored Dupanloup for claiming on little evidence that Saint Charles Borromeo and Bossuet offered good justification for the study of the classics. He went on at length about the influence of the humanistic writers of the Renaissance and the errors of contemporary education, which ought to be influenced by the church fathers rather than the classical authors. He recoiled against the glorification of Socrates and maintained that the teaching of the importance of Christ was being erased by the sort of study advocated by the Archbishop of Orleans with the support of the *Journal des Débats* and *Le Siècle.* Closing this opening round of the exchange, he declared: "It seems to us that the question is resolved."[53] That line was very far from describing the situation. Already the battle lines were formed. On 19 May 1852 he had written an article attacking Charles Lenormant, editor of *Le Correspondant*, who had advocated the ideas of Dupanloup and received the backing of the *Journal des Débats.* In this piece Veuillot had quoted Dupanloup's own earlier studies of education to the effect that the students learned little Greek or Latin anyway, and had attacked Dupanloup quite as much as Lenormant.[54] The struggle had already begun.

On 30 May Dupanloup sent out a pastoral letter forbidding his clergy to read *L'Univers*. Veuillot responded, attempting to defend himself against the charge that he had "slandered" the Bishop of Orleans,[55] but surely he could not have believed that he was doing no more than respond to charges. Veuillot had assumed a tone of certainty in taking the opposite position from that of a learned bishop who was giving official instructions to his clergy, not simply as an educator, but as their bishop. Veuillot was apparently attempting to stimulate divisions within the Catholic clergy. Already the Archbishop of Paris had written Dupanloup, agreeing with his views on *L'Univers.*[56] Thus Veuillot was entering again into conflict with his own bishop.

Dupanloup took the initiative. His plan was to gain the adherence of as many other bishops as possible to a declaration he drew up against Veuillot. While this declaration did not name Veuillot or *L'Univers*, it was aimed squarely at them. It specified that episcopal acts were not subject to adjudication by the newspapers. It stated that the use of the classics was proper in the schools, though they should be expurgated and used along with study of the Christian fathers, and in no case were journalists to influence the choice of studies in the seminaries.[57] The statement was very carefully trimmed so as to be acceptable to as many bishops as possible. However, Dupanloup, though hoping to get the endorsement of a large part of the eighty-one French bishops, was knowingly bringing a conscious division in their ranks, since he was well aware of the support that Gaume, Veuillot, and other intransigents had.

The bishops of France were divided into Gallicans, ultramontanes, and liberals, ideologically speaking, and in politics and in social background they formed various other groups. However, with regard to ideological differences, often it was hard to classify any given bishop. The ideologies themselves were not sharp, particularly liberalism and ultramontanism. The best statements of this situation were letters written in 1853 by Sibour and Montalembert to each other. They were acutely conscious that only a few years before the ultramontanes had been Catholics seeking liberty from secular forces, who in rallying around the pope were seeking freedom of religion. Now they could see that there was a new ultramontanism, which they identified with Veuillot.[58] Montalembert went so far as to say: "Men weakly servile in the temporal order and insolently oppressive in the spiritual, strive to establish between ultramontane Catholicism and despotism an abominable solidarity."[59] Allowing for Montalembert's bitterness and overstatement, he was right about the transition, since the days of Lamennais, in ultramontanism. Though these orientations, Gallican and ultramontane, were very real, they often defied definition in given situations, and the individual bishops were often difficult to categorize. Attempts have been made in this regard, but oversimplification is a danger.[60] Dupanloup was nevertheless determined to rally the bishops as a group against the pretensions of the lay journalist who dared to challenge him in his own bailiwick.

Even before Sibour wrote Dupanloup of his support, Clausel de Montals, Archbishop of Chartres had indicated his.[61] For a long time he had been alone among the bishops in his public support of *L'Univers*. He had differed with Veuillot on several political matters, but this stand in direct opposition must have hurt Veuillot. He did not learn of the prelate's position for some time, and did not write about it for *L'Univers* until 1 August.[62] Many bishops indicated their support of Dupanloup's declaration, but the stand of many others was either unclear, or in favor of Veuillot. The Bishop of Blois continued to regard Veuillot as a defender of religion.[63] The Archbishop of Avignon, while agreeing with the principle of episcopal authority, the point that necessarily appealed to all of the episcopacy, declared he hated to see divisions. "Alas! Why disunite the soldiers when the enemy is so close!" As for Veuillot and the lay religious press, he said, "In spite of its vagaries, the religious press has rendered and will be able to render valuable services. Will not defiance solemnly pronounced against it furnish the bad press an occasion for triumph and applause humiliating to the episcopacy?"[64]

Perhaps the most significant letter was from the Archbishop of Reims, Msgr. Gousset, who wrote in a careful way: "I agree that *L'Univers* has its faults; it has made errors, notably concerning the law of 1850 about public education. But if one can reproach it for being too ardent, may one not reproach other journals, likewise estimable, for not being enough so, or for confounding prudence with fear, moderation with feebleness?" Msgr. Gousset made it clear that he thought the issue over the classics was just a pretext for the enemies of *L'Univers*. He then laid down the rule for Dupanloup, "in necessariis unitas, in dubiis libertas, in omnibus charitas."[65] It is interesting to see someone other than Veuillot reprimanded for lack of charity, but Dupanloup of course was not entirely to blame. His very position had been defied by Veuillot, and Dupanloup may well have been thinking more of defending episcopal rights than of taking offense against Veuillot personally.

Dupanloup accompanied his correspondence with his episcopal brothers with a great deal of persuasion through various agents, hoping to gain backing in his project of the declaration. He had vicars-general and various clergymen at his disposal, among them the Abbé Charles Place, whom he sent on many personal missions to persuade the bishops to look with favor on an expression of episcopal solidarity. Place visited a number of key bishops, although not always with success. He was particularly rebuffed by Msgr. Gousset.[66] Place not only worked positively for Dupanloup, but also kept his ear open for reports of what was being done for Veuillot, which was considerable, as it turned out. He noted that Du Lac and Veuillot had spent a good many hours with the Bishop of Toulouse, and reported that they had made a favorable impression. Moreover, he pointed out that steps were being taken on behalf of Veuillot and *L'Univers* to gain the support of other bishops.[67]

In Veuillot's eyes it was strictly the Gallican element who were his enemies. "It is the coalition of Gallican bishops," he wrote *L'Univers'* man in Rome, the Abbe Bernier, "which bursts forth against the organ of ultramontanism. Msgr. Dupanloup, who is only a very lukewarm ultramontaine, if indeed he heats himself up to lukewarmness, exploits this feeling to gain his ends, which are of two sorts: 1) To avenge himself against *L'Univers*, of which he has always, and always vainly, sought to get the upper hand. 2) To replace *L'Univers* by journals of his own: *L'Ami*, which is still, I believe, his own, and *L'Union*, where he has garrison troops." Obviously, episcopal prerogative did not appear to Veuillot to be an essential ingredient in the altercation. Actually, Gallicanism was hardly the whole explanation of the support that Dupanloup received, as perhaps not more than fourteen, or less than a third, of those supporting Dupanloup's declaration were clearly Gallican.[68] As for the ultramontaines, Louis Veuillot felt they were timid.[69] At the time he made this claim, before the death of his daughter Thérèse, he may have been enjoying the fight. He made the remark to his sister Élise, who did not yet have the burdens she shortly inherited. While Louis was away on a trip to Alsace, the Rhineland, and the low countries, he wrote unusually fully about his combats to his wife. He also wrote, in pious and flamboyant words, to a number of other ladies, including Mme Thayer, the Comtesse Montsaulnin, and the Baroness de Mosfart.

As letters came in to Dupanloup giving him support, a good many also came in backing Veuillot. One letter from Rome described *L'Univers*, as "admirable."[71] The Archbishop of Avignon did not contest the need for affirming the principle of episcopal authority, but did not like the form of the declaration.[72] The Archbiship of Reims stated that episcopal authority did not extend to people outside the bishops' diocese.[73] It is interesting to remember that Veuillot had been born in the Bishopric of Orleans, although he never had returned to the Gatinais after leaving it as a boy. The position of Msgr. Parisis was not exactly clear with regard to the classics, but he was very clearly opposed to the declaration. He also published a letter in *L'Univers* and while conceding that the journal had its faults, gave it his strong praise.[74] Doney, Bishop of Montauban, and Dreux-Brézé, Bishop of Moulins, both strongly opposed the declaration. The Bishop of Moulins pointed out that church organization was not like a constitutional state, where the majority decides.[75] Msgr. Doney of Montauban called Dupanloup's project "inexpedient."[76] The Bishop of Gap, Msgr. Depéry, was bitter in his opposition. In what would appear to be rather bad taste he intermixed the Creed with his observations: "I believe in God, creator of the universe, but not in the good faith of those who want to destroy *L'Univers*. I believe in Jesus Christ, who has established His church with his Christian doctors, and not with the doctors of paganism. I believe in the Holy Spirit, who speaks by the prophets, and not by the sibyls. . . .I believe in the communion of saints, but I do not want to belong to that of the *Gazette, Siècle, Débats, Presse,* and *Charivari. . . .*"[77] The responses coming to Msgr. Dupanloup obviously varied widely.

Dupanloup kept close track of the results, and so did Louis Veuillot. Dupanloup seems to have gone out of his way to pass information to Veuillot about the support he was getting. When his list still was not complete he nevertheless sent it to Veuillot. The most remarkable episode, however, was the visit of the Abbé Place to the office of Louis Veuillot on 24 July 1852, to read him the declaration and tell him the names of bishops and other clerics supporting it. Veuillot described the visit of Place as in the character of sergeant-at-arms for his bishop, but the interview took place in a courteous way, and no doubt the Abbé Place was very careful. For example, he pointed out that the Bishop Coadjutor of Chartres (but not yet Msgr. Clausel de Montals) had adhered. Veuillot counted 25 or 30, but a document in the Veuillot papers, communicated no doubt by Place and dated 6 July 1852, included 32.[78]

The full import of this information must have weighed heavily on Veuillot, who immediately contacted the papal nuncio to determine whether the Roman cardinals were against him.[79] He was told that they were not, but the new papal nuncio, Msgr. Garibaldi, unlike his predecessor, gave the general appearance of a desire to be neutral.[80] The support that Veuillot received from Parisis (Bishop of Arras), Salinis (Bishop of Amiens), Debelay (Archbishop of Avignon), and Gignoux (Bishop of Beauvais), therefore, meant much to him, and he thanked these prelates profusely for their stands.[81]

Dupanloup insisted that he wanted to avoid publicity, and he wrote his adherents to make an effort to avoid it.[82] When the Abbé Place visited Veuillot on 3 July he stressed this desire.[83] Whether he would have continued seeking quiet if he had prevailed cannot be said, but at this point secrecy did indeed seem the most advantageous course of the bishop in conflict with a journalist. However, even though he did avoid mentioning the declaration, at this phase of the struggle Veuillot still had plenty to say about the issue of teachıng the classics. Cardinal

Donnet, Archbishop of Bordeaux, took a position similar to Dupanloup's, and Veuillot did not hesitate to respond to this prelate's article after it was published in *L'Univers.*[84] Perhaps even more astonishing in a way than his assault on the teaching of the classics in church schools was Veuillot's assault on the French and Latin of the University, scathingly picking out errors that appeared in print.[85] Who were these people anyway, as little qualified to state what was good taste as to pronounce on religious questions!

The question as a whole slowly tapered off in the late summer and fall of 1852, but Dupanloup had rounded up at least partial support from a majority of the French episcopacy. Of the 81 bishops, Veuillot at first heard that 63 had adhered. This figure was clearly wrong.[86] The list as recorded in the dossier on the classics issue in the library of the Compagnie de Saint-Sulpice shows 44 names, the same figure Eugène gives.[87] It is hard to categorize the nature of the support, because many of the bishops who agreed with Dupanloup's desire to defend episcopal authority also had sympathy, in varying degrees, with Veuillot. The show of strength however, was very great.

Now the episcopacy had divided itself, something neither Rome nor themselves wanted. Dupanloup suddenly decided not to follow up on the advantage he appeared to have when a letter from Cardinal Antonelli reached Cardinal Gousset. Gousset had announced his support for Veuillot, and the attention of Pius IX had been directed to the matter. In effect, therefore, the very carefully written letter of the cardinal secretary of state was the answer of the pope. Episcopal authority was of course spoken of as fundamental, but fear was expressed as to the deplorable results that could follow the issue.[88] In diplomatic language the message told Dupanloup to call off the fight and not to bring out any declaration which would show the division of the bishops on the question. It was, in effect, a mild victory for Veuillot, but not one which he could exploit. There had been some expectancy of a declaration, but *L'Ami de la Religion* carried a note by Dupanloup himself, dated 3 August, deploring "discord among brothers," and also deploring those who blocked unanimity,[89] so that one would no longer be expected.

Of course, the question of teaching the classics in the schools did not go away. Louis Veuillot wrote that he still felt Dupanloup wanted war.[90] He had plenty of reason for discouragement, particularly after the public letter of the Cardinal Archbishop of Bordeaux. The thing that seemed especially to trouble him was that some of his own support from the prelates was disappearing rather than growing. He believed that even Parisis and Gousset were temporizing, and that they were not supporting Gaume, or therefore *L'Univers.*[91] But although a respite seemed to come about the time of the death of his wife, the affair of the classics only paved the way for further trouble with the same bishops as soon as another pretext for difference should arise.

Louis Veuillot was not in good physical condition for further struggles. In September he exclaimed "quel rhume!" in writing his brother. His description of his troubles even exceeded what one might expect in fraternal correspondence, and "I am not dead" was about the best he could say.[92] Veuillot was very open about everything, his health or lack of it being no exception, but even allowing for his tendency to complain, he was not well at the very height of his problems with Dupanloup. The death of his wife was hard on him. The pathetic notes he wrote at the time of her death sound very hard on himself. Although many sent their condolences: "I merit but a very small amount of compassion, like all guilty people who receive their just chastisement. . . .My consolation is to hope that having contributed to the proofs and merits of this good soul, she will be more powerful with God in gaining my conversion."[93] Even to Montalembert Veuillot had a penitential approach when in responding to condolences he declared: "Forget that I have said too much and believe that if my *appréciations* differ from yours, I do not have any other *résolutions.*" Montalembert wrote the word *précieux* after these lines.[94] Veuillot would hardly have written in such a vein had he not been badly shaken, but, despite the temporary rapprochement, Veuillot's distress did not bring any reconciliation between the two men.

As the battle over the classics reached a stalemate, a new phase of Veuillot's troubles with the hierarchy opened in January 1853. Louis Veuillot and *L'Univers* are automatically associated in the minds of those who study the religious history of France of the nineteenth century, but the very voluminous series, *Bibliothèque nouvelle*, brings no such immediate response today. Nevertheless, the volumes published in it were widely read, in their day many of them were controversial, and Veuillot was its director and principal editor. One such volume was *Essai sur le catholicisme, le libéralisme et le socialisme*, by the ambassador of Spain to France, Juan Francisco Donoso Cortés, the Marquis de Valdegamas. By its very title one can see that the eighty pages of this small book were dealing with key considerations of the day, but it was not so much the book itself as a key review that stirred up the hornets' nest. *L'Ami de la Religion* was intellectually élitist, in general somewhat oblique, from the point of view of controversy, and hardly the organ one might have expected to touch off the storm that followed. However, the learned Abbé Gaduel, a leader of the Sulpician school and, significantly, vicar-general of the diocese of Orleans, attacked the book in a sweeping way. He also picked at it with regard to theology, maintaining that it erred in various ways. Drawing from the theologian Witasse, whom Veuillot, incidentally, dismissed as a heretic, Gaduel leveled the charge of tritheism at Donoso Cortés. He further accused him of Lutheranism, Calvinism, and Jansenism. As though these were not enough, he brought forth a final charge of pseudo-traditionalism. This last point was the one that particularly rankled Veuillot. In late January and early February Veuillot drew on all the information he could muster to attack this church scholar from Dupanloup's jurisdiction who presumed to attack the theories of the godfather of his deceased child, the man whose ideas he so admired.[95] Veuillot thrashed in a desperate way in four long editorials. He cited the Council of Trent, Bossuet, Bourdaloue, and the Bible itself. He cited particularly a tract by Msgr. Parisis written in 1847 to justify his concept of the role of the lay religious press in engaging in such polemics.[96] He attacked the theologians who had given ammunition to Gaduel, and he attacked the Abbé Cognat, editor of *Ami de la Religion*, and the Abbé Sisson, also associated with that journal. The secular press and the legitimist journals, the spectrum from *La Presse, Le Siècle,* and *Journal des Débats* to *La Gazette de France*, including the Abbé Chatenay who wrote for it, were not spared. Veuillot's ranging assaults reached out as far as they had ever gone. During these tirades in behalf of Donoso Cortés and against Dupanloup's vicar-general he even found the opportunity to attack the controversial Abbé Michon. Veuillot never showed conspicuous restraint, but the articles he wrote on 24, 26, 30 January, and 2 February 1853 were no doubt his most audacious. And the resulting clash with the hierarchy was no doubt the most severe.[97]

Shortly before the review and Veuillot's wild attempts to demolish with words all associated with it, his old friend, Msgr. Rendu, Bishop of Annecy had written Gustave de La Tour a letter, suggesting ways that *L'Univers* might in the future avoid controversy by placing more emphasis on articles dealing with foreign countries. In this letter the bishop declared, "It is very deplorable to see the children of the light understanding each other so little with respect to the means of spreading it. It is a pitiful side of human weakness."[98] Although Veuillot not only had such words from his friends, but also corresponded himself directly with the good bishop at this very time, he showed no sign of being influenced at all by these worthy sentiments.

Hardly had Veuillot finished the last of this series of articles attacking Gaduel and the rough treatment given Donoso Cortés than he departed for Rome! There is no indication that he went there to gain papal support. Eugène denies that he had any idea of the next blow that would be struck against him.[99] The Bishop of Amiens was going to Rome to deliver the acts of a provincial council, and he asked Louis Veuillot to go with him. Apparently without any long reflection Veuillot decided to make the voyage.[100] It would have been an exciting time to remain in Paris, since the Emperor was about to be married to Eugénie de Montijo, but the allure of going to Rome, which he had not visited since his conversion, proved greater. To La Tour he wrote: "The Gallicans will put a political construction on this trip, especially after the lively polemic with *L'Ami*. The truth is that I go to pray to the Good Lord and renew my old vow of servitude to Saint Peter and his works as long as I live." He said he had intended to do this for a long time, and especially was he so moved after losing his wife.[101] There is no good reason for questioning his sincerity, but it is remarkable that just at the time he most needed the direct intervention of the pope he found himself in Rome.

Times had changed in the fifteen years since he last had been in Rome. In 1838 there had been many days of stage coach travel. In 1853 he got into a railroad car the evening of 1 February, and two days later he was in Marseille. His records tell nothing about railroad travel in those days, except that he saw fit to say that they had had no misadventure. However, they missed their steamer connection for Civitavecchia, and had to wait a few days in Marseille. He had little to say about the Bishop of Amiens except that the bishhop had that *je ne sais quoi* which made it pleasant for all. Not often did Louis Veuillot speak of rich people, or of how rich they really were, but in Marseille he spent some time with a rich banker, named Chuit, who was a Catholic militant and devotee of *L'Univers*. He had a home "like a palace in *A Thousand and One Nights*, and promenading around with Veuillot all day, he bought him some shoes and cigars. "He is a friend," concluded the journalist who often sounded a bit hard on the middle class. In Marseille was also the Abbé Gaduel, but nothing came of this coincidence. For the benefit of the children he reported that he had crossed over the bridge at Avignon. Seven days after the departure of the steamer they missed they caught another, and by 12 February Louis Veuillot and the Bishop of Amiens reached Civitavecchia. On the way he was careful to notice whether the people with whom he talked seemed Bonapartist or not, concluding that they did. He was particularly struck with a young American woman who said that she was *enchantée et très contente* with Napoleon, since he had brought back long riding boots. He also enjoyed hearing her sing some French songs.[102] Obviously there were other things in life besides the right blend of politico-religious talk.

By 18 February Louis Veuillot had exchanged some words with the pope when his audience was being arranged, but by this time the major development affecting him had already taken place in Paris. Dupanloup had spent a week in Paris where he had seen Sibour,[103] preparing the way for a letter which the Abbé Gaduel then wrote to Archbishop Sibour. Perhaps Dupanloup could not tell diocesans of Paris what not to read, but Sibour could. The letter the Abbé wrote to Sibour dated 10 February 1853, was calculated to impress Sibour, and many others who would subsequently see it in print. His very first words, "I am a priest," were perhaps the most effective words he used. The book of Donoso Cortés contained a "multitude of evident and very serious errors against *saine* theology and against Catholic doctrine." Veuillot was the director of *Bibliothèque nouvelle* which had published the book, but his articles that had appeared in *L'Univers* of 25, 27, 31 January and 2 and 3 February 1853 were particularly the object of his complaint. These, he maintained, were "injurious, defamatory, and scandalous." He asked no less than that Veuillot should be punished for "satire, violence, injury, *colère, mépris,* and calumny."[104]

The answer of Sibour was not long in coming. He issued an ordinance on 17 February, which, among other things, made reference to his *mandement* of 24 August 1850 and Louis Veuillot's "submission" of 3 October 1850. He accepted completely the complaint made by the vicar-general of Orleans, and he forbade ecclesiastics of his jurisdiction from reading *L'Univers*. He forbade *L'Univers* and other religious journals from using the terms "ultramontane" and "Gallican" as "injurious qualifications." He accused Veuillot of violating both Christian love and simple honesty. He declared that such theological matters had been discussed as were not to be treated of in daily journals. He included the whole of Gaduel's letter in his ordinance.[105] He could not have done much more. Probably the most significant part of his statement was the point about the unsuitability of the discussion of theological matters in the daily press. With the accelerated rise of the power of the press as a whole, and in particular the lay religious press, Sibour was falling behind the times, at least with regard to expediency.

Simultaneously with the landing of this blow in favor of Dupanloup, the Bishop of Viviers, Msgr. Guibert, sent out a circular to the clergy of his diocese, dated even before Sibour's ordinance but not appearing until two weeks after its date, saying that he was canceling his subscription to *L'Univers*. This blow too must have hurt Veuillot, since the Bishop of Viviers had been friendly in the past. However, Veuillot's use of the terms "Gallican" and "ultramontane" had particularly rankled the bishop, who also felt Veuillot was undermining the episcopacy.[106] The

Bishop of Viviers, who was later to become the Archbishop of Paris, had signed Dupanloup's declaration, but not as an enemy of *L'Univers*. He was very tactful, and the language he used in his circular was moderate. As an oblate in the Order of Mary the Immaculate he had submitted his circular to his superior, who happened to be the Bishop of Marseille, which circumstance had caused the two-week delay. This delay was beneficial to *L'Univers* and Louis Veuillot. Because of it the circular appeared publicly only one day before the harsh words of Sibour. The very comparison of these two pronouncements put the ordinance of Sibour in a bad light in the eyes of other bishops, and prevented him from getting the kind of support he might have received otherwise.[107] However, Veuillot had plenty of reason to worry, had he been the type of man prone to do that.

In England in the summer of 1852 the future Cardinal Newman had used strong language with reference to an apostate priest, who had then brought civil proceedings against him and been awarded heavy damages. Veuillot knew all about the case, since *L'Univers* had raised around 100,000 francs in Newman's behalf.[108] Were Dupanloup or Sibour going to back Gaduel in a suit like this against *L'Univers* which had just shown itself very capable of raising a large sum of money?

Louis Veuillot was lucky in this respect, and he was also lucky in the kind of people who carried on the offices of *L'Univers*. Veuillot's "crew" (C.S. Phillips' word) was a particularly able group.[109] There were Eugène, Melchior Du Lac, Roux-Lavergne, and Coquille as the regular editors. La Tour by this time had joined the inner group, and together with Léon Aubineau, who had already participated while still archivist of the Department of Indre-et-Loire, rounded out the editorial staff. Taconet remained the cooperative owner, and Barrier the dependable *gérant.* In fact, in a day when all articles had to be signed, Barrier's name was often used for pieces by special correspondents whose names, for one reason or another, could not be used.[110] Du Lac was still the *maître,* and Eugène a competent alter ego for his brother, who himself wrote little in the three-month period of his stay in Rome. Obviously *L'Univers* had become the force that it was under the leadership of Louis Veuillot, but even without his leadership it might have been of much the same importance, given the competent group of like-minded editors who produced it. This is not to deny that Veuillot was a great force in French Catholicism, but there were many other avenues, literary as well as personal, through which he wielded influence in addition to his role as editor-in-chief of *L'Univers*. His absence, from February through April of 1853, gave *L'Univers* a dramatic backdrop for its ardent editorial policy, but it was functioning without him. And loyal Élise was taking care of his correspondence as well as his children.

Just at the time when Louis Veuillot was seeking an audience with the pope he was receiving encouragement from others to get direct papal support. Dom Guéranger, Abbot of Solesmes, wrote him that he ought to appeal to the Holy See, and that if only this were done the ordinance of Sibour would be canceled.[111] Others, like Canon Desgarets, urged him on: "Obviously in France you are the flag of priests and laymen who love Roman doctrines and want to see them develop and reign supreme among us to the greater glory of God and for the good of souls." Gallicanism, he said was desperate about its situation and was about to use "brutal force."[112] Gustave de La Tour sounded both hopeful and also somewhat desperate. A few days after the ordinance of Sibour he felt things were going a bit in favor of *L'Univers*, but he added: "Rome must save *L'Univers*, or we will perish under the blows of the episcopal Gallicans." An adjournment gained by submission to the archbishop would only ensure our ultimate death, he said. He called *L'Univers* the "watchdog of the house" which the Gallicans are trying to enter, and deduced that they wanted to kill the dog.[113] An air of gravity and a feeling of need for immediate action gripped contestants in both camps. Sibour whipped up feeling on both sides with a letter to all ecclesiastical editors written a week after his ordinance about *L'Univers*. "Demagogy in the church," he warned, "– is presbyterianism and laïcism seeking to substitute themselves for the episcopacy in matters of education and shepherding of souls."[114]

With this pressure building up, Louis Veuillot, who may well have started for Rome with a desire for a vacation and a chance to renew his 1838 feeling and vows, must have been growing most eager for an audience about business affairs with Pius IX. His activities from his arrival were all directed toward that end. He put up at a hotel called the "Minerve," on the fourth floor in a room without heating. Thereafter he complained throughout his stay of the snow, rain, and freezing weather. He also complained that the room was expensive, but at the time of his departure in April he was speaking of financial arrangements in terms of a few hundreds of francs (three-hundred of which he borrowed from the Bishop of Amiens!), so his expenses could not have been extremely great. He spoke of himself as being "Spartan," but quite probably he did not want Taconet to think he was overspending on this mission, vacation, or whatever he may have called it to the owner of *L'Univers*.[115] It is remarkable that a man who was helping shape the direction of nineteenth-century Catholicism was so penuriously franc-conscious about his expenses while on one of his two most important trips as editor of *L'Univers*, and that when aspiring to stand so close to the papacy he felt it necessary to justify his recommendation that Cardinal Fornari, secretary for Latin letters and keen supporter of *L'Univers*, be given one complimentary copy of *L'Univers*![116] At first he dined with the Bishop of Amiens, but soon, in order to save money, he began taking meals with the Abbé Bernier, the regular representative of *L'Univers* in Rome. However, although the weather treated Veuillot badly, the many friends of ultramontanism, and indeed others not primarily so identified, treated him very well, inviting him to many meals throughout his stay. One of these hospitable people was Msgr. Falloux, brother of the French royalist leader and a member of the Roman court.[117] When he was about ready to return to Paris in April he was frank enough to refer to himself as a "sponger" after having been so extensively entertained.[118] But although he may have seemed petty about his personal arrangements, the little man from the Loiret, editor of a modestly financed journal, not only saw the pope, but grandly immeshed his personal struggles with the large new tendencies of world Catholic organization.

By 18 February the formal audience was not only assured, but Veuillot had already had a chance to exchange a few words with the pope informally. His association with the Bishop of Amiens gave him this opportunity. He managed to be with the five abbés in the entourage of the bishop, who were themselves to have an audience. When Louis Veuillot was presented to the pope, the pontiff appeared to recall his meeting with Eugène, who had visited Rome in 1850. This fact must have been pointed out to him by someone. Then, to Veuillot's delight, the pope raised his voice, at least according to Veuillot he did, and declared for others around to hear: "*L'Univers* is a journal which has done some good; it has performed great services, many services, and like all good things it is put to the test."[119]

The arrival of the Bishop of Amiens and of Louis Veuillot, of course, had not taken place unnoticed by the ambassador of France to Rome, the Comte de Rayneval. Despite the fact that the ultramontanes potentially could present problems to the Second Empire, they did not seem to be an immediate problem, and Napoleon fully appreciated the support *L'Univers* had already given him. Nevertheless, quite a number of persons "more or less actively involved in the exaggerated ultramontane direction" had coincidentally arrived at the same time, including the Abbé Gaume and the Bishop of Versailles. Rayneval thought it his duty to suggest that the pope and Cardinal Antonelli be on their guard. According to Rayneval, the pope almost seemed to reproach Gaume for his stand on the classics. Reporting on 20 February, Rayneval seemed to think Veuillot had already had his audience, referring to the exchange of remarks of the pope and Veuillot of 18 February. He informed the foreign minister that Veuillot was representing the pope as completely approving of his doctrines, whereas, he said, a witness to their talk took things differently, saying that the pope had only uttered some inconsequential words, "which were far from having the meaning that he [Veuillot] sought to give to them."[120] Rayneval believed that Msgr. Salinis, Bishop of Amiens, was working for moderation, and he thought that, despite the agitation going on, the pope and Antonelli would take care of the troubles in such a way that the French government need not be disquieted. No doubt the same episode can appear very differently to different observers, but Rayneval seemed not to be aware that, whereas French supporters of the classics were often not associated with extreme ultramontanism, the papal court was of course oriented in such a way as to combine these two currents. Also, while Veuillot undoubtedly made the most of every favorable word the pope may have uttered, the pope was indeed disposed from the start to sympathize with him, despite his defiance of his bishop (who was not associated with the new ultramontanism), and despite some of the things the pope had said during the quarrel over the classics. Rayneval probably tended to say what was expected of him, and draw the conclusion which he might naturally have reached, without much inside information. He reported the day after Veuillot had his private audience that the pope "deplored such passions about matters so elevated in themselves and which required to be settled with all the calm of cold reason." While admitting that the pope praised the efforts of *L'Univers*, Rayneval said that the pope recognized that the journal often hurt the position of the bishops.[121] These points cannot be contradicted, but, at least according to Veuillot as he reported in personal letters to his sister and brother, the pope showed that his feelings, whatever his reasoning might have been, were on the side of Louis Veuillot.

An interesting view of politics at the papal court of the nineteenth century is offered by Veuillot's account of the presentation of his cause,[122] and in those days arranging an audience with the pope was not simple. First he had an audience with Cardinal Antonelli, but according to Veuillot there was no special significance to this meeting. However, he next saw him again together with Cardinal Fornari, former nuncio to France and a sympathizer with his cause. He then saw various other key ecclesiastics and tried the best he could to take advantage of the comings and goings of others.[123] On 23 February he was finally presented to the pope. He had to wait an hour, but this was nothing to him in view of the previous efforts and the expectation. The only thing that seemed to disappoint him was that after a previous fortnight of rain, it had to rain again on *this* occasion![124] He entered the pope's presence at last, and, as he told the story to his sister Élise, the pope declared, "Ah, there you are, Monsieur Veuillot; I am happy to see you!" Approaching the pope, Veuillot dropped to his knees. The pope then indicated for him to rise, but Veuillot replied, "No, Holy Father, let me remain at your feet." He knelt thus, one hand on the pope's desk and the other on his armchair, the pope turning a bit towards him, and they talked. He gazed fixedly into the pope's eyes. "Never have I had such pleasure contemplating the face of a man," he wrote. He loved those fine, dark eyes, reflecting paternal serenity. Veuillot was unquestionably under the spell of the pope. Nevertheless, the depth of his submission may be questioned. The pope indicated that he should rise. Perhaps he might quite properly have said something about having thought he should stay kneeling, but if his purpose were really to submit himself to the Vicar of Christ, why did he not rise when told to do so? He wanted an absolute pope, and he was demonstrating the way a churchman must be before him. His gesture, intended as a sign of complete submission, may actually show something quite different.

His first words after asking to remain on his knees were, "Very Holy Father, here I am at your knees." He spoke with emotion, but he was not timid, because, according to his own account, one could not be timid before such a face. The pope asked him if this was his first visit to Rome since his pontificate, and he replied that had he been to Rome before during it he would have come to him. Fifteen years ago he had come, and the pope referred to this trip as his confirmation. "Precisely," Veuillot replied to the pope. Pius IX was a warm person, considerate of the feelings of those talking with him. No doubt he liked to hear such agreement. Nevertheless, it is interesting to note this because as has been noted there were bishops who resented agreement, since freedom to agree implied there might also exist disagreement. "Presbyterianism" it had been called. Was not the warmth of Veuillot's agreement to be compared with his disagreement with the Archbishop of Paris? "You know the work I perform," said Veuillot; "this work is combatted. I come to place it at your feet. We do not want to do anything but serve God and the church. My collaborators and I are your most submissive and devoted children." "Si, si," said the pope, who seems to have used alternately French and Italian, according to Veuillot's account. Veuillot said that all they wanted to do was follow the pope's will, to death itself. "It is with these sentiments," Veuillot continued, "that I come to ask of you, for the satisfaction and peace of conscience, whether this work should be continued, or modified, or interrupted." The pope told him that the work should be continued. Here Veuillot won a victory. However, the pope told him, "The best things are capable of being bettered. Always seek to do better. Be prudent, avoid quarrels; but the work is good and renders service to religion." His praise was thus considerably qualified, and a measure of modification certainly was indicated by the pope. "Very Holy Father," responded Veuillot, "we avoid quarrels as much as we can," blaming others for starting them. Veuillot described the pope as saying "si, si" at different points, although this was what he himself might be expected to have been answering. The pope told him that it was necessary to be patient. "When a bishop writes something that may seem strange to you, let it pass. The bishops are a respectable body. In France the bishops are very good." To this good advice Veuillot replied, "Yes, Holy Father, those who love you!" The pope smiled, said something that Veuillot did not catch, and, after something about ultramontanism was injected, declared: "*Dupanloupe* (*sic* – Louis Veuillot, on his knees, noted the pope's pronunciation of the terminal "p") himself is a good bishop. He has vivacity like you. You Frenchmen want to do everything right away. You cannot abide an obstacle. Be respectful to your bishops." Veuillot then insisted he was respectful to bishops, but added: "All the same sometimes they are very hard on us. Anything serves the Gallicans as a pretext for persecuting us. Look at the suit this abbé of Orleans is filing against me right now." The pope had not heard about the case, and Veuillot told him that the vicar-general thought that such as he should not be writing about such subjects, but that he himself felt he knew enough theology to defend religion. The pope smiled and raised his shoulders. He further admonished Veuillot to be more moderate toward bishops.

The discussion then turned to the classics. According to the pope the whole matter was very simple: "To want to banish pagan authors from education would be *une sottise*, not to introduce Christian authors a fault, *una colpa*." Veuillot insisted that he would only call for the expurgation of the pagan authors, and that what the pope had outlined was his program. He maintained that young people were not reading the Christian authors. The pope uttered words of agreement, but went on to say that the bishops, not others, should regulate education. Veuillot argued that his people were not trying to regulate education, but were simply raising their voices as citizens (*sic*) and fathers of families.

He then turned the discussion to the Little Sisters of the Poor in Paris, and claimed that the archbishop had not done right by this group in certain particulars. The pope showed interest and said he would think about what might be done for them. Veuillot then cast aspersions on

Fourtoul, minister of education. At this point, after about twenty minutes conversation, Veuillot wrote his sister, he, Veuillot, thought the audience had lasted long enough. Hereupon he made the request of the pope to be allowed to attend the pope's private mass and to receive communion from him. The pope, who also sympathetically heard Veuillot tell about his five orphan children, told him that he might. Veuillot then kissed the pope's hand, and the pope gave his blessing. He followed Veuillot to the door with an affable smile and a look of good will. Veuillot was transported by it all, and convinced that the pope was on his side. Msgr. Mérode, attached then to the papal court, who although brother-in-law of Montalembert was a constant friend over a long period to Veuillot, let him know that the pope was pleased to have seen him, but he also said that the pope never wanted to hurt anyone's feelings. He further told him that the critical things the pope had said about *L'Univers* had to be weighed doubly heavily for this very reason.[125] Nevertheless, Veuillot was ebullient from then on, buoyed up by the belief that the pope, with his beatific smile and warm eyes, was on his side. Victor Cousin once remarked, "Veuillot will always have the pope and grammar on his side."[126] Already he had shown by dint of hard work he could hold his own in the French language with anyone, but now indeed he had, truly, the support of the pope. No matter what admonishments the pope may have given him, how could a mere archbishop trouble him now!

The battle was turning, but yet much had to be done to follow up the advantage. At first the French ambassador to Rome did not seem to think Veuillot was winning. He reported that the pope and Antonelli found the religious press in general and Veuillot in particular very inconvenient. He thought they did not want to intervene in this local French ecclesiastical quarrel, and that Veuillot was being warned.[127] Whereas at home in France the Emperor, Ségur, and General Cotte, among others, leaned to the side of Veuillot, Rayneval apparently assumed the government inclined against him. Instructions on the matter were slow in coming to him, and when they did they were vague.[128] The affair was a church question, and the pope and his curia would decide it without any advice from the French government.

Not long after Veuillot had felt the ecstacy of the papal smile he received word of Archbishop Sibour's sentence against him. Mail often took ten days to two weeks to reach Rome, and Veuillot complained a good deal about the Roman post.[129] Sibour's sentence of 17 February only became known to him on 2 March. When he heard it, he took it pretty much in his stride. He complained also about the weather that day, but he visited several churches and engaged in other activities. The

Bishop of Amiens greatly encouraged him: "What are you complaining about? Never has a journalist made more noise! You preoccupy the pope and the Sacred College; you are certainly the subject of many diplomatic notes; ambassadors are informing themselves about your doings; you have here many prelates who go to great lengths to serve you or oppose you. Just see to it that you do not get any big ideas about yourself!" Veuillot replied that fundamentally he was modest and would like nothing better than to avoid making a stir. However, as a fight seemed to be unavoidable, he gave every appearance of enjoying the prospect. He said he agreed with all that Salinis told him, particularly that his affair with Dupanloup was becoming the center of attention. "The Bishop of Orleans has important puppets here who certainly are not asleep. My side is fencing around. My friends are circulating; the Bishop of Amiens is everywhere; I myself am seeing cardinals, and the most important of them are for us." It all reminded him of the *jeu de boules* on the Rue du Bac.[130]

No doubt, the Archbishop of Paris believed he had struck Veuillot down by his sentence of 17 February. Shortly afterwards he must have realized differently. Gustave de La Tour in Paris wrote Veuillot that the nuncio and the prelate had been having serious conversations. At this juncture Msgr. Garibaldi began to appear less neutral than he had formerly seemed to Veuillot. He spoke of Roman rights, which the archbishop had to assure him he was not attacking. La Tour believed that the nuncio was displeased. The affair was further complicated by the Bishop of Moulins, Msgr. Dreux-Brézé, who wrote to Sibour, complaining that the press should not be interfered with as it was being in this case, despite the irritating ways of *L'Univers*. The Archbishop now determined to defer to Rome in the matter, which facilitated bringing matters to a head. La Tour spoke disparagingly of the letter from the Bishop of Moulins and of other legitimists like him in the clergy,[131] but although the letter attacked *L'Univers* for its polemics and for political stands taken according to expediency, the main thing it did was to question whether Sibour was authorized to take the measures he had taken against a journal. Sibour therefore referred the whole question to the Holy See, thus facilitating a prompt papal review.[132] Had the question not been brought to a review by this episcopal move, a papal statement might not have been elicited. Even so, there was some legalism involved.[133] Nevertheless the Holy See moved in a surprisingly swift fashion in this matter.

The situation came to be solved in the following way: 1) Veuillot pleaded his case in a formal way to Cardinal Fioramonti, secretary for Latin letters, by a letter of 3 March 1853.[134] 2) Cardinal Fioramonti then answered in such a way as practically to be speaking for the pope, and, without using any names, nevertheless made it clear that the Holy See was in general sympathy with Veuillot, without wishing to destroy any more of the dignity of the episcopacy than could be helped in this case.[135] 3) The Cardinal Secretary of State Antonelli wrote a simultaneous letter to Archbishop Sibour asking him to withdraw the ordinance against Veuillot. He was unwilling initially to do this, just as Veuillot was reluctant, even at the behest of the Holy See, to ask Sibour to do so. However, Veuillot ultimately did write a letter to Sibour, which satisfied the pope, although in it he requested the withdrawal of the ordinance without speaking of submission.[136] 4) Sibour then decided to accept the situation, and he canceled the ordinance on 8 April 1853.[137] Veuillot thereby won the battle, although his feud with Sibour continued until the latter's death, as the Gallicans continued their long-drawn-out struggle with the ultramontanes.

These steps did not come about easily, and with slow communications, the tide of the contest was difficult to visualize. Veuillot himself experienced several changes in expectations about his chances. On 4 March he wrote his brother: "Things are going well and even rapidly. Everyone in Rome is indignant, especially the pope."[138] He seemed to be walking on air. The same day he wrote a letter to the editors of *L'Univers*, which he intended for publication in the journal, summarizing his appeal and just what was going on at the Holy See. He stated that he was appealing for the honor and liberty of *L'Univers*, and made public his battle against the sentence. Later he had reason to wish he had not made public his counterattack against Sibour, particularly when *L'Ami de la Religion* began immediately to counter it.[139] By 6 March he heard that Fioramonti had sought views on his character, and that a Father Rubillon in particular had caused the cardinal to ask whether Veuillot really were a Christian! "The chances appeared very good this morning; they are less so this evening," he wrote his brother. In the same breath then he quipped that the Bishop of Amiens was going to the Quirinal to see "cette fleur des montagnes."[140] However, he may have underestimated at the time the influence of Salinis, even on Fioramonti. The bishop's influence was great throughout the crisis.[141]

Even the role of the French government, although quite indirect, was not without significance. The ambassador to the Holy See, Rayneval, was as we have seen initially not favorable to Veuillot. However, he soon came to see the favor in which the pope held Veuillot, and informed the Quai d'Orsay of the nature of the letters that would be written to Veuillot and Sibour.[142] He also emphasized the vigorous support for the government that *L'Univers*, unique among the religious journals, had shown. And then, he added, after Veuillot wrote and made peace with his archbishop, perhaps the two would mend their ways. The archbishop might give up his unwise assertions of episcopal authority, and Veuillot might renounce treating as enemies others who espoused the Christian cause. He anticipated the archbishop's permitting Veuillot to be "more Catholic than the pope," and Veuillot's ceasing "to accuse his archbishop of heresy."[143] When Fioramonti wrote his letter to Veuillot on 9 March, Rayneval apparently did not hear of it immediately, but when he did he said that it was "the most striking approbation of the doctrines of *L'Univers*."[144] Thereafter, Veuillot was able to write: "His [Rayneval's] conduct has changed; he has just paid a very long and very friendly visit to us, and we have conjectured that the latest news from Paris is not foreign to this politeness. De Cotte and Ségur have written the Emperor as our friends."[145] Imperial favor was something Veuillot had hoped would be forthcoming. He had written his brother two weeks earlier: "A word from the Tuileries would do a great deal."[146] In any case, his former support of the coup was not now hurting his cause.

The nuncio, Msgr. Garibaldi, was out of sympathy with Sibour, if for no other reason than that the French regime wanted an end to the troublesome situation.[147] The pressure from this quarter on Msgr. Sibour must have been great as the archbishop was made to realize the displeasure of both the pope and the emperor. However, his episcopal dignity was very much at stake and he wanted to receive something in the way of an entreaty from Veuillot so that he could seem to be retiring the measure against the journalist as an act of his own, and not simply as a result of directions from the Holy See in response to Veuillot's appeal. Veuillot was loath to write, and when he did he avoided making any statement which could be regarded as submission. He had voluntarily gotten on his knees to the pope, but he was not going to do this to the Archbishop of Paris. He complied with the papal wish, however, and wrote Sibour, though in submitting a copy of his letter to Sibour to the pope shortly before Easter he still spoke of being "unjustly struck" by Sibour.[148] The pope had already said of Fioramonti's letter to Veuillot, which was couched in general terms, did not mention names, and only indirectly was made to seem to reflect the pope's sentiments, "But poor Veuillot will not be satisfied."[149] Not surprisingly there was also some question whether the Holy See or Sibour would be satisfied with what Veuillot wrote in satisfaction of the pope and Sibour. His letter was dispatched on Easter Monday, 27 March, and Veuillot heard that Cardinal Antonelli said to Cardinal

Fornari: "I do not know whether Veuillot's letter will please the archbishop at all, but it suits us and is all that is necessary." Veuillot had spoken of the enemies of religion rejoicing over their division, but he was hardly submissive. He had heard that the archbishop was aware through the nunciature that the encyclical *Inter multiplices*, which was then being prepared, would say some of the same things that had been written by Cardinal Antonelli, and that the archbishop would accordingly have to lower his flag.[150] By 31 March the encyclical had been completed and sent out, and Veuillot's attitude was growing ever more confident. He called the Archbishop of Paris "the Parisian" in a letter to his brother. In addition to expressing satisfaction with what he believed to be the nature of the encyclical, he reported with pleasure the way that, he had heard, Cardinal Piccolomini, *très rond et très simple*, had cut down two Gallican legitimists from Nantes.[151]

The compromise sought by the pope had indeed involved at least some sacrifice on the part of Veuillot in writing to his archbishop. Rayneval declared that "the sacrifice has appeared painful, but it has been executed." He further noted that the archbishop was imposing himself over the press, though of course not all of the French religious press was in Paris.[152] The archbishop must have been much chagrined over his situation. He wrote to Bishop Dupanloup, "The motives for which one blames my order do not have any appearance of reason." He was bitter over the importance of the journalist Veuillot, who was throwing his weight around in Rome, and declared that the pope would only have had to give the word to make Veuillot subject to him.[153] Indeed there was general prejudice against journalists even at the Holy See, a fact Veuillot himself knew well. The pope, of course could also have taken much clearer actions in supporting Veuillot's ultramontanism. He might simply have pronounced in favor of *L'Univers* and not sought a compromise. "The reason," according to Veuillot himself, "is that we are journalists, good journalists without doubt, but finally just journalists. To pronounce between an archbishop and a journalist! There is no audacity nor sense of justice that would not be stricken dumb and stop short at that."[154] But journalist though he was, Veuillot had been favored by the Holy See over the archbishop, to the distress of many.[155] The pope certainly did what he could to save the dignity of the prelate, but the latter when caught up in a struggle with the rising lay press had taken the side of declining Gallicanism.

The quarrel, of course, was awkward for everyone, as Drouyn de Lhuys, French foreign minister, pointed out to Rayneval, when expressing his hope that Veuillot's letter would prove satisfactory to Msgr. Sibour.[156] Sibour at this point of frustration was ready to permit a detente to set in. He was in touch with Rayneval, who in turn showed his letters to Cardinal Antonelli, and he told Dupanloup that he saw signs that Veuillot and *L'Univers* were going to be more moderate, at least with respect to the issue of the classics.[157] The pope had made himself clear about the classics, and Veuillot himself could see that he had to be careful about attacking the study of the pagan authors in the future. With the arrival of the encyclical *Inter multiplices*, there was nothing Sibour could do but lift his ordinance of 17 February 1853, which had been a major blow at the status of the lay press as well as Veuillot personally. His first words in lifting the ordinance on 8 April were, "After having taken into account the encyclical letter," and early in the statement he used the word "voluntarily."[158] The fact that he received the encyclical the same day he lifted the sentence against Veuillot slightly diminished the meaning of the word, "voluntary."

Louis Veuillot was sure of victory before he actually heard about it. He wrote to Eugene on 3 April telling about the role of the Bishop of Amiens and the encyclical. He admitted then that Sibour had asked, through the nuncio, that he himself write on his own behalf for relief, though Antonelli was not sure yet whether the ordinance would be suspended or retired. However, through Salinis he was able to see the encyclical, especially words that the pope privately indicated were written especially for Veuillot. These were:

> This is why, in encouraging you to keep away from the faithful committed to your care the mortal poison of evil books and evil newspapers, we most insistently ask you to try also to foster with your good will and with all marks of your favor the men who, inspired with the Catholic spirit and conversant with literary and scientific fields, consecrate their labors to writing and publishing books and journals in order that opinions and attitudes contrary to the Holy See and its authority may disappear, in order that the darkness of error may be dispelled and minds may be flooded with the pure light of truth.
>
> Your charity and your episcopal solicitude ought therefore to further the enthusiasm of these writers, inspired with a good spirit, so that they may continue to defend the cause of Catholic truth with attentive care and knowledge; if perchance in their writings they should happen to be wanting in some respect, you ought to tell them about it with fatherly words and with prudence.[159]

Veuillot wrote his brother that the pope said to Salinis: "It is for Veuillot that I have done this; is he satisfied with it?" "How not to be satisfied with such generosity?" was his answer. Although he was not sure yet what Sibour would do, he had won a victory, and now he would like to return to Paris. However, everyone else, except Elise, wanted him to remain in Rome until things were definitely arranged.[160] The view of the French ambassador in Rome was that if Veuillot returned before Sibour retired the sentence there would outbursts.[161] But Veuillot was eager to go home, and he wrote Msgr. Mabille, even before he heard of Sibour's action, that he was remaining in Rome only until he could obtain the benediction of the pope, and that then he would return to Paris.[162] Drouyn de Lhuys thought that if only Veuillot would answer in the way in which he had been counseled to do it, the archbishop would respond by lifting the sentence.[163] The fact that he responded at all, personally asking relief, was probably less important to Sibour than the encyclical. Sibour had need of getting out of the mess, and acted accordingly.

Veuillot was not the only one to have a personal victory in this affair. The pope had ordered the examination of Donoso Cortés' book about socialism, the immediate cause of the clash, and the results reported to him were that "three or four slight inexactitudes" were encountered, which loomed bigger in French translation than in Spanish, while four serious heresies were noted in Gaduel's article. Moreover, the pope was advised to have a good translation made in Italian, since it was found to be the best book available against socialism.[164] The Holy See thereby had spoken in favor of Veuillot in both the general and the specific causes of the trouble and had vindicated the Spanish thinker-diplomat whom Veuillot so admired. Unfortunately, Donoso Cortés did not live to hear of or to enjoy the victory, as he died during the month of May.[165] By 14 April Louis knew of the retirement of the sentence, but in writing his brother said he had had so many things to do that he had been unable to find time to write to Donoso Cortés.[166]

The formalities of his pilgrimage were all the more important to Louis Veuillot, because he was engaged in such a struggle. He had made visits to many of the important churches and climbed the Scala Santa. He had asked the staff of *L'Univers* to arrange a special mass at Notre Dame-des-Victoires before the issue was decided.[167] Obviously now he could not leave Rome until he had sealed his victory with another pontifical benediction. Before receiving this blessing, however, he had to do one more unpleasant thing: write again to the Archbishop of Paris. When it was indicated to him that he should write this second letter, he was most reluctant, and he told his brother that he had answered, "I do not intend to let myself be conquered by generosity."[168] However, he could not refuse, and he must have summoned some magnaminity at this stage of the game, because the letter which he addressed to Sibour on 16 April was more conciliatory than could have been expected, even referring to the editors of his journal as "your devoted children."[169] After this last inspired gesture of reconciliation to his archbishop, Louis Veuillot had an audience on 18 April and now nothing stood between him and his return to Paris.

The Archbishop of Rouen had let Salinis know of his distress over the outcome of the case, saying that the episcopacy was thereby erased and that Veuillot would return to Paris through a triumphal arch.[170] Veuillot must have been somewhat concerned about this reaction, and he wanted it known among the bishops he was not seeking such a result. He wrote Salinis shortly after his arrival in Paris in late April: "I arrived Wednesday evening without having passed through any arch of triumph or any trimumphal gate." There were none of the drums that the Archbishop of Rouen feared, and the first thing that he did was to arrange an interview with the Archbishop of Paris. According to Veuillot Sibour opened his arms, and he fell into them. When the conversation came to a touchy point, Veuillot said, "That is all past." He told Salinis that the meeting even had its comical side, and that he would not be surprised if some day he found himself sitting at dinner at the archbishopric, "asking water from M. Cognat, and offering wine to M. Gaduel." He was speaking too soon, because despite the apparently conciliatory attitude of Veuillot after his victory, the group over whom he had triumphed was only waiting to turn on him again.[171] However, he was home, after a victory, and the foreign ministry was under the impression that the pope and everyone involved in the trouble were satisfied.[172] Veuillot himself probably believed for a time that there was indeed this happy outcome. He wrote the Baroness de Mosfart: "The storm which kept me in Rome is calmed. I am now reconciled with Monseigneur de Paris, who has received me very well. . . ." He was however, genuinely bereaved by the death of Donoso Cortés,[173] the advancement of whose ideas was at the center of his dispute in the first place, and to whom Veuillot had been looking for intellectual leadership.

On his return to Paris, Veuillot's correspondence seemed to return to normal channels. Literature, religion, and other topics were treated more for their own sake and not subordinated to the daily exigencies of the battle that had been taking place. Even a letter to the Abbé Bernier reflected little of the recent strife, and his comments on the encyclical sounded pious and detached.[174]

Late in August Cardinal Fioramonti wrote Veuillot again stating papal satisfaction with *L'Univers* and referring to a decoration for Taconet.[175] Veuillot was known to care nothing for decorations and such marks for himself. On many occasions however, in spite of this attitude, he had the opportunity to get ribbons for his buttonhole. For example, in the early spring of 1854 the papal nuncio took steps to arrange for the minister of public instruction to bestow the croix d'honneur on Veuillot, but Veuillot told him that if this honor were offered, "I would refuse it very politely and very decidedly." He did not feel that in this refusal he had made any sacrifice, because the prize itself was not something for which he yearned. Anything that he had done was for love of the church, he explained to Msgr. Parisis, to whom he told the story of this project. The nuncio understood,[176] or so Veuillot thought, but late in the summer of the same year he spoke of "escaping" a decoration again.[177]

Veuillot, as usual, continued to get into controversies in the period after his return from Rome in 1853, but he actually seemed to be in a somewhat more cautious mood in this era than was his wont. Throughout the history of *L'Univers* the staff was tightly knit and working harmoniously. Not only was Du Lac the "mentor" and "brother" of Veuillot, the others were also called "brother." Special contributors like Segrétain and Rupert joined themselves closely to Aubineau, Roux-Lavergne, La Tour, and Taconet, and their zeal may have at least equalled that of Veuillot. In these days the offices of *L'Univers* were on the Rue de Grenelle, and in good weather the editors would play at *boules* outside instead of at dominoes. After contesting together with thrown metal balls on the hard dirt, they often went as a group to Notre Dame-des-Victoires, the church where tens of thousands of soldiers' hearts hung from the walls in brass cases, and where they felt that benediction descended upon the militant role they were playing.[178]

At all periods in his life Louis Veuillot was alternately introspective and outgoing by nature, and he was particularly so at this time. "Il faut qu'on me brise. . . ." he wrote in his private journal in June of 1853.[179] Not long after that he wrote: "You will see no other refuge than in the Cross. . . . For myself as for others, outside of that I see nothing. The rest is illusion, deception, egoism, remorse, dispair."[180] Despite this melancholy introspection, however, Veuillot could step directly into an active world and vigorously lead the battle of what he regarded as good against evil in a remarkable change of pace. Nevertheless, he seems to have had somewhat more doubts about the role of the literary man and journalist during these days than at some other periods. To one clergyman he wrote: "May it please God that I never contribute in pushing a young man into a literary course!"[181]

His attitude on the classics continued to be what it had been, although the admonitions he had recently heard in Rome restrained him from getting involved any further in this matter. To Blanc de Saint-Bonnet, the Christian philosopher, he said that he could not understand how people could try to develop a taste in the young for Homer, Virgil, and Horace, when they had hardly come to appreciate Racine, La Fontaine, and Bossuet. Further, whatever these pagans had to say, their significance could better be studied in history than in literature.[182] However, although he was obliged to avoid quarreling with Christian defenders of the classical literary pagans, he still could, and did indeed, become involved in political arguments with the *Catholiques parlementaires*. His high point in defending the Napoleonic regime was 1853-1856, when he managed to associate persons involved in undermining Napoleon with persons disliking his defense of papal orthodoxy. Small wonder that formal decorations would have been his had he not avoided them. At about this time he became embroiled in a disagreement about political liberty with the *Journal des Débats* and *Le Siècle,* and also with *Le Correspondant*, which seemed to be taking sides with the secular press. *L'Ami de la Religion* received support from Montalembert, but it really was not of great consequence; and it was *Le Correspondant* that Montalembert reorganized in 1855. In early June Veuillot's legally-minded friend Foisset wrote about Catholicism and freer laws in a careful way in *Le Correspondant*, bringing a strong response from Veuillot against parliamentarianism and the sort of liberalism *L'Independence belge* could now more freely advocate than any of the French journals under the present regime.[183] The Abbé Delacouture, writing in the *Journal des Débats* in July, brought a similar response from Veuillot, who became ever sharper as the exchange involved an attack by Delacouture on a book by Du Lac, *L'Église et l'État*, written in 1850 to refute ideas of Catholics, revolutionary or democratic, supporting revolutions.[184] Many attacks were directed at Veuillot during this time, including those by the notorious Abbé Michon. *Le Siècle,* Veuillot particularly noted, made a habit of likening him to Tartuffe.[185] But Veuillot's responses to all were such as to bring ecclesiastical criticism – not from Sibour or Dupanloup, who were not yet ready to take up the struggle again – but from the Bishop of Angers, Msgr. Angebault. This prelate's criticisms were on the grounds of Veuillot's want of charity, for which Pius IX eventually censured him, but Veuillot came back with a strong defense:

> Permit me to say this: for the maintenance of peace it is not solely to me that reproaches should be made; it is to those who first broke it, and in such a disloyal way that it became impossible to remain quiet and not to answer them, and a bit harshly. *Duris dura responsio.*

Responding harshly to the harsh was not turning the other cheek. Nevertheless this was the way in which Veuillot began his letter to the bishop of one of the most intensely and conservatively Catholic areas of France. He went on to explain that he could not endure Delacouture's attack on Du Lac's demonstration that the ideas of *L'Ère nouvelle*, which confused democracy and Christianity, were wrong. There was no room for debate in these matters, he said, and his epistle was another striking example of his telling a bishop that he (a layman) was perfectly correct in firing back at his assailants, Catholic as well as secular. He did excuse himself for not having answered the bishop's letter promptly, a failure for which some would have felt Veuillot should be criticized. His excuses were that several of his collaborators were absent and that four of his children were sick.[186]

In addition to standing his ground against still another bishop, he attacked many other Christians. Sylvester de Sacy, editor of the *Journal des Débats*, perhaps was more in the secular camp. Veuillot called his paper "the journal of Jews, protestants, *universitaires*, Voltaireans, the most perfidious and constant enemies of the church."[187] But Louis-Félix Danjou would seem to have been a bird of a different feather. He had been organist at Saint-Eustache (the second largest church in Paris, which had probably the best organ in Paris) and composer of sacred music. He had been a librarian at the Arsenal before going to Montpellier, where he had launched *Messager du Midi* in 1848. In this journal in late 1853 he attacked as "semi-pagan" both Constantine and Louis XIV.[188] His views on the classics were acceptable to Veuillot, but basically Danjou was attacking those who take liberty from Christians, and at this point in his career Veuillot was particularly defensive against the assertion of democratic ideology on the part of Christians. Veuillot was far from being on his own in this respect. Coquille, Segrétain, Aubineau, and the rest wrote articles that were at least as strong as what Louis Veuillot himself had to say. The general tenor of them all was practically to the effect that to worry about liberty was to take an anti-Christian stand.[189] Veuillot was, reasonably enough, accused by his enemies of being concerned about liberty only when his opponents were in power. In the mid-fifties he was still satisfied with Napoleon. So, despite a certain sympathy for some of the ideas of Danjou, Veuillot attacked him sharply, blasting him for holding up the United States as an example of a free land where religion could freely be practiced, countering that America was a land where slavery and polygamy existed.[190]

While Veuillot thus returned to his normal journalistic controversies he became the object of expressions of annoyance from quarters other than secular or liberal-Catholic journals. Already obscene pictures of Veuillot had been picked up by the police, including one drawing showing him with the pope.[191] Poetry about him began to appear late in 1853. When poems are published about one, answers are harder to make than answers to editorials. Francisque Tapon, who as an extremist reformer called for a universal republic as the proper expression of Christianity, under the name F.-T. Fougas wrote verse which depicted the editors of *L'Univers* in a scathing way. He put into their mouths such words as:

> Par nos articles bigots
> De notre France nouvelle,
> Faisons un nid de cagots
> Selon Rainn'ville et Villèle!
> Le billet de confession
>
> Bientôt redevient d'obligation;
>
> Déjà, grace a notre saint zèle,
> On voit tout le peuple aux processions.
>
> *Très solennellement, avec les gestes:*
>
> Nous vous bénissons,
> Et rebénissons! . . .
> Bien vite à genoux. . . vilains polissons!

This sort of jingle could easily be chanted by the enemies of *L'Univers* and Louis Veuillot, but he probably did not take Fougas-Tapon very seriously. His brother called him "one of those imbeciles on whom revolutions dote."[192] At the time Louis merely pointed out that he was one of those refugees of whom France was well rid, though he suggested that *Le Siècle* was harboring his illegal writings.[193] However, another author, who could not be so easily dismissed, Victor Hugo, in his refuge on Jersey now wrote some verse about Veuillot and *L'Univers* that was published in Brussels and was part of his *Châtiments.* He savagely described Veuillot and his *journal frénétique,* accusing Veuillot of being in the pay of the police, among other things:

> Armé d'un goupillon, il entra dans la lice
> Contre les Jacobins, le siècle et le péché;
> Il se donna le luxe, etant de la police,
> D'être jésuite et saint par-dessus le marché.

> Pour mille francs par mois, livrant l'Eucharistie,
> Plus vil que les voleurs et que les assassins,
> Il fût riche. Il portait un flair de sacristie
> Dans le bouge des argousins.

On and on Hugo went in this vein, including the following quatrain:

> Depuis dix-huit cents ans, Jésus, le doux pontife,
> Veut sortir du tombeau qui lentement se rompt,
> Mais vous faites effort, o valets de Caîphe!
> Pour faire retomber la pierre sur son front![194]

The great romantic stung and hurt Veuillot. He was not fair at all in his accusations that Veuillot had profited from his activities, any more than in the inference that he was making the stone roll back on the tomb, but these words hurt Veuillot nonetheless. Perhaps the very fact that he was malevolently apprized of Hugo's writings in the first place by the editors of *Le Siècle,* who said that Hugo was calling the editors of *L'Univers* "spies, thieves, assassins, and *crapules*," may have had something to do with his reactions.[195] Of course he responded violently in *L'Univers*, although he did not press this attack long. As for the role of the rival journal he declared to a supporter: "Le Siècle, with twenty-five thousand subscribers, is still but the voice of one imbecile. If I had need of encouragement to continue the struggle to which I have vowed my life, I would draw more than enough force from the feeling which these stupid and savage attacks raise up. . . ."[196] However, the wounds inflicted by Hugo, who struck at him on several occasions, wounds into which *Le Siècle* rubbed salt, hurt him badly.

The Catholic church in Europe and the whole world got particular attention from Louis Veuillot on the eve of the Crimean War, which was consistent with the religious situation at the outbreak of the war. The schism in Goa, the troubles of Catholics in Switzerland, persecutions in the German states, the Anglican-Catholic problem in Great Britain, and the oppression of Roman Catholics in the Russian Empire, especially in Poland, were favorite topics of the editors of *L'Univers* in this era. They seemed almost like a team in the way each specialized in particular parts of their general attack. L. Rupert would write, for example, on the situation in Piedmont,[197] while La Tour would immediately follow with a discussion of the religious situation in Russia.[198] Then N.-J. Cornet would follow with an attack on the persecution of Catholics in Baden,[199] a subject dear to the heart of Louis Veuillot, who was raising thousands of francs for the Catholics of Baden at this time.[200] But despite the breadth of the concern of Louis Veuillot and the other editors of *L'Univers* for the plight of the Catholic Church in many lands, the Crimean War meant, of course, that the greatest concern for oppressed Catholics was directed toward Russia and those areas the Russians intended to dominate in the Near East.

On 16 January 1854 Veuillot wrote a powerful editorial, bringing together things that he himself and other editors had already said, and likened the whole struggle to the Crusades:

> By the Crusades Europe was saved, not only from Islam, but from itself. It was, as today, full of troubles, factions, revolts, devoured by anti-social sects. There are places where one is unable to gather the people together except by precipitating their energy in glorious perils. This torrent of bad passions becomes the flood of the Crusades, which, sweeping along much mire and much pure gold, stops at the stone of the Holy Sepulchre, after having cut between Europe and the Orient an abyss Islam cannot pass.
>
> The Greek schism is the Islam of our times. Between it and Europe France can yet again cut the chasm; she will save herself, and she will be rewarded by the peoples and by God.[201]

The Crimean War had begun in the fall of 1853 when Russia put such pressures on the Ottoman Empire that the latter was obliged to defend itself, and in so doing found no difficulty in gaining extremely powerful support. Austria "shocked the world with her ingratitude" (for Russian aid in 1849), and nearly joined the coalition that was built up against Russia. Both France and Great Britain came early to the aid of the Turks, and particularly in the case of France, the traditional Western defender of the Holy Places, the Russian pretensions with regard to the whole area were intolerable. After the war was well along, Sardinia under Cavour, seeking to enlist the aid of the powerful Western nations for the unification of Italy, also joined the coalition. The Russians were forced to sue for peace in 1855. It really was surprising that Veuillot could speak of this pro-Turkish alliance as a crusade. Veuillot, of course, was filled with dislike for Russia, a feeling intensified by his association with Donoso Cortés, and a dislike also shared by Pius IX.[202] The allies of France, however, made up a rather unsatisfactory crusade. Veuillot wrote Gustave de La Tour that he did not care for the "entente cordiale with England,"[203] and before the peace was made he came to regard Sardinia and Cavour as the most immediate of all dangers to the papacy. In the case of the Turks, he was forced to rationalize that they were simply something left over from the past and that in comparison to them schismatic Russia was the greater danger to Catholicism and the enemy against which Western Europe would have to move. At best his logic in the matter of the Crimean War left something to be desired.

L'Univers was not as full of editorializing on the war as one might have expected, but the articles that Louis Veuillot wrote were passionate. His two articles contrasting Napoleon III and Nicholas I in early March were dramatic in the extreme. "Posterity will thank the Emperor Napoleon III for having seen the dangers with which Russia threatens Latin civilization." Humanity owed him the further debt of forestalling revolution at the same time.[204] Nicholas I, on the other hand, the persecutor of forty million Catholics, who was threatening the tomb of Jesus Christ, had evoked a true crusade that would not only check schismatic Russia but also perhaps break Islam in the process. Veuillot branded him "the persecutor of the Church."[205] The desultory operations of 1854, which had produced such discouraging battles as Balaklava and the Charge of the Light Brigade, finally saw the French and the English break the defenses of Sebastopol under the able defender Todleben, to the exultation of Veuillot. He saw the will of God being carried out against the emperor who had exiled innocent people, including Catholic priests, to Siberia, and he also saw the rising star of Napoleon III in this victory.[206] Veuillot saw the hand of God again in the death of Nicholas in March 1855, relating this development to the other good things that were bound to happen. after the proclamation of the Immaculate Conception of Mary which had been made the preceding year.[207] Veuillot hoped that the fall of Sebastopol would end the war immediately, but Alexander II continued the struggle until the fall of 1855. The brother of L. Rupert of *L'Univers* had died as a chaplain with the French army in the Crimea. Veuillot glorified General Canrobert, and the overall commander at the end of the war, Pélissier,[208] as he had already glorified Saint-Arnaud, and he rejoiced over the return of the Garde Impériale at the end of the year with a triumphal re-entry into Paris. He hated the point of depature of this parade, the Place de la Bastille, but nevertheless he made the whole thing symbolic of a Christian victory for which everyone was indebted to Napoleon III.[209]

Perhaps the reason that there were not more editorials of this sort was explained in the appearance of one of his most exciting books, *La Guerre et l'Homme de Guerre*, in late 1854. Probably few pieces of literature have been more explicitly written for the purpose of supporting a given policy of a given government, and few have been more satisfactory to the régime supported. He traced the development of warfare in the whole of human history in very short order, but showed surprising knowledge in his abridgement. The title of his second chapter, "La Guerre est un Phénomène divin," tied in well with his crusading theme for describing the Crimean War. Perhaps most striking to Napoleon III must have been his sketch of the mission of Napoleon I, whose costly campaigns he completely justified. He dramatized Judith and the Maccabees, and plunged ahead through centuries and civilizations in very few pages to the Christian warrior of the West, and preeminently of France. The last chapter dealt with the priest and the soldier in such a way as to make clear the close alliance of the two. Napoleon III was still protector of the church, and Veuillot dramatically buttressed his support of the régime by this theme.[210] Small wonder that he was much in favor at this period in the Tuileries.

At the very time he was engaged in writing this glorification of the warrior, at least the sort of warrior Napoleon III might be sending against Nicholas, he was also finishing another book that grew from the afterglow of the Revolution. Monsieur Dupin, a high functionary in the July Monarchy who had maintained his position and prestige through the events of the succeeding years, had given a paper at the Academy of Moral and Political Sciences which cast calumny on the Old Régime by resorting to the questionable charge that the Old Régime had tolerated a supposed "law" known as *droit de seigneur*.[211] Stories that immoral lords had taken advantage of peasant girls, particularly brides, had somehow been crystalized into the belief that they had done so under sanction of a "law." A certain M. Bouthors of Amiens had written a refutation of the existence of any such "law," and this piece was the occasion for the discourse of M. Dupin.[212] Veuillot was quick to turn himself to writing an answer for this charge against the old order. His *Droit de seigneur au moyen âge,* however, was one of Veuillot's most carefully documented studies. Despite the other preoccupations of the period, he took all pains to muster as much evidence as he could to refute Dupin. Veuillot drew heavily on the Abbé Rohrbacher's multi-volume work, *L'Histoire de l'église,* Charles Guérard's *Condition des personnes et des terres au moyen âge,* the Bible, Bossuet, and a variety of other sources. He quoted Ozanam to support his own thesis, and referred to this man, whom he had often criticized, as a "great Christian, great scholar, and great writer."[213] This praise is an example of Veuillot's generosity toward former opponents if they chanced to be on his side of a current issue. Michelet's *Origines du Droit français* he also used extensively to his own purposes and without any of the same generosity toward the author. In addition to Veuillot's own efforts, which were certainly scholarly albeit undertaken with the sole purpose of sustaining his refutation of Dupin, he had the aid of his brother-in-law, Arthur Murcier, younger brother of the deceased

Mathilde, who found much of the material for him. Veuillot's relations with "Mon-Carthur," as he often called him, were very close. A year after they had finished *Droit de Seigneur au Moyen Age* Louis said to Élise in a letter about other matters that when he wrote *je* she should read *nous* (Louis and Arthur).[214] Arthur, who was later to marry the niece of the Abbé Gaume whom Louis had defended so ardently, attended the École des Chartes in Paris, which was under the direction of Guérard. Arthur graduated from school at the same time *Droit de Seigneur* was finished, and Veuillot sounded like a proud but confident father in expressing his desire to hear the results of the young man's examination.[215] It would be impossible to say just how much Arthur contributed to Louis's ammunition. Veuillot had drawn heavily from a work written in 1807 by Louis de Sainte-Marie for his *La Guerre et l'Homme de Guerre*, so much so that Eugene acknowledged the influence later,[216] but Veuillot in the introduction to *Droit de Seigneur* spoke of the aid of his "relative and friend" Arthur.[217]

The book was finished in relatively few months, despite the extensive citation of sources, and on 16 July 1854 Louis wrote *fin*. Together with "Mon-Carthur" he went to Notre Dame-des-Victoires, as was his wont on such occasions, and lit "un beau cierge de vingt sous." He wanted to dedicate the work to some nobleman, but was refused by the Comte de Berry, who did not want to be "compromised" by it.[218] He had already sounded out the Comtesse de Montsaulnin about her husband, and evidently had been discouraged in this regard.[219] But although he had trouble in getting anyone to accept the honor of the dedication of the work it was both a financial and a disputative success. He felt that he had been fighting the good fight for the church. "Thanks be to God," he wrote to a curé late in the year, "*Droit de Seigneur* has been a great success, and I do not believe our adversaries will return to the subject, although M. Dupin and some others are always saying they will answer. Completely to discourage them in this respect, I am preparing a second edition, buttressed with a great number of ancient and modern authorities which will show still more clearly what the Middle Ages were with regard to liberty, civilization, and morals."[220] He had also been busy at the same time with a work of piety, *La Vie de la Bienheureuse Germaine Cousin*, which was widely read and admired by thousands of the faithful, but ignored by intellectual and political circles.[221] *Droit de Seigneur*, however, certainly was not ignored, and Veuillot had the last word in this debate for quite some time.

At about the time when the doctrine of the Immaculate Conception of the Virgin Mary was proclaimed, an event which gave great satisfaction to Veuillot,[222] an election took place that was greatly to his displeasure. The classical scholar Tissot, also a man of the Revolution, had died, and Msgr. Dupanloup was elected to fill his place in the Academy, to Veuillot's great disgust. Had Veuillot ever been elected to the Academy, he would very likely have refused the election, but it is amazing how closely he followed the proceedings of the Academy and the elections to it, an interest which no doubt demonstrates the importance that was attached to these elections.[223] This election gave him an opportunity to open the old question of the study of the classics and to associate his enemy Dupanloup with the old revolutionary Tissot, for they were in harmony at least with regard to Virgil. It gave him the occasion to quote Bossuet against the literary circle of Molière. It gave him a chance to talk about the classical style of French writers, as opposed to the ancients, and to deplore the century that had seen the passing of Bossuet and the coronation of Voltaire.[224] Whatever contempt Veuillot may have had for the Academy, it certainly irritated him to see this public mark of literary distinction accorded late in 1854 to the bishop who would like to have brought him down.

During 1854-1855 Veuillot continued to be attacked as usual by various shades of the press, but the moderate Catholic press proved the chief source of distress to him. Montalembert was patron of *L'Ami de la Religion* at the time when that sheet and *L'Univers* differed over the attitude French Catholics ought to adopt with regard to the Catholic reawakening in England.[225] *L'Univers* was assertive of the rights of Wiseman, Archbishop of Westminister, who was being sued by certain clergymen in England under his supposed jurisdiction. *L'Ami de la Religion* advocated a policy of gentleness towards adversaries, which, although certainly Christain in general tenor, did not fit the purposes of *L'Univers.*[226] *L'Ami*, however, was read by so very few people that it did not appear to Montalembert to be a vehicle potentially capable of battling with Louis Veuillot. Late in 1855 Montalembert conceived of the idea of revitalizing *Le Correspondant*, mostly by giving it new leadership. Charles Lenormant had been a professor of history at the Sorbonne at the time when Michelet and Quinet were suspended in 1846. Radical students in revenge had forced him out, and he had become editor of *Le Correspondant* then dominated by Dupanloup. Despite the way in which he had gotten into journalism, Lenormant was not a writer who could match editorials with Veuillot, and Montalembert moved to impose new leadership in 1855.[227] Thereafter *Le Correspondant* became a source of trouble for Veuillot. Broglie, Augustin Cochin, Foisset, and Gratry were its editors when it came out under the new impetus on 25 October 1855. *L'Univers* was soon complaining of it. Lacordaire wrote to Montalembert that he was not surprised at the opposition of *L'Univers* – which was calling for the moderation of *Le Correspondant*![228] But Lacordaire's judgment was not always good. Over a year earlier he had written Montalembert that he had heard from a Jesuit priest in Rome who said that eyes in Rome were being opened to the danger that *L'Univers* and "its so-called ultramontanism" were coming to pose for the papacy.[229] There was little astuteness in this observation, although it contained a measure of truth. Some of Veuillot's staunchest supporters detected a desire on the part of the pope for some moderation. Msgr. Depéry, the Bishop of Gap, wrote Veuillot in June of 1854 that his clergy were devoted to *L'Univers*. He praised Veuillot for his devotion to orthodoxy and his courage in combatting doctrines he felt had to be crushed. However, he said that during his visit to Rome many bishops, including friends of Veuillot, had asked him to speak to the pope about intervening against the kind of pressures that were being brought to bear on the Gallicans. According to Depéry the pope said that France ought to be careful about *furia franchese*, which, of course, meant the fury of the campaign of *L'Univers*.

Veuillot deplored the unfriendly things he presumed Montalembert was saying about him,[230] while Montalembert lamented the damage Veuillot and his disciples were doing.[231] Writing to Lacordaire early in 1855 Montalembert spoke of what he considered to be the sinister influence of *L'Univers*. He spoke of the liberty and virility of some peoples "in contrast with this fanatical and servile spirit which transforms men into executioners or eunuchs, and which is tending to be reborn in France after having reduced Spain and Italy into the state that one knows. His main point was: "This spirit has its principal base in *L'Univers*. It has just produced a significant manifestation in a book entitled *La Guerre et l'Homme de Guerre*, and especially in the chapter, "Prêtre et Soldat." However, he complained, "the clergy has remained deaf to my voice because of *L'Univers*." Despite the defection of some of the laity, Montalembert believed, the clergy remained faithful to Veuillot – and, for the most part, he certainly was right about the lower clergy. He quoted the venerable curé of Notre Dame-des-Victoires, who told him: "When one attacks *L'Univers*, one attacks the pope, who has decided in favor of him against his adversaries."[232] Later in the year, Montalembert wrote Lacordaire, "We have the very same enemies, Louis Napoleon and Louis Veuillot, who personify political despotism and religious fanaticism."[233] Thus spoke the former head of the Catholic party about the editor from whom many of the clergy were taking their cues for sermons.

Veuillot resented the new *Le Correspondant* because he felt it would divide Catholics further,[234] which of course it did, particularly on occasions when *L'Univers* became embroiled with the secular press about religious matters. Even before the revitalizing of *Le Correspondant* Veuillot had spoken of the "allies of *Le Siècle*" among the religious press, aiming his guns primarily at the Abbé Cognat of *L'Ami de la Religion.* One of the key issues in the polemics between *L'Univers* and *Le Siècle* was the matter of latter-day miracles. Just how an intelligent person accepts, rationalizes with regard to, or thinks and feels about spiritual manifestations in the physical world is elusive in any case, and certainly was so in the case of Louis Veuillot. Cruel jokes had been made about Veuillot's faith.[235] It can indeed be said that Veuillot wanted to believe whatever the Catholic church believed and that he truly hated those who ridiculed faith in any accepted beliefs of the church. Much of the furor over miracles in 1855 revolved around a vision seen by two children at Salette. The attack on the validity of this episode by Pierre Clément-Eugène Pelletan, editor of *Le Siècle,* and the support given him by the writer he had once admired, Jules Janin, occasioned an immediate counterattack by Veuillot in *L'Univers*, which he broadened to include *L'Ami de la Religion* because of its indulgent attitude towards the secular press.[236] The matter deeply troubled Veuillot. He would not cease his argumentation, and would certainly not let the other camp get in the last word. Particularly during the month of May he wrote a series of articles on mystical matters in which he went to great effort to cite the leading medieval scholastics and the pronouncements of numerous popes in defense of his stand about belief in latter day miracles.[237] In the course of his polemic he paused to deplore Guizot, who despite his "grand esprit " had he felt contributed to the frame of mind he was attacking.[238] On Veuillot's tomb the words "J'ai cru, je vois" are aptly carved; the warmth of his argumentation in this debate demonstrates how much he wanted to accept the miracles.

Veuillot's troubles with *Le Siècle* broadened, and as they did the regime of Napoleon III began to lean towards *Le Siècle.* During the course of the year *Le Siècle* participated in the glorification of the poet Béranger, who was still alive. Beranger had been imprisoned as a revolutionary more than once in the days of the restoration, but he had also been a glorifier of Napoleon. It was therefore very acceptable to the bureau of the press and to Napoleon III himself that this extolling of Béranger take place. *Le Siècle,* which Eugène characterized, as "part Napoleonic, part republican, and completely impious,"[239] was part of the chorus which Veuillot attacked.[240] He picked apart the skill of

Béranger as a poet as well as the things he personified. "In four verses the poet (Béranger) simultaneously outrages decency, age, love and death," Veuillot maintained. "Ah," he declared addressing Jourdan of *Le Siècle,* "you are right to cherish him; he's your man!"[241]

As *Le Siècle* and other journals quarreled more and more actively with *L'Univers* over these and other subjects where religion and secular impiety came into conflict, the régime became anxious to calm things down, since it derived support from both quarters. It has been estimated that anticlerical journals in 1855 had 90,000 subscribers, while the Catholic press had only about 30,000.[242] Evaluating the press in this way is difficult, however, since some journals did not neatly fit into the pattern. *Journal des Débats,* for example, was supposedly Christian, but Eugène considered that M. de Sacy, its editor, "gave full license to Voltairean collaborators."[243] *La Presse* and *Le Siècle,* the leaders of the secular press, had plenty of imitators, but whereas *L'Univers* had provincial echoes, *Correspondant* and *Ami de la Religion* often took the side of the secular journals when they engaged in polemics with *L'Univers.* Within the limits tolerated by the régime, sharp dueling occurred among all these journals, and Napoleon's bureau of the press had reason to be distressed and to try to calm down the inflammatory columns, for they were capable of causing great divisions in the Second Empire even without any direct attack on governmental policy.

The bureau of the press was under the Director-General of the Sûreté-Générale. In mid-1855 the Director, M. Collet-Meygret took steps to quiet the warring parties without using the cruder devices of the direct warning or the suspension. Veuillot poured out his heart to Gustave de La Tour. "Eh bien, the minister of the interior takes the side of *Le Siècle* against us; at least he invites us in a very urgent way to be quiet, and we have reason to doubt that the same injunction has been made to *Le Siècle.*" He had the impression that the defense of Béranger by his rival might have had something to do with this one-sided pressure.[244] He complained increasingly of unequal pressures by the régime. Writing to a priest just ten days later he declared: "It appears clear to me that the government, if not the emperor, inclines to the left." He felt *Le Siècle* enjoyed a protection that the Catholic papers no longer had. "These papers are warned for the smallest things against the governments – of Sardinia and Spain – while *Le Siècle* can say what it likes against the pope." Particularly was Veuillot uneasy about the rising influence of Prince Napoleon (Jerome) at this period.[245] Whatever Napoleon III's private attitude toward the church may have been, he was very discreet in his public utterances, but his cousin, Prince Napoleon, was famous for his anticlericalism. He later became an embarrassment to the emperor, but at this period he was being used in various important capacities, and his anticlericalism may well have had some influence as Veuillot believed. The situation did not however signal any actual deterioration in the relations of *L'Univers* with the government. The régime was more neutral than Veuillot felt, and it tried to calm both sides. It would not be until Napoleon began to abandon the pope, much later on, that the good relationship would come to an end.

Louis Veuillot has frequently been called a "bigot." Amusingly, the *régisseur des annonces* for *L'Univers* in those days was a M. Bigot, of 8, place de la Bourse. Also, as militancy of the journal rose at this time, advertisements of Eugène's books on the religious aspects of war were conspicuous. The business side of *L'Univers* was in harmony with the rest!

Louis Veuillot lived and worked with an intensity that called for rest on occasion. If nothing else tired, his eyes which suffered from inadequate lacrymal supply gave trouble. In his letters very incidental references to this situation are frequent. For example, in writing about fears of paganism which troubled the wife of the Préfet of Besançon, he explains that he ran into her at the oculist.[246] On other occasions he explains that sister Élise, is writing because of his eyes.[247] In addition to his problems with his eyes he needed vacations from the intense activity in which he immersed himself. He had many friends, like the Comte and Comtesse de Montsaulnin for instance, who invited him to distant parts of France for vacations. In 1854 he accepted the hospitality of Gustave de La Tour to come to Brittany, where he was fêted both at Tréguier, the home of La Tour, and in other places.[248] Early in 1855 he went on a rather extensive trip that carried him to Poitiers and Limoges, during the course of which he had occasion to visit the town where he had risen to fame in journalism and letters, Périgueux. This visit had some sentimental pleasure for him, though he was shocked at some of the changes. He hastened to tell his brother that the first person he visited was the bishop, Msgr. Georges Massonnais,[249] a gesture consistent with his devotion to the church despite his own troubles with bishops. He seemed the most satisfied with seeing old friends, some of whom had changed less than the town itself, but he found that it was as narrow in outlook as ever. He was gratified, however, that he was by now forgiven by those who had felt that he made caricatures of them in *Pierre Saintive*, the novel he had written in 1840. He wrote a description of the town to Madame Testas, a native of Périgueux whose family he had known there, and with whom he kept up a close correspondence much of his life. "Périgueux is no longer mine nor yours. . . .," he reported.

"Nothing is as we have known it. It is much nicer looking and much less charming. The streets are lighted with gas, and the shoeshine boys speak French; there are houses and statues where we used to see gardens, and the little girls have become mothers of big boys. Your house is a café. One enters by what was the window, and where you used to sew one sees the face of a drinker smoking. Do not ever come here; it is too sad."[250] So spoke Louis Veuillot, who true to his own advice never returned to his native home in Boynes.

In the summer of 1855 Louis Veuillot made plans to visit his friend Théodore de Bussierre[251] at his large and beautiful château at Reichshoffen in Alsace. He sent Élise ahead with all the children, and anticipating a happy reunion soon on vacation, he wrote the usual letters about the children's doings, lessons, singing, and so on. Practically at the same time that he expressed a wish, in a letter to Élise, that God spare the children's health, he received word that his eldest daughter, Marie, then nine years old, had died from diphtheria on 18 June 1855. He hastened to Reichshoffen where he found that the youngest, Madeleine, was also stricken by the same disease. He remained there with her, sending Eugène, who had also come, back to the Murcier grandparents in Versailles with the other three, hoping that they might be spared the infection. Hardly did Eugène get there, however, than six year old Gertrude became ill. Hearing of her condition Louis hastened to Versailles. When he left Reichshoffen he thought that Madeleine was recovering.[252] "Madeleine is better and even completely well, after having had a very bad night," the harassed father wrote to his brother on 24 June.[253] She had been dosed with calomel, which appeared to have brought results, but unfortunately they were illusory. At this point he heard of the turn Gertrude had taken and dashed off for Versailles. Gertrude died before his arrival. And then Madeleine's condition changed after several days, though as late as 1 July he wrote as though he still believed she had been spared.[254] Such was not to be the case however. She was brought back from Alsace apparently well but worsened again and died on 2 August. The whole experience must have been terrible for Veuillot. His letters reflect great anguish. He never departs from the pattern of the thorough Catholic, and describes what he had been told about how Gertrude had held a crucifix at her death, kissing it many times, making the sign of the cross while taking the most repugnant medicines.[255] In writing thus to the Comtesse de Ségur and Élise, Veuillot could hardly have been guilty of conscious exaggeration, but one may wonder whether some signs of piety, natural enough on the part of the desperately sick child, had not made an undue impression on an overwrought father who was looking for such signs, because in his account he made her seem like a dying saint. The formal announcement of the deaths of his three daughters which he sent out on 4 August was a pathetic one indeed, and brought many expressions of sympathy from friends and supporters.[256]

He went back to Brittany to recover peace of mind, staying part of the time with La Tour. While in Brittany he wrote one of his better poems, appropriately entitled *Le Cyprès.* The last stanza went like this:

> Mes pas suivent encor le char qui les emporte;
> Dans la fosse mon cœur tombe encor par lambeaux:
> Et comme les cyprès plantés sur les tombeaux,
> Ma douleur chaque jour croît et devient plus forte.
> J'ai vu le Champ romain, de ruines couvert,
> Poussière de splendeur sans retour écroulée;
> Rien ne vit dans la plaine a jamais désolée;
> Le cyprès seul est toujours vert.[257]

Louis Veuillot did not hide his grief, or much of anything else, for he was a thorough-going publicist, but there was undeniably the deepest grief in the heart of this man who had now lost four of his children and his wife. Only Agnès and Luce were left. His religious faith had been severely tested, and he stood up very well. There is no doubt his underlying zeal for the battle buoyed him. He must have felt a calling in his work, for a never-flagging ardor kept him going even after so much sadness. However, within a short time, the halcyon days with the Second Empire were to be over, and personal attacks on him and *L'Univers* were to strike anew and in a grievous way. Although he had been already tested, some of his worst trials still lay ahead.

CHAPTER VI

POPE AND EMPEROR

The brilliant international exposition of 1855 was kept open in the spring of 1856 as the peace concluding the Crimean War was about to be signed in Paris, already in the throes of rebuilding and beautification. The emperor was at the zenith of his reign, France was clearly the grand power of the continent, and Paris the fulcrum of diplomatic dealing. What a time to enjoy the favor of Napoleon III! Such a time Louis Veuillot chose to break from him.

Camillo Benso, Count of Cavour, to the chagrin of some of the more short-sighted of his fellow Sardinians, had arranged that Sardinia would join France and Great Britain in fighting for the Turks against the Russians. Thousands of Piedmontese soldiers had been sent to fight in the Crimea, a move which must have seemed at the time like madness in Turin. They participated successfully at the Battle of Traktir. However, this latter-day Machiavellian statesman, who frankly admitted that if he did for himself what he would do for his country he would be a rascal, was looking forward to rewards from France and Great Britain in a most calculating way.[1] He was not long in beginning to seek repayment of his favors, and during the next several years ensnared Napoleon III into supporting his Italian policy. It was this development which brought the complete hostility of Veuillot towards the Second Empire.

On 8 April 1856 Cavour arranged a session of the Congress of Paris which gave its attention to the situation of Italy. Consistently with his masterful ways, he managed to get Comte Walewski, natural son of Napoleon I and the Comtesse Walewska, and now serving as foreign minister of France, to introduce the matter. Louis Veuillot was alarmed.[2] Supposedly the discussion was to center on matters that could in the future endanger the general peace. For these problems the powers were to consider what principles would be useful in forestalling potential troubles. Walewski, who himself might be classified on the clerical side, started the discussions by introducing the situations of Greece, the occupation of the Papal States, troubles within the Kingdom of the Two Sicilies, and revolutionary propaganda emanating from the Belgian press. He did not mean to open the Pandora's box of Italian nationalism to the extent that transpired. His attention to the Belgian press was, of course, something that pleased Veuillot and French Catholics in general. But in mentioning the Papal States and the Kingdom of the Two Sicilies he paved the way for Lord Clarendon, British foreign minister and plenipotentiary to the congress, to attack the government of the pope. As Veuillot concluded, "Lord Clarendon proposes to dethrone the pope." His lordship did not use those words, but the separate lay regime he did propose amounted to the same thing. "It is all too natural that an English minister speaks thus," said Veuillot in an editorial dated 2 May 1856 when the protocol of the session had been released. "It is the usual language of England, revolutionary and protestant at the same time; it is the fatal role this power ceaselessly plays in Italy." According to Veuillot the papal régime had been secularized as much as it could safely be, and as for the brigandage that plagued the Papal States, there was more of this curse in the city of London alone than in all of the papal realm.[3]

Clarendon's attack on the Papal States, Veuillot felt, was particularly dangerous, since in his opinion revolution there would mean revolution everywhere, and to this situation he closely associated the Kingdom of the Two Sicilies. Not often was Veuillot a defender of the Prussians, but in this debate Baron Manteuffel, plenipotentiary of Prussia and a traditionalist (who later became a Catholic and retired from the Prussian service), won his praise for his warning to the congress with regard to the revolutionary dangers that could result from meddling in the affairs of the Neapolitan kingdom. Veuillot ended an editorial with a warning to the emperor that Europe could save itself from revolution, and that the defeat of Russia had shown that it had the power to do so without Russia. The situation of France was now splendid, and the greatest promise for the future could be seen.[4] With some delicacy Veuillot told the emperor that he would be throwing away the fruits of victory if he now espoused Italian nationalism and abandoned the pope. The emperor's attention was brought to the article, and, through General Cotte, Veuillot was informed that he was displeased. In the opinion of Eugène Veuillot the "truly conservative and almost Catholic phase of the Second Empire reached its end."[5] Veuillot's rupture with the emperor came slowly and not without attempts on the part of Napoleon to woo him back. The Empress Eugénie in due course bid well to do this very thing. But the new French policy of supporting the national aspirations of Cavour and Sardinia rendered any reconciliation impossible. Veuillot's troubles with the régime began in earnest in May of 1856.

Drifting into disfavor with the emperor was a serious development for Veuillot, but he had other troubles in 1856. Of course he continued to exchange barbs with the secular press and to criticize the liberal Catholics, but in addition he was the object of attack by three different tracts which appeared in order of increasing seriousness and weight. First a lightweight and weak-charactered popular biographer wrote a patently-false and scurrilous sketch of his life that was serialized in the *Moniteur du Loiret*, possibly with the awareness of Dupanloup at some point in the affair. Then Falloux wrote his *Le Parti catholique, ce qu'il a été, ce qu'il est devenu*, which attacked Louis Veuillot quite craftily and blamed him for the break-up of the Catholic party because of his support of Bonapartist authoritarianism. Then appeared a tract, *L'Univers jugé par lui-même,* signed by an obscure priest, but almost certainly inspired by Dupanloup himself. The third of these attacks became very complicated and nearly involved a suit by Veuillot in the court of law.

On his return from Switzerland in 1838 Louis Veuillot had met an aspiring author named Eugène Jacquot who had tried to press himself on Veuillot. Not liking him, Veuillot had avoided him. Eighteen years later the man had his revenge. He had become a writer of short, popular biographies, and he ground out one about the now well-known editor of *L'Univers.* He knew nothing really of Veuillot's life, but living in the general area where Veuillot had grown up he patched together something for public sale that thoroughly maligned him and included slurs on Veuillot's mother, who, it will be remembered, had long operated a tavern that catered to the bargemen who brought their wine to Bercy. This trashy author for some reason called himself Mirecourt, the name of the town where he had been born. Veuillot must have gotten his hands on a copy of the sketch as soon as it appeared, because even in January of 1856 he wrote jokingly about it to his friend Segrétain: "Try to get a copy of the biography of Louis Veuillot for yourself. What an abominable man! I mean Louis Veuillot."[6]

When Léon Lavedan, a rising journalist who later was to become editor of *Le Figaro*, began to serialize this biography in the pages of the *Moniteur du Loiret*, Louis Veuillot became angry. No doubt he disliked being held up to ridicule and scorn before the people with whom he had lived a happy, though different, phase of his life. However, what most roused his anger was the intervention of Bishop Dupanloup in the affair. Dupanloup intervened perhaps because he feared he might be thought to be behind the whole thing.[7] Late in life Veuillot wrote that perhaps the so-called warning Dupanloup sent to the editor of the *Moniteur du Loiret*, a journal which was always in the camp of the Bishop of Orleans, had been prepared by an inexperienced secretary, but nonetheless he still believed that the whole episode reflected badly on the prelate.[8] What the note said was that whatever the *wrongs* Veuillot might have done, for reasons of *charity* he was asking Lavedan to cease the publication of Mirecourt's (Jacquot's) biography. These words inflamed Veuillot, who thereupon lost sight of all humor. He immediately wrote a protest to Lavedan, which he insisted be inserted in the *Moniteur.* The very way Lavedan had accepted the bishop's plea for *charity* added fuel to the fire, and in his protest Veuillot blasted away at Lavedan, primarily expressing his anger over being accused of having been subsidized by Louis Philippe up to 1848 and by "grandes dames du faubourg Saint-Germain" thereafter. He suggested that Lavedan did not understand the word *condottiere*, but in any case justly protested against this libel. Of course, he had received a subvention from Guizot in the early 'forties, but certainly not up to 1848. He was also favored in various ways by respected ladies like the Comtesse de Monsaulnin, but he was not "subventioned."[9]

Veuillot's strong words in the letter were addressed to Lavedan, but his jibes were really intended for the benefit of Dupanloup, who, he felt certain, had originally approved the piece. Most of what he said was by careful and indirect implication. But speaking of the slurs on his mother, he pointed out that she, like her husband, had worked hard to raise four children who were not ashamed of her or her name. "Know and publish, to expiate the injury you give, that in her humble condition this valiant woman was able to teach her children love of justice and courage in poverty."[10] Veuillot was doing more than defend his own mother. He was by inference attacking Dupanloup, the illegitimate son of a woman who did not raise him and whose name he did not bear. Everyone in the Loiret must have known this fact, and the sharpness of the dig must have been widely noticed, but especially by Dupanloup.

The serial was stopped, and later on Mirecourt (Jacquot) apologized, and even dropped this item from his collection of writings. Eugène Veuillot says that from 1866 to 1876 Jacquot wrote Veuillot ten letters, and, a fact which was of importance to the editor of *L'Univers*, he dropped out of the circle that supported Dupanloup. The affair probably worked in favor of Veuillot in that important Bonapartist officials in the area of Orleans, including Vicomte Louis de Loverdo and court councillor Leroux, reacted against Lavedan and let *L'Univers* know of their support.[11] Msgr. Angebault, Bishop of Angers, who claimed to remain "outside of the debates of the press," volunteered his sympathy to Veuillot for the way in which he had been attacked,[12] and Msgr. Thibault, Bishop of Montpellier, was among other prelates who expressed their support.[13]

Louis Veuillot was hardly thrown from his stride by the

Jacquot-Mirecourt biography, though such a brush would have loomed much larger to a person not accustomed to public exposure. However, hardly was this matter simmering down than the next damaging publication appeared, *Le Parti catholique, ce qu'il a été, ce qu'il est devenu*, presumably a study of the Catholic party by no less an authority than the Comte de Falloux, but also an attack on Louis Veuillot and *L'Univers*. It appeared first in the columns of *Le Correspondant*, and therefore with the blessings of Montalembert and his circle, and then as a separate little book. To an uninitiated and simple-minded person the piece would seem relatively unobnoxious, and so it had to seem in order not to be suppressed by the régime. In fact, however, Falloux was trying to demonstrate that the break among the politically active Catholics was all the fault of Louis Veuillot and *L'Univers*. He claimed that Veuillot had rallied to the emperor for self-serving reasons, and that he had helped deal freedom a great blow by his stand. The brochure was written very craftily from the point of view of words chosen, for example, *Impérieuse alliance*, to describe Veuillot's support of the Empire, but was very vulnerable to attack from the point of view of accuracy, since it was an assault by insinuation. Veuillot, upon first seeing the thing, confessed to the Comtesse de Ségur, that he thought it *effroyable*.[14] A response to this was not so simple to formulate as a response to Jacquot. Falloux was a big man, and he had used his pen cleverly. Veuillot could not simply overwhelm him, as he had Jacquot. He would have to match him with a carefully written answer. Between June 19 and July 2 he wrote six long articles, each of which filled a page. These were then put together and published shortly as a separate small volume, together with certain letters of prelates that particularly supported his counterthesis.[15] He entitled this work *Histoire du Parti catholique*, as if to say, in contrast to the tricky title of the brochure of Falloux, that this work was the straight story. Neither writer, of course, was really interested in history for its own sake; both were only using historical background to support their own present positions. Falloux was trying to appeal to parliamentarian sentiments in blaming Veuillot for the existence of the Second Empire, and Veuillot was blaming parliamentarians for playing games with the world position of the Catholic church. However, Veuillot brought in many more angles in this exposition, and he showed the selfishness of his enemies over quite some years. Soon he saw with resentment the intrusion of Henri de Riancey, his former collaborator, now editor of *L'Union*. Montalembert's description of *L'Univers* and Veuillot's role as leader of *une école fanatique et servile* had been taken up by Riancey, and Veuillot countered his accusation by publishing a long letter of

Msgr. Parisis, dated 2 August 1856, which cited the stand of the pope in favor of Veuillot.[16] Since Veuillot was not yet writing in any way that the government would resent, he had an advantage. He certainly may be said to have won the debate. He was not writing for anyone but Catholics, which was not the case with Falloux, and it appeared in this era that *L'Univers* and Veuillot were still gaining strength. The directness and the fullness of Veuillot's answer themselves were enough for the verdict of most Catholic readers to be given to him. It had taken two to make the quarrel, and the liberals had broken with Veuillot as much as he had broken with them. The very points with which Veuillot began his answer to Falloux were decisive: "As a witness his memory fails, as a historian he produces no documents, as a writer he masters neither his style nor his ideas."[17] Eugène conceded that Falloux's brochure was a success in the salons and in the liberal and Gallican press, but claimed, though he may have overstated the matter, that Falloux was discredited elsewhere.[18] Louis Veuillot had come out well from a second battle.

By the time Veuillot had put his best efforts forward to combat Falloux, he found that he not only could not rest on his laurels but on the contrary was faced by the most serious challenge yet, in a situation where he was going to have to face his most implacable enemy within the Catholic church – Dupanloup. Veuillot, together with his two daughters and his sisters had gone to the château of the comtesse de Ségur at Nouettes for a few days vacation during which he intended to check proof for his answer to Falloux. Here he heard toward the end of July 1856 of a 201-page book put out by Dentu, *L'Univers jugé par lui-même, ou Études et Documents sur le journal L'Univers, de 1845 a 1855.* Eugène wrote him on 22 July further details about the matter, and painted a desperate picture for his vacationing brother. He told him that Msgr. Parisis and their friend Bonnetty, editor of *Annales Catholiques*, had given him information showing that the book was *un produit-orleano-parisien* – the work of Dupanloup with the connivance of Sibour. The haste with which *L'Ami de la Religion* announced this collection of texts from *L'Univers* which, with the accompanying commentary, would purport to show that *L'Univers* was inconsistent and opportunistic, proved, according to Eugène, the complicity of Dupanloup. He further claimed that it was being distributed from a property that belong to Sibour. Quoting Bonnetty, Eugène claimed that the bulk of the material had been ready to come out in 1853, but that because of the encyclical of that year and the victory Veuillot apparently had won, his enemies had not dared to publish at that time this indictment of the editorial stands of *L'Univers*. Now, however, with the assault of Falloux paving the way, they dared to bring the stuff out of the drawer into which it had been put in 1853 and to act as a "rear-guard" for Falloux. The book had several collaborators, who were unnamed, but from the great similarity of its language to that of an *avertissement* of Dupanloup which had been prepared in 1853, suppressed at the time of the encyclical, but of which a copy had fallen into the hands of *L'Univers*, Dupanloup was regarded as the real author of the libelous book.[19] That a bishop should have been even the inspiration of such a project is the notorious part of this episode, for *L'Univers jugé par lui-même* was a very dishonest book. Early in it was the completely false statement: "C'est toujours le meme esprit, l'esprit revolutionnaire."[20] It maintained that *L'Univers* stimulated revolution in Austria and Russia,[21] and quoted it as saying that "democracy is the very daughter of the church."[22] The book was made up of seven chapters, the bulk of which were devoted to establishing the revolutionary nature of *L'Univers*. After the coup d'etat, according to this book, *L'Univers* became demagogic, and therefore it had over the years the greatest of contradictions in its positions. The book was too extreme to have any credibility, and Veuillot might have treated it with even less seriousness than the biography of Jacquot – except for his belief in the episcopal origin of the volume. It was an extreme example of lifting bits out of context, and even lifting quotations from other quotations and from other journals quoted in *L'Univers*. Among other things it used capitals and italics where the originals had had none, but quoting the enemies of *L'Univers* from the very columns of the journal was among the worst of the abuses. Eugène tried to trace down certain quotations, and could not even find them.[23] All these purported quotations, now in false contexts, were strung together by scurrilous writing, much of which was strikingly similar to the *avertissement* of 1853. As he perused the material this similarity struck Louis Veuillot, who found some very considerable chunks almost identical.[24] Of course, an underling could have been using this already well-known attack on Veuillot, but in that case at least the inspiration of the book seemed to be identified. Convinced of this fact, Veuillot felt the powerful bishop was after him in an underhanded way. He took mortal offense, with the result that one of the stormiest chapters of his life began to unfold.

When *L'Univers jugé par lui-même* appeared, Veuillot was still fuming about Falloux. In fact, he had already thought about publishing his principal articles in two or three volumes when this new attack convinced him to go ahead.[25] Not that Veuillot was not usually ready for a battle, but at this juncture he was unusually ready. His correspondence reveals him to have been especially sarcastic during 1856-1857, and both terms and names he used for people and his plays on words seem unusually inventive. For example, he saw the hand of Montalembert in his presumed persecution, and his professions of special affection for Montalembert at other times are somewhat undermined by the fact that he constantly referred to him not as Charles, but as "Charlotte," during 1856.[26] He restricted his references to Albert de Broglie to a simple disrespectful "Albert," but he lumped some of the others in a common enemy group as "Talembert, Falloutembert, Dupanloubert."[27] He spoke of *fallopinerie* and *falloupinage*;[28] he made a verb, *fallouciser*, and an adjective for Félix Dupanloup, *féliciennes.*[29] For the Abbé Sisson, who also played a role in the affair of *L'Univers jugé par lui-même,* he invented the word *désissonne.*[30] The most shocking of his word tinkerings, however, was speaking of writings emanating from Dupanloup not as being "in-jésus" (the printing term), but "in-Félix."[31] This sort of thing, even though only written to friends and relatives, was unusual, and certainly indicated his great agitation. Feeling, over *L'Univers* and the issue of being for or against it, was now running high in the public arena and was not confined to Veuillot. Many extreme things were being said in the press and elsewhere. The dean of the cathedral chapter at Dijon said that what Veuillot wrote seemed to have been composed while on the knees and that one ought also to read it this way! Veuillot's acquaintance Foisset attested to Veuillot's fanaticism in this period,[32] and the latter's willingness to go to the uttermost never was more striking. No doubt the fervent support he received from various prelates greatly strengthened his desire to fight uncompromisingly. During 1856 Louis Veuillot received at least 77 letters from ecclesiastical figures no lower than the rank of monsignor[33] – an amazing testimony to the importance of a Catholic layman.

Louis was seconded throughout his life by various able people, and he himself never ceased to acknowledge the leadership of Du Lac. But Eugene was his alter ego at the outbreak of this battle. Almost as soon as he heard of the publication of *L'Univers jugé par lui-même* he rushed to see the papal nuncio. Msgr. Sacconi had replaced Msgr. Garibaldi in 1853 and was to remain nuncio until the critical year of 1860. When he first became nuncio Msgr. Sacconi, understandably, had seemed to want to avoid taking sides in the quarrels centering around *L'Univers*, but by 1856 it was clear that he sympathized with the militant journal. He expressed disbelief that any bishop (Dupanloup) could be behind such a book as had just appeared, but, aside from this point, he indicated his clear support. Eugène did not hesitate to let the nuncio know he believed quite differently, and asked him whether he thought there might be a conspiracy of bishops trying to bring about the suppression of *L'Univers*. Msgr. Sacconi told him candidly that it was too soon after the encyclical of 1853 for such a move.[34] All considered, *L'Univers* could feel it had the backing of the representative of the pope, and therefore, of course, the pope himself. Although the initial reaction of Louis Veuillot was one of satisfaction with the nuncio, feeling, in August, that he was "completely for us," he complained in October to the Abbé Bernier in Rome about the nuncio's weakness.[35] The nuncio wanted to bring about as much conciliation with as little fuss as was possible, and any such conciliatory attitude was bound to be unsatisfactory to a man who believed he was battling for right against evil masquerading in ecclesiastical robes.

The first major public support *L'Univers* received was from the Bishop of Arras, Msgr. Parisis, who had already come so strongly to its aid during the troubles of 1853. Msgr. Parisis wrote a letter to *L'Ami de la religion* in early August, complaining of the backing that journal had given to the libelous book. He said about everything that could be said positively on behalf of *L'Univers*. He denied the accusations against it. He volunteered that if *L'Univers* were actually what the authors of the libel maintained it was, it would indeed have to be suppressed. However, he insisted, "I am not afraid to proclaim, as a profound conviction, that the suppression of *L'Univers* would be a public misfortune for religion." Parisis, unlike another prelate who supported Veuillot, Bishop Pie of Poitiers, seemed to enjoy the battles of the press. He went as far as any prince of the church had done in this period in the line of supporting the lay press. "The services rendered to the cause of religion by *L'Univers*," he said, "are those rendered everywhere by Catholic journalism, of which no one today underestimates the importance or the necessity." Having done homage to the press in general he said that *L'Univers* was the journal preferred by prelates in Italy, England, and Ireland, as well as in France. "Ask missionaries in America, the Indies, or China what journal they see, and all will answer *L'Univers*." He demanded what would replace it if it were to disappear? "When will any other Catholic sheet have gained such a position?" After thus letting the readers of *L'Ami de la religion* and others know what the situation of the Catholic press was, he turned to the ridiculous nature of the whole question. Almost everything that was alleged about the positions *L'Univers* had supposedly taken referred to articles before the encyclical of 1853. The statement of the pope was "the most glorious, gentle, and extraordinary that a journal had ever received." He feared there was a project within the church to destroy this "grand institution," and as a bishop he raised his voice in the defense of it.[36]

Following this a great debate arose about *L'Univers*, and as the secular press and part of the Catholic journals were seen to attack it, many ecclesiastics, including prelates, and others sprang to its defense. Among the first to applaud Parisis' defense of *L'Univers* was Cardinal Gousset, Archbishop of Reims, who wrote to Msgr. Parisis directly to this effect.[37] He regretted the divisions that had threatened before the encyclical of 1853, and he defended the orthodoxy of *L'Univers*. Many others also wrote to Parisis of their support, and these included Msgr. Doney, Bishop of Montauban, Msgr. de Ségur, Msgr. Nanquette, Bishop of Mans, various abbés, including Gaume, the Comte de La Tour, the Comtesse de Souchet, and the Vicomtesse de Pitray.[38] Many wrote directly to Louis Veuillot. Msgr. Jolly-Mellon, Bishop of Sens, said that an undeclared war had been undertaken against *L'Univers*. Like the Bishop of Arras he would regard the suppression of *L'Univers* as "an irreparable misfortune," because its suppression would "deprive religion of a defender full of courage, zeal, and light, and completely appropriate for the times in which we live."[39] Cardinal Bonald, Archbishop of Lyon, wrote in a similar vein, also calling *L'Univers* a defender of religion, "full of courage and zeal."[40] The Bishop of Fréjus deplored the "miserable pamphlet" which attacked *L'Univers*.[41] From all over the country important prelates indicated their backing. One of the very strongest statements came from Canada, where the Bishop of Canada-West wanted to be included among those "praising you and blessing you for all the eminent services you render to the sacred cause, of which you are, in the realm of the press, the most powerful, intelligent, and courageous defender."[42] An impressive list of *L'Univers* supporters was promptly mustered. To it were added the reassurances of Cardinal Villecourt, who wrote Veuillot twice from Rome. The cardinal told him that the princes of the church were generally in favor of him and that all the truly faithful were indebted to him "for the constant, indefatiguable, often heroic, zeal with which you defend the sound doctrine and divine authority of the Holy See."[43] Dom Guéranger congratulated him on winning a victory in avoiding being censured by his bishop, which could not very well happen after all the episcopal praise that he had won.[44] In short, Veuillot had won the backing of much of the church, and he was able to write Msgr. Fioramonti that a large part of the church in France embraced Roman doctrine.[45]

Louis Veuillot during his career gave much evidence of familiarity with the Bible and often quoted it in putting forward his various causes. However, notably in the Epistle of James, Christians are told in the Bible not to go into gentile courts, but to settle their troubles among themselves. Louis Veuillot overlooked, forgot, or never comprehended this prohibition. He decided the only thing to do was to take the case of *L'Univers* to court to maintain its honor. True, he did not seek damages, for which he could have made a very good case indeed. Despite the evident caution of the nuncio in the matter, Louis Veuillot believed he had his backing, at least in a general way. "The nuncio is completely for us," he wrote to Msgr. Mabille, Bishop of Saint-Claude.[46] To Msgr. Parisis he spoke in the same tone, and he looked forward to a legal victory – which he would celebrate with a pilgrimage to Notre Dame-des-Victoires as he had celebrated his victory in 1853.[47] He was still willing to let the matter be settled by other means, including particularly ecclesiastical arbitration, but he felt he had to explain to Du Lac that "at present we cannot back down without appearing to doubt our cause." He was disappointed that the nuncio would not intervene, and this nonintervention determined him to persist in his suit. And while he made the decision to press his case in the civil courts rather than to settle the matter as an internal Catholic problem, he greatly resented the criticism that Montalembert and his *Le Correspondant* directed at him.[48] Having brought the case before the state court, he had to wait for its sessions to open. Therefore his decision of August could not have fulfillment until late November, when the court recess would be over.

The person who probably had done most of the work in preparing the ill-conceived and ill-executed *L'Univers jugé par lui-même* was the Abbé Cognat. However, he was replaced as editor of the journal dominated by Dupanloup, *L'Ami de la religion*, by the Abbé Sisson, who became thereafter the special target for Veuillot. Sisson was actually a dioscesan of the Bishop of Strasbourg, but he was for the time being under Archbishop Sibour, who defended him, while Msgr. Roess of Strasbourg reprimanded him for the role he was playing.[49] As time went on he deserved the reprimand even more. Various ecclesiastics favorable to Dupanloup and Sibour stepped into the case, and late in the year it appeared that an exchange of notes, whereby the troublesome book would be dropped in exchange for the dropping of the case against those who put out *L'Univers jugé par lui-même* and for the non-publication of documents by *L'Univers* to refute the warped picture created by it, would be the solution. Somewhat carelessly Veuillot signed such an agreement, and as part of the bargain the notes were to appear simultaneously in *L'Univers* and *L'Ami de la religion*. *L'Univers* published the notes three days before they appeared in *L'Ami*, and when Sisson put in his columns he did so with an explanation that made it seem as though the shoe were on the other foot, and the suit were reversed.[50] This perversion of the truth was too much for Veuillot, and by mid-December the legal process was more alive than ever. Bitterness was deepening and spreading. One clergyman wrote Veuillot about the conspiracy against him, referring to *L'Ami* as *L'Ennemi de la religion.*[51]

The identity of the plaintiff in the case was obvious: *L'Univers* and Louis Veuillot. However, *L'Univers jugé par lui-même* was anonymous, and its author-editor was only indicated under the vague line in the preface, "plusieurs avaient du s'employer a ce travail." Who were these "plusieurs"? The Abbé Cognat, an obscure priest, stepped forward at this juncture as the sole author-editor.[52] He was no more worth all the fury than Jacquot-Mirecourt had been. The real defendants were Dupanloup for what may have been his direct inspiration, or possibly even his authorship, and Sibour, for his support and complicity. Indirectly, Montalembert and the whole group, including Broglie and Falloux, who hoped to rid French Catholicism of this extreme ultramontane force were also defendants. Some of the very same people who had criticized certain past Jesuit tactics of letting the ends justify the means were now engaging in a crude attack on their chosen enemy. *L'Univers* had not gained its enthusiastic following by the moderation of its views, and it had been politically fickle in advancing what it saw as its constant goal by supporting anyone of any party who would come to the aid of ultramontane Catholicism. It was indeed vulnerable on the charge of extremism, if that were the charge. However, violation of every rule of handling quotations in print was not a proper way in which to discredit it.

It must have been exciting to sit in the courtroom of the *sixieme chambre du tribunal correctionnel* when pleadings actually began on Christmas Eve of 1856. The simple, and presumably poor, priest, Cognat, was represented by a former minister of Louis Philippe, of Cavaignac, and of Napoleon III, Me Dufaure. *L'Univers*, the plaintiff, was represented by an unknown, Me Josseau, practically starting his career against the celebrated barrister. Dufaure ripped into his case with all the hard skill of which he was capable, and the Belgian as well as the French press covered the case extensively. Josseau did what he could in two long pleadings, but appears to have been outclassed by Dufaure. In December and January the columns of *L'Univers*, of course, were full of the case and its background. Veuillot already had done a good job of showing the dishonesty of *L'Univers jugé par lui-même* in its use of quotations, and he went far in demonstrating the duplicity of Sisson. He rounded up all sorts of support from prelates and from the Catholic press in France, Italy, and elsewhere.[53] He was ready to do much more, both in and out of the courtroom, in this battle which was pitting ecclesiastical-liberal elements against lay-reactionary-ultramontane forces. The battle, however, was cut short by a tragic event. A crazed priest, who had absolutely no connection with the case, murdered Archbishop Sibour in the church of Saint-Étienne du Mont on 3 January 1857. Catholics all over France were shocked. Suddenly the atmosphere became much less tolerant of a continuation of divisive in-fighting. Veuillot's anger could not resist the tide, and, of course, as a man of order quite as much as a Catholic, he too was repelled by the event. Accordingly he agreed to sign notes along with Cognat, similar to those already negotiated, for putting the case to rest.

The case was hard to put to rest, however, and for many weeks after the signing of the notes in mid-January related matters kept the issue warm. Louis Veuillot had not liked the idea of suing a priest, but Cognat had stood up as the sole author. He had seemed to be taking all responsibility from either Dupanloup or Sibour. However, after Sibour was killed, the Abbé Cognat appeared much less heroic. In a letter dated 16 January 1857 Cognat wrote Msgr. Bonnechose in a different sense. He now gave the impression that he had become involved against his will, and that he really had wanted no part of the work of making up the book *L'Univers jugé par lui-même.* Sibour now appeared to have been the big force behind the libel, though Cognat did not deny his editorial work. Veuillot, of course, had been impressed from the first with the similarity of the language of the Dupanloup *avertissement* of 1853 and this recent book, but in any case Cognat and Dupanloup were in the same camp, and the little man no doubt was much influenced by earlier words of the big man against Veuillot. To see the departed Archbishop Sibour depicted as the principal force was too much to bear for his cousin, Msgr. Léon Sibour, Bishop of Tripoli and former vicar-general of the archbishopric of Paris. Cognat's letter had gained wide publicity, and Msgr. Léon Sibour replied to it in such a way as to undermine its validity. He particularly attacked Cognat's accusation that Archbishop Sibour, personally, just before his death, had asked for Dufaure's defense of him. Léon Sibour was quite ready to throw Cognat to the tender mercies of Veuillot, but Veuillot, who still fundamentally blamed Dupanloup for the whole thing, had no special desire to take revenge on Cognat.[54] He had much resented the fact that Cognat had been reassured in November he would keep his post even if condemned,[55] but the inspiration of the book he was certain had come from Dupanloup.

The continuation of charges and countercharges in the press was an ugly feature of the affair. Veuillot particularly resented the overlapping of efforts of the secular press with the liberal Catholic journals, especially in the wild charge that he, Veuillot, was responsible for the assassination of Sibour. *Le Figaro* that *feuille boulevardière* in the words of Eugène,[56] carried an article to that effect, and the Abbé Sisson reproduced it in *L'Ami de la Religion,* to the amazement of Louis Veuillot.[57] He also felt that Cognat had not stuck to his agreement of mid-January, and he much resented later assertions of Cognat about *la pureté de sa cause*. Veuillot declared he never would have yielded to the armistice if Cognat had spoken of the purity of his cause in January.[58] Nevertheless, while hostile journals kept up their jibes and insinuations, *L'Univers* remained comparatively restrained. Various prelates lamented to Veuillot about the attack of *L'Ami de la religion* of 15 January 1857,[59] and Msgr. Thibault of Montpellier congratulated him on his moderate attitude toward Cognat.[60] Veuillot may not have been very moderate in the usual sense of the word, but, for him, he actually did show some restraint considering the nature of Sisson's insinuations and the publicity his articles received, even in Belgium. Moreover, although *L'Univers jugé par lui-même* ostensibly went out of print as a result of the understanding, a M. Gaultier de Claubry, a friend of Dupanloup and Sibour, re-edited it (badly, according to Eugène) under the new title *L'Univers en présence de lui-même.*[61] Thus the substance of the dishonest attack was still on the market. To Catholics, in general, however, this assault on Veuillot had largely boomeranged. It was obvious to many both of the clergy and of the laity that Veuillot and his journal had been victims of foul play. Just what role Dupanloup and Sibour had played could not be fully ascertained. Cognat had shown weak character as well as lack of skill in the whole affair, and his attempt to pass blame on to Sibour after the death of the latter should be given no credence. What Sibour had done was probably confined to giving the support of his office to a project which turned out to be inept as well as malicious. Dupanloup, however, probably had known much more about what was being done than had Sibour. At the very least he was the inspiration of the attack. *L'Univers jugé par lui-même* was prepared under his auspices. Many thought it had been prepared by seminarians in the *Évêché* itself. This point was made by Maynard in his biography of Dupanloup in 1884. A priest named Thoinard, curé of Cravant, wrote to Eugène that he had been one of the seminarians, and that the copying of the manuscript had been done at the seminary. This clergyman volunteered that from that time he had become attached to *L'Univers.*[62] No doubt quite a few other people reacted that way as a result of the nature of the attack and the strong defense of *L'Univers*.

Liberal Catholicism as a whole in France was suffering a loss of adherents at this time, and the episode of *L'Univers jugé par lui-même* was associated with the general tendency. The trend, however, did not mean that things were going well for Louis Veuillot and *L'Univers*, although his troubles with the episcopacy were at an end. Cardinal Morlot, who replaced Sibour as Archbishop of Paris, was already a distinguished prelate. He became the imperial almoner and part of the council of state. He wanted no trouble with Veuillot. According to Eugène, he said to Louis Veuillot, "I appreciate your services as well as your fine talent, and you will not see me join your adversaries."[63] Morlot was a careful man, as this statement would indicate, and to all intents and purposes he was no special factor in Veuillot's troubles with the empire that subsequently developed. The statement made by Morlot might almost have been made by the Emperor himself. However, Napoleon III in trying to stay ahead of his people had to reflect the forces that were popular, and political liberalism again was in the air. Liberals of the press and other sectors were not directly opposing the empire, and when it suited their purposes they backed it against whatever other forces they did not like. This is the general situation that confronted Louis Veuillot in the late 1850's.

Hardly was the trouble with Dupanloup and Sibour over than, early in 1857, *L'Univers* took up the defense of another bishop, and as a result drifted into trouble with the regime, partly because of the growing liberal sentiments within it. The Bishop of Moulins, Msgr. Dreux-Brézé, endeavoring to maintain his authority in his diocese, had disciplined certain priests, who then appealed to the council of state. *L'Univers*, with a strong article by Du Lac, sprang to the defense of the bishop, who had been obliged to give account of his actions to the government. *Le Moniteur* took official notice of this article, and of the reprimand the bureau of the press gave *L'Univers* on this occasion. The combination of an official warning and an officially inspired article strongly defending the government's proceeding in the case of the venerable bishop should have been enough to silence any paper.[64] Louis Veuillot, however, simply would not take his cue and be quiet. He knew a second warning would be followed by suppression if he continued to oppose the policy of the government, but he chose nonetheless to defend episcopal prerogative and to defy the government. He was proving he was "Catholic before all." Some of the priests involved in the case tried to have an interview with him, but he rudely rejected their request. "It is not for me to judge between the Bishop of Moulins and his priests; and these people are not the judges of their bishop. If they are to complain of him, it is not to the secular tribunals or less still to the journals that they should bring their complaints," he wrote one of them.[65] Louis Veuillot did not try to defend the Bishop for his inept handling of his priests, but he lamented the damage they were doing the church by their opposition to their bishop. He himself had just brought suit against a clergyman who had the obvious support of two bishops, including his own, but then that had been an entirely different matter, he must have felt. In this case a bishop had been defied, and he must be supported. Veuillot was a proponent of order, and the assassination of Sibour had greatly disturbed him on this score.[66] As for those upstart priests he wrote with sarcasm to Msgr. Parisis: "They find it very bad and inconceivable that a bishop should be more entrenched in his position than a functionary. If this haughty spirit continues, it will carry us far, and even further those who pretend to lead us in this way. The future is very black. All the councils around the emperor are bad."[67] He saw the government showing signs of undermining the church, the one source of true order. Veuillot at that era had no affection for the Bishop of Moulins, and even said as much to one of the priests embroiled with him, though he later was on friendly terms with him.[68] Personality had nothing to do with this case. Veuillot was willing to run great risk for any bishop against those who would undermine episcopal authority by replacing it with the intervention of the state.

The Moulins case could have brought the suppression of *L'Univers* when the journal squarely retorted to *Le Moniteur's* obvious siding with the priests. Veuillot's enemies in the government were primarily the ministers of interior and of religion, MM. Billault and Rouland. These two were determined to get rid of Veuillot, but as yet the emperor was not willing. Even a simple monk, the Capuchin Father Laurent, wrote Veuillot that the ministry was just waiting for the right occasion to strike him,[69] and Veuillot himself certainly realized his danger. Rashness was one of his charms, the one by which he kept his readers enthralled, and he believed that he yet could go as far as he did in this matter. However, he was perfectly willing, even eager, to go down to martyrdom in the right battle. Napoleon still wanted the support of Veuillot, and, despite Billault and Rouland, was unwilling to permit the second warning or a suppression order to go out. Veuillot had a conversation with Napoleon's aide, General de Cotte, who revealed a good deal about the régime and its policy toward the press. When it had been reported to Napoleon that *L'Univers* had taken its stand on the Bishop of Moulins' case, and the pressure was applied by its enemies, General de Cotte had replied that *L'Univers* really had been quite moderate (he did not say *for it*), and that were it to be *frappé,* one of the best friends of the emperor would be gone. "If *L'Univers* is reviled by a certain number of Catholics, it is not for the manner in which it defends religion; it is because it defends you yourself." According to Veuillot's report to his sister of what De Cotte said about the meeting, the emperor replied, "It's true."[70] According to Eugène, Marshal Vaillant, minister of war, also came to the aid of *L'Univers*. He was not a devout person, but he hated *Le Siècle* and that segment of the press. He is said to have told the emperor that if *L'Univers* were to be suppressed, he would ask for the suppression of *Le Siècle*. The emperor then got up, saying: "Things will rest here; I have need of *Le Siècle*." He may indeed have been desirous of hanging onto Catholic support for as long and to as great a degree as he yet could, but clearly he was hoping to have the support of the secular liberals, even in 1857, which by usual school-book classification was still part of his "authoritarian period."

Billault took advantage of the aftermath of the Moulins affair to make things uncomfortable for Veuillot. He charged Collet-Meygret of the bureau de la presse to ask him in a personal interview whether he held anything against him, Billault. "Quelles pauvres gens!" exclaimed Veuillot to his sister. To Collet-Meygret he replied that if he did indeed have personal resentment, he would not use his paper for its satisfaction – a very frank answer, but hardly the sort for which Billault was waiting, unless, of course, he was setting a trap. Veuillot, not surprisingly, brought up the matter of *Le Siècle* on this occasion, saying that "it was a disgrace and a danger to see this miserable journal daily insulting the church." He maintained that its line was going to have to be stopped, and that if not the imperialist sentiments of every Catholic would wither. "Ceasing to protect religion, the government would no longer be anything." Veuillot declared "We would blush to support it, and we would await the judgment of God upon it."[71] He could scarcely have said anything stronger.

During this conversation with the man who could have been the instrument of the suppression of *L'Univers*, Veuillot discussed the matter of Gondon and the new journal, *L'Universal*. He learned that his former colleague, his London correspondent, whom he branded an "intriguer," had seen Collet-Meygret with supposed authorization of Veuillot about government authorization in case he were to purchase *L'Univers*![72] The possibility of buying out *L'Univers* and transforming it had been thought of by others. One individual, described only as a *farceur* by Veuillot, had told the Abbé Sisson that he would buy the journal for him, but only on the condition that Veuillot were kept at its head![73] However, what could have been a more serious threat to *L'Univers* was this project of a considerable number of Catholic supporters of the empire who preferred a more liberal voice for Catholicism to launch a journal to give it the sort of rivalry that *Le Correspondant* and *L'Ami de la religion* were unable to offer. The group backing Gondon included the Abbé Dauphin, vicar-general and dean of Sainte-Geneviève, Viollet-le-Duc, Charles Calemard de Lafayette, and various members of the council of state and of the legislative body. They declared in a program that: "The religious conviction professed by the grand majority of men of order is represented in the press by only one journal. However, everyone knows that *L'Univers*, by its passionate interpretation of the doctrines it wishes to defend, by the violence and the tone of its polemics, has alienated the great majority of the public for which it speaks. If journals hostile or indifferent to the Catholic faith smile over its paradoxes and gloat over the intemperance of its language, wise spirits in our ranks groan about its faults." The program went on to say that Catholic opinion, whatever that was, wanted an organ "more moderate and more Christian" than *L'Univers*. Without naming them, the program stated that "numerous bishops" desired such a sheet. Gondon claimed the support of the director-general of the Sûreté and of the minister of interior, Billault. He also claimed that the journal's name was proposed by the minister.[74] No doubt the minister did support the project of this new journal, which it was hoped would undercut *L'Univers* seriously. Whoever proposed the name, *L'Universal,* was engaging in a cheap trick by suggesting so similar a name. The new paper, however, was a failure. A few numbers appeared, but insufficient funds had been raised, and it completely failed.[75] In a way it is too bad that it did not get adequate backing, because the contest might have aroused interest, and the air might have been further cleared as to what the spirit of French Catholicism in this era actually was. Gondon completely faded from French journalism after this episode, while Veuillot's paper won an ever-tighter grip on the Catholic public.

While *L'Univers* was being threatened once again with competition, it was also having its own problems with regard to ownership. For years Taconet had been the principal owner and Barrier the *gérant.* The pair had been perfect for Veuillot's purposes, just as was Bailly who handled the printing of the journal. While the imperialist-Catholics were backing Gondon and the project of *L'Universal*, the possibility of *L'Univers* falling into other hands by being bought out was one of the threats mentioned to Louis Veuillot as we have seen. However, Taconet managed one way or another to buy out the other owners, and *L'Univers* became his sole property, to the great relief of Veuillot. "M. Taconet is sole proprietor of it," he wrote a friendly priest. "It is as though I were. My position is freer, surer, and even a bit improved. Many combinations were made to exclude us; we have made others only to put ourselves in the hands of God, and we have won. Alas! There was a traitor among us. He is gone."[76] The maneuvering by which all the outstanding shares were sold to Taconet can hardly be traced,[77] but afterwards Veuillot's base was as firm as could be hoped for: "*L'Univers* is the property of Taconet, that is to say, mine," he wrote the Comtesse de Ségur, to whom he made the further observation that he was "married" to *L'Univers*.[78]

However firm it may have been from most pressures, it continued to come into conflict with the régime. Béranger, already in his lifetime a great ideological cause, died in 1857. The government expected public manifestations commemorating the popular poet, and wanted to identify itself with him. Veuillot had been watching for his death also, and managed to describe his last hours in such a way as to suggest that the once irreverent *chansonnier* had, practically speaking, died the death of a confessing Catholic.[79] It is doubtful whether Veuillot convinced many people in this respect. *Le Siècle* of Louis Jourdan, which carried much of what the famous literary idol and politician, Lamartine, had to say about Béranger's death, made much of the matter. Veuillot could not sit back and watch this flood of romantic excess without answering. Béranger, according to Veuillot, was far inferior to Alfred de Musset in the same type of poetry. The national celebration of the passing of the "national poet" was most inappropriate. Lamartine spoke of Béranger as a "man of glory and a man of good," claiming that the homages rendered to him would "resuscitate" France. "The people and the army," wrote Lamartine in his *Méditations,* "heard themselves feel, think, love, hate, and breathe in Beranger. He is a man-nation. He has made the soul of a people." How could Lamartine, who himself had recently been critical of Dante's *Divine Comedy*, carry on thus over this Paris song-writer? How could he even drag in "Lisette"? What a policy on the part of the government! How could it give this "impromptu canonization, subject to revision," to a revolutionary of little talent! In this vein Veuillot treated the readers of *L'Univers* to a rare attack on romantic poets in general and a well-coordinated attack on Lamartine, Béranger, and the régime, in particular.[80]

The régime did not take any notice directly of Veuillot, but replied to this only in a guarded and disguised way. The principal reply was considerably later, in early 1858, in the form of an article in *La Patrie*, and not in *Le Siècle, La Presse,* or *Le Moniteur*, and it was written by an unknown with the signature of "Brémond." Veuillot could have avoided a confrontation, but instead he made this article the target of a savage editorial. He recognized "Brémond" as Alfred de la Guéronnière, councilor of state, head of the *services de l'imprimerie, de la librairie, et de la presse*. Eugène called him "brochurier officiel de l'Empereur," a particularly significant phrase in view of the article on the unification of Italy he was shortly to write, which would put Veuillot in the untenable position in which he would find himself in 1860.[81] The article in *La*

Patrie was an extreme attack on Veuillot, but Veuillot replied in a still stronger vein. Had he simply replied to "Brémond," all would have seemed quite normal, but Veuillot spent pages asking the question, "Who is M. Brémond?" His repeated use of the name is probably the most striking use of repetition in all his editorials. Of course, after introducing all sorts of derogatory terms for the non-answering Brémond, including *bâtard,* he conspicuously throws in the name of Alfred de la Guéronnière, and repeats it as often as he can while still using the name Brémond.[82] By this time Veuillot had put aside Béranger, and the romantics and was openly making war on the functionaries of the régime, and already running the severest risk of being closed down, but this way of operating was his stock-in-trade. A temperate Veuillot would not have been Louis Veuillot.

L'Univers survived this exchange, largely because La Guéronnière had indeed attacked under the cloak of what he thought was anonymity, and could not now very well admit that Veuillot was correct in identifying him as Brémond. Also there were other preoccupations of the régime, which could have dulled the desire to invite trouble by so rash an act as bringing things to a head with the popular *L'Univers.* There had been an attempted assassination of Napoleon III by Orsini, a fanatical Carbonaro, whose desperate act was part of the program to force France to do something for the unification of Italy. *L'Univers* was of course an active foe of the unification of Italy. The minister of interior, Billault, had been replaced by General Espinasse, but still pressure to do something about *L'Univers* persisted in the council of state. The desire to avoid trouble was also there, however, plus, perhaps, some amusement on the part of the other councilors about La Guéronnière's embarrassment. General de Cotte saw Veuillot in early February, and he told him that he had spoken strongly in defense of *L'Univers* in inner circles. Veuillot noted with satisfaction in a letter to Msgr. Parisis that La Guéronnière had not answered his last article, and despite the things that other journals, from *Le Siècle* to *L'Ami de la religion*, might say, the affair was over.[83]

In mid-1857 there were elections for the legislative body. It was not very easy for Louis Veuillot to see just what to do. He still regarded the régime as a bulwark in the cause of order, but increasingly he feared what liberal-imperialists within it might do with regard to the Catholic church. The situation of the Catholics, therefore, was serious but not yet hopeless. Veuillot's role in politics was still considerable, though largely as a molder of Catholic opinion through *L'Univers.* As usual, there was some talk that he himself might be a candidate for the legislative body, but he did not let this talk come to anything.[84]

Judging from various of his writings, we know he had completely renounced a political career long before this time. He may have welcomed a certain amount of consideration for public office for the effect it might have on his general position; this factor would be difficult to assess. Throughout his life he wrote many letters of recommendation, and it is interesting to see the kind of advocacy he gave for the Comte de Montsaulnin in seeking official backing for him. He wrote General de Cotte, describing what a fine person his frequent host was, identifying him with the oldest traditions of the country, and showing how much more practical it would be for the régime to give its blessings to him than to his opponents. He was also able to close the letter with a *Domine, salvum fac Napoleonem.*[85] At the time of the elections he could still, with some effort, give the general blessings of *L'Univers* for the official candidates. Nevertheless he deplored some of the tendencies of those in the régime and the fact that some secular liberals had gained influence within the ranks of the régime. He regretted the influence of *Le Siècle* and the *Journal des Débats,* especially the advocacy of the latter of the monopoly of the university. However, he could still advocate that Catholics not abstain, but rather show their strength by voting. "Catholics will therefore go to the elections. In spite of the complaints that we have just enumerated, we believe that they will vote for the candidates of the government. That is what we shall do here ourselves, and what we advise them to do, except in the rare cases where they have to choose between a candidate of the government and a man who offers more for the security of the true order. At Besançon, for example, who would be able to blame a Catholic elector for preferring Monsieur de Montalembert, in spite of his faults, to an opponent, without doubt honorable but very new, who opposes him?" He mentioned others who might be favored over official candidates, including a relative of his friend, Théodore de Bussières,[86] but it is interesting to observe that he took a who-could-blame attitude about voting for Montalembert rather than giving an outright endorsement, as he would have done in the 1840's. Montalembert was thoroughly trounced. "For Montalembert," Veuillot wrote afterwards to Élise, "it is a disaster; fewer votes than the socialist." Indeed, he received less than one-sixth of the ballots, and Veuillot declared, "The clergy completely abandoned him, saying nothing against him, but also saying nothing for him, and refusing even to pass out his circulars."[87] Several of Veuillot's friends were elected, notably La Tour who easily won in Brittany,[88] but so far as Veuillot was concerned Montalembert's complete defeat must have been the most remarkable thing about the elections. There were some opposition victories, including that of Émile

Ollivier, but generally the elections left the official party with overwhelming numbers. Montalembert complained about the lack of support he received from the clergy. No doubt the Besançon clergy were sympathizers with Veuillot and could see that he really was not endorsing Montalembert. Veuillot insisted that he had supported him as best he could and had written some letters recommending his candidacy.[89] However, had Veuillot truly wanted to see the election of Montalembert, Montalembert might have done better in the race. Veuillot still rankled at what *Le Correspondant* had been saying about his recent troubles, and the deep differences between the two men, which had opened up in the forties and intensified after their split over support for Napoleon in 1852, had become still worse in the late fifties.

Veuillot had had much to say about Montalembert during the attacks the *Journal des Débats* and *Le Siècle* had launched against miracles in the spring of 1857,[90] and his disapproval again became great in December when he accused Montalembert of giving support to nationalist aspirations in Italy against the pope. When the *Indipendente* of Turin published letters from Montalembert on 11 December, Veuillot expressed his anger in several numbers of *L'Univers*. In criticising the former chief of the Catholics-before-all, he focused on his liberalism and the ill-advised attempt he seemed to be making as a conciliator. He attacked what he called his eclecticism and confusion. He bewailed his stand about Belgian politics of the day, but he particularly compared his line on Italy to that of *Journal des Débats* and *Le Siècle*. He accused Montalembert of seeking an *Eldorado catholique*, and in four numbers generally hacked him to pieces for the readers of *L'Univers*.[91] In this stand, however, he was not without plenty of support. Gustave de La Tour supplemented Veuillot's enumeration of Montalembert's bad stands. Agreeing that *L'Univers* should be close with the Italian Jesuit journal, *Civiltà Cattolica*, and with *Armonia*, he then shifted the consideration to Germany, where he feared Montalembert and *Le Correspondant* might be winning friends.[92] Not that the fight between the two Catholic leaders was not important, but, in fact, it was being waged between two journals that were very small, particularly *Le Correspondant*. However, as the two dueled editorially, Lacordiare, finding himself in the town of Sorèze, wrote to Montalembert that he could not get ahold of a copy of *L'Univers*![93] Msgr. Xavier de Mérode, his brother-in-law in Rome, tried to get Montalembert to stop attacking *L'Univers* and Veuillot when the latter warmed up the classics debate late in 1858, but Montalembert squarely resisted the attempt.[94] To an attempt on the part of Veuillot for a rapprochement as the Italian situation worsened, he replied that he hardly could see how such was possible "after the language you have used about me for eighteen months publicly."[95] Writing to the protestant Guizot in the summer of 1859, the worst thing he could say about Lamennais while generally treating him sympathetically was that he saw a link between him and Veuillot. He said that the "fanatical and servile school, of which M. Veuillot and P. Ventura are the *coryphées,* proceeds directly from him; however, Lamennais could never have called the emperor *un homme simple et bon*, as Veuillot had.[96] Even when *L'Univers* was suppressed in 1860, when the Alsatian Catholic leader Keller tried to effect a reconciliation, Montalembert said that the profound differences between them were such that he wanted no reconciliation – which might make him look like an accomplice of Veuillot's![97] Thus even desperate events for Catholics in the late 1850's could not accomplish what the Revolution of 1848 had done by way of reconciling the leaders of the old Catholic party.

Among all the questions which confronted Veuillot, Napoleon III was in the very center. Veuillot needed no reminder of the importance of the Emperor, particularly with regard to the question of threats to the Papal States as the movement for Italian unity grew stronger. The attempt on his life by Orsini brought the full spotlight on Napoleon III. Orsini was a Carbonaro who wanted the former Carbonaro, Louis Napoleon, to do something for Italy or die for his failure to live up to his youthful rash commitment.[98] Although some of his accomplices escaped judgment, Orsini philosophically accepted his own condemnation in the belief that he had done something for the Italian national cause. He did not misjudge, because within months a very uneasy Napoleon met with Cavour, and, at a good price, arranged for French participation in war against Austria, the power which presented the prime obstacle to Italian unity. In the cause of Italian nationalism, papal interests and sovereignty, of course, were to be sacrificed.

When Orsini set off his bomb on 14 January 1858, as Napoleon and Eugénie got out of their carriage on the Rue Lepelletier, a number of people were killed or injured, but the imperial couple escaped injury. Veuillot's editorial comments, emphasized the thanks that were being offered to Providence that the imperial couple had been spared. Then he quickly pointed a finger at Victor Hugo, who from his asylum under the union jack in Jersey had said, "in the name of conscience you can kill this man in tranquillity." Hugo, Veuillot insisted, had encouraged "types of bandits for whom even the dagger had become too noble an arm." This "cosmopolite" kind of revolution, harbored by England, Belgium, and Piedmont, had to be stopped.[99] Obviously Veuillot hoped that the attempted assassination would have a salubrious effect on the emperor.

Although he was very wrong as to what Napoleon's future course would be, he struck while he believed the iron was hot enough to effect some changes in the government's policy toward the press, and, of course, toward the general position of the pope. He flailed with great ardor trying to strike at all manifestations of the forces of revolution. January 21 coming just one week after Orsini's attempt offered a good occasion, for example, for a general blast at regicides, the Jacobin slayers of Louis XVI, and the Girondins who paved the way for them. He condemned France both for the way she had permitted regicides to kill Louis and Marie Antoinette, and for subsequent attitudes on regicide.[100] Rachel the noted actress died at the age of 37 at about this time, and the popular sensation was great. Louis Veuillot, however, did not join the loud chorus of her mourners. He did not admire her as an actress. Scorn for her as a symbol of romanticism and radical currents was his main reaction, and her popularization of the *Marseillaise* during the empire had particularly annoyed him. He resented the fact that various literary figures, notably Béranger, had exalted Rachel. Why did Béranger, her lover, not also exalt Mesdames du Barry and de Pompadour? These ladies were generous to literary men, hated the Jesuits, and it was not their fault they were not born in an era of popular sovereignty.[101] He blasted at all his political-literary enemies in a rolling barrage that covered many journals, including the *Journal de Débats, Le Siècle, Patrie*, and even *Le Moniteur*. He fired back especially at Hippolyte Rigault, who undertook to defend Hugo from Veuillot's attacks in the *Journal des Débats*. This young *universitaire* received quite a literary working over from Veuillot, who frankly admitted he liked his light style – a lightness which also extended to his reasoning! But Veuillot was constitutionally unable to refrain from delivering his heaviest blows on Hugo, the peer of France and Member of the Academy, who in exile under the British flag was now a base provocateur of assassination. While lumping him with other sons (or "bastards") of '93 who incited the Carbonaro to set off the bomb, he could not resist ridiculing as well Hugo's plays, many of which he had written before being banished (the word "exiled" annoyed Veuillot). *Hernani, Marion Delorme, Marie Tudor, Ruy Blas* – all these had to do with humiliation of crowned heads.[102] While he was engaging in this broadside against all he deemed detrimental, one of the targets of Veuillot's pen was Brémond – La Guéronnière, with whom he was to clash so spectacularly in the course of the next year. Attacks on a councilor of the emperor were perhaps not the best preparation for a meeting with the emperor, but with Veuillot's past record this manoeuvre was not inconsistent.

Msgr. Salinis and Msgr. Pie, Archbishop of Auch and Bishop of

Poitiers, respectively, the one not far from the end of his life, and the other with many years lying ahead, were both important supporters and advisors to Louis Veuillot. No ecclesiastic, however, had more influence on Veuillot or was in closer touch with him than Msgr. Parisis, Bishop of Arras. Veuillot corresponded with him about approaching the minister of interior, Billault, personally, and even Napoleon III himself. The prelate approved of the move. Salinis also corresponded with Veuillot about the direct approach. Therefore it cannot be said that he was precipitous in the matter, or that he acted completely as a layman, proposing to speak with the emperor about the church and its problems with the lay press without first conferring with approving prelates. The initiative, however, was strictly his, and the stance he was taking was bold. With Billault, the minister of interior, whom he met in early January, there was little satisfaction. Billault listened to him, and, like most other politicians, tried to calm Veuillot and to sympathize with him where he could, acting, for example, as though he shared Veuillot's distress over *Le Siècle.* In reporting this interview to Parisis, it is interesting to note, Veuillot did not give the appearance of having any great feeling for the relative importance of matters. For example, he told Parisis about his general attempt to defend the church from the assaults of its enemies in the press, and then he informed the bishop that despite the formation of the new *L'Universel*, *L'Univers* had gained 150 new subscribers during the month. Slightly more significantly he announced that *L'Univers* had been granted authorization to be sold in the railway stations and on the streets.[103] The editor of a journal in France who was impressed with addition of 150 subscribers, and who noted that it had been arranged without difficulty that his newspaper be sold in the street, hardly seems like the same man who takes it upon himself to go before a cabinet minister and to be issuing statements on behalf of the whole Catholic church.

When Veuillot told Msgr. Salinis that the minister of religion, Rouland, had told him that he had spoken against Billault to the emperor, Salinis replied, "I do not believe any of it."[104] Actually, what the emperor may have thought of Billault made little difference, for as a result of the Orsini situation the emperor replaced Billault with General Espinasse, who in turn only remained in the ministry until June when he was succeeded by Delangle. Veuillot still hoped in early 1858 that the emperor would return to the clerical policy he had demonstrated in his earlier days, and his interview with Billault was simply a preliminary for the bigger meeting. He arranged the meeting as secretly as he could, and instead of going through more regular channels had his friend General de Cotte make the arrangements. He asked Parisis for his prayers and counsels and promised him that he would say nothing about the meeting either before or after it occurred. He made good on the promise, saying nothing of the interview until the fall of 1871, well after the passing of the Second Empire, and on an occasion when the publication of various papers found in Tuileries made it seem desirable for Veuillot to explain what his relations with the emperor had been.[105]

General de Cotte made an appointment for February 19, and then Veuillot seemed to suffer from doubts as to whether he should thus be plunging ahead, right down to the moment when he encountered the emperor personally.[106] Veuillot admitted that he was a bit nervous when being led to the anteroom to wait to talk with the ruler of France, but while sitting there his thoughts drifted from what he was going to say to what he had felt like when waiting to have an audience with the pope. His nervousness then passed away, and he compared the whole situation unfavorably with the surroundings and feelings he had had before meeting with Pius IX. "In short, if it had been possible, I would certainly like to have gotten out. But I had come. I thought that this first time would be the last time."[107] Assuming Veuillot actually did write these lines at the time of the interview, and did not make any later insertions, he was quite prophetic about his relations after 1858 with Napoleòn. When the emperor made his appearance, he almost swept Veuillot off his feet: "The emperor was standing. He advanced toward me and held out his hand. I expected a gloomy face, a sphynx without eyes of which I had so often heard spoken. I found none of this, but rather an open and welcoming air and a good voice."[108] The emperor himself plunged right into the very topic Veuillot wanted to discuss, the troubles between *L'Univers* and *La Patrie*, in whose columns La Guéronnière had been attacking Veuillot. The emperor regretted that these attacks had been made, and he just about disarmed Veuillot from the very start. True, the emperor was in a position of great power, but it is amusing to see the man who normally could so easily seize the initiative in any sort of exchange lack thunder from the very beginning.

Of course Veuillot did bring the emperor around to some of the things that were bothering him. As he told Parisis, he planned to discuss "general affairs, the press, the church, and society."[109] He did indeed have things to say about all of these general topics, but somehow it would certainly seem that his "game-plan" was either not too well thought out or he was unable to follow it in the way he would like to have. As he was building up his exposition to the emperor along the line of general matters, the Empress Eugénie entered the room. The emperor rose and presented Veuillot to the beautiful empress (who appeared to

Veuillot to look like twenty) "in kind and even flattering terms," and the empress responded with kind words for *L'Univers*, which no doubt were sincere. The discussion became literary, and the empress praised the literary quality of Villemain's study of Chateaubriand. The emperor then asked Veuillot how long he had been a journalist, and Veuillot gave a vague answer. The emperor told him how honorable his work was, with Veuillot replying to the effect that he would hope so. The empress now retired, after having thoroughly won Veuillot. To Parisis he called her "Her Gracious Majesty (one can say Gracious)." At this point he turned the discussion to *Le Siècle,* but without much chance to gain any advantage, since Napoleon immediately indicated his displeasure with this journal also. They talked about institutions and men, and Napoleon gave Veuillot to feel that as always it was men who made the problems. Veuillot could not very well start reciting a list of ministers and functionaries who did not please him, and the skillful politician Napoleon thoroughly carried the day – no mean trick, since Veuillot was a good talker as well as a good writer. Writing to Parisis he concluded: "In sum, Monseigneur, I retired very satisfied, personally and politically."[110]

For some time after this interview Veuillot showed no opposition to the policies of the régime, and even echoed some of the men he would like to have brought down. A brochure entitled *Napoleon III et l'Angleterre*, inspired by Napoleon himself and written by La Guéronnière, had come out with the purpose of trying to force the British to do more about preventing plots against foreign sovereigns from being hatched on their shores. British liberalism was in such a strong position at the time that the French got no satisfaction. When one of Orsini's comrades was acquitted in England, Veuillot had occasion for another of his denunciations of English ways.[111] Veuillot, of course, had a good deal to say in the columns of *L'Univers* about the officially inspired brochure, but he emphasized the general idea of trying to make the British mend their ways, rather than criticizing La Guéronnière's exposition.[112]

In the summer of 1858 the emperor went on a trip to Brittany which won Veuillot's approval, at least for the time. On his way he went first to Cherbourg, where, in the presence of none other than Queen Victoria, he dedicated a statue of Napoleon I. "The emperor did a deed and pronounced words which were worth more than winning a battle," said Veuillot. The words were pronounced at Sainte-Anne d'Auray, where the emperor declared his pleasure at being "in the midst of the Breton people, who are, above all, monarchical, Catholic, and soldierly."[113] Veuillot was delighted, and felt that the Empire was a safeguard of order in the anarchy that was threatening. The only trouble was that the emperor must have been thoroughly insincere. Very shortly after appearing as a Catholic sovereign among his strongest church supporters in such a dramatic way, he went to the resort town of Plombières, where he met Cavour incognito. Here they plotted to get Austria to attack Piedmont, which France would then defend, to be rewarded with Nice and Savoy after the new Italian kingdom would receive Lombardy and Venetia. As Cavour and Napoleon rode around the streets of Plombières, quite unknown to the world, and of course to Louis Veuillot, they talked of events that might take place in central Italy and what would become of the States of the Church.[114] The sinister deal was sealed by an arrangement for the marriage of Prince Napoleon, the emperor's cousin, with Princess Clotilde, daughter of Victor Emmanuel II, which was to take place the following year. However, Veuillot, no more than anyone else, knew nothing of these arrangements; consequently what appeared to be a rapprochement between him and the emperor continued for some time. Not only did Napoleon III take up the one course of action that was certain to make an enemy of Veuillot, but he allowed him to continue to support the empire while the new direction was secretly being arranged.

In this era when Veuillot was temporarily won back to the emperor he had at least the usual number of new interests. His daughters were growing up as students at the Couvent des Oiseaux, and Élise watched over all that concerned them, as well as over the many dinners that were held at the Veuillot establishment, 44, Rue du Bac. Eugène married a young American woman in early October, to the great interest of Louis, who wrote Parisis that this Louise d'Aquin was the daughter of a *grand chrétien, grand abonné de L'Univers* (apparently not all subscribers were equal!), now deceased.[115] He left the family well fixed, however, and Louise had a dot of 100,000 francs, which Louis told the prelate was *un peu pauvre*! The family d'Aquin had already contracted a marriage with a family prominent in Catholic circles, when Louise's older sister had married Dr. Charles Ozanam, a physician and younger brother of Frédéric Ozanam. To Blanc de Saint-Bonnet Veuillot said: "This marriage has been the object of a rapprochement that is most pleasant to me. Because I have opposed Ozanam on certain occasions, on courses of action, it has been thought we were personal enemies. I am, thanks to God, the least guilty man in the world in regard to this fault, and I protest that I have neither enemies nor friends. On a matter of doctrine, I would battle my brother, and I would love my murderer."[116] This strange-sounding statement was actually a true one, since Veuillot was always more excited by issues than by people, and it was observed that he could engage in a major public quarrel with someone and then talk with him in a drawing-room as though they were the best of friends. Blanc de Saint-Bonnet, incidently, was an interesting thinker whose ideas began to take a very strong grip on Louis Veuillot during 1858. At the start of the year Saint-Bonnet had presented him with a book, entitled *L'Infallibilité,* of which Louis Veuillot published excerpts in *L'Univers.*[117] Even Donoso Cortés had not confronted him with a more stimulating idea than this of the infallibility of the pope. Events of 1870 were already being influenced as this idea settled into his mind. In Madame Eugène Veuillot, Louis now had still another young friend, and even on her wedding trip he was writing to her, concerned about how she would get along on a ship![118]

Louis took a trip himself in the summer of 1858, almost at the time of Napoleon's trip. He went to several religious shrines of the south, including the house of the Virgin Mary of Betharram, about which he dutifully wrote to Eugène and to Sister Èlise from the Pyrenees.[119] But much the most important visit he made was to Lourdes. Lourdes was not yet a pilgrimage site, only an obscure place recently astir over reports of a fourteen-year-old girl who had seen a strange vision of the Virgin Mary in a grotto there. By arriving almost immediately after the reports spread Veuillot showed himself a leader abreast of popular forces in Catholicism as well as of Catholic politics. There is no doubt that he was interested. He talked with the curé and with officials and townspeople. "People believe in it, and the unbelievers as well." He talked with the procureur-général, whom he knew, and who gave him "ridiculous explanations." To Eugène he wrote: "It is a miracle, which the administration does not want, in spite of the people, who do want it."[120] When Veuillot returned to Paris, he again became engaged on that old theme of his, miracles, now heavily influenced by the controversy that ensued over Lourdes. The secular press, led by *Le Siècle, Journal des Débats,* and *La Presse*, launched an attack on this miracle, as an example of doubtful miracles in general. Veuillot got into all the special quarrels between Catholic sheets and the secular press and introduced many arguments of his own. He wrote with much passion, but he tried to use logic and reason, and succeeded in doing so to a remarkable degree, to sustain his case – that something quite beyond logic had occurred.[121] He was determined to believe, and to convince others, or at least to get the better of the unbelievers in debate. There was a similarity, however, between the way in which he sustained this psychic-religious thesis and the way in which he had defended various practical policies he had supported.

During this time Veuillot barely escaped being drawn into another debate over the teaching of the pagan classics which would have caused him more trouble with the episcopate. Generally speaking the columns of *L'Univers* were open to all prelates who had something they wished published, but Veuillot made exceptions to the rule. Msgr. Landriot, Bishop of La Rochelle, reacted against an article by an Abbé Bensa, who had reviewed a study of the Revolution by Msgr. Gaume, which reopened the debate about the classics of several years standing. Veuillot did not care for the tone of Msgr. Landriot's article, and told him so.[122] Not content with ruling the bishop's study out of order, he published an editorial on the subject himself, taking the bishop to task on a number of points and then closing the debate by citing the encyclical of the pope on the matter.[123] The nuncio approved of the refusal, but understandably he was nervous about what might follow.[124] Not surprisingly this period was one of many during which episcopal voices lamented the power of the "lay-pope." Msgr. Guibert, Bishop of Tours, wrote another prelate: "If you knew how great the illusion was in the very regions where one is supposed to be most enlightened! That it is very well educated people, in a better position than others to make this evil cease, who seem persuaded that the safety of the church is attached to *L'Univers*!"[125] Msgr. Cœur, Bishop of Troyes: "Great courage is needed to attack *L'Univers*! . . . Some laymen, without any mission and without any importance, have usurped the most sacred rights of the episcopate." He accused the editors of *L'Univers* of pushing the church this way and that way and adding themselves to the constitution of the church as though they had been ordained to have such power.[126] But as had been the case five years earlier, although Veuillot had serious enemies among the prelates, he also had many friends, and most of the bishops probably had a warm spot in their hearts for him as a champion of the church, although a considerable number simultaneously had qualms of varying degrees about the extent of lay usurpation of clerical functions. The very application of the term "clerical" to such men as Veuillot no doubt troubled a good many, though it would be difficult indeed to assess with accuracy the reaction of the clergy to this new use of the term. The strength of the new force, however, was incontestable, and Msgr. Guibert asked "how to fight such a party, which is supported by practically all the clergy of the second order, which does not foresee the consequences of lowering the bishops, a very adroit party which skillfully cloaks itself with the appearances of devotion to Rome."[127] Guibert was not fair in questioning the sincerity of Veuillot's feelings for Rome, for devotion to Rome was certainly the key to his outlook.

L'Univers' representative in Rome in 1858 was a new one. The Abbé

Bernier had first been replaced by Henri de Courcy, but de Courcy's health being bad, he had turned out to be only a temporary correspondent. Henri de Maguelonne, who went to Rome early in 1858, was an excellent choice. He had edited a diplomatic sheet for Guizot before 1848, and was an extremely skillful and original writer. Although a layman, he was a personal friend of Cardinal Pecci, future Leo XIII, and thus from several points of view Veuillot had certainly picked the right man for this key assignment at a critical turn of affairs.[128] Veuillot was accustomed to work intimately with strong collaborators, many of his own choosing, and one can only speculate that had he succumbed at any time to the temptation to go into the government, his ability to pick men might have contributed to success.

A very peculiarly Roman episode now prepared the way for the Second Empire to be able to turn much French public opinion against the pope, and this episode also brought the rupture between Veuillot and Napoleon's régime. A well-to-do Jewish family living in Bologna in the States of the Church had hired as a nursemaid for their five-year-old son a Christian girl. The simple girl became distressed when the child happened to be taken sick, because she feared he might die without having been baptized and thus not be saved. She took the Mortara child to a priest, who ought to have known the repercussions a baptism not authorized by the parents might have, but nevertheless baptized the child. The baptism was not kept secret, and when authorities in the States of the Church heard that a Christian child was being raised by a Jewish family, a circumstance which was against the law, the child was taken away from his parents, and brought to Rome, where he became a special ward of the pope. The resulting furor in France, Italy, and the whole Western world may be imagined. During late 1858 and early 1859 the Mortara Affair was the scandal of the day, and, in fact, few other affairs in the entire century equaled it in notoriety.[129]

The secular press of France of course played up the case, blaming the church for going to such inhuman lengths where it ruled, even to the point of breaking up families. The entire liberal press lamented for the poor Jewish family to the point that European Jews must have wondered at this unaccustomed concern for them on the part of great numbers of gentiles. The Jews also had some able and outspoken advocates of their own cause in the persons of Alexandre Weill, Simon Bloch, Salomon Cahen, and Isidore Cahen. The liberal Catholic sheets were circumspect in this affair, but their aims now particularly included not offending Napoleon III. Lacordaire sarcastically wrote to Salinis on Christmas Eve, "*L'Univers* was and has ever been authorized in the name of Jesus Christ."[130] but the liberal wing of Catholicism was now in the process of making a rapprochement with the emperor. Napoleon himself wrote some articles for *Le Constitutionnel* under the name "Boniface,"[131] and part of the general assault on the papacy was launched from the columns of *Le Constitutionnel. Le Siècle* and *Journal des Débats* were naturally in the forefront, but practically the whole of the liberal press, as well as all journals close to the régime, and a wide variety of other papers combined to try to make the Papal States seem hateful to the French people.

Veuillot plunged into bitter polemic. He was aided by a former rabbi named Drack, now converted to Christianity, who felt that the Jews were ungrateful to the pope for what he believed they owed him.[132] Veuillot easily could have thought up a line of argument like that himself, but in his exchanges with the Jewish, official, and liberal journals he benefited a great deal from the technical aid of ex-Rabbi Drack. Many terms he used revealed at least secondhand familiarity with the thought of the Talmud, in articles particularly concerned with the Jews.[133] Some of the columns of *L'Univers* indicate an interest in Jewish conversion quite beyond even the complicated problem presented by the Mortara Case. For example: "A free-thinking Jew told us the other day that the authors of the Talmud are the Jesuits of Moses-ism. No, they are the protestants," replied Louis Veuillot. Veuillot just could not keep a mention of protestantism out of even such an affair as that of the Mortara child! Further reflecting on the parallel he concluded that the Jews one fine day might be converted, in which case they would see that the way of Jesus was the way of their own prophets, whereas the protestants, such as saw the light, would have to come back one by one.[134]

However, it was not in the nature of Louis Veuillot to become interested in any matter for its own sake, and most of his writing about the Mortara Affair was for the pragmatic end of defending the papal government in an action taken. He crossed pens with many. Among those contesting with him were MM. Louis Jourdan, Amédée Renée, de La Bedollière, Alloury, and Plée. M. l'Abbé Delacouture of his own diocese attacked him in the *Journal des Débats.* Before the debate was to quiet down he had been called a good many uncomplimentary things, including "the Mazzini of the church" in *Le Constitutionnel*, an epithet which particularly irritated Veuillot when *L'Ami de la Religion* broke its silence by reprinting the offensive piece.[135] The liberal Catholic press thus was already making a clear swing toward support of the Second Empire as it began favoring the dismemberment of the Papal States. When Abbé Sisson of *L'Ami de la Religion*, who kept the pressure off Dupanloup by claiming to be sole owner of the journal, proposed in

November of 1858 to make the paper a daily, the régime had every reason to favor him, and granted this authorization as a reward.[136]

Much about the whole Mortara episode was very stormy, but the most dramatic part of the storm in France was a protest to the régime on the part of important French Jews who took offense at a *L'Univers* editorial of 18 November 1858 which went on at length about Jewish characteristics. In it Veuillot maintained that there were Jews, and then again other Jews, but he concluded that they all had similarities, and that one of them was the way they did not become true citizens of the lands where they lived. He spoke about interesting acquaintanceships he had had with Jews in Algiers, and he also spoke of rich bankers in the highly developed countries.[137] In neither case was he very flattering about them. Not surprisingly a group of important French Jews, including Alphonse de Rothschild and F. Halévy, resented being called *déicides* and being held up to scorn for the tenacity with which they clung to their identity. They expressed outrage at the hatred they believed was directed against them, and they appealed for the protection of the government against such assaults.[138] Nothing came of the protest directly, though Prince Napoleon, now minister for Algeria, subsequently went out of his way to appoint Jews to colonial councils. The government was growing apprehensive about the way things were going in the press, and began putting pressure on all journals to end their polemic.[139] Although the Mortara Affair and related angles involving the Jews continued to be discussed by Louis Veuillot down to the early days of 1859, to all intents and purposes the ministry of the interior was able to choke off newspaper discussion at this time. It is easy enough in viewing the affair with twentieth-century eyes to conclude that Veuillot was antisemitic, but such a conclusion is not entirely correct. For one thing, racial antisemitism as opposed to religious prejudice was not yet developed in Europe. Veuillot seems to have had a thoroughly medieval attitude toward the Jews, as toward all unbelievers, seeking only their conversion. In his hot editorials in the Mortara Affair he quoted the Old Testament with such frequency and fervor that he obviously held the closest of bonds to exist between the Jewish Scriptures and Christianity. He thought of the Christians as the true continuers of Old Testament revelation, and only seems to have held the characteristics of tenacity and blindness against the Jews because they did not accept this view of themselves. His association with the Israelite Christian Drack would tend to illustrate the point. Indeed, he was no racist, and if twentieth-century racism had been known then, he would not have shared it. He was a citizen of his Heavenly City, a Roman Catholic. His feelings towards even Englishmen and Germans could be very warm – if only they were devout Catholics! It is wrong to think that Veuillot would have been a part of the *Action française*,[140] had their existences overlapped, despite superficial characteristics of both that would suggest it. As for the little Mortara child, Veuillot was eager from the moment of his arrival in Rome, on a trip he took early in 1859, to see the object of all the excitement. While watching a religious procession, Veuillot had his attention directed toward the boy. "I was truly enchanted to meet him at the chair of St. Peter. On the order of his superior he kissed my hand. What a sight for M. Plée of *Le Siècle*, if he had been able to see that! I myself heartily kissed the student of the *Rochettini*, and Élise did likewise. He is well, and he has an open and *spirituelle* face, and the best-looking eyes in the world."[141] Young Mortara for his part throve under the guardianship of the pope, and despite efforts to get him back, made by his parents through the government of Italy after unification, he became an ever more enthusiastic part of his new life. When he was grown he decided to become a monk. After the complete collapse of papal government in 1870 Mortara moved to Poitiers, France, where he lived for decades, a respected churchman. Thus he fulfilled the fondest dreams Veuillot could have had for his complete conversion. Veuillot had plenty to say about Mortara from time to time in the years to come. Whatever twentieth-century critics may have to say about Veuillot and the legal aspect of the Mortara Case, it is obvious that the child for whom so many tears were shed was himself actually thankful for what the nursemaid and priest had done! It is also obvious that the conversion of this little Jewish child gave Veuillot one of his greatest pleasures.

Feelings and attitudes that could not be expressed precisely in the way that, say, his foreign policy views might be outlined, Veuillot expressed in poetry. In his less busy hours he often composed poetry as an amusement, and even walking around the familiar streets of the Seventh Arrondissement he would be seeking the right word or poetic phrase. When his eyes bothered him he would give them a rest in this way. In this general period he did not complain as much as usual about his eyes, although in one letter he mentioned that he did have to use some sort of pommade every night on them.[142] Some of his poems of this time reflect his preoccupation with the Jews. One piece, *Les Filles de Babylone*, loomed importantly in Veuillot's eyes, and he showed great interest in what various people, such as Msgr. Parisis, would think of it.[143] *Les Filles de Babylone* is a long subdivided poem of over forty pages. In it his feelings are much wound up with the Israelites in their troubles with the other peoples of the Fertile Crescent, and the words of the Lord are used in a fully Semitic way.[144] The shorter poem, *Ave*

Rabbi!, reflects the same spirit. Whatever one may say about how narrowly Veuillot interpreted Christianity, he certainly did not try to overlook its Jewish roots.

Things were not going well for the ultramontanes in France as the year 1859 dawned. At the imperial New Year's reception for the diplomatic corps, Napoleon III told the Austrian ambassador that he regretted relations between the two countries were not what they had been, strongly suggesting by his comment the imminence of a war, which almost inevitably would have disastrous results for the Papal States. The division between the liberal and the ultramontane French Catholic press with regard to relations with the Second Empire bothered Veuillot. The obvious influence of the Abbé Maret, one of the founders of *L'Ère nouvelle* and dean of theology at the Sorbonne, was a threat. Maret was a brilliant man, and his Gallican fears about interference from Rome were being very much encouraged by the régime of Napoleon III. Enemies of Veuillot, like Msgr. Cœur of Troyes, gave Maret encouragement in his representations to the ministry of the interior to the effect that *L'Univers*, in its opposition to revolution in general, also opposed the principles of '89 and hence the very principles upon which the Second Empire claimed to be based, whatever its practices might be.[145] Maret was a very dangerous enemy of ultramontanism, and his influence was at its zenith at the start of 1859. Indeed, the very next year he was named with approval of the régime to be Bishop of Vanves, though Pius IX did not ratify the choice.

It was now nearly six years since Veuillot had been in Rome. He had always felt certain of the pope's personal support, but he began to wonder about the situation around the pope. Would liberals like Msgr. Mérode and Msgr. Falloux have influence on the pope? Would the pope be persuaded to make the kind of concessions that would be convenient to Napoleon? Veuillot could not be sure. He had based everything on Pius IX and the papacy, and he wanted to make sure of his base. Accordingly he betook himself to Rome to see the true shape of things. Conditions of travel had changed since his last visit, and Veuillot made practically no mention of the mode of his getting there and returning. In 1838 and 1853 he had written in detail about the nature of travel and of accommodations for the traveler, but in 1859 travel must have been routine. He probably went directly by train to Marseille, and almost certainly he took ship there for Civitavecchia. However, the steamers must have been faster and better than formerly, because he had no more to say about this trip than would a preoccupied personage of the 1970's.

When last in Rome, in 1853, Veuillot had been under terrible pressure from Dupanloup and Sibour, and had been aware that as yet the pope really did not know of him. In 1859 on the other hand, there was every reason to suppose that the pope had not forgotten him, and the initiative was now his. His reports from Rome uniformly reflect that he saw what he hoped to see. He had told his correspondent in Rome, Maguelonne, well before he left Paris that the policy of *L'Univers* would continue to be the same as it had been despite pressure on it by the régime.[146] Increasingly he realized how closely La Guéronnière was watching it.[147] Nevertheless, if reassurance was what he wanted, it was what he found. Msgr. Falloux he found was such an insignificant and vain figure that people laughed about him.[148] Mérode, on the other hand, who differed with his brother-in-law Montalembert about Veuillot,[149] made an excellent impression on Veuillot, who reported to Eugène shortly after arrival: "Mérode is perfect, and already has had us to dinner three times." In the same breath he expressed similar satisfaction with the warm reception of the Cardinals Fioramonti and Antonelli. But transcending all, of course, was his happiness at the sentiment the pope himself expressed for *L'Univers*. "I bless Monsieur Veuillot, Monsieur Eugène, their sisters, the sister-in-law, and the little nephews, when there are such." Giving gifts for them all, especially for Élise, he stood there with Veuillot and his sister, with moist eyes and, leaning on him as he did so, according to Veuillot, called his journal "pauvre cher *L'Univers*," the "child on which the mother supports herself."[150] Thus even in January, shortly after Veuillot arrived, he was already reassured after two audiences with the Holy Father. What more could he have wanted? Nevertheless he remained nearly two months longer and solidified his position still more. Of course Veuillot loved Rome. He was still a sight-seer and had plenty of sights to report to his brother, including the aforementioned meeting with the Mortara child.[151] Before leaving Rome he had still another audience with the pope, and this time was able to pass on the pope's highest compliments for an article *Eugenio* had written in answer to an officially inspired imperial brochure on French policy in Italy. Veuillot did gather that the pope was somewhat sad about Father Ventura, and no doubt Veuillot was eager to take any hint here about direct support of *L'Univers* in this direction. He also noted that his "triumph continues, with Mérode at the head."[152] He had no reason to stay longer, and by early March was back in Paris, where problems had multiplied during his absence.

Various personal traits of Veuillot were reflected by his reports of this latest trip to Rome. He had not forgotten his old friend the Abbé Gaume, however much trouble the latter had caused him, and went out of his way to get certain items for him. Of course, he sandwiched in with these reports of his own good deeds observations about his indigestion and about the cost of things in Rome.[153] He went to considerable lengths in an effort to secure the title of Commander in the Order of Saint Gregory for Taconet.[154] To please the proprietor of *L'Univers* in such a matter was no doubt important, but the title was not simple to obtain. It is curious, however, to see again how Veuillot would make a serious effort to get a title or honor for someone else, when such formalities meant nothing to him personally. Shortly before returning home he found among his effects a book by an obscure young author. He then asked his friend, Msgr. Bastide, canon of Santa Maria Maggiore, to see if he could not get Fioramonti to arrange for an expression of papal benediction to be sent to this young man.[155] Attention to little gestures of this sort, or to making sure that certain special people received subscriptions to *L'Univers*, sounds trifling to recount, but besides revealing that Veuillot took a personal interest in those with whom he was associated, it probably goes rather far in accounting for the cooperation he commanded in his endeavors. Though he kept personalities and principles in very separate categories, the powerful loyalty he received from his associates was in many ways traceable to his personal relations with them.

While Veuillot was still in Rome the significant brochure, no doubt inspired by Napoleon III himself and written by La Guéronnière, *Napoléon III et l'Italie*, had made its appearance. This piece traced the situation in which France had moved into Rome in 1849 and Austria into other provinces. The question was asked, what would happen if France and Austria were to have a war? Obviously the position of the States of the Church would be altered, and certainly not for the benefit of papal sovereignty. In addition to this brochure, there appeared in the official *Moniteur universel* a series of articles by Edmond About which attacked weaknesses in the papal government, preparing Frenchmen for a reversal in policy with regard to the Papal States. A large part of the total press gave support to the imperial policy, and against this imposing array Louis Veuillot was now inspired to launch a counterattack on behalf of the pope.

Veuillot's foreign policy campaign of 1859 had been anticipated by a series of articles he had written in the spring of 1858. Obviously echoing the teachings of Donoso Cortés in those articles, he had bewailed the un-Christian policies of the European countries in Asia. He had said much about England and the fallacies of Louis Philippe's policy of cordiality with the English, but yet made clear Russia was the greatest danger to Europe so far as he was concerned. While France and the rest of Europe would be continually plagued by revolution, Russia he feared would be seizing wealth and power in Asia, later to use these gains against a divided Europe.[156] France, as Veuillot believed, had no natural allies, therefore what she should do was form an alliance of Catholic nations, to defend both herself and all of Europe from the dangers that would beset Europe from revolution, Russia, and the influence of the English.[157] The idea of a Catholic alliance was still at the center of his thinking in 1859, and naturally Austria would have to be the key ally, and not an enemy! To fight against Austria, to take land from the pope to be given to a revolutionary state – this was a plan for disaster, unthinkable to Louis Veuillot.

Before Veuillot went on his trip to Rome in 1859, he had written an article asking the question, "Is France still a Christian nation?"[158] One negative part of his answer was that in any case much of the press certainly was not. Thus mentally prepared to do battle with a large part of it, he now attacked Edmond About and his articles. His attack was partly *ad hominem*. He held up About as "a flower of the university type, the type of literary man trained by the state." He listed all of About's academic distinctions gained in the university system as though they were serious defects about which an innocent reader should be warned. His books had "nothing in common with what is serious, nothing in common with what is honest."[159] Veuillot, of course, also found a wide variety of specific things to criticize in the writings of About, particularly those writings that had been gathered in a book and published in Belgium under the pretentious title, *La Question Romaine*. This book was being sold in France, although it had not been authorized and went somewhat beyond what About had published in *Le Moniteur*. Veuillot took advantage of the situation, discussed the book as though it were indeed authorized, and thus let it appear as though his attack on About could be taken as directed against the cabinet. The book was therefore no longer permitted, because it was embarrassing to the régime, and an announcement to this effect in *Le Constitutionnel* was particularly interesting because it was signed by "L. Boniface," who may in fact have been a certain obscure writer who contributed to that journal, but who may also have been Napoleon III himself as he was known sometimes to use that man's name in that paper.[160] Veuillot was now summoned, in early April 1859, by the minister of interior, the Duc de Padoue, who, with great care in what he said, let Veuillot know that at least unofficially he was receiving a warning for unacceptable statements.[161] Although Veuillot thereafter was careful not to be quite so obvious, his general line was no different during the spring of 1859, while the Roman question remained his great preoccupation. Napoleon III, of course, was not directly committed to destruction of the papal territories, but he was obviously not preparing to defend anything more than a limited area around Rome in the very likely case that Italian forces were to seize the lands of the pope.

The episcopacy in France seemed to draw closer to Veuillot during the spring of 1859. Msgr. Sibour, for example, not someone particularly expected to rally to Veuillot because of his relationship to the late archbishop, told him in a letter dated 23 February that the situation had completely changed, and that French Catholics should make some sort of manifesto.[162] Later in the spring he complimented him on one of his usual blasts, saying that it was "full of reason, wit, and particularly courage."[163] Msgr. Doney, Bishop of Montauban, gave him encouragement to continue to write about the Papal States, saying that the Catholic powers of Europe had an obligation to do something for defense of the pope.[164] Later on Msgr. Fillion, Bishop of St. Claude, summed up the situation: "*L'Univers* has just finished a tough but glorious and useful campaign. It is a duty for me to send you congratulations and thanks."[165] The bishops as a rule seemed to be impressed with the close connection of the temporal power of the pope with the whole position of the pope. This was the point particularly emphasized by Msgr. Dreux-Brézé, the Bishop of Moulins.[166] Msgr. Cousseau, Bishop of Angoulême, gave Veuillot his assurances that he was in the right in his polemic against E. About.[167] Even though Veuillot had recently been told by the pope himself: "You have always been on the right course; you do not stray from it,"[168] it must have been very reassuring to receive this episcopal approval closer to home. He replied sharply to one C. Lefevre, who tried to maintain in *La Patrie* that the opinion of the bishops of France supported that of the emperor.[169] Whatever the attitudes of the individual French bishops might happen to be on the matter of the lay press, and *L'Univers* in particular, the bishops in general could sense that the days of pontifical temporal power were near an end, and that the Italy envisaged by Cavour would not be good either for the papacy, or for the church in France.

Napoleon made a show of worshiping at Notre Dame Cathedral before his departure for Italy and the war against Austria. Veuillot, still faintly hoping that it might be worthwhile to praise anything that appeared to be good about the emperor, reported this to the readers of *L'Univers* and wound up the article with the words, "Let us pray that God may protect France and the Emperor!" Some of the liberal Catholics professed to see this as Veuillot playing the emperor's game, but Du Lac did what he could to banish the idea.[170] Veuillot was, in fact disgusted with the emperor. In a letter to one of the friends with whom he regularly corresponded, Madame de Cuverville, he said: "So far as I am concerned, my dreams are cruelly dashed. Where now is my Charlemagne? Although my neighbor (Montalembert) is in the country, I am not able to cast my eyes on the terrace from my window without seeing him, without hearing him congratulate himself, 'I certainly was right.' That horrible 'I certainly was right,' which exults in its hateful perspicacity, is one of the things that poisons our spring in Paris. I do not reproach myself, however, for having hoped for something better. Whatever bad may come, I will rejoice, on the contrary, for having always hoped, for having wanted the best, and for having more easily believed in it than in evil."[171]

The war was short. French victories over the Austrians at Magenta (4 June 1859) and Solferino (24 June 1859) told the story. The crafty Cavour had managed to goad Austria into attacking Sardinia, and the French army, with Napoleon III physically present but actually under the command of MacMahon, defeated the Austrians in the difficult terrain of northern Italy. Veuillot was thus left in a very bad position. A patriot against a short and victorious war! To Maguelonne in Rome at the time of news of the victory at Magenta Veuillot admitted: "French [national] spirit has completely gained the upper hand, and the war is now popular. There goes the whole idea of an alliance of the Catholic lands now."[172] With great excitement everywhere about the success of the army, Veuillot did not have much to talk about. Almost the only subject on which he agitated during the conduct of operations was the inadequate provision for military chaplains with the army, and even this complaint was taken amiss by the ministry of the interior.[173] The public, despite the extensive casualties of the two hard battles, gloried in the victories. Actually, Napoleon's hand was not as strong as it appeared. He hastened to make an early armistice with Austria for fear that the Germanic Confederation might move against him if he moved too near those borders of Austria which were covered by the Confederation. In making peace he allowed Austria to keep Venetia, though not Lombardy. Cavour, not consulted about this, was quite beside himself with disappointment. Napoleon as a consequence did not get Nice and Savoy until later.

As soon as the war was over, Veuillot felt he could start criticizing the policies of the regime again: France, by fighting Austria, was weakening the papacy. This theme of Veuillot's was attacked by *La Patrie* at the start of July. *L'Univers* was called "more Austrian than Catholic," an even more unjust tag than "Mazzini of the Church." The author of the new epithet was Théodore-Casimir Delamarre, director of *La Patrie*, regent of the Bank of France, and a big force in business circles. He sneeringly observed that Cardinal Antonnelli was not a priest, and blamed him personally for the troubles between pontifical troops and Italian nationalists in Perugia. His tone drove Veuillot to make fanatical statements in reply. Veuillot declared "Christianity is the papacy." If the term Christianity were used without this definition understood, it might be used to cover "Anglicanism," "Prussianism," or "Muscovitism." The Holy See is Christianity, Veuillot maintained.[174] The Roman Question came to be ever more emotional. Veuillot dug into Latin to bring out Charlemagne's most appropriate title: *Carolus gratia Dei rex, regnique Francorum rector, et devotus Ecclesiae defenso, atque adjutor in omnibus Apostolicae Sedis.* He noted that the "pious Empress" had distributed religious medals to the officers going off to the war, but by implication one could conclude that Napoleon III compared very unfavorably to Charlemagne.[175]

The disfavor of the government was soon expressed, in the form of an official warning concerning a piece he published 10 July 1858. His comments on this date had opened with discussion of an article received by *Le Siècle* from some critics of the régime entitled "Une enquête sur le 2 décembre et les faits qui le suivent." Veuillot picked the article to pieces, but in a manner even more derogatory of the government. He dwelt on the authors' criticism of pontifical troops who fought back at "patriots" who attacked them. These authors' presumption that revolution was undoubtedly correct brought from him the most stinging sarcasm.[176] In this case the régime felt the sting, and a formal warning was issued. Louis Veuillot had long known he was being watched by La Guéronnière.[177] This "Grand Master" of the press, as Veuillot had called him, explained to the minister of the interior that "since the establishment of the empire *L'Univers* has shifted from giving support to the government, on many occasions, to visibly creating a party within the church against the Concordat and the independence of the civil power. It has succeeded. The bonds of this journal with Rome, the audacity of its polemics, the talent of its principal editor, have given it a truly directional influence over a large part of the clergy. Before the war *L'Univers* defended the rights of Austria in Italy and the Treaties of 1815. Since the arms of France have taken up the struggle for Italian independence, it has been unable to hold this ground, but there is one point upon which its resistance has been absolute; that is it holds it to be the duty of the papacy to refuse these reforms in the exercise of its temporal power." La Guéronnière went on to maintain that the article in question was "perfidious" in regard to the "glorious campaign that France has just made for the freeing of Italy." He objected to what Veuillot said about the bad effects of revolution on French society. He claimed Veuillot was fomenting class struggle. "He disquiets consciences, deceives the clergy, calumniates the government, compromises the august character of religion in speaking of avenging the papacy, which France protects and respects," La Guéronnière went on.[178] Several of these points were enumerated in the formal warning, which Veuillot then published in *L'Univers*, together with a letter to the minister of the interior in which he maintained that he had been the first among the men of the press to hail the government in December of 1851, a fact which, he said, the *rédacteur* of the *avertissement* (La Guéronnière) should remember. Since there was no delay, no debate, and no appeal, those who put out such a warning should be just, he declared in closing.[179] Taconet had been named as *gérant,* but Veuillot as author of the article in question. The points which were enumerated in the warning were those La Guéronnière had outlined to the Duc de Padoue, but of course the incidentally flattering points the former had made about Veuillot's influence were not included in the warning.

The terms of the armistice with Austria were not announced until the day after the warning issued to Veuillot. Thus there was little that he could write about for the rest of the year. He hinted in a letter to Maguelonne that the real cause of the warning had not been given, but he admitted that he had not been following the official line on the war,[180] which was the ostensible reason for the warning he had received. Many people gave their sympathy to Veuillot at this juncture, and he showed a certain gallant pleasure about it all. To the Comtesse de Ségur he said: "If the valiant and triumphant La Guéronnière could read your letter, I would be well avenged for the warning." He also declared, less chivalrously, that what Rouland and La Guéronnière had not been able to pardon was that he had said Antonnelli was as honest as any of the ministers of Napoleon III. He represented Taconet to the Comtesse as having noble courage, maintaining that when he was told that, if he asked, the warning would be rescinded, according to Veuillot, Taconet replied that the warning was unjust, but since it had been given, he would just keep it. "Ah!" exclaimed Veuillot, "this manufacturer of cartridge boxes has a stouter heart than a large number of gentlemen and academicians of our acquaintance!"[181] Then he spoke as though he did not think *L'Univers* was in any greater danger of suppression than it had been a bit earlier, but perhaps he said this because he felt the fundamental situation was no worse, and for the immediate future he did not anticipate committing any too direct provocation of the régime.

During that summer and fall many of Veuillot's activities fell outside the realm of *L'Univers*. He was greatly interested in the fact that Eugène had a son, and he seemed very much absorbed in the poetry he was then writing, particularly the part of his *Filles de Babylone* which he called "Vocation d'Isaie." He seemed to value the reactions of Msgr. Parisis to his poetry, as much as his advice about editorial policy, and when the good bishop let him know he did not like the poem, Veuillot decided to publish it anonymously! "I submitted to him as judge, and he condemned me; I am executed. I hide ignominiously my ignominy. . .," he wrote his literary friend, Segrétain.[182] In one of his letters to the Comtesse de Ségur he stated that he had become a poet at the age of 46.[183] He had written, in point of fact, a great many poems before this age, but, curiously, at this particular one of the critical points in his life he did indeed appear for the first time to have become seriously and primarily absorbed in his poetry.

In editorials, Veuillot now depended on the tried and true themes. Donoso Cortés was a safe topic, as was criticism of Russia. Metternich could safely be spoken of, and Veuillot's formerly unpublicized interview with him at the end of 1849 was an acceptable subject.[184] In August, when a number of political criminals and opponents of the government, ranging from Félix Pyat to Victor Hugo, were given amnesty, warnings issued to the press were also revoked. Veuillot did not enjoy being in the company of the other recipients of this amnesty and declared to his brother, "I am proud of *L'Univers* for not having shed the slightest tear of sensibility at this amnesty."[185] To be sure, it was not long before official censure was again applied to *L'Univers* and its principal editor. In October of 1859 he was held responsible for twofold irritation of the authorities at the bureau of the press. In the first place, he had reverted to a theme of criticizing the policy of the government for cooperating with the British in China to the detriment of the Christians there. General Montauban was made Marshal Palikao as a mark of imperial favor, for success in pacifying the Chinese, but Veuillot voiced all manner of objections to the expedition, with the result that his long article of 7 October 1859 brought another formal warning.[186] Then Veuillot invited further trouble by telling the readers of *L'Univers* in so many words that the regime had ordered the journal to publish no more episcopal letters.[187] The journal was expected simply to desist, through normal prudence, from a practice which had resulted in embarrassing criticisms of the government's policy in Italy, but Veuillot unmasked the degree and nature of the censorship.

Not all pressures on Veuillot were solely from the regime, but some were by-products of the liberal press. In early October he was exploiting what should have been a "safe" topic, holding up to public ridicule the sordid life of a notorious Englishman, Lord Henry Seymour, who had just died in Paris. *Le Siècle,* which had recently been treating with great consideration the revolutionaries of Italy, and their atrocities in Parma and elsewhere, came now also to Seymour's defense in such a way as to stir up some of its more violent readers.[188] An agent for wines, one Perdriou, living at 32, Rue Gallois, in Bercy, wrote a letter that Veuillot published. The letter, taking Veuillot to task for criticizing Seymour for leaving some of his wealth to his hosts in France, called Veuillot "un crétin et un homme sans conscience."[189] The letter was violent enough for the police to take note of it. The agent reporting the episode to the prefecture said that this Perdriou "enjoyed a certain reputation for intelligence." Moreover, upon thus breaking into print, "he received the congratulations of a large number of neighbors, inhabitants of the commune of Bercy." Some of the congratulations were said to have come from very high sources. Adding insult to injury, the agent further suggested that the apparent misspelling of "Seymour" by Perdriou might have been the "invention of the editor-in-chief."[190] Whatever the prejudices of the police informant may have been, it was evident that not everyone in Bercy liked Veuillot. It is also possible that Veuillot had a stronger base in the Faubourg Saint-Germain than in rough-and-ready Bercy where his mother had been hostess to the winebargers.

As the end of 1859 approached, Veuillot's position with respect to the régime became completely untenable. Napoleon was interested in whatever compromise he might effect with ultramontanes, but Veuillot was far from alone in taking an uncompromising stand. Even Dupanloup published a pamphlet in defense of papal rule. Montalembert had gotten into serious trouble with the régime for an article in *Le Correspondant* on 25 October entitled "Pie IX et la France en 1849 et en 1859." Veuillot did not display any special sympathy for his old leader in this regard,[191] but he did express sympathy for the former minister of public instruction, Villemain, who had written a brochure entitled *La France, l'Empire et la Papauté.*[192] He felt that all the bishops except Cousseau (Angoulême), Cœur (Troyes), and Berteaud (Tulle) were solidly supporting the rights of the pope against the Italian nationalists and their patron, Napoleon.[193] In this conviction, he raised his voice loudly against an "anonymous" brochure, *Le Pape et le Congrès*, written there is little doubt by La Guéronnière, and obviously the direct work of Napoleon III.[194] The brochure was evidently preparing the way for more demands to be made on the pope. Exactly at Christmas the anonymous brochure was countered by not only an article by Veuillot, but also a letter he dispatched to the pope and published in *L'Univers*. "As for us, your children of France, we believe that your authority is only to be defined by you yourself, and we recognize as yours all the rights you recognize for yourself."[195] He left no room for Napoleon and Cavour. *Le Constitutionnel* carried a reply by "L. Boniface," who one way or another was certainly speaking for the emperor, but the main answer was a technical second warning (the one of July presumably having been sponged away with the amnesty). This warning was for having attempted "to organize in France, under a religious pretext, a political agitation."[196]

For Veuillot politics and religion were inseparable, so the charge, whether made in a fair spirit or not, had a certain logic. Along these lines another episode tied in very appropriately. The general who was in charge of French forces in Rome, General Goyon, was entirely disposed toward the pope, and on a ceremonial occasion at the start of 1860 exchanged complimentary speeches with the pope. In this favorable circumstance, the pope added to his friendly words for his supposed French defenders an attack on the imperial brochure, *Le Pape et le Congrès*. By 10 January Veuillot had received the pope's words, but he had also received an order from the government not to publish them. He did not print the pope's allocution, but instead wrote an article of his own that was the strongest advocacy possible of the pope's rights. He ended by posing the question which, he said, was before Europe: Pius IX or Garibaldi. "Who can doubt the choice of France," he concluded.

The stage was completely now set for the dramatic last number of *L'Univers*. In this number which appeared on 29 January 1860, there were plenty of other fireworks, beside the principal bombshell which the pope himself provided. Veuillot managed to get in some of the most shocking quotations he could find, from the pens of both Quinet and About, as well as from others, in an effort to fill the reader with horror at these revolutionaries who were trying to destroy the pope. He also copied from *L'Union Bourguignonne* a letter from his somewhat liberal Catholic friend, Foisset, who occupied a court post in Dijon. Foisset, who defended the temporal power of the pope, wrote primarily about the unfair way in which Lacordaire had been misrepresented by the press that supported the imperial policies. Along with the sympathies Lacordaire had for Italy, he also had supported the pope's rights to territory, according to Foisset.[197] Veuillot thus made demonstrable all claims of the broadest Catholic backing for it when he published the encyclical *Nullis certe*.

Although Veuillot had spoken lightly to the Comtesse de Ségur of *L'Univers'* precarious position, privately he must have contemplated its desperate position throughout the fall of 1859. Probably the most dangerous part of his speculation concerned aid for a volunteer army to support the pope. In October he talked about raising money for this purpose, in writing to Parisis,[198] and in December he informed Maguelonne of specific plans for recruitment.[199] Men like La Tour and others urged Veuillot on[200] – as though he needed any urging. Veuillot meanwhile knew the seriousness of defying the governmental decree governing the publication of episcopal letters.[201] His very avoidance of publication of the pope's allocution at the start of the year showed the heed he had paid to the specific prohibition with regard to that matter. Even though Veuillot was disposed to avoid any move that would surely bring immediate suppression, he found himself boxed into such a position, on 28 January 1860, that he had to take the fatal step.

As late as the day before he had been expressing hopes of being able to walk the tightrope. On the twenty-eighth, however, the encyclical *Nullis certe* reached him. In it the pope spoke of "criminal rebellion" and of his rights. He was speaking in response to what the Emperor of the French had said and done, and he did not want his words buried. So far as Veuillot was concerned there was no question at all as to what to do. *Le Pape et le Congrès* was not going to be the last word, and if the pope asked to express himself with regard to the threat to his own sovereignty, the columns of *L'Univers* were his, whatever the price. There was little discussion among the editors, who were all like-minded. Only Taconet, who had hundreds of thousands of francs tied up in *L'Univers* dragged his feet. But, as Veuillot explained to Maguelonne, Taconet was confronted with the threat of mass resignation, and however "little decided for sacrifice" he may have been,[202] he would scarcely have been any better off without his staff, so he gave in to the general desire. Actually Veuillot appreciated the difficulty in which Taconet found himself, and the real sacrifice that Taconet was making, although it was ameliorated later with the launching of *Le Monde* which in a very restricted way filled the gap left by the suppression of *L'Univers*. As Veuillot explained to a sympathetic clergyman, *L'Univers* was valued at 500,000 francs, and he was in danger of losing 200,000 out of his own pocket.[203] However, economics do not go very far in explaining the decisions of partisans like those running *L'Univers*, including Taconet. In explaining the situation to his colleagues, Veuillot referred to the encyclical as the "death warrant," and pointed out that inevitably the forthcoming number would be the last.[204]

He could not have been more correct in his prognostication. Napoleon III signed the order of suppression on 29 January, and a well-prepared letter accompanied the move.[205] *L'Univers* was charged with being an organ of "a religious party" which made daily opposition to the state, "sapping the fundamental bases upon which the relations of the church and civil society are established." It made open war "on our oldest national traditions, and was dangerous to religion itself, which it compromised by mixing with it passions unworthy of it, and associating with it doctrines irreconcilable with the duties of patriotism." Moreover, *L'Univers*, or more properly Veuillot, was "insensible" to warnings. The true interests of the church, and of public order, according to the minister of the interior, required its suppression, because the doctrines and pretensions which *L'Univers* was attempting to resuscitate were not up-to-date. Even the old French monarchy had combatted the stands of *L'Univers*, and the empire would continue to do this.

The best proof that the editors of *L'Univers* knew what they were doing is the letter that they collectively wrote immediately to the pope. Their "great consolation" they told the holy father was to be able to throw themselves at his feet. They reminded him that it was "an encyclical of Pius IX which had given life to *L'Univers*, and it was for an encyclical of Pius IX that life was given up." They asked forgiveness for their past faults, and they insisted that they would stay together in the future in order to be able to serve him in any way they could.[206] The gesture resulted from a tearful meeting held at the time of the decree of suppression,[207] and the letter was drafted by Veuillot. Actually there is no way that the sincerity of the author or the group can be challenged. They meant what they said, however dramatic and out of harmony with the prevailing outlook of the twentieth century it may sound. It is significant to look at the order of the signatures. The names appended are: "Louis Veuillot; Du Lac; Eugène Veuillot; Coquille; Aubineau; Rupert; Chantrel; Courcy (De La Roche-Héron); le Comte de La Tour, deputy in the Corps Législatif; le Comte de Maumigny; l'Abbé Cornet; Barrier; Taconet." Taconet, and even Barrier, whose name was appended to so many articles written by others, were appropriately at the end, and even more appropriately so in view of something less than precipitate action on their part. Du Lac, the clergyman and Veuillot's "master," signed before Eugène. It is also interesting to see a member of the legislative body among the group in the person of the Comte de La Tour. If one is looking for a significant collection of ultramontane names, it would be hard to find a document more indicative of the hard core of this group. The pope responded, but not until 25 February. He wrote to "Our dear sons, Louis Veuillot and other editors of the religious journal entitled *L'Univers*" and he said about all that could be said by way of acknowledgment of the sacrifice.[208] It is also interesting to note that Pius IX went out of his way to write two letters to Élise in the course of the spring and summer.[209] Eugène heard that the pontiff exclaimed "Caro Veuillot! Caro *Univers*!" on hearing the news of the suppression.[210]

When the journal was suppressed, Veuillot was both realistic in accepting the situation and also over-dramatic about it. He admitted that not only Taconet was in financial danger, but also he himself, Du Lac, his brother (this order!), Rupert, and others were in an awkward way. "Thanks be to God, we all have quiet and even happy consciences in our sadness. . . .It was the publication of the encyclical that killed us, but we could not have escaped for long," he now confessed to Msgr. Gignoux.[211] More dramatically he announced to another bishop: "*L'Univers* is quite dead. It was established, it lived, by a miracle; only a miracle will bring it back." Forgetting apparently what he said about conscience the same day to Gignoux, he added in this other letter that he was willing to go into exile voluntarily – "in expiation of my faults."[212] Small inconsistencies, however, could only be expected in his agitated state of mind. He had sealed the death warrant of *L'Univers* himself, and he had made his journal an international cause in thus opposing the policy of the French empire. Had he bowed to censorship at this point, he would not have been Louis Veuillot, or under the circumstances, even normal.

The suppression of a daily newspaper that had fewer than 20,000 subscribers would hardly seem to be an important step for an authoritarian state to take. *L'Univers* had done the unallowable in directly opposing the policy of the regime and also had disregarded specific instructions to it. What *L'Univers* in the hands of Veuillot had done was to choose, and clearly choose, between the French empire, for which he had the highest hopes and in whose emperor he had once seen a modern Charlemagne, and Catholicism. He chose between a ruler, and an increasingly secular one, and the church. He became a Guelf among Ghibellines. In choosing the church he was making no vague choice. His Christendom was not some vague world movement such as might be defined by Maret or protestants. It was Catholicism, centered in Rome. Even taking travel problems into account it is worth noting that he went many times to Rome, but never to the Holy Land. After taking ship at Marseilles, as he had to do for a trip to Rome, he could have spent a few more days on the calm Mediterranean and gone to Jerusalem. But for him Rome was the center, and the Vicar of Christ on earth was indeed the pope. A bitter liberal Catholic spoke unjustly of Pius IX, when he declared that Pius IX outdid Louis XIV, that his actions proclaimed: "L'Église, c'est moi!"[213] This saying does, however, justly describe the attitude of his adherent Veuillot. The pope really was the substance of the church for Veuillot. In addition, Pius IX was the anchor of all Veuillot had advocated and all he represented. In the words of Montalembert to his brother-in-law Mérode, "Pius IX has made Veuillot; Veuillot has made Napoleon III, and Napoleon III has paid back Pius IX in a way that you know better than anyone."[214] Veuillot had only helped, to be sure, to make Napoleon, but Veuillot would not have been the influence that he was without Pius IX. Most serious for Catholicism, and for all of Christendom, was the fact that Veuillot may have made Pius IX and Roman Catholicism appear more militant than was the case, and may have done so in such a way as to leave the special imprint of the outraged journalist from Boynes on the whole image of the church that was presented to the French public. On the other side of the coin, so far as Catholic solidarity was concerned, Veuillot himself made a good target for many who otherwise might have criticized the hierarchy or the pope. Veuillot was not a doubter in any regard, and surely he had no doubt that the Lord had come to bring not peace but the sword. In his case the sword was a pen (he used a goose quill), and the emperor could only end a decade of peace between them by snapping it.

CHAPTER VII

THE MAN WITHOUT THE JOURNAL

All sorts of people, including those who had not been friendly to Veuillot, sent condolences on the suppression of *L'Univers.*[1] One had the impression that death had struck, an impression to which Louis himself heavily contributed. On Louis' passports he had always been described as an *écrivain* or *homme des lettres*, however, rather than a journalist. He liked to call himself an "ouvrier en chambre."[2] The years 1860 through 1867 showed that he was not only a journalist. He wrote as extensively and to equal effect as when he had been principal editor of *L'Univers.* In a way his life became even more dramatic in this period, because he had become suspect in the eyes of the régime, and was watched as a potentially dangerous figure in a way that he had not been before. His time was freer for special interests, and it was more possible for him to travel without the pressure of returning to the offices of *L'Univers.* Nevertheless, he was always somewhat at loose ends. He seemed more unstable in these years, and without *L'Univers* he was more conscious of himself and his relations with others. The idea of reviving *L'Univers*, or some substitute for it, remained a dominant preoccupation for him. He never forgot it, and his regular requests to be allowed to revive it were more than perfunctory.

At several times of crisis in his life Veuillot hastened to Rome, as though memories of the inspiration of 1838 and perhaps some new words of Pius IX would somehow give him clear direction. February 1860 was no exception, but even as he set out for Rome the ashes of *L'Univers* were his main preoccupation. He worried a good deal about Taconet and the hundreds of thousands of francs involved, as well as what would fill the vacuum for the readers of his beloved organ. Taconet and others stirred around, and within a very short time the ultramontane manufacturer and publisher was able to buy out *La Voix de la Vérité,* the little sheet of the Abbé Migne – founder of *L'Univers*! He was allowed by the regime to do this and to change the name to *Le Monde*, with the proviso that neither Louis nor Eugène were to be associated with the editorial board.[3] The régime,apparently did not rule out Du Lac, or any of the other editors, who solved their employment problem by moving over to the new venture of Taconet. Its first number appeared on 15 February. Louis Veuillot, though proscribed from participation, followed its early days with great interest. He wrote Parisis from Paris, before departing for Rome, that he doubted Taconet would get the authorization, and he even advised Taconet to plead bankruptcy. He thought that the existing religious journals were out of the question, *L'Ami* because it too was suspect now, *La Gazette de France* because it was still Gallican, and *L'Union* because it was clearly legitimist. He knew that the condition would be posed in any case that neither he nor his brother could participate, and he added, "I do not think that I could or should edit any other journal than *L'Univers*."[4] Veuillot, during his trip to Rome, worried about how *Le Monde* would fare, and he feared that even though it was no *L'Univers* it too might be silenced by the régime, and his friends would again be out on the street.[5]

Louis Veuillot cannot be said to have been guilty of heeding the morrow with respect to his own finances. His big concern was the Denier de Saint-Pierre,[6] and secondarily to raise funds for a future journal.[7] There did exist wealthy partisans eager to look out for Veuillot, notably the Comtesse de Ségur, "Maman Ségur," who was taking steps to organize a subscription for Veuillot personally, one that would give his life a fairy-tale-godmother twist.[8] Veuillot joked about these benevolent schemes, and obviously did not accept any such personal gift. The police heard conflicting reports as to whether or not Taconet continued to pay Veuillot 6000 francs as a pension,[9] which certainly Veuillot deserved. It was probably true that the dowry of his wife, which may have been 50,000 francs, was altogether exhausted by now. Money, however, except for immediate arrangements, was never a concern of Veuillot's, however gleefully he may have counted new subscriptions and cast a petit bourgeois eye on affairs of *L'Univers*.

Veuillot was determined to touch base again in Rome, and by 12 February he was on the way, stopping at Marseille to change from the train to the boat. Five or six smokers had apparently bothered Veuillot on the trip (though he himself puffed cigars), but at the station he forgot these irritations when he was greeted by his rich businessman friend Chuit, with whom he was now invited to stay, as earlier, until boarding ship. On the platform also was a representative of the banker-publisher Mirès, who owned Granier de Cassagnac's *Pays*, which currently was being favored by Veuillot. Mirès was an extraordinary man, a Jew whose friendship Veuillot was enjoying at the very time of the recent protest by leading Parisian Jews against some of his writings. What this man's true religious beliefs and feelings were, of course, one cannot say, but he was *commanditaire* of the papal railroads. He obviously had warm feelings for the pope and for his strongest supporters. In any case, "his man" on the platform had made arrangement for handling Veuillot's baggage, passport, and other details of his voyage. Veuillot attempted to reimburse him for the price of his passage, at which Mirès' man made such a *geste indigné* that Veuillot did not press any further, with the observation in his note to Élise that with the choppy sea he would no doubt be paying his debt, to the fish. He was traveling alone, although he had intended to take Eugène with him, because Eugène's newborn-son Pierre was sick.[10]

Veuillot kept close notes about what he did all during this stay in Rome, which lasted from mid-February until late March 1860. It was his fourth visit to Rome. He knew his way around in the Eternal City, and within a very short time had met with many of the key prelates. He listened closely to what they had to say, especially Cardinal Marini, who felt that the secular aspects of the papal government had become too important, and who regretted that despite the growing bureaucracy the ways of the papal court were still too old-fashioned.[11] He also had several interviews with the pope, including a very long one on the 18th of February, shortly after his arrival. There is no doubt that Veuillot did have some influence in Rome. Montalembert wrote to Mérode, shortly after Veuillot arrived, quoting his friend Léon Corudet to the effect "that the greatest misfortune of Pius IX at this moment would be to have such a personage near his throne."[12]

In mentioning his first long interview with the pope, Veuillot, who did not customarily repeat himself very much, even to different people, for a man who wrote perhaps two-thousand letters a year, did not neglect to repeat to all his correspondents that the pope began by tearfully declaring to him: "Blessed are those who are persecuted for rightousness sake, for theirs is the Kingdom of Heaven." The pope, according to Veuillot, wept several times more, especially when Veuillot told him of the Denier de Saint-Pierre, which Élise was collecting. They talked of many lesser things, including a decoration for Segrétain (a deputy and mayor of Laval), and then the pope did not spare Veuillot the fears he had for the near future. He was apparently expecting to be driven from Rome. But he also said: "We shall return; but for the glory of truth and for the éclat of its triumph, it is necessary for us to be beaten, I say beaten; the pope does not die." Thoughts along these lines were the last Veuillot heard during this initial interview. Leaving the pope he went to Saint Peter's, where he saw small children boosting each other up to kiss the toe of the time-honored bronze statue of Saint Peter, a favorite of pilgrims through so many centuries. "Vive Jesus!" he closed his report to Élise.[14]

Primarily Veuillot had come to Rome for this sort of experience. The charm of Rome was in being in Rome, he told Segrétain, even though he did not like his hotel, even though he was cold. It was raining, and his usual physical complaints were with him.[15] But another more practical motive bringing Veuillot to Rome was to talk about what to do about a journal. *Le Monde* was something, but endangered as it was, it was not the strong voice Veuillot wanted lifted. What in its place? While talking with the pope, Veuillot noted that the pontiff had placed on the table where *L'Univers* usually was to be found (or so Veuillot thought) the new *Le Monde*. The pope gestured sadly toward it and said that it contained a good article by *Dou Lac* (so Veuillot imitated the pope's pronunciation in his letter to Du Lac), but obviously it was not the same paper – and Veuillot did not bother to point out that already the frail successor-sheet had received an admonition from the regime.[16] The question was whether or not to establish a journal somewhere outside of France. The régime in France was also concerned about this possibility. A report of 3 March says in so many words that officials had opened Veuillot's letters to his sister which included observations that the pope did not trust anything about the French government. These officials also did not believe that *Le Monde* was succeeding, and they were curious as to what use would be made of Veuillot's talents by the papacy.[17] Even before Veuillot left for Rome one agent had heard that Veuillot was prepared to take a post abroad.[18] By the time he had talked to the pope Veuillot was writing Du Lac that he might go to Brussels, or Geneva (Rupert of *L'Univers* was Swiss), or even London, offensive though that last assignment might be to him. A new *L'Univers* would be set up outside of France to invade France some way or other.[19] On 20 March 1860 he wrote Élise cryptically that the matter had been "regulated,"[20] but in actual fact nothing had been decided. *L'Univers* was dead, or at least asleep for seven years, and the journalist was going to have to be "man of letters" for that period of time.

Not only was Louis Veuillot not to be an editor, he was not even to be director of the papal railroads! From the very moment of the suppression of *L'Univers*, the financier Mirès had offered this post to him, but he had steadily refused it.[21] Nevertheless, there was still talk about the possibility during Veuillot's stay in Rome, and during the month of May the security officials were still hearing that the post was being offered to him.[22] Veuillot seems to have had railroads on his mind when, in complaining by mail to poor Élise about his health and his plans going awry, he exclaimed: "Like a railroad, I am completely derailed."[23] But although Mirès did not in fact persuade Veuillot to associate himself with running the pope's trains he, Mirès, continued to be associated with Veuillot in the minds of the police.[24] He was thought to be writing something for Mirès, or to be receiving money from him – and also from the Duc de La Rochefoucauld.[25] The suspicions of the police were not without some foundation, since Veuillot's correspondence shows Mirès did give 10,000 francs to Elise for the Denier de Saint Pierre.[26] Veuillot was more generous with his words for Mirès than almost anyone about whom he wrote. He repeatedly called him "gentilhomme Mirès" to his sister and referring to him said, "Jews and Judaizers conduct themselves better toward me than certain Christians."[27] Again, to his sister: "All that you say to me about this son of Israel gives me great pleasure. I like him very much, and if he becomes poor some day, I will tell him this and make him see it. Saint Peter will not fail to notice what is put in his bourse."[28] In the heartless modern sense Veuillot was not antisemitic!

One French clergyman whom he noted with great interest in Rome was the Abbé Lucien Bonaparte, grandson of Napoleon I's brother Lucien, who was later to become a cardinal. He was interested to see that the Abbé Bonaparte had no leaning toward Napoleon III politically, and that he did not personally resemble his illustrious relative either. Moreover, the other French clergymen at the papal court also seemed to be far removed from Napoleon III.[29] Veuillot had much contact with certain of the pope's officials, and it was even suggested that he was helping Cardinal Antonelli draft a reply to a message sent to the Holy See by the new French foreign minister, Thouvenel, who had, significantly it seemed, just replaced the more clerically oriented Walewski.[30] Veuillot had little confidence in the work of the papal minister of arms at this time, Mérode, whose relations with Veuillot again seemed to be clouded. No doubt the persuasion of Montalembert was a factor in this estrangement. General de Lamoricière, in command of the army, was on the other hand highly rated by Veuillot.[31] As volunteers for the papal army trickled in from Ireland, Belgium, France, Canada, and elsewhere, the problem of supply began to develop.[32] Even after he had left Rome Veuillot was concerned about the procurement of cloth and was writing *L'Univers'* former agent in Rome, Maguelonne, about the services his old friend Augustin Testas could render. He was trying also to see what could be done about getting a decoration for this friend on the Île Saint Louis.[33]

Politics and practical matters would have seemed to be the proper sphere for Veuillot's discussions with the prelates and, of course, the pope, while he was in Rome, but he did not confine himself strictly to such matters. One might even have questioned, if he loved the pope as much as he professed, the advisability of his seeing the pope on so many occasions. Was not he, a person in bad odor with the French government, compromising the pope in the eyes of foreign governments? Surely it was good for Veuillot to be with the pope, but was it good for the pope to be reported, even by French agents to the French régime, to have been in such constant touch with Veuillot? Could not Veuillot have accomplished his own general mission without allowing it to appear as though he might be trying to exercise a directional influence in Rome? In conversation with the pope, Veuillot injected the subject of hypocrisy on the part of the enemies of the church, which led the pope to say that he had personally excommunicated the King of Piedmont. The pope recommended silence on the matter of excommunications, when Veuillot asked him. But Veuillot foolishly wrote all this down in his notes,[34] and scarcely more than a week elapsed before these notes were seized by French authorities. How well did Veuillot serve Pius IX in this respect? Had he led the pope to make some remark about the suitability of excommunicating Napoleon III, he might have caused still more trouble. He wrote to his friend Ségretain deploring that "the horizon is covered with clouds,"[35] but his ill-advised note-making can be said to have raised still more clouds.

Veuillot took leave of the pope on 26 March, and not long afterwards departed from Civitavecchia on a Neapolitan steamer, the *Capri*, large, quiet, and several hours faster than the others, he had heard.[36] Apparently the trip was as good as expected. He arrived at and departed from Marseille the same day, and reached Paris on 1 April 1860. There a suprise was in store for him. He certainly must have known that there was surveillance on him, and that his trip to Rome at a critical time, when the new foreign minister Thouvenel was letting it be known that the Papal States and the temporal power were not going to be defended, rendered him doubly suspect. The régime expected that he might be bearing a bull of excommunication against Napoleon III![37] Why did it suspect this step was being taken? – and that Veuillot would be bringing word of the step? In any case, what a time to have in his possession written evidence of discussions with Cardinal Antonelli about general foreign policy and also that memorandum about discussing with the pope the excommunication of the King of Piedmont! On reaching home he was greeted by three police officers, in plain clothes, who contented themselves with digging through his luggage and taking all of his papers![38] Nothing arbitrary or illegal was being done. These officers were there on order of the minister of the interior. But here was the information – all those views of prelates, the pope himself, and the thoughts Veuillot had recorded while in Rome. There was the evidence also of who was contributing to the Denier of Saint Peter, generosity which might be very ungenerously interpreted by the secular officials of the Second Empire.

Veuillot protested strongly to the agents that they were taking his private papers. In fact, he was also the bearer of papers to the nuncio, though not the particular ones suspected by the régime. It was easy indeed to find and seize the papal correspondence in the three small trunks of Louis Veuillot. The material was of course promptly given to the nuncio, but not before it had been carefully extracted by the régime. The agent making the report of Veuillot's distress over the seizure was obviously amused at his embarrassment, and particularly thought the joke was on Veuillot for having been betrayed to the police by a fellow-traveler who had won his unsuspecting confidence on the trip.[39] After a few days his personal correspondence, letters from his children included, was returned to him, but other material was retained for some time and copied. Publicity for his plight was not easily obtained, though courageous Mirès and Granier de Cassagnac carried a statement in *Pays* of what had been returned to him – and what had not.[40] When he went to see the minister of the interior, Billault, to protest the matter, Billault went out of his way to be polite, even complimenting him generously, as Veuillot himself had to admit,[41] but it was quite some time before all the material was out of the government's hands. Practically all of his notes had been extracted and copied in the interval. Veuillot's incoming mail was opened for some time after his return. Well into May he was still complaining of his letters being opened, and the police were hearing of and making note of his complaints.[42]

Veuillot furnishes a good example of the vulnerability of a private citizen presuming to dabble in public affairs under an authoritarian régime. Actually, this sort of surveillance was applied to persons even more prominent than he under the Third Republic, such as the emperor's own cousin, Prince Napoleon. The idea of carrying compromising papers in his effects was most unsound. He knew that he was, in fact, subversive to the régime, which perhaps deserved such treatment, and he was lucky that he got off as lightly as he did. For reasons of expediency the régime would have had little to gain, and perhaps considerable face to lose, by prosecuting Veuillot for his act. After his papers were indeed taken and held, one can only note a gentleness on the part of officialdom, which did not press the search of his effects beyond what he had just brought back from Rome. Veuillot not only had not been careful, but also he was out of character with the image he held of himself as the good soldier of the church. The good soldier is expected to eat secret orders rather than allow them to be captured. He apparently had made no precautions for the destruction of his notes. He could easily have carried the papal correspondence in such a way, with appropriate seals, that the régime would not have touched it. Here is one of the best examples of the way Veuillot from time to time embarrassed the church and compromised it with his pen.

The episode of the seizure of his papers brought no further direct consequences. No doubt it impressed on Veuillot that caution has its place. It also must have helped discourage him from any further speculation about establishing a journal outside of France. Under the censorship being applied to him, there really was no opportunity for him to do such a thing. The régime suspected that despite the provision that he not be on the editorial board of *Le Monde*, he would be writing for this journal. Even rather late in the summer of 1860 one observer for the police, whose observations in this case were inaccurate, speculated that *Le Monde* would pass into his hands under a pseudonym.[43] It was also reported that he sought the opportunity of writing for *L'Union*, but that Henri de Riancey, with the plea of tight finances, would not give Veuillot this outlet because Veuillot had not helped Riancey become a senator in a period when his support would have been important.[44] In point of fact, Veuillot was practically excluded from any chance to write for the press even under a pseudonym. Montalembert's biographer, Lecanuet, maintains that he did contribute to *Le Monde*,[45] but Eugène, who had a high regard for Lecanuet, points out that his brother contributed only two obituaries and one strictly religious piece to the new Catholic journal during his days of banishment from the press.[46] In fact, he completely broke off relations with Taconet during 1860 over this issue, with Taconet understandably holding Louis Veuillot at arm's length for fear that his new venture would be closed down.

Veuillot was depressed. His brother pointed out that throughout his career he had always spoken as though he wished he had the time to be able to write at his leisure about his favorite topics, but now that he had the opportunity he was not happy.[47] Of course, the trying circumstances may have had something to do with his low spirits, but, in truth, *écrivain* though he was, he missed the daily warfare of the press. For that matter, it was suggested that the world of the press, including his enemies, missed him. What, for example, was *Le Siècle* to fill its pages with now that Veuillot had been removed from the scene?[48] His sadness, however, transcended personal reasons. As one police observer said: "Louis Veuillot is discouraged; he sees the greatest misfortunes about to descend on the world, socialism accepted, supported, and regularized by the emperor, undermining the church, and demolishing old Europe."[49] This one report was accurate. But Veuillot did not sit back and allow his darkest thoughts to overwhelm him. He traveled widely in France during the early sixties. Apparently he never revisited melancholy Boynes. He went to the pleasant country or seaside homes of various well-to-do and well-born friends. During July of 1860 he spent some weeks at the Château of Époisses, which belonged to Charles de Guitaut. He also visited the Comte and Comtesse de Montsaulnin, the Comte and Comtesse d'Esgrigny, Vicomte de La Tour, Vicomte de Bussierre, and others. He even visited the Abbey of Solesmes for a period of time. During 1860 he had close touch with the nuncio, Msgr. Chigi, who was also a visitor on occasion at the same friends' country and seaside places. The police were shadowing him closely, and according to their records, he saw the nuncio no fewer than fifteen times during April, as well as twice in May, not counting the visits to the nuncio of Élise,[50] who, in spite of the extent of her collections for the papacy, hardly could have had conversations with the nuncio without also mentioning the affairs of her brother.

Veuillot visited spas where one might have been taking the waters, but by his own observation was taking in fresh air rather than drinking or bathing in medicinal water.[51] He reached Lyon on his travels, and stayed a while with one of his old friends and collaborators on *L'Univers*, Léon Aubineau. At Lyon he was recognized by a crowd of people on the street and cheered, an event that was not unnoticed by the authorities.[52] By and large, however, there was nothing tumultuous about his peregrinations, and he seems to have kept himself in a state of comparative calm. He could not forget Montalembert through all this, but during the summer of 1860 remarked that he heard nothing of his former leader one way or the other.[53] Before very many months, however, Montalembert's *Les Moines d'Occident* appeared, with cutting remarks about Veuillot in the introduction. Even these Veuillot took calmly enough, observing that Montalembert was "one of those adversaries who do not disarm before dying."[54]

The great sorrow that oppressed Veuillot during 1860 was the total collapse of the old order in Italy. By revolution and by plebiscite the duchies of north Italy were taken over by enthusiastic nationalists, and the spectacular Garibaldi swept across Sicily and into Neapolitan territory. Fearing that once he controlled all of the Kingdom of the Two Sicilies he would next take Rome and the Papal States, Victor Emmanuel of Sardinia sent his army into the papal territories on the way south to forestall and deal with Garibaldi. This action brought a clash of the papal forces with those of Victor Emmanuel II. During the spring, as we have seen, Veuillot had been seriously concerned about the defense of the Papal States. Now, with the actual opening of hostilities, he sounded somewhat immature, exclaiming in the florid literary fashion of the day, "With what joy I would give up my pen and all that it has produced to be twenty-five years younger with a sabre."[55] From this point on he often spoke as though he wished he were a zouave and could fight for the pope. No doubt these were his honest feelings at the time, but it is interesting to contrast his current reactions to Lamoricière, with his observations of nearly a score of years earlier when Lamoricière had held a command in Algeria. General de Lamoricière now was a hero, whereas Veuillot had not thought highly of him in Algeria.[56]

One of the things that distressed Veuillot was the antagonism between Cardinal Antonelli, the secretary of state for the pope, and the minister of arms, Mérode. The former was against preparing for military action at all, while the latter turned to the chores of throwing up a line of defense.[57] Veuillot was confident that if given a free rein, General de Lamoricière could get the troops disciplined and ready for battle, but how could he do this if the papal government was divided against itself? The pope himself shrank from the idea of bloodshed. Yet he permitted his ministers to go ahead with preparations for defense in spite of Antonelli's reservations. It must have given Veuillot second thoughts about the whole situation in Rome to see Mérode, the liberal, boldly preparing the defense, while Antonelli, who had seemed to symbolize the institution of ultramontane authority, was unwilling to use the forces of the pope against the Piedmontese. The official entrusted with papal finances, Corcelles, had been viewed by Veuillot as an unreliable liberal, but now that he was bending every effort to provide resources for the defense of the Papal States, Veuillot saw his merit.[58] But despite the work of Mérode, Corcelles, and Lamoricière, he papal forces of fewer than thirty thousand were overwhelmed. The principal battle they fought with Victor Emmanuel's troops occurred at Castelfidardo. There the tiny but multinational army of the pope was badly beaten on 18 September 1860. General Pimodan was killed, and the survivors withdrew to Ancona where ten days later in another engagement they were destroyed as an army.

Veuillot was thoroughly upset. He saw the ideas of Garibaldi spreading in Europe, and, in fulfillment of the predictions of Donoso Cortés, paving the way for the eventual takeover of the Russians. More immediately he saw the anguish of his friend the nuncio.[59] He himself felt frustrated. He wrote an article about Lamoricière and the papal forces and gave it to Du Lac, who no doubt would like to have inserted it in *Le Monde*, but Taconet absolutely refused to let him do it. The rupture between Veuillot and his former publisher was complete.[60] Ambroise Petit, editor of the *Gazette de Lyon*, was willing to open his columns to Veuillot, but Veuillot realized the truth of the matter: One could utter small unimportant truths, but not big ones. Within the course of the year he slipped the article into a new edition of his *Mélanges* and got away with it, but this kind of article would have been impossible in the daily press. "Pimodan was very lucky!" exclaimed Veuillot,[61] professing to envy the fallen hero.

Veuillot was exaggerating in this matter. While Pimodan lay in the ground, a silent symbol for the clerical party that Veuillot had done so much to mold, he himself was still able to write and even to publish most of his work in various forms. By the start of 1860 he had collected various earlier writings, plus some new material, in a miscellany called *Ça et La*, to be published by Gaume Frères et Duprey. The book is one of the most heterogeneous imaginable. It includes pleasant sketches with autobiographical material in them, such as his *Du mariage et de Chamounie*, which tells of his early days and travel. It also includes in various parts epigrams in the traditional French style of the seventeenth century, putting tersely his political ideas. "Civil equality has nothing at all to do with liberty. Civil liberty has nothing to do with nobleness. Democratic France has no more of true equality and true liberty than had noble France. One finds in France today more villeins, serfs, and slaves than one-hundred years ago." "In France they like to imitate England, take its customs, morals, and trade, become protestants and shopkeepers. England, where Jesus Christ has had true altars for only thirty years, they say is the land of liberty!"[62] This was Veuillot at his worst. Often he had good information for his editorials and other writings, but at other times his maddest feelings controlled his pen. He defined words according to his current outlook, and "true equality" and "true liberty" could only be understood in terms of freedom for the pope. As for England and its "dark satanic mills," he lost all balance when writing of England. Just where he got the "thirty years" from would be hard to say. In offering this book to his admirers he was closing the ranks of the ultramontanes, and making the hard core of the group ever harder. Yet at the same time he still appreciated delicacy and sentiment. "Do you remember Meg Merillies, the immortal sorceress? I will always love Walter Scott, even though a Baronet. Of all men in the world he has given me more friends, has best used my youthful passion for reading." Without Walter Scott, he asked, how did he know that he might not have come to enjoy such writers as Sue? Scott's heroes and heroines had an antique nobility about them. Love led to marriage. If marriage was impossible, they parted, shedding great tears. Here one saw "primitive innocence" and the "purifying flame."[63] Veuillot hated "les anglais," but when it came to this "noble Englishman," here we find an explanation of the way Veuillot came to be Veuillot. He would never admit to being a romantic, for romanticism meant the stirring of national wills which would bring the subordination of the good German and Italian Catholics to men filled with the godless spirit of the French Revolution. But in many ways, particularly in his liking for medieval times, he was a romantic. *Ça et La* was collected expressly for partisan Catholics, like everything else Veuillot ever wrote, but in the wide variety of offerings, and in the occasional distillations of what he felt to be the noble essences of life, one can see the wide range of Louis Veuillot, illustrated here perhaps better than in any of his other works.

Even from Veuillot's correspondence it is hard to be sure just what he was working on at any given time. He hopped from project to project. His personal papers contained many sketches that were never completed.[64] Even his brother makes no attempt to connect works with one exact time or another. He points out that Louis intended to write a major work about the persons around Jesus, but in this hectic period of his life only a one-page plan ever resulted.[65] Some of Louis' notes at first look naïvely simple, but any study must begin with some clear idea, which in its inception may appear oversimplified. We find notes outlining how he planned to develop the theme that religion is not a philosophy, but an act of faith.[66] He left a sketch developing the idea of how hard it is for the rich man to enter Heaven, like a camel passing through the eye of a needle.[67] He wrote on miracles. "Miracles were necessary," Veuillot informs us, "but the great miracle was His Word."[68] It is impossible to date his undated sketches, but it is a safe assumption that any given one of these plans might have been made during the early 1860's when in his enforced idleness, after being deprived of *L'Univers*, he made starts in all directions in trying to give expression to all the pent-up projects about which he had been thinking during the years when his world had been mostly confined to the issues of the day.

Two particular works, very different in form from each other, can be assigned to 1860 and 1861. These are the book, *Le Parfum de Rome* and the brochure, *Le Pape et la Diplomatie*. At the turn of the year 1860-1861 Veuillot had seen Persigny twice in long interviews in an attempt somehow to get the new minister of the interior to permit the reestablishment of the journal. Judging from the book and the brochure which shortly followed it, one can understand why Persigny did not give permission for the revival of the daily publication of such an irreconcilable line. His conversation with Persigny was friendly enough, and of considerable duration, but both men understood each other all too well. Persigny returned still more of the papers that had been seized at the start of the year, but he was not disposed to consider the revival of *L'Univers.*[69] Veuillot found the conversations "interesting," if not satisfactory. He saw a striking resemblance between Persigny's answers and what the emperor himself had been saying with reference to the religious question: "fundamentally nothing clear, nothing reassuring." He heard Persigny representing the triumphs of Napoleon as the culmination of the Revolution. Persigny complimented Veuillot on his literary skill, but he was not going to let him use it in a daily organ against the triumph of the kind of Caesarism which he himself represented so well.[70]

While *Le Parfum de Rome* was the best romantic glorification of papal Rome which he, or probably anyone else, ever penned, the brochure *Le Pape et la Diplomatie* was the most challenging point-by-point defiance of the government.[71] The latter was first published in February, 1861, *chez* Gaume, and opened fire directly on Arthur de la Guéronnière by name in the very first line. It identified him as councilor of state as well as author of the brochure *La France, Rome et l'Italie.* According to Veuillot the brochure reflecting the emperor's views did not even have its terms straight. By Italy the author really meant to say revolutionary Piedmont, and by Rome it really meant the papacy.[72] He did not hesitate to cite the words and writings of Montalembert generously, nor did he hesitate to attack Thouvenel many times by name. "The pope is the bearer of what humanity has honored, desired, and hoped for for twenty centuries. La Guéronnière, however, seems to think that he is supposed to deal rather with the wills of those presumptuously claiming to be this artificial Italy."[73] Of course Veuillot manages to bring protestant influence into the picture, and he sees Luther in the background – as though Victor Emmanuel could be really very directly influenced by the sixteenth-century German. He ends on a very negative note picturing the world, without the pope, sinking into paganism and returning to antique Caesarism. It is amazing that the brochure was permitted to be sold at all, probably much less surprising that within a few weeks all thirty-five thousand copies of the first printing were exhausted.[74] No doubt the regime contemplated steps against Veuillot, particularly with reports filtering in to the effect that he was engaged in the organizing of Catholic-legitimist committees of resistance.[75] However, other reports indicated that the political forces of Henri V were not behind Veuillot.[76] Persigny and others apparently did not feel that clericalism was the enemy. The régime appears to have believed that however much excitement an occasional broadside might stir up, it was better to overlook Veuillot than to make him any more of a rallying point. Veuillot himself followed the reaction to *Le Pape et la Diplomatie* rather closely, keeping a file of clippings. He noted the sarcasm of what he termed the "revolutionary press," and he also noted that the religious press, understandably, avoided much comment.[77] These journals were muzzled and had his example to keep before them.

Back in March of 1860 Veuillot had begun to plan *Le Parfum de Rome*, at a time when he had many other immediate preoccupations. He had written to Du Lac about this project. The words of the pope to him were part of the inspiration for the book. The pope had said Rome was about to die. It would be reborn, but meantime its death was approaching. Not his friend, Pius IX, but the *pope*, the Vicar of Christ, was speaking to him in these words.[78] Obviously, he felt, it was his Heaven-appointed mission to help with the rebirth of Rome by giving an intimate description of his own personal experiences of rebirth in the eternal city.

How much he had written or planned in 1860 is difficult to know. The book did not appear until the turn of the year, 1861-1862. It is clear that his greatest efforts during 1861 were expended on this major work, which was lengthy enough to require being printed in two volumes.[79] The same publisher that brought out his brochure, Gaume Frères et Duprey, produced it. He wrote at various places besides his own home: on his travels of that year, which were again extensive, and particularly at Solesmes, where he found the atmosphere conducive to this effort. On 2 June 1861 he wrote Dom Guéranger, "I have need to breathe monastic air, and to rest my poor spirit between the chants of the monks and the songs of the birds." He said that it was *un petit ouvrage* (though there were 547 pages of text in the definitive edition of it), and that it would be entitled *Le Parfum de Rome*, which he felt constrained to advise the reverend father would "be only a piece of pure literature, but the kind of literature which could not be without utility at this moment."[80] Veuillot's idea of "utility" was to present a thesis quite the opposite of the dominant imperial thesis, but Dom Guéranger was not hesitant to allow his friend to do his writing at the abbey over which he presided. He stayed over a month there, and was able to write to Segrétain at the end of his visit: "Ah! How charmed and uplifted I am, and how I feel myself remade!" He really did seem transported. He heard singing Italian voices calling him back. He wrote poetry in prose form.[81] He went on to other places, including Le Pouliguen, home of the family d'Esgrigny, where he had a similarly fine stay with his aristocratic friends before moving on to the Château de Craon *chez* La Marquise de Champagné until well into September. He complained a little of his lumbago at the latter place,[82] but on the whole maintained the ebullient attitude he had expressed after leaving Solesmes. He had had more sadness early this year, the death of his sister, Annette,[83] but personal sadness, even combined with seeming disaster all around would not overwhelm Veuillot. He was one of the most hopeful people to be found, and the book he was writing was about the grandest of cities, which in the words of the pope himself would surely come to life again.

Despite distractions Veuillot had the book finished by late 1861, and, considering the size of the work, it sold very rapidly. The first printing of 5500 copies was soon gone.[84] Veuillot himself was well content, and figuratively laid it as a pious tribute at the feet of the pope, who was well enough pleased to make Veuillot a large gift of money, which was the papal custom in such matters. Veuillot, needless to say, lumped the five thousand francs the pope had given him with the ten thousand he himself had organized for the Denier de Saint Pierre,[85] an amount shortly surpassed by Élise, who turned over another sixty-seven thousand to the cause.[86] The Veuillots showed themselves to be proficient fund-raisers along the way.

The work itself defies description. It is a miscellany somewhat similar to *Ça et La*, but it has geographical unity, and an intimacy between the place, Rome, and the protagonist, Veuillot. It is extremely subjective, with the author seeing, but seeing only what he wants to see and in the way he wants to see it. No one more deliberately made use of his time than Louis Veuillot, and at the outset of *Le Parfum de Rome* he says: "One reads in the American language: 'Time is money!' "[87] To Veuillot no time is better spent than in going to Rome and drinking from its Catholic fountains. His pious – and militant – thought begins on the trip to Rome while he makes comparisons of the travelers he sees on the way – including some unfavorable observations, even at this early date, of Americans seeing the sights.[88] He brings the reader into the Eternal City and early in the work begins a series of epigramatic observations in Saint Peter's Square. Here the idiom becomes very French, and the comparison is immediately with the Place de la Concorde. "La Place de la *Concorde*. A pretty word! The altar of the Concorde was the guillotine." The priests of this goddess were divided into three colleges: infantry, cavalry, and artillery. What a nice, regulated, balanced French place! None of the flavor of Rome there. "There is not a stone in Rome that does not say something, and something grand!" But what do those of the Tuileries, the Corps legislatif, and the Arc de Triomphe have to say? No doubt at heart Veuillot was a French patriot, but not when France was opposed to Rome of the pope. "Place de la Concorde! Speak French, say: *place de la cacophonie*."[89] In this spirit Veuillot wanders about Rome, seeing the right sights the right way, and telling his readers about his intimate feelings on history, Christianity, and the troubles of the popes. He shifts from contemporary political situations to the Rome of Peter and Paul. He looks at all the traditional pilgrimage and tourist points, but in the way he wants to see them. He accompanies Mozart and Goethe sympathetically to certain places, and gives his meditations on them to the right-thinking nineteenth-century Frenchman. Touching the Roman question of his day, he gets into very dangerous ground, disguised only by burying it among his distillation of Christian thoughts on the stones of the Caesars. From the Coliseum he takes his reader to the little church of the German College, where the Roman chant is done in a simple way, better than the way in which those flowery Italian musicians and singers in other churches clutter up religious chants with vocalization. His thoughts go to that young English monk Wilfrid, whom Gregory II renamed Boniface, and who went out to Christianize the Germans. As for the singers: "The Germans sing with valiant voices; they have loyal blond heads, resplendent with simplicity." Alas, Luther too came from Germany. If only Goethe, Hegel, and Fichte could have known this singing![90] Not only was Veuillot not antisemitic, he was not even anti-German – so long as Germans could outdo Italians in raising their chants to God and their voices in defense of the pope.

Veuillot was uninterested in esthetics. But he subscribed to the theory, widely accepted in his day, that singing, painting, architecture, and all the arts ought to add up to something inspirational. The beauty which he saw must correspond to beauty of an inner sort. Thus he could see especial beauty in "a poor church, for a long time without glory, history, or name" – Sant' Andrea delle Frate. Here a friend of Veuillot's, Théodore de Bussière, in 1841 had led a young Jew, Alphonse Ratisbonne, whose father was president of the Israelite consistory of Strasbourg; he had led him into this uncelebrated church, and subsequently the young man became a Christian. Together with his brother, young Ratisbonne became a priest, and the two brothers founded the Company of Notre Dame of Zion. This episode is celebrated as a miracle by Veuillot in *Le Parfum de Rome*, and for this attention the gratified Jesuits later erected a Latin plaque in Sant' Andrea delle Frate to "Ludovicus Veuillot cujus nomen Posteritas admiratur."[91]

Le Parfum de Rome reflects, as Veuillot promised, the kind of literature that would be of utility to the cause of the pope and the church. There is no evidence that the régime did anything to impede its production or distribution, though along the way its writing was known to the authorities. As early as August, 1861 a police informer was able to report its title to the préfet.[92] Its sale, however, occasioned no particular sensation. Veuillot watched for reaction to the book in the press, which, after papal reaction, loomed next in importance in his eyes. He did not detect much immediate reaction, noting on the first of January, 1862 to Parisis that both friendly and enemy journals so far were quiet. Parisis seems to have helped Veuillot with the book, and Veuillot thanked him for the "small corrections" which he made.[93] His friends, of course, largely congratulated Veuillot, because they liked the spirit of the book and no doubt were favorably impressed with it. But Dom Guéranger was an exception. He did not have to flatter Veuillot, and he was a strong literary critic as well as a student of Roman religious rites. He had allowed Veuillot to write in the peace of his abbey, and he was now entitled to criticize the fruits of Veuillot's efforts. "When one reads your *Ça et La*, one sees that you know *France of today*, but in reading *Le Parfum de Rome*, it is easy to see that you have seen only *grosses realités*. . ." He told him that he had missed the details, the delicacy of Rome. Literarily he criticized a style which he described as bourgeois dialogue, which might be acceptable in an article or two, but was boring in two volumes.[94] Who could have been more ultramontane in sympathy than Dom Guéranger? And who could have set himself up more authoritatively as connoisseur of the Rome Veuillot was trying to convey? Perhaps this very knowledge and feeling for Rome account for Dom Guéranger's sharp criticism. All things considered, his reaction indicated Veuillot could not count on carrying along with him even those most aligned with his cause.

Before he finished *Le Parfum de Rome* Veuillot had many diversions and interruptions. He gave his attention to the project of one of the women with whom he often corresponded, who herself was thinking of writing about Rome. He told her that nothing was more opportune, and gave her every encouragement. Moreover, with little more than a plan yet in mind for his own book, he proceeded to tell her all about what he himself was going to write.[95] Apparently he had no hesitancy in sharing his ideas and he discussed the matter with a woman who was herself planning to write on the subject in the same way in which he might have written to Msgr. Parisis. Perhaps Veuillot was fanatical, but he certainly was not selfish or little. All one had to do was to be on his side, and he was ready to share the very ideas some authors would want to keep under wraps, reserved for themselves. But attention to other people's literary efforts was only a small part of the diversion of his time. He did some editing, and writing, of material for his *Mélanges*, for which he now had the time that had been so short while he edited *L'Univers*. Certain of his religious articles, especially his *Portraits de*

Saints, he pulled together and polished up, largely from pieces that had appeared in *L'Univers*. This he did particularly at the behest of the Comtesse d'Esgrigny.[96] As an amusing guest he must usually have livened his stay at country places, but again especially with the d'Esgrignys, because poems, plays for the children, and amusing but light-weight bits of writing which he left there were good enough so that he eventually let some of these appear in his collected works.[97] His principal distraction in this era, however, was his new brochure, *Waterloo*.

Le Pape et la Diplomatie had been a big success. Moreover, he had managed to get away with its publication. Here seemed to be the best substitute for the daily editorial in *L'Univers*. Eugène had become editor of a religious journal, the *Revue du Monde Catholique*, and Louis published various pieces in it anonymously, and was even thought to have been the editor by one of the ladies with whom he corresponded,[98] but Veuillot was not going to ruin Eugène's situation by introducing there the brand of militancy that brought suppression. The occasional big blast from a brochure did indeed seem to be the best way to try to fill the gap left by the decease of *L'Univers*. The *Waterloo* brochure, published in the spring of 1861, while it was only twenty pages,[99] did more than the usual editorial could, even one that might be divided over two or three numbers, because it permitted a concerted build-up of the force of his argument within the compass of one piece in the hands of the reader at one sitting. Despite the title, the subject matter was the position of the papacy. Superficially Napoleon I was made to seem a hero, and superficially the issue in the brochure was made to be the struggle between the Catholic and protestant principles. When Napoleon I was defeated at Waterloo, the protestant powers were held up as the victors. Russia, ever the villain in Veuillot's writing, seems to have been overlooked, and the role of Austria was not discussed. Protestantism had overwhelmed France. What Napoleon I had done to the papacy likewise did not come under fire. The object of attack was the settlement made by 1861 for Italy. The "decapitation" of Catholicism was presented here as victory by the "protestant diplomats." His guns could not be trained directly on Napoleon III, but "protestant diplomats" were fair enough targets. His conclusion was: "The first Waterloo was a catastrophe, the second would be a cataclysm."[100] To a priest to whom he sent a copy, he referred to the brochure as "an arrow against the devil." If he were to fall in this second Waterloo, he said he was going to ask for the place of a martyr.[101] The régime apparently must have realized that it is not a good thing to make martyrs out of people like Louis Veuillot, and no special steps were taken against him at this time. The brochure was another success, and Veuillot was still getting in his blows, albeit thinly disguised.

On completion of *Waterloo*, Veuillot sent copies to prelates including Msgr. Guibert, who was later Archbishop of Paris. Although 1860-1867 was his worst period for relations with the government, his standing with the episcopacy improved. Veuillot showed he was still a militant. "The world much deceives itself: The Church which is believed beaten marches toward an era of glory, and already we see the dawn,"[102] he wrote Guibert. Without *L'Univers* Veuillot was in a weak position and needed good relations with the bishops. He wrote of his efforts to seek permission for the revival of the journal, and when there was still another new minister of the interior two years later in mid-1863 he predicted, that if this authorization were to be given, it would be "Farewell to poetry!" But Veuillot deemed it wise to defend the role of the lay religious press meanwhile, and to do so without admitting that he could before have been wrong in his policy. "Since the suppression of *L'Univers* I have had occasion to reflect about the press. I have not lost any of my opinions about it; far from that. Indeed, more than ever, I believe that it is the sole efficacious weapon in the hands of laymen to fight the present evil. A journal is needed against journals, like cannon against cannon."[103] Veuillot had not changed; he was only trying to fortify his position.

Veuillot had a variety of private interests, old and new, to pursue during the years of public journalistic inactivity. He could write letters to Maguelonne recommending a papal zouave.[104] He could follow with interest splinter journalism even in England that took up the old line of *L'Univers*, and even the police knew of his feelings for English ultramontanes.[105] He could still correspond with prelates about the old classics debate,[106] though this question must have lost some of its zest. By this time the possibilities of running for the Corps législatif had lost their appeal. But, of course, there was always the possibility of another trip to Rome. In mid-1862 Veuillot set off again for the Eternal City on what was to be his fifth trip. Veuillot must be counted an inveterate traveler for the nineteenth century, but his travels were almost all strictly in line with his profession. He visited the centers of ultramontane Catholicism in France and its fringes, but as a traveler his distinguishing characteristic was the bee-line he so frequently made between Paris-Marseille-Civitavecchia-Rome. He received his passport in late April, and, according to police reports, which noted his connections not only with councils in Rome but also with officers in Paris, he departed with the Duc de La Rochefoucauld from Marseille to Rome.[107]

Having arrived in Rome, it did not take Veuillot long to arrange an audience with the pope. He did note how many bishops there were in Rome from foreign lands, and his letters home had a freshness about some matters that would indicate his still genuine enthusiasm for these outward signs of the majesty of the church. Strictly speaking, the French bishops according to the concordat were supposed to go back and forth only when authorized by the régime, and within a year this practice came to be enforced by the French government.[108] But other matters were unimportant compared with the papal audience, and on 13 May 1862 he was again with the pope – for an hour. He described the pope's reception of him as "incredibly affectionate and gracious." He said that the pope was "calm and resolute," and that he went forth from the audience "full of security and *allegresse*." As usual, he obtained special blessings for his family, notably Élise and Eugène, and he arranged with the pope, himself, for an audience for Du Lac, who the pope assured him would be treated *en évêque.* As the ecstatic Veuillot was leaving the pope's presence he had yet another request – to kiss the feet of the pope, which Pius IX allowed *Caro* Veuillot to do.[109] It has been remarked by scholars of the French church that Veuillot had called the pope "Christ on earth,"[110] and by his own account of his actions he seems to give justice to this description. But the audience was something more than just a benediction for Veuillot and those close to him: toward the end of the audience the pope began to speak in Italian, which Veuillot curiously called "the language of his heart," and he took Veuillot to task for his pride. When Veuillot had published *Le Parfum de Rome* the pope had sent him 5000 francs, which Veuillot had added to the Denier de Saint Pierre. Apparently the pope had intended to let this be a gift in order that in his dignity he need not be solely the receiver of charity, especially when Élise and her cohorts were sending so many thousands to Rome. Veuillot fell to his knees insisting that he was not governed by pride. But the pope had told him that he was! Now here he was, on his knees to be sure, but telling the pope he was not governed by something by which the pope had said he was! Perhaps he did indeed want to make the gift to the pope as large as possible, but he might have found another way to do that. Had not pride made him less than graceful in handling a gift from the pope? As in 1853 he was on his knees before the pope but presuming – even in a spiritual matter – to tell the pope that he, Veuillot, was right. He wanted to be the absolute servant of the pope – his way.[111]

While with the pope Veuillot made some practical observations about the man's condition. He observed that despite fatigue, "Pius IX bears with increasing vigor the weight of his 72 years and the weight of the world."[112] His judgment must have been good. Despite illness that lay ahead, Pius IX lived another sixteen vigorous years, standing by his principles to the end. As long as this pope lived, Veuillot's life had great meaning for him, and the base of his stands was strong. He even had someone who could give him deserved admonishment, such as he would receive again, even a dozen years later. After the death of Pius IX Veuillot, like the Comte de Chambord, the patient pretender to the throne of France, would find his life no longer oriented. But in 1862, when Veuillot could see strength in the pontiff, he felt confirmed in his ways and purpose.

Veuillot stayed in Rome the better part of two months, from early May until late June 1862. He had a great deal to interest him, and of course he did not feel the familiar call to get back to the offices of his beloved *L'Univers*. He could enjoy at leisure reading in *Civiltà Cattolica* words of praise for his *Le Parfum de Rome,*[113] and enjoy being appreciated without dashing back to the editorial room. He was exposed to the fine arts in general, when in Rome, in a way that made him more receptive than he was in Paris, where he was ever suspicious of the invasions of the profane. Rome was appealing to a man who had been a theater critic in his early days. His time was well taken up. He could mention that he had been *chez* Liszt without any other comment, so many other things he had to say.[114] He thought a great deal about the finer things of life, and here they were, in the city of the pope, to be enjoyed.

The special role of the literary man, nevertheless, seemed to him to transcend most other functions. Sometime in this general period he wrote:

> The architect, the sculptor, the painter, the creator of gardens have more pleasure in creating. They address themselves more to the crowd. They see their work and it is seen. It exists, and it has a name. People know the architecture of Vitruvius and that of Palladio, and Michelangelo's, and so on. These statues and paintings have their father; the style of a garden belongs to Le Nôtre, and so on.
>
> The poet and the musician do not see all that they have dreamed about. Their creation remains immaterial, but it is higher, more powerful, and more desirable. Time has not attacked Homer, [though] it has corroded the marbles of Phidias. . . .[115]

Veuillot loved beauty and hated the bizarre ugliness that was glorified by certain schools of the nineteenth century. Veuillot had his eyes and his mind as wide open during this stay in Rome as at any period in his life, and he combined this outward sensitivity with some introspection of himself. Fundamentally Veuillot had always been more of an extrovert than anyone else around him, but as with others past the prime of life he began to take stock. Ten years earlier he had not been able to think that as he approached fifty he would have much left in him,[116] but as he reached his fiftieth year he revised his thinking somewhat, and at least saw the mellowness of this age. Without dating his notes he no doubt wrote at about this time: "Autumn is a season made for people of fifty years. . . .The flowers of autumn are beautiful but somber and almost without perfume."[117] He dreamed about the resurrection and about knights in armor, according to his personal papers,[118] but he also had some of the romantic thoughts more conventionally associated with human beings. "Love is a substance here; union is the expression, the definitive form of love. Love is the base, union is the coronation."[119] Just as he had thought of marriage as a bachelor, so was he now as a widower thinking about it. Louis Veuillot was a prominent man with a conspicuous family, but without a wife. He corresponded with many ladies, and was highly regarded by many of them, if for no other reason than that he flattered their intelligence and appealed to them for his personal virtues. He was certainly not much to look at; his main appeal was in his words, written or spoken. Not surprisingly, many gossiped about the possibility the man of letters might remarry. In his biography of his brother, Eugène Veuillot found it necessary to disclaim at some length the basis of rumor that Louis would marry one particular lady,[120] and his case would seem to be strong that Louis Veuillot was a strict monogamist and had no intention of remarrying at all. On her death-bed Mathilde had indicated to him that it would be good for the children if he remarried. Veuillot, however, reporting these words to his brother later declared: "I want to reassure you at least on this point, and I say to you that in any case our daughters shall have no other mother. I experienced a kind of joy in taking this vow."[121] These words sound very much like Veuillot, and there is no reason to think that Eugène did not report him correctly.

Before his going to Rome there was much talk about Veuillot remarrying, among others the wealthy Marquise de Champagné. Veuillot emphatically denied he had any idea of such a marriage, and he resented what the press had done to her reputation as a result of its rumor-spreading. For twenty-three years this fine woman had been true to the memory of her husband, and it was disgraceful that papers like *Le Figaro* were saying she might marry a poor, fat, grey, literary man.[122] He was upholding the idea of strict monogamy for others, and no doubt he held to the principle for himself.

The person about whom there was the most talk, at least in Veuillot's lifetime, was a woman for whom Veuillot admittedly had the greatest of sympathy and admiration, Madame Gjertz, a widow of Norwegian origin. She had little money, four children, and considerable literary talent and intelligence.[123] Despite her Lutheran background she had become a Catholic. His compassion for her was of the highest order. Just when he came to be interested in her is hard to determine, but as early as 1857 he was publicly taking her side against Hector Berlioz in a literary dispute over religious music. Mme Gjertz had written a piece on rhythm that Veuillot had published in *L'Univers*. Mme Gjertz had taken the stand that rhythm had a relation to theology, and that certain rhythm was essential to church and liturgical music. Berlioz came back at her in the *Journal des Débats*. Berlioz had written successful religious music and was not a man Veuillot was eager to attack. However, when Berlioz denied the theory of Mme Gjertz, despite praising her originality, Veuillot sprang into action. Citing composers from Palestrina to Beethoven he produced a very strong defense of Mme Gjertz's theory, and in any case demonstrated very extensive, if superficial, knowledge of music.[124] Berlioz had denied there was any specially Christian music. Although this stand would not be expected to be one that Veuillot would like, it is doubtful whether he would have gone out of his way to attack such a tangential argument had there not been a personal reason.

By 1862 Mme Gjertz, now in failing health, had written portions of a book described by Eugène as a "Scandinavian novel, very doctrinal and passionate." She had turned to Veuillot for help. The title she had given the work was *L'Enthousiasme*. Veuillot was enthusiastic, but not for the title. He proposed some alternates, including *La belle Norvègienne, La Fille du Préfet* and *La Neige enfin fondue*, all of which might be said to suffer from the same drawbacks as could be ascribed to *L'Enthousiasme*.[125] The author, however, seems to have persisted in her original intention without diminishing the enthusiasm of Louis Veuillot for her work. Early in 1862 Veuillot negotiated with the Bishop of Strasbourg to obtain financial aid for Mme Gjertz, who was struggling to support herself and children by translating. Her German was good, but Veuillot could not resist joking about some of the renditions by this pathetic and appealing woman. It seems she thought "Rom's Aroma" was the way his new book was to be translated. By August of 1862 there were no more jokes. The poor woman was dead. Upon receiving the "cruel news," he pushed his brother-in-law to start arrangements for the orphans and for the publication of still another book written by Mme Gjertz.[126] As the summer wore on he continued to press his efforts in behalf of her children and for publication of her work.[127] Few persons even of his own family received more conscientious attention from him during the course of his life. However, his interest in her apparently never included plans for marriage, and only wagging tongues gave cause for the need to deny such a possibility. The fact that as late as 1864 he was still concerned about translations of her book into Scandinavian tongues tends to show the character of his interest in Mme Gjertz.[128]

The fact remains that Veuillot was without the immediate preoccupation of *L'Univers* and was lonely, at least in a certain way. Correspondence with leading Catholics and ultramontanes brought many sorts of gratification to him, but even here there must have been something lacking for the fiery man of the world. It was not surprising that when Juliette de Robersart, a Belgian noblewoman with church connections, and Louis Veuillot met toward the end of his stay in Rome, Veuillot, who would always deny that he was a romantic, accompanied her on a moonlight visit to the Colosseum and along the Appian Way. Juliette, very intelligent, and though in poor health a great traveler, was just the sort of woman who could converse endlessly with Veuillot. The man of fifty apparently conversed with her about numerous subjects, not recorded in documents. However, in the next six months he wrote her at least 59 letters, and she responded with at least 26. She was said "not to have been beautiful but of a physique that would not pass unnoticed," and "indocile à toute proposition matrimoniale." She was in her thirties, probably thirty-seven.[129] Technically she should have been addressed "Madame," since she held the title of canoness in a noble Hungarian order.[130] She does seem to have been a person who would interest Veuillot. One thing notable about the correspondence that followed was that the letter writers became "Gilbert" and "Jacqueline," Versailles became "Marly," and so on. Actually, his correspondence with her is not strikingly different in subject matter from that with other interesting ladies with whom he exchanged letters. Obviously he was interested in her personally, and the matter of how Christian marriage compared with pagan marriage was among the subjects they discussed, though there was nothing specific arrived at about themselves. Throughout the correspondence Juliette's close friend, Charlotte de Grammont, knew of the exchange, since Juliette early in the game showed Veuillot's letters to her.[131] Charlotte, who lived in Versailles and never traveled, expressed a great all-consuming desire to read Louis Veuillot's letters. She made copies of them all. But then, in order to understand them, she said, she would have to have the other part of the correspondence. In this manner she managed to get Veuillot to send her what Juliette had written.[132] Veuillot sent the letters, but since he and Juliette had discussed, among other things, rumors of what was being said of them,[133] Veuillot was not happy about the situation when Charlotte announced that some day they ought to be published! There is no accurate assessing of what Charlotte de Grammont's motives may have been. Perhaps she thought that the two were getting in rather deep, and that Veuillot did not sufficiently understand that Juliette was not interested in marrying. In any case, the return of Juliette's letters effectively ended the affair which had begun in Rome, although Veuillot still heard from Juliette de Robersart from time to time at later dates.[134] The letters Charlotte had assembled were set aside not to be opened until twenty years after the death of Juliette, and when this date had been reached, it is not surprising that considering the mysterious circumstances, including the fictitious names, the curiosity of the public did cause their publication. However, it is doubtful indeed that they represent anything more than an exchange of friendship between lonely intellectuals. It is interesting in this connection to note that Veuillot seemed irritated with Juliette for not thinking highly of Mme Gjertz's *Enthousiasme.*[135] He mentions Juliette in cordial terms to his brother-in-law in the same letter in which he is showing the greatest interest in the status of Mme Gjertz's book.[136] Many months after the "Gilbert-Jacqueline" correspondence was collected he mentions to Charlotte de Grammont, with whom he continued to correspond frequently, receiving a certain letter from "Ronda" in Spain which he describes as a "jewel," making him want more like it. He tells Charlotte he does not like to make copies of letters, but is doing it anyway with Juliette's. Their joint purpose at this point was to publish all that Juliette had written them about Spain, and to do this, unknown to her, for the benefit of an orphanage.[137] Their object was to provide Juliette, who they agreed was far too modest about her literary talent, with a pleasant surprise. The eventual publication of the letters between Veuillot and Juliette de Robersart may be regarded as an answer to this project. The main thing that the letters show is that Louis Veuillot was very susceptible to the influence of intelligent ladies,[138] provided that their intelligence was expressed along the lines of Catholic orthodoxy.

During early 1863 Veuillot busied himself with an answer to a controversial play that had been produced with great success in Paris at the end of 1862, but which had been less well received in the provincial towns. The play was called *Le Fils de Giboyer*, and had been written by Émile Augier, presumably encouraged by that *César déclassé,* Prince Napoleon. The dialogue and the drift of the story were outrageously insulting to the traditionalist and to the religious elements of the population.[139] Insulting legitimists and Catholics was, however, at this stage of the shift in imperial policies, something that could be done with impunity. In the words of Eugène, Augier had become the *insulteur officiel.*[140] However, Montalembert's *insulteur publique*, the master of the game, stepped in to write an answer. The result was a brochure in the form of a play entitled *Le Fond de Giboyer*. The dialogue between various stock types in Veuillot's piece probably would not seem very interesting except in reference to the currently popular play it was lampooning. The words he put in the mouths of his characters were answers to specific slurs that were dropped in Augier's play. The brochure was not an overwhelming success, but Veuillot found that many of the journals normally on the other side of the fence, such as *Le Figaro* and its editor Jouvin, were this time on his side.[141] In the development of terminology the use of the term "clerical party" began to take on significance in the Augier-Veuillot exchange.[142] To answer the anticlerical favorites of the régime, Veuillot was reaching back into his arsenal of the 1830's, when he had been the forthright and fearless theater critic.

During the mid-sixties there was a general upswing of activity among Catholic liberals again that paralleled the resistance activity of ultramontane forces. Had *L'Univers* only been coming out, Veuillot would have been having a field-day with some of the happenings of 1862-1864. Probably the most dramatic episode in liberal Catholic annals in this period was known to Veuillot only long afterwards, and not until the overthrow of the Second Empire was he able to publicize and make politico-religious capital out of it. Msgr. Gerbet and others resisting the emperor's foreign policy were drawing up a list of modern errors, which was eventually published as the *Syllabus of Errors* in 1864, and knowledge of the possible consequences of this work distressed the liberals of French Catholicism. Dupanloup, Montalembert, Théophile Foisset, Albert de Broglie, Augustin Cochin, and Alfred de Falloux were leaders among those who did not want to resist modern political tendencies, but, rather, desired to bring about an accommodation of the Catholic church to these new conditions. To cement their determination this little band had a meeting, described in due course by Veuillot as the birth of a "secte des Catholiques sélon Cavour,"[143] at Montalembert's beautiful old estate, La Roche-en-Brény,[144] a far cry from the first story of 40, rue de Bac, where he had to see Veuillot and the bourgeois sights of that bustling Parisian street. Although Broglie could not make it at the last minute, Dupanloup said a mass in the presence of the others, on 12 October 1862, and the event was commemorated with a plaque that said: "In this oratory Félix, Bishop of Orleans, distributed the bread of the word and the bread of Christian life to a small troop of friends who for a long time were accustomed to fighting together for a free church in a free land, and who have renewed this pact to devote the rest of their lives to God and to liberty." It was not until 1871, one year after the death of Montalembert, that Veuillot "penetrated" the chapel, copied this inscription, and made an issue out of this particular pact.[145] However, Napoleon III's adoption of Cavour was from the first clearly seen to have a bearing on the role of Veuillot's antagonists within the French church.

The congresses of Belgian Catholics held at Malines in 1863 and 1864 fell in the same category as the meeting at La Roche-en-Brény. They served as rallying points for Catholics, including the French, who sought to liberalize the direction of the church in line with the desires of Cavour. Of these episodes Veuillot learned quite a bit despite being out of Paris much of the time in 1863. Montalembert, unable to speak from a legislative rostrum for a dozen years, now at this congress was in his element again and gave a dramatic speech. The English Cardinal Wiseman and the Abbé Mermillod, without directly attacking Montalembert's speech, countered with more conservative views of change within the church, and of ecumenism.[146] Veuillot was distressed to hear about the appeals of Montalembert, but he derived some satisfaction in quoting to Mermillod Donoso Cortés' views of Lacordaire, views which he thought applied to Montalembert: "I do not fear for him; he will save himself by inconsequence."[147] But despite Veuillot's professed lack of belief in Montalembert's effectiveness, he did fear that liberalism was again on the rise. He felt frustrated in not being able to combat it through the columns of *L'Univers*.

Montalembert's influence no longer in any way matched his eloquence, but other manifestations appeared at this time which could not so easily be dismissed. Both the novel of Victor Hugo, *Les Misérables,* and Ernest Renan's *La Vie de Jésus* made enormous impact on the reading public not only of France but of the Western world. Both had fresh vitality in their approach. Both reflected sensitivity to man's religiosity, and both introduced aspects that were not part of the accepted Catholic attitudes. Veuillot had much to say about *Les Misérables.* He could not deny the force of the book, or even its importance in centering the good things in life on the church.[148] Certainly people were miserable creatures without the church in his eyes. It is possible that Veuillot might have tried to match novels with Hugo on the theme had it not been for publication of Renan's biography of Jesus, the man. It would be hard to name a book that stimulated a greater diversity and intensity of reaction than did this work.[149] Among the reactions to it was Veuillot's *La Vie de Notre-Seigneur Jésus-Christ.*

Veuillot had been watching Renan's progress for some time, seeing his apostasy coming on. Despite the excitement he caused, quickening interest in religion for many people, Veuillot could only take his book as a diminution of the divinity of Christ. Veuillot had long been a Bible-reader, but one is apt to get the impression that he was particularly interested in using it for support in this or that argument. Now he was going to defend the divinity of Christ, and for this awesome duty he had to prepare himself by examining the sources with such skill that he might undo the effective work of Renan. He did not underestimate the task, but he did plunge into it with zeal. He worked in various places, including Solesmes, but not in a hasty manner, and although he did most of the work in 1863, it was not until 1864 that the book appeared. Despite the fact it was not overly long, 330 pages in the definitive edition of his works, it shows detailed study of the whole of the New Testament, plus considerable study of the subsequent history of the Christian church.[150]

Veuillot exclaimed that he had found "one-hundred thousand beauties that he had not seen." He described himself as smiling, loving, admiring, and weeping. "Oh! how this poor devil Renan has worked to my profit. Perhaps I have only produced something very ordinary for others; but for myself I have made a chef-d'œuvre, I have amassed mountains of faith, I have converted myself."[151] One cannot see evidence of any greater charity on Veuillot's part after all his Bible-studying, but apparently he did reinforce his general Christian faith, and he even began to think more of Christ as having been in Galilee and Jerusalem. Veuillot's tomb has on it the words, so important to him, "J'ai cru, je vois." Preparing his answer to Renan certainly deepened his faith. The book itself makes a twentieth-century reader think of Papini.[152] But while forceful, it really does ring quite true to the Gospel stories in tone. There is absolutely no attempt at higher criticism, but he blends the Synoptic accounts with that of John in a very skillful way, harmonizing the Gospels with what Acts and Paul have to add. Jesus is completely Our Lord in Veuillot's book, and the inclusion of those two words even more than the addition of the word Christ in the title gives the key to the book. He refers to the Old Testament significantly and artfully, and he even uses later writings, such as those of John Chrysostom, to shed light on the life of Jesus Christ. But with the Resurrection he does not end the story. He carries the church down to the present in a ninety-page section called "Jesus

Christ Continued in the Church." In this work Veuillot wrote with delicacy. He left no doubt of his thesis that Jesus is divine, but he wrote with a positive touch, avoiding the contentious tone of a polemicist. This book deserves to stand at the head of his works. If Veuillot had written nothing else, it would have been a great memorial.

When Veuillot published his *Vie de Notre-Seigneur Jesus-Christ* in the spring of 1864, the popular response was immediate and great. It went through many editions, eight having been produced by 1874. He received another letter of praise from Pius IX, who was well pleased that Veuillot had avenged the "outraged divinity" of Jesus. The pope expressed his satisfaction with all the writings of Veuillot, and never had the pope been more solidly behind him than in July of 1864.[153] Pius IX's voice, however, was one of many. Cardinal Sacconi had written a week previously with his highest praise for *Carissimo Signor Veuillot.*[154] Various prelates, like the Archbiship of Reims, particularly congratulated Veuillot on being so honored by the pope,[155] and this time even Dom Guéranger sent congratulations rather than criticisms.[156] Gustave de La Tour, who in 1863 had beaten Thiers and a considerable coalition of opposition for reelection to the Corps législatif,[157] wrote to Veuillot that one could not have had a better recompense than the letter of the pope, "so full of thanks and affection." He added: "Here is a new affirmation of the doctrines of *L'Univers*." His conclusion was that this letter from the pope would open the eyes of their adversaries.[158] Veuillot enjoyed all this praise. While thanking his bourgeois friend Madame Testas for some cigars, he declared in practically the same breath that the pope's letter "has done me an honor of which I am happy, proud, and overwhelmed."[159] Veuillot could write a book that was graceful in the true sense of the word. It was also characteristic of him that he could enjoy what amounted to a victory celebration after its publication with an earthy couple who also seem to have kept him well supplied with wine.[160]

During the period of writing and publishing *La Vie de Notre-Seigneur Jesus-Christ*, Veuillot had his quota of private troubles and sadness. In December 1862 he wrote to Maguelonne: "I have been in a state of lethargy for a good six months, and it is only with effort that I go out." He reminded his old correspondent in Rome of a famous cold he had once caught in the catacombs and said that nowadays that was the way he was all the time.[161] Complaint of poor health was frequent on the part of Veuillot, and in 1864 he did not hesitate to go into details about his migraine headaches and rheumatism while writing even to the admiring Charlotte.[162] Allowing for possible exaggeration, it is still safe to conclude that Veuillot did not feel well throughout much of his life, and the early sixties was no exception. In September of 1863 his mother died, at the age of 73. He told Msgr. Parisis that she had died in the way he hoped to.[163] He never seems to have been the least embarrassed by her humble existence. She had remarried, but he was on good terms with her second husband, and he wrote special letters to several prelates, such as Msgr. Pie, to tell of her passing.[164] He was much saddened by her death. His children, Luce and Agnès, the only ones left, had some illnesses, which loomed ominously to Veuillot.[165] Several of his friends had trouble, including his generous friend, Mirès, the Jewish banker, who had been wrongly convicted of fraudulent financial operations and sentenced to five years in prison. Two years later his appeal was upheld, and he was exonerated,[166] but this was not a pleasant affair for Veuillot to watch, particularly since Mirès had been so involved in financial affairs with the States of the Church.

Even the American Civil War did not go to his liking. Had Veuillot been writing for *L'Univers*, he might have had a good deal to say about the Civil War in America, but as it was his observations were incidental and personal. Eugène's wife was from New Orleans, and his closeness to Eugène extended to her. On occasion he had deplored certain barbarous aspects of America, including slavery, but while the war was taking place he was for Louise d'Aquin Veuillot's side – the South. To Eugène he wrote on 4 October 1862: "The first thing I look for in the paper is the despatch from America. Jackson does not want to be in Washington any more than I want to see him there. Guitaut [his friend] is just as passionate a secessionist as I am. The [Catholic] Bishop of New Orleans is expected to pass Époisses today on his way to La Roche-en-Brény. If we encounter him, we will want to shout: 'Jackson for ever [*sic*]!' How is that, belle-sœur?"[167] By the summer of 1864 the war had taken its final direction, and there was nothing more to shout about. However, in telling Élise of reports of the death of "Msgr. le general Polk, a Protestant Episcopal bishop, he could not resist a macabre pun: "Pauvre homme, quelle chance il a de présider une eternelle polka dans l'église d'en bas, c'est-à-dire dans l'église à l'envers!"[168]

Hope sprang eternal for Veuillot that somehow, sometime, the régime would allow the resuscitation of *L'Univers*, with himself as editor. A young man named Auguste Roussel wrote Veuillot that several young people, including himself and an associate, Arthur Loth, wanted Veuillot's advice about founding a paper, the *Revue de la Jeunesse Catholique.*[169] Whatever the insubstantial source of his hope during the summer of 1864, Veuillot had the optimism to ask the Bishop of Arras, Msgr. Parisis, to appeal to the emperor on his behalf. Parisis wrote a masterful letter, which showed that he understood very well the importance of the press in general and of the religious press in particular. There was nothing vague about his approach to the subject, and he appealed to the emperor's sense of balance concerning the total state of public opinion. His appraisal of the different segments of the press is wrothy of the attention of students of the press today, because he surveys the whole scene as it appeared to an interested observer of that era. He pointed out that the great daily journals which regularly attacked religion were numerous and powerful. The oldest were the *Journal des Débats, Le Siècle,* and *La Presse*, which between them had more than 90,000 subscribers. With the addition of *Le Temps, La Nation*, and *Le Globe*, the total subscriptions in this category would come to at least 140,000. His estimate was that the additional readers of these papers, including those in the cafés and so on, would be more than a million. There is no way to check the accuracy of his estimate, but it is significant to note how many more readers he claimed there were of these papers than their actual subscriptions. To balance this side of the scales there were only three important religious journals, *L'Union, La Gazette de France*, and *Le Monde*, the first two of which were as much political as religious. Between them these journals had only 23,000 total subscribers. Parisis reminded the emperor that when Veuillot had edited *L'Univers* this paper had circulated in the cafés and been sold in the railroad stations. *L'Ami de la Religion* had now atrophied, and the restrictions placed on *Le Monde* were such that a great imbalance had occurred with respect to the treatment of religion in the press. How was a healthier situation to be restored? Obviously, *L'Univers* should be re-authorized.[170] The assessment of the situation was very well put, and the case for *L'Univers* and Louis Veuillot was put in a most persuasive way, since the emperor himself, despite his lack of religious belief, realized the possible consequences of a too dominant influence of the antireligious – and radical – press. Nevertheless, when the emperor personally answered Parisis' appeal about a month later, he refused, with regrets, to approve authorization of *L'Univers*, on the grounds that Veuillot and *L'Univers* had not confined themselves to religious matters but had attempted to bring about division among his ministers.[171] Veuillot was not easily discouraged, and by April of 1865 he had again sent a formal petition to the minister of the interior for authorization,[172] but this in due course was treated in the accustomed way.

Veuillot was offered a chance for participation in journalistic activities at the best literary level, when Villemessant of *Le Figaro* offered him 24,000 francs for regular contributions along the lines Villemessant would decide, but Veuillot refused such conditions.[173] In fact, it was really unthinkable that Veuillot would have consented to be regularly associated with the journal he had dubbed "boulevardier." A work he had prepared on *Molière et Bourdaloue* was now largely completed. This comparison of the great preacher with the dramatist who created the rascal priest Tartuffe had appeared in six numbers in *Le Revue du Monde Catholique*, but it was not until late in 1864 that proofs of it were ready for publication in 1865.[174] The situation in Rome was changing, and the pope was said to be ready to issue a great statement. What was there to keep him from going to Rome for a sixth time?

On 15 September 1864 Napoleon signed a convention with Victor Emmanuel by which the new King of Italy promised he would not attack the present territory of the pope, while Napoleon promised to withdraw the troops from Rome within two years. "When our master no longer gives to the pope the miserable protection that he had not dared to refuse up to the present, what further use will God have for him?" asked Veuillot?[175] The pope seemed suddenly in a much worse situation. Also, the encyclical, *Quanta Cura*, and the accompanying *Syllabus of Errors* were shortly to be released. Work had proceeded on the *Syllabus* for some time, and only in 1862 did its preparation pass from the realm of secrecy. Knowledge of its preparation had occasioned the secret meeting at La Roche-en-Brény, and the issue of modernism had again brought liberal and conservative Catholics into conflict. Veuillot felt he had to be in Rome to bring himself abreast of the new developments. He arrived on 30 November 1864 with Élise and his two daughters. He was destined to stay three months in Rome, and the police were aware of his intentions from the beginning.[176]

This visit to Rome was in some ways like his previous visits, but in some ways a bit different. He seemed to be an observer this time more than an actor in the scene. His arrival in Rome was hailed, and attention was given him during his stay by a wide variety of people,[177] and again he had a "good long audience" with the pope,[178] at which the pope not only had his usual kind words for Veuillot, but also blessed Élise, his children, and the servants whom Veuillot had brought along. "I have seen their fixed gazes on him, I have seen the love of these simple hearts, and I have felt where lies the force which will triumph over all. The Holy Father is in good health, steady, and tranquil. He is and he will remain master of the world," Veuillot wrote Léon Aubineau.[179]

The Catholic church of France had troubles within its bosom, including renewed resistance to the Roman rite and suspicion between ultramontane and Gallican prelates. The issuance of the encyclical *Quanta Cura* and the *Syllabus of Errors* was therefore a dramatic episode. The latter was made up of sixty-one propositions bearing on the modern world, and the whole stand of the pope was against the very presumptions which were the basis of modern thought and those who wished to compromise the time-honored assumptions with "new" conditions. Veuillot, of course, was delighted with the stand taken by the pope.[180] Now he had ammunition, and he would use it, for his *L'Illusion libérale*, which he was not to be long in writing. Dupanloup, too, published a brochure at this time, and Veuillot was his opponent again. Just as Veuillot had recently brought himself to grips with the story of the four different Gospels of the life of Christ, now he had to measure the field of theology as he prepared to attack Dupanloup, *Le Correspondant*, and the whole liberal school on this ground. He began comparing unlimited liberty and liberty to go to perdition, and trying to pick holes in the arguments of the liberals.[181] Whatever one may say of Veuillot's arguments, he certainly was gaining a speaking acquaintance with a broad number of concepts in involving himself in these matters.

During his stay in Rome he had the opportunity of observing much activity and excitement. He observed the situation of the beleagered King of the Two Sicilies, heard news about the problems of the Emperor Maximilian in Mexico, and took notice of the trip of Prince Napoleon to Rome.[182] He was entertained by the French ambassador to the Holy See, and from him he learned still more of French foreign policy. "Alas! I can only say," he wrote to Eugène, "that at present I know Drouyn de Lhuys [foreign minister] better than he does himself."[183] He well knew the increasingly secular orientation of the Second Empire, and was most disconsolate about it. To one of his correspondents he wrote: Here I am, *ravi* and *désolé*. Rome is so beautiful that one is unable to believe that God would allow such a great work to be touched by the catastrophe that seems so inevitable and imminent. . . ."[184] He put no faith in men in general to do anything about this or other threatening tragedies. By April of 1865 Veuillot was back in Paris, but shortly afterward he felt the need to retreat to Solesmes again, from which he wrote to his sister that "most men are not strong and seem made solely to fulfill some given function."[185] Except for the pleasure of meeting a monk born very near Boynes, Veuillot seemed to be complaining of everything, including the quality of "modern" paper![186] It was in this frame of mind that he planned and eventually wrote, between considerable interruptions for other projects, his *L'Illusion libérale.*

L'Illusion libérale was Veuillot's most striking and personal denunciation of liberal Catholicism. It appeared in brochure form, *chez* Palmé, at the start of 1866. Although it was not very long,[187] it was the result of much thought – and overwhelming feeling. Fundamentally, he attacked the terminology of liberal Catholicism. "The liberal Catholic is neither Catholic nor liberal. I mean by this, even without doubting his sincerity, that he has no more true notion of liberty than he has of the church. *Catholique libéral tant qu'il voudra*! He has a well-known character, and in all of his traits is a personage all too frequent in the history of the church: sectarian, there is his true name."[188] The assertions of the liberal individual he attacked at some length, and various evil beings, such as Frederick the Great and Cavour were dragged into his story of the development of liberalism in religion. He concluded with a play on the revolutionary motto of France: "The world is about to lose with Christ all that Christ has given it. The Revolution dissipates this royal heritage in boasting of conquering it. Everything is heading for tyranny, for the humiliation of man, for the sacrifice of the weak, and all this is being done in the name of liberty, equality, and fraternity. Let us conserve the *liberty* of proclaiming that God alone is God, and that it is necessary to obey and to adore only him, no matter what masters his wrath allows to stalk the earth. Let us conserve the *equality* which teaches us to fold our arms neither before force, nor before talent, nor before success, but only before the justice of God. Let us conserve fraternity, this true *fraternity*, which exists and can only exist on earth if we maintain the *paternity* of Christ."[189]

The appearance of this brochure was duly noted by the régime. It was well summarized by the authorities in Marseilles, who described him as the "implacable foe of liberal Catholicism." But while paying close attention to the brochure, the police assessment minimized its potential influence.[190] While there were no official repercussions from the writing of this brochure, Veuillot's liberal opponents in the church believed they had grounds for denouncing it to the Congrégation of the Index. Some points about grace could be criticized theologically, and this was done. The move, however, came to nought, for the sympathy of the pope and the curia in general were too well known for any measure to be taken against the brochure. One of Veuillot's defenders let him know that the pope himself had said: "I am very pleased with this piece. Louis Veuillot has expressed all my ideas, because they are absolutely my ideas; but Louis Veuillot is always Louis Veuillot and his pen strikes like a rapier."[191] Maguelonne said that the pope observed to him that Veuillot was the *vero defensore del mio pontificato.*[192]

The appearance of *L'Illusion libéral* would have been more timely had it come sooner after the issuance of the encyclical and the *Syllabus*. The strategically bad situation of Rome in the middle of the new Kingdom of Italy, and other threatening developments in international affairs that pointed to war between Austria and Prussia, as well as Italian and German unification power plays caused diplomatic and military affairs to take over the spotlight. In mid-1865 Veuillot launched his most serious criticism yet on the whole foreign policy of the empire when, again *chez* Palmé, he published the brochure *Le Guepier Italien*. Italy certainly was a "hornet's nest," and France had indeed stirred it up. He traced the development of the present situation in Italy, showing what a mess Napoleon's policy had created.[193] He had every reason to expect to be in trouble[194] as soon as *Le Guepier Italien* appeared in print, and even used the word "prison" when writing to Charlotte de Grammont.[195] The temper of the régime might be said to have been thoroughly tested by this brochure, and it became obvious that the régime did not proceed as hastily against this kind of publication as it did against journals. Emboldened by getting away with *Le Guepier Italien* (if Veuillot were a man who at all required to be emboldened), he wrote for publication the next year another very dangerous pamphlet about the war between Prussia and Austria, *À Propos de la Guerre.*[196] Napoleon III would like to have been able to mediate this struggle between the two Germanic powers, in which Italy was the ally of Prussia, but he could not because events moved too quickly, and too decisively in favor of Prussia and Italy. Napoleon's relative power was greatly diminished by the outcome of this war which ended the old Germanic Confederation and practically united North Germany. Veuillot did not directly open fire on the past weakness of French policy so much as talk of future generalities. He was impertinent enough to ridicule the idea that Antwerp and Cologne might become French territory in a day when all real freedom appeared to him to be receding. His biggest idea was that Donoso Cortés' prediction was right: the Western countries were destroying themselves; freedom itself was being destroyed by the new "liberating" movements; and in due course some Eastern despotism threatened. Donoso Cortés' concept of a coming decline of the West seemed to him to be taking place. The regime carefully noted the appearance of this broadside,[197] but again Veuillot was not made the object of any judicial action.

Next, turning from foreign policy to domestic affairs, Veuillot published his *Les Odeurs de Paris, chez* Palmé, late in the year 1866. The police watched the preparation of this work, which was of book-size, again with interest.[198] As soon as it came out, it was a big success, quickly selling the first 3500 copies, and exhausting 35,000 before very long. It had been well known that he was preparing a description of Paris and Parisians that was going to contrast that city unfavorably with the beauties of Rome. Parts of the book had already appeared in various journals. The police reaction was that it was not to be regarded as a serious undermining of the régime, despite the fact that Veuillot maintained in it that Napoleon had carried out the programme of Victor Hugo, and that in it Veuillot made a few more bitter observations about contemporary foreign affairs. The police were surprised to see the author's change of pace, from inspired prophet to *misérable gazetier* dredging up scandals about the great city.[199] Not surprisingly the intimate nature of the description of Paris caused a great stir in the press and people rushed to get their copies.

The book itself is a minute inspection of the life of mid-century Paris, its boulevards, its theaters, its press, its artists, poets, writers, and painters. Possibly the boldest touch in the book was to call the city "Bonifaciopolis" – making allusion, as he had done before, to the articles signed "Boniface" written or inspired by Napoleon III himself.[200] The press in general came under mordant attack, and Buloz, Rochefort, Jourdan, and many other journalists were maltreated individually and at some length. Henri Murger, author of the popular novel, *La Vie de Bohême,* was given sarcastic treatment, and Paris as a whole was contrasted with Rome for its degeneracy. Some of the people personally attacked were referred to by name, and others by obvious pseudonyms, for example, Albert Wolff, a frequent contributor to *Le Figaro*, and a perfect example of what Veuillot termed "the boulevardier," became "Lupus."[201] He ridiculed, in passing, the strange juxtaposition of statues in the public squares, and contemplated the national heroes thus commemorated. While he did not like the location of the statue of Joan of Arc, his was one of the first pleas in the drive to bring about her canonization. "It is sweet to think that one day Catholic France will solicit in the court of Rome the canonization of Joan of Arc, martyr of God and of country, liberator of her people. But it will first be necessary to let the century of the liberator Garibaldi pass away."[202]

After the publication of the Paris book, Veuillot became involved in a busy exchange of letters with men he had annoyed, among whom were Villemessant of *Le Figaro*, Wolff, and Jouvin.[203] No legal actions resulted, but feelings against Veuillot in some quarters were no doubt intensified. One reviewer, Armand de Pontmartin, who at first praised the book in *La Gazette de France*, later reversed his opinion and declared that in fact Veuillot was too hard on the present epoque, which was actually better than its predecessors.[204] If even his friends felt this way, it is certain that his enemies became, after reading *Les Odeurs de Paris*, still more committed, especially since Veuillot was not talking about politics or religion, but about daily life as they were enjoying it. One individual physically menaced Veuillot, but Arthur Murcier, his faithful brother-in-law, chased the man off with his cane.[205]

In his privately expressed reactions to life around him Veuillot constantly included many complaints about the disreputable tone of Paris. The same man who had been brought up in dockside Bercy wrote frankly to the discriminating lady of Versailles, Charlotte de Grammont, of his reactions upon going to the theater and seeing more than a hundred nude women on the stage.[206] Apparently he had no inhibition about describing to her the specifics of what he did not like. After the publication of *Les Odeurs de Paris* he sent Charlotte a copy of a cartoon by Morland, showing Veuillot, labeled "Gutter Writer," ascending from a sewer with a bucket labeled "les odeurs de Paris."[207] Any attack on institutions of the French capital was sure to please Englishmen. One who wrote Veuillot of his pleasure over the book was Cardinal Manning, who told him that the columns of the *Westminster Gazette* were henceforth open to him.[208] Manning subsequently wrote Veuillot that he wanted to meet him,[209] and good relations with English Catholics dating from this time became important to Veuillot later on.

One rather exceptional reaction to the publication of *Les Odeurs de Paris* was a flattering sonnet written about Veuillot by one of his former enemies, the "boulevardier" Arsène Houssaye. Houssaye was much impressed with Veuillot's assault on the Paris of the day. Eugène Veuillot was not sure that Houssaye had produced a good sonnet, but he appreciated his good intention. At least the line about fighting Paris with the weapons of Rome was descriptive:

LOUIS VEUILLOT

Il lisait Bossuet dans sa virile enfrance;
Aux Pères de L'Église, homme il est remonté;
Pour la foi, cette veuve, il a tout affronté,
De l'orphelin Jésus, il a pris la défense.

Chevalier qui s'en va de par le chrétienité,
Chaque mot contre Dieu lui révéle une offense:
Le vieux catholicisme est, sous son éloquence,
Jeune encor de miracle et d'immortalité.

Athlète, il s'est mis nu comme le premier homme,
Pour combattre Paris par les armes de Rome·
Pamphlets tout pleins d'odeurs, parfums tout pleins d'espirt!
La Lutèce moderne a roulé jusqu'à terre:
Mordant Proudhon, blessant Rousseau, piquant Voltaire,
Il a fait son épée avec les clous du Christ.[210]

In the fall of 1866 Louis Veuillot had in mind among other things a reconciliation with Montalembert. Veuillot could easily let bygones be bygones, but Montalembert apparently had a much harder time forgetting his wrongs. Msgr. Mermillod took the initiative to try to bring the two men together, and Veuillot would have been very happy if this could have been done.[211] With the further schism between liberals and ultramontanes in the Catholic church, 1866 was a favorable time. But Montalembert dashed cold water on Mermillod's attempt. He repeated many of the terms of contempt he had used about Veuillot in the past, "calumniator," "traitor," "insulter," and "madman." He lashed out at his latest book, and in sum he made it clear that there would never again be a reconciliation between the two.[212] Veuillot had continued to provoke Montalembert's anger over the years, and his attitude toward Rome was basically very different from Montalembert's. However, Veuillot had never ceased to concern himself in a friendly way about his former chief and, despite his famous shortcomings in the matter of charity, did seem to have mastered his animosity better than Montalembert.

Veuillot had more new projects to occupy him during the winter of 1866-1867. One of these was a second edition of Juliette de Robersart's *Lettres d'Espagne.*[213] In fact, one of the longest letters Veuillot ever wrote to the *indéchiffrable* Juliette was in 1866.[214] To his own writing he also gave much thought. According to François Veuillot, there were plans for three more books that never were completed.[215] *Raphaël, Philosophe et Théologien* did appear in an abbreviated form, but *Les Choses de la Vie* and *Figures d'à-présent* were fated to remain unfinished projects.[216] Political situations again were changing. Napoleon III could see the trouble developing for France in the growing strength of Prussia, and within his own country he feared the popularity of the liberals. By several stages in the sixties the authoritarian nature of his régime had been progressively modified and liberalized as the emperor sought to ride the waves. Suddenly, in January of 1867, the régime decided to relent with regard to its strict policies for authorization of publications. The actual legislation was not effected until 1868, but on 19 January 1867 the Emperor gave directions to Rouher in a letter that changed the whole situation.[217] Veuillot now had the unexpected opportunity to come forward again as an editor! Within only a few weeks his whole life reverted to the pattern of seven years earlier.

Hope is a cardinal virtue, and Veuillot had generally been hopeful and sometimes even overly optimistic during his life. However, just before this new opening in the clouds, he had sounded quite pessimistic. To naval Captain Maisonneuve, a longtime friend, he wrote: "The world has tried to beat down Christianity, and it has done this from a social point of view." Just how long this "most ignoble kind of despotism" was going to be the master he did not know,"[218] but ever since 1860 he had been infected with this outlook. Writing to a young would-be crusader, the writer Quid'bœuf, even after the emperor's letter to Rouher was known, he said: "Your vocation can only develop in Paris. It is necessary that you be here and that I have a journal. In spite of the news of the day, I do not think it will affect us. I expect some knavery which will exaggerate the present troubles soon. This system cannot sustain even the appearance of liberty of the press."[219] Events promptly showed that Veuillot was wrong in his initial appraisal of the situation.

During Veuillot's life he wrote tens of thousands of letters which have been preserved, and a large part of these have been published. In late January and early February he seems to have written fewer letters than usual. Perhaps he simply did not have the opportunity for copying, or possibly he spent more time than usual dashing around to see people. For whatever reason, there is less evidence preserved of his activities at this critical point than at other comparable periods. Eugène's biography of his brother tells us that by 19 February 1867 La Vallette, the minister of interior, had authorized the right of Louis Veuillot to be editor-in-chief of a journal. Permission to revive the title *L'Univers* he was more reluctant to grant, but eventually that, too, was authorized.[220] Both in Louis' own correspondence and in his published works is preserved a letter to Napoleon III, thanking him for the authorization of a journal under the old title *L'Univers.*[221] His formal request had been submitted to the minister of the interior only on 15 February, and in that letter he had said that he would be willing to accept the title *L'Unité* in case *L'Univers* were not authorized.[222] Apparently it was the decision of Napoleon III himself to allow the old title to be revived. If France was to be permitted to read the sometimes-daily harangues of Louis Veuillot, it might as well be reading *L'Univers*, the emperor must have reasoned. Even before the formal authorization, Veuillot parodied in triumph, to one of the ladies with whom he corresponded, the old nursery rhyme:

> La nouvell' que j'apporte
> (Vos beaux yeux vont briller)
> La nouvell' que j'apporte
> Malbrough est deterré.

"Yes, Madame, *L'Univers* is rising from the dead and will astonish the world here on 15 April. The troops are under arms, the corporal is at his post, he only lacks cartridges, which is to say a bit of money, but I will have it, if I believe in the signs."[223]

Many things had to be resolved before *L'Univers* could be launched again. What about *Le Monde*? What about Taconet? What about all the former editors of *L'Univers* now working for Taconet? What about other Catholic journals, including new ones that might now be created? Of course, what about the money? If money were lacking, would it be possible for *Le Monde* and *L'Univers* to be somehow fused? Although many practical questions had to be resolved, the biggest question in Louis Veuillot's mind was: What were the wishes of the pope? The important thing was to obtain the blessings of the pope for *L'Univers*. While exulting to his friend about the revival of *L'Univers*, he had said that he did not doubt he would obtain these blessings, "even though unworthy."[224]

Within a few days he was on his way to Rome, following his usual tracks through Marseille and his friend Chuit's palace, always conscious now that he might be followed by the police.[225] The police, to be sure, were collecting reports from as early as 22 February 1867 concerning the pope and his possible sponsorship of Catholic journals in France.[226] The police were aware that Émile Keller was considering launching an ultramontane journal at this time, and that both Veuillot and Keller had been in contact with Msgr. Mermillod about the matter.[227] Veuillot engaged in various feverish activities on arrival in Rome. The papal audience, nevertheless, was the key to all.

By 25 February 1867 he had seen the pope. He had gone before the pope feeling badly, but come away cured. He had had a cold and his eyes had troubled him, but after seeing the pope he felt nothing but joy. "I am transported, radiant, blessed with a goodness, I might almost say with a tenderness, which made me ashamed more than ever before not to be a saint, but determined to make the attempt. He is very well, of a serenity which seems to increase with peril, truly gay, truly merciful. I had leisure to tell him all my plans; he approves, he blesses. The resurrection of *L'Univers* gives him a true pleasure, he said so several times to me." Veuillot left the pope delighted. He had been re-blessed and called *Caro* Veuillot. "Oh! how good it is to be blessed by Pius IX!" The pope extended his blessing to Du Lac, Aubineau, Eugène, and others. According to Veuillot the pope also remembered his servants. And with this great all curing benediction he went off to dine with the zouaves.[228]

Veuillot stayed two or three weeks in Rome, consolidating his position with various prelates, paying attention to *Civiltà Cattolica*, and doing the other things he usually did while in Rome, but now that it was clear that the pope specifically wanted the resurrection of *L'Univers*, as such, and in his hands, all other Catholic editors and ultramontane forces were going to have to adjust themselves accordingly. Keller, who had been thinking of entering the field, decided to leave it open for *L'Univers* now that the pope had spoken, and apparently also as a result of the persuasion of Msgr. Mermillod.[229] Veuillot did not care for the printer now used by Taconet, but he was determined to negotiate with his old publisher nonetheless.[230] Veuillot did not underestimate the value of Taconet's contribution in having kept the Catholic press alive during the years 1861-1867.[231] However, he long had had mixed feelings about Taconet and did not regard his talents highly. "In him the Christian and the merchant are continually at war,"[232] and this time the merchant won the battle. Taconet had an investment tied up in his paper and of course required reimbursement if he were to yield to Veuillot and go out of business in favor of the revived *L'Univers*. Veuillot found that he was able to raise money, now that the pope had given his blessings, from people like Madame de Pitray, for instance, who offered as much as 10,000 francs for the cause.[233] The régime heard that the pope himself had given money.[234] Certainly the position of *Le Monde* was overshadowed,[235] but Taconet was a businessman as well as a Catholic, and he did not want to lose his investment. In late March there ensued an extensive correspondence between Taconet and Veuillot, in which Veuillot offered to give Taconet 350,000 francs, "cash on the table," for *Le Monde*. Taconet was willing to sell, but he pointed out various reasons why the sum should be over 500,000. Veuillot was not persuaded. Taconet, after stalling, finally would not give in, and negotiations between them broke down.[236] On 3 April 1867 Veuillot wrote Taconet to this effect, nevertheless he closed by saying "I remain yours very affectionately."[237] Veuillot did not believe that *Le Monde* could survive. Again he was wrong; both journals functioned independently, and thirty years later they eventually were merged.[238]

More important than the hundreds of thousands of francs that were in question were the men who had served Louis Veuillot and who during the dark years of 1861-1867 had served Taconet. Du Lac was the key figure, and he watched the negotiations carefully.[239] For him there was no question about what to do, and he joined *L'Univers* as soon as it was definitely reconstituted and remained with it until his death in 1872.[240] Louis Veuillot only completed a short sketch of his life, but it is apparent that throughout his life Veuillot had always looked up to this devoted and self-effacing cleric who had made *L'Univers* "clerical" in the strict sense of the word. Coquille was the only one of the old group who did not come back. According to Eugène, he gave as his reason for staying with *Le Monde* his feeling that this journal had rendered good service, and that if he too left it at this point it would collapse. Apparently he did not see any necessity to avoid competition or to give absolute preeminence in the ultramontane camp to the revived *L'Univers*. Aubineau, Serret, the Abbé Morel, and Chantrel made the change, as did the various correspondents in distant places, notably Maguelonne, who had continued to exchange letters with Veuillot throughout the intervening seven years in quite the same way as before the suppression. New editors also soon joined, including Loth, Roussel, Buët, and Petit.[241] The total transformation for Veuillot had been quick. Almost before he could get accustomed to the idea, *L'Univers* was his again and all his – without Taconet.

CHAPTER VIII

L'UNIVERS REVIVED AND VICTORY FOR ULTRAMONTANISM WITHIN THE CHURCH

Veuillot had been surprised when *L'Univers* was authorized. Despite the terms of the September Convention (1864), which had provided for the withdrawal of French troops from most of the pope's territory, relations between France and the papal government actually improved a little, particularly after the creation of the Légion d'Antibes for defense of Rome. The emperor's anticlerical cousin, Prince Napoleon, overstepped his position in 1865 when he made a speech at Ajaccio saying that to all practical purposes Napoleon I had never been a Catholic, and after Prince Napoleon's disgrace (this speech was not all that he did to make himself a laughing stock) his sister, Princess Mathilde, and her salon, gathering place of free-thinkers, had less influence. The Duc de Morny had died in 1865, and the presidency of the Corps législatif had been given to the former foreign minister, Walewski, whose sympathies were still with the clerical orientation.[1] Montalembert had been rousing and brilliant in his speech at Malines, but now the question of orthodoxy was raised in respect to his words.[2] The influence of men like the protestant Émile Ollivier was rising at home, and in foreign policy the situation grew ever more shaky after the victory of Prussia over Austria. The emperor was already embarrassed by the Mexican venture, which was turning into a disaster. Veuillot was under no illusions now, as he had been in his early days of support for Napoleon III, but again he could hope that an ultramontane journal might be a force in French life. It was a more mature but still determined man who now picked up his journalist's pen, a man with a skill that had been polished by seven years of hard work as an *écrivain.*

There was joy in the camp of the ultramontanes, and in a large segment of French Catholicism. Msgr. Guibert, Archbishop of Tours and after 1871 Archbishop of Paris, was one of the first to write Louis Veuillot of his pleasure on hearing of the provisional authorization. Essentially ultramontane, but very sensitive to various local considerations, Msgr. Guibert hoped that an understanding could be reached with Taconet.[3] Even before the definite word had come Msgr. Mermillod was rejoicing over *L'Univers*' resurrection.[4] Even without

Taconet's participation, raising money proved no problem. Subscriptions began promptly to mount. The day after the first number appeared, Veuillot wrote Maguelonne that 5000 subscriptions had been taken, and that shortly there would be 7000.[5] Within two months the figure had reached 8000, and it was felt that the influence of the revived journal, as in the past, far exceeded the number of its subscriptions.[6] By early 1868 it had over 10,500 subscribers,[7] which by the standards of any paper of that day could be regarded as substantial.

But not everyone was happy. The Archbishop of Paris, Msgr. Darboy, Gallican, circumspect, in some ways difficult to classify, was not in the joyous group. On the surface there was no open trouble between the archbishop and the journalist, but Darboy was vexed to have the journal coming out again. Veuillot told Charlotte de Grammont: "I assure you that my archbishop in his quality of senator is not happy with me. All the same, I obey his commands as well as I can or I will have to pay. But as for respect, I do what is necessary."[8] While Veuillot's good relations with his own pastor were thus faltering, the old hostility of Msgr. Dupanloup came forth again. From the early to the mid-sixties it had appeared as though imperial policy toward Rome were driving the two together, but this situation did not develop. Hearing of expressions of satisfaction from a large part of the episcopacy, including the Archbishops of Bourges and Poitiers and the Bishop of Beauvais,[9] Dupanloup immediately wrote to other bishops reviving his old objections to Veuillot. He said he was dangerous, prone to perpetrating antagonisms not only among the laity but among the clergy. He criticized him for joining the liberals in 1848 (whom now he so often insulted as though he had never been one of them), then accepting the coup and abdicating to Caesarism. According to Dupanloup, Veuillot would inevitably put the priests and bishops into opposition, and even the bishops and the pope. By his doctrines and language he would "dig a veritable abyss between the mass of the laity and the clergy." On the other hand, somewhat inconsistently, Dupanloup asserted that too many priests had themselves been affected by "an intemperance of language" growing from reading Veuillot's narrow doctrines, "in his polemics of almost every day, in these floods of calumnies and injuries, in an equal obliviousness of Christian sentiment and of the simpler conventions, truth, justice, and charity."[10] In short, Dupanloup warned the episcopacy of what in his eyes was ahead for them. There was other opposition to Veuillot on a cruder plane. Insulting things were said and drawings drawn for popular consumption of which Veuillot was the butt. As early as May of 1867 one Daniel Lévy was fined 100 francs and given a suspended sentence for publishing an unauthorized drawing of Veuillot in *La Lune.*[11] Veuillot had to be able to take abuse while handing out abuse to others.

The first number of *L'Univers*, appearing April 16, 1867, had some interesting aspects. The feature editorial by Louis Veuillot was one of these. It included a rather frank summary of the fate that *L'Univers* had suffered and its problems in gaining provisional re-authorization. Skating on rather dangerous ice, he then changed his direction somewhat and focused on the pope. Not too modestly, but with papal authority behind him, Veuillot declared: *Qui perdiderit animam suam propter me, inveniet eam.* Like a Christian martyr *L'Univers* was now raised up from the dead, and it would say aloud for its readers what *Le Monde* had only suggested. In identifying the papacy as the highest authority of Christianity Veuillot could not have gone much further than to say:

> There is no other base for civilization than the Gospel, no other architect of the social order than the Vicar of Jesus Christ. To believe this is reconciliation. The world, after pagan barbarism, which was slavery, has crumbled, and will only be rebuilt when it has generally accepted these words of one of the church fathers: "Christ is the solution of all our difficulties."[12]

Veuillot's whole stand would be for Christianity, as interpreted by the Vicar of Christ, and he had sounded the key note of support for this highest authority's infallibility. *L'Univers* would be the same as in the past, "except for improvements from experience."[13]

The other notable feature of the first number was a review of Montalembert's *Les Moines d'Occident*. This review was written by one of the new men, A. de Lansade, and since Montalembert had only recently rebuffed Veuillot, it might have been expected that the editor of *L'Univers* would at least allow the reviewer to say whatever he pleased. Montalembert had even insulted Veuillot in the preface. But Veuillot wanted to consolidate as much support from Catholic ranks as he could, and any gratuitous slap to the former chief of the Catholic party would lose him friends. Perhaps also he either still dreamed of a reconciliation with his old chief or in some way was haunted by a lingering loyalty to him. Writing to Lansade to make sure that this article would be ready for the first number, he gave this subtle indication of what he wanted: "Please make it something general which will let you return to the work. I would particularly like to see a little praise for the worker. The job is solid; that will not be repugnant to you. If you want to make some reservations, do so in a veiled way. I am sure you know what I mean. It will require a delicate touch, no affectation of generosity, no mention of the past, and just between you and me, you have every right to ignore, without giving the appearance of forgiving, what has been bitter in the past. Farewell. I leave you to that charming and kind angel who throws planks across ditches."[14] The resulting article followed Veuillot's instructions very well, giving further evidence of the skill available at the offices of *L'Univers*. In addition to showing Veuillot's policies and his preoccupation with Montalembert, this instruction to Lansade also illustrates the care with which Veuillot now considered the tone of all articles appearing in his journal – although his opponents may have had the impression that *L'Univers*, as before, just blasted away. It is impossible to reconstruct the extent of influence Du Lac and others had on the journal's editorial line, but once the line was decided it was carefully carried out.

While the editors were being careful not to collide too directly with the régime, despite their intensified emphasis on Catholic allegiance to the pope himself, the nature of the articles and editorials of the revived journal was very similar to that of former days. Foreign policy could be treated in such a way as to serve the cause, particularly if the emphasis were kept on the position of the church rather than on the blunders of the Second Empire. At the time of negotiations over the neutrality of Luxembourg it was proper enough to attack protestant Prussia, bringing Frederick the Great and Voltaire to life again, if such attention was paid particularly out of concern for Pius IX.[15] There was no need directly to criticize French foreign policy, which clearly was losing its lustre in everyone's eyes. The sad mistake of the man who had offered the crown of Mexico to Emperor Maximilian was a fair topic,[16] and the readers of *L'Univers* might affectingly be told of how the pope wept when he heard the emperor had been shot.[17] Witty things might be said about the visits of crowned heads from round the world to Europe at the time of the Exposition of 1867,[18] without rubbing in too directly the contrast between France's awkward position and the grandeur that was being displayed. During the period of the exposition, on 6 June 1867, a Polish revolutionary named Berezowski fired at Tsar Alexander II in the Bois de Boulogne narrowly missing him. Naturally a tirade against regicide followed that permitted Veuillot to write on one of his favorite topics. Napoleon III might of course be reminded of Orsini, but the influence of men like the anticlerical Alphonse Peyrat could also be brought forth and blamed. A variety of themes, even from sixteenth-century English history, could be blended to serve the thoroughly acceptable line against regicide.[19] Veuillot had no higher opinion of Alexander II, oppressor of Polish Catholics, than he did of the would-be assassin, but he exploited the situation and used it as an opportunity to say what he wished, in a proper way.

Steadily after revival *L'Univers* sniped away at *Le Siècle* and *Le Figaro*. Veuillot no doubt hated the factions that these journals represented, but he may have been glad for their presence as targets. As a matter of fact, he served the same purpose for them. In the rebuilding days of *L'Univers*, petty quarrels between it and the secular press may have done more for journalism itself than for any of the individual causes. Strictly literary matters had always been a feature of *L'Univers*, and after 1867 its interest in this field was continued. At the death of Beaudelaire, Veuillot, wrote the mother of the author of *Fleurs de Mal*, a touching letter of condolence,[20] in which however he avoided saying anything more about his poetry than that it had caused *un bruit regrettable*. Instead, he stressed the happy thought that God had taken pity on this oppressed soul and had allowed Beaudelaire time to repent and to receive the sacraments.[21] Veuillot thus found many little ways of giving spice to his positions and yet avoiding trouble directly with the régime.

Veuillot had excellent men for his purposes around him, but it is noteworthy that he also was eager to use the talents of women. Many of the women with whom he corresponded were able literary people, and he wrote to Msgr. de Segur about their role.[22] He did not know where to put the "h" in *Landwehr*, so he asked Charlotte. He told her: "I regret bitterly that *L'Univers* has taken so firm a resolution as to be exclusively masculine," adding with a light touch, using Italian, as he often did when trying to be amusing, "L'ingresso e proibito alle donne solto pena di scomunica,"[23] as though it were all right to joke about excommunication if only signs posted in the Papal States might be invoked. Actually, he did open the door to her participation. On 3 May 1867 there appeared an unsigned article describing the enthusiasm over the lenten preaching of the Dominican Father Matthieu, which could be easily identified by its opening words, "One writes from Versailles [Charlotte's home]."[24] Louis Veuillot disliked Madame de Sévigné,[25] and he hated the scheme of liberal education for girls that was one of Victor Duruy's leading projects, and one which was not altogether alien to Dupanloup,[26] but women with his approved brand of ideas he never underestimated. He sought their advice and help whenever he could get it.

L'Univers had hardly been relaunched when Louis Veuillot took yet another trip to Rome! The year had been declared to be the eighteen-hundredth anniversary of the martyrdom and triumph of Saint Peter, and Bishops from all over the world came to the Eternal City for this anniversary. Veuillot accepted the figure of 440 of them.[27] He had just recently been to see the pope, but still he could not pass up this great occasion. Reaching Rome by 20 June 1867 he wrote Élise:

> . . . .I did well not to go by sea, because it would have been terribly rough. I made a mistake going by land, because the fatigue is horrible, the dust unbelievable, the inns overpriced, the countryside scorching and totally unattractive. Nonetheless we arrived safely, without accident, or loss of baggage. It is terribly hot, there is unending noise, and our Via Frattina is as busy as a carnival. In short, one is better off on the Rue de Bac.[28]

But the bishops and the pope were not on the Rue de Bac, and he knew that something big was in the air, quite apart from the celebration of the martyrdom of Saint Peter.

Plans were already being laid for a great ecumenical council to be held 1869-1870. The reunification of Christendom would have been a great thing, though it is hard to see how arrangements for it could have brought joy to Veuillot, unless, of course, the protestants were to submit completely to Rome. The Vatican Council of 1869-1870 turned out to be simply a great council of approximately 800 Catholic prelates, and although provision was made ahead of time for consideration of various theological matters, even in 1867 it was clear that the question of papal infallibility was going to be the central interest and concern of the council. This subject was central and fundamental to everything in Louis Veuillot's schemes, and even though he had only recently been in Rome, and even though the press of business ought to have kept him in the offices of *L'Univers*, he simply had to be in Rome when it was being discussed. His observations during the two weeks that he spent in Rome in midsummer were geared to this issue. He watched the doings of Dupanloup and Darboy closely. Since already he was in the thick of a struggle with Dupanloup, it was with joy that he noted reactions of various foreigners, such as a young Spanish priest and editor, in favor of him and against the Bishop of Orleans.[29] Had Louis Veuillot known of public opinion polls, he would have been using the techniques of this device for his purposes.

The pope, ever busy, had hundreds of bishops and other dignitaries on hand in Rome, and only recently he had received Louis Veuillot intimately. Nevertheless, Veuillot made arrangements right away to have an audience with the pope, although Darboy got to Antonelli first, denouncing, according to what Veuillot heard, his moves.[30] Despite whatever denunciations Darboy may have made of Veuillot, the determined editor got his audience, albeit not alone – he had to go in the company of the Belgian Cardinal Berardi. Veuillot realized he had gone rather far in his demands on the Holy Father's time, but he pleaded the example of the leper who had been healed. The pope wittily replied that when the Lord asked Peter for a third time whether he loved Him, the questioning was not solely for information but also to test Peter's patience! As usual Veuillot was delighted with the pope, but the pope had a question for him: Did he have need of presenting himself to his bishop (Darboy)? Veuillot replied he would certainly go if ordered to do so, and that if he had been so ordered, his bishop would receive him. Through all this exchange, according to Veuillot, the pope smiled.[31] However set in his course Pius IX had become, and Gallican as Darboy most certainly was, it seems safe to assume that Pius IX would have been pleased had Veuillot done exactly what he asked him about. Eugène assures us that Pius IX gave no such order,[32] and no doubt the pope was wise in doing no more than asking a question. Of course the pope wanted Veuillot's backing for the ultramontane position, but that Veuillot might help to make things smoother along the way was also within the scope of his wishes. Veuillot, the "sergeant of Jesus Christ," only responded to orders of His Vicar, and not to hints of gratuitous charity toward an antagonist.

When the celebrations of the eighteen-hundredth anniversary of the martyrdom of Saint Peter were over, Veuillot returned to an existence that was very similar to his old routine before the suppression of *L'Univers*. He seems to have thrived on the problems of his journal and to have felt invigorated by the excitement of being back in affairs of the day again. Other people attributed greater influence to him and to *L'Univers* than he did himself,[33] but it is unmistakable that for him the frustrations and sad mood of 1861-1867 were past. His letters to friends, especially Charlotte de Grammont, during the summer of 1867 reveal this new frame of mind, and although none of his letters to Juliette of this period are available, he was hearing from her with pleasure at this time.[34] An exchange with "this poor devil" Wolff of *Le Figaro* – this "Jew, Bohemian, vain sot, and laughing-stock" only added zest to his continuing duel with that "boulevardier" journal, Villemessant, Villemot, and all the rest of those well-established cynics, according to Veuillot.[35] The stands of *Le Siècle* against the scaffold – and against marriage – of course troubled Veuillot, and he defended both.[36] However, despite his concerns over the social order in France, Rome again dominated his attention.

The troops Napoleon III had promised to withdraw in the September Convention of 1864 were indeed recalled. Their recall by the end of 1866, of course, was a signal to Garibaldi, who rapidly threw together a revolutionary force after leaving his island home on Caprera. The government of Victor Emmanuel was slow to move, but finally, as Garibaldi was ready to invade the Papal States, he was arrested and taken back to Caprera. He eluded the Italian authorities there, rejoined his forces, and Victor Emmanuel II had to seem ready to oppose him. So did Napoleon III, who dispatched a force from Toulon under General Failly.[37] The French forces finally stopped the Garibaldians at Mentana, a town about thirteen miles northeast of Rome, on 3 November 1867, but in the meantime the pontifical troops, especially the Zouaves, had been engaging the Garibaldians, notably at Monte Rotondo. *L'Univers* reproduced the speech of Father d'Alzon, founder of the Assumptionists, in honor of the Pontifical Zouaves and Veuillot started out a letter to Father d'Alzon with the words, "Bravo! Bravo!"[38] The whole thing was like an inspired crusade, and the Zouaves had now won a victory over the Garibaldians, aided, of course, by the French troops. Garibaldi was out of the way for a little while, and Veuillot could rejoice in the three thousand casualties, killed, wounded, and prisoners, which the Garibaldians had suffered.[39]

Veuillot's joy followed much apprehension. He had pictured the worst developments possible for Rome, and great as was his admiration for the Papal Zouaves, he had not been able to envisage quite such a happy turn of affairs as took place at Mentana. He went surprisingly far in the columns of *L'Univers*, not only in picturing Prussia as an ally of Garibaldi, but also in picturing the government of Victor Emmanuel as conspiring with him. Looking back further, Veuillot bewailed the way that France had enfeebled Austria, built up Italy, and set the stage for a collapse of the Papal States.[40] Especially through October of 1867 he had followed the ominous situation, and with the victory at Mentana he bitterly hurled back the Garibaldian cry, *Rome ou mort.*[41] Throughout his career Veuillot had partaken of victories and defeats, and with all of them he had strong feelings, but the victory at Mentana was more strongly savored by him than almost any other.

The success of the papal forces at Mentana and the obligation Napoleon had felt to send an army to defeat the Red Shirts seem to have caused Veuillot to lose the restraint he had at first maintained on being reauthorized to edit *L'Univers*. Napoleon III delivered a speech from the throne on the subject of the Roman Question, in which he was not reassuring as to the future. Veuillot immediately said about the idea of a completely united Italy:

> The unity of Italy is the cause of all the evil. It menaces the church and the monarchy alike. The expression *one* Italy is not that

> of Victor Emmanuel, it is of Garibaldi and even more of Mazzini, the prophet of the universal republic.
>
> Revolutionary Italy only wants Rome in order to drive out the pope; it only wants to abolish Christianity to reintegrate at Rome a Caesar-emperor, pontiff and god of earth. All this is completely out of range of Victor Emmanuel. For a long time that which calls itself the "monarchical party," in Italy, has been no more than a docile agent of the Revolution. Who can count on whom for the safety of the monarchical principle and the salvation of the European order?[42]

Napoleon III was obviously being held responsible for what had taken place in Italy, but the régime no longer chose to silence such criticism.

In his outspoken attacks Veuillot fired at some of the most established figures of the régime, and at some of the people only recently coming strongly to the fore, as well. Haussmann and Ollivier were good examples. Much of the prosperity of the Second Empire had been associated with the rebuilding of Paris under the celebrated préfet of the Seine, Baron Haussmann.[43] Prosperity declined in the sixties from the flourishing level of the fifties, but still his great projects continued unabated, with great blocks of old buildings being demolished to make way for the wide boulevards and elaborate structures that replaced them. In order to accomplish his ends Haussmann, although he was a protestant, had the work pushed on seven days a week, violating Sunday, to the distress of Veuillot. This matter was the subject of a quarrel with *Le Siècle.* Haussmann, in Veuillot's eyes, was not only demolishing the old Paris for new markets, barracks, and *cafés chantants*, but he was demolishing the Ten Commandments.[44] In the meantime, another protestant was rising, making his peace with the emperor, and working his way into such a position as to be ready to take over the reins as the government headed in its new more liberal direction – Émile Ollivier. Ollivier once said that Montalembert was a protestant without knowing it,[45] and Veuillot in his turn said that Ollivier was Caesarian without knowing it,[46] despite his professed liberalism. Veuillot seems not to have doubted Ollivier's intentions, and Ollivier, for his part, felt that Veuillot had let him off easier than he might have done.[47] In his observations Veuillot treated none of the ministers or servants of Napoleon III lightly, whether they represented the local establishment of Paris or the new order of things to come in the whole country.

No one could deny that Veuillot had foreseen the danger of Prussia, but in the late sixties the columns of *L'Univers* were relatively quiet about Bismarck, the North German Confederation, and danger to France from that quarter. Wherever the religious side of international issues loomed large, the attention of *L'Univers* would be fixed. There was indeed something rather precious about its emphasis, ever recalling the collapse of the Sonderbund and fixing on the victory at Mentana. Perhaps because of the influence of Donoso Cortés over the years, and perhaps because of the mixture of the religious question with practical politics in Spain, Veuillot attached much importance to the chain of events that began there in 1868 with the overthrow of Queen Isabella II and the substitution of a military dictatorship. He was hardly an apologist for Isabella, but he saw revolution and danger in the action of Prim and Serrano. He was horrified when Victor Hugo supported the changes that were under way.[48] Although the Carlists were not the easiest element in the world to defend, Veuillot seemed to identify Don Carlos with the cause of the Catholic church. As usual he emphasized the importance of the church as the solution of that country's trouble, and since the church had suffered such attacks there in recent years he could dramatically hold up Spain as a warning. He called for the destruction of revolution,[49] and he bickered with such monarchist journals as *La Gazette de France* about the dangers of any compromise.[50] But whatever other journals might say about Spain, throughout the years *L'Univers* and Louis Veuillot gave relatively more attention to that country than the general run of Parisian journals.

Although Veuillot had to be careful what he said about the imperial family, it was both safe and convenient for him to come to the defense of the prince-imperial, when various journals criticized him for immature clerical views. The twelve-year-old boy, son of the devout Spanish-born empress, was said to have declared: "When I become emperor, I will demand that everyone fulfill his religious obligations. I will not tolerate people without religion." *L'Opinion nationale* and the *Journal des Débats* were foremost among the many journals which could not let this observation pass without comment. Veuillot got into debate with them, and while Veuillot did not insist that the prince imperial had said these words, he made it clear that such an utterance would have been most promising for the future.[51] Such an emperor as that would have rekindled 1852-like devotion, in a certain quarter.

One of Veuillot's articles started off on the theme of the emperor's addiction to tobacco. One of Napoleon III's many physicians had declared publicly that the emperor smoked too much, and immediately many began to talk about the matter and what effects the emperor's addiction could have for France.[52] This vice of the emperor's was of small importance, Veuillot thought, and, likening tobacco smoke to incense before idols, he attacked the idols and sins of the day in a tirade which probably seemed a good example of what some who did not enjoy reading him thought of as his crudeness. He sounded like an Old Testament prophet and a modern puritan at the same time. There was much justice in his observations, but what was remarkable was that a peccadillo on the part of the emperor had served as the starting point for his widely attacking both public and private morals.

Whether tobacco materially hastened the development of physical troubles for the emperor as his doctor warned, or not, many prominent French personages did sicken and die in 1868. Depending largely on whether they had made open professions of the Catholic faith or not, Veuillot would write moving obituaries, or articles pointing out the errors of their ways. Veuillot tended to emphasize death and dying as one of his themes in writing. Necrology became a useful device for journalizing. Lamartine, the Comtesse de Gontaut-Biron, Berryer, Havin, Rothschild, and Rossini died in rather close succession, and Veuillot was able to make some comparisons, at least for the latter four.[53] Havin could be described as an *ultrafigarotique*, even in death. The dead were treated pretty much like the living in the uninhibited appraisals of Louis Veuillot. The royalist political leader, Berryer, had been criticized from time to time by Veuillot, without any special retorts, but Veuillot came under fire for his harsh obituary. It happened that Berryer's own organ, *L'Union*, had reported his death prematurely, and not surprisingly Veuillot had assumed he was dead. But not quite, and now Veuillot could be accused of attacking Berryer *mourant*. Attacking a dying man was not considered cricket. Henri de Riancey, *L'Union* and various royalists took Veuillot to task, for remarks that were comparatively mild albeit premature.[54]

Veuillot had other troubles with the legitimists in 1868. Ever more he had come to admire the Comte de Chambord personally as well as to endorse his principles, but his relations with many of the more practical of the established supporters of monarchy were not always good. The church was not always the be-all, end-all for these people. Veuillot wanted a completely traditional church, and as long as a traditional monarchy would make the church the keystone of the social and political order, that was what he wanted. Charity, at least of a material sort, was something in which Veuillot was not wanting, and the fulfillment of social and economic obligations of the church, and society as a whole, to the poor he had always advocated. The "men of good will," Albert de Mun and La Tour du Pin, had not yet founded their Œuvre des Cercles des ouvriers,[55] but Maurice Meignen and the Brothers of Saint Vincent des Paul already had a circle in Montparnasse at that time which was a forerunner of the associations of upper-class traditionalists and laboring-class people of the seventies. Anticipating the emphasis of this noble-sponsored social Catholicism, Msgr. Mermillod preached during Lent of 1868 at the Church of Sainte Clotilde in the Faubourg St. Germain on the need for Christian economic aid to the poor. Msgr. Mermillod sounded like a socialist to some of his auditors, and he was accused of being such. Veuillot sprang to the defense of the prelate. After all, Veuillot had been a worker in Paris, like his father before him. He had defended the rights of the well-born and admired their nobility whenever it was nobility of character. But charity in the form of sharing with the poor was as old as Christianity, and when Mermillod pointed it out to the well-to-do legitimists, he was only reminding them of their Christian obligation. There was no place for economic slavery in the Christian world, and the representatives of old France were no exception to the rule.[56] Veuillot was on strong ground in this matter, and he was in the vanguard of the clerical-legitimist economic and social thought that came to the fore in the days of the Third Republic. He had to share the label of socialist that had been applied to Mermillod, but the circumstances of this charge of socialism probably enhanced his general popularity, and that of the legitimists who inclined to the side of the workers of that era. Nevertheless, many conservatives seemed outraged with him, and looked for other issues on which to criticize him. For example, at this period some of the clergy and legitimists had decided to have vengeance on Victor Duruy, and because on occasion Veuillot avoided hostility with the emperor, one of the Rianceys called him a *canaille* for not turning on the emperor![57] The explanation of Veuillot's actions, or lack of same, was the old one: he was *Catholique avant tout*, while the Rianceys and their like were primarily royalist, content to assume that the church would have its proper place under the monarchy.

Veuillot continually made reference to the fine arts, particularly if they had some bearing on religion. Music seemed to please him next to literature, and Gounod he especially admired. During the fall of 1868 he enjoyed Gounod's company when vacationing in the country. He wrote his sister: "Gounod is very cheerful, very gracious, very sparkling, with a touch of the feverish." Veuillot had particularly come to know him in the years 1842-1845 when Gounod had been organist at the Church of Foreign Missions on the Rue de Babylone in his parish.[58] They knew each other on intimate terms over a long period, and we find Veuillot writing to his friend, Émile Perrin, director of the opera, to get tickets for the Comte de Ségur to the first performance of *Faust* that took place in Paris on 4 March 1869.[59] Gounod wrote music for a poem of Veuillot's, which took the form of his last testament. Veuillot was thoroughly charmed by Gounod, who could tell good stories by the hundred, as well as play Mozart and Beethoven by heart![60]

Painting was not usually of particular interest to Veuillot, but when his boyhood friend, Émile Lafon, who had painted members of the family and friends, and who had the same religious outlook as he, painted a large picture of the Battle of Mentana, which was displayed in Paris in 1868, he thought it worthy of note. Lafon had gone about the work carefully, using the new method of working from photographs. Veuillot had shown much interest in the production of the painting,[61] even sounding impatient about how things were going, and when the work was finally brought to public view, he wrote a long discussion of the canvas, with some of his usual comparisons with other great artists.[62] Art criticism was out of the usual line for Veuillot, but if the subject involved were one Veuillot considered worthy, he would tackle it. And here it was worthy – the Pontifical Zouaves firing on the Garibaldians, driving the impious revolutionaries from Rome, and, in some instances, dying heroically. Even painting had to be given the fullest attention if the right artist were depicting the right scene. As for sculpture, however, Veuillot was sure of one thing: it mattered not whether Houdon or someone else had made a statue of Voltaire, that man ought not to be memorialized anywhere. Without saying much about the actual product, Veuillot bewailed the prospect that a statue of Voltaire was to be placed at one of two prominent places in Paris. Ironically the installation did not take place until August 1870, when Prussian troops were on the move against France, a coincidence exploited in due course by Veuillot.[63]

Whatever Veuillot's strong and weak points in the appreciation of the arts may have been, and he was much more sensitive in these areas than most journalists of the time, politics naturally were his greatest interest. In 1868 and 1869, after a good many concessions had been made to liberalism within the Second Empire, the emperor prepared for the third elections of the Corps législatif. In view of the changing political kaleidoscope, legitimists and clericals troubled themselves a good deal about their relationships with each other. A good many legitimists were thoroughly put out with Veuillot, especially since the episodes of Mermillod's preaching and the premature article about Berryer. However, Veuillot's base of popular strength seemed greater than ever. Simple priests were behind him as never before, and legitimists wanting to broaden their purely monarchical appeal could not forget that they needed the support of the peasants. Veuillot received many protestations of support from parish priests. Typical of them was a message from an Abbé Boisson of Vessoul who complained of those who were criticizing Veuillot about the Berryer article. He told Veuillot that his articles proved that "more and more you are Catholic-before-all, exclusively Catholic, Catholic like the pope and with the pope, in the manner of Saint Ambrose and Saint Francis de Sales: *Ubi Petrus, ibi ecclesia.* The pope and the church are completely one."[64] Maurice de Bonald lent his support to Veuillot from a more elevated quarter, attacking those "so-called legitimists" who were giving him trouble.[65] Other legitimists, while deploring past stands of Veuillot, appealed to him for support for legitimist candidates who would back the program of the Comte de Chambord, especially with regard to the temporal power.[66] It seemed as though the legitimists had need of Veuillot, but, while he was generally sympathetic with them, he regarded them as only incidental to his cause.

Since Veuillot had often been spoken of as a potential candidate for parliament, it is not amazing that in early 1869 the rumor started again. *L'Union de l'Ouest*, organ of Falloux, picked up the rumor that he was to stand for election in Anjou. Veuillot was complimentary of the journal, but he wrote an article denying that this was the case.[67] Of course it is doubtful that he ever was seriously tempted to seek election, but at a time when *L'Univers* was functioning effectively he certainly had too much practical judgment to consider the possibility. However, he used the journal for the support of the Catholic cause very extensively during the spring of 1869 in a campaign that, except for Paris and a few other cities, brought general support for the empire in its liberalized form.

While Veuillot had a lot to say,[68] perhaps his main point was expressed thus: "For us, without denying the more or less good intentions of men, we do not count on journals, the tribune, nor on the *Union libérale* (royalist and moderate republican opposition), nor Ollivier, nor Rouher, nor even on the emperor or the dynasty. We count on the love of Christ, our eternal master, and on the social institution of his love, the papacy."[69] Veuillot went on, further identifying the church and the papacy, and calling for a return of loyalties to the pope from Caesar. Veuillot's appeal to the electorate was indeed a strange one. He spoke of the monkey which got ahold of a razor, and trying to fix his beard, cut himself badly. Though various explanations have been made of this ancient fable, Veuillot insisted that the razor was universal suffrage.[70]

So far as Veuillot was concerned, the monkey gave himself some bad cuts in the elections of 1869, especially in Paris. Adolphe Guéroult, who had given Veuillot so much trouble in the past, had been the representative of his arrondissement since 1863. His elimination in the first round of voting was certainly not to be bewailed, but the resulting run-off produced something much worse. Augustin Cochin was a liberal Catholic associate of Montalembert, indeed, one of the group which had met at La Roche-en-Brény in 1862. But he was a serious churchman, and in Veuillot's eyes an essentially honorable man. He was opposed by the positivist newcomer to Paris, Jules Ferry. Ferry was to become as clear an opponent in politics as Veuillot ever had in the next decade, and Veuillot unfailingly spotted his qualities as a secularist as soon as he presented himself. Nevertheless, despite the apparent abundance of Catholic sentiment in the district, Ferry won the election, to the great chagrin of Veuillot.[71] He could now foresee his future targets.

Veuillot resented the clear-cut denial Ferry had made of any association with the administration or with the church – Ferry the *pure*. Like many politicians, Ferry had made appeal to his *concitoyens*, but Veuillot insisted he was no *con-citoyen* of Ferry's.[72] Veuillot's bitterness about the election was great, but it was not solely reserved for Ferry. He had barbs for the old Persigny, who made an appeal for the support of young people. He resented the influence of the Jewish Péreire brothers, one of whom was elected to the Corps législatif. And he also foresaw the kind of inept leadership the empire was to have with the rise of Clément Duvernois. He felt the program the government would offer was poor, and he resented the way the conservatives were being pushed aside.[73] In general he held out little hope, and he was making it easy for himself to say in the near future "I told you so."

Far transcending practical politics, even issues that concerned the church, was for Louis Veuillot the question of ultramontanism as opposed to Gallicanism and liberalism. The question was nearly a generation old in the 1860's in the form that it took then, but a new round opened in 1867 which caused Veuillot's clashes with Dupanloup, Montalembert, Falloux, and the whole of that group to begin afresh. In December of 1867 Veuillot wrote to Cardinal Chigi: "Your excellency is not ignorant of my thinking about the Bishop of Orleans. I have sympathy neither for his talent nor for his person."[74] It was hard to say much more, but Veuillot's opponents at least matched him in invective. Montalembert bewailed the state of consciences and honor of Catholics in France and elsewhere who were "under the direction of the man whom the pope has given them for their chief and oracle."[75] Not only was Montalembert going far in attacking Veuillot, his identification of the latter with the pope would seem to have transcended the usual care to maintain an appearance of respect for the papacy. He recriminated Veuillot strongly and was dismayed by the exchange between *L'Univers* and articles by Lavedan in *Le Correspondant.*[76] Falloux declared that "the Christianity of Bossuet gave peace, but that of Veuillot a fever."[77] Falloux, however, sounded a hopeful note: "...The papacy did not indeed perish with the Constable de Bourbon, no more did the church perish with Luther than with Arius, and it will not perish with Msgr. Mercurelli and with Veuillot," to which Montalembert noted in the margin, "No, but we, *we* will perish."[78] Montalembert may have been the closer to the truth.

Veuillot seemed to have no restraint as he attacked the liberals in the late 1860's and outraged men like Dupanloup. A rather impartial observer, Ollivier, while saying that Veuillot was "one of the most remarkable writers of this period," and giving him credit for making a contribution to the way the French language was used, likened him to a very different sort of person – Proudhon. He criticized his exaggeration and personal attacks while praising him for "his marvelous suppleness and rich variety," but he particularly noted in the affairs of the church that, because of Veuillot, to the trio of pope-bishop-priest a fourth element was added – the layman.[79] As the ecumenical council of 1869-1870 approached, and then took place, this observation was especially true.

Soon Msgr. Maret, dean of theology at the Sorbonne, became a new target for Veuillot, though Dupanloup remained his greatest adversary among ecclesiastics. For some time Maret had been preparing a book, which was eventually published in 1869, well before the council met, under the title *Du Concile générale et la paix religieuse*. The work was worthy of its author's position, but it was known from the start to have an ulterior purpose – that of combatting the doctrine of papal infallibility. During 1868, especially during the month of November, Veuillot became involved in a great exchange of editorials with a number of other journals, largely secular, and in an exchange of letters with Maret himself. Maret was not allowed to become Bishop of Vanves only because of the opposition of Pius IX, and he had been made Bishop of Sura *in partibus*. Thus Veuillot was taking a risk openly to confront the learned bishop in a heated exchange. He showed, however, no hesitancy in citing various authorities against the dean of theology, who fundamentally was bringing forward the weight of the bishops of the church in council in their role of determining theological questions.[80] In engaging in such a debate Veuillot was going about as far as a layman conceivably might go.

When Msgr. Maret's book finally came out, the antagonists were at it again. Veuillot treated the book as something that was calling for usurpation of papal power, and he likened the councils of bishops about which Maret wrote to a sort of senate intended to check the power of the pope. He said that Maret was trying to wipe off the tomb of the

Apostle Peter the words, *Tu es Petrus et super hanc Petram. . . .*[81] The previous year Maret had become very angry at Veuillot, and he had been encouraged by another of Veuillot's old opponents, Gratry, who told Maret that "this great curse of the church is asking to be warned (*averti*) more often."[82] He came back at Veuillot strongly again in the fall of 1869, but he also attacked the various bishops who defended Veuillot. Msgr. Pie of Poitiers was consistently Veuillot's mainstay by this time, but Msgr. Plantier, Bishop of Nîmes, came in for a special attack by Maret. During the summer of 1869 Msgr. Plantier had sent out a pastoral letter that was essentially a defense of the doctrine of infallibility. He was an able man who had written other religious works. This latest study had particularly pleased Veuillot, who had written a special article about it.[83] That article was perhaps as important to Maret as a letter that Plantier himself published in *L'Univers* against Maret's position. Maret was moved to write a hot reply in early October to *L'Univers.* Veuillot had a policy of printing all letters of bishops in his journal, but surely he wished he did not have to publish this one. Because of the strength of Maret's attack Veuillot wrote to Msgr. Plantier in advance, telling him the nature of the letter, and taking the position that the two together were under fire because together they had championed the truth.[84] In a way Veuillot was showing consideration for the susceptibilities of the Bishop of Nîmes, but it is remarkable to see the role that he was playing in causing bishops to confront each other in sharp opposition and in taking sides in such a way as to make it the layman who had the last say, at least in the columns of his journal. Dupanloup's epithet for Veuillot, *Accusator fratrum* was appropriate for he made practically impossible an atmosphere of conciliation among the French bishops before the meeting of the council. Normally his differences with some of the bishops did not affect the overwhelming backing he had among the parish priests. While some had on occasion taken exception with him, it was not common for this to happen. However, because of the reproaches he had cast on the idea of power for a council, he was sharply criticized by one young man at this time, a curé named Lamaron. Veuillot seems to have resented the presumption of this mere priest in taking him to task, and, in answering, primarily lectured him on manners towards a man of fifty-six years, telling him that others had differed with M. Veuillot but had been polite about it.[85] It was all right for a man like himself, with little formal education, to attack the dean of theology at the Sorbonne, but who was this mere priest who pretended to be able to take him to task? Veuillot could be touchy.

The attackers of Veuillot became more strident during 1869, not surprisingly, but somehow the initiative passed so clearly to Veuillot that he was able to take their attacks calmly. His normal role was to be rather relaxed in a battle, and he seems often, though not always, to have thrived in such situations. Moreover in the fall of 1869 things were falling his way. The victory of the infallibilists at the Vatican Council has been presented as his triumph,[86] and already before the Council met he seemed to be acting like a person on the verge of seeing a great goal attained. Probably his greatest goal was to see ultramontane Catholicism rigidly established in France, but first this kind of Catholicism would have to have its victory within the church itself.

One episode that facilitated the strengthening of his position among French Catholics was the case of Father Hyacinthe. Father Hyacinthe, an able man and a fine speaker, was a Carmelite and had been made preacher at Notre Dame by Darboy. His ideas, however, became conspicuously very liberal, and he took a stand against infallibility. Had he been somewhat more careful in his words and deeds, he would have been a significant force in the struggle. However, neither his words nor in particular his deeds, were careful. His closeness to a woman, and a protestant at that, became notorious. The fact that he would later marry her after leaving the priesthood did not affect his situation in 1869. He went to Rome in the early summer of 1869 and would admit there to doing nothing wrong. Moreover, he branded the régime there "the worst of personal governments." Veuillot followed all this to his advantage, eliciting a letter of reply from Father Hyacinthe to the effect that he retracted nothing that he had said.[87] Father Hyacinthe may not have been entirely truthful about what had taken place between him and the pope, but he told enough for Veuillot to declare: "How can he differ with the pope, but not want anyone to take exception with him!"[88] Within a short time, despite the attempts of other liberals to get him in line, Father Hyacinthe left his post, his order, and his church. He became Monsieur Loyson. Veuillot exploited the situation to the full in September,[89] to the great embarrassment of the liberals. He declared that Père Hyacinthe had formerly had influence which had emanated to him from the church, but that as Monsieur Loyson he would henceforth have none. This was true certainly within the Catholic church, and although he started a sect of his own before long, he had done about all that he could to play into the hands of the forces he had opposed within Catholicism, particularly Veuillot.

Dupanloup, in the meantime, had not been idle, but had something to do with the publication of a brochure, not a pastoral, *Observations sur la controverse soulevée relativement à la definition de l'infallibilité du prochain Concile. Le Correspondant* on 15 October had issued what appeared to Louis Veuillot to be a manifesto on the subject of infallibility.[90] This piece obviously had the assent of Dupanloup, if not perhaps his direct inspiration. The matter of declaring papal infallibility was adjudged "inopportune," the key word for the opposition at the council. Jousting with the manifesto of a journal was one thing, but to engage in a public quarrel with the bishop who was to be the effective leader of the opponents of infallibility at the council was another, but Veuillot became so engaged. He wrote an article that associated Dupanloup's *Observations* with Maret's book, with the attitudes of Montalembert, with the German opponents, including Bishop Doellinger and lay groups, and, of course, with Père Hyacinthe. Although the tone of Veuillot's article was more guarded than some he had written, he did describe Dupanloup as the opponent of the Vicar of Jesus Christ in so many words.[91] Dupanloup now trained his guns on Veuillot, as he had done in 1853.

Dupanloup immediately issued an *avertissement* to Veuillot that had an almost unprecedented vehemence. Both he and the journalist were preparing to leave for Rome, and the prelate hoped to demolish Veuillot at this juncture. Actually he fell victim to his own hatred of Veuillot and wrote of the troublesome journalist in a way that Veuillot hardly ever did of others. The warning had the appearance of a political manifesto. There were short-sentence paragraphs of the variety that Mazzini might have turned out for the relatively unlettered. Veuillot, practically speaking, was called the devil three times. Among Dupanloup's charges were:

> You give yourself a role in the church which is no longer tolerable.
>
> You, simple layman, one of those writers of whom one of the bishops said recently in your very columns that "they have no authority and are nothing in the church," you strangely usurp it.
>
> You agitate and trouble spirits in the church.
>
> You make a sort of pious riot at the door of the council.
>
> You trace for it its course; you pose questions that the Holy Father has not posed; you speak of definitions, which according to you are 'inevitable'; you define the mode and the form.
>
> You insult, denounce, and put under the ban of Catholicism all Catholics who do not think or speak as you do.
>
> It is too much, monsieur. It was time to answer you. That is why I have spoken.
>
> . . . . .
>
> I accuse you of usurpations from the episcopacy, and of perpetual intrusion in the most serious and delicate matters.
>
> I accuse you especially of excess of doctrines, deplorable taste for irritating questions, and violent and dangerous solutions.
>
> I accuse you of accusing, insulting, and calumniating your brothers in the faith. No one ever deserved more than you the scriptual word: *accusator fratrum*![92]

Not long after Veuillot reached Rome he wrote that the *avertissement* had had the opposite effect from what Dupanloup intended. The very violence of the bishop had brought about a reaction.[93] Veuillot's assessment no doubt was right. He was clearly on the ascendant side, and although he had gone far in involvement in ecclesiastical matters, his tone had not been as strident as in some previous situations. The tactics of Dupanloup had become those of desperation, and when it was clear that the overwhelming majority of bishops were leaning to the side of the doctrine of infallibility of the pope, it was more inopportune to attack the popularizer of the doctrine than to pronounce the doctrine itself. Veuillot understood his role better than his opponents did. Back in the summer of 1867 he had written: "I write for a Catholic journal not as one having a *mission* but because I have a *permission*; this serious nuance must be grasped."[94] This permission of the pope himself gave him latitude in the age of the broadening of the bases of government in the world to bring before the growing forces of public opinion the wishes of the pope, at least as he interpreted them.

Veuillot was more correct in judging general Catholic sentiment of the late 1860's than in moulding it, though he was not unimportant in the latter regard. In an impressionistic and amateurish way Veuillot had refreshing insight into history. He could see that associations of working men were more affected by the changes of the nineteenth century and Louis Philippe than they were by the French Revolution, even including the "freedom" it gave the worker. He believed that the Revolution really began with the introduction of revolutionary ideas during the Enlightenment, and that the counter-revolution had begun in 1789. But this self-educated, unprofessional historian's most interesting idea was that the Vatican Council of 1869-1870 ended the Middle Ages, an idea he propounded shortly after the pope formally called for the council in 1868. "The 29th of June, 1868, the promulgation of the bull *Æterni Patris*, is the date of its extreme end, of its last gasp. Another era begins." He went on to explain how church and state had been separated de facto, and that everyone recognized it. The state was "laïc," according to Guizot, or "free," according to Cavour, two revolting ideas to Veuillot.[95] The governments had not been called upon to send representatives, despite the fact that most of the European states were officially Catholic, and almost all of them had treaties with the papacy for the regulation of church matters within their borders. The church was now free from these régimes, which would not henceforth be able to influence the stands that the church would take. There had not been a great council since the Council of Trent, when

Christendom, albeit divided, was still the thesis, and the concept of separation of church and state impossible. By most standards of thinking the modern age was the age that was drawing toward an end, having been in existence since the time of the Council of Trent, but in line with Veuillot's emphasis on the Catholic church as the key institution, there was some logic in saying that the disappearance of a vestige of the medieval period, the close association of church and state, was marking the end of the Middle Ages. If nothing else, Veuillot was giving historians something to think about with regard to periodization.

The régimes of Europe had for some time been concerned about uncontrollable directions of the Catholic church, and in the increasingly secular nineteenth century still wished to exercise some influence. When the pope became ill in 1861, there had been a meeting of many of the key statesmen to try to influence the choice in favor of a pope who would present the secular governments with fewer problems. The pope had lived, however, even outliving the men who were providing for his demise.[96] Napoleon III was concerned about what would occur at the meeting of the council, but he tended to avoid taking a stand in this affair. The foreign minister whom Ollivier shortly chose, Daru, was a friend of Montalembert and a liberal, and would much like to have seen some participation by the lay rulers for the benefit of the liberal forces at the council, but there was not much he could do about it, particularly since the protestant Ollivier, who soon became the prime minister at the start of 1870, was disposed to keep hands off this Catholic matter.[97] Various foreign governments, notably Catholic Bavaria, were distressed as to what it would mean if the pope were declared to be infallible, and there was one notable example of German laymen of Coblenz trying to bring about the inclusion of governmental representatives in the council,[98] but the papacy refused to invite ambassadors of any sort to Rome. Veuillot, paraphrasing Charles Albert of Sardinia, declared that the *Santa Chiesa farà da se.*[99] So it was to be, and the pope was to guide the church with the powers of infallibility.

In mid-November 1869 Veuillot disclosed his plans for still another trip to Rome over his well-beaten path, signing himself *Fra Luigi* in a light-hearted vein to one of the ladies with whom he corresponded.[100] He now had two routes, to Marseilles by train and then the boat to Civitavecchia, or to the Simplon, not yet completed, a train route with a small interruption. He must have remembered the cinders of his most recent trip, and this time he decided to go to Marseilles and on by boat. He had no good idea how long the council might last, so he decided to take with him his children and Élise, servants and household effects. The council had many matters it might develop, and there was no clear

(Wesmael-Charlier)

Louis Veuillot with Élise

warning yet of the coming of the Franco-Prussian War. It was reasonable for him to assume that, while infallibility might have been dealt with in an even shorter time than it was, other great decisions might have kept the bishops for a long time in Rome. Obviously Veuillot attached paramount importance to the meeting of the council. He had an excellent correspondent in Henri de Maguelonne, and it might have been sound to let him keep the journal informed and to visit Rome only briefly. However, the entire church seemed to be going to Rome, along with over seven hundred bishops.[101] Veuillot simply felt he could not be absent from Rome while there were such momentous proceedings. He traveled as quickly as he could, with no rest at Marseilles, and he arrived in Rome still feeling sick.[102] He took up residence, with Élise as *padrona di casa*, at 79 Via de Due Macelli, where he had a large dining room, large study, and plenty of place to receive people. All this space he needed in view of the comings and goings of prelates and others interested in the cause of infallibility which he intended to set about assiduously to publicize.[103] A great supply of good Bordeaux wine arrived not long after the Veuillots, which was to be used not only as consolation to Veuillot and others, but as part of the resources to rally the infallibilists. During the fifth week of the council Veuillot was host to over fifty bishops,[104] and by this time he had had to lay in additional supplies and get a larger table. Throughout the council Veuillot's residence served as a meeting-place for infallibilists, and he joked on several occasions about this special function of bringing prelates together at his groaning board. One of his first letters from Rome he signed, "Le premier moutardier du Concile,"[105] and after three months he spoke of "running a hash house (*gargotier*) for the Holy Spirit."[106] From his mother in Bercy he knew all about the function of "running a hash house," but this one in Rome was far from that of Bercy. Apparently Élise more than rose to the occasion. To his brother he wrote not long after the opening of the council: "You would be amused to see how *la fille du peuple* conducts herself in presiding over bishops. She was born in Bercy, but Rome is her *air natal*. She questions, she listens, she remembers. She has an unaffected enthusiasm, unnoticed by her but visible to others, which makes a great impression. And this is an excellent asset for a brother and a journalist."[107]

During his stay in Rome Veuillot often mentioned the comings and goings of Msgr. Mercurelli, papal secretary of state for Latin letters, and of Msgr. Nardi, auditor of the rota. These men went back and forth from the office of *L'Univers* in Rome to the Vatican. The question can certainly be raised as to whether Veuillot became one of the real shapers of the course followed by the council, or whether he was merely an observer and an indirect rallier of support for the cause of infallibility.[108] There really is no definite answer that can be given. The incomplete official history of the council would not have shown that a lay journalist had a direct influence.[109] All histories of the council show the closeness of the editor of *L'Univers* with many bishops, notably leaders of the "opportunists,"[110] but none really reflect evidence that he did much more than operate a sort of journalist's salon. Important ladies in Rome on both sides of the major issue also exerted themselves in this manner, often being called *mères de l'église,* and less reverently referred to by Veuillot as *commères du concile.*[111] Veuillot's function, aside from getting the inside word on a council not attended by reporters, of course, and providing a journal that was widely read and quoted in Rome during the council, was not unlike that of these ladies who held salons. Word was passed from prelate to prelate through this friendly journalist, and from Mercurelli and Nardi Veuillot was hearing reports from close to Pius IX. The evidence is circumstantial, but at least indirectly the role of Veuillot was important and one that Maguelonne could scarcely have performed. If Veuillot was indeed a shaper of the course taken by the infallibilists, layman that he was, the subtleties of indirect influence are difficult to fathom. However, the nature of his reporting of the council is a plainer matter. He has been accused of presenting the council to his readers as essentially one-sided, and as much more harmonious and simple than it was.[112] Actually, it was not in those days the way of journalists to present the news as impartial observers, but rather as advocates of their causes. If Veuillot felt rather calm about the way things were going, it was because he felt sure that the "inopportunists" were defeated before they ever got started. Regardless of the feelings of many elements of the public, he could see that the council was overwhelmingly going to declare itself for infallibility, and he wanted to see a harmony in the council that could be reflected in his accounts. To Eugène he wrote in December: "Orleanism is strongly and even furiously bestirring itself, nevertheless the Holy Father seems to me to have tranquilly put it in a cage, and the bars are strong. The difficulty is to explain this to the public. We will try. Be assured that the proceedings of these people will never be given as the perfect model of Christian life in the Council."[113] However, the bishops themselves at the council were not the ones whom Veuillot specially singled out for criticism, preferring to go at the anti-infallibilist forces from other angles. Since he actually saw great sentiment growing for the pope, he tried to overlook the opposition faction of bishops in the hopes that he could present the council as buttressing the wishes of the pope and presenting unity to the world.

On arriving in Rome Veuillot went as directly as possible to the Vatican to arrange a meeting with the pope. Seven hundred princes of the church, many of whom had had less opportunity to see the pope than Veuillot, notably bishops from Asian and other remote parts, were also desirous to see the pontiff, but Veuillot wanted to be in direct touch with him right away in any case. Veuillot arrived in formal attire, and Antonelli was "charming, even affectionate" to him. All was arranged. Dupanloup, "ce terrible Msgr. Félix,"[114] had not reached Rome yet, and Veuillot, now ahead in the contest, toured some of the familiar squares of Rome with pleasure despite the press of affairs. The pope received Veuillot on Sunday morning, 4 December, and Veuillot was able to report to the readers of *L'Univers* that he had turned over a large subscription, 75,000 francs, to the Holy Father for the benefit of the Council. He also reported to his readers that although he had not seen the pope for over two years, the pontiff was vigorous despite the immense work which he had had to do. Veuillot contented himself with informing those who read his columns that the pope gave him his benediction, but privately he recorded that the pope had declared: "You have done very well in this whole affair, as in all others. Dear *L'Univers*, always in the breach and always victorious."[115] What greater encouragement could he receive?

While the praise and blessings of the pope were the main concern of Veuillot, he also received a broad vote of confidence from other levels of the Catholic world both before his departure from Paris and after his arrival in Rome. A layman from a small town in Lot-et-Garonne, a customs official, wrote Veuillot: "How others can accuse and condemn you! As for me, from the first time I had the pleasure of reading you, I have not ceased admiring and loving you."[116] A canon in Annecy told him the *Observations* of Dupanloup "have strongly wounded sincerely Catholic hearts in our religious country."[117] An abbé in the Somme stated that he was distressed to see the *Observations* of Dupanloup, a prelate who had done much for the church in the past.[118] A curé in St.-Illiers-le-Bois wrote that Dupanloup's thesis came fifty years too late.[119] Many such letters from the rank-and-file of French Catholicism came in. The very growth of *L'Univers* itself to approximately 14,000 subscriptions was an endorsement.[120] But in Rome Veuillot received attention that exceeded the hommage rendered to many of the most important prelates. On 6 December he wrote his brother, "I have now the aureole of clerical and even episcopal popularity. People stop me on the streets, encircle me in the salons. The prompt and private audience given [by the pope] has produced this effect.[121] Veuillot had felt very tired ever since his arrival, but yet he was apparently at the peak of his influence. Accordingly, his old opponents in France were distressed. Falloux sounded somewhat less extreme than Montalembert, but he spoke of "the sad leaders of the majority, the lack of intelligence, lightness of character or covetousness of [cardinals'] hats, pontifical favors, and the smiles of M. Veuillot. . . ."[122]

Veuillot's tone about Dupanloup at the time of the opening of the council varied greatly. For public consumption he said that on leaving his audience with the pope, he went to pray in Saint Peter's where he recognized Dupanloup near him, on his knees, reciting his confession. "Visibly the prelate prayed in good heart, and I too. . . ."[123] On the other hand for his intimates, by mid-December, at a time when he was complaining of the rain and bad weather, remembering his sad days in Rome in 1853 when he felt like crying, he wrote: "I attributed this misfortune to the influence of Msgr. d'Orleans, who persecuted me then. But today there are compensations! Outside of my flourishing household, which gives me such good company, I am another person, and Félix, thanks be to God, in another situation. . . .He is not the same man. He is little heard and less surrounded. He has seen neither the pope nor the leading Frenchmen. For the first time the man of triumph is embarrassed of his own person. I doubt that he will find enough people to sit before the plates he has so pompously prepared, – and I, I am buying table settings!" In a word, "Félix is finished."[124] During the stay of the Veuillots in Rome, Louis wrote 145 public letters and 37 private ones, while Élise wrote 180 back to Eugène and *L'Univers*,[125] and her testimony sounds much like that of her brother with regard to Dupanloup.[126] Quite apart from the great matters before the council, Veuillot enjoyed a triumph over his enemy from the start.

The council itself formally opened on 8 December 1869. Committees were chosen, and a variety of matters for consideration of the church could have come to the fore. The big undercurrent, however, was whether there would be a pronouncement of the doctrine of papal infallibility, and how it would be introduced. The pope himself might have made the proceedings simple if he had simply asked that the council declare the doctrine. As with the proclamation of the Immaculate Conception in 1854, however, the pope wanted the council to be guided by the Holy Spirit, and he waited for the proposition to come from the council itself as a result of inspiration.[127] The group that was especially to deal with matters of faith was constituted by Msgr. Manning, Archbishop of Westminster.[128] Veuillot was thoroughly satisfied with Manning's ultramontanism, but he did not altogether trust him, thinking him somewhat underhanded.[129] Manning stacked this commission in such a way that there was only one person on it who was not a known infallibilist, and that person was only accidentally included. Because in fact, there was surprising harmony at the opening of the council, and the Jesuits, for example, and other factions contributed to a spirit of moderation, most of the displeasure of the council fathers was felt over the choice of this *De Fide* group.[130]

Had Veuillot been a reporter in the usual sense of the word, there was much that he could have said about the choice of the *De Fide* group alone. As time went on, various writers of the liberal Catholic, royalist, and secular journals had plenty to say about the "opposition." From the start, however, Veuillot did his best to let the pope's *Unum sint* be his keynote. He stressed the theme, "The pope and the people," from the opening of the council.[131] He sounded almost like 1848, though his motive was to stress the exclusion of the governments through which the liberal Catholics, notably in France, would wish to bring opposition to the monarchical principal for the church. From the beginning Veuillot made incidental reference to the day when the pope would announce the dogma of papal infallibility,[132] but he did it in such a way as to suggest there was little question but what the council would shape the pronouncement spontaneously and unanimously. The Holy Spirit had brought the council together by an infallible order, and the council was busying itself in following the dictates of the Holy Spirit, Veuillot explained to the readers of *L'Univers.*[133] Early in his reports Veuillot did indeed say that "a bishop" had accused "certain people" of misusing the expression, *Ubi Petrus, ibi Ecclesia*, but he minimized that sort of reference, and he avoided naming the bishop – Dupanloup.[134] The arrival of the Bishop of Orleans, when it took place, was announced as something the readers of *L'Univers* would want to know, and at the same time they were also told that the Bishop of Sura (who was simply called Maret when Veuillot launched attacks at other times) was looking well despite his seventy-two years.[135] He could not deny that all views were not quite the same. The council was not however a parliament, and "I will always deny there exist in the council elements of anything violent or opinionated such as the word 'opposition' denotes."[136] The bishops were searching for the true teachings of the church, and they would find it as a body. Such was the spirit of the articles Veuillot produced for *L'Univers* in the early phases of the council.

Veuillot was, despite the lofty platitudes he was penning for the readers of *L'Univers*, an able reporter. He distinguished sharply between information he was sending Eugène for their own consumption and the pieces he was sending for their columns. He chafed at the fact that elections were announced only three days after the fact. Reporters could not go to the place of the council meetings, and one of his more interesting pieces about the early days of the council was a description of attempts on the part of the press to slip into the meetings in disguise.[137] Veuillot actually learned key information with the appraisal of certain bishops by simply waiting for them to disclose things to him as soon as they might be known. To Eugène he wrote: "If I learn anything for sure before the time, you will know by telegraph," speaking of an election. "I prod Maguelonne to instruct you better, but he is ill, and I do not have the time always to be on his back," Veuillot told his brother. In the one surviving written communication between Veuillot and Maguelonne in this period, Veuillot interestingly, and perhaps significantly, asks for a concordance and a Bible.[138]

One of the ways Veuillot played down the struggle at the Vatican Council between the infallibilists and their opposition was simply to provide articles that often had nothing to do with the work of the council itself. He was in Rome, and he had an audience who had acclaimed his *Le Parfum de Rome.* A number of interesting and picturesque pieces written at this time describe such matters as Christmas in Rome, and various churches and sights, livened by the intrusion of M. Coquelet, his fictitious figure whose views could be used to emphasize whatever Veuillot wished to bring out. The Villa Borghese, the Pincio, and the departure for home of Canadian zouaves who had served for two years, were topics that Veuillot brought colorfully and emotionally to the attention of his readers. Some of the articles were on generalities such as could have been treated just as well in Paris, and some of them focused on individuals who represented the Gallican, "inopportunist," or liberal camps – persons other than the bishops involved in the work of the council. But the issues of the council could not be avoided altogether, and Veuillot had to deal with them as best he could, while trying to preserve the picture of a growing spirit of unity among the bishops that was going to produce the statement of papal infallibility.[139]

At the council the infallibilists and the "inopportunists" were very unequal from the beginning. The ratio was about three to one, with another considerable group being somewhat difficult to fathom, including the Oriental bishops and others who had special reasons for wishing to seem aloof. Guibert, Bishop of Tours, Lavigerie of Algiers, and particularly Forçade of Nevers were significant among the pivotal group of French bishops. Cardinal Donnet of Bordeaux, Pie of Poitiers, and Plantier of Nîmes were especially conspicuous among the infallibilists, while Dupanloup was strongly supported by Cardinal

Mathieu of Besançon, Darboy of Paris, and Ginouhliac of Grenoble. Veuillot hoped that divisions would not be generally as noticeable as they turned out to be and that somehow the council could reach the desired ends with as little stir as possible. Not long after the opening, however, connections between the "opportunists" and the several governments of Europe, but primarily France, brought these divisions much more into the open.

There were several situations that developed during the council that demanded the attention of an observer. Despite the importance of the implications of infallibility for all governments of Europe, France was the country most concerned, not only because of the question of the Catholic church within France, but because France was in the position of guaranteeing Rome from Italy, whose monarch was under excommunication. Indeed, Ollivier understood from Antonelli that this situation was the key consideration in not inviting the monarchs to be represented at the council.[140] From the start, as Ollivier could see, the pope took the initiative in all the proceedings and arrangements of the functioning of the deputations in a way not done at the Council of Trent.[141] By papal instructions the deputations were to bring out *schemata* for public sessions only after secret sessions had adopted them. By 28 December 1869 an issue had developed over certain matters brought before the deputation *De Fide*, and the first test between the two poles had developed. The collection of signatures on *postulata* for the deputation at the turn of the year was the first positive indication of strength.

By the start of 1870 Ollivier was prime minister. A protestant who was more objective toward the ultramontanes and Louis Veuillot than his foreign minister, Daru, a friend of Montalembert's, he countered Daru's desire for intervention, which Darboy tried to bring about. Lavigerie impressed on the French cabinet how strong the infallibilists were. As it began to appear in February that the soon to be declared independence of the Catholic church was going to affect church-state relations, more pressure from the liberals was brought to bear on the French régime for intervention in some form. Banneville, ambassador to the Holy See, said that many French bishops were giving in to a kind of "presbyterianism" encouraged by *L'Univers* and other such journals,[142] and Daru was disposed to do what he could, but the Vatican was well aware of divisions in the French cabinet and of Ollivier's disposition to follow the same aloofness as most of the other European régimes. Daru had proceeded in such a way as to appear to be somewhat independent of Ollivier. When in April he sent a memorandum to the pope asking that a "protector of the crown" be accepted as a representative to the council, only to have the request refused, he resigned. This expedient had been suggested by Msgr. Forçade. Next Darboy and Pie took extreme stands on the matter of infallibility in May. In mid-June the question of infallibility was brought before a session of the whole council, less a large group of "inopportunists," who had decided to boycott the session rather than to vote against it.[143] Such was the general scene that unrolled before Veuillot, who learned at the "Hôtel Veuillot" (as his apartments were called) a large part of what he wrote about so brilliantly, yet in so slanted a fashion.

As the division of the bishops came more into the open at the start of 1870, Veuillot publicly complained of the attempt of *Le Français* to claim that influence of *L'Univers* was resented.[144] While he continued to present such subjects as "Epiphany in Rome," he was forced also to treat the politics of the council as the liberal Catholics tried to bring French governmental intervention. Ridiculing the idea that "opportunity" had anything to do with the acts of God, he saw hope in the attitude of Ollivier, who seemed to be breaking with the traditions of the régime.[145] In supporting the case for nonintervention Veuillot brought out some refreshing argument. Things were different now, he said. "No longer is there a monarchy, an aristocracy, nor a democracy, neither in a state, in a corporate way, nor even in seed. There are no longer kings, great secondary situations, nor people. There are only multitudes and administrations, at the head of which is an emphemeral employee whom one still calls a king, but of whom the true name is Caesar, force." Further supporting his case and speaking in general terms very much aimed at the political order of France he maintained: "Liberalism is the enemy of liberty; liberal Catholicism is the enemy of authority in the church, that which leads it to love or at least to serve the authority of Caesar. Whoever is hostile to the authority of the church is Caesarian. . . ."[146]

Despite his desire to keep to generalities about the opposition, with the possibility that Daru and his school might bring pressure on the council, Veuillot became more open about the "opposition" and the infallibilists. Nevertheless he showed care in more ways than one. To his brother he gave the instruction: "Cite the Orleans group, but always support well what you cite. There are those who read these citations to others and say to them: 'See what this *L'Univers* dares to say!' "[147] But, at least for a time, Veuillot's own articles largely avoided mentioning Dupanloup or other French bishops by name. As the "opposition" became more difficult to avoid treating as such, he gave much attention to the situation, but put his specific attention on the doings of the Bavarian Bishop Doellinger, who by late January had brought all of his anti-infallibilist efforts clearly into the open, to the Croatian Bishop Strossmayer, to Cardinal Rauscher of Vienna, and to non-Frenchmen as much as possible. In due course the French ambassador to the Holy See accused Veuillot of having conducted a "revolutionary campaign against half the bishops of France,"[148] but the tone of Veuillot's articles certainly did not indicate opposition to bishops as such, especially not French bishops. The Bishop of Sura, *in partibus infidelium*, came in for some harsh mention in early 1870, but as Msgr. Maret. But for an object on which to focus his attention, Veuillot found Father Gratry to be a most convenient person.[149]

Gratry, who had been almoner at the École Polytechnique and director of the Collège Stanislas, was a man of such intellectual and literary ability that he had been elected to the Academy. He was the most notable spokesman for the "inopportunists" outside of the council. When he published a series of partisan brochures early in 1870, he created a great stir. In his attack on the cause of infallibility he used excessively strong terms, and he got into such specific matters as the Roman breviary, about which he also used immoderate language. Nevertheless, while the infallibilists blamed Darboy and Dupanloup for his words, at least one of the "inopportunists" stood behind Gratry with a letter of support.[150] Many of Veuillot's articles made Gratry the cynosure of attention, and the fact that his arguments came out in several letters or brochures, made him an appropriate object of long-range attack.

The most spectacular support that Father Gratry received was from the ailing Montalembert. The old leader had become incensed at being accused of being a Gallican and wrote a letter that was published 8 March 1870 in the *Gazette de France* and subsequently was carried in many journals. He reproached the ultramontanes, and *L'Univers* especially, for creating "an idol in the Vatican."[151] The letter went remarkably far in what may be regarded as open criticism of Pius IX and the association of *L'Univers* and, *Civiltà Cattolica* with him. It was the last gasp of Montalembert, who died 13 March. Eugène wrote a very measured reply to the letter on 9 March, about which Louis expressed his great satisfaction: "You have responded perfectly to Montalembert. The applause is unanimous and ardent. As for me, I find you even better as a journalist than an entrepreneur."[152] Eugène had to write the article about Montalembert's death, which appeared the next day, and again he did the job in the way Louis would have wanted. The journal was edged in black, and no one could have wanted a more graceful recognition of the passing of a rival.[153] The feature article, which had been written by Louis, was an attack on Gratry, who had made common cause with Montalembert, but at least so far as externals were concerned, *L'Univers* had been extremely proper and charitable.

Veuillot had feelings which amounted to a complex about Montalembert. There is no question that he very much liked him and had accepted him as the leader of French Catholics. Veuillot had no objections to following a leader, if the leader were only right. But in the 1840's Montalembert showed tendencies which Veuillot could not accept. Their reconciliation in 1848 was a great thing to him, and he was haunted in later days by the idea of another reconciliation after their rupture in 1852. This was not to come. Dupanloup, Falloux, and many others he regarded as adversaries, even enemies, but Montalembert was someone with whom he wanted a reconciliation. In his last letter Montalembert had spoken of the "poor clergy" in France. Veuillot now spoke of "poor Montalembert, poor humanity!" To none other than the brother of his wife, whom he really loved, he made a very strange disclosure. He said he had been struck by lightning without even seeing the flash when he heard by telegraph of the man's death. "I can no longer believe in dreams. On the faith of a persistent dream, the only one of this kind I have ever had, I had obstinately hoped for another end. Have I told you this, I who have never been able to dream of anyone I have ever known or loved, not even Mathilde or our dead little girls; I have a score of times dreamed of Montalembert, and always fundamentally the same dream in sequence, regular, reasonable, and very clear on awakening. I would see him, we would talk about the situation and characters, each explaining himself a bit, and we would embrace openly and tenderly. J'avais fini par compter tout de bon là-dessus." It is interesting to hear Veuillot say he no longer believed in something. Veuillot was particularly tantalized by the question of whether Montalembert had begged forgiveness of God before he died. "He bears this terrible secret."[154] Veuillot's attitude toward Montalembert was forgiving, and whatever wrongs he in fact did his former leader, his own soul was perhaps less troubled by this relationship than might have been expected. Veuillot, seems to have assumed that Montalembert was the one who was completely wrong, and that asking God for pardon was the thing that Montalembert particularly had to do. In any event, an important phase of Veuillot's life came to an end with the death of Montalembert, his lasting estrangement from whom may be regarded as one of his main disillusionments.

Veuillot closed out his differences with Montalembert on an appropriate note, and he managed to keep his debate with Dupanloup on relatively high ground. Various letters Dupanloup had written since his *Observations* and warning to Veuillot practically obliged Veuillot to answer. One of his best articles saw Veuillot having differences of a literary sort with Dupanloup, avoiding theology. "I leave the Council Father. I deal only with the Academician."[155] He managed to connect another Academician, Gratry, with Dupanloup, and with reference to Dupanloup's residence in Rome, the Villa Grazioli, he called Gratry a "pronounced *graziolino*," and managed by this means to send some of his arrows tactfully in a non-episcopal direction.[156] Just as in the case of his exchange with Montalembert, the editors of *L'Univers* totally satisfied Veuillot in his dueling with Dupanloup. In a piece dated 24 March that was published in *L'Univers*, he went out of his way to speak of his brother, Leon Aubineau, Joseph Chantrel, and two younger men, newly associated with him, Arthur Loth and Auguste Roussel. However, the first mentioned was "my dear and venerated Du Lac, my master," whose "forty years of good work for the church" was something to be held up in an article aimed at Dupanloup.[157]

While Veuillot might call Gratry a "fallibilist" in the columns of *L'Univers,*[158] he never called Dupanloup anything like this. Certain prominent ladies in Rome who worked for the "inopportunists" had been referred to as *Matriarches* of the council, and Louis wrote his brother to see to it that *L'Univers* avoided such references in the future. "Do you know what this does to us," he asked? "You will see that they fall on your sister and nieces who are at least *puellarches*."[159] The boys who had grown up in Bercy had to be careful in what they said not only about bishops, but those who were close to bishops of the opposition. However, Gratry, and especially those in the French régime unsympathetic to infallibility, were not to be treated quite so carefully. At one point Veuillot, in speaking of Father Gratry in *L'Univers*, explained mockingly that he called him "Father" because he had *quelques enfants intellectuels.*[160] He had said that he did not like to hear a bishop (Dupanloup) mock another (Msgr. Dechamps), especially when the latter was in the right,[161] but at least he never made light of Dupanloup or any other bishop in the way he handled this priest. Members of the government, however, had no protection from him by their office. Veuillot on 2 April 1870 called Napoleon III himself a "blind agent of the revolution."[162]

Darboy, influential in Paris though not in Rome, had tried to persuade Napoleon to intervene. Napoleon had hesitated because of inertia and the example of the rest of Europe, and Ollivier had seen even less reason to intervene. Daru had sent off notes to Rome on 20 February and 6 April to try to gain concessions for the French government with regard to the council, but as we have seen despite the intervention of the non-aligned Msgr. Forçade, nothing had been obtained. When Ollivier took over Daru's function of foreign minister for the time being, even he seemed prone to consider some of Daru's plans to influence the council, for which Veuillot labeled him a *daruiste.*[163] However, the chances of the French government to get its foot in the door at Rome had passed, if they had ever existed at all, and Veuillot was well aware of the relative security the council now had to carry out the will of the large majority of bishops. Somewhat ironically he even used an expression he had once detested to his own purposes now. He said in a published article that he did not have any "big objections" to the phrase "a free church in a free state" if that described the situation of the church's ability to define its own dogma for all time.[164] Veuillot could never tolerate a government divorced from the church, but the untrammeled situation of the council as it headed toward defining the infallible nature of the pope's official declarations seemed a satisfactory expedient.

One delicate matter that Veuillot rather than someone else at *L'Univers* treated during the council was the attitude of Father Newman. In spite of terrible things he was accustomed to say about England over the years, Veuillot had derived joy from the movement most identified with Newman. *L'Univers* made a practice as we have noted of announcing notable conversions. The quiet and altogether sincere course that Newman followed may have been compared privately by Veuillot with the success story of Cardinal Manning's rise, however satisfactory Manning's position on infallibility was to Veuillot. In early February Newman's friend Moriarty wrote him that he was a voice crying in the wilderness in Rome with regard to the great question,[165] and Newman must have thought about the matter for some time when he wrote Manning that he was distressed about infallibility and did not think he was going to be able to accept the decision of the council. In stating his feelings he used language akin to Montalembert's. Veuillot gave full credit to the great figure of English Catholicism, but he thought he should have been more careful about his words.[166]

Veuillot ever looked for authority, and as the pope would not speak officially, only privately, about his belief with regard to papal infallibility, the appearance of a book by Dom Guéranger in early 1870 that refuted the writing of Maret, delighted him. Its very title, *La Monarchie pontificale*, suggested the nature of the work, and Veuillot used it in attacking Gratry.[167] That was the kind of thing he associated with the term "church dogma." As the debates proceeded toward a conclusion it therefore irked him to hear infallibility called "his dogma." Yes, he believed in infallibility, but it was the true teaching of the church, as the fathers at the council would declare, and it was not *mon dogma*. However, Veuillot's logic was equally shaky about Gallicanism in saying that that purely French ecclesiastical concept would die "in the civil arms of Daru and Beust (Austro-Hungarian chancellor)."[168] However, this was not a time when Veuillot was notably exact in what he had to say about various matters, including the plebiscite that was held on 8 May in France.

The choice of Ollivier at the start of the year had signalled a new era for France. Yet the constitution of the new liberal empire had not been prepared and submitted to the people for approval until this date. Napoleon was hoping to ride with the new liberal wave, and Ollivier had calculated that he could gain Catholic support by following a policy of hands-off for the Vatican Council. Veuillot, however, was not to be taken in either by action or by inaction on the part of Ollivier. In effect Veuillot advised Catholics to abstain from voting. To his readers he posed the question of what to do, and he made it clear that the association of the dynasty with the Daru memorandum was the decisive thing: "For me, not being able to vote *no*, since I do not wish to precipitate disasters which will come quickly enough, I am not able to resign myself to say *yes*, because I do not wish to give myself in perpetuity to princes who refuse to take any engagement toward the church, even that of respecting its liberty."[169] Banneville, French ambassador in Rome, not surprisingly, did not like this role of Veuillot, and writing to the new foreign minister, Gramont, after the plebiscite, complained of "the inexactitudes *audaciously* edited by M. Veuillot in the journal *L'Univers*" with regard to the attitude of the bishops during the period before the plebiscite.[170] No doubt his policy with regard to this political question was his own, and he was somewhat freer about saying what Catholics should do in such a political affair than he was in discussing some aspects of theology.

Probably the furthest Veuillot went in discussing a precise heresy was in the matter of Febronianism. Febronius was an eighteenth-century prelate whom Veuillot described as an example of Josephism. He declared that Febronius had fallen into "Wyclifian democracy" as a result of the "natural weight of error."[171] Febronius indeed had been labeled a heretic, so he was on safe ground in attacking him this way, but what made his attack significant was that the pope had warned Darboy in 1865 that he was on the verge of Febronianism,[172] and Darboy had not responded in such a way as to give satisfaction. Early in 1870 Darboy had written the emperor that "the liberty of the bishops is not complete,"[173] and thereby had proven that both the pope and Veuillot had good grounds for their assessment of him. Despite the fact that Darboy deliberately tried to steer an unaligned course at the council, he was in fact extremely independent of the pope in his attitudes, as Veuillot could easily discern. Dwelling on the very heresy of which the pope had warned his archbishop, however, was a bold thing for Veuillot to have done.

At the very time the plebiscite in France was taking place the pope gave "twenty good minutes" to Veuillot, his sister, and his daughters.[174] Louis Veuillot was able to hand over to the pope at this time one-hundred thousand francs in addition to what he had already presented as a result of the campaign of *L'Univers* in December. With this large sum of money Veuillot presented the names of the subscribers to the gift. He had been urged to be less direct in this kind of support and to soft-pedal the near-daily announcement of the contributors in the columns of the journal. However, after an initial indication to his brother about restraint in this matter, he had given the signal for full-steam-ahead in late 1869, implying that he was doing what the pope wanted.[175] He would appear to have been correct.

Veuillot and the pope discussed politics and the plebiscite which was taking place in France. Placet or abstention they agreed were the alternatives.[176] When the bishops were to vote in the council they could indicate *Placet, Non placet*, or *Placet juxta modum*. Supporting the emperor under conditions, notably a change in religious policy, was indeed what would have pleased the Holy Father, and therefore Louis Veuillot. Of course the main thing they discussed was the matter of the proclamation of infallibility. The pope indicated that although people desired him to proclaim it himself, he would not do it. It must be the work of the Holy Spirit. He told Veuillot of his personal belief in papal infallibility, but that the council must proclaim it. Nevertheless he strongly indicated by his manner his confidence.[177] Veuillot was cautious in his reporting to the readers of *L'Univers*. He made an allusion to "eternal things," but he did not report what he recorded himself of their talk on this matter.[178] He did, however, pass on to his readers his impressions of the pope's appearance. The pope told him that in a few days he would be entering his seventy-ninth year, and exclaimed, "What is an old man of nearly eighty able to do!" Veuillot reassured his readers that the pope's condition was like the Roman sun in the "vigor of a new spring." The pope complained to him of a "bad book" which had newly appeared, attacking his authority. Veuillot was not long in turning his attention to this book.

The "mauvais livre" to which the pope referred was a pamphlet coming from Paris, entitled *Ce qui se passe au Concile*, which Veuillot believed to have been written by several authors.[179] He believed it was a product of Maret's school, and without naming those who might have written it, he condemned the anonymity. He contrasted the honesty of Father Gratry, whom he now said he respected, with the underhanded ways of these authors.[180] He denied the truth of the criticism in the "bad book," and he professed to see in it the publication of the program of the "opposition." But despite the vigor with which Veuillot pursued the sneaky pamphlet that had irritated the pope, he reserved some of his sharpest barbs for yet another piece of this same sort that appeared also at this time. His old target the Abbé Gaduel, grand vicar of Orleans, wrote a pretentious piece with the Latin title, *Disquisitio moralis*, which presumably was a warning to the bishops about what might happen to their souls if they voted for infallibility. Again the tract was anonymously published, but it was not hard to detect that Dupanloup's man was the author, and Veuillot's attack was appropriately unrelenting. If something can be laughed at, it can be demolished easily, and in a Voltairean way he gave his first article on the subject the heading, *Une petite pièce pour rire*. He declared "the bishops are amused with this plate of theological macaroni, not however without finding themselves a bit insulted."[181] He quoted the tract extensively for his readers, and he picked the Latin apart, as he enjoyed doing assaults on academic enemies. Veuillot knew some Latin, but no doubt he had clerical assistance in this respect. Possibly his best phrase was that in which Gaduel, whom he said everyone had guessed was the author since he had been Dupanloup's mouthpiece in the affair of 1853, was called a *disquisiteur* who composed his piece from "the Latin of the Gauls" and "the French of the ostrogoths."[182] Veuillot's side was winning, and he was enjoying making as much as he could over the impending victory.

One of the marks Veuillot received of the pope's special approval was a letter to him (he was addressed *Dilecto filio Aloisio Veuillot* – not *Ludovico*) dated 19 May 1870. By it the pontifical blessing was given in the strongest tones.[183] It had become the practice of the pope to write many letters along these general lines to people who had contributed to the cause, and Veuillot took advantage of this practice in asking the pope during his 8 May audience to write to three priests of the diocese of Orleans who had specially supported the cause of *L'Univers* in the face of the opposition of Dupanloup.[184] Veuillot incurred the displeasure of some of the clergy of the diocese by his attempts to make them appear to be persecuted by their bishop. One priest wrote him that the clergy did not have to be afraid of supporting infallibility since Dupanloup had relaxed his earlier order to them to be silent. This man took exception to the strength of Veuillot's language in his articles and generally defended his bishop.[185]

The episode of the papal letter to Veuillot, and his letters to clergymen in the diocese of Orleans, had other repercussions. The French ambassador in Rome was distressed over the encouragement this act had given to the "most violent champion of the most exaggerated ideas."[186] But not only Veuillot himself irritated French diplomats with the public expressions of papal favor which he received, his journal, too, actually overstepped the bounds of diplomatic propriety, perhaps as a result of the way papal officials favored him. Supporters of the doctrine of papal infallibility had been invited officially by the Vatican to write of their support. The letter from the Vatican was directed to Msgr. Chigi, the nuncio in Paris. *L'Univers* published this letter on 20 June 1870 as though it had reached the nuncio and come into the hands of the journal from that source. In fact, it had not, and Gramont promptly protested to Rome. The papal government, of course, gave satisfaction, and the episode had no other repercussions. However, the semi-official position Veuillot held among the ultramontanes is well illustrated by the incident.

Louis Veuillot, his children, and his sisters spent nearly eight months in Rome. The expense must have been very considerable. Élise wrote and copied letters for him, but he wrote hundreds of pages of articles for *L'Univers*. He visited, or was visited by, hundreds of different people. He had to use tact because of the delicacy of the situation, and surely the strain told on his nerves. Even to a person who had so long been in Rome the city had its allures, but at last in March he told Madame Testas he was bored.[187] His long-standing complaints of the Roman climate, especially the cold rain, punctuated his correspondence. This very correspondence greatly diminished during his busy days. He noticed things in Rome he felt had been brought in by revolutionary elements. The grafitti on the walls irked him, and even became a subject for one of his articles.[188] He kept on grinding out articles on the celebrations of the church, on heretical brochures, on missionaries in Korea, on the work of the council, minimizing the differences, while attacking outside elements that opposed infallibility. During May and June other matters were largely put aside unfinished by the council fathers, who turned to direct, and secret, discussions on the great question at hand. As debates continued and the weather became warm Veuillot could see that he was in for a longer siege yet, and he wrote his brother that he had heard June would have forty days.[189] About international affairs Veuillot seemed much less perceptive than usual at this point, but he darkly suggested to his brother the idea that Dupanloup might be hoping the forces of Garibaldi would interrupt the council.[190] They did not end the council, but they did pave the way shortly afterward for the Italian government to end a millenium of papal rule of Rome.

Letters poured into *L'Univers*, and to Louis Veuillot, in the early summer in support of infallibility. The journal was still publishing editorials advocating its proclamation, but the publishing of letters from priests and others in its columns seems to have been at least as impressive as the editorials by this stage of events. When the priests of Metz sent in 500 francs for the expenses of maintaining a papal zouave for a period of time,[191] what further editorializing was needed? Veuillot liked to pick apart the writings and speeches of others, but in July he was able to comment even on the silence of people like Strossmayer. He concluded that Dupanloup and others had given up the fight.[192] In an article written 30 June and published a week later he attacked a Prussian writing in the *Gazette de Bonn* for predicting terrible consequences of the proclamation of infallibility,[193] but he did not seem to be aware of the immediate Franco-Prussian troubles that were approaching. "All is going well," he wrote on the sixth. "The month of July will give the world an immortal fruit which has only been able to mature in eighteen and a half centuries. *Tu es Petrus*."[194]

By 13 July there was a preliminary vote on infallibility. Veuillot received inside word on the outcome and telegraphed the results back to his brother. Of 601 prelates voting, only 88 had indicated *Non placet*; 62 were *Placet juxta modum*, and some of these preferred not to make any of the carefully worked out concessions (which were essentially disregarded by Veuillot) that limited the proclamation of infallibility to matters of faith and morals declared *ex cathedra* by the pope; and 488 cast ballots of *Placet*. Veuillot had a scoop, but he wanted none of these figures to come out, although he well knew it was a great victory and that the "inopportunists" had lost out badly. He wanted to be able to announce unanimity and to maintain the secrecy of all but the final figures when the cannons of the Castel Sant'Angelo announced the results. Eugène was ordered to hold two numbers of *L'Univers* in readiness for the big moment. Veuillot reported happily the weakening of bishops like Msgr. Landriot (Reims), who voted *Juxta modum*, and various others who came all the way to *Placet.*[195] The rage of the "inopportunists" came to nought, particularly when the pope rejected the request of Msgr. Rivet that the council be permitted to retire without voting at this point.[196] The inopportunists held a caucus and decided that it was better to retire to their dioceses without voting than to vote *Non placet*. Dupanloup was largely responsible for this decision, though not all like-thinking bishops were altogether satisfied.[197] The Bishops of Cajazzo (Two Sicilies) and Little Rock did not get the word, and when the great vote was taken on 18 July there were two *Non placets* to mar what would otherwise have been unanimity among the over 500 bishops who remained. Veuillot would have loved to be able to say *unanimity* in the brief report that he fired off to Paris on hearing the final vote, and he pointed out in the first sentence that they had "submitted" directly after the vote. "Te Deum laudamus! It is done. Except for two dissenting voices, now submitted, the dogma has gained unanimity. By their abstention the opponents have made this unanimity," Veuillot admitted. "They have already done many things by their opposition. *Quod inopportunum dixerunt, necessarium fecerunt.*"[198]

Veuillot announced the triumph on 20 July in a number decorated with a triumphal arch. This number did not resemble the usual format. He had been the spokesman for a victorious group. Nevertheless his article was very short. True, it had been sent by telegraph, but also the edge had been taken off the unanimity by the abstention of about a hundred bishops. Moreover, he now knew that war would be declared shortly against Prussia. However, the triumph which he briefly described he likened unto the Exodus. The world had been *de-pharoah-ized* in his word. "To speak the truth, the route we will follow from here will be a long one. But we have Moses, something better than Moses."

For reasons of his own, Veuillot did not take the boat from Civitavecchia to Marseille, or even the same rail route back that he had considered following in late 1869. Instead, he followed a more circuitous itinerary by rail, which took him to Florence, Venice, Milan, Lyon, and then back to Paris. His departure was emotional. The very weather at the time of the vote had been ominous, with a terrible thunderstorm taking place, about which one had to be optimistic in order to regard it as a sign of change perhaps for the better.[199] He paid a last visit to Saint Peter's Cathedral, but he had no visit to the pope. "Twenty times I kissed these marbles more precious than gold." His thoughts turned to Lamennais when he reached Florence, that genius who had been insubordinate.[200] It was probably a good thing for Veuillot to see the diverting gondolas and the canals of Venice, especially since he had to see the monuments to Manin, Cavour, and the achievement of Italian unity.[201] In due course, an exhausted man, he reached Paris, now gripped in war.

Veuillot has a monument in the collection of articles he wrote while in Rome which was issued just two years later under the title *Rome pendant le concile*. Although the collection was somewhat edited, it reflects the purposeful and favored journalist in a way that is almost unique. Here was a man who had made common cause with the victorious side in a struggle he was both participating in and reporting. Here was a fighter trying to shift the scene of the battle so that his victor could seem to have had a still greater victory.

While on his way home a group of priests in Meaux wrote him:

> The day so impatiently awaited has finally arrived. The Holy Spirit has spoken by the Vatican Council, and the Mother Church counts a new victory. We understand the happiness you enjoy, and we wish to share it with you from the bottom of our hearts. . . .
>
> Not only have you fought the good fight, with the rare talent God has given you, but in opening the columns of your estimable journal to the free expression of our faith, the public manifestation of our desires, you have furnished the means to the clergy of our land to produce one of those glorious acts which will shine forever in history and which has brought consolation to the heart of the Supreme Pontiff.[202]

The declaration of papal infallibility was one of the most striking pronouncements in church history. As the pope was on the threshold of losing all temporal power, he gained formally the power previously only implied, that when he spoke officially on matters of faith and morals he could not be wrong. Veuillot had contributed to the movement. He shared in the victory. Then, just when he gained the opportunity of savoring the victory, he had to see his own country go down to miserable defeat.

CHAPTER IX

DISASTERS AND THE CHANCE FOR CATHOLIC MONARCHY

Napoleon III, while trying to stay on the crest of the popular wave in France, not only was beginning to lose his grip at home but badly losing the struggle to remain dominant in Europe. The victory of the Prussians over Austria in 1866 made his situation very serious, and his poorly planned attempt to organize a triple alliance with Austria and Italy came to nought because he was under such pressure from clerical elements in France, notably the empress, that he could not yet abandon Rome completely. This factor caused Italy, and indirectly Austria, not to join France in a scheme against Bismarckian Germany.[1] Veuillot had paid little attention to foreign policy in the period before the Franco-Prussian War, largely because of his preoccupation with the proclamation of papal infallibility. Prussia, of course, he had consistently branded an enemy in those days, because of the protestantism and rationalism it symbolized rather than because of the worsening diplomatic situation. Suddenly, just as the constitution *Pater Æternus* (proclaiming infallibility), was about to be voted, the Spanish throne question came to a head, and French diplomacy bungled into Bismarck's hands. Napoleon III found himself in such a position that there was nothing else to do but to declare war on Prussia on 19 July 1870.[2] Defeat, revolution, and the most trying part of Veuillot's career lay ahead as he took his return trip from Rome to Paris. However, as the terrible days came, a clean sweep of much that Veuillot disliked took place, and the hope that something much better might fill the vacuum created by the fall of the empire gave an immediacy to his polemics that had been lacking as long as Napoleon remained on the throne.

When Veuillot left Rome he believed the battle ahead for the establishment of the new dogma would be heavy, and he was prepared to engage in polemic with journals of different colorations that would surely attack the dogma. Not surprisingly his first article on returning to Paris dealt with lack of satisfaction with the role the clergy of Paris were playing in this regard.[3] Had there been no war with Prussia, his preoccupation would have been to quarrel with the secular press, and with what was left of liberal or Gallican journalism. France did not experience an "Old Catholic" secession like that which took place in

Germany, but he would have had plenty of opportunity, no doubt, to carry on the good fight for the cause of Rome. However, he could see that suddenly the whole picture had changed, and another sort of war had to be fought. Prophetically he wrote from Rome as early as 17 July 1870 words that were published five days later:

> It is tomorrow! Great joy is mixed with great sorrow. This day will not be as sweet as it should have been. War and opposition are cruel *nuages*! When the church will proclaim the very principle of order and peace, at that very moment war will perhaps bring the shedding of blood, and a more unforeseen rebellion will sadden and scandalize souls. A sad contrast which will show what inspires faith and what pride imposes, what God demands and what man inspires.[4]

Eugène set the tone for *L'Univers* that prevailed throughout the struggle, that it was war between protestant Prussia and Catholic France, and the journal was pledging support for the emperor in this kind of war.[5] Louis soon penetrated somewhat deeper into the currents of foreign affairs, even before any decisive battles were fought. He knew that there was a chance of a triple alliance, a secret that the French foreign minister had only come to know when affairs got out of hand, but he realized that Rome was the key. He knew that Beust, the protestant foreign minister (and the only person ever designated chancellor of the Dual Monarchy) of Austria-Hungary, wanted to come to the aid of France, but would do so only at the expense of France abandoning Rome. This Beust wanted, because Austria-Hungary could not join France without having Italy in on the coalition for fear of another attack such as had occurred in 1866. However, the prospect of allies on such a basis had no appeal for Veuillot. Quite the contrary, since for him the war would have no meaning if it could only be won in such a fashion.[6] His fears, however, were beside the point because even though Ollivier would have been glad enough to withdraw the French troops from Rome, had the clericals allowed him to do so, the chances of so doing in exchange for the support of Italy and Austria-Hungary promptly vanished. Engagements fought the first week of August clearly showed those governments that France had little chance of winning the war, and their policies became those of neutrals.

The initial military defeats brought the collapse of the cabinet of Ollivier, and its replacement by one under General Montauban, the Comte de Palakao. Veuillot, however, could see rising on the horizon the three men named Jules – Favre, Simon, and Ferry. Ferry even then seemed to him the worst of them, and in an article written within a week of the defeat at Wissembourg Veuillot suggested the meaninglessness of asking soldiers to die for Jules Ferry![7] Still his articles were not defeatist. He expected that although the tests would become ever worse, courage also would grow. Nevertheless, as was his wont, he preferred to shift the spotlight to Rome. He told his readers that the pope "had lost none of his perpetual calm." He quoted the pope as saying to a Frenchman: "I have done what I could to forestall the war. . . .I have said what I could to decide the French not to abandon papal territory. People give me political reasoning of which I am able to understand nothing. God will provide."[8]

Before the collapse of the main French army and the withdrawal of troops from Rome, permitting the collapse of papal defense, Veuillot had fired many shots at the rising fortunes of Gambetta, Ferry, and the others who were to dominate the Government of National Defense that filled the vacuum that the Second Empire left. In fact, it is remarkable that these people, once they came to power in a desperate war situation, allowed him to continue his journal after the blasts he had aimed at them. But in August of 1870, with all the impending disasters, Veuillot focused great attention on the dedication of a statue of Voltaire, and he kept returning to this theme from time to time during the fall.[9] The rejuvenation of the cult of Voltaire took place at a time favorable to these assaults of Veuillot, as he was able to associate the initial two Prussian victories with the dedication ceremonies which took place on the 14th of August. He was able to quote a variety of slurs on the French which Voltaire had uttered to his Prussian patron, Frederick the Great, and then to associate this official endorsement of Voltaire, with the régime which had brought France into such a bad situation.[10] Just as *L'Univers* had conducted a great subscription for the pope, so *Le Siècle* had raised money for this "god of imbeciles," as Veuillot called Voltaire. That there should be a statue erected by *popular* support under *governmental* auspices to "the most wretched knave who ever dishonored literature" was more than Veuillot could stand.[11] He reached something like apoplexy in reacting against the impiety of it all, especially as the dedication was being perpetrated in the face of the approach of the Prussian armies. There was a project to put up a statue also to Joan of Arc, but so far as Veuillot was concerned, he wanted none of that in such company. "A statue of Joan of Arc in Paris next to Voltaire! . . ..Voltaire would be amused, Havin (former editor of *Le Siècle*) would rejoice, but Joan would weep." Symbolism can be important, and for Veuillot the Voltaire statue was "an outrage to religion, decency, and patriotism,"[12] something that could not be offset by anything else.

The imminent withdrawal of French troops from Rome distressed Veuillot, who declared to his readers that "if France declines the honor of protecting the Vicar of Christ in the future, our sacrifices will be without consolation and even victory without hope."[13] His patriotism demanded putting the church first. Early calling for "no treaty, no sedition, no blasphemy," he attacked those "protestants, Jews, and free-thinkers, types dominant in Vienna, who would counsel the French to treat. . . ."[14] But while lumping Vienna Jews with others he blamed in his desperation here, he held up the rebellion of the ancient Israelites against their "legitimate king," Rehoboam, as an example of something from which Frenchmen must profit.[15] Moltke was likened unto Holophernes, the Assyrian general;[16] Veuillot never lost his Biblical frame of reference.

What else could a journal do besides inflame and try to shape public opinion? The subscriptions for the council had shown what a financial factor *L'Univers* could be, and during August Veuillot's journal set about raising funds for the relief of soldiers and for chaplains.[17] A large sum was raised for this purpose. Veuillot meanwhile was already laying the groundwork for the movement of national expiation of the post-war period. He reacted violently to the phrase that was voiced about, "Christianity *idiotifié* by the pope and the council," and concluded that France could be *deidiotifiée* by getting rid of the influences of Voltaire, Quinet, and others. He incidentally pointed out that *idiotifier* was not a good French word, but something that a Prussian might use.[18]

The terrible day came. On 2 September 1870 the army of Marshal MacMahon was badly defeated at Sedan. The hapless emperor was captured. By 4 September the empress had to flee Paris, and Gambetta set up the Government of National Defense. What was Veuillot to say? The journals had been ordered weeks earlier not to report details of troop movements, and now a revolutionary provisional régime had taken over. New as the régime was, it did not have an altogether new look to Veuillot. "Old Monsieur Crémieux re-enters his old ministry of finance." As for the Second Empire, "nothing remains except universal suffrage, which baptized it, confirmed it, and blessed it." Universal suffrage appeared to Veuillot to be the thing that had taken on divine qualities, but he declared: "The country will rebuild itself around the altar. The altar is its native land, and it has nothing of its fecundity. Whoever lifts his hand against the altar will be a parricide."[19]

Except for General Trochu, commandant of the Paris military district and president of the government, those in power were essentially hostile to the Catholic church. How could Veuillot in any way be sanguine? Throughout the sad days of 1870 Veuillot identified the disasters of

France with those of the papacy. He did this more by instinct than anything else, because he lacked news reports as the Prussians closed in on Paris. In 1871, however, he pulled events together in pairs. On 20 September, Rome, from which the French troops had been withdrawn, and which was defended only by the pontifical troops, fell to the Italian army. Almost at the same time the investiture of Paris was complete. The withdrawal of the Pontifical Zouaves (who then distinguished themselves as the Volunteers of the West in action at Patay and elsewhere which Veuillot would have reported with relish if only he could have) Veuillot paired with the surrender of Toul. Congratulations which the French ambassador in Rome gave to the King of Italy on 25 September at the takeover of Rome he associated with the Prussian seizure of Bougival, Rueil, and Nanterre. The formation of a Roman government by General Cadorna on 27 September he linked with the report of Favre's failure to get terms for France at the interview at Ferrières. The removal of marks of papal sovereignty on 28 September Veuillot recapitulated in the same breath with the collapse of Strasbourg and the loss of 27,000 prisoners. On 5 October the plebiscite overwhelmingly endorsed the Italian national annexation of the papal territories, while the Prussians moved into Versailles and the French régime, now at Tours, made Crémieux minister of war. The various steps to make Rome the capital of Italy were paired by date with French disasters. The passing of the Spanish crown to the son of Victor Emmanuel came at the same time as the surrender of Metz.[20] Had Veuillot heard of all these things as they happened, he would hardly have been able to contain himself. In a general way, however, in 1870 he knew that such events were, or would be, taking place, and so he wrote of Job and other such themes for those who still were able to find and read newspapers.[21]

The Prussians did not completely seal off Paris and begin a siege proper until the early fall in 1870, but by the time of the rout at Sedan the likelihood of this situation was pressing. Veuillot had been able to foresee the dangers even before the collapse of MacMahon and the Empire. In a note to Auguste Roussel of 28 August he said: "Penitence will bring miracles. France will live again, but is dying."[22] His daughters were taken in late August to the Daughters of the Visitation at Le Mans by Élise, who then returned to be with her brother during the hard days ahead.[23] Those days were to be very hard, even without the privations of a siege. As he wrote on 28 August to Madame Bacon de Seigneux: "My administrative and editorial sections are disorganized by the war; and my brother and I and two other older people are obliged to do double duty, I should say triple, because of the subscriptions."

But despite such practical preoccupations he typically exclaimed: "If France is beaten, the church will re-enter the catacombs."[24] One of his editors, Ernest Schnaiter, a former army officer, went with the army as a war correspondent and was feared lost in August after the Battle of Forbach.[25] Eventually he turned up again unharmed and, though he had various duties that took him from *L'Univers* at times, was able to contribute articles to the journal. Aubineau left the country, and Loth and Roussel, younger men, had to perform service for the guard. They did, however, contribute articles when they could. Although *L'Univers* continued as a daily sheet, it was just about that – only two pages in length.[26]

The dramatic escape of *L'Univers* from Paris was carried out by Rastoul. He left on one of the last trains from Paris on 17 September, taking 15,000 francs with him, and headed for Le Mans where he thought he had arrangements for starting a provincial edition of *L'Univers.* He found there that matters could not be arranged as he had thought, and after visiting several other cities finally launched a two-page edition at Nantes.[27] This edition continued through the war and until the government moved from Tours to Bordeaux. Early in 1871 the Nantes edition ceased. It had had problems in issuing numbers, but it is fascinating that the Nantes edition did get communications by balloon from Paris, including some copies of the Paris edition, and Louis Veuillot's articles were then reproduced in it. By 10 January Leon Aubineau set up a Bordeaux office and began issuing an edition from that city. By mid-February Louis Veuillot moved to Bordeaux, which briefly was the seat of the journal. In due course the editor of *Liberté* of Bordeaux, Gregory Ganesco, declared that of all the papers that had two editions, *L'Univers* was the only one in which both editions hued to the same line.[28] Rastoul had kept *L'Univers* alive outside of Paris reflecting Veuillot's doctrines, while the editor-in-chief addressed himself to generalities and to special matters in wartime, besieged Paris.

Early acts of the Government of National Defense were to end the stamp tax on the press and to grant it full freedom.[29] Although news reports were hard to get, Veuillot at least for the moment was under less legal constraint than he had ever experienced. He declared that France had been punished after Sedan for her sin, and he looked for a crusader to lead her.[30] Militant patriotism was perfectly in order under Gambetta, though editorials about Judas Maccabbeus were hardly what he would have prescribed.[31] Before outside communication was choked off Veuillot had received an edition of the *Civiltà Cattolica* of Rome in which he was delighted to read an article by Father Margotti to the effect that Napoleon's policy toward the German states, Mexico, and

Rome accounted for his downfall.[32] Despite his preoccupation with Rome, when not discussing the sad situation of France, Veuillot also warned that Spain, Belgium, Holland, and Italy herself were targets of Prussian ambition. He could see that Alsace and Lorraine were gone with Sedan.[33] One expression that he liked to repeat was that "Unfaithful France is whipped and humbled, but still does not want to repent."[34] It was against France, not the Empire or the republic, that Bismarck was making war, Veuillot insisted, in one of his typical patriotic cries,[35] and his appeals were for France, not the existing power-holders.

Veuillot had many specific complaints about the régime. He criticized the attempt of Favre in late September to negotiate with the Prussians,[36] and he attacked the minister of beaux arts for suggesting the destruction of the Arc de Triomphe.[37] Despite the terms of Trochu's acceptance of the presidency – the maintenance of three great principles, God, the family, and property – Veuillot saw the régime attacking all of them.[38] He bewailed what he called lack of leadership, and in particular he felt that the choice of unsuitable generals like Garibaldi was deplorable.[39] The Hôtel de Ville he labeled the "mortuary" of France, and for the sins committed there and elsewhere God would chastise France, he maintained.[40] The dominant figures Arago, Flourens, Blanqui, and Pyat he especially attacked,[41] but all officials in the city and national government came in for some kind of attack by Veuillot, though he tended to be lenient toward Trochu. The degree of freedom of the press that allowed Veuillot to lament so much at that lametable point was amazing.

Abbreviated versions of most journals were published during the Prussian siege, and there was also a considerable group of brand-new radical sheets, such as Pyat's *Combat* and Blanqui's *Patrie en Danger*. With all comers Veuillot crossed swords about the anticlerical tendencies of the régime and about the conduct of the war. None of the journals, and notably *L'Univers*, were more than vestiges of their former selves, but in a small compass the journalistic battle had never been sharper. One of the most inflammatory acts of a governmental official was the secularizing of schools in the Eleventh Arrondissement by the mayor, Mottu, a move which brought the strongest criticism by Veuillot,[42] and which served as a point of argumentation for all the journals. A plebiscite held by the régime in early November, as a vote of confidence, likewise threw the journals into quarrels. Veuillot, as we have seen, had no love at all for the régime, but with Trochu at its head, and with complete anarchy as the alternative, he counseled endorsement.[43] A violent exchange with Delescluze of *Le Réveil*, who accused the Catholics of being subjects of the pope rather than of France, was typical of the kind of polemics in which Veuillot became involved while the Prussians slowly wore down the French forces outside of Paris.

Veuillot was ever the cavalier, and not only did he defend the pope whenever attacked by various hostile journalists, he also came to the defense of the Empress Eugénie. In an open letter to Favre dated 22 November he bewailed untrue slurs made on the former empress,[44] and for these kind words the empress wrote him three months later a letter of thanks. Veuillot declared the empress was like "a bird which escaped from a falling tree."[45] He also showed a certain magnanimity toward a former journalistic enemy, Adolphe Guéroult, with whom he had a friendly meeting in mid-fall,[46] though no special entente developed with the director of *L'Opinion nationale*.

A group of radicals representing the city government had briefly taken members of the national government captive on 31 October 1870. In view of this Veuillot could insist with much justice on the dangers of the direction things seemed to be taking politically.[47] As the armies steadily were losing the war the menaces of these Parisian radicals seemed to confirm Veuillot's words describing their attitude: *Vive la fraternité! Sois mon frère ou je te tue!* Their religion, or rather their lack of it, of course was the trouble: they did not even accept the Supreme Being of Robespierre, he concluded.[48]

By December Paris was being shelled by the Prussians. One of Veuillot's longest pieces in the short *L'Univers*, which was still making a daily appearance, was an imaginary trip to Rome. In his private papers are even more extensive details about this fantastic Christmas voyage than appeared in *L'Univers.*[49] This long piece was featured to provide revitalizing end-of-the-year fare for its weary readers in beleaguered Paris.[50] When the departmental edition was set up in Bordeaux, this material was published again there, in its first number on 10 January 1871. Veuillot wrote in an unpublished paper, "The ideal is real, veiled, and disfigured by the visible."[51] This imaginary trip challenging the reader to transcend his visible circumstances was close to this category of thought.

France was seized by a wave of defeatism and a desire to reach an armistice with the Prussians in December and January, 1870-1871. Gambetta still wanted to fight on, and Veuillot, who had much criticism for the conduct of the war by Trochu,[52] was also of a mind to hold out, though already bombs had fallen heavily on the Left Bank. Trochu resigned in late January, to be replaced by General Vinoy, but the change was to no avail. With confusion in the government, and with much of the countryside crying for peace, resistance against the now united German Empire became ever less possible. Eventually terms of armistice had to be accepted. Veuillot lamented the "vile excuses" of the government,[53] but there was nothing he could do about it. The fighting was over, and at last there were to be no more secular or civil burials of soldiers to berate. He now could turn to politics, at least for a few weeks, as a National Assembly was to be elected to come together at Bordeaux to try to patch up the cracks of a vanquished nation and to form a permanent government.

Louis Veuillot had had a hard time during the siege, eating what odds and ends he could get, and existing in an area under bombardment. His zeal for trying to continue his defense of the church, even under these circumstances, had helped sustain him. France was being chastised for sins he had pointed out, and he no doubt even felt a certain satisfaction in the process. He missed his children badly, and was practically out of communication with them, though he did send at least one letter by balloon which reached them at the Convent of the Visitation in Mans. In this letter he told them of his prayers, particularly those made at the object of his dreary walks, the church of Notre Dame-des-Victoires.[54] After the fighting ceased travel was still hard. *L'Univers* had to be kept functioning in Paris, and when he felt free to leave Paris, it was to Bordeaux, full of the confusion of the coming together of the National Assembly, that he went first. Agnès and Luce, he felt sure, were in the best of hands at the Visitation.

The elections to the National Assembly took place so quickly that little campaigning could take place before them, and many of the candidates were little known. For the most part members of established conservative families carried the day, swept in by the general desire for peace and order.[55] In a situation like this, even Louis Veuillot had little opportunity to launch much of a campaign in the press. As had been the case on various other occasions, there was talk of Veuillot himself as a candidate, but he made it clear, although just shortly before the elections, that he was not to be considered for the post of deputy.[56] He formulated his principal ideas in a long article dated 31 January 1871.[57] In so doing Veuillot showed some political astuteness, and in effect he made the clerical-monarchical platform of his "Everyman's Republic" as palatable as possible.

First and foremost, "Henry (with a 'y') de Bourbon is asked to accept the regency of the French people. . ." He is asked as "head of the most illustrious French family, under which France grew, was consolidated, and rebuilt. . . .which notably gave us Lorraine, Alsace, and Algeria." His "striking personal honesty" Veuillot held up to Frenchmen as his prime asset.

The Government of National Defense had called for the elections, but in launching his own legitimist campaign Veuillot wanted the regent, the Comte de Chambord, to do this. As a concession to modernity perhaps, he did not care what the title of the chief of state would be, but national unity would be maintained by the principle of heredity! The National Assembly would be elected by the indirect means of the provincial assemblies, which would themselves be elected by universal manhood suffrage. Each province (he did not say what would happen to the departments) would administer itself "freely." The "moral bases of the constitution" would be religion, the family, property, and liberty. He explained that every Frenchman was a soldier, and that that was why decentralization was necessary. Bachelors were to be taxed. Revolutionary laws affecting wills were to be abolished. Civil and religious liberties were to be proclaimed.

The church was to have many liberties, including the right to establish universities. "The state will in no way interfere in the government of the church."

Corporations ouvrières exist by right, Veuillot declared. None of these would be socialist labor unions, of course; what he had in mind were the old associations whose vestiges had been still surviving at Boynes when he was born. France was to become a Christian nation, and there was to be no work on Sundays.

Although the money would bear the face of the Comte de Chambord, the one thing Veuillot did not seem to care about was his title. Perhaps he feared that "king" was just the word not to use in the nineteenth century. In any case, once the National Assembly voted the constitution he was proposing, Henry would be asked by it "to accept for himself and for his descendants in direct line or by adoption the function of supreme chief of France, or rather, *of the Franks*." This Christian chief was to be free to choose the title of president or king, and also whether to be anointed at Reims or at Saint-John-Lateran.[58] Presumably Saint Peter's would have been acceptable!

Obviously Veuillot was talking in terms of idealism. In the election he endorsed no candidates. Sarcastically he proposed "Coquerel," his fictional personification of all that was stupid.[59] He regarded the whole thing as an "electoral carnival."[60] There was no way for a journal to try to influence people in the provinces, where the candidates were locally known figures, often political novices.[61] In Paris the situation was very serious, but who was to persuade revolutionary spirits there not to vote for Gambetta, Pyat, Delescluze, Rochefort, and such? The radical left greatly outdistanced even moderates like Favre, to the distress of

Veuillot, when the votes were counted.[62] An ideological stand, even of a general and not immediately practical sort, was about all that he could take. Many years later, when Veuillot died, the Comte de Chambord declared that Veuillot had been the only person who had understood him.[63] Veuillot's words at this juncture in 1871, even despite his peculiar position with regard to the title of the pretender, do indeed sound like words that the Bourbon claimant would understand, or even say himself.

The National Assembly, with about two-thirds monarchists of one coloration or another, and including some extraordinary figures, even Garibaldi, came together promptly in Bordeaux in the second half of February. It chose Thiers, who had been elected from no fewer than twenty-six departments, to be the chief of the executive power. By 19 February he had constituted his cabinet.[64] France was now ready to give herself a permanent constitution, after first attending to making peace, and liquidating the immediate problems brought on by the war. *L'Univers* of the provinces had already been moved from Nantes to Bordeaux by the versatile Rastoul. He had the collaboration of several of the journal's best men. Louis Veuillot could not stay in Paris now any more than in the spring of 1870, so off to Bordeaux he went with sister Élise, at just about the time that Thiers' cabinet was being selected.

Eugène, who stayed in Paris, needed help for the Paris edition, but who was to be sent? Rastoul, whom Veuillot regarded as a soldier, deserved to remain at the base he had established. Aubineau was in charge when Veuillot arrived, and he said proudly, "Not me." Chantrel? Only if he were forced to go. Du Lac? Veuillot could not ask him.[65] The result was that Eugène was shorthanded, and Louis had the cream of the staff. Nevertheless, he had to be in Bordeaux. Just to exist in Bordeaux, however, was very difficult at this time. Military units were being broken up there, and people were scrambling for quarters. The arrival of hundreds of deputies alone made accommodations tight, and only the hospitality of various sympathizers made his stay tolerable. Élise was briefly sick, and for quite a few days Veuillot had unsettling problems as a result of the most unusual conditions.[66]

While in Bordeaux Veuillot, although pressed for quarters and meals, seemed to get back into the swing of writing letters. There had not been much sense in his trying to correspond from besieged Paris, but after leaving Prussian-occupied territory he could turn to this happy function again. It was from Bordeaux that he had his exchange with the Empress Eugénie, and not only did he have to write to Eugène, but also he could even pick up his exchange with Charlotte de Grammont, who had written him in early February about the great zouaves and the terrible Gambetta.[67] He had imagined her off in Normandy, or even England, but found she had remained in the Château Craon. How much worse it would be, he said, in Paris with Mottu.[68] He spared her the details of how *enrhumé* he was, but these he did not spare Eugène,[69] and he let the children know what the search for quarters was like.[70] At last on the eighth of March the journal carried the announcement that henceforth there would be just one edition, since the National Assembly was moving to Versailles.

Before moving to the theater at the Palace of Versailles from the Grand Theater of Bordeaux, the deputies, under the leadership of Thiers, had decided by the Pact of Bordeaux to suspend discussion of the form of government and to pull together for the solution of more pressing problems. The greatest necessity was to come to terms with the Germans, and on 26 February Thiers had signed preliminaries. The main subject about which Veuillot had written during his stay in Bordeaux was this. This "humiliation" was the result of the mishandling of Thiers, Favre, and others, and the very worst thing had come to pass. The real cause of the disaster was the change that had come over France since the Revolution.[71] Now, according to Veuillot, France was paying. He prepared a balance sheet in early March for his readers:

> Five billion to be paid to the Germans,
> Around four billion for the cost of the war,
> A previous debt of fourteen billion,
> The territory shamefully diminished,
> Disorder and sedition everywhere,
> Good public sense diminished worse than the territory,
> The general conscience more devastated than the soil, more ruined than the treasury, more sullied than the history;
> On the other side of the ledger:
> A political, civil, and religious alliance with Garibaldi;
> There is the balance sheet of the "immortal" principles of '89 in the 82nd year of their reign.
> If they go on at this rate, what do you hope for the immortality of France?
> And under what masters and what languages will Frenchmen celebrate the centennial of their "regeneration"?[72]

Veuillot felt passionately on all these points, and no doubt even the implication that disasters might lie ahead for the French language was a major concern for him. Nothing troubled him more, however, than the territorial losses. Émile Keller, the Alsatian Catholic leader, personified the situation, and publicly Veuillot expressed the sympathy of France for him. "Exiled from France in Alsace, or exiled from Alsace in

France, he will not be exiled from the church, and he will ever defend it, and ever with *éclat.*"[73] Keller, of course, was touched by these words, and in his reply stressed the role of the pope "in the great Catholic family of which Pius IX is the father."[74]

On 18 March 1871 the insurrection of the Paris Commune erupted. In effect the city of Paris began a secession from the rest of France, when the Parisian radicals, much reinforced by outside leaders like Dombrowski, defied the essentially conservative elements of much of the rest of the country.[75] As early as 17 March Veuillot prophetically wrote: "We have known the illusion of our military force; we are about to know the illusion of our civil force."[76] Thiers mismanaged matters. True, the situation was difficult, but he neither took the steps that might have prevented the insurrection from getting out of hand, nor, having fled Paris after a quick visit, did he proceed in an effective, or even by some lights honorable, way in dealing with the Communards. Guardsmen by the thousands went over to the insurrectionary regime, and France was confronted with civil war.

L'Univers was in Paris when the disorder began, and Louis Veuillot was in Versailles. He had just arrived there when matters became serious. Whether he arrived after the execution of Generals Thomas and Lecomte, which Veuillot declared even the Prussians would not have carried out,[77] or just before their execution is hard to say. According to François, he took his daughters to the home of his brother-in-law Arthur Murcier, who now resided in Saint-Germain, and from there he went to Versailles to follow proceedings of the National Assembly.[78] On his arrival in Versailles he had found connections with Paris still in effect. *L'Univers* was being sent to readers outside the city, and reports, such as those from the editor-in-chief, were able to come into the city. It was not until 11 April that he established a Versailles edition, first at one address, then at another. This sheet, much like the edition in besieged Paris of the fall, was literally a two-page sheet, even smaller than the war-time product, and, like the other, poorly printed. However, over three weeks elapsed before Veuillot got out this Versailles edition.

On his arrival in Versailles Veuillot seems to have misjudged the extent of the insurrection. He wrote his friend Madame Bacon de Seigneux that he gave the republic of Paris one week.[79] In view of his many complaints of the ineffectiveness of Thiers, and the way he had generally magnified the bad fruits France was harvesting, it is a little surprising that he said what he did. He was full of complaints, including complaints of the postal service, about which he lamented to his brother in Paris.[80] His most serious problem was his eyes, which were especially alarming him at this time. Along with the discomfort of his eyes he could not stand the noise where he was quartered. He had been put up at the *petit seminaire*, which in itself was agreeable to him, but there were many other people there, including a "thousand sailors." The place was a *très bruyante caserne*. Although bad news was to be heard all around, he told Eugène he was bored with his *métier.*[81] During the next few weeks his articles reflected a bit of this feeling.

His old friend Gustave de La Tour wrote Veuillot from Brittany that liberal Catholics were dominant in the ministry, and even in Brittany,[82] hardly words to lift his sagging spirit. One of his articles stressed the general sterility of the situation,[83] and his tone was one of fretful quibbling about little things. For example, to the proposal to erect an expiatory monument on the site of the execution (assassination was Veuillot's constant term) of Generals Thomas and Lecomte, he objected that a simple cross would be better.[84] He became bitter over the motto, *Liberté, Egalité, Fraternité,* and resorted to whipping one of his tried-and-true whipping boys, Crémieux.[85] He did write one article on Thiers becoming a republican, which was somewhat prophetic,[86] but even so the generality of the piece had something a little tired about it. He picked at the departed empire, and he wrote articles on the theme, "M. Thiers is unable to grow." He resorted to the feminine form, Adolphine, and complained he did not like the *ragoût* this cook was serving.[87] Veuillot could write well about events, but March and April of 1871 did not inspire him.

At the start of April Louis wrote Eugène in a most casual way about dining with Taconet, who likewise had taken refuge at the petit seminaire, but who did not plan to try to have a Versailles edition of *Le Monde*. Louis himself had not yet gotten his own edition under way, and his main bit of news was about his right eye. He feared that he really did have something seriously wrong; he was not just complaining as he often had. The right eyelid hung down from the eyeball, as though paralyzed.[88] He sounded like an old man at the end of his career, not someone about to publish a sheet almost alone. He spent much time during these days on the grounds of the Palace of Versailles. He thought about grand things, and he called Louis XIV "the author of the only French epic poem." François conjectured that a considerable portion of Louis Veuillot's poetry of this period was either written or rewritten while sitting in the park at Versailles. Indeed, a new edition of his *Filles de Babylone* was not long in coming out, and his newest poems were to be gathered and published under the title *Chants de 1871* the next year. His custom of long-standing had been to write poetry when his strained eyes were not up to the functions of the editorial office, and the trying spring of 1871 was another example of the disabled editor resorting to the role of poet. The poem which gave its own title to the new collection included the verses:

Chansons de sang et d'esperance,
Refrains à redire en pleurant,
Allez a ce pauvre mourant
Qui fut le grand pays de France.

. . . . .

Chansons de sang et d'esperance,
Parce que nous avons dormi
La gloire passe à l'ennemi;
Ne laissez plus dormir la France.

. . . . .

Chansons de sang et d'esperance,
Parlez de devoir et d'honneur;
Que Dieu nous fasse un sang meilleur
Et qu'il recouronne la France![89]

That God recrown France! This line was written at approximately the same time that the Comte de Chambord wrote a great bit of poetic prose to a supporter, letting it be known he was ready on the right occasion to assume the functions of kingship. Chambord stated very clearly that the independence of the pope was dear to him, and that liberty for the church was the prime condition. "The old sword of France" was in his hand, and in his bosom was "the heart of a king and of a father who has no party." He was only bringing back religion and peace. "The word is for France, and the hour for God."[90] Nothing could have sounded better to Louis Veuillot than the words Henry [*sic*] de Bourbon used. In fact, Veuillot himself was the author! Veuillot emphasized the gulf between the Comte de Chambord and the royalist politicians, whom he lumped with the rest, and drew a parallel between the pretender and the Good Lord. When Chambord spoke of bringing back God, it was like the sensation Jesus caused among the Jews in speaking with authority, Veuillot said. What a choice French people had – they might choose Citizen Delescluze and the guillotine or Henry of Bourbon and the cross! Oh, yes, between these two extremes would be a "happy" medium, such as France had had in the past – Adolphe Thiers![91]

Meanwhile at Versailles Veuillot was most unhappy. He reported that he was eating beefsteak, but that "Sainte Inopportunité" was with him.

"I am growing fifty years older each day."[92] It was while he was in this situation that Chambord wrote his letter, and that the worst events of the Commune took place. The Versailles government, so slow to act, finally had been reinforced with soldiers released by the Germans, and the assault to retake the city was underway. Curiously, it was not until 12 May that the Commune suppressed those six journals, including *L'Univers*, that had been pursuing their independent critical lines. The embattled staff of the Paris headquarters of *L'Univers* worked desperately to get out a final number, to the great concern of Louis Veuillot, who particularly feared that Loth and Roussel would be objects of revenge of the vengeful regime of the Hôtel de Ville. Veuillot gave full credit to the whole group in Paris for fighting the battle of *L'Univers* in the most difficult of conditions and the greatest danger.[93] If there ever was a time when *L'Univers* showed that it was a vital organ quite without Louis Veuillot, it was during the siege of the Commune. Things were so bad in Paris that old enemies taking refuge in Versailles were temporarily drawn together. As the fighting drew to an end, Louis wrote Eugène, who had departed for Angers to retrieve his family, that he had been "fraternizing" with Arsène Houssaye and Buloz of the *Revue des Deux Mondes*. While he was so doing, the two offered him praise, but their sort of praise he found "detestable."[94] The fact was that *L'Univers* was a remarkable journal even without the Veuillot brothers.

Probably enraged by the Versailles decree of 8 May 1871 governing public prayers, the Communards launched full-scale destruction of many landmarks in Paris. At the same time they took revenge on many hostages, most notably executing before the end of hostilities the Archbishop of Paris, Darboy. The Archbishop died the night of 24-25 May at the hands of a firing squad, when an exchange for Auguste Blanqui was not effected.[95] Tremendous damage to the city was brought about. The Préfecture, the Palais Royal, the Hôtel de Ville, Saint Eustache, the Tuileries, and many blocks on both sides of the Seine and on the Île-de-la-Cité were devastated. For some reason the item of destruction that seems to have evoked the most comment from Louis Veuillot was the pulling down of the Column Vendôme. Perhaps it was the earliness of this destruction, the sympathy Victor Hugo had shown for the idea, and the fact that it had been the project of the minister of beaux-arts of the Government of National defense, Gustave Courbet, to do just this, as well as to dismantle the Arc-de-Triomphe, that prompted Veuillot's reaction.[96] At any rate, Veuillot made special public comment on the destruction of this imperial symbol.

At length, the Versailles troops moved into the areas evacuated by the desperate Communards, cornered them on Montmartre, and brought about the worst slaughter in the history of Paris as sequel to the greatest destruction and killing of hostages the city had seen. The National Assembly, on Thier's announcement of 22 May that troops had entered Paris, voted that he and the troops had *bien mérité de la patrie*. Veuillot declared in his edition of *L'Univers* that Thiers merited the *indulgence* of the country.[97] Many Frenchmen wanted revenge for the terrible deeds of the Communards, and were disposed to condone the atrocities connected with the massacre of Communards and the summary decrees of execution that sometimes accompanied the acts. Some of the royalist officers who led troops into Paris, like the Comte de Mun, were disposed to have pity for the victims of the Versailles soldiers, and Veuillot, despite his enormous hatred of these Paris rebels, was so minded. He did not rejoice at the vengeance, and he feared that the suppressors of the Commune were doing the same sort of thing that had been so shocking. "The Commune therefore is dying faithful to itself. It began assassinating generals, and it ends in assassinating priests. Diabolic instinct has indeed guided its hand. It has planted the dagger where the intelligentsia of the Revolution have thrown the most ink stains."[98] However, Veuillot did not want an eye for an eye. Darboy was hardly dead before he wrote: "Summary executions equally frustrate justice, which is a human need, and great Christian humanity, of the necessity for which no crime deprives any criminal."[99] These executions were unworthy of soldierly honor and Christian government in Veuillot's estimation. It was of course one thing to sit in Versailles and pen noble lines and another to restore order against the most desperate men of disorder. However, Veuillot's moderation contrasts very well with what many others were saying at the time, and of all people Veuillot might have been expected at least to have a different emphasis.

Louis Veuillot returned to Paris the first week of June 1871. Rastoul had been to Paris a few days previously, and he was to have reported on "our poor old 44,"[100] as Veuillot called his dwelling on the Rue de Bac, but there is no evidence any word got to him before he laid eyes on the place himself. No damage had been done, but great damage had occurred nearby. The smoke was still a problem on 7 June, but Veuillot did not seem to want to go into detail in his correspondence. He had plenty to do in getting the journal going again from its regular base in Paris, and he had plans to reissue some of his older works, such as *Le Lendemain de la Victoire*. The aftermath of 1870-1871 seemed to him to have a precedent in the period of 1849. He seemed like an old man who wished he could be doing something other than his immediate duties, but he had no choice except his duties. "My *métier* weighs on me terribly. But what good is there in complaining? Alas! When will the time come back to write sonnets?"[101]

Even in the smoky situation of Paris, Rome was ever on Veuillot's mind. He took up communication with the Vatican from Paris by a letter to Msgr. Mercurelli sent in the hands of young Arthur Loth, whom Veuillot highly commended to Mercurelli. The future editor and historian of the royalist movement was praised not only for his role as a soldier in the first siege and a resister of the Commune in the second, but as the author of a piece on Pope Honorius. Veuillot described him as a "young scholar, modest, courageous, very pious and very pure, one of those on whom I particularly rely to carry on the battle for me."[102] The young man so eulogized, who did indeed carry on with *L'Univers* was the representative of the journal to the twenty-fifth anniversary of the election of Pius IX as pope. He bore a collection of nearly 650,000 names of people protesting their fidelity to the pope.[103] Such signatures were, of course, more a protest against the seizure of Rome than anything else, since presumably good Catholics normally would demonstrate their fidelity in a more usual fashion.

The sending of Loth with this singular list gathered by Catholics throughout France would have been a notable episode in Veuillot's life, even if it had stood quite by itself. However, the letter which Arthur Loth also carried to Mercurelli contained as well strong and presumptuous advice for the Vatican from the lay editor. He warned that the Gallican-inopportunist party was still a major danger:

> . . . . . Believe me, Monseigneur, the church is not finished with this party. We see from near that nothing is changed. Moreover, I shall continue to await the attack, twofold rather than just one, before answering it.
>
> I fear this battle is not finished. At this very moment a great effort is being made to elevate Msgr. Dupanloup to the See of Paris. This would be, I believe, his misfortune and ours. Paris more than any other diocese in the world has need of an apostolic man, and one who on arriving would inspire neither apprehension nor enthusiasm. Such is not the case of Msgr. Dupanloup, who is before all a party man. He would make it a triumph of party, in rubbing out the other, and the unfortunate see would remain more abandoned than ever.[104]

So wrote the lay editor to one of the key prelates in the Vatican.

Veuillot had Dupanloup overly much on his mind. The pope would never have appointed Dupanloup to the great post at that time. He already had an important see, and his role in 1870 had not been such as to make such an appointment within the realm of possibility, even if the régime had urged it strongly. Veuillot noted that the "truly good Paris, some thousands, perhaps [only] hundreds of souls," wanted the Archbishop of Bourges, despite support he had given Napoleon. He also thought well of Freppel, Bishop of Angers, but he realized there was no real hope for the appointment of either of these prelates. By late July he thought Dupanloup was abandoned and had renounced his bid, and he wrongly supposed that the Archbishop of Tours, Msgr. Guibert, had also been dropped from consideration. "My choice," Veuillot declared to Msgr. Nardi, "would be a monk or a simple priest who would arrive at the office directly and with the purpose of dying in it."[105] Nardi had of course shown his strong sympathies for Veuillot during the Vatican Council, but again it is astonishing to see the editor trying to influence the Vatican.

Msgr. Guibert had remained a monk, and Veuillot may have been on the right track when he thought the choice might be made in that direction. Jules Simon, ever careful in such matters despite his own outlook on life, declared to a hesitant Guibert, "Ah! Monseigneur, never have I doubted that you were made to be Archbishop of Paris." Guibert accepted. There were reasons for thinking that Guibert might not like Veuillot, but Veuillot accepted the choice as though it were the best. His old friend, the artist, Émile Lafon, wrote him at this period that during a visit with Msgr. Guibert he had been assured that the prelate had great esteem for Veuillot. Lafon said that if the new Archbishop had ever had any differences with *L'Univers*, they had concerned not a matter of principle but only the form of its polemics.[106] So far as Veuillot was concerned, the period when Guibert was at the head of the archdiocese turned out to be a particularly placid one in his relations with his bishop.

A prelate with whom Veuillot developed very close relations in 1871 was Msgr. Freppel, Bishop of Angers. Freppel was from Alsace, now lost to the Germans, and he had been named Bishop of Angers only after the start of the Vatican Council. It might appear that a clergyman from Strasbourg, who had become bishop in the devoutly Catholic area of Brittany, would have been a long time friend of Veuillot, like Salinis, Parisis, or Pie, but such was not the case. The connection of the two had begun in 1852 when Freppel as a young teacher had asked Veuillot to protest against the giving of *Le Prophète.* François Veuillot's statement, "It is true their subsequent relations were a bit strained," is a mild way to put it.[107] Freppel, who as dean of the chapter of Ste. Genevieve had preached before the emperor, was recommended by the president of the senate, Troplong, in 1862 to the minister of the interior, Rouland, as "an ecclesiastic of the old Gallican school, rendering unto Caesar what is Caesar's, and avoiding all extreme opinions." He was sent as a theological consultant to Rome in 1869, and as late as that time still pronounced himself against the stand of *L'Univers* on infallibility. At the death of Msgr. Angebault in 1869, Darboy was among those who recommended Freppel for the vacant see in Angers. Freppel had ardently wanted to be a bishop, and now his ambition was fulfilled.[108] It was after this point that Freppel made a great reversal in his previous stands and switched to the ultramontane camp. His relations with Louis Veuillot now became very warm, and the two remained close through the rest of Veuillot's life. In fact Freppel assumed the aspect of one of the pillars of the church in the eyes of Veuillot.

Elections were scheduled to be held for the National Assembly on 2 July 1871, and the conservatives of Paris decided to include an ecclesiastic among those on their slate. Eugène Veuillot persuaded Freppel to accept the nomination which *L'Univers* had pushed,[109] and Louis was now in the position of giving his principal political support to a man who only months before had opposed his main interest. However, Veuillot was ever willing to overlook the past if a former opponent came around to his position and had something to offer. Freppel was just such a person.[110] Dupanloup was elected a member of the National Assembly at this time, and later he became a senator; but on this first occasion Freppel, who later represented so militantly the church in the parliament, went down to defeat. In general, the conservatives did well in Paris, but Freppel, although he received around 84,000 votes, had to wait for another era before making his entry into the parliament. Freppel had been in close touch with Veuillot from the start of his short candidature.[111] As soon as he lost, he wrote Veuillot that, although defeated, he felt the loss was not without some glory. He blamed *Le Français* and the rest of the monarchist press, as well as "maneuvers of the last hour."[112] Veuillot was not quite able to put a candidate into parliament without other support, but it is interesting to see how many votes Freppel, practically unknown previously in Paris, did get with little other than the backing of *L'Univers*.

The Comte de Chambord is a difficult figure to understand unless one considers that his ideology was of another age, and that he was more interested in his way of ideologically representing the monarchical principle than in any immediate achievement of power.[113] The monarchy could have been restored in France in 1871 had Chambord been willing to accept a "fusion" with the Orleanists, but that was not the nature of the reconciliation he desired. Veuillot and Chambord were like-minded in this respect. Whereas the purely or largely royalist journals hoped for some "transaction" between the princes, *L'Univers* supported the divine-right stand of the pretender. On June 3 Veuillot advocated in his article: "We need a head! France, lying as though dead, will recover, raise itself, and walk." He called for an "independent" king, not an absolute monarch in the previous tradition; a military, but not a Napoleonic leader; a king *au peuple*, but not *du peuple*; a king recognized by the people, but not created by them. "Ah, well, France, if she will, has all this in one man alone, who alone has all this. It is Henri de Bourbon, son of France, of the race of Saint Louis, the first Frenchman and at the same time the first gentleman of the world."[114]

This person arrived in France on 2 July 1871. The Comte de Paris wrote him just at this time to try to effect a meeting for a formal reconciliation, but Chambord was not receptive. Just why he came to France, when significant elections were underway, when his cause was at its zenith, and never let his presence be known is something of a mystery even considering his attitude of letting things follow the divine scheme. He went to the Chateau de Chambord, where he announced himself to the caretaker as "the proprietor." But there he penned quite by himself a manifesto that shocked the royalist world. He spoke of being ready to help France recover from her ruination by insuring decentralization. His observations on social conditions were benevolent, but in terms of an older period. He denied that he was bringing back feudalism or its abuses, but "I will never allow the standard of Henri IV, Francis I, or Joan or Arc to be snatched from my hands." He mentioned that this was the flag that had conquered barbarism in Algeria, and he closed with the line, "Frenchmen, Henri V cannot abandon the white flag of Henri IV."

Many newspapers expressed the view that irreparable damage had been done to the cause of royalism by this intransigeance regarding the revolutionary flag on the part of Chambord, but Veuillot hailed his subordination of all matters to the church and his defiance of fusionist politicians. Veuillot gave examples of the untruthfulness with which the enemies of the Comte de Chambord had been implying that all the evils of the old régime would come back with him.[115] Friends of Veuillot like Gustave de La Tour reinforced him, further expounding upon the obvious reasons why Chambord was the natural king.[116] Very shortly after the startling manifesto the pretender granted an interview to Gabriel de Chaulnes, to whom he reiterated that he was not a "revolutionary king." He bewailed revolutionary currents and said that "in order to save France, it is necessary to react against these ideas, against liberal Catholicism." De Chaulnes reported all this to Veuillot directly,[117] words that were exactly what Veuillot wanted to hear. Veuillot had been out of step with royalism in 1840, and in 1850, and now in this period he took a stand which most of the royalist leaders wanted to soft-peddle; but in fact he was in complete harmony with the pretender. Chambord's right-hand man, Henri de Vanssay wrote him to this effect on 19 September 1871.[118] Belcastel, the most reactionary member of the legitimists in the National Assembly, in the approbation he showed to Veuillot also emphasized this unity.[119]

De Chaulnes was not only a bridge between the pretender and Veuillot, but also played a role in a related ecclesiastical issue in which Veuillot became involved at just this time. A group of pilgrims from Nevers were given a private audience by the pope on 18 June 1871, during the course of which the pope spoke strongly about the recent events that had taken place in France. He said in so many words that Catholic liberals had helped bring on these disorders, and he warned the pilgrims about the error of their ways. The allocution was reported in *L'Univers*, and was copied elsewhere. The *Annales religieuses* of the dioscese of Orleans treated the topic, but in so doing it suppressed the term "liberal Catholicism" and generally shortened the statement in such a way as to distort it. Gabriel de Chaulnes reported this to Veuillot,[120] and Veuillot turned sharply on the journal.[121] De Chaulnes had emphasized that the journal was closely tied to the archbishopric, so the old duel between Veuillot and Dupanloup showed signs of beginning another sharp round. The two journals exchanged editorials, but then to all intents the *Annales religieuses* gave ground,[122] and despite the entry of many other papers into the debate, *L'Univers* may be said to have won. Dupanloup and Veuillot had some further differences, but Veuillot also came to support Dupanloup on a number of occasions during the seventies, and the day of open warfare between them was thereafter in the past.

Having re-entered the lists for a brief time in Paris after the Commune, Veuillot with his suffering eyes was ready for a vacation. During the last week in July and most of August he divided his time between the country homes of his old friend of the thirties and forties, Mallac, and of Dr. Imbert. The first at Changy-les-Bois and the second at Royat both afforded him rest and quiet: His nerves must have been in at least as bad condition as his eyes. From Mallac's he reported that there was a woman whose talk was like "a castanet solo which never ends." He also apparently could not get a proper *plume* with which to write, only *plumes de fer,* which caused him to start a letter to Élise with a blast against typewriters.[123] He developed his article on *Adolphine* for the pleasure of Mallac,[124] but for the most part was on vacation. As he was in the Loiret, where rain particularly stands in the furrows of the fields, perhaps he had a little more reason than usual to complain of the weather, but his complaints here fully matched his complaints from

Rome. Despite this sojourn near his own birthplace, he apparently made no effort to go to Boynes. After the better part of a fortnight of quiet life at the Château de Changy, he moved on for a stay with Dr. Imbert at Royat. There is no evidence of his seeking any medical treatment, only rest. No doubt the change did him some good, but he sounded dejected nonetheless when he wrote to Madame Testas "You are one of the three or four terrestial things which make me remember that I am not dead."[125] Despite the sad ring of such words, Veuillot had the unusual pleasure of being on vacation in company with his brother. Normally one or the other of them was on duty all the time in Paris, but apparently on this extraordinary occasion neither could wait for a vacation.

During the absence of the brothers Veuillot *L'Univers* became the object of a suit by the government on the charge of false news. The paper had discussed the doings of revolutionaries in Lyon, suggesting that a rebellion like that of the Paris Commune was in the making there. The position the journal took was that they had simply said what everyone knew anyway,[126] but in any case Louis Veuillot had to engage a lawyer and face the charges of the régime. The militant Catholic from Caen who took on the case, Professor Carel, carried it through successfully, and *L'Univers* was cleared on 12 September. Veuillot thanked Carel publicly.[127] The journal had the backing of a large part of the press,[128] since, after all, other journals were also vulnerable to such charges, and *L'Univers* had really done nothing that the others did not do also.

During the fall of 1871 France was preoccupied with the questions of what to do about the pope, who was at the mercy of the Italian régime, and the royal question in France, speculation as to whether the Comte de Chambord would compromise his principles sufficiently to permit some sort of solution. The first problem would become particularly acute in 1872, and the second in 1873. Meanwhile, Louis Veuillot also had various lesser matters that attracted his attention. For one thing, the publication of the papers that had been seized in the Tuileries included letters showing Veuillot's support of Napoleon III in the 1850's. Veuillot had written of his desire in 1854 that Napoleon III equal the roles of Charlemagne and Saint Louis, and he had some explaining to do on the score of why he now had turned elsewhere for the fulfillment of this desire. Veuillot's answers were simple enough, reflecting the Catholic-before-all role he had always played, but he had to fill many columns with explanation during October and November.[129] He particularly blamed *Le Français* for the attack, and he suspected that this supposedly monarchist journal was really an organ of Thiers, written for Catholics, but against the church.[130] He blamed *Le Français* in December for the break-up of the solidarity, such as it had been, of journals that had formed a union for political order.[131] Thiers, of course, was a continuing object of Veuillot's sarcasm, while a wide range of other people were raked over the coals, including Falloux, the Princes of Orleans, and the Abbé Michaud, whose doctoral degree in theology Veuillot questioned.[132] Michaud came back at him with the charge that Veuillot was trying not only to refute him, but to injure him, and he maintained that the Catholic church was a new one since 1870,[133] meaning that Veuillot had helped to change it. He spoke of the burning of Paris partly as retribution, but destruction of Paris was a delicate subject. When Chicago was destroyed in the fall of 1871, Veuillot could be more hard-boiled about what retribution would come to materialists, even using Nineveh as a frame of reference.[134] But despite the diversity of his interests, Veuillot still kept the Roman question uppermost in his mind.

During 1871 and 1872, despite guarantees the Italian government made to the papacy, the position of the pope was both perilous and pathetic. He lived in the greatest of simplicity and feared that he might be driven out of even the little that was left to him.[135] Legitimists in the National Assembly launched a movement to gather petitions to request that the French government as an expression of support for the pope not send an ambassador to the government of the King of Italy. Veuillot threw himself fully into this conflict. The role of Thiers was one of compromise in the whole matter. His foreign minister, Remusat, was pro-Italian, but Thiers would like to have avoided trouble, if possible. Throughout the whole period the French frigate, *Orénoque,* stood ready at Civitavecchia to carry the pope into exile. The pope, in fact, had considered a number of possible places of exile, including Malta and Avignon. In due course Thiers even made available to him the Château de Pau,[136] but offering refuge is quite a different thing from giving support. Veuillot regarded this willingness to open the doors to the pope as a refugee in France as simply underlining the abandonment of the pope by France.[137]

L'Univers and Louis Veuillot were directly involved. *L'Univers'* correspondent in Rome, Henri de Maguelonne, so neglected during the council, was now in a very sensitive spot. The Italian régime was putting pressure on him, and might have forced him to leave because of the articles that *L'Univers* was publishing. Veuillot wrote him a long letter in November, commiserating with him, and sharing his own complaints with him.[138] Eventually the matter of the petitions pushed by Belcastel and Abbadie de Barrault with great support from *L'Univers* brought matters to a head. In the spring of 1872 the involvement of *L'Univers* and Louis Veuillot in the affairs of the pope developed in such a way as to bring what amounted to censure of Louis Veuillot by the pope.

The Italian government enraged Veuillot. Even the physical completion of the tunnel under Mount Cenis, finished in the fall of 1871 after about a dozen years of work, distressed him.[139] By February of 1872 the empty post of ambassador at the Quirinal was to be filled by an obscure French diplomat, Fournier, who for some time had been at the relatively unimportant post in Stockholm. Fournier was known as an anticlerical, and already the French ultramontanes were against posting any ambassador in Rome. Veuillot bewailed the sending of an "ambassador to Herod."[140] He continued this line, bringing Barrabas and Pilate into the picture. He became involved in the very sharpest exchanges with other journals, and never had he been shriller than in expressing his bitterness as Fournier departed for Rome.[141] The affair came to a head on 22 March, when the question was debated in parliament, and many eyes were focused on Dupanloup, deputy of the Loiret.

Veuillot was ready to attack various people, particularly Thiers, but in this affair his greatest bitterness was toward Dupanloup. As in the matter of infallibility, Dupanloup's position on the matter of diplomatic representation in Rome was that it would be inopportune to leave the post vacant. The parallelism of his positions, of course, affected Veuillot. This time, however, Dupanloup was sitting not as a bishop but as a simple deputy. In his capacity as deputy he had denied the Vatican the gesture Veuillot wanted, and in this same capacity it would be appropriate to attack him, so reasoned the editor. Even though Dupanloup were only a deputy, Veuillot declared to his readers after this debate, "it is horrible for us, we avow it, to see implicated in the denial of justice so important a personnage, who was seated two years ago on the same day at the ecumenical council." He went on to bring up the last words of Montalembert about the "idol in the Vatican," and to repeat the words of Pius IX on 23 March 1870, when the pope had talked about Pilate having been forced by the Pharisees and the multitude (Veuillot must have misquoted the pope some way, since the Saduccees were the primarily guilty ones) to condemn Christ. Veuillot even recalled a gesture of disdain the pope had made during his discourse. He went as far as possible in turning the plea for support of the pope against Dupanloup.[142]

For a fortnight Veuillot continued along these lines, attacking particularly the deputy from the Loiret. Veuillot had always a trenchant tone, but never more than in these days. On totally different subjects he cut sharply, and arrogantly, and Dupanloup was not the only Christian he attacked. Upon the death of Mazzini Veuillot gave free rein to his least charitable side.[143] On the occasion of the exhibition of the paintings of Henri Regnault, which Veuillot, though admittedly not a qualified critic, did not like, he made pride the subject of his scathing exposition.[144] Whether the pope read any of these editorials, even those directed against Dupanloup, is questionable, but the pope had long been familiar with the general position of *L'Univers* and many of the other leaders of the French ultramontanes. He had seen the zeal of the zouaves, among other things. On 13 April 1871 the pope granted an audience to the nobles of Rome and some other distinguished visitors, during the course of which he pronounced the following words:

> There is a party which fears too much the influence of the pope. This party, however, should recognize that without humility there is no just party. – There is another party, opposed to it, which totally forgets the laws of charity; however, without charity, one cannot be truly Catholic. Therefore, to the first group I counsel humility, and to the second, charity; to all I recommend unity, concord, and peace in order that, reunited in solid and powerful phalanxes, Catholics may continue to fight in France incredulity, impiety, the desire for unjust gains, which are attempting new ravages, to the great damage of justice and truth.[145]

For Veuillot those words were a "thunderbolt."[146] They were quickly reproduced, and because they were so apt in describing the situation in France, they were widely discussed by various journals. The pope had not made any official statement, and was only speaking in an incidental way to a group of Catholics, but his words were closely studied and even treated almost as though he had issued an encyclical. Two particular conclusions may be reached about the reactions to them: little attention was given to the liberals and their lack of humility in comparison with the attention that was given to the party which "totally forgets the laws of charity"; also, none of the first group took the reproof of the pope personally, whereas Louis Veuillot took the blame of the second group on himself. Love is the greatest of Christian virtues, and to be found to lack it was to him a very serious matter. However, the pope had mentioned the group lacking in humility first, and they were the people opposing his influence. The second group was opposed to the first, and therefore at least trying to seem to be on the side of the pope. Nevertheless, the liberal Catholics produced no spokesman from their group to accept the blame either for himself or for the others, while Veuillot hastened to assume that he was the one whom the pope intended to censure.

The first words of Veuillot for the public were:

> The speech of the pope inflicts an unexpected blame on the opinion which we represent, and we are not able to hide that this blame will be considered as falling exclusively on us. The same speech blames our adversaries also, but that is not something with which we will occupy ourselves at the moment. Our adversaries will do that which they judge fitting. Our duty is to obey, and to seek by whatever means are available, for our part, to reach the accord which is recommended to us. We will do our best. We will soon see whether we will succeed. For the present, it will suffice to say that we will not make ourselves only judges of our efforts, and that we will not even consider our own judgment.
>
> We are children of obedience; our principal and our unique business is to obey. If therefore The Judge deems our work no longer able to claim the interest of the church, it will be terminated and we will disappear.[147]

These were dolorous words indeed, and Veuillot had in fact reached a depth to which he had never before descended. He had built everything on loyalty to the pope and papal approbation, and now he had been publicly censured for lacking the prime Christian virtue. The event was an *accident*, Veuillot wrote to Prosper Dugas, using the word in its Thomist sense. There was no undoing it: *Vox emissa, emissa est.* The pope, for whose infallibility Veuillot had fought to bring about recognition, had spoken. "I have not written to Rome, I will not go, I will not send anyone. The thought of retiring runs through my spirit." Despite the fact that he was down, however, he was not out. He told Dugas that he had not hated these people, for lacking charity toward whom he was censured, and he questioned whether he could tolerate doctrines which were against the influence of the pope.[148] Of course the only way to understand something is to ask questions about it, but one may wonder whether Veuillot was not in fact already quibbling over the pope's choice of words within a week of his censure. Veuillot had worked in a law office as a boy, and something of the lawyer may have been in him when he found the words of the pope as reported in *Voce della Verità* slightly more favorable to his situation.[149] A Jesuit priest in all good spirit sent Veuillot documents to prove that he could profit from the reprimand. Veuillot accepted the point with good grace, but he made an interesting rejoinder: when Peter struck Malchus with a sword, the Lord told him to put his sword back in the scabbard – but not to hand the sword over to Malchus![150] All shades of journalism soon had had something to say about the reprimand, and Veuillot had no intention of letting *Le Français* disarm him! For Louis Veuillot, Veuillot took his reproof with humility, but from a time shortly after the first sting he was able to quibble with the other journalists while accepting the blame that had been cast on him.[151]

Veuillot told Dugas that "since the *accident*, I have terribly many letters to write..."[152] To Madame Bacon de Seigneux he said: "I especially suffer from the abundance of my consolers, because I am not able to answer them all."[153] Letters poured in, and no doubt he derived much consolation from what almost amounted to a vote of confidence. The Bishop of Tulle, Msgr. Berteaud, writing to "mon bien aimé et noble Louis," stated that "a pope by the name of Gregory condemned the use of the arquebus, but he did not intend to paralyze courage or to weaken warriors."[154] Hardly was the report out on what the pope had said than Père d'Alzon, founder of the Assumptionists, wrote Veuillot, lecturing him on both charity and pride. Yes, he had been censured, but he could show the world that he was the true son of the church by his wholehearted submission.[155] Veuillot obviously accepted this advice. The legitimist Gabriel de Chaulnes wrote Veuillot the day after Père d'Alzon, saying much the same. He also pointed out the little dignity the liberal Catholic press had, and he particularly condemned the "rude" words of *Le Correspondant* in the immediate reactions of the press.[156] Gabriel de Belcastel gave him prompt praise for his submission.[157] Many parish priests wrote Veuillot of their sympathy and support. One especially significant letter began:

> We feel ourselves struck with you by the word of Him who so many times chose to encourage and bless your works. Every heart truly Catholic shares your experience. Your pen has too often consoled and avenged the defeats which brute force has inflicted on our cause for us not to recall today in what manner you have been able to fortify our faith. Profoundly attached to holy doctrines, of which you have always been the eloquent defender, I thank you for the good you have done to my soul.[158]

Such was the nature of the widespread support for Louis Veuillot.

Veuillot realized, however, that he had somehow incurred displeasure in the one place where he wanted to be approved. Quite indirectly he heard it said that Cardinal Berardi had remarked that his sarcastic line about "Adolphine" Thiers was not approved.[159] He knew, however, that somehow the pope must have heard more than criticism of a certain series of articles, and consequently that what he wrote was not automatically favored. He suffered as a result, and appropriately talked of Job when writing to Charlotte de Grammont.[160] He found his situation bitter, cruel, and embarrassing.[161] He practically withdrew from writing, which made the words of *L'Union de l'Ouest* that his "zeal had slackened," words which were copied by other journals, notably *Le Français,*[162] seem to be true. Veuillot particularly resented the editor of *Le Français,* Gustave Janicot, for Janicot hated Veuillot and obviously was taking advantage of the situation. One police agent, no friend of Veuillot, said that Janicot was jealous of Veuillot with good reason.[163] Not until mid-June did Veuillot get back into something like his usual activity, and even then he did so mostly to try to show his fidelity to the pope.[164] His embarrassment was still great, and his spirits were at a low ebb.

Veuillot wrote and received certain letters during May that made it seem he was trying to elicit some further word from the pope that might exonerate him. From April 20 through 26 July Cardinal Nardi wrote him no fewer than thirteen letters, the burden of which showed the essentially favorable disposition of the pope toward Veuillot. Father Freyd, the superior of the French seminary in Rome, saw the pope and assured Veuillot of the same thing.[165] Father Freyd pointed out that Belcastel was in Rome as a simple pilgrim, but that he was pleading for him. He also noted that Thier's influence was being exerted.[166] Despite the flood of support he received,[167] Veuillot finally resolved to do something decisive. He therefore wrote the pope himself directly, after letters to Mercurelli, Nardi, and other prelates had produced only general assurances of the esteem of the pope. The letter dated 5 May 1872 which he sent the pope was built around the question of whether he was being blamed or condemned. Freyd, Nardi, and others had given him strong assurances that he was still in favor, but Veuillot took this dolorous line. If he were condemned, he would just give up his activities, he told the pope. He emphasized that his role was to fight for all the rights of the Holy See, and he signed his letter that he prostrated himself at the feet of the pope, from whom he sought indulgence and benediction.[168]

By the sixteenth of May the pope had answered Veuillot's letter. The pope quoted Proverbs and Ecclesiastes to the effect that acceptance of reprimand was the essence of true support for the Holy See. He went on to say that he had never found anything wanting in the principles for which Veuillot had fought, but only in the "bitter zeal, foreign to the charity of the Catholic man."[169] The letter had begun and ended with words of love and benediction. However, Veuillot was not really satisfied. He received further letters of support, one of which was from Cardinal Bilio,[170] but the pope had left an important qualification in his letter of blessing. Veuillot had indeed been found wanting. As matters had stood after 13 April, Veuillot could have avoided assuming he was all by himself one of the two parties blamed. As it now was, he had endeavored to regain the sort of personal mark of favor he had received in 1853, and for his efforts he was reminded of a true principle against which he personally had offended. Veuillot was worse off now, in his own eyes, than he had been.

Did Veuillot stop at this point? No. On 27 May he wrote Msgr. Mercurelli: "In his letter of 16 May the Holy Father not only bore down his reproaches of 13 April, by recalling former counsels that he found badly obeyed, but in reality he presented me as a relapser. Thus are annulled all old and new encouragements, and my situation becomes worse than it was before."[171] He compared his situation adversely with that of 1853, and he complained of the lack of charity of his enemies. His tone was bitter, and again he used the word "condemned." Through Du Lac he heard that the reception of his letter to the pope had been "dolorous," and he thereafter wrote a letter in a similar tone to Cardinal Pitra.[172] He misrepresented the pope in making these complaints. Instead of bearing his chastisement for what it was, and continuing to fight for the same ends but with a different tone, as so many had at least hinted he ought to do, he seemed to be taking the position that he was not understood fully. He wanted the infallible pope to give him complete endorsement, not simply of his principles but with a personal and almost immediate expression of his love. Cardinal Pitra wrote him from Rome some words of encouragement, telling him to "get up and walk,"[173] but without results for Veuillot was as nearly staggered at this point as he had ever been. Finally, in January of 1874, a year and a half later, Veuillot was able to go back to Rome. Again he saw the pope's smiling face and heard himself called *Caro* Veuillot.[174] Only then did his feelings return to normal. Veuillot certainly had demonstrated his acceptance of the idea of submission. The pope had also shown that he would not automatically give a complete endorsement of Veuillot whenever the editor desired. All things considered, even by Veuillot's own admission, he appeared at his worst when confronted with papal displeasure.

During the spring and summer of 1872 Veuillot returned to his usual work with editorials that had much of the same "bitter zeal," although other Catholics did not come in for the blasts which he had delivered in the past. Despite the hint that articles on "Adolphine" were not well received in Rome, Veuillot continued to fire away at Thiers. Thiers had taken a stand for a conservative republic, but Veuillot attacked the very concept of such.[175] He scanned the whole French and European scene, but tended to keep to the themes of his favorite generalities, including of course the position of the pope. He came out very squarely for Don

Carlos, or Charles VII of Spain, as he chose to call him.[176] But even while he was trying to bury his own sadness in returning to journalism-as-usual, *L'Univers* suffered a heavy blow in the death of Du Lac.

If *L'Univers* was a "clerical" journal in the truest sense of the word, it was Melchior Du Lac who had made it so. As a cleric, he was somewhat restricted in what he could do perhaps, but had Louis Veuillot never come on the scene it is quite possible that Du Lac would have inspired the various other able laymen associated with the journal to perform in much the way that they did under Veuillot. Throughout his life Veuillot had called Du Lac "mon maître," and he was sincere. Du Lac had the same ideas Veuillot had, but he managed to keep out of direct confrontations. The strength of Veuillot's position in the eyes of his readers, and probably more importantly, his associates, lay in his close association with Du Lac. For forty-six years Du Lac had been engaged in battling for the church. When he became ill during the summer of 1872, Veuillot felt apprehension of a great loss approaching. Although Du Lac did not die until 7 August, Veuillot told Dom Guéranger he knew he was dying as early as 10 July.[177] Later in the month he likened him both to an ancient hero and also a great Christian. "The holy Church has not had in our times a firmer worker, one more disinterested, more solid, or purer. It is he who has veritably made *L'Univers*."[178] When Du Lac died Veuillot wrote one of his longest and best articles, which Dom Guéranger, who was not free with his praise for Veuillot, called a "full, true, eloquent, Christian funeral oration."[179] Even from the immediate point of view of manpower at the offices of *L'Univers*, Du Lac's loss was felt,[180] but in the long view Du Lac had made a valuable contribution to *L'Univers* in quietly complementing the more spectacular role of the layman, Louis Veuillot. As Canon Pelletier wrote to Veuillot, the death of Du Lac was going to create a real *lacune* in the staff of the journal.[181]

Despite the situation at *L'Univers*, Louis Veuillot spent the late summer and early fall of 1872, as well as the early winter, traveling and visiting. Before he took this break, he moved from his apartment on the Rue du Bac which he had so long occupied to a much grander place at 21, Rue de Grenelle. He did not give a clear reason why he made this shift after twenty-five years at 44, Rue du Bac. Perhaps he had the girls in mind, who were young ladies now. He had to pay 4500 francs, in good gold coins, quarterly for the new residence. As a young man in Rouen he had moved fifteen or twenty times in the space of a year, and ever afterwards had hated moving, so he took up temporary quarters now in Versailles while Élise had to do the work! Once she had moved all effects, Louis Veuillot found it safe to return to what was *une vielle grande maison, l'on dit même un hôtel,* with gardens, and silence. There had been a good deal of noise from the omnibus at the Rue du Bac. He put up on the walls portraits of his family, including not only Mathilde in her bridal gown, but also his father in worker's clothes. But despite this touch, he found his palatial quarters much more appropriate for the classics on his shelves.[182] He was referring to French classics, but he scarcely sounded at this point like one who had fought the sort of teaching Dupanloup had advocated.

He had hardly made the move when, after the death of Du Lac, he received invitations to go on a vacation. In late August he visited Dom Guéranger at Solesmes; then he went on to Le Pouliguen in Brittany to stay with the d'Esgrigny family. There he spent most of the month of September. He received other invitations, including one from Msgr. Peyremale of Lourdes, who called Veuillot "the first to make known and to defend Notre Dame de Lourdes."[183] Had Veuillot no other claim to fame, he might have been remembered solely for this one. Msgr. Freppel was very insistent that Veuillot come to Angers,[184] and Veuillot did visit him briefly. Freppel tried to induce Veuillot to purchase a property there, and he nearly succeeded, it would appear, because in November Veuillot was speaking of a deal he might make to buy a place for 40,000 francs.[185] However, as on other occasions, the deal was not completed. Veuillot never came to own land other than a plot in the cemetery of Montparnasse.

Veuillot had gone to the country for his health, and his sister took his health seriously, worrying about the fact that he smoked too much. At least in this one respect he may have had something in common with Napoleon III. A Doctor Sales-Girons of Compiegne had given quite a lecture in the hearing of Élise about the dangers of tobacco, and Louis was impressed with her remonstrances.[186] In a letter to Luce he assured her he had not smoked while writing![187] He wrote many letters to his family, but he also wrote to Charlotte, and while writing to her he asked about "your Netherlander," an obvious reference to Juliette Robersart.[188] It is hard to say just what these two ladies meant to Veuillot, but clearly they continued to be important to him. Letters to Juliette from this period are not available, but presumably they were similar to those to Charlotte. The pleasures he had he liked to pass on to her, and while in this area that was so to his Catholic tastes, he remembered friends with whom he could share his thoughts.

While on this recuperative visit to Le Pouliguen Veuillot was not out of touch with *L'Univers* and journalism, and he contributed a number of articles to the journal. One was the first of a series he continued after his return on the marriage of the former Père Hyacinthe, now M. Loyson.[189] He pulled no punches in this matter, and the full import of a defrocked priest going about the business of taking a wife was brought home to his reading public. He had written extensively during the summer on the whole subject of marriage,[190] so he had an ideal with which to contrast this situation, just as he seized on the marriage of Henri Rochefort, who, on the way to exile in New Caledonia, was permitted to marry a woman by whom he had had a child.[191] He also wrote on a wide range of other topics, including the plight of the Catholic church in Geneva, the role of Gambetta, and the meaning of Lourdes.[192] These articles were pretty much his standard sort of thing, though the extensive attack on Père Hyacinthe, now Monsieur Loyson, might be held up as questionable in view of the recent admonishment he had received from the pope with regard to charity.

After returning from this vacation Veuillot was back at his desk in Paris for only a relatively short time before he went on another trip, to the South this time. After stopping briefly in Lyon, where he saw Dugas and others on 18 December, he went on to Nice, where he had a most extraordinary visit. No doubt his health was the reason for this sojourn, as it had been for his summer stay in Brittany, and it is possible that Doctor Imbert, who practiced in the winter on the Côte d'Azur, was behind the move. However, what made the stay in Nice extraordinary was the circumstance that Veuillot met there Léontine Fay, Madame Volnys, the actress whom he had admired in 1831. Just how the arrangements were made cannot be said, though one of the persons in Nice about whom Veuillot talked was a Père Lavigne, who may have been connected with the lawyer for whom he worked as a boy. No doubt the visit was the work of a conspiracy of old friends. Veuillot had not seen the actress since 1831, and she now was sixty-two and white-haired. However, he told his sister, he would have recognized her. Years of militant Catholicism had not erased the impressions of the young theater critic. "Elle est *charmante*, dans mon genre," Veuillot wrote his sister on arriving in Nice.[193] After having made a reputation at an early age on the stage in Paris, she had gone to the Russian empire, where she had become a reader at the court. Despite the time she had spent living in Saint Petersburg, this rather mysterious lady was still a devout Roman Catholic, who was eager to discuss matters of communion with Louis Veuillot as soon as she had met him. François Veuillot assured his readers that Madame Volnys had "severe virtue,"[194] and it seems safe to assume that such was the case, despite her earlier profession's frivolous reputation. Veuillot now had a new friend to add to the Grammont-Robesart-Esgrigny-Testa list, and in the next years corresponded with Madame Volnys extensively.

While in Nice, or Nizza, as he enjoyed saying, staying in a house built for Englishmen to vacation in, listening to people saying "Orem*ous*" in the churches, and gazing on the wonder of macadamized streets, as well as the southern beauty,[195] he was pretty well out of affairs until his return in mid-January. During the year he had worked on new editions of some of his books and his *Mélanges,* but he does not seem to have been engaged in any work at this time. Even his poetry seems to have been neglected. Speaking in November of poets, he declared that Pegasus was still alive in the nineteenth century, but that he was "hitched to an omnibus!"[196] What Veuillot wanted to do, as always, was to go to Rome. It was cold and rainy in Nice, but it was the desire not to escape the weather, but to see the pope that motivated him. On New Year's Day he wrote his sister and daughters to this effect.[197] However, he got word from different sources that January 1873 was not a good time for such a trip. The officers of the *Orénoque* had visited the King of Italy as well as the pope at the start of the year, and the church-state crisis had become very sharp. Since the pope's words of 13 April Veuillot, as we have seen, had felt "in disgrace." He felt misunderstood. However, he thought he understood the pope. "The pope has been too much tormented on my account. It is not my fault, because I have been unjustly accused; it is not his fault at all, because I have been accused subtly."[198] He felt banished from Rome by circumstances. "I am not able to go to Rome without seeing Pius IX; and I am not able to see Pius IX without risking disagreeable things, which nothing would justify. Therefore I am banished from Rome."[199] So went the logic of Veuillot. However, the subjectivity in his line of thought here was very great, and he magnified his own problems and situation. Despite the pleasure of having his boyhood theatrical idol as a new friend, he returned to Paris not long after these expressions of frustration to take up his familiar causes. People had been gossiping about him, and he assured Charlotte that he was not *amoureux*, only distressed about his relations with the pope.[200]

During 1873 the interests of Louis Veuillot were heavily absorbed by the monarchical campaign, but of course there were other matters which on occasion occupied his attention. He met Captains de Mun and de La Tour du Pin Chambly de la Charce, who were organizing their Cercles Catholiques des Ouvriers. He was much impressed with them, though he could not resist telling Eugène that the second was indeed a man, though his name sounded like a sentence.[201] *L'Univers* over a period of time would come to raise a good deal of money for their social work. He had grief also. Early in February 1873 Arthur Murcier died at the age of 40, leaving a widow and four children. Veuillot eulogized him for the readers of *L'Univers* both for his assistance, which had included helping him with *Droit du Seigneur*, and for his Christian life.[202] He explained to *Ma très chère amie, Ma Léontine,* that Arthur was practically a son to him,[203] as indeed he was. "Mon Carthur" was much more to Louis Veuillot than most sons are to their fathers, and his death was a great loss.

Veuillot showed interest in some matters in his own special way. The trial for treason of Marshal Bazaine is a good example. In the summer of 1871, when the captives were home, the case of the Marshal had arisen. Charlotte begged Veuillot "on bended knee" not to come to the defense of the general who surrendered Metz.[204] He nevertheless later nearly met with him during July, 1873,[205] and when Veuillot saw the pope after Bazaine's conviction both spoke sympathetically of the Marshal.[206] Veuillot never was convinced that the old Foreign Legion commander and Bonapartist had been treated fairly, and he hoped that he would offer his sword to some good cause,[207] presumably that of Carlism. However, Bazaine disappointed Veuillot in this regard. But despite the diversity of Veuillot's interests, during 1873 he managed to tie most affairs quite directly to the monarchical campaign.

In March 1872 Louis Veuillot had met Comte de Monti de Rezé, the special adviser of the Comte de Chambord. He was much taken with the fine manner and appearance of this nobleman. Monti spoke to him of "his King, who more than ever is mine," Veuillot declared to Charlotte. "But, alas! by what means to hope that the Good Lord would wish to have enough pity on us to give us such a master."[208] However, despite that note of fatalism, by early 1873 Veuillot sounded hopeful, not for anything good to come out of the National Assembly, but for a restoration in spite of it. To a Belgian gentleman he wrote: "It is true that God is with the big battalion, but the big battalion is the one where Jesus Christ is. Since '89 God has worked to reassemble this battalion, to which he will give his standard. In my view it is ready."[209] Veuillot wanted to close up its ranks and move against the enemy. Chambord was his Christian king, but Veuillot would have been happy if he had had something also of the Joshua or Gideon in him.

During 1873 Frenchmen did not fight each other, but Spaniards did, one group waving the Bourbon banner and pleading the cause of the Catholic church. Naturally Veuillot could not separate the Carlists from the cause of Chambord. *L'Univers* pushed to raise money for their cause, and Veuillot did what he could with his pen.[210] Amadeo of Savoy gave up the kingship which he had so imperfectly held, and early in the year a republic with Emilio Castellar as premier was established.

Veuillot particularly trained his guns on him, since such an attack was probably easier to conduct than an advocacy of Don Carlos, a person whose private life was distasteful to the Comte de Chambord. One form that Veuillot's attack on Castellar took was to contrast him with George Washington, greatly to the favor of the latter. Although he brought in a few criticisms of an adverse sort against Washington, he pictured him mainly as a unique figure, honest, religious, aristocratic, and like a Christian king.[211] His assault on Castellar thus worked to the enhancement of Washington in the eyes of Veuillot's readers.

Following the Spanish parallel, Veuillot called Thiers the "Serrano of France."[212] He hammered away at the fusionists steadily, and singled out Dupanloup particularly for his letter to the Comte de Chambord in which he tried to get the Bourbon pretender to accept the Tricolor.[213] Louis Veuillot heard that "someone, an immense someone" was displeased with Dupanloup for just such attempts to give advice, and for Charlotte put these words in the pope's mouth: "This *Vescovo* of Orleans speaks to the bishops as though he were pope, to the pope as if he were Jesus Christ, and to Jesus Christ as if the Father Eternal were his vicar-general, and the king were his Swiss [Guardsman]."[214] True, Veuillot was writing most confidentially to a close friend who could allow for his imaginative exaggerations, but he was speaking against one of the very people the pope had in mind when he uttered his reproving words about the two parties in France. Veuillot simply did not put into practice what he had been told by the very authority he insisted was infallible.

Veuillot also attacked Falloux at this very time; régimes had come and gone, but his old enemies were still around. He especially took exception to a letter of Falloux in which the latter had spoken of "blind legitimists."[215] He published a very long article by Belcastel, who attacked the fusionist movement and the idea that Chambord should give up the white flag, and gave this ultra-legitimist leader space for several days.[216] From the point of view of social background it was curious to see two men of such different origins as Belcastel and Veuillot so close in their politico-religious efforts. They both were behind the movement for the establishment of the special status of the Church of the Sacré-Cœur and for the dedication of France to the Sacred Heart. Likewise they both were associated with the manifestations at Paray-le-Monial, where Marie Alacoque had had her vision in 1675. Belcastel had led the delegation of more than 150 deputies, and Colonel Charette of the Zouaves brought the banner this unit had carried at the Battle of Patay.[217] Chambord's cause and the cause of the Catholic church were identified as one and the same by both men, as Veuillot fought against the attempt to water down the significance of the Christian monarchy. Veuillot even quoted an English protestant to the effect that the eucharist was the basis of political order. "Liberty, equality, and fraternity were born the day the eucharist was given to the world,"[218] he declared in *L'Univers*.

While Veuillot loved generalities and such grand projects as the dedication of France to the Sacred Heart, he threw himself meanwhile into immediate political situations, although not in such a way as to choose the lesser of what appeared to him as two evils. In the spring of 1873 much attention was focused on an election in Paris for the National Assembly in which Rémusat, who as foreign minister had distressed Veuillot in 1871, and who had gone over to the brand of republicanism that Thiers represented, was opposed by a radical republican, endorsed by Gambetta, Barodet.[219] Most Parisian conservatives supported Rémusat, who was willing to play the political game with the Orleanists, and the Duc d'Aumale in particular, but the hard-core of the right-wing Bonapartists and the legitimists supported a Colonel Stoffel. Veuillot opposed both Rémusat and Barodet, throwing his support to Colonel Stoffel.[220] Barodet received over 180 thousand votes, Remusat over 135 thousand. Colonel Stoffel gained fewer than 27 thousand votes, not even the difference between the two. This election represented a trend in the country, one which Veuillot was to hate, but despite his hatred of the radical republicans he wanted nothing to do with any conservatives who had a Thiers-orientation. He wanted the true monarchy, and even a Stoffel was not exactly the kind of representative he had in mind for the National Assembly. He held off any endorsement until two days before the voting.[221] During the course of the election Veuillot employed some amusing expressions. He insisted that if Voltaire were to come back at that time, he would be a moderate republican.[222] As for Falloux in the background, he was a *quartre-vingt-neuviste* and would try to make a fusionist of Joan of Arc.[223]

Thiers made much over bringing about the liberation of the territory, but Veuillot maintained at the announcement by the German emperor that the troops were being withdrawn that he did not feel liberated with Alsace and Lorraine gone.[224] Veuillot was not exactly a man of revenge, but he was one of those who could never forget that these were French territories. In any case, Thiers gained nothing in his eyes by expediting the whole business. Despite the trend in the spring elections, the country as a whole was still monarchical, in one hue or another, and Thiers's policies lost favor. He fell by late May and was replaced by MacMahon. Veuillot was encouraged by the change. He was glad to see Thiers fall on general principles, and as yet he had not come to see the full import of MacMahon's limitations. He hoped the practical nature of the old Marshal would be sufficient, and he liked some of the things which he believed were associated with him. He felt he was the most appropriate head of state France had had for a long time. However, he saw the way the Marshal was accepting the parliamentary nature of things, and he particularly flinched at the appointment of the Duc de Broglie as the premier.[225] How much Veuillot really expected of MacMahon is hard to say, but before very long he was much disillusioned with the old soldier.

During the summer of 1873 the monarchical campaign began in earnest. Had Chambord only gone along with the politicians, he would have been put on the throne – where he might have been able to stay until his death.[226] It would seem as though the leaders of the Orleanist group were very blind in thinking he would return under their terms of compromise, but the whole country seemed confidently to expect some sort of transaction. Early in August, however, Veuillot told his readers "Henri of France remains true to himself."[227] He realized that although France was in a state of provisional government, there were no signs of a definitive arrangement. In any case, there would be no monarchical fusion.[228] Reconciliation of the cadet family to the chief of the Bourbons was what Chambord would accept, and when the appealing Comte de Paris made his trip in August to Chambord's residence at Frohsdorf in rural Austria, many thought the restoration would be the result. Veuillot was skeptical about the optimism of much of the press, and dismissed the trip with the observation: "Let us wait in silence for authentic and complete news."[229] Authentic and complete news was just what the French public did not get. Optimists and wishful thinkers heard what they wanted to, and interpretations were placed on the words of Chambord that suited the needs of the fusionist politicians, who wanted a monarchy, even if not quite the right kind.

Veuillot made much of the theme that both the people and the king wanted to end the revolution, and that the people wanted a republic under Broglie no more than under Thiers.[230] On the score of revolution, Veuillot put forth an interesting theory: the Revolution did not start in 1789; it really ended there, having been started in 1682. Its purpose was to de-Catholicize France. The nineteenth century, in his eyes, was a "century of faith" in working to undo the Revolution. Of course, he especially singled out the Vendeans in this process.[231] From the point of view of those who recognize in ideas the central force in history, Veuillot was right that the eighteenth century was a revolutionary era before 1789. He was also right in understanding that Chambord had no special desire to feel a crown on his brow, but only desired to see his concept of traditional monarchy being established. The fact that his concept of Christian monarchy was the distillation of the noblest essences of the old establishment was what the *politiques*, as Veuillot liked to describe the fusionists, did not appreciate. Veuillot told his readers that the trip of Lucien Brun and Charles Chesnelong to Frohsdorf changed nothing, and Frenchmen would have done well to heed these words. The supposedly astute Broglie attacked Chambord's stubbornness for not abdicating, but this fine nobleman did not understand Chambord as well as the peasant Veuillot did when he said that "M. le Comte de Chambord is King of France. That is his title."[233] Veuillot understood that in Chambord's mind a king does not abdicate.

Veuillot recapitulated in his career many walks of life. He was born in the country, and his ancestors were peasants. However, his father, a maker of barrels who moved to Bercy, really Paris, to do this labor, he called an *ouvrier*. He became thoroughly bourgeois in his personal pattern of life, and he had the virtues of the bourgeoisie. However, his foot was in the door of the church, and though not a cleric, his stock-in-trade was his interpretation of ecclesiastical affairs. More and more he was associated with the old nobility, and his ideals were theirs. He could take on the colors of any of these groups quite easily. However, at this era of the monarchical campaign he liked to be thought of as a peasant. He associated the peasant with Catholicism, and he defined French patriotism in Catholic terms. Bismarck was aware of all this, and he called France the "land of Véuillot," of which Veuillot was happy to remind his readers in the day of the Kulturkampf and the making of the League of the Three Emperors.[234]

While the *politiques* were reconciling the various shades of monarchists and making arrangements for the restoration, Veuillot had plenty of other concerns. During 1873 there were many large pilgrimages in France which had a political as well as a religious aspect. Many papers discussed this subject, but Veuillot was especially upset by the sort of concern that Saint-Genest of *Le Figaro* was showing in saying that these manifestations were disturbing to the public order and not conservative. Veuillot said Saint-Genest disregarded both Habakkuk and the New Testament when he deplored these pilgrimages.[235] In coming to the aid of De Mun, La Tour du Pin, and others of the Cercles catholiques d'ouvriers, he particularly cited a pilgrimage of theirs to Liesse.[236] He pushed the Carlist cause in Spain, and received special thanks from Alphonso of Bourbon whose army in Catalonia was in special need of money.[237] Not only in focusing attention on other Catholic concerns but in the general tone of *L'Univers* toward the negotiations among the monarchists Veuillot seemed to indicate that he could sense what the outcome of the whole affair would be. Certainly the readers of *L'Univers* were not led into thinking that some happy compromise would be reached. Veuillot's only inconsistency would seem to have been in taking *L'Ordre* to task for spelling "Roy" in sarcasm,[238] when, in fact, he himself had spelled the pretender's name "Henry" only recently.

The flag question loomed as importantly to Veuillot as to anyone. "The last memory of the white flag," he declared, "is the conquest of Algeria, and the last memories of the tricolor are Sedan and its consequences."[239] He went to some lengths early in October to cite various letters of Chambord to show that he would never give up his banner,[240] and he flatly predicted that Chambord's answer to the whole proposition of returning with the tricolor would be unacceptable to those who provoked it.[241] "Some old Huguenots, faithful to Henri IV, said, to excuse his abjuration, 'Paris is well worth a mass.' Henri V is visited by politicians who tell him that Paris is well worth an engagement with the Revolution."[242] When the Comte de Chambord wrote Eugène Veuillot at the death of Louis that his brother was the only person who really understood him,[243] he was very correct.

On 27 October 1873 the Comte de Chambord wrote a letter from Salzburg to Charles Chesnelong clearly stating that his person was nothing but his principle was everything and that he would never relinquish the lily banner.[244] Veuillot told his readers quite calmly I-told-you-so. "Our skillful *politiques* have brought about results which surprise no one, except themselves. The king has always expressed himself very clearly and very nobly, but they did not understand. They wanted to *make* the monarchy, not according to the needs of the country and the honor of the prince, but according to their views. . . .He refused them, and their plans are upset."[245] Even as great changes were quickly being made by the same men who were thwarted by Henry V, Veuillot proceeded to give something of a lesson in history to his readers. He went into the background of the pretender's training, identifying his ideas with the religious orientation of the white flag.[246] Alexandre de Saint-Albin, once a supporter of Falloux, but now in Veuillot's camp, at that time had just prepared a lengthy study on the Comte de Chambord.[247] He promptly wrote Veuillot in praise of his understanding of the pretender.[248] One might almost say that Louis Veuillot understood Chambord better than he did the pope, which would be ironic, since His Most Christian Majesty existed in the eyes of Veuillot only to defend Christianity and its leader, the pope.

During the month of November the National Assembly busied itself with making the strongest provisional measures possible. It established

Marshal MacMahon as president for seven years, many of the deputies hoping that he would keep the throne warm for the king, and that the Comte de Chambord would die, facilitating the establishment of the Comte de Paris on the throne. Veuillot was well enough satisfied with MacMahon for such a provisional chief of state, but he had fears for the church. He was especially afraid of that arch-liberal Catholic, the Duc de Broglie. The prime concern of a king of France should be to protect the pope, and he saw little hope for that approach now. One of his subtler articles was about the Duc de Broglie, who, Veuillot said, was ruling while MacMahon was reigning.[249] Eventually Veuillot came to have more doubts about MacMahon, and spoke of the arrangement of November being perhaps a *MacMahonnat* rather than a *septennat*, but to begin with Broglie was his chief concern after the white-flag letter from Salzburg.

The failure of the monarchist campaign marks a turning point in the career of Louis Veuillot, as it did in the careers of many other public figures. During the first two and a half years of the existence of the National Assembly *L'Univers* had been, as usual, in the extremist category, but it was on the extreme of what might well have been the future mainstream of French politics. Had Chambord been restored, *L'Univers* would have become perhaps the official organ of the king! Of course the republican, secular trend had set in as early as the summer of 1871, and by the spring of 1873 the trend seemed clearly away from the Christian monarchy. Until 1873 the police had not looked upon the monarchists as potential enemies of the state, since they appeared to be potential inheritors. After 1873 the legitimists were increasingly viewed as troublemakers, particularly when they were strongly clerical. Louis Veuillot naturally fell in this category. His attacks on Thiers and on the Princes of Orleans in 1872 had been noted by the police.[250] One agent had believed Veuillot to be trying to bring about a clash with the radical republicans in order to force the hand of the monarchist Commission of Thirty to act in a strictly legitimist fashion.[251] In any case the Christian monarchy had not been established in 1873, and in clinging to this lost cause Veuillot was again becoming an object of police surveillance. During the 1870's Catholic-legitimist militancy of a conspiratorial and potentially violent sort developed, but close scrutiny shows that Veuillot had no hand at all in the projects of men like Charette to strike at the republic with force.[252] With the decline of royalist hopes he appeared, as did the Comte de Chambord himself, more than ever a Catholic-before-all.

CHAPTER X

DECLINING YEARS AND LEGACY

Following the voting of the *Septennat* Louis Veuillot was very discouraged. He believed the majority of legitimists had become Orleanists and had abandoned the Christian monarchy as he and the Comte de Chambord had conceived of it. He wanted to go to the countryside and get away from it all. He feared that Broglie would take reprisals against the die-hard legitimists – and events proved that he was right. What he finally decided, he told one of his friends, was that "it is necessary for me to see Rome in the condition that it is in under Victor Emmanuel."[1] Shortly afterwards he also wrote Madame Volnys about the perfume of some violets she had sent him and that he hoped to see her, though his plans were to go directly to Rome first.[2] Together with a young secretary named Paul Lapeyre who had recently come into his employ and to whom Veuillot increasingly dictated his writings, he left 5 December 1873 for Rome. Veuillot dictated each morning his impressions to Lapeyre, who added a few notes of his own, with the result that one can see in detail what Veuillot did and thought on his trip to Rome.[3]

Travel was ever improving, and Veuillot had little to say about it any more except to indicate the general route, which this time was through the tunnel at Mount Cenis. His first visit was to Geneva and nearby Ferney, where Msgr. Mermillod had to live, having been banished from his diocese. Here was Louis Veuillot in the land of Calvin, and still worse, Voltaire! Msgr. Mermillod ironically lived in the house that had been the residence of Voltaire's friend, Madame Denis. Mermillod had converted one of the rooms into an oratory, and Veuillot wanted to look in the works of Voltaire to see if he could find whether that room had been occupied by Diderot, La Harpe, or d'Alembert. He admitted that Voltaire's chateau was "magnificent." He found the churches of Geneva interesting, and especially was struck with the "unique Temple," the temple of the freemasons which had been bought by Catholics to replace a church confiscated by the protestants. He thought that the Church of Saint Peter, seized by the protestants, was the only "monument" in the city, though he described the Catholic cathedral as *belle*. He noted gossip about "the infamous and ridiculous" Loyson, who was conducting services in a room of a library in Geneva. Mermillod, he concluded, was the "only Genevan who does honor to Geneva and loves his land."

Veuillot, while casting scorn on the words of the French minister of public works, Victor Lefranc, who had hailed the tunnel as a symbol of Franco-Italian friendship, noted a few things about the project. Only two years old, it now needed repairs. He admitted, though, that there were no jolts or terrors, or even disquietudes, and that in thirty minutes the train took one at a trot through the eight or so miles. To what end? It was as dismal on one end as the other. Soon he came to Turin. What statues! But among other things he was amused by the representation of Cavour. "He is beginning to lose his glasses, and he is in a toga," Veuillot noted. His route carried him through Bologna and Florence. His entry into Rome was sad, and he thought of Gibbon and his slurs about Rome in the hands of the church. He saw various personnages, including Maguelonne and Msgr. Mercurelli, and even caught an initial glimpse of the pope. He dined with Msgr. Bastide, and picked up the story that Jews were forming associations to buy ecclesiastical property. He met General Kantzler, who commanded papal forces in the tradition of Charette, and he visited principal sights, including Saint Peter's, before the audience came. What better way to face a changing situation in France than to have the blessing of the pope?

One circumstance had no doubt added a touch of sadness for Veuillot on arriving in Rome, beside the loss of papal sovereignty: his friend Féburier, who together with his wife Élisabeth had by example inspired Veuillot to become an active Christian while he stayed with them in Rome in 1838, had died shortly before his trip. Veuillot had been perhaps more lastingly influenced by them than anyone else in his life, and his subsequent article on Féburier's life was one of the most sincere pieces Veuillot ever wrote.[5] However, he had some pleasant experiences on the way back. He had a good visit in Florence, where he saw many works of art, and he made it to Nice for Christmas. In Nice of course he saw Madame Volnys again. Unfortunately, his host, Pére Lavigne was not well, nor was Madame Volnys,[6] but despite the shortness of his visit there, he had something to talk about in the letters that followed. He seemed still to be vexed over the fact that only iron pens, not real *plumes*, were to be found anywhere these days.

Reaching Paris in time for the start of 1874, Veuillot immediately entered into one of the most fiery of all his journalistic battles. Apparently he must have felt fully absolved and fully in the good graces of the pope. Apparently also he was no longer much troubled about the need to be charitable toward other Christians, because he certainly did not turn the other cheek to his old enemy Dupanloup. True, Dupanloup seemed to show himself even less interested in being charitable than Veuillot. The good words of the pope of 13 April 1872 apparently had little influence on either of these Christian leaders at the start of 1874. The immediate flare-up was occasioned by a memorial service held in Orleans for soldiers who had been killed in the war. Flags and various escutcheons had been placed on the walls of the cathedral for the occasion, but for some reason the committee decided not to put up Charette's, perhaps because the Sacred Heart was superimposed on it. The old battle of the ultramontanes and Gallicans was thereupon joined again. Some journal other than *L'Univers* started the expression the "scandal of Orleans" referring to this exclusion of the standard of the zouaves. *L'Univers*, of course, joined in the melée, but Louis Veuillot at first had nothing to do with it all, since he was in Rome. Dupanloup, however, took up his pen and directed a letter to Veuillot, accusing him of outraging good Catholics with *un profond rafinement d'injures* and of ruining the efforts to bring about a monarchical restoration.[7] Dupanloup himself was not in Orleans during the episode in question, but the staff of *L'Univers* saw Dupanloup behind it all. Veuillot, of course, had left no orders to observe forbearance in case of attack, but Dupanloup went about as far as he could to provoke Veuillot to retaliate.

Veuillot's main answer to this attack was to re-introduce the matter of the inscription of La Roche-en-Brény. The Bordeaux edition of *L'Univers* of 5 March 1871 had brought to light the episode of 1862 when Dupanloup, Falloux, Cochin, Montalembert, and the absent Broglie had dedicated themselves to a free church in a free state. Dupanloup, in celebrating mass in this connection, had made himself the central figure in an act that was really enshrining words of Cavour. The absent Broglie (present in spirit, according to the inscription), however, was now principal minister under MacMahon in 1874, and likewise a principal target of articles that Veuillot wrote on 2 and 13 January 1874. The greatest excitement was stirred up by these articles. It was hardly by chance that Veuillot chose this time for the publishing of these editorials.

At the time Veuillot departed for Rome the police already had been watching him.[8] Many of his articles were already in their files. The authorities noted that some of the hostile press had thought he was up to something. They noted that the Rome correspondent of *Le Temps* wrote the very day Veuillot was having his papal audience: "He has the mental condition of Peter the Hermit. – He would like to have a crusade in forty-eight hours. – The name of M. de Broglie excites him in the highest degree."[9] He was suspected of trying to stir up trouble against the cabinet when he was in Rome, and on his return he was not long in making good on the suspicion. At the conclusion of his 2 January 1874 article, after taking a good swipe at Dupanloup for his attempt to develop the conciliar movement against the pope, and also blasting Falloux, Veuillot wrote:

> There remains M. Albert de Broglie, who has become vice-president of the council of ministers and second personage in France at the moment. What he thinks today of a free church in a free state we do not know; but we know what ambassadors, by his will, represent France in Italy and Switzerland, lands where the state is free and the church is in prison.
>
> The hour when M. le Duc de Broglie governs France will be that of the most cruel anguish in history for the papacy, not simply beaten, but abandoned by France.[10]

These were very menancing words, but he went just as far on 13 January when he spoke of "this canonization of the maxim of M. Cavour," firing again at the Bishop of Orleans, the chief of the cabinet, and the deceased Montalembert.[11] By this time the press had published Dupanloup's letter to Veuillot,[12] and many had joined the fray. Dom Guéranger congratulated Veuillot as early as 3 January for taking such a stand against "this sect."[13] The key man in the sect, however, had been able to reform the ministry, and he had power to deal with Veuillot. He wanted only a good pretext to act, and that pretext promptly presented itself, with none other than Bismarck, the German chancellor obliging.

In Germany the Kulturkampf was raging. Moreover, the German ambassador in Paris, Count von Arnim, had been playing monarchical politics, and Bismarck was determined to have none of that. For his purposes a republican France, which would be anticlerical, and in Bismarck's judgment weaker, would be much better. It would also be easier for Germany, a monarchy, to have an alliance with Russia and Austria-Hungary if France could be held up as a danger to the monarchical principle.[14] France as the "land of Veuillot" was to be thwarted. Accordingly, Bismarck went into a towering rage for the benefit of the French ambassador, Gontaut-Biron. He thundered about the French clergy and "their allies," especially *L'Univers*. Gontaut-Biron informed the Duc Decazes, the foreign minister: "I told him that *L'Univers* was a journal of little influence, one which only represented the French episcopate. . . ." He went on to minimize the influence of the French bishops, saying they were "innocuous, like the Comte de

Chambord." He admitted he did not convince Bismarck.[15] Bismarck made a speech to the Reichstag on 16 January about the dangers of South Germans joining a pontifical legion under Henry V,[16] and fully exploited the situation. Broglie, of course, was not pro-German, but relations had certainly become better with Germany, and he was anxious to avoid trouble. To give satisfaction to Bismarck in such a matter would be to kill two birds with one stone. Accordingly, on 19 January 1874 the government suspended *L'Univers* for two months. The reason for this "arbitrary ukase" (to use Eugène's words at the reappearance of *L'Univers*) was that the number of 19 January 1874 contained articles and documents making it of such nature "as to create diplomatic complications."[17]

The articles in question, like many pieces that Veuillot had written in the past, were insulting to Germany, but Veuillot had no monopoly on that sort of thing. There was only one document involved, and as Belcastel pointed out to Broglie, it really was little other than a pastoral of the Bishop of Périgueux promulgating a papal encyclical.[18] Veuillot was right when he told everyone that the Broglie-Dupanloup-Falloux team had used Bismarck as an excuse to strike at him for beginning his attack on the "free-church-in-a-free-state" movement. To Maguelonne in Rome Veuillot wrote: "Prussia has not demanded my head rather than some other. It has been offered for the satisfaction of La Roche-en-Brény church. Arnim has said to Decazes: 'Assuredly we are glad to be rid of M. Veuillot, but we would like to have greater satisfaction for ourselves.' I conjecture that the true motive of M. de Broglie has been to assure the silence of *L'Univers* for the evil blow that is being prepared for Rome. I would be surprised if the thing did not take place before 20 March."[19] To a priest Veuillot wrote: "The famous inscription [of La Roche-en-Brény] that I have made known is the true *document* which has brought about this diplomatic complication, and the goal is silence during the *coup de nuit* which they are trying to carry off against Rome."[20] Veuillot was at least partly right about Bismarck; the Germans were probably at least as concerned about the bishops as they were about his journal, though he may have been underestimating Bismarck's concern about the forces he himself influenced. As for a coup of some sort, he may have had in mind the worsened relations between Italy and France that threatened to bring about the recall of the *Orénoque.* As it happened the *Orénoque* was not recalled until the fall of 1874, when it was replaced by another vessel for the same purpose of standing ready to be of service to an escaping pope.

As soon as the suspension was announced Decazes telegraphed

Gontaut-Biron about it, exclaiming, "What more manifest proof of the correctness of our intention!"[21] He further said to his ambassador in Berlin, "We will not hesitate to employ means under the laws to satisfy the preoccupations of the German government." He said that the measure already taken had been voluntary, and that he wanted to calm spirits in Berlin.[22] Despite various observations about Bismarck, Gontaut-Biron reported that the chancellor was "very satisfied" with what had been done.[23] Whatever the motivation of Broglie, and whatever the weight Bismarck gave to *L'Univers* and Veuillot, the episode had the effect of improving the relations of the two régimes, which, of course, was not something Veuillot wanted to do.

Had the suspension been longer than the customary two months, Veuillot might have done something special with the time. One of his correspondents suggested that he go to Frohsdorf – after all he had just been to Rome, and the closeness of Chambord's stand with Veuillot's position would indeed seem to suggest that the two should concert together closely. Veuillot, however, did not believe anything would be gained by such a trip. He said that he would really like to catch up on his sleep, or better still, to finish his long poem, *Cara*, which he had begun years earlier, and which he never finished.[24] As it was, Veuillot mostly wrote and received letters about his situation. First and foremost among the letters Veuillot wrote was a simple statement of what had happened that was addressed to the pope. However, the emphasis here was different. Veuillot said that Bismarck demanded the suspension, and that the government had not blamed any individual for transgression of laws. He said nothing about the liberal Catholics being out to get him. He stated that beginning 20 March 1874 *L'Univers* would again consecrate itself to the "defense" of the Holy See. "Humbly prostrated at the feet of Your Holiness, my colleagues and I implore the Apostolic benediction," Veuillot closed his letter.[25] The pope himself had called the French liberal Catholics a "veritable curse" in June of 1871,[26] and there was no need to say any more about them, particularly after what he had said in December 1873. As for the "defense" of the Holy See, Veuillot certainly subscribed to the theory that the best defense is an offense. The letter produced the desired results. Within three weeks the busy and harried pope, whose very existence in Rome was in question, addressed a letter of commiseration and benediction to Veuillot. This time there was no reservation in his praise for the editor and his journal.[27] The pope completely satisfied him this time.

Veuillot received all sorts of condolences and encouragements. He busied himself collecting money for the Carlists, and one of the most sincere of the condolences was from a Carlist officer.[28] He received money from priests for the Church of the Sacré Cœur.[29] On 14 February 1874 he heard the Comte de Mun speak for the first time, and immediately wrote to him words of praise and encouragement. He became dramatic about frustrations and declared his admiration for the dragon who had the right to die fighting![30] For the most part he hammered away at the theme of the "sect of La Roche-en-Brény." To bishops, priests, and others he insisted that the blow really did not come so much from Bismarck as from this group. He told Msgr. Mercurelli: "The instances of Prussia are a pretext. Bismarck did not demand this sacrifice; it was offered to him." He went on: "M. de Broglie, Msgr. Dupanloup, and M. de Falloux are the three survivors of the heretical pact of La Roche-en-Brény where the free church in the free state was sworn."[31] Cardinal Pitra offered *L'Univers* money, but Veuillot told him to keep it, since he believed the journal would not be hurt by the suspension.[32] In general, Veuillot was indeed little discouraged by this suppression, and he insisted on his hopeful attitude in writing to Père d'Alzon. Speaking of the great things that were to be done, he exclaimed: "Long live God, long live the pope, long live France! And I add: Long live hope!" He told the founder of the Assumptionists that he had only been using his rights as a citizen, and he closed saying: "All will go well, and we will carry on the struggle by the grace of Our Lord and King Jesus, who has not ceased to love the Franks."[33]

During the suspension the police kept an eye on Veuillot. Some of his letters got out and were published in other journals. *Paris Journal* published one he addressed to priests at Servières,[34] and *L'Assemblée Nationale* printed an exchange between him and the legitimist General Cathelineau.[35] But despite surveillance and a collection of clippings about him, they were able to suspect no more by early summer than that he was going to write a pamphlet.[36] Veuillot was no conspirator; he wanted to make all clear in *L'Univers*. In due course, 19 March 1874, St. Joseph's Day, the suspension was off, and Veuillot plunged back into the fray, not the least tempered by two months of idleness. In fact, he picked up exactly where he had left off in January.

He began by "saluting the discretionary power of M. de Broglie," as well as giving thanks to Saint Peter. Practically speaking, he denied the validity of the charges made against *L'Univers.*[37] If ever a journal and editor recovered after a blow by a régime, *L'Univers* and Louis Veuillot did in March 1874. His defiance of the same régime that suspended the journal was remarkable, and he seemed to be courting another blow, which, to be sure did come later in the year. "It has always appeared to us that *L'Univers* was destined to die a violent death, not that it seeks such an end, but because it truly has many enemies." Louis Philippe had struck *L'Univers* with "judicial hypocrisy," Napoleon III with "authoritarian hypocrisy," and the commune had driven it "into the catacombs" with logical hypocrisy," but the action of Broglie, "without warning, reason, pretext, or responsibility" was beyond description, Veuillot told his readers shortly after the journal reappeared.[38]

As for the matter of the inscription at La Roche-en-Brény, suspended along with *L'Univers*, this polemic was revived with additional force. During the suspension, the future biographer of Dupanloup, the Abbé Lagrange, vicar-general of Orleans, took up the cause of Dupanloup in the columns of *Le Correspondant*. Afterwards Veuillot attacked the concept of the free church in the free state from every angle that he could. A response from Lagrange, of course, brought more from Veuillot. Veuillot got in the last words in an article at the end of May entitled "Un Dernier Mot," in which he played games with the original Latin used by the pretentious liberals in their marble inscription.[39] For him this battle cry of the enemy, the liberal Catholics, was to be fought with every weapon, even including such knowledge of Latin as he had.

Veuillot had the satisfaction of seeing the Broglie cabinet fall shortly after the reappearance of *L'Univers*,[40] but the victory was a hollow one, because the Goulard cabinet was neither significantly different, nor inclined to treat *L'Univers* with much greater tolerance. His editorials in the summer of 1874 continued to set forth the same political principles he had enunciated in 1873, but the situation of Henry V was rapidly becoming hopeless. Indeed, one of Veuillot's articles was entitled, albeit sarcastically, "Henri V Impossible,"[41] *L'Union*, the principal royalist journal, was suspended in early July, and it is rather surprising that in the wake of a manifesto by the Comte de Chambord *L'Univers* was not struck by the same measure. *L'Univers* defended *L'Union* stoutly on this occasion,[42] but Veuillot missed a second suspension this time, probably because the line of *L'Univers* at this time was more general in nature than at its suspension.

On the reappearance of *L'Univers* Veuillot had repeated the words of Chambord, "La parole est à la France, l'Heure est à Dieu," adding bitterly, "Mais la France semble n'avoir plus de parole et Dieu n'avoir plus l'heure."[43] Veuillot had not given up on France, but some of his special attention for the battle between Catholicism and the secular forces of the world was devoted to Spain in this era. Spain had always attracted a larger part of his attention than that of most other Frenchmen concerned about affairs of Europe, but 1874 was critical for the cause of Carlism. He saw the Spain of the Cid fighting against forces using the "canons of Krupp."[44] By May he could see, with the defeat by Marshal Concha of the Carlist army besieging Bilbao, that the cause was nearly desperate.[45] The Carlists held on for some time, but by the end of the year Isabella II's son, Alphonso XII was able to return and to consolidate the Spanish government under him. De facto, Marshal Serrano, who had replaced Castellar as the real leader in Spain, had things under control by September, and measures were even being taken for the exchange of ambassadors between the two countries. Veuillot exploded at this point. "Spain, great Spain, formerly people of Christ, today officially people of Serrano!" Of course he was bringing someone to the throne, and this was "Monsieur Alphonse," as Veuillot called the future Alphonso XII.[46] Not surprisingly the representative of Serrano in Paris protested to the government of MacMahon. Not only this, but two young Spaniards arrived the next day to challenge the aging editor to a duel! The honor of their king was at issue. Veuillot did not merely call the police or tell them to go away, but took pains to point out that they were not the ones who should be making the challenge, that Serrano in any case ought to content himself with the vengeance he had already had, and that they, in effect, had already discharged whatever chivalrous duty they had in pointing out to him that they thought he should be challenged to a duel. In the face of these arguments they withdrew.[47] Rumors of this episode got about however, and the police took note of it.[48] The ministry of the interior acted quickly, and this time *L'Univers* was suspended for two weeks, until 23 September 1874. The publication of insults to an "established government" constituted the basis of the suspension. Veuillot doubted that Serrano had received as many testimonies of sympathy in the matter as he had. Many of the subscribers of *L'Univers* wrote Veuillot at this time, and he regretted that because of his poor health he was unable to answer them.[49] He probably enjoyed this type of martyrdom. The very suspensions of *L'Univers* no doubt enhanced its stature in the eyes of many.

At about this time, Marshal Bazaine, whose death penalty had been cut to twenty years imprisonment by MacMahon, escaped from the country. Veuillot wrote to congratulate him on his escape, but he also told him he wanted to see him go to Spain to fight the good fight.[50] One, of course, might question whether the man who handed Metz over to the Germans would have done the Carlists any more good, but Veuillot must have had some reason to think Bazaine might have the will for such a war. He was wrong, however. Veuillot was generous toward Bazaine, but he was less than generous with regard to Guizot, who died just as the journal reappeared on 23 September. Throughout his life Veuillot had been interested in what Guizot was doing and writing, and had often sent him copies of pieces he had written. He never forgot Guizot's patronage during the forties, despite their differences of opinion about laws on education and other matters. He must have cared what Guizot thought about him. Guizot was always considerate of Veuillot and polite to his former protégé. Veuillot in turn had high esteem for Guizot, except for the fundamental matter of his protestant outlook. The two could make common cause against secularism, and indeed such was their bond and the bond that Veuillot had with other protestants on occasion. One of the longest obituaries Veuillot ever wrote, if not absolutely the longest, was understandably the obituary of Guizot.[51] Veuillot gave him credit for "superb gifts," having been especially impressed with him as a speaker and a writer. "Personally M. Guizot had the most attractive qualities." But he lacked two things, "two essential forces": "These two forces are the force to dare to do good, and the force to abstain from evil." As a public figure he did not equal the private man. Veuillot resented the way in which Guizot identified himself with the bourgeoisie, almost as though he had created it. Most strikingly he declared that "neither in religion nor in politics did M. Guizot have what might be called an idea." He summed up Guizot as a sterile product of protestant liberalism. Despite his talents, despite his skill in amassing information and in presenting it, Guizot offered, Veuillot thought, a certain emptiness. Obviously Guizot had had an influence on Veuillot, and Veuillot had been at times preoccupied with him almost as much as he was with Montalembert, but at the time of Guizot's death, whatever personal sympathies he had always felt for him, Veuillot could not resist sternly telling his readers the specific ways in which the great protestant leader presented an example of talents wasted on a wrong foundation. However, it is hard to see how he could have been more generous to Bazaine than to Guizot. In some way Bazaine had become a symbol of a soldier abused by the régime in power, and a police agent reported that "in legitimist circles people are astounded at the persistence of M. Louis Veuillot in supporting Marshal Bazaine. . . ."[52] Veuillot's attitudes toward these entirely different men give something of a hint of his outlook on life.

Just before the suspension of the journal for the second time a woman of Veuillot's acquaintance entered a convent, and Veuillot wrote almost as much on this event as he did on the life and false premises of Guizot. The woman, however, was Élisabeth Féburier, who with her late husband had had such decisive influence on him in 1838. She had long been a supporter of convents, and now she chose to enter the order of the Little Sisters of the Poor, an order to which Veuillot gave the highest tribute.[53] Throughout his life, at least since 1838, monastic idealism had seemed the highest to him, and when this ideal of a Christian wife took the veil, Veuillot wrote with a positive ardor that equaled even the ardor of his assaults on Dupanloup, Broglie, and all those whom he found wanting. Moreover, it was not only because of the inspiration of Élisabeth Féburier that he was so specially interested in religious orders at this time, but also because of his own daughter Luce, who had decided to become a Visatandine.

Apparently Luce had first made up her mind to enter a convent during 1873, but had been persuaded by her father to wait a year.[54] Enemies like Henri Rochefort tried to spread the idea that the wicked Veuillot had forced his daughter to take the veil,[55] but such, of course, was not the case. He told Madame Bacon de Seigneux in terms that sound somewhat exaggerated of the virtues of Luce, but when he declared that with her departure joy had fled his life, and that his "heart was cruelly torn" he sounded thoroughly sincere. "Nature is created to obey," he declared. *Fiat voluntas tua.*[56] He wrote to Msgr. Mercurelli as though God were demanding too much of him, and he asked that he request the pope to bless his daughter's entry into the convent – and also request a benediction for a former servant-girl who was entering another community.[57] Luce was expecting to enter on 25 March 1874, Annunication Day, but she was delayed a couple of days. Writing to Madame Volnys's son-in-law, Alexis Fay, Veuillot described the scene accompanying her actual departure, an affecting scene complete with her kissing the windowsill of her room and the door of the house. She kissed the servants and her father a final time. "A thousand nothings become solemn when they are done for the last time. . . ." I will see her again, but I will kiss her no more. She is no longer my daughter. The grill is between her and me." Veuillot played on the words of Rousseau, of all people, when he wrote Dom Guéranger. In the saying *L'animal qui pense est un animal dépravé* Veuillot made the last word *décavé,* which seemed to him to describe his "horrible and irreparable loss."[58] Allowing for a number of things, Veuillot was sad about Luce's taking the veil, though certainly it must also have been a satisfaction. Perhaps he felt he *had* been responsible for her taking the veil, but if so he must have had a certain satisfaction in that also.

The touching scene was perhaps a bit premature, for Luce did not finally take the habit of a Visitandine until 21 December 1874. Her father, although then in bad health, went to see her do this in the Visitandine chapel in Paris.[59] He already of course was addressing her "Sœur Marie-Luce" and signing his name "Ton Ancien Père," but while writing her he called her "Lulu."[60] Luce's departure seems to have driven the father closer to his elder daughter Agnès, because the two went on an extended trip in the late spring together. They first went to

Touraine, returned to Paris, and then spent considerable time in Brittany. Obviously *L'Univers* ran itself meanwhile without the presence of Louis Veuillot. Louis spent many hours at the Convent of the Little Sisters of the Poor, of which order Élisabeth Féburier was a member.[61] Going into a convent may have seemed like a major break to Veuillot, but in a way those of his circle who had entered religious orders were not removed from him in the way in which they would have been for many.

Having "lost" Luce to the Visitandines, Veuillot next lost Agnès by marriage. Again the loss must have been one that was very satisfactory. Suppose that Agnès had married a free-thinker! She made a good marriage, on the contrary, to a devout army officer, Commandant Pierron. Veuillot knew his new son-in-law well. He had introduced him to Prosper Dugas as "loyal as a blessed sword" as early as March 1873. He had further called this able battalion commander a "priest of the sword," and added that "All his *ideas* are ours." Commandant Pierron had written some well-regarded articles in *L'Univers* about army reorganization under the signature of "Officier Supérieur."[62] Louis Veuillot could scarcely have found a better son-in-law, or so at least he made it appear, if he had gone looking for one himself. In fact he may well have been the matchmaker, though this can scarcely be documented. Just when the plans for the marriage were made also cannot be said, or whether father and daughter were aware of this approaching event when they took their trip. As soon as Pierron asked for the hand of Agnès, François tells us, he received "cordial felicitations." The marriage was held on 3 December 1874 at the Chapel of the Nunciature, where it happened that Msgr. Meglia took the spotlight off the bridal couple to pay hommage to Louis Veuillot.[63] The newly-weds, however, must not have minded, and probably expected such a situation. Veuillot sent most cordial letters to them to Clermont-Ferrand, where the Commandant was stationed, and they seem to have been sending him gifts, rather than the other way around, for he mentions cheese and other products of Auvergne reaching him.[64] Pierron lived until 1907, became a member of the Conseil Supérieur de la Guerre, and was designated for command of an army in case of mobilization.[65] Veuillot had every reason to be satisfied. If his public life was stormy, his domestic affairs were the opposite.

The celebration of Agnès' marriage was quiet largely because of the health of Louis Veuillot. Since Élise had been able to be hostess for cardinals in Rome, presumably she could have staged an elaborate wedding for her niece, whom she had raised almost as her daughter. However, on 15 October 1874, while working on revisions of his *Vie de*

Jesus-Christ in his study at home on the Rue de Varennes, Louis had suffered what François called an *attaque*. He had been under some pressure to complete this work, and it is interesting to note that in his published correspondence there is a gap between 17 September and 26 November. Perhaps he was already ailing when the attack, or stroke, occurred. François, who of course was not a witness, says that his body was not paralyzed, nor was his mind clouded at the time. His confessor was called, and, according to the family tradition, told Agnès the next day that her father was a saint.[66] Louis Veuillot no doubt seemed saintly under such conditions, but when in sound body impressed some as being more apt to wield "the crucifix like a club," to use the words of Hanotaux.[67] He slowly recovered, but it is apparent that he was thereafter a man of impaired health. He had driven himself hard, smoked and perhaps eaten too much, and been in the midst of one fray after another for decades. Now he sounded like an invalid when he wrote to Madame Volnys, who seems to have taken the lead away from Charlotte as his favorite correspondent by this time.[68] He wrote almost no one else during the rest of 1874. The wedding of Agnès and the final vows of Luce kept him in Paris until nearly Christmas. Then he went, through Bordeaux, in company with his sister to the seaside at Arcachon, where he stayed about a month. He eventually recovered enough to get back into his old routine, or something like it, and to get into some bitter engagements. Nevertheless, he gave "the impression of progressive enfeeblement" from this time onward. In the spring of 1875 Élise noted that while the stiffness he had exhibited in one of his legs seemed better, his speech became "more defective."[69] Veuillot had always done quite a bit of complaining about his health, but his complaints of lumbago seem to have reached a crescendo at this period, along with a "nervous condition."[70] Clearly he was never to be his old self again, but he swung back into his old battles anyway.

While still on his recuperative vacation at the start of the year Veuillot wrote a few articles, mostly about Spanish affairs.[71] It was while he was on the coast that Dom Guéranger died, leaving a great gap in the ranks of the ultramontanes. The very fact that Veuillot wrote no long article on Dom Guéranger on this occasion was indicative of his own condition, because he unquestionably felt this loss as a major blow. Increasingly Veuillot was to see big men, on his side and on other sides of his battles, pass away. However, he had plenty of petty but significant matters with which to be occupied. It was nothing new to become embroiled with *Le Figaro*, but this *boulevardiste* journal added a new wrinkle when it offered reduced rates for clergymen and claimed 4200 among its subscribers. The battle between the two journals became very sharp and extended,[72] and, to be sure, since this blow was a hard one for *L'Univers*, Veuillot wrote most of the key articles himself. Msgr. Freppel, claiming that he was not intervening, wrote a letter to Villemessant of *Le Figaro* in which he said not one of those 4200 was in his diocese, practically questioning the figures themselves.[73] Various other ecclesiastics wrote of their support to Veuillot, who blasted any clerics who read such a sheet. One supporter wrote: "Permit a little vicar to take the liberty to express his thanks to you and to speak of his satisfaction with the polemic undertaken against *Le Figaro* and its *troupeau* of subscribing ecclesiastics."[74] No doubt Louis Veuillot increased his stature, at least with the hard core of his followers, by the strength of his responses to that journal which tried a new trick.

Veuillot had always hated the enemies of Sunday repose, but even here another new wrinkle was injected. A hat shop for ladies on the Rue Bonaparte, not far from the offices of *L'Univers* (10 Rue des Saints Pères), put up a sign on a Sunday in March 1875, that it was *fermé pour cause de réparations.* Closed on Sunday for repairs! *L'Univers* could not let this slap pass, and Veuillot made the attack on this insinuation his own. The hostile press, not surprisingly, took up the cause of the merchant, M. Valentin, whose store was known as "À la Mère de Famille." Emboldened by such support, and no doubt desiring to gain cash from the situation, M. Valentin sued *L'Univers* for 20,000 francs.[75] The case went to court in April, and Veuillot retained Me Oscar Vallée, a Bonapartist, to represent him. According to *Le National*, the crowd interrupted him while he quoted Falloux and Montalembert in defending Veuillot's cause.[76] A police report said that the award of 4000 francs was "just and merited," but further observed that juries were rarely on the side of journalists in suits like this one.[77] Veuillot appealed, but in late summer the award of 4000 francs was upheld. The sum was not excessive, and *L'Univers* probably gained devotion from its supporters to a degree to justify the expense. Veuillot was also similarly involved at this very time in a case where he was accused of false news about radicalism in the army.[78]

Veuillot's extremism and willingness to fight out of principle and without regard for the expediency of the battle was further illustrated by an assault on the ex-Abbé Michaud in April of 1875. He represented him as a man who had thrown away a most promising situation in the church for radical ideas.[79] Michaud answered him directly in some of the hottest language even Veuillot had ever received. Michaud quoted Montalembert in calling *L'Univers le journal de la canaille cléricale,* but he went much further himself. It was moderate enough for him to claim that he was a "Christian Catholic" instead of a "Roman Catholic," but then he went on to maintain that "... The Roman Church of 18 July 1870 did not reject me. It is I, on the contrary, who have kept nothing of it and who rejected all that is in the sewers of *papisme veuillotin*. Do not invert the roles."[80] Veuillot quoted a few other lines from Michaud's epistle, including Michaud's reference to Veuillot's article as a "firman permitted by the Idol of the Vatican."[81] Not content with engaging in an unnecessary public fight with Michaud, Veuillot also published an article not long afterwards against the Jews.[82] Generally speaking, after a notable article Veuillot would receive letters re-echoing whatever he had said. In this instance it would seem that he may have been led to the article by his correspondence. A certain Madame Ferry de Pigny wrote Veuillot a notable assault on the Jews, blaming them for everything, including Bismarck, Andrássy, Victor Emmanuel, and Garibaldi. Obviously she had been inspired by other things Veuillot had written, but here was an example of a letter, complete with fleur-de-lis, which evidently inspired Veuillot.[83] Certainly there was no trace of what can be called emergent racial anti-semitism in Veuillot's subsequent article. It was an old-fashioned not to say mediaeval attack on Jews from a religious and ideological point of view. Nevertheless the choice of this sort of subject would show a certain desperation on his part as the tide of events seemed to be going against his cause. It is worth noting that the police were maintaining surveillance of the offices of *L'Univers* in the summer of 1875,[84] though there is no evidence that they watched 21, Rue de Varennes.

After surveillance of Veuillot was increased, one of the more reliable agents reported that many legitimists were distressed with Veuillot, as the elections for the two houses of the parliament that would replace the National Assembly approached, because he was evoking the spectre of feudal institutions. These legitimists desired that Veuillot "moderate his Catholic zeal."[85] Veuillot was increasingly sounding like an extremist at a time when evidence was beginning to mount that ultra-right-wing plots might be an actual danger. Veuillot never was implicated in any such doings, but as a precaution "Monsieur Marseille" was requested by the head of the Paris Préfecture to prepare a sketch of his life.[86] The agent produced the job by fall. On the whole an accurate summary was made, which ended with this characterization:

> M. Veuillot, who appears to be a man who accommodates himself to all governments, provided that these seem to him to have the ideal of full rein for the temporal power, and full power for the clergy directed by the papacy, is drawn by numerous intimacies into the bosom of the clerical party, the moderate members of which accuse

> him of doing more evil than good for religion because of the vehemence of his polemics, his intolerance, and the extreme nature of his language. Nonetheless, he has a great influence on the Vatican, where he is regarded as one of the most zealous and eloquent defenders of ultramontanism.[87]

Such was the official view the ministry of the interior and the police took of the Catholic editor, and in a number of ways the summary was not inaccurate.

Veuillot enjoyed an unexpected victory in 1875, the passage of a bill by the National Assembly that established the right of Catholic universities to grant degrees.[88] By 1880 this right was taken away,[89] but for a brief period Catholic faculties, which came to be formed, were able to grant degrees themselves, albeit subject to mixed juries, and the monopoly of the *universitaires* was briefly interrupted. Veuillot was rather late in entering the battle, but he did what he could and was overjoyed with the success.[90] As always he showed willingness to give credit where it was due, and along with Lucien Brun and Charles Chesnelong he especially praised Dupanloup.[91] Dupanloup had been willing to accept the compromise on the juries, something that seemed bad to Veuillot, but he knew a victory when he saw one, especially a surprise victory. This episode was not the first example of Veuillot applauding Dupanloup. When the atheist Littré was elected to the Academy, Dupanloup had resigned rather than sit in the same body with him, an action that brought high praise from Veuillot for his enemy.[92] Veuillot almost invariably could praise actions without regard for the person who did them. Littré, incidentally, was received with pomp into the Masonic Order at this very time, an event which evoked the expected reaction from Veuillot.[93]

Notable in the movement for higher education on a Catholic basis was Msgr. Freppel, who strove to organize a faculty at Angers.[94] Freppel succeeded, and during the fall was able to describe to Veuillot the inauguration of a Catholic university.[95] Freppel was grateful to Veuillot for his aid, and among the few names of laymen inscribed in his *livre d'or* at Angers was the name of the journalist.[96]

The achievement of the legal right for some higher education to be under Catholic direction was of such importance in Veuillot's eyes that he listed it among the gains of the century. Despite the terrific damage of the French Revolution and its continuing effects, Veuillot even in his declining years saw the positive gains made by his cause. He enumerated 1) the return of French churches to the Roman liturgy that Dom Guéranger had championed; 2) the liberty for religious orders, for which he especially credited Lacordaire; 3) liberty of primary and secondary education; 4) the defeat of Gallicanism brought about by the *Syllabus* and the Council; 5) and now the victory for higher education.[97] Veuillot had a well-known tendency toward bitterness, but he also had the capacity for seeing successes and good things, even when they were mixed with the bad. Paul Lapeyre, who because of Veuillot's declining physical condition was closer to him than a secretary would have been otherwise, later reported words of Veuillot in 1876: "Young Catholics of today," he quoted Veuillot as saying, "have a chance. When Lacordaire and Montalembert began their struggle for freedom of instruction, and after that, when my brother and I entered the battle, *la France croyante* was almost a desert. Now the desert is populated. One sees there a crowd, life, activity. Now men of faith who want to serve the church are joined together in a body. To fight indifference, mistrust, and hate they find support and resources which their predecessors did not know."[98] Veuillot could see the rosy side as well as give credit to those with whom he had quarreled.

If the general situation appeared to Veuillot to be not all bad, his family seemed to be almost entirely a source of happiness to the aging man. He had had no son, but now he could speak to Madame Volnys of "ma militaire et ma militante."[99] Although he said he was able to see Luce very little, he also played on the word "réglementairement" to describe the way he could indeed visit her,[100] and he corresponded very regularly with her, signing himself "Papa," almost seeming to forget all the door-kissing and so on. Lieutenant-Colonel (as he shortly became) Pierron and Agnès came to Paris on occasion, and in the meantime Veuillot corresponded extensively with them. In fact, a large part of his correspondence beginning in 1875 was with his family and intimate friends. Then in the spring of 1875 Agnès told her father she was going to have a child, which hope for the future interested Luce as well. Veuillot said it was all right with him if the child were a girl. If a boy, he would like to have a soldier – or, even better, a priest.[101] He was greatly interested in the coming event, and signed himself, "Grand-Papa" months before its occurrence.[102] Luce, was born in early December, and he declared he had had no anxiety, but was glad the child was delivered. He went to Notre Dame-des-Victoires, and he reported: "Already Luce the Second is *chargée de prières*.[103] Eventually Agnès had seven more children, of whom three were boys.

In late 1875 the National Assembly, which had constituted France a republic and provided for elections to a two-house parliament, declared its own demise. In early 1876 these elections took place. Veuillot, of course, was much interested in the ultramontanes seeking office, but he was definitely distracted from the elections by a purely ecclesiastical battle that was taking place. Msgr. Pelletier, canon of Orleans, but an enemy of Dupanloup, had published a tract entitled *Mgr. Dupanloup, Épisode de l'Histoire contemporaine*. Essentially Msgr. Pelletier made the bishop the personification of liberal Catholicism. However carefully written, it is hard to see anything but insolence in such a piece. Cardinal Guibert backed Dupanloup, and when Pelletier appealed to Rome, the tract was condemned on technical points.[104] Veuillot and *L'Univers* took Pelletier's side in the matter, and Veuillot's letters to Pelletier gave him the strongest encouragement. He told him to disregard the journals of Dupanloup that "turned bloody purple" over the matter. "The moment of retribution has come," he said. "Show your teeth and they will be quiet."[105] Veuillot, however, was wrong about the support that Rome and the nuncio would give Msgr. Pelletier. Despite the strong language he used to Pelletier, he had not gone to the forefront of this clerical struggle, and when Rome had spoken, he let the matter drop. He complained in June that Pelletier was not satisifed with what the pope had said, and observed that "the disciple is not greater than the Master."[106] To a degree he had learned a lesson since 1872.

While the senate that was elected contained a majority of conservatives, largely because of the nature of the elections, the chamber of deputies was heavily republican. Soon Veuillot was attacking Jules Ferry,[107] and before long Freppel was imploring the support of *L'Univers* for the scarcely established Catholic university system,[108] but the first issue that developed from these elections was the matter of whether Albert de Mun could take the seat to which he had been elected from Pontivy. On the charge that undue clerical influence had been used to obtain this victory, De Mun had been denied his seat pending an investigation. Veuillot, not surprisingly, wrote one of his sharpest articles.[109] When De Mun's wife wrote to Veuillot of her gratitude, Veuillot praised her husband as made "of the stuff of a *better* Montalembert."[110] The blessings of Veuillot had obviously been given to De Mun, La Tour du Pin, and their little band of "Men of Good Will." Indeed, that group, and particularly the thinking of La Tour du Pin, was probably influenced by Veuillot.[111] In due course the parliament invalidated the election of De Mun, to the great disgust of Veuillot.[112] In the politics of the Seventh Arrondissement in Paris, where Veuillot had tried to persuade the legitimists to support a Bonapartist, Bartholoni, as the most satisfactory conservative standard-bearer, he had been most unsuccessful and uninfluential.[113] Therefore, the sad lamentation about what republicans would do with a church-supported candidate applied to his own experiences as well as the case of De Mun.

On 3 July 1876 the papal nuncio, Cardinal Guibert, and a total of thirty-three archbishops and bishops went to Lourdes for the crowning of Our Lady of Lourdes. The Bishop of Poitiers, Msgr. Pie, spoke at the ceremonies. Veuillot used the occasion to criticize the railing tone of journals which still went out of their way to deny that any miracle had occurred. Veuillot had often been ridiculed for the nature of his faith, including his faith in miracles, but still he did not hesitate to refer to the event at Lourdes as the greatest miracle of the day, after that of the existence of the pope as a prisoner in Rome.[114] Msgr. Pie had come to be for him what Parisis and Salinis had formerly been, and when he wrote him about his speech, he referred to it as *Belle Écriture,* "more than canonized," and "much loftier than the Pyrenees."[115] Veuillot had not been present for the ceremony, curiously, but he had visited Lourdes just beforehand. He said that he was not cured, but that he had been deeply interested.[116] Obviously, religion was something much more to Louis Veuillot than any personal prayers that might be answered. Lourdes was miraculous for him quite apart from any effects on his physical state at that time. His physical condition was bad. When Veuillot wrote to Pie on 9 July he said "I have neither legs, nor hands, nor pen."[117] He was nearly worn out.

In 1876 the Abbé Jules Morel, who had collaborated on *L'Univers*, and whom Veuillot had known sympathetically for years, published a *Summa*, or *Somme contre le catholicisme libéral.* Veuillot treated the tract with care,[118] but did not give it a blanket endorsement, although he devoted many pages to his comments. In developing his thesis Morel had made observations about certain Catholics which Veuillot corrected. Salinis and Du Lac were not treated in the way Veuillot believed was proper, and he strongly came to their defense, especially in the case of Du Lac. As for "our master," as he called him again: "We can not bear that one speak of him without witnessing the extreme consideration that he merited. M. Du Lac was the true founder of this journal. . . . Good and dear Du Lac! A man who was truly grand, a man of solid gold, and whom I would dare to say was made by the hands of God to be a journalist, if one can say that God ever made a man for this purpose."[119] Du Lac had remained in the background, but the testimony of Louis Veuillot must be regarded as sincere about him, especially at this point.

Of all the ecclesiastical figures who influenced Veuillot in the latter part of his life, Freppel, the recent-comer to ultramontanism, was the greatest force, and one who might have involved Veuillot even more deeply in his battles had Veuillot been in better health. "We must take the offensive and bring fear to our adversaries," wrote Freppel, trying to bring pressure to bear on the center-left.[120] Not only in the matter of education, the situation of which Freppel thought with good reason was grave, but also in his quarrel with the Bishop of Gap over matters of liberalism, Freppel did his best to inflame Veuillot.[121] It would almost seem as though the young and vigorous bishop was trying to fire up the inflammatory layman in an unparalled way.

Veuillot was not strong enough for battles, though he still tried to fight. Writing in a mournful way about the passing of Cardinal Antonelli in the fall of 1876, a man whose ways had brought much trouble to the pope but one whom Veuillot did his best to present in a favorable light at his death,[122] was more the sort of thing for which he was suited now. He came to the defense of Paul Granier de Cassagnac,[123], fiery deputy and editor who was under great legal pressure from the liberals. Cassagnac was tried on charges they brought against him, but was acquitted. *L'Univers* called him a hero, a description bringing great exultation from some of his readers, and of course Cassagnac's thanks,[124] but Veuillot did not really get very deeply involved in the affair. He attacked Hyacinthe Loyson when the latter held religious conferences in the *Cirque* during the spring of 1877,[125] but this sort of thing he could do almost in his sleep. He did show some of his old fire during the crisis of 16 May 1877, when Broglie and MacMahon brought about the dissolution of the republican and increasingly anticlerical chamber of deputies,[126] but although he was able to keep on writing editorials even after the elections went against the conservatives, bringing a still more republican chamber, there was nothing especially fresh about his line. He praised a manifesto of Chambord at this time,[127] but Chambord was giving him little about which to write in these days. Otherwise Veuillot's negative side generally prevailed. When Thiers died in September 1877, Veuillot was most uncharitable. He played on the theme that the republicans, and not the state, footed the bill for the occasion. He found it fitting that the ceremonies were at Notre Dame de Lorette, which was small in comparison with other likely churches for such an event, and to all purposes he passed hard judgment on him.[128] Again it must be noted that the pope had spoken to him little more than five years earlier about this sort of thing.

In the fall of 1877 Veuillot in writing to his old friend, the Comtesse d'Esgrigny, declared "I am raging" in thinking about the political situation.[129] It is easy enough to see how the victories of the men who were to follow Gambetta and Ferry enraged him, but the fact that in his rage he had actually supported the Broglie forces probably added a good deal to his bitterness. However, he seems to have softened on

MacMahon. "He does his best," Veuillot concluded to another friend. "Let us resign ourselves to dying far from Paradise." There was no hope of reviving the empire, but he believed the monarchy still was possible because it had something of the divine in it.[130] The general political situation, which was deteriorating rapidly so far as he was concerned, and was to do so even more clearly after 1879, was bringing dismal thoughts to Veuillot as he grew old.

Photographs, none very flattering, of Louis Veuillot at younger ages exist, but descriptions of what he looked like when young are scanty. There is more to be found in documents about his looks near the end of his life. He had many passports, but those in the police records at earlier dates are very incomplete. The only one that contains anything of interest was dated 14 April 1879. Since it shows his residence as 11, not 21, rue de Varennes, it may also be inaccurate in other details. As a 65-year-old man he was described as 1.70 meters (Élise was 1.69) which was not far from 5 feet 7, his hair and beard not surprisingly gray, his eyes, brown, though nothing is said about sagging lids and inflammation. His forehead was high, his chin round, his nose "strong." His *visage* was full, and the color of his skin brown. Nothing was indicated about special marks, and however deep his smallpox scars still were, they were apparently not regarded as worthy of mention.[131] His secretary, Paul Lapeyre, gives some impressions of the man, especially as he sat writing at a terribly fast rate to a wide variety of correspondents,[132] who included people from Father Mortara to journalistic rivals. Louis Veuillot too had something to say about himself. In 1875 a writer for a Belgian journal named Bernard Lozes turned out a piece that for some reason Veuillot felt was overly flattering. Veuillot also thought it did not truly picture him, and he set about to correct the impression it gave. In correcting his "portrait" Veuillot insisted, "I have a bigger nose, paler skin, I am more pockmarked, etc., etc." Lozes had described the room in which Veuillot was to be found, but even this not correctly, and Veuillot went on to point out that over the fireplace was nothing but a crucifix, and to make certain other observations which, along with his admission to having a big nose, eventually delighted his enemies.[133] The police noted clippings about a year later in various papers that had obtained this letter. He was laughed at for saying that though he admired Boileau, he did not want to imitate him in following Time with a watch in hand, a remark Veuillot made in explaining that he did not have a clock on the wall. He had only the crucifix to look at, which told him of his eternal hour. The most interesting observation of Veuillot's that was brought out as a result of this letter's becoming known was what he said of enemies: "I have passed sixty, dear sir. At this age one knows that enemies do little bad, and that they are of much service. For my part I have never had a single one who was not of great use. I seriously believe that no one has ever arrived in Heaven without having been pushed and sustained by some enemy."[134] If enemies were needed in order to get to Heaven, Veuillot would have no problem on this score.

While the episode of more than a year's standing was coming to light, Veuillot was off on the west coast of Arcachon for his health. *La République française* observed at this time, "Let us sincerely wish him good luck and long life, because he would be truly missed in the *galerie excentrique* of our day."[135] Others mocked the sick man in an even more bitter fashion. *Ralliement* declared at the end of 1876: "Bad times seem to be near. Rome is the capital of Italy, and France regains the lead in the scientific world. Antonelli is dead, and the pope is dying. Poor Jesuits, poor Veuillot, poor *L'Univers*. Your impotent rage will not save you, and you will celebrate next year [referring to 1878] the glorious centennial of the great Voltaire."[136] Meanwhile a police official seemed to delight in reporting that the windows of Eugène's residence were illuminated with Venetian lanterns on the fiftieth anniversary of Pius IX's entry into the church.[137]

At the start of 1878 Victor Emmanuel II died, and not long after him Pius IX. Veuillot wrote one of his best articles on the death of the pope and on the miraculous nature of the choice of popes.[138] He followed it with other articles about Pius IX and the election of Leo XIII, but his underlying sadness was inescapable. As was the case of the Comte de Chambord, and even more so, Louis Veuillot had lost the pope around whom he had built his outlook on life. The election of Cardinal Pecci as Leo XIII brought a good, but rather stylized piece from Veuillot's pen.[139] The popes, whose choice was miraculous, were men none the less, and Veuillot was disposed to wonder what course Leo XIII would follow. In any case, he would not be the warm Giovanni Mastaï-Ferretti who had smiled on him and called him *caro* Veuillot. Journals like *L'Union de l'Ouest* had dwelt on Leo's liberalism, while even *La République Française* expressed satisfaction with him, but Alexandre de St. Albin reassured Veuillot by citing a pastoral of Cardinal Pecci, which he had written in his capacity as Bishop of Peruggia.[140] Several princes of the church, including Cardinal Bonnechose and Cardinal Pitra,[141] had recently been corresponding with Veuillot about liberalism, and from them perhaps Veuillot had higher assurances than the historian of legitimacy could give. Among Veuillot's writings at the time of the election and coronation of Leo XIII was an article drawing a parallel between Leo the Great and Leo

XIII. No doubt it reflected Veuillot's hopes for the future of the papacy. Actually a future encyclical which Leo XIII would come to issue on human liberty in 1888 would have been in a number of ways most satisfying to him, but in 1878 Veuillot did not look ahead with unmixed confidence.

Veuillot was not well enough to go to Rome for the coronation, at least without knowing how he might be received. He therefore sent Eugène to Rome for him. Eugène was in fact the real manager of *L'Univers* at this time. Msgr. Mermillod had given personal assurances that Leo XIII would be all that Veuillot hoped, but still uncertain, Louis Veuillot wanted to hear what his brother would say. Apparently it was not easy for Eugène to arrange an audience, and several times the appointment was adjourned, which must have distressed Louis considerably. The new pope, of course, was extremely busy, and early 1878 was not a time when it was easy for him to grant private audiences. Eugène received the attention due the second editor of a journal of such small size. However, the day finally came, and Eugène was able to say the things which Louis prayed he would be able to say.[142] On 2 March 1878 *L'Univers* published the highlights of the audience the pope had granted Eugène. According to the report the pope said: "I have long known *L'Univers*; I read it and appreciate its services; I encourage your perserverance, and I give you the blessings you ask." Then the pope inquired about Louis Veuillot's health and gave his benediction for him. Eugène then told him his brother was coming to Rome, and the pope said that he would gladly see him, adding: "Continue your good work, continue it with firmness. Religion is attacked strongly, and it has to be defended. Everything is there. It is society that one will save in defending religion. The Catholic press, sincerely submitted to the teachings of the Holy See, is more useful than ever, and I want to encourage you in it." With the special benediction for the ailing Louis Veuillot, Eugène was sent on his way rejoicing.[143]

The new pope was crowned shortly after this interview, and Louis Veuillot could write heartily about the event.[144] Louis Veuillot was really in no sense fit for travel, but his big desire was to make a final trip to Rome and to receive the blessings of the new pope personally. He wrote to Msgr. Mermillod that much as he wished to see him, and the beauties of Lake Geneva, he was not physically up to such a stop. Apparently his legs particularly troubled him. However, no matter how bad his health, "the tomb of Pius IX is the gate to the future world," and together with his sister he had to go to Rome.[145] He truly sounded like a relic of himself when near the time of his departure he said he would present arms in saluting Freppel, except that the arms of this soldier of the church now were not worth much.[146] With his sister and the Abbé Louis, Veuillot traveled by train through Turin and Pisa to Rome, and by 28 April 1878 he was comfortably put up at the Hotel Minerva. His sister wrote back to Eugène in Paris that Veuillot had arrived, however, without the joy he had usually felt on his previous arrivals. He seemed bitter, partly over his sickness, and partly over the passing of old supporters like Msgrs. Bastide and Nardi. He could look forward to seeing Cardinals Chigi, Sacconi, and Pitra, Msgr. Mercurelli and Maguelonne. Mercurelli made arrangements for the papal audience, and on 4 May Veuillot had the satisfaction of a cordial greeting from the new pope. Veuillot was able to bring an offering of 74,000 francs, largely from the subscribers of *L'Univers*, but also including 10,000 which he stated had been given to *L'Univers* by Pius IX.[147] The pope repeated the same things he had said to Eugène, but he did go a little farther by mentioning the good work of *Le Monde, L'Union*, and *La Défense* and adding: "But *L'Univers* stands at the head." According to Élise in a letter to Eugène, the pope talked in this vein fifty-seven minutes. The pope gave his blessings to all the subscribers of *L'Univers*, and he told Veuillot to report this fact in its columns. As usual, Veuillot managed to bring someone else into the pope's presence, this time the Abbé Louis who had accompanied them to Rome.[148] Élise denied that Louis Veuillot wept after the audience, but he provably was in a high state of nervous tension during the day.[149] He stayed a few days longer in Rome, but he had done the one thing he had desired to do – receive the blessings of the pope. He then returned by Genoa and Nice. It is obvious that Veuillot attached the fullest positive meaning to papal benedictions, and that he must have believed that thereby he and his journal were thoroughly endorsed. Christ had taught His disciples to bless those who had used them ill, but Veuillot saw in the good wishes of the pope something more like a vote of confidence. Leo XIII, like Pius IX before him, had Christian love no doubt for Veuillot and those who followed his lead, and Veuillot, of course, could see it. Veuillot's response to all these benedictions certainly suggests that the import of blessings is not a simple matter.

Veuillot still had a few more good articles left in him, and he worked also on the revision of some of his already published works, an activity that had busied him a considerable part of his long career. He also began classifying some of his miscellaneous papers, and few men have ever been more careful about preserving their literary legacy than he. Various current events, such as the Congress of Berlin, the provisions for the centennial of Voltaire, and more controversies over the nature of the pilgrimages of the day, brought forth the kinds of comments from Veuillot that might surely have been predicted. One interesting obituary was notable, for its brevity rather than for what it said. On 11 October 1878 Msgr. Dupanloup passed away. This event brought from Veuillot not much over 400 words. He could about as well have ignored the bishop's death altogether. He spoke as though time alone would tell what the judgment on his merit would be. He stated in the most matter-of-fact way: "The disagreements of Msgr. Dupanloup and *L'Univers* have been frequent and public, and we shall restrain ourselves from adding anything at this moment." Veuillot gave Dupanloup credit for taking good stands on occasion, but he pointed out once more that he had taken a stand at the Council that was to be regretted.[150] The matter, however, was not at an end here. Several papers, led by *Le Figaro* attacked Veuillot for such a curt dismissal of the great bishop. Their attacks drew five more articles from Veuillot.[151] In one of these Veuillot speculated on what would have happened to the church, *humanly speaking*, had Catholics in general followed the lead of Dupanloup. He concluded that 1) "the immense grace of the *syllabus* would have been adjourned, if not lost." 2) The declaration of the infallibility would have been found inopportune. 3) Liturgical reform would have been thwarted. 4) The whole cause of Catholic liberalism would have been victorious.[152] Veuillot was thought by many to hate Dupanloup and others. Veuillot, however, insisted that he did not hate Saint-Genest, Lavedan, and others who loved Dupanloup – maintaining that he only hated their ideas.[153] There is every reason to believe Veuillot. He distinguished, as he believed, between men and their ideas. If there is any good defense for him against the charge of lack of charity, it is that he hated ideas rather than persons. Nevertheless, men and ideas do become inseparable – just as Veuillot and militant ultramontanism were inseparable.

While Veuillot had been in Rome, the police had noted his announcement of the blessings the pope had bestowed on the readers of *L'Univers* as well as on Louis Veuillot.[154] They maintained a file of clippings about the aid the journal had afforded the pope at the very time when right-wing extremism was increasingly regarded as a threat to the government by the republicans who were consolidating their position. The police tended to confound Veuillot with the Jesuits, and they noted that the latter were anxious about the intentions of Leo XIII.[155] One agent, who speculated unreliably on various occasions, claimed that "poor old Veuillot is falling into ruin," and suggested that Paul Granier de Cassagnac was going to take his place.[156] This shallow report overlooked the different ideals of the two reactionaries, but nevertheless reveals the confusion of republican officialdom. For all his ranting Veuillot remained primarily a religious man.

1879 was the last year of Veuillot's active role as a journalist. He wrote some of the more important editorials carried in *L'Univers*, but most of his pieces were short. He dealt with the death of the Prince Imperial, the resignation of MacMahon, the return of the parliament to Paris, and the twenty-fifth anniversary of the proclamation of the Immaculate Conception. These he treated relatively briefly and in quite predictable fashion. His importance as a journalist at this time continued partly because of the influence of more vigorous people like Msgr. Freppel who were close to him personally. Belcastel and Lavigerie corresponded with him during the year, and even though his letters were few, Veuillot clearly remained the guiding light of the journal. Actually, some of the things Veuillot wrote for the journal in 1878 probably reflect his feelings in his last years, as well as anything he wrote near the end of his life. In July 1878 he proclaimed the country sick. He did not speak of a *malaise* but of *notre maladie.*[157] He even spoke of hastening death. Another article was entitled "La Fin." In it he maintained "France is ceasing to be a society, it is becoming a mob."[158] When a man writes like that, his career as a journalist would seem to be nearing an end. He did manage to come out of retirement in May 1880 to pen a few lines on the death of Cardinal Pie,[159] quite the opposite sort of comment from what he had said of Dupanloup, but this was absolutely his last contribution. At the end of 1879 he wrote in shaky hand to his brother, resigning from *L'Univers.* In this remarkable epistle (how many people resign formally to their younger brother?) he expressed satisfaction at having spent forty-five years (he was a bit inaccurate) with *L'Univers.* He spoke of the simplicity of his purpose and of some of the great men, Salinis, Guéranger, Gerbet, Parisis, Donoso Cortés, Bugeaud, and Guizot (he did not mention Montalembert) with whom he had been associated. However, it was Melchior Du Lac whom he called the greatest. He had found him at *L'Univers*, and there he had died "in his arms."[160] To the world Louis Veuillot and *L'Univers* seem synonymous, but to Veuillot it was to the end Du Lac and *L'Univers.*

Plans were made in the nineteenth-century fashion for extensive travel for the ailing Veuillot in early 1880. According to François Veuillot the "great silence" began at this time,[161] and a break like this was to have pointed up his retirement from the world of letters. As an intimate wrote him in mid-1879: "Everyone abandons us! You no longer have the consolation of writing, and we do not have the *soulagement* of reading you."[162] Not being able to write, he was almost obliged to run away from himself, if his health permitted. He planned to go to Spain, and even to go to the baths at Mannheim. He rested a while with Madame Arthur Murcier (wife of his deceased brother-in-law) at Gatigny, which demonstrates something of the closeness of his family connections. He reached Spain during the spring, and traveled about visiting Burgos, Avila, Madrid, Cordova, Granada, and Seville.[163] Records are incomplete for all of these travels. By August he was stricken at Saint-Pair by what was probably a combination of troubles related to his general condition. The police, who still regarded him as worth watching,[164] noted that he had been gravely ill and was returning in September from Granville.[165] As late as 1881 they believed he was handling a large subscription for the Denier of Saint Peter,[166] but in fact he was a complete invalid by this time. Travel and the general exhaustion of an extremely strenuous career had taken their toll.

The year 1882 is practically a blank in his life. Some undated notes survive from his last years, but mixed with them are papers he must have written considerably earlier, though with an awareness that the end was coming. Apparently he never tried to write an autobiography, though one undated encyclopedia-length piece, probably written around 1870, survives.[167] In this brief item he has included such touches as the fact that he never owned a piece of land in his life, except the family burial plot in the Montparnasse Cemetery, which he bought for 500 francs. He also sharply recalls his month in prison and the 3000 francs he paid in fine for his defense of the church. The fact that this item breaks off in the midst of a sentence suggests the possibility that rather late in life he thought of writing at greater length. However, sometime in his last years he made the testamentary decision that his papers were to go to Eugène for the obvious purpose of editing them. One of his last notes is a lament about not having hot water. Another simply says, *je souffre.*[168]

On 5 April 1883 lung and respiratory trouble overtook him. At first it appeared he would survive the attack, but by 7 April his death seemed imminent. Cardinal Jacobini at the Vatican was notified by telegram of his situation. Luce was notified, but as a nun she prayed at her convent. Agnes was called, but got there too late. Faithful servants, the family of Eugène, Élise of course, and a large number of friends and supporters in Paris stood by. His confessor arrived, as did a telegram from Rome expressing the pope's sorrow. Louis Veuillot died in the afternoon, having lived not far from the three score and ten he might have expected.

During 1883 the Comte de Chambord also died, as did Wagner, Karl Marx, General Chanzy, Gustave Doré, Manet, and Prince Gorchakov. Gambetta had died just at the end of 1882, but it was not known generally until 1883. A striking group of great figures passed from the European scene in 1883, a year of deaths. Veuillot deserves to rank with this group.

When Louis Veuillot died he left behind him two main legacies, a journal and a school of ideas, as Édouard Hervé observed in *Le Soleil.*[169] Important as *L'Univers* was in bridging the nineteenth and twentieth centuries for ultramontane Catholicism, the school, however vague, was probably more significant. Louis Veuillot worked all his life in keeping all his papers, letters, and works of all sorts together so that the full effect of his ideas might be saved. As soon as he died his school proper began. His last minutes were dramatically brought to the readers of *L'Univers* by Auguste Roussel, who then quoted the poetic testament of Louis Veuillot,[170] which contained the words *J'ai cru, je vois* that were to be inscribed on his tomb and even set to music by Gounod.

Louis Veuillot's legal will was not published until nearly four weeks later, when his brother Eugène described its contents. The willing of his papers to Eugène was the most important practical point, but his deliberate expression of forgiveness to every one of his enemies, written late in his life but while he could be said to have been in full possession of his faculties, was also significant, since it was important to try to undo the heritage of his religious battles. He blessed his religious enemies, notably Montalembert and Lacordaire. He declared he loved them – "especially Montalembert." According to Eugène, he had burned a large number of papers that tended to enhance his role and to put others in a bad light. "Why prolong the battle after our death?"[171] It would indeed have been interesting to see what he chose to burn, especially when so many of his surviving letters are as strong as they are in opposition to some of his opponents. But Veuillot was unusually generous to those who would study his career and battles, so we cannot complain if he burned some of his papers.

The bereaved family promptly sent out an announcement of his death to appropriate people, and the police braced themselves for what might have been a tumultuous occasion. Violence had accompanied the funeral of Pius IX, and it was only wise to anticipate trouble at the burial of Louis Veuillot. One police observer, notable for imagination but less so for accuracy, predicted that the legitimists would forget their old grievances and, together with the Jesuits, would send out collective invitations to the religious orders and to the Catholic workers in order to have a "significant" procession. All sorts of messages would be read at the cemetery, he warned, including a benediction from the Vatican, to which the crowd would shout: *Vive le Pape-roi! A mort les jeoliers du Saint-Père*! Then, on departing from the cemetery, the same people would engage in manifestations against the republic.[172] This was not a bad guess, but another observer, writing on 9 April also, predicted that nothing would happen the next day, saying that the crowd would not be apt to become unruly and that Veuillot was not generally liked, especially among the bishops, because he was too ultramontane.[173] The police, nevertheless, watched the funeral closely.

When Eugène published the *Hommages* to his brother on the first anniversary of his death, he was able to include an impressive list of persons who were in the procession. These included the Marquis de Dreux-Brézé, the Comte de Vanssay, Comte de Mun (with a numerous deputation from the *Cercles catholiques d'ouvriers*), Comte de La Tour du Pin, Vicomte de Chaulnes, the Marquis de Ségur, Paul Granier de Cassagnac, Henri de Pène, the Duc de La Rochefoucauld-Bisaccia, Comte de Damas, Comte de Blacas, Emile Keller, General Kantzler, the Prince de La Tour d'Auvergne, Baron Baude, and, far from least, General (he preferred his title of Colonel, which he held in the Pontifical Zouaves) de Charette. Large numbers of clergymen of different degrees of importance were present, but only one bishop, Msgr. Perraud of Autun. Msgr. Guibert was not present, but he was represented. The press was represented by a few notables, including Thureau-Dangin of *Le Français,* Louis Teste of *Le Gaulois*, and Drumont, then of *Liberté.*[174] The police took careful note of these people besides observing that there were students and children from Alsace-Lorraine. They watched closely, sending in reports about every half-hour from mid-day. The body arrived at 12:30 at Veuillot's church, St. Thomas d'Aquin, followed by about 1500 mourners on foot and thirty carriages. St. Thomas d'Aquin is not one of the larger churches of Paris, and this number of persons made for quite a crush. The 1 p.m. report still predicted speeches at the cemetery, and indicated the ceremonies in the church would be long. Finally at 1:35 the procession began to go toward the Cemetery of Montparnasse by way of the Boulevard Saint-Germain and the Rue de Rennes. The mourners reached the cemetery at 2:15, but reports of 2:25 and 3:10 still indicated no incidents. Only when a brigade of police arrived was there grumbling among the mourners. No speech was given there, and in a tone of surprise the last of these reports declared: *Absolument rien à signaler.*[175]

Among the Veuillot papers is a stirring "Funeral Oration" by the Abbé Paul Bruchesi, future Archbishop of Montreal, and formerly a student in Paris and Rome. This oration was no doubt given in Montreal, but it would have been most appropriate for the eulogy at St. Thomas d'Aquin. It contains some most descriptive phrases, including what might be regarded as the best title Veuillot could have –

"SERGEANT OF JESUS CHRIST" – a title which, according to Father Bruchesi, "he liked to call himself."[176] That was exactly what Veuillot was, a sergeant, and not a recruiting sergeant, either. He kept the Catholic ranks closed up, kept in line a large part of the rank-and-file, and was completely devoted to his commander-in-chief – the pope. He barked cadence at his Christian army, and he did the best he could to prevent straggling. Particularly he was the sergeant when subordinate commanders tried to deviate from the supreme commander. The analogy of the Bruchesi funeral oration, was not only fitting, it would also have been likely to stir up the hearers had it been delivered in Paris.

The Bruchesi oration had some other good phrases. Veuillot was called a *Lutteur indefatigable.* He was called a "soldier" and an "intrepid athlete of the faith." "Who has defended more valiantly than he the temporal power of the Holy See?" asked Bruchesi. His career was recapitulated with identifications with the working and bourgeois classes. Veuillot was said to have had "theological sense" without being a theologian. He was said to have represented infallibility as a doctor and master. Saint-Beuve was quoted as saying that "nothing more beautiful has been written in our beautiful French language" than Veuillot's piece on the *Chambre nuptiale.* And, in another good phrase, he was the "Lamoricière of the press." These things did not have to be said aloud. The 1500 who walked to the cemetery felt them. Hearing them, the more excitable might have made the afternoon of 10 April 1883 more eventful.

Letters poured in to the family. The three most important, at least in the eyes of Eugène, were from the Comte de Chambord, Don Carlos, and Cardinal Jacobini. The letter from the pretender, dated Goritzia, 23 April 1883, was perhaps, as Eugène maintains, his last significant act. He spoke of his emotion at Veuillot's passing and of the battle Veuillot had fought against atheism. His most important point, however, was: "Especially in 1873, when we touched port, and when the intrigues of a policy less concerned with corresponding to the true aspirations of France than in ensuring the success of a combination of parties, obliged me to dissipate the equivocals in breaking the bonds destined to reduce me to the impotence of a disarmed sovereign, no other person was able better to penetrate my thought, none better able to give my protestation its true sense."[177] The Comte de Chambord has indeed been a much misunderstood person, and this letter shows the closeness of Veuillot's thought to that of the pretender. Don Carlos, son of Don Juan and grandson of the original Don Carlos, also wrote, but had no such interesting point to make.[178] However, Carlism too had been entirely to the tastes of Veuillot, and the importance which Eugène attached to Don Carlos's letter reflects an aspect of his brother's outlook. Eugène had addressed a letter on 14 April to the pope, but it was Cardinal Jacobini who answered it on 2 May. He answered for the pope, speaking of the pope's recognition of Louis's devotion to the church which he had "courageously defended for long years," but the pope himself did not write.[179] Veuillot died with papal tribute, but this tribute was delegated to be expressed by a prelate. No doubt the family wished Leo XIII had signed the letter himself, but he did not. It seems safe to assume that Pius IX would have done so.

Hundreds of other people wrote condolences, many of them very moving. They came from all levels of social importance,[180] but the testimonies of the lower clergy definitely established Louis Veuillot as a religious leader, just as such letters throughout his life had done. Men like Lucien Brun and Albert de Mun showed their deep sympathy.[181] Over eighty prelates, approximately half of whom were bishops or archbishops, including nine cardinals, expressed their sympathy. Cardinal Guibert did not write, although he was officially represented. It is not insignificant that the Bishop of Gap, no reactionary, chose to call Veuillot a "great Catholic" who had rendered services for the church.[182] No small amount of poetry was produced to commemorate Veuillot.[183] The religious press, of course, particularly mourned Veuillot's death. Many of the things said in the columns of Catholic or legitimist papers were predictable, but a few ideas were significant. Coquille, writing for *Le Monde*, beside saying that the effects of Veuillot were "immense," brought up an interesting angle: Would not the pope have stopped Veuillot if he had not fully approved of him?[184] Actually, Pius IX had often not fully approved of Veuillot's line. Nevertheless, both friends and foes of ultramontane Catholicism liked to associate Pius IX and Veuillot, and this was done at the time of Veuillot's death.

The most interesting observations about Louis Veuillot were made by journals that were not particularly Catholic, including the most secular parts of the press. *L'Union* said he had the *verve gauloise* of Rabelais. Further, it quoted Charles de Rémusat as saying that he so admired the talent of Veuillot that if his name had been presented for election to the Academy, he would have voted for him.[185] *Le Siècle* told the tale more impressively, having Saint-Beuve quote Rémusat as saying: "This devil of a Veuillot has so much talent that, if he presented himself at the Academy, I would not have the courage to refuse him my vote!"[186] *Le Figaro* compared his style to Bossuet,[187] though Rochefort's journal, *L'Intransigent*, said he was only a pamphleteer.[188] Eugène included many slurs among the published *Hommages* to his brother, for such words from Rochefort he no doubt thought added to the picture. Many people had loved Veuillot for his enemies. André Treille in *Paris*, who believed that religion was ever incompatible with progress, called Veuillot the "true pontiff" of Catholicism, "severe, intolerant, cruel, inexorable." [189] Éduoard Drumont in *La Liberté* pronounced Veuillot a *grand écrivain* comparing him to Bossuet, Molière, and Bruyère: "He often climbs as high as the first, he amuses like the second, he portrays like the third."[190] Many writers at that time did not hesitate to speak of him in the same way in which they referred to the great names of French literature, including Voltaire. *République Française* said he shook the Catholic church to its foundations, and only the future could tell what his effects on it were. This secular journal further judged: "He was not a Christian of ancient times; he was a Catholic of the *belles époques* of the Inquisition and the Holy League, a misguided figure in our century. . . ."[191] While *Le Siècle* said he had "too great a place in journalism," it also declared: "In truth, he deserves better for his gifts than he received."[192] Paul Granier de Cassagnac in *Pays* exclaimed: "France loses its greatest *écrivain*, the church its most valiant support, journalism its master." Along with such praise he put his finger on a key to Veuillot's personality: "horror of concession."[193]

The death of Veuillot produced great repercussions in the world of journalism. Nearly everyone admitted that a great force had passed. *L'Univers* still had able editors, including Eugène and the younger men, Loth and Roussel, and it had many years of influential journalism ahead. However, it faced certain difficulties, and the personality of Louis Veuillot was no longer even in the background as a resource for difficult situations. One document in the papers of Léon Lavedan, who had been in the press bureau of the ministry of the interior, described *L'Univers* not long after Veuillot's passing as "without movement, without action." In addition, it was thought to be finanically moribund.[194] Veuillot's personal contacts with great personages were missed. The journal and the "school of Veuillot" went on, but its greatest days were over. It is significant that Père Vincent de Paul Bailly founded *La Croix* in 1883.[195]

Father Mortara possibly made the most striking gesture of all those admirers writing to the family. He wrote to Élise and proclaimed Veuillot a "true martyr." He went further. He asked for some memento of Louis Veuillot which for him would be "a relic" which he would keep with something he had that had belonged to Pius IX.[196] Some of those who had been so upset nearly thirty years previously by the removal of the "infant Mortara" from his family must have had troubled reactions on learning of this letter. Eugène noted that a number of the letters called for a monument. Already a commemorative plaque existed in Rome, and a school had been named for Louis Veuillot in Burgos, Spain. A group representing the *Cercles catholiques d'ouvriers* and professors at the seminary of Gap were among those suggesting a monument. The latter thought there ought to be a column in the "Église de Montmartre."[197] A curé from Oran wrote supporting a monument, saying: "Their [brothers-in-arms] device will ever be that of their dead general, that of Louis Veuillot: 'Conquer or die for the cause of God and the Church of Jesus Christ.' " The spirited curé sent "a modest offering to cooperate in the erection of a monument to the memory of the lay prince of the Holy Church and of the papacy."[198] An ecclesiastical student at the Institut Catholique of Toulouse wanted the "marble of a rich monument" to perpetuate Veuillot's memory. For this he dug into his pocket to the extent of 72 francs,[199] which probably was digging deeply.

Eventually a monument was erected in Boynes, which Veuillot had never revisited in his lifetime, and on 29 November 1899 a bust of Veuillot was placed in the Chapel of St. Benoit-Labre of the Church of Sacré-Cœur in Paris,[200] doubly significant since Labre, canonized in 1883, was a very extreme person and Sacré Cœur's founding and building had been pushed by Veuillot. On the bust in bronze, done by Léon Fagel, are the words, *J'ai cru, je vois.* Beside the bust are two figures representing faith and force, and at the bottom are some dreadful creatures, presumably being crushed. This recognition of a fiery layman in such a conspicuous way sixteen years after his death was most remarkable. It was strong testimony to the continuing influence of his personality and school.

The year 1913 was the centennial of Veuillot's birth (and also Ozanam's), and the family and the rest of the hard core of Veuillotism could not let this occasion pass without doing their best to glorify the memory of the man. In 1913 there was a measure of reaction in the air that was beneficial to this cause. A journal in Bordeaux pointed out the admiration of followers of the *Action française* for Veuillot, calling him "one of the masters of the Counter-Revolution."[201] Another aspect of Veuillot's life came to light, with the *Revue des Deux Mondes* publishing some of his correspondence with Madame Volnys (Léontine Fay), which Oscar Havard said "breathes a love, ever more living, ever more etherial."[202] Clemenceau, during the elections of 1913, recalled the saying attributed to Veuillot to the effect that he wanted liberty on the grounds of the principles of others when they were in power, but when his group would be in power he would refuse this liberty on the grounds of his own principles.[203] Albert de Mun and Jules Lemaître were behind the movement to honor Veuillot,[204] and Ernest Daudet lent his pen. Of the French Catholic leaders of the nineteenth century, Daudet pointed out, Joseph de Maistre, Bonald, Chateaubriand, and Montalembert were aristocrats, and Lacordaire was of a comfortable bourgeois background. Veuillot, however, was from the peasantry and from a "milieu in which one only put on gloves to fight." Veuillot armed for a crusade and thought only of "exterminating the Saracens."[205] In September a big subscription had been launched, and by November an impressive list, including De Mun and Jules Lemaître, had contributed.[206] People were readied for celebrating the birth of the militant Catholic.

Invitations were sent to key persons to participate in the celebrations that were going to center at Sacré-Cœur. Some like Pierre de La Gorce said, "with great regret," that they could not participate.[207] Éduoard Drumont, who described himself as "sick and outside of the militant life," sent "enthusiastic admiration."[208] Maurice Barrès accepted, calling Veuillot a "maître écrivain."[209] At first Cardinal Amette, Archbishop of Paris thought his commitments would prevent him from attending,[210] but he eventually made it, as did many other prelates of the church.[211] No doubt a big reason for the success of the centennial was the blessing Pope Pius X gave to the Veuillot family at this time and the strength of his words in a letter to François Veuillot. If ever the papacy gave approval to the general work of Veuillot, it was at this centennial, in a time when the prestige of Pius X was at its greatest. He was then in the last year of his life, and his canonization followed in due course. On 22 October 1913 he wrote:

> . . . In the example of two popes who have preceded us at the Apostolic See, and principally Pius IX of hallowed memory, it is our pleasure to give testimony to that great man of good, unyielding defender of the rights of God and of the Church. With the flame of his apostle-like zeal he entered the lists adorned with precious gifts which made him a writer, artist and thinker of genius, by which he has equaled and surpassed the most illustrious masters, because, in the holy battles in defense of sacred principles, his pen was at the same time a cutting sword and an illuminating torch. . . . With what noble frankness he knew how to unmask liberal theories, such baneful deductions, sophisms disguised under the name of liberty. . . . The whole of his illustrious career is worthy of being presented as a model to those who struggle for the church and holy causes and who are exposed to the same contradictions and the same unbridling of passions. May they be proud of their titles of Christians

> and servants of the church with the example of Louis Veuillot. May they know that God will fight with them and give them victory at the time chosen by Providence.[212]

More than this could hardly have been said. Another feature of the commemoration of Veuillot's birth, however, added to the symbolic solidarity of the occasion, when Cardinal Touchet, Archbishop of Orleans, accepted the invitation to speak at the ceremonies.[213] That a successor of Dupanloup's spoke at Veuillot's centennial, 26 November 1913, was a point especially noted by *La Libre Parole.* Before other cardinals (including Amette and Luçon of Reims, who called Veuillot an "intrepid champion") and many other prelates,[214] Touchet intoned against liberalism. He quoted Victor Cousin about Veuillot's having had the pope and grammar on his side, but his discourse, based on Second Timothy 2:3, "Work like the good soldier of Jesus Christ,"[215] left no doubt of his stand on militancy. Cardinal Andrieu, Archbishop of Bordeaux, added a few words after the speech, noting it was "vibrant like the note of a bugle."[216] Catholic journals in France reacted very solidly to the glorification, as did many foreign journals.[217] Veuillot thus enjoyed a major triumph thirty years after his death.

Of course there were discordant notes sounded at this time. Naturally *La Lanterne* carried an article speaking of "the eternal *Tartufferie* of the Catholic Church," and quoting Lacordaire to the effect that Veuillot had brought back the flag of the Inquisition.[218] A few other journals reacted to the commemorative occasion in predictable ways. The most significant sour note was sounded by Julien de Narfon in *Le Figaro* and elsewhere. He wrote an article entitled "La scandaleuse apothéose," in which he expressed the view that Veuillot had not been useful to the Catholic church. He pointed out that he was politically a skeptic.[219] In this second matter he was right. Veuillot did not really care deeply about politics, though at least one ideology, that of the monarchical principle, an impractical one at the time, seemed to him in tune with the kind of theocracy he desired. Various ecclesiastics who were contemporaries of Veuillot also had thought he was not useful to the church. But as Veuillot himself would have pointed out, who was an editor of *Le Figaro* to be talking about the needs of the church? The great Hanotaux was really not quite accurate when he said that Veuillot "distributed holy water as though it were vitriol and handled the crucifix like a club."[220] He did not handle either, though he once might have been a priest had his bishop only responded to his youthful application. What Veuillot did was to try to keep the ranks of Catholics closed by attacking only those he believed to be the enemies of the church. He did not wield a club. Pius X himself said his sharp pen was a sword and a torch. He represented the church militant. His technique may be questioned, but he had volunteered as a Catholic soldier, a "sergeant of Jesus Christ." Do armies not need sergeants?

FOOTNOTES

INTRODUCTION

[1] C. Lecigne, *Louis Veuillot* (Paris: Lethielleux, 1913), p. 438.

[2]*Fonds Veuillot, Nouvelles Acquisitions Françaises,* Bibliothèque Nationale, 24622 (hereafter cited as "BN NAF"), pp. 209-220.

[3]Gabriel Hanotaux, *Contemporary France*, 4 vols. (Westminster: A. Constable, 1903-1909), vol. 2, trans. E. Sparvel-Bayley, p. 622.

[4]Jacques Chastenet, *Histoire de la Troisième République,* 7 vols. (Paris: Hachette, 1952-1963) 1:118.

[5]Charles S. Phillips, *The Church in France, 1848-1907* (New York: Russell and Russell, 1967 [first published 1936]), pp. 14-15.

[6]Gordon Wright, *France in Modern Times* (Chicago: Rand, McNally, 1974), p. 237.

[7]Paul Gagnon, *France Since 1789* (New York: Harper and Row, 1964), p. 189.

[8]Philip Spencer, *Politics of Belief in Nineteenth-Century France* (London: Faber and Faber, 1954), p. 217.

[9]BN NAF, 24622, p. 40.

[10]11 September 1913, BN NAF 24624, p. 99.

[11]Jules Rénault, *Louis Veuillot, 1813-1883* (Paris: Lethielleux, 1929), p. 13.

[12]Jules Lemaître, *Les Contemporains* (Paris: Boivin, 1893), 6th ser., pp. 2, 4, 69.

[13]Edmond Schérer, *Études critiques sur la littérature contemporaine*, 10 vols. (Paris: Michel Lévy, 1863), 1:203-220.

[14]BN NAF 24620, p. 218.

[15]Spencer, *Politics of Belief*, p. 218.

[16] A. Latreille, E. Delaruelle, J. R. Palanque, R. Rémond, *Histoire du Catholicisme en France*, 3 vols. (Paris: Spes, 1962), 3:585.

[17]Spencer, *Politics of Belief*, p. 217.

[18]BN NAF 24620, p. 166.

[19]BN NAF 24619, p. 134.

[20]*Ibid.*, 24620, p. 249.

[21]*Ibid.*, p. 226.

[22]*Ibid.*, p. 297.

[23]Roger Aubert, *Le pontificat de Pie IX, 1846-1878* (Paris: Bloud et Gay, 1952), p. 227.

[24]Alexis Crosnier, *Louis Veuillot, Apologiste* (Paris: Beauchesne, 1913), p. 38.

[25]BN NAF, 24618, p. 457.

[26]Crosnier, *Veuillot*, p. 38.

[27]James Ward and Bertil Grezzi, "Pius IX's Voltaire," *Thought*, XLV (1970), 346-370.

[28]BN NAF 24620, p. 346.

[29]Emmanuel Gauthier, *Le Vrai Louis Veuillot, étude psycholgique et morale de l'écrivain d'après sa correspondance* (Paris: Alsatia, 1938), pp. 250-276, 291-333.

[30]Schérer, *Études critiques*, 6: 219-220.

[31]Charles A. Sainte-Beuve, *Causeries du lundi*, 15 vols. (Paris: Garnier, 1890), 1:67-68.

[32]BN NAF, 24620, p. 127.

CHAPTER I

[1]The opening paragraph of *Rome et Lorette* (Œuvres complètes, 40 vols. (Paris: Lethielleux, 1924-1938), (hereafter cited as "O. C."), 3:7-8) is an example of poetic prose from the pen of Louis Veuillot. "Il y avait une fois, non pas un roi et une reine, mais un ouvrier tonnelier, qui ne possedait au monde que ses outils. . . .," and "Un jour, traversant une bourgade du Gatinais, il vit, a la fenêtre encadrée de chevrefeuille d'une humble maison, une belle robuste jeune fille qui travaillait en chantant; il ralentit sa marche, il tourna la tête, et ne poussa pas sa route plus loin" are descriptions that cannot be avoided. His brother Eugène incorporates Louis' words into his own voluminous *Louis Veuillot*, 4 vols. (Paris: Lethielleux, 1913), ("hereafter referred to as "*Vie*"), 1:1-2. There is no reason to question the date of Louis Veuillot's birth, but when his centenary was celebrated in 1913 cases were put forth for two different houses. Veuillot family tradition at that time favored a place near the old Porte de Pithiviers as being the structure built by maternal grandfather Jacques Adam, but a review of the matter by Albert Sibot, "Louis Veuillot et Eugène Veuillot," *Notice biographique* (Pithiviers: Imprimerie moderne, 1913), p. 4, favored a building on the Rue de l'Echelle.

[2]The archives of the Mairie of Noyers contained a birth certificate of an aunt of Louis Veuillot who was called the daughter of the miller of the town. This aunt, Marie-Edmée Veuillot Desmaisons, was described by Eugène (*Vie*, 1:7) as "la lettrée de la famille" and the one who taught Louis to spell the name "Veuillot", rather than "Veluot, "Veliot", or "Veuliot." It is interesting that Louis Veuillot seems to forget her when he says ". . .je suis le premier de mon nom et du nom de ma mère qui ait su lire, ou tout au moins qui ait su un peu d'orthographie (*Rome et Lorette, O.C.*, 3:8). The registers at Boynes were spelled "Veillot", and as late as 1831 Louis spelled it this way. *Vie*, 1:46.

[3]*Vie*, 1:5-6.

[4]*Ibid.*, 1:3, 7; *O.C.*, 3:7.

[5]Eugène tells us that he "ne conserva de sa vie militaire que l'amour de la pipe." *Vie*, 1:4.

[6]Naturally, such a family tradition has been recounted in such ways as to suggest discrepancy. In 1913 pictures were circulated of the cross at Boynes (see *Chronique picarde* (Amiens), 4 Oct. 1913, BN NAF 24624, p. 176). But what was pictured in the press was an ornate iron cross and not the wooden crucifix referred to by Eugène in *Vie*, 1:4. Also, Louis, who originally told the tale in *Ça et La, O.C.*, 8:420-421, spoke of the crucifix being on the Place de l'Église, while Eugène, *Vie*, 1:5, has it on the edge of the village, as it seems to be in the picture of 1913. These are small details, but in view of the probable influence of the event on Louis's militancy, the episode is worthy of consideration.

[7]François Veuillot, *Louis Veuillot, sa vie, son âme, son œuvre* (Paris: Alsatia, 1948), p. 3.

[8]*Vie*, 1:3.

[9]*Ibid.*, 1:4; *O.C.*, 3:8.

[10]*Vie*, 1:7.

[11]Eugène in his biography (1:4) says Louis was taken at first and then returned to Boynes. Louis' own words in *Rome et Lorette, O.C.*, 3:8, say he was taken, but the footnote to the 1913 edition repeats that he was returned.

[12]*Vie*, 1:7.

[13]*Ibid.*, p. 11.

[14]*Ibid.*, pp. 8-9.

[15]*Ibid.*, 1:9. In addition to this piece, cited from *Libres penseurs*, vol. 5, *O.C.*, Veuillot has other sketches of his family's life in the same work (pp. 5-7 and 270-274).

[16]*Ibid.*, 1:9-10.

[17]*Rome et Lorette, O.C.*, 3:9.

[18]*Ibid.*, pp. 10-11.

[19]*Vie*, 1:12.

[20]*Ibid.*, 1:12-13.

[21]*Fragments de Mémoires, O.C.*, 10:517.

[22]*Vie*, 1:19.

[23]*Fragments de Mémoires, O.C.*, 10:517.

[24]*Rome et Lorette, O.C.*, 3:9.

[25]*Ibid.*, p. 9; *Vie*, 1:16.

[26]*Rome et Lorette, O.C.*, 3:11.

[27]*Vie*, 1:14.

[28]*Ibid.*, p. 28.

[29]*Rome et Lorette, O.C.*, 3:12; *Vie*, 1:27.

[30]*Vie*, 1:24-25.

[31]*Ibid.*, pp. 27-28.

[32]*Ibid.*, p. 29.

[33]*Ibid.*, p. 29.

[34]*Ibid.*, p. 30-31.

[35]*Ibid.*, p. 38.

[36]*Ibid.*, p. 41.

[37]*Ibid.*, p. 32.

[38]*Ibid.*, pp. 38-39.

[39]*Ibid.*, p. 37.

[40]*Ibid.*, pp. 25-26.

[41]*Ibid.*, p. 26.

[42]*Ibid.*, p. 47.

[43]*Ibid.*, p. 57.

[44]*Ibid.*, pp. 46-47.

[45]Louis Veuillot to Mr. Émilien, 15 April and 15 May 1831, BN NAF, 24220, pp. 1-5. The nature of the criticism is discussed in *Vie*, 1:41-46.

[46]Report by M. Marseille, 8 Nov. 1875, Archives de la Préfecture de Police de Paris (hereafter cited as "APP"), B/A 874; *Vie*, 1:41. For his eventual meeting with Léontine Fay, see below, pp. 380-381.

[47]*Vie*, 1:40.

[48]*Ibid.*

[49]*Rome et Lorette O.C.*, 3:13.

[50]*Ibid.*, pp. 13-14; *Vie*1:47-51. Some of Veuillot's writings in *L'Écho de la Seine Inférieure* are gathered in *O.C.* 27:1-43.

[51]*Vie*, 1:53.

[52]*Rome et Lorette, O.C.*, 3:13-14.

[53] *Vie*, 1:53-54, 66.
[54] *Ibid.*, p. 56.
[55] *Ibid.*, p. 68-69.
[56] *Ibid.*, p. 70.
[57] *Ibid.*, pp. 70-72; *O.C.*, 3:18.
[58] *Vie*, 1:72-73.
[59] *Ibid.*, 1:76-77. Some of Veuillot's writings in the ***Mémorial*** *de la Dordogne* are found in *O.C.*, 27:44-80.
[60] *Ibid.*, p. 74; *O.C.*, 3:18. Louis Veuillot later referred to the bishop as "un saint viellard" (*O.C.*, 3:18). Eugène spells the name of the abbe two ways in his biography: "Guines" (1:74) and Guigne (1:91).
[61] *Vie*, 1:76.
[62] *Ibid.*, pp. 95-96.
[63] *Ibid.*, p. 82. Some of these pieces are in *O.C.*, 27:81-105. "Sylvain" and "L'Aspre" were other names he used.
[64] *Ibid.*, pp. 88-90. See Pierre Fernesolle, *Pour qu'on lise Louis Veuillot* (Paris: Lethielleux, 1928), pp. 21-42; Hector Talvart, *Louis Veuillot et la monarchie* (Paris: Rupella, Charles Millon, 1927), pp. 15-29.
[65] *Ibid.*, pp. 85-86. Eugène points out that even in the archives of Périgueux only a few runs of the Mémorial were to be found, and that there was no published account of this encounter. In a letter to Gustave Olivier, 19 Sept. 1836, he said he fought *two* duels within twenty-four hours, *O.C.*, 15:20.
[66] Louis Veuillot had corresponded with Gustave Olivier during his stay in Périgueux, and some of his letters are in *O.C.*, 15:10-23.
[67] *Vie*, 1:98-99.
[68] *Ibid.*, 1:101; *O.C.*, 3:21.
[69] *Vie*, 1:101-103.
[70] *Ibid.*, p. 107.
[71] *Ibid.*, p. 108.
[72] His letters to the father of Dr. Henri Parrot, a doctor in Périgueux also, and to Armand d'Hautefort, *O.C.*, 15:21-25, indicate his affection for the people there.
[73] *O.C.*, 15:47, 68; *Vie*, 1:116.
[74] Louis to Eugène, 24 May 1838, *O.C.*, 15:47.
[75] *O.C.*, 3:21-22.
[76] *Ibid.*, p. 23; *Vie*, 1:109, Douglas Johnson, *Guizot* (London: Routledge & Kegan Paul, 1963), pp. 148, 173.
[77] *Vie*, 1:109, 112.
[78] *Ibid.*, pp. 111-112; *O.C.*, 3:23.
[79] *Vie*, 1:117; *O.C.*, 3:24.
[80] *O.C.*., 3:19.
[81] Louis Veuillot to Gustave Olivier, 19 Sept. 1836, *O.C.*, 15:19-21.
[82] *O.C.*, 3:22.
[83] Louis to Eugène, Rome, 19 March 1838, *O.C.*, 15:27.
[84] *O.C.*, 3:23-24.
[85] *Ibid.*, p. 24; *Vie*, 1:117-118.
[86] His father, whose portrait was painted by Émile Lafon, could be said to have been converted to Catholicism by Louis immediately after his return from Rome. He lived only until the next year, but his mother lived until 1863. At this time she and her daughters lived at the Port de la Rapée, 14, in Bercy, where she operated a tavern for bargers with the sign "Au Gigot" on the door. *O.C.*, 15:47, 68; *Vie*, 1:119.

[87] *Vie*, 1:119.
[88] *O.C.*, 3:24.

CHAPTER II

[1] *O.C.*, 3:15.
[2] *O.C.*, 15:26-78.
[3] *Ibid.*, 3:7.
[4] *Vie*, 1:121.
[5] Louis to Eugène, 19 March 1838, *O.C.*, 15:27.
[6] *Ibid.*, 3:25-26.
[7] *Ibid.*, p. 28.
[8] Louis to Eugène, 19 March 1838, *ibid.*, 15:28.
[9] *O.C.*, 3:29.
[10] Louis to Eugène, 19 March 1838, *ibid.*, 15:28.
[11] *O.C.*, p. iv. Adolphe died after forty years of married life, and Élisabeth, although rich, became one of the Little Sisters of the Poor. See below, p. 398.
[12] *Vie*, 1:131.
[13] BN NAF 24220, pp. 6-7.
[14] *O.C.*, 3:32-40.
[15] *Ibid.*, p. 22.
[16] *Vie*, 1:126.
[17] Louis Veuillot to Armand d'Hautefort, Albert de Calvimont, Henri Parrot, Justin Peyrot, Léonce Pessard, Eugène de L'Isle, and Eugène Veuillot, Naples, 3 April 1838, *O.C.*, 15:29-38.
[18] It certainly would not have been felicitous for him or his brother to have mentioned it, but Good Friday was Friday the Thirteenth that year.
[19] *O.C.*, 3:59-72.
[20] Not many modern conversions have been more fully described. See especially *O.C.*, 3:88-98, but Veuillot and those treating him make much in various places. Lucien Christophe, *Louis Veuillot* (Paris: Wesmael-Charlier, 1967), especially stresses his conversion.
[21] *O.C.*, 3:94-97.
[22] *Vie*, 1:132.
[23] Louis to Eugène, Ancona, 12 June 1838, *O.C.*, 15:52-56.
[24] *Ibid.*, 3:98.
[25] Louis Veuillot spoke little of this important interview, his principal mention being less than one page in *Rome et Lorette, O.C.*, 3:98. Eugène likewise gives little attention to it in his biography (*Vie*, 1:136). Louis does not mention it in his correspondence. He did have an interview with Cardinal Fesch, aged uncle of Napoleon, and Olivier gives an account of this interview, writing under a pseudonym in *L'Univers*, 15 Nov. 1840.
[26] Louis to Eugène, 12 June 1838, *O.C.*, 15:56.
[27] *O.C.*, 3:161-168.
[28] Phillip Spencer, *Politics of Belief*, p. 217. E. Schérer, *Études critiques*, 1:203-220, ridicules his belief, but does not quite use these words in this piece.
[29] *O.C.*, 3:171-174.
[30] Louis to Eugène, 3 June 1838, *O.C.*, 15:51.
[31] *Vie*, 1:135.
[32] Louis Veuillot to Gustave Olivier, 2 July 1838, *O.C.*, 15:59.

[33]*Les pèlerinages de Suisse, O.C.*, 2:11.
[34]*Ibid.*, pp. 11-22.
[35]*Ibid* , p. 23.
[36]*Ibid.*, pp. 151-152.
[37]Louis Veuillot to Gustave Olivier, 11 July 1838, *O.C.*, 15:67.
[38]Louis to Eugène, 9 July 1838, *ibid.*, p. 63.
[39]Gruyère was one of the areas he visited. It is curious that at least before he went there he referred to its principal product as "ce cruel fromage" (*ibid.*, p. 66).
[40]*O.C.*, 15:67; Vie, 1:139.
[41]*Vie*, 1:139.
[42]Charles Foucauld was a dissipated nobleman who became an ascetic who worked with the Berbers in the Sahara.
[43]16 June 1838, *O.C.*, 15:56-58.
[44]*Ibid.*, pp. 58-75.
[45]*O.C.*, 2:118-119.
[46]*Ibid.*, pp. 236-241.
[47]*Ibid.*, p. 241.
[48]*Ibid.*, 15:74. A man named Jacquot, who called himself Eugène de Mirecourt, gave "lessons in literature" at the place his sisters had been staying. He was the same one with whom Louis Veuillot later had trouble. See below, pp. 219-220.
[49]*Vie*, 1:145-148.
[50]Louis Veuillot to Armand d'Hautefort, 5 Sept. 1838, BN NAF 23223, p. 11.
[51]Louis Veuillot to Mme X, Paris, 1839, *O.C.*, 15:84-85.
[52]Louis Veuillot to Mme de Wailly, Paris, 1839, BN NAF, 24223, pp. 3-6.
[53]*O.C.*, 15:55.
[54]Eugène Veuillot has dozens of titles in the Bibliothèque Nationale. His most notable work is his four-volume *Louis Veuillot*, but his *La Cochinchine et le Tonquin* (1859), *La Croix et l'epée* (1856), *Les Guerres de la Vendée et de la Bretagne* (1847), and *L'Église, la France et le schisme en Orient* (1855), plus his editing of Louis's correspondence and works, make him a significant literary figure in his own right.
[55]Louis Veuillot to Supérieur du Seminaire a Fribourg (Suisse), 11 Aug. 1838, *O.C.*, 15:75-78.
[56]Same to Father Roshaven, 1 Oct. 1838, *ibid.*, pp. 79-80.
[57]In fact, Gustave Olivier was the publisher, and he simply used this name. *Vie*, 1:155.
[58]*O.C.*, 2:iii.
[59]*Ibid.*, p. iii; *O.C.*, 15:75.
[60]H. Talvart, *Louis Veuillot*, pp. 15-29; P. Fernesolle, *Pour qu'on lise Louis Veuillot*, pp. 21-42.
[61]*O.C.*, 2:192-193; Adrien Dansette, *Religious History of Modern France* (New York: Herder and Herder, 1961), 1:241, errs when he says that Veuillot had not reached this stage under the July Monarchy.
[62]*Vie*, 1:162-163; for trouble with Sibour, see below, pp. 143-161
[63]*Vie*, 1:163; *O.C.*, 2:192-194.
[64]*Vie*, 1:183-187; *O.C.*, 2:iii-iv.
[65]*Vie*, 1:187-189.
[66]*O.C.*, 15:62.
[67]Édouard Pontal, *Louis Veuillot et son frère, employés au Ministère de l'intérieur*, (Angers-Bordeaux: Siradeau, 1925), p. 80.

[68]*Vie*, 1:165-166.
[69]Undated sketch of his life by Veuillot, BN NAF 24632, p. 486.
[70]For Guizot as a protestant, see D. Johnson, *Guizot*, pp. 377-431, esp. p. 384.
[71]*Vie*, 1:191.
[72]*Ibid.*, pp. 193-194.
[73]*O.C.*, 3:143-144.
[74]BN NAF, 24622, p. 38.

CHAPTER III

[1]Claude Bellanger, Jacques Godechot, Pierre Guiral, and Fernand Terrou, *Histoire générale de la presse française,* 4 vols. (Paris: P.U.F., 1969-), a projected four-volume study, the second of which deals with the period 1814-1871, is the leading general work, while the standby for more than a century was Louis Eugène Hatin, *Histoire politique et littéraire de la presse en France,* 8 vols. (Paris: Poulet-Malassis et De Broise, 1859-1861). Georges J. Weill, *Le journal; origines, évolution et role de la presse périodique* (Paris: La Renaissance du Livre, 1934) is a useful account told from a liberal point of view. Anita M. R. May, "The Challenge of the French Catholic Press to Episcopal Authority, 1842-1860: A Crisis of Modernization," a University of Pittsburgh dissertation of 1972, is a very informative and perceptive study of the role of *L'Univers* and other Catholic journals.
[2]See especially Waldemar Gurian, "Lamennais," *Review of Politics*, IX (April, 1947), 205-229.
[3]*Vie*, 1:356-357.
[4]*Ibid.*, 1:357.
[5]*Ibid.*, 1:364.
[6]*Ibid.*, p. 359.
[7]*Ibid.*, pp. 168-171; *O.C.*, 80-81.
[8]*Vie*, 1:171-172; *O.C.*, 80-81.
[9]*O.C.*, 27:107-11.
[10]*Ibid.*, p. 113.
[11]See especially Veuillot's *Histoire du parti catholique, O.C.*, 6:407-480.
[12]*O.C.*, 27:117-122, 343-411.
[13]*Vie*, 1:203-204.
[14]*O.C.*, 2:iii.
[15]*Vie*, 1:205.
[16]BN NAF 24223, p. 17.
[17]*Vie,* 1:215; *O.C.,* 7:101-133; *ibid.,* 15:131.
[18]*O.C.*, p. 99.
[19]*Ibid.*, p. 111.
[20]*Ibid.*, p. 115-116.
[21]*Vie*, 1:218.
[22]Louis Veuillot to Abbé Morriseau, 10 Dec. 1840, *O.C.*, 15:131.
[23]*Vie*, 1:225; *O.C.*, 4:vi.
[24]*O.C.*, 15:135.
[25]*Vie*, 1:225.
[26]Louis Veuillot to Edmond Leclerc, 18 Feb. 1841, *O.C.*, 15:137.
[27]Louis to Eugène, 18 Feb. 1841, *ibid.,* p. 138.
[28]*Vie*, 1:225.

[29]Louis Veuillot to Abbé Morisseau, Alger, 3 March 1841, *O.C.,* 15:142.
[30]Same to same, 18 Feb., 1841, *ibid.*, p. 141.
[31]*Ibid.*, p. 143.
[32]*Vie*, p. 232.
[33]Louis Veuillot to Abbé Aulanier, July, 1841, *O.C.*, 15:212.
[34]*Vie*, 1:230.
[35]Louis Veuillot to Dumast, 1 Aug. 1841, *O.C.*, 15:221.
[36]*Vie*, 1:236.
[37]Louis Veuillot to Leclerc, end of March, 1841, BN NAF 24220, p. 22.
[38]*Les Français en Algérie, O.C.*, 4:22-29.
[39]*Vie*, 1:242.
[40]Louis Veuillot to Dumast, Easter, 1841, *O.C.*, 15:149.
[41]Louis Veuillot to Leclerc, April, 1841, *ibid.*, p. 167.
[42]*Vie*, 1:233-234.
[43]Louis Veuillot to Abbé Morisseau, 3 Mar. 1841, *O.C.*, 15:143.
[44]Same to Leclerc, 7 Aug. 1841, *ibid.*, p. 224.
[45]Same to Eugène Veuillot, 27 July 1841, *ibid.*, pp. 215-216.
[46]*Ibid.*, p. 215.
[47]*Ibid.*, p. 224.
[48]*Ibid.*, p. 215.
[49]*Vie*, p. 244.
[50]Louis Veuillot to Aulanier, 14 June 1841, *O.C.*, 15:195.
[51]Same to Leclerc, 7 Aug. 1841, *ibid.*, p. 224.
[52]Same to same, 26 March 1841, BN NAF 24631, p. 35. Veuillot observed the Moslems closely, and in his *Notes intimes* (BN NAF, 24620, pp. 409-452) are extensive observations on the Algerians.
[53]*O.C.*, 4:3-13.
[54]Louis Veuillot to Leclerc, Alger, 26 June 1841, BN NAF, 24220, 35-36.
[55]Same to same, Alger, 28 July 1841, *ibid.*, p. 43.
[56]Same to Eugène Veuillot, 1 May 1841, *O.C.*., 15:170.
[57]Same to Dumast, Alger, 9 May 1841, *ibid.*, p. 178.
[58]*O.C.*, 4:12.
[59]*Ibid.*, 15:195-196; 4:94, 200. In these references the name is G'Stalter, and in *Vie*, 1:233, G. Stalter. Most likely it was "Gstalter."
[60]His reports of 8 March and 19 April 1841 are published, *O.C.*., 4:244-256.
[61]Louis Veuillot to Leclerc, 5 May 1841, *ibid.*, 15:177.
[62]*Ibid.*, 4:250.
[63]*Ibid.*, p. 251.
[64]*Ibid.*, p. 256.
[65]*Vie*, p. 264.
[66]Louis to Eugène, 20 April 1841, BN NAF, 24631, p. 39.
[67]Same to Leclerc, 20 June 1841, *ibid.*, 24220, p. 33.
[68]Same to Eugène Veuillot, 10 July 1841, *ibid.*, p. 54.
[69]*Vie*, p. 266.
[70]*Ibid.*, p. 412.
[71]*O.C.*, 15:230, 245, 266.
[72]Louis to Eugène, 25 Jan. 1843, BN NAF 24220, p. 79. The carefully edited *Œuvres complètes* do not show the date in January, but the place, Nancy, was inserted, where Veuillot was at the time, although the original does not show this information.
[73]*Vie*, 1:viii.

[74]In addition to the obvious sources on the relations of Veuillot with Guizot are the private archival material of Guizot in the Archives nationales.
[75]Louis to Eugène, 25 Sept. 1841, *O.C.*, 15:234.
[76]Same to same, 6 Nov. 1841, *ibid.*, p. 244.
[77]Same to same, 25 Sept. 1841, *ibid.*, p. 235.
[78]*Vie*, 1:266.
[79]Louis to Eugène, 6 Nov. 1841, *O.C.*, 15:245.
[80]Undated sketch of his life by Veuillot, BN NAF 24632, p. 486.
[81]Louis to Eugène, 12 July 1842, *O.C.*, 15:311.
[82]Same to same, 20 April 1841, *ibid.*, p. 153.
[83]*Ibid.*, 4:xii-xiii.
[84]Louis Veuillot to Eugène, 12 July 1842, *O.C.*, 15:311.
[85]Extract of a report of 13 April 1842, dossier 7273, *Archives nationales* (hereafter referred to a "AN") 305, AP 5. This is the earliest of the documents Lavedan, Veuillot's enemy, who later became director of the Bureau de la presse, extracted.
[86]*O.C.*, 27:276-296.
[87]*Ibid.*, 15:236.
[88]See notes by Eugène and François Veuillot, *ibid.*, pp. 271, 363.
[89]Louis to Eugène, 11 July 1842, *ibid.*, p. 310. See note, p. 306 for Taconet.
[90]Same to same, 12 July 1842, *ibid.*, p. 311.
[91]Maurice Vallet, Louis Veuillot. *Sa Vie, ses idées sociales, ses idées politiques, ses idées littéraires* (Paris: Société française d'imprimerie et de librairie, 1913), pp. 22-23.
[92]Louis Veuillot to Abbé Morisseau, 13 March 1843, *O.C.*, 15:363.
[93]One of the best treatments of this subject is by Eugène Veuillot, *Vie*, 1:328-383.
[94]*O.C.*, 27:236-246; *O.C.*, 15:19; *Vie*, 1:177-181.
[95]*O.C.*, 15:119.
[96]See below, pp. 356-358, 362-363, 385-388.
[97]*Vie*, 1:307.
[98]*Ibid.*, pp. 307-315; *O.C.*, 15:336-348.
[99]*Vie*, 1:313-315.
[100]Louis Veuillot to Dumast, 13 March 1843, *O.C.*, 15:364.
[101]Louis to Eugène, 28 March 1843, *ibid.*, p. 368.
[102]Same to Foisset, 9 April 1843, *ibid.*, p. 372.
[103]Same to Eugène, April 1843, BN NAF, 24220, p. 81.
[104]There were other Catholic journals in Paris beside *L'Ami de la Religion* and *Le Correspondant*. Among them were *L'Université catholique, Annales de philosophie chrétienne, Revue de Saint-Paul, Revue catholique,* and *Mémorial catholique.*
[105]*O.C.*, 15:240.
[106]Louis to Eugène, 24 April 1842, *ibid.*, pp. 284-285.
[107]*Vie*, 1:271-272.
[108]Louis to Eugène, 31 May 1842, *O.C.*, 15:301.
[109]*Ibid.*, 3:308.
[110]*Ibid.*, pp. viii-ix.
[111]Louis Veuillot to Abbé Morisseau, 29 July 1842, *ibid.*, p. 314.
[112]*Vie*, 1:407-411.
[113]Louis to Eugène, April 1843, BN NAF, 24220, p. 81.
[114]Same to same, 22 April 1843, *ibid.*, p. 83. Annette was married in 1845 to Stanislas Desquers.

[115] Same to same, June 1842, *ibid.*, p. 69.
[116] Dansette, *Religious History of Modern France*, 1:241.
[117] *Vie*, 1:373.
[118] Dansette, *Religious History of Modern France*, 1:212.
[119] *Ibid.*, pp. 214-217.
[120] *Vie*, 1:343-358. See Waldemar Gurian, "Lamennais," *Review of Politics*, IX (April, 1947), 205-224.
[121] Dansette, *Religious History of Modern France*, pp. 217-218.
[122] *Ibid.*,.pp. 220-224.
[123] *L'Univers*, 8 Feb. 1843.
[124] *Ibid.*, 24 Feb. 1843.
[125] *Ibid.*, 28 Feb. 1843.
[126] *Ibid.*, 8 Oct. 1843.
[127] *Ibid.*, 25 Nov. 1843.
[128] *Ibid.*, 12 Oct. 1843.
[129] *Ibid.*, 30 Jan. 1844.
[130] *Ibid.*, 12 Feb. 1843.
[131] *Ibid.*, 18 Feb. 1843.
[132] *Vie*, 1:391; Dansette, *Religious History*, 1:147-148.
[133] *Vie*, 1:440; Dansette, *op. cit.*, pp. 232-235.
[134] Dansette, *op. cit.*, pp. 232-233.
[135] *Vie*, 1:367-405, 415-426; Dansette, *op. cit.*, 1:232-240.
[136] *O.C.*, 27:427-433.
[137] *Vie*, 1:416.
[138] *O.C.*, 15:386. So were Cardinal Bonald, the Archbishop of Lyon, and the Bishops of Chartres, Arras, and Strasbourg.
[139] *O.C.*, 15:416.
[140] Dansette, *Religious History*, 1:242.
[141] *Vie*, 1:376-383. See especially Louis Veuillot's own *Histoire du parti catholique, O.C.*, 10:407-480.
[142] *L'Univers*, 23 July 1843.
[143] Veuillot to Foisset, 20 June 1843, BN NAF, 24223, pp. 38-40.
[144] Same to Parisis, 9 Nov. 1843, *ibid.*, 24220, p. 72.
[145] See unpublished dissertation of Anita May, "The Challenge of the French Catholic Press to Episcopal Authority, 1842-1860): A Crisis of Modernization." University of Pittsburgh, 1972.
[146] Préfet of the Seine to the Garde des Sceaux, 8 Sept. 1843, AN, BB[18] 1415, Dr. 7117.
[147] Lettre a M. Villemain, Ministre de l'Instruction publique, sur la Liberté d'Enseignement, *O.C.*, 27:482-514.
[148] *Ibid.*, pp. 514-517.
[149] François P. G. Guizot, *Mémoires pour servir a l'histoire de mon temps,* 8 vols. (Paris: Michel Lévy, 1858-1867), 7:376-385.
[150] *O.C.*, 28:29-30.
[151] *Ibid.*, p. 37.
[152] *Ibid.*, p. 47.
[153] Dansette, *Religious History*, 1:243.
[154] Montalembert to Louis Veuillot, Madère, 13 Jan. 1844, BN NAF, 24633, pp. 58-65.
[155] Same to same, undated, *ibid.*, p. 66.
[156] *Vie*, 1:429. For an anticlerical interpretation of Combalot's rashness, see

Antonin Debidour, *Histoire des rapports de l'église et l'état en France, 1789-1870* (Paris: Alcan, 1898), p. 456.

[157] *Vie*, 1:429-430.

[158] Mgr. Affre to Veuillot, 21 Feb. 1844, BN NAF, 24633, pp. 54-55.

[159] *Vie*, 1:430-432.

[160] See *L'Univers*, especially 23 Jan., 7 March 1844.

[161] The Bishop of Chalons was a notable protester; *L'Univers*, 30 Jan. 1844.

[162] *Ibid.*, 5 Jan. 1844.

[163] *Ibid.*, 10 Jan. 1844.

[164] *Ibid.*, 19 March 1844.

[165] *Ibid.*, 16 April 1844.

[166] *Ibid.*, 30 Jan. 1844.

[167] Veuillot to Parisis, 10 March 1844, BN NAF, 24220, pp. 96-97.

[168] *L'Univers*, 7 March 1844.

[169] *Vie*, 1:436.

[170] Note for the minister of interior, AN 305, AP 5.

[171] Note, cabinet du Préfet de police 22 April 1844, *ibid.*

[172] *L'Univers*, 7 March 1844.

[173] Veuillot to M. Lelièvre, and Msgr. Parisis, 12 May 1844 *O.C.*, 16:59-61.

[174] Report of inspector, 11 May 1844.

[175] Note of Veuillot, 7 June 1844, with report of 12 June 1844, APP, EA/15.

[176] Veuillot to Lelièvre, 12 May 1844, *O.C.*, 16:59.

[177] Note of Lebel to Préfet, 11 June 1844, AN 305, AP 5, Dr. 7.

[178] *O.C.*, 16:59-81.

[179] Darboy to Veuillot, Langres, 19 May 1844, BN NAF, 24633.

[180] Veuillot to Dupanloup, 11 June 1844, Bibliothèque de Saint-Sulpice, Veuillot dossier, 2.

[181] Montalembert to Veuillot, Madère, 17 Feb. 1844, cited in *Vie*, 1:486.

[182] *Ibid.*, p. 442.

[183] Extract of police report, AN 305, AP 5, Dr. 7.

[184] Édouard Lecanuet, *Montalembert d'après ses papiers et sa correspondance*, 3 vols. (Paris: Poussielgue, 1895-1902), 2:230.

[185] *Vie*, 1:485.

[186] *Ibid.*, p. 493.

[187] Phillips, *The Church in France, 1789-1848*, pp. 292-293.

[188] *L'Univers*, 2 Feb. 1844.

[189] *Ibid.*, 3 Feb. 1844.

[190] *O.C..*, 16:96.

[191] Dansette, *Religious History*, 1:239; *Vie* 1:504.

[192] Dansette, *op. cit.*, p. 239.

[193] *L'Univers*, 9 Aug. 1844.

[194] *Ibid.*, 10 Aug. 1844.

[195] *Ibid.*, 20 Aug. 1844.

[196] Throughout Veuillot's life he received letters from priests in different parts of France thanking him for his expression of ideas that appealed to them. The pastoral letters of the dioceses of Paris and Orleans were good examples at different periods of the absence of the militant tone.

[197] *O.C.*, 16:110; Lecanuet, *Montalembert*, 2:231.

[198] *Vie*, 1:511; *O.C.*, 16:104.

[199] *Vie*, 1:511.

[200] *O.C.*, 16:110.

[201]Veuillot to Léon Aubineau, 22 Jan. 1845, *ibid.*, p. 119.
[202]Same to Montalembert, 5 Jan. 1845, *ibid.*, p. 113.
[203]Same to Foisset, 4 March 1845, *ibid.*, p. 126.
[204]Same to same, 25 Jan. 1845, *ibid.*, p. 116.
[205]Undated statement about his life, *Notes intimes*, BN NAF 24632, pp. 486-487.
[206]Philip Spencer, *Politics of Belief*, pp. 213-214.
[207]Phillips, *Church in France, 1789-1848*, pp. 292-293.
[208]*Vie*, 1:470-472.
[209]*Ibid.*, p. 471.
[210]E. Gauthier, *Le Vrai Louis Veuillot*, p. 32.
[211]*Vie*, 1:519-520.
[212]One of Annette's children married Eugene Tavernier, secretary to Veuillot and an editor for *L'Univers. O.C.*, 16:131.
[213]*Vie*, 1:522-524.
[214]*O.C.*, 29:534.
[215]*Ibid.*, 536-537.
[216]*O.C.*, 16:148.
[217]Louis to Eugène, 15 Sept. 1845, BN NAF, 24220, pp. 101-102.
[218]*O.C.*, 8:13-53.
[219]*Ibid.*, p. V.
[220]*Vie*, p. 527.
[221]*O.C.*, 8:25.
[222]*Ibid.*, p. 14.
[223]Veuillot to to Dom Gardereau, Aug. 1845, *ibid.*, 16:147.
[224]Gauthier, *Le vrai Louis Veuillot*, p. 146.
[225]François Veuillot, *Louis Veuillot, Sa vie*, p. 77; Philip Spencer, *Politics of Belief*, p. 214. All of Veuillot's references to Mathilde emphasize her demure nature.
[226]August 1845, *O.C.*, 28:269-292.
[227]9, 26 Nov., 3 Dec. 1845 *ibid.*, pp. 323-342.
[228]10 May 1845, *ibid.*, pp. 355-360.
[229]Louis Bascoul, *Louis Veuillot, sa jeunesse*, p. 56.
[230]Veuillot to Dumast, start of Oct. 1845, *O.C.*, 16:149-150.
[231]Same to same, 21 Dec. 1845, *ibid.*, 16:156.
[232]Same to Foisset, 28 Ap. 1846, *ibid.*, p. 168.
[233]Same to Commandant de Maisonneuve, 4 July 1846, *ibid.*, pp. 185-186.
[234]*Vie*, 2:90-98.
[235]*Ibid.*, p. 91.
[236]*Ibid.*, pp. 92-93.
[237]*Ibid.*, p. 98; Lecanuet, *Montalembert*, 2:291-292.
[238]7 June 1846, *O.C.*, 28:365.
[239]*Ibid.*, pp. 366-371.
[240]*Vie*, 2:101-104.
[241]Veuillot to Montalembert, 24 June 1846, BN NAF, 24223, pp. 68-70.
[242]Same to same, 4 July 1846, *ibid.*, pp. 72-74.
[243]*Vie*, 2:118.
[244]*Ibid.*, p. 125.
[245]Veuillot to Montalembert, 11 Nov. 1846, BN NAF, 24223, 89-101.
[246]De Coux to Montalembert, Nov. 1846, BN NAF, 24633, 83-85.
[247]Veuillot to Du Lac, 10 Nov. 1846, BN NAF, 24220, pp. 107-108.
[248]*Vie*, 2:130-133.

[249]24 June 1846, *O.C.*, 28:377-383.
[250]Veuillot to Du Lac, 4 Dec. 1847, BN NAF, 24220, p. 131.
[251]*Vie*, 2:151-153.
[252]*O.C.*, 28:572-602.
[253] *Vie*, 2:153-154.
[254]*Ibid.*, pp. 138-139.
[255]Bishop Wicart (Fréjus) to Veuillot, 4 Feb. 1847, BN NAF, 24225, p. 44.
[256]Bishop of Périgueux to Veuillot, 17 March 1847, *ibid.*, pp. 37-38.
[257]Archbishop Bonald (Lyon) to Veuillot, 28 Feb. 1846, *ibid.*, p. 30.
[258]*Vie*, 2:139.
[259]*O.C.*, 16:242.
[260]Louis Veuillot to Msgr. Gousset (Reims), 8 Dec. 1846, BN NAF, 24223, pp. 108-119.
[261]*O.C.*, 28:502-512.
[262]Lecanuet, *Montalembert*, 2:320-323.
[263]Veuillot to Du Lac, 4 June 1847, BN NAF, 24631, p. 69.
[264]Same to same, May 1847, *ibid.*, p. 65.
[265]Same to same, April 1847, *ibid.*, p. 62.
[266]*O.C.*, 28:502-545.
[267]13 March 1847, *ibid.*, p. 509.
[268]15 Nov. 1847, *ibid.*, 16:326.
[269]Veuillot to Dumast, 24 Oct. 1847, *ibid.*, p. 317.
[270]Guizot, *Mémoires,* 8:517.
[271]Johnson, *Guizot*, pp. 377-431.
[272]Veuillot to De Coux, 8 Nov. 1847, BN NAF, 24223, pp. 176-182.
[273]*Vie*, pp. 153-154.
[274]*Ibid.*, p. 84.
[275]*O.C.*, 16:176-177.
[276]Veuillot to Du Lac, May, 1847, *ibid.*, p. 283.
[277]*Ibid.*
[278]Veuillot to Du Lac, 24 Oct. 1847, *ibid.*, p. 315.
[279]Same to same, 25 Dec. 1847, 17 Jan. 1848, BN NAF 24220, pp. 132, 135.
[280]Louis to Mathilde, Aug. 21, Aug. 26, Aug. 1846, *O.C.*, 16:195-200.
[281]*Vie*; 2:147-148.

CHAPTER IV

[1]*O.C.*, 29:61.
[2]28 Jan. 1848, *ibid.*, p. 92.
[3]Phillips, *Church in France, 1848-1907* pp. 14-15, states very well the separation in Veuillot's mind between the public and personal sides of his antagonists. On Guizot's death in 1874 Veuillot's article on him, *O.C.*, 38:491-500, certainly returned to his early 1848 line.
[4]21 Feb. 1848, *O.C.*, 29:149.
[5]29 Oct. 1847, *ibid.*, 16:321-322.
[6]8 Nov. 1847, *ibid.*, pp. 323-325.
[7]*Ibid.*, pp. 326-328.
[8]*Vie*, 2:204.
[9]*Ibid.*, p. 200.
[10]Veuillot to De Coux, 8 Nov. 1847, *O. C.*, 16: 323-325.

[11]Same to Same, 11 Feb. 1848, *ibid.*, p. 346.
[12]*Vie*, 2:200.
[13]*Ibid.*, p. 206.
[14]*Ibid.*, p. 207. Most of Louis' letters to Du Lac begin "Mon cher frère."
[15]See footnote, *O.C.*, 16:341.
[16]Veuillot to Dupanloup, 14 Jan. 1848, BN NAF, 24223, pp. 195-197. The original of this letter is in the Bibliothèque Saint-Sulpice under Correspondance Veuillot, p. 5.
[17]Veuillot to Montalembert, 18 Dec. 1847, *O.C.*, 16:333-334.
[18]*Vie*, 2:202.
[19]*Ibid.*
[20]Phillips, *Church in France, 1789-1848*, gives a good survey of religious revival, pp. 259-285, and Dansette, *Religious History*, 1:242-244 summarizes the situation.
[21]*Vie*, 2:218-219.
[22]Louis to Mathilde, 25 Feb. 1848, *O.C.*, 16:348.
[23]Same to same, 22 Feb. 1848, *ibid.*, pp. 349-351.
[24]26 Feb. 1848, *ibid.*, 29:166-169. A curious note that Louis Veuillot added in 1857 was: "The Church was free in fact and in law in the United States. Since the invasion of European socialists this situation has changed." (p. 167)
[25]29 Feb. 1848. *ibid.*, p. 171. For French press reactions to the American republic, see Msgr. Joseph N. Moody, "The French Catholic Press of the 1840's on American Catholicism," *The Catholic Historical Review*, 60 (July, 1974): 185-214.
[26]*Ibid.*, pp. 155-160.
[27]23 March 1857, *ibid.*, p. 164.
[28]11 March 1848, *ibid.*, p. 176.
[29]*Vie*, 2:214.
[30]*Ibid.*, p. 279.
[31]*O.C.*, 29:188-197.
[32]Veuillot to Comte de La Tour, 24 March 1848, *ibid.*, 16:361.
[33]Same to Rendu, 4 April 1848, *ibid.*, p. 362.
[34]Same to Dumast, 26 April 1848, *ibid.*, p. 366.
[35]*Vie*, 2:231.
[36]Georges Duveau, 1848: *The Making of a Revolution* (trans. Anne Carter) (New York: Pantheon Books, 1967), pp. 179-180.
[37]*O.C.*, 29:197-201.
[38]*Ibid.*, pp. 206-216.
[39]Veuillot to Abbé Boucheny, 14 March 1848, *ibid.*, 16:359-360.
[40]*Ibid.*, p. 360.
[41]*L'Univers*, 6 April 1848.
[42]*O.C.*, 29:185-187.
[43]*Vie*, 2:229.
[44]Veuillot to Rev. Père X, 18 March 1848, BN NAF 24631, pp. 84-85.
[45]Same to Rendu, 4 April 1848, BN NAF, 24223, p. 213.
[46]Montalembert to Veuillot, 29 May 1848, BN NAF, 24633, p. 179.
[47]Duveau, *1848*, pp. 96-100; René Arnaud, *The Second Republic and Napoleon III* (trans. E. F. Buckley) (London: Heineman, 1930), pp. 12-13.
[48]30 April 1848, *O.C.*, 29:217.
[49]7 May 1848, BN NAF, 24620, pp. 37-38.
[50]4 May 1848, *O.C.*, 29:219.

[51]*Ibid.*, p. 224.
[52]Duveau, *1848*, pp. 117-124, gives a colorful account.
[53]*O.C.*, 29:241-247.
[54]*Ibid.*, p. 252.
[55]*Ibid.*, p. 212.
[56]*Ibid.*, p. 256.
[57]Frederick A. Simpson, *The Rise of Louis Napoleon* (London: Frank Cass, 1968) (first printed, 1909), presents the qualities of the man as a claimant that were not necessarily those of a ruler.
[58]*O.C.*, 29:262-264.
[59]*Ibid.*, pp. 262-274.
[60]*L'Univers*, 4 May 1848.
[61]*Ibid.*, 11 May 1848.
[62]*Ibid.*, see especially lead editorials of 6 and 14 May 1848.
[63]*O.C.*, 29:241-250. Duveau, *1848*, pp. 117-124.
[64]*L'Univers*, 16 May 1848.
[65]*Ibid.*, 19 May 1848.
[66]*Ibid.*, 23 May 1848.
[67]Duveau, *1848*, pp. 145-146.
[68]*L'Univers*, 29 May 1848.
[69]The printery of E.-J Bailly, Divry et Cie. was located at 2, Place de Sorbonne.
[70]*L'Univers*, 25 June 1848.
[71]*Vie*, 2:259-260.
[72]*Ibid.*, p. 260; *O.C.*, 5:331-377.
[73]Dansette, *Religious History*, 1:258-259.
[74]*L'Univers*, 27 June 1848.
[75]For general appraisals of the role of the press, see Jean-Baptiste Duroselle, *Les débuts du catholicisme social en France (1822-1870)* (Paris: P.U.F., 1951), pp. 299, 303-304 and Ross W. Collins, *Catholicism and the Second French Republic, 1848-1852* (New York: Columbia University Press, 1923), chapter 2.
[76]*Vie*, 2:277.
[77]*O.C.*, 29:316-321.
[78]*Ibid.*, pp. 325-327.
[79]*Ibid.*, pp. 368-369.
[80]*Ibid.*, pp. 368-390.
[81]Veuillot to Foisset, 19 Nov. 1848, *ibid.*, 16:394-396.
[82]Same to Montalembert, 19 Nov. 1848, *ibid.*, pp. 396-398.
[83]Duroselle, *Catholicisme social*, pp. 304, 317.
[84]Veuillot to Blanche-Raffin, 21 July 1848, *O.C.*, 16:370-371.
[85]Same to Dumast, 19 Aug. 1848, *ibid.*, p. 374.
[86]*O.C.*, 29:294-308.
[87]Veuillot to Msgr. Clausel de Montals, Sept. 1848, *ibid.*, 16:385-388.
[88]*O.C.*, 5:1-328.
[89]*Vie*, 2:304.
[90]Veuillot to Montalembert, 19 Nov. 1848, *O.C.*, 16:396-398.
[91]*Ibid.*, 5:331-377.
[92]*Ibid.*, pp. 379-533.
[93]Arnaud, *Second Republic and Napoleon III*, p. 33-34, gives a thumbnail appraisal. Simpson, *The Rise of Louis Napoleon*, gives considerable treatment.
[94]*O.C.*, 29:336-367. Anita May's valuable article, "The Falloux Law, the Catholic Press, and the Bishops: Crisis in Authority in the Catholic Press," *French*

Historical Studies, 8 (Spring, 1973):77-94, strongly emphasizes this neutrality.

[95]*O.C.*, 29:338.

[96]*Ibid.*, p. 350.

[97]*Ibid.*, p. 340.

[98]*Ibid.*, p. 331-335.

[99]Veuillot to Foisset, 19 Nov. 1848, *ibid.*, 16:396.

[100]*Ibid.*, 29:338-339.

[101]The role of France is traced by Pierre de La Gorce, *Histoire de la Seconde République*, 2 vols. (Paris: Plon, Nourrit, 1898), 2:151-248.

[102]*L'Univers*, 29 Nov. 1848.

[103]*Vie*, 2:287-288.

[104]Louis Napoleon to Veuillot, 2 Dec. 1848, BN NAF 24633, p. 187.

[105]*Vie*, 2:288 quotes a letter of Louis Napoleon to Prince de Canino, 7 Dec. 1848.

[106]*Ibid.* La Groce, *Seconde République*, 1:457-484.

[107]Veuillot to Dumast, around 16 Dec. 1848, *O.C.*, 17:7.

[108]*Ibid.*, footnote, pp. 7-8.

[109]*Ibid.*, 29:363-364.

[110]Veuillot to Aubineau, 5 March 1849, *ibid.*, 17:32.

[111]Veuillot to Dumast, 19 April 1849, *ibid*, p. 41.

[112]Same to Foisset, 23 March 1849, *ibid.*, p. 35.

[113]Same to Montalembert, 23 Feb. 1849, *ibid.*, p. 28.

[114]Same to same, 18 April 1849, *ibid.*, pp. 40-41.

[115]*O.C.*, 25:491-505.

[116]Montalembert to Veuillot, 21 Feb. 1849, BN NAF, 24633, p. 198.

[117]Same to same, 24 April 1849, *ibid.*, p. 203.

[118]Veuillot to Dupanloup, 24 Feb. 1849, Veuillot Dossier, Bibliothèque Saint-Sulpice.

[119]Veuillot to Editor, *Liberté de Penser*, 5 Feb. 1849, *O.C.*, 17:23.

[120]Johnson, *Guizot*, pp. 7-9.

[121]Veuillot to La Tour, 29 Dec. 1849, *O.C.*, 17:12.

[122]Veuillot to Guizot, 28 Dec. 1848, *Fonds Guizot*, AN, 42 AP 150, Dr. 31.

[123]*L'Univers*, 11 Jan. 1849.

[124]Veuillot To Guizot, 17 Feb. 1849, BN NAF, 24223, pp. 236-237.

[125]*O.C.*, 17:45, see footnote.

[126]Veuillot to Guizot, 28 April 1849, BN NAF, 24223, p. 252; also in AN *Fonds Guizot*, 42 AP 150, Dr. 150.

[127]Veuillot to Guizot, 16 Dec. 1849, AN, *Fonds Guizot*, 42 AP 150, Dr. 31.

[128]Considering his influence, not much exists on Donoso Cortés. See J. T. Graham, "Donoso Cortés on Liberalism," doctoral dissertation, Saint Louis University, 1957.

[129]*Vie*, 2:340-341; *O.C.*, 17:51-52.

[130]*O.C.*, 29:534-536.

[131]*L'Univers*, 6 Jan. 1849.

[132]*Ibid.*, 21 Jan. 1849.

[133]*Ibid.*, 2 April 1849.

[134]*Ibid*, 5 April 1849.

[135]*O.C.*, 30:24-28.

[136]*Ibid.*, pp. 8-11, 28-32.

[137]La Gorce, *Seconde République*, 1:151-248.

[138]*L'Univers*, 9 March 1849.

[139] *Ibid.*, 9 May 1849.
[140] Veuillot to Dumast, 21 May 1849, *O.C.*, 17:46.
[141] Roger Price, *The French Second Republic: A Social History* (Ithaca: Cornell University Press, 1972) pp. 246-250.
[142] *O.C.*, 17:52, 29:537-543.
[143] Alfred de Falloux, *Mémoires d'un royaliste*, 2 vols. (Paris, Perrin, 1888), 1:559-572. For the central figure, Falloux says somewhat less than might have been expected.
[144] *Le Parti catholique, O.C.*, 6:430.
[145] See Anita R. May, "The Falloux Law, the Catholic Press, and the Bishops: Crisis of Authority in the French Church," *French Historical Studies*, 8(Spring, 1973):77-94, especially p. 86, and John K. Huckaby, "Roman Catholic Reaction to the Falloux Law," *French Historical Studies*, 4(1965):203-213. The former puts emphasis on Catholic opposition to the university rather than the state as such.
[146] May, "The Falloux Law," pp. 78-80.
[147] *L'Univers*, 21 July 1849.
[148] Alfred de Falloux, *Le Parti catholique, ce qu'il a été, ce qu'il est devenu* (Paris: A. Bray, 1856).
[149] Louis Veuillot, *Le Parti catholique, O.C.*, 6:413-480.
[150] *Ibid.*, p. 424.
[151] *Ibid.*, p. 431.
[152] *Ibid.*, p. 432.
[153] *Ibid.*, p. 433.
[154] May, "The Falloux Law," *FHS*, 8:86, uses this point in sustaining the position that Catholic opposition was not simply on the part of the conservatives.
[155] *Vie*, 2:356, Arnaud, *Second Republic and Napoleon III*, p. 44-48; Dansette, 1:265-271.
[156] Veuillot to M.X., 1 June 1849, *O.C.*, 17:48.
[157] Same to La Tour, 27 April 1849, *ibid.*, p. 42.
[158] Same to Montalembert, 2 June 1849, *ibid.*, p. 51.
[159] C. Lecigne, *Louis Veuillot*, p. 229.
[160] Veuillot to Msgr. Rendu, 2 Aug. 1849, *O.C.*, 17:61-63.
[161] *Vie*, 1:358-359.
[162] *Ibid.*, p. 357; A. de Falloux, *Mémoires*, 1:571.
[163] *O.C.*, 6:437.
[164] May, "The Falloux Law," *FHS*, 8:77-94, develops the subject effectively.
[165] *Ibid.*, p. 86.
[166] *Ibid.*, see especially quote from *Le Correspondant.*
[167] Veuillot to Dumast, 26 June 1849, *O.C.*, 17:55.
[168] *Ibid.*, 22:240, see note; E. Gauthier, *Le Vrai Louis Veuillot*, p. 72.
[169] *Ibid.*, 29:544-549.
[170] *Ibid.*, p. 551.
[171] *L'Univers*, 2 July 1849.
[172] *Ibid.*, 3 July 1849.
[173] *Ibid.*, 19 July 1849.
[174] *Ibid.*, 7 July 1849.
[175] *Ibid.*, 9 July 1849.
[176] *Ibid.*, 28 July 1849.
[177] May, "The Falloux Law," *FHS*, 8:87-94.
[178] *L'Univers*, 1 August 1849.

[179]May, "The Falloux Law," *FHS*, 8:87, says they were being "blackmailed."
[180]*Ibid.*, p. 89.
[181]*Ibid.*, p. 91.
[182]*L'Univers*, 15 July 1849.
[183]*O.C.*., 29:554-557.
[184]*Ibid.*, pp. 554-563.
[185]*Ibid.*, p. 558.
[186]*Ibid.*, pp. 561-563.
[187]*O.C.*, 6:434.
[188]*L'Univers*, 16 July 1849.
[189]*Ibid.*, 6 August, 4 September 1849; 4 Jan., 23 Jan., 23 Feb., 17 March 1850. This list may not be complete.
[190]*Ibid.*, 14 July 1849.
[191]*Ibid.*, 21 July 1849.
[192]*Ibid.*, 1 Sept. 1849.
[193]*O.C.*, 29:568.
[194]*L'Univers*, 28 Oct. 1849.
[195]Louis Veuillot to Guizot, 16 Dec. 1849, AN, *Fonds Guizot*, 42 Ap 150, Dr. 31. This letter does not appear in Veuillot's published correspondence, which contains little from Veuillot to Guizot in this period.
[196]*L'Univers*, 23 July 1849.
[197]*Vie*, 2:376-377; Lecanuet, *Montalembert*, 2:466-473.
[198]Veuillot to Morisseau, 28 July 1849, *O.C.*, 17:58.
[199]Same to La Tour, 11 Aug. 1849, *ibid.*, p. 68.
[200]Veuillot to Dumast, 25 Oct. 1849, *ibid.*, p. 102.
[201]*Vie*, 2:380-381; Lecanuet, *Montalembert*, 2:467.
[202]Veuillot to Foisset, October 1849, *O.C.*, 17:100.
[203]*Vie*, 2:383-384.
[204]*O.C.*, 29:578-579.
[205]*Vie*, 2:382.
[206]*O.C.*, 29:579.
[207]*Ibid.*, p. 580.
[208]*Ibid.*, p. 581.
[209]*Vie*, 2:368.
[210]*L'Univers*, 15 Jan. 1850.
[211]*Vie*, 2:368.
[212]*O.C.*, 29:581.
[213]*Ibid.*, pp. 582-583.
[214]*Vie*, 2:372.
[215]*L'Univers*, 19 April 1850.
[216]*Vie*, 2:385.
[217]Lecigne, *Louis Veuillot*, p. 229.
[218]*Vie*, 2:387; Anatole Leroy-Beaulieu, "Études politiques et religieuses: Le mécomtes du liberalisme," *Revue de Deux Mondes*, 3e per., 69(May 15, 1885):421-450.
[219]*O.C.*, 30:173-177.
[220]*Ibid.*, pp. 83-89.
[221]*Ibid.*, pp. 90-106.
[222]*Ibid.*, pp. 93-94.
[223]*Ibid.*, p. 100.
[224]*Ibid.*, p. 105.
[225]*Ibid.*, p. 108.

[226]*Ibid.*, p. 109.
[227]*Ibid.*, p. 118.
[228]*Ibid.*, p. 119.
[229]*Ibid.*, pp. 106-147.
[230]*Ibid.*, p. 129.
[231]*Ibid.*, pp. 141-142.
[232]Marvin L. Brown, Jr., *The Comte de Chambord: The Third Republic's Uncompromising King* (Durham, N.C.: Duke University Press, 1967), pp. 58-80.
[233]Falloux tells his own story, *Mémoires d'un royaliste*, 2:7-42, 153-185, 343-381.
[234]The principal theme of Brown, *Comte de Chambord*, is the ideological split on the ranks of the royalists and the unwillingness of Chambord to compromise his principle in any way.
[235]*O.C.*, 17:108.
[236]*Vie*, 2:394-395; Chambord to Veuillot, 20 Feb. 1850, BN NAF, 24633, p. 221.
[237]*O.C.*, 30:186-203.
[238]*Ibid.*, p. 203.
[239]*L'Univers*. 1 May 1850. See *O.C.*, 30:155-159 for Veuillot's assessment of the election of Eugène Sue.
[240]*Vie*, 2:390.
[241]*Ibid.*, pp. 390-391.
[242]Louis Veuillot to Eugène, Brussels, 20 Dec. 1849, *O.C.* 17:111.
[243]*Ibid.*, pp. 113-116.
[244]*Ibid.*, p. 115. The account he published ten years later says he had four conversations of two to three hours. *O.C.*, 34:360.
[245]*Ibid.*, pp. 111, 113.
[246]*O.C.*, 34:337. Veuillot maintained he changed nothing. If that is the case, Metternich's vocabulary alone is interesting for an early use of the word "nihilism," *ibid.*, p. 344.
[247]*Ibid.*, p. 343.
[248]*Ibid.*, pp. 343-345.
[249]*Ibid.*, p. 357.
[250]*O.C.*, 17:112; *Vie* 2:426-428.
[251]*Ibid.*, 34:361.
[252]*Vie*, 2:397.
[253]Phillips, *Church in France, 1848-1907*, pp. 1-3; Lecanuet, *Montalembert*, 3:103-110.
[254]*Vie*, 2:397.
[255]*Ibid.*, pp. 398-399.
[256]*Ibid.*, pp. 399-400. The order of events indicated on p. 400 would seem to be in error, at least the reference to the letter of 24 Nov. 1848.
[257]*O.C..*, 30:204-247.
[258]Veuillot to Abbé Bernier, 10 May 1850, *O.C.*, 17:152-155.
[259]See note of Eugène, *ibid.*, p. 152.
[260]*Vie*, 2:411-413.
[261]Veuillot to Abbé Bernier, 6 August 1850, *O.C.*, 17:182.
[262]For Veuillot's attitude on medals and decorations, for himself and for others, see *ibid.*, 17:182, 18:189, 20:200, 21:9, 26:31.
[263]*Vie*, 2:414. Eugène to Louis Veuillot, Rome, 17 July 1850, BN NAF, 24633, pp. 231-234.
[264]*Vie*, pp. 414-416.

[265] Louis to Mathilde, 31 Aug. 1850, *O.C.*, 17:191.
[266] Same to Abbe Bernier, 17 July 1850, *ibid.*, p. 169.
[267] Same to Mathilde, 31 Aug. 1850, *ibid.*, p. 191.
[268] Same to Msgr. Clausel de Montals, 2 Aug. 1850, *ibid.*, pp. 176-177.
[269] Same to Aubineau, 3 June 1850, *ibid.*, 17:160.
[270] *Avertissement* dated 24 Aug. 1850, Archives de l'Archévêché de Paris (hereafter cited "Archévêché") 4, E, II, 1, p. 23; BN NAF, 24239.
[271] *Mandement*, pp. 21-30.
[272] *L'Univers*, 2 Sept. 1850; *Vie*, 2:402-403; Charles Guillemant, *Pierre Louis Parisis*, 2 vols. (Pas de Calais: Brunet, 1916-1917), 2:418.
[273] Veuillot to Parisis, 4 Sept. 1850, BN NAF, 24220, p. 178.
[274] Same to Mathilde, 2 Sept. 1850, *O.C.*, 17:196.
[275] *Ibid.*, pp. 204-220.
[276] Veuillot to Abbé Bernier, 4 Sept. 1850, *ibid.*, p. 199.
[277] Same to Aubineau, Sept. 1850, *ibid.*, p. 210.
[278] *Ibid.*, p. 209.
[279] Veuillot to Curzon, 11 Sept. 1850, *ibid.*, p. 214.
[280] Same to M. "G.", 5 Sept. 1850, *ibid.*, p. 204.
[281] Same to Abbé Bernier, 7 Sept. 1850, *ibid.*, pp. 207-208.
[282] "B" to Veuillot, Tours, 15 Sept. 1850, BN NAF, 24225, pp. 78-79.
[283] Rio to Veuillot, 24 Sept. 1850, BN NAF, 24633, pp. 235-236.
[284] Donoso Cortés to Veuillot, 3 Sept. 1850, BN NAF, 24225, p. 117.
[285] *O.C.*, 17:192, see note.
[286] Veuillot to Abbé Bernier, 4 Sept. 1850, *ibid.*, pp. 198-199.
[287] Same to same, 28 Sept. 1850, *ibid.*, p. 229.
[288] Same to Parisis, 8 Sept. 1850, BN NAF, 24220, p. 180.
[289] Same to Bernier, 26 Sept. 1850, BN NAF, 24631, p. 109.
[290] Same to Parisis, 14 Sept. 1850, *O.C.*, 17:223.
[291] Same to Bernier, 26 Sept. 1850, BN NAF, 24631, p. 110.
[292] Parisis to Sibour, 12 Sept. 1850, *ibid.*, 24239, p. 31.
[293] Veuillot to Parisis, 27 Sept. 1850, *O.C.*, 17:35.
[294] Blanquant de Bailleul to Veuillot, Rouen, 25 Sept. 1850, BN NAF, 24225, p. 91.
[295] Veuillot to Parisis, 27 Sept. 1850, *O.C.*, 17:235.
[296] *Ibid.*, p. 234-235.
[297] Same to same, 28 Oct. 1850, BN NAF, 24220, p. 196.
[298] Same to same, 30 Sept. and 28 Oct. 1850, *ibid.*, pp. 192, 196.
[299] *L'Univers*, 5 October 1850.
[300] Louis Veuillot to Abbé Bernier, 5 Oct. 1850 BN NAF 24220, p. 169.
[301] Donoso Cortés to Veuillot, 11 Oct. 1850, BN NAF, 24225, p. 121; Msgr. Blanquard de Bailleul to Veuillot, 5 Oct. 1850, *ibid.*, p. 93; Msgr. Guibert to same, 12 Oct. 1850, *ibid.*, p. 143.
[302] Msgr. Dreux-Brézé to Sibour, 24 Sept. 1850, BN NAF, 24239, p. 40.
[303] Anon. to Veuillot, 17 and 31 Oct. 1850, *ibid.*, 24225, pp. 68-72; Msgr. Dufêtre to Veuillot, 30 Oct. 1850, *ibid.*, p. 122.
[304] Veuillot to Parisis, 20 Oct. 1850, *O.C.*, 17:250-251.
[305] Anon to Veuillot, Rome, 17 Oct. 1850, BN NAF, 24225, pp. 68-70.
[306] Veuillot to Sibour, 1 Nov. 1850, Archévêché, 1, D, IX, 3.
[307] Same to Fornari, 5 Oct. 1850, 5 Oct. 1850, *O.C.*, pp. 244-249.
[308] *Vie*, 2:420.
[309] Ernest Sevrin, *Msgr. Clausel de Montals*, 2 vols. (Paris: Vrin, 1955), 2:602.

[310]Sibour to Veuillot, 27 Feb. 1851, Archévêché, 4, E, II, 1.
[311]Veuillot to Fornari, March 1851, BN NAF 24220, pp. 224-225 (this letter is unpublished); *O.C.*, 17:271, see note; *Vie*, 2:439-440.
[312]*L'Univers*, 18 March 1851.
[313]*Ibid.*, 19 March 1851.
[314]Clausel de Montals to Veuillot, 19 March 1851, BN NAF, 24225, pp. 249-250.
[315]Same to same, 21 March 1851, *ibid.*, p. 251.
[316]Msgr. Rendu to Veuillot, 30 March 1851, *ibid.*, pp. 312-313.
[317]Veuillot to Fornari, 7 April 1851, *O.C.*, 17:278-279.
[318]Same to Bernier, April 1851, *ibid.*, p. 281.
[319]*Ibid.*
[320]Msgr. Gignoux to Veuillot, 29 April 1851, BN NAF, 24225, p. 281.
[321]*Vie*, 2:443-444.
[322]*Ibid.*, p. 445.
[323]*O.C.*, 30:484-509.
[324]*Ibid.*, pp. 491-494.
[325]*Ibid.*, pp. 484-490.
[326]Clausel de Montals to Veuillot, 7 Sept. 1851, BN NAF, 24225, pp. 271-272.
[327]Veuillot to Clausel de Montals, end of March 1851, *O.C.*, 17:277.
[328]Same to Combalot, 9 Sept. 1851, *O.C.*, 17:303-304; see note, p. 303.
[329]*Vie*, 2:447-451.
[330]Veuillot to Sibour, 1 Oct. 1851, *O.C.*, 17:304-305.
[331]Same to Foisset, 12 Oct. 1850, *ibid.*, p. 250.
[332]Same to Bernier, 10 May 1850, *ibid.*, p. 153.
[333]Lecanuet, *Montalembert*, 2:413, 416-417.
[334]Anon. to Veuillot, Rome, 31 Oct. 1850, BN NAF, 24225, p. 270.
[335]Veuillot to La Tour, 15 Feb. 1851, *O.C.*, p. 270.
[336]Montalembert to La Tour, 19 Feb. 1851, BN NAF, 24236, p. 25.
[337]*Vie*, 2:435-436.
[338]Montalembert to La Tour, 19 Feb. 1851, BN NAF, 24236, p. 25.
[339]Brown, *Chambord*, pp. 58-68.
[340]*O.C.*, 30:255-316.
[341]24 Sept. 1850, *ibid.*, p. 269.
[342]Montalembert to La Tour, 1 Sept. 1851, BN NAF, 24236, p. 50.
[343]8 Jan. 1852, *O.C.*, 31:15-16.
[344]2 Oct. 1850, *ibid.*, 30:275-278.
[345]11 April 1851, *ibid.*, pp. 408-417.
[346]18 Aug. 1850, *ibid.*, pp. 260-264.
[347]22 May – 20 July 1851, *ibid.*, pp. 514-545.
[348]Montalembert to La Tour, 6 Aug. 1851, BN NAF, 24236, p. 40.
[349]Same to same, 11 Sept. 1851, *ibid* pp. 50-56.
[350]*Vie*, 2:454; La Gorce, *Seconde République*, 2:444-497.
[351]Montalembert to La Tour, 14 Nov. 1851, BN NAF, 24236, p. 74.

CHAPTER V

[1]*Vie*, 2:462-464. For events of 2 December 1851 see also La Gorce, *Seconde République*. 2:444-538.
[2]*Vie*, 2:464.
[3]*Ibid.*, p. 437.

[4]*Ibid.*, p. 465.
[5]*O.C.*, 31:1. Veuillot was referring to Cher.
[6]Veuillot to Mme Thayer, 9 March 1852, *ibid.*, 17:341.
[7]*Vie*, 456-457.
[8]*Ibid.*, p. 466.
[9]Falloux, *Mémoires d'un royaliste*, 2:128-133.
[10]*Vie*, 2:462.
[11]*Ibid.*, p. 469; Lecanuet, *Montalembert*, 3:8-13.
[12]*Vie*, 2:471-472. This article appeared 14 Dec. 1851 in *L'Univers*.
[13]*O.C.*, 31:1-3.
[14]*Ibid.*, p. 3.
[15]*Ibid.*, pp. 4-8.
[16]*Ibid.*, p. 8-15.
[17]Pie to Veuillot, 13 Dec. 1851, BN NAF, 24223, pp. 308-309.
[18]P. Dugas to Veuillot, Lyon, 30 Dec. 1851, BN NAF, pp. 277-278.
[19]Veuillot to Abbé Demiau, Jan. 1852, *O.C.*, 31:336-337.
[20]Same to Bernier, 15 Jan. 1852, *ibid.*, 17:331-332. See note p. 331.
[21]*Ibid.*, 31:31-33.
[22]*Ibid.*, pp. 33-36.
[23]Veuillot to Saint-Albin, 18 Jan. 1852, *ibid.*, 17:333-334.
[24]Damas to Veuillot (Antézy-Nièvre), 14 Dec. 1851, BN NAF, 24225, p. 275.
[25]Same to same, Antezy, 17 Jan. 1852, *ibid.*, p. 407.
[26]*O.C.*, 31:39.
[27]*Ibid.*, p. 48.
[28]La Tour to Veuillot, Tréquier, 4 Feb. 1852, BN NAF, 24225, pp. 523-525.
[29]*Vie*, 2:480-481.
[30]*La Bretagne*, 22 Jan. 1853, BN NAF, 24631, p. 3.
[31]Veuillot to Albéric de Blanche-Raffin, Dec. 1851, *O.C.*, 17:328.
[32]*Ibid.*, see note p. 329; *Vie* 2:484.
[33]Lacanuet, *Montalembert*, 3:42-59.
[34]Charles de Montalembert, *Des intérêts catholiques au XIX*[e] *siècle* (Paris: J. Lecoffre, 1852).
[35]*O.C.*, 31:265-279.
[36]*Vie*, 2:491.
[37]See below, pp. 337-338.
[38]*O.C.*, 18:380, see note.
[39]*Vie*, 2:513-514.
[40]Veuillot to Msgr. Gignoux, 19 Nov. 1852, *O.C.*, 31:19.
[41]Same to Guizot, 25 Nov. 1852, AN, 42 AP 150, Dr. 31 (Fonds Guizot).
[42]*O.C.*, 18:20, 24.
[43]Veuillot to Montalembert, 30 Nov. 1852, *ibid.*, p. 24.
[44]Same to Cuverville, 29 Nov. 1852, *ibid*, p. 22.
[45]Same to M. "X", 2 Dec, 1852, *ibid.*, p. 28.
[46]*O.C.*, 31:58-167.
[47]For Veuillot's side in the affair of the classics see *ibid.*, 176-243 and *Vie*, 2:493-511.
[48]Montalembert to La Tour, 25 Feb. 1852, BN NAF 24236, pp. 125-126.
[49]Veuillot to Sibour, 23 April 1852, Archévêché, 1, D, IX, 3.
[50]Jean Joseph Gaume, *Le Ver rongeur des sociétés modernes, ou le paganisme dans l'éducation* (Paris: Gaume frères, 1851).
[51]29 Sept. 1851, *O.C.*, 31:171-177.

[52]The background and character of Dupanloup have intrigued many. The monumental study of him is in Francois Lagrange, *Vie de Mgr. Dupanloup*, 3 vols.(Paris: Poussielgue, 1883-1884). Lagrange was a great admirer of Dupanloup, and an ultramontane, Michel U. Maynard, criticized the book in his own *Mgr. Dupanloup et M. Lagrange son historien* (Société générale de librairie catholique, 1884). G. Hanotaux, *Contemporary France*, I:241-242, is one of many to include a sketch of Dupanloup. Even Ernest Renan, who decided to leave the church after talking with Dupanloup, has a study of Dupanloup in his *Souvenirs*.

[53]6, 7, and 9 June 1852, *O.C.*, 31:176-196, esp. 178.

[54]*Ibid.*, pp. 197-205.

[55]Veuillot to Dupanloup, 19 June 1852, *ibid.*, pp. 205-208.

[56]Sibour to Dupanloup, 10 May 1852, Bibliothèque Saint-Sulpice, *Classiques*, II, 1053-1058.

[57]*Vie*, 2:500.

[58]Lecanuet, *Montalembert*, 3:104-106.

[59]Montalembert to Sibour, 23 Sept. 1853, *ibid.*, p. 105.

[60]Anita May's dissertation, "The Challenge of the French Catholic Press to Episcopal Authority," p. 399, is the best summary of the groupings of the episcopacy.

[61]Clausel de Montals to Dupanloup, 9 May 1852, Bibliothèque Saint-Sulpice, *Classiques*, I, 459-460. The aged Bishop of Chartres had a most difficult hand to read.

[62]*O.C.*, 31:211-212.

[63]Bishop of Blois to Dupanloup, 18 June 1852, *ibid.*, pp. 571-572.

[64]Bishop of Avignon to same, 27 June 1852, *ibid.*, pp. 97-98.

[65]Msgr. Gousset to same, 30 June 1852, *ibid.*, p. 105.

[66]*Vie*, 2:501-502.

[67]Charles Place to Dupanloup, 24 June 1852, Bibliothèque Saint-Sulpice, *Classiques*, 2:1206-1207.

[68]Veuillot to Bernier, 25 June 1852, BN NAF, 24220, p. 242; J. Maurain, *Politique ecclésiastique*, pp. 46-52; A. May, "Challenge of the French Catholic Press," p. 399.

[69]Same to Élise, 3 July 1852, *ibid.*, p. 259.

[70]*O.C.*, 17:354-359, 362.

[71]Pierre La Croix to Dupanloup, 14 July 1852, Bibliothèque Saint-Sulpice, *Classiques*, 1:412.

[72]*Vie*, 2:503.

[73]*Ibid.*, p. 502.

[74]*Ibid.*, p. 504.

[75]Moulins to Dupanloup, 20 July 1852, Bibliothèque Saint-Sulpice, *Classiques*, 1:211-213.

[76]Montauban to Dupanloup, 31 July 1852, *ibid.*, pp. 237-256.

[77]*Vie*, 2:205.

[78]6 July 1852, BN NAF, 24225, p. 457.

[79]Veuillot to Abbé Bernard (Avignon), 24 July 1852, *O.C.*, 17:383-385.

[80]*Ibid.*, see note, p. 385.

[81]*Ibid.*, pp. 373-375, 388-389, 396-398, 401-403.

[82]Form letter, 15 July 1852, Bibliothèque Saint-Sulpice, *Classiques*, 1:157.

[83]*O.C.*, 17:384.

[84]*Ibid.*, 31-238-242.

[85]*Ibid.*, pp. 244-261.
[86]*Ibid.*, 18:3; *Vie*, 2:507-508.
[87]Bibliothèque Saint-Sulpice, *Classiques*, 1:119-121; *Vie* 2:507.
[88]*O.C.*, 17:385; *Vie*, 2:507-508.
[89]BN NAF, 24225, p. 677; *Ami de la Religion*, 7 Aug. 1852.
[90]Veuillot to Abbé Gibert (vicar-general of Msgr. Dreux Brézé, Bishop of Moulins), 13 Aug. 1852, BN NAF, 24220, pp. 250-252.
[91]Louis to Eugène, Amiens, 1 Oct. 1852, BN NAF, 24631, p. 134.
[92]Same to same, 19 Sept. 1852, *O.C.*, 18:8-9.
[93]Note of Veuillot, 30 Nov. 1852, BN NAF 24620, p. 48.
[94]Veuillot to Montalembert, 26 Nov. 1852, *O.C.*, 18:20. Lacanuet, *Montalembert*, 3:383.
[95]*O.C.*, 31:344-375; *Vie*, 2:531-536.
[96]*Ibid.*, pp. 362-363.
[97]R. Aubert, *Pontificat de Pie IX*, p. 306; E. Sevrin, *Clausel de Montals*, 2:687; F. Hayward, *Pie IX*, pp. 154-155.
[98]La Tour to Veuillot, 19 Jan. 1853, BN NAF, 24226, p. 41.
[99]*Vie*, 2:539.
[100]*O.C.*, 18:45.
[101]Veuillot to La Tour, 1 Feb. 1853, *ibid.*, p. 46.
[102]Same to Eugène, 5 and 12 Feb. 1853, *ibid.*, pp. 47-49.
[103]*Vie*, 2:540.
[104]10 Feb. 1853, Bibliothèque Saint-Sulpice, *Affaire de Classiques*, 2:1679-1684. Gaduel to Archbishop of Paris, Archévêché, 4, E, II, 1.
[105]Ordinance of Sibour, 17 Feb. 1853, AN, F^{19} 5594; Archévêché, 4, E, II, 1.
[106]Circular of J. Hippolyte, Bishop of Viviers, 2 Feb. 1853, Bibliothèque Saint-Sulpice, *Classiques*, 2:1625-1643; AN, F^{19}, 5594.
[107]*Vie*, 2:543-544.
[108]*O.C.*, 17:404.
[109]*Vie*, 2:429; P. Spencer, *Politics of Belief*, p. 211; C. S. Phillips, *Church in France, 1848-1907*, p. 63.
[110]*O.C.*, 17:330.
[111]Dom Guéranger to Veuillot, 21 Feb. 1853, BN NAF, 24633, p. 303.
[112]Canon Desgarets to same, 22 Feb. 1853, *ibid.*, 24226, p. 18.
[113]La Tour to Veuillot, 23 Feb. 1853, *ibid.*, p. 44.
[114]Sibour to ecclesiastical editors, Archévêché, 4, E, II, 1.
[115]*O.C.*, 18:51, 111.
[116]Louis to Eugène, 9 March 1853, *ibid.*, p. 80.
[117]*Ibid.*, pp. 52-53.
[118]*Ibid.*, p. 111.
[119]Louis to Eugène, 18 Feb. 1853, *ibid.*, p. 50.
[120]Rayneval to Drouyn de Lhuys, 20 Feb. 1853, AE, CP 1000 (Rome), pp. 82-83.
[121]Same to same, 24 Feb. 1853, *ibid.*, pp. 87-88.
[122]*O.C.*, 18:49-124.
[123]*Ibid.*, pp. 49-55.
[124]*Ibid.*, p. 59. Veuillot quickly gave the essence of his audience in a postscript to his letter to Eugène of 23 Feb. 1853. To Élise he wrote a long letter on Feb. 25, telling his full story, *ibid.*, pp. 59-63.
[125]*Ibid.*, p. 63.
[126]L. Christophe, *Louis Veuillot*, p. 11.

[127]Rayneval to Drouyn de Lhuys, 28 Feb. 1853, AE, CP 1000 (Rome), p. 98.
[128]J. Maurain, *Le Saint-Siège et la France de décembre 1851 à avril 1853* (Paris: Alcan, 1930), p. 175.
[129]*O.C.*, 18:67.
[130]Louis to Élise, 2 March 1853, *ibid.*, pp. 65-66.
[131]La Tour to Veuillot, 1 March 1853, BN NAF 24226, 46.
[132]Sibour to Saint-Siège, 9 March 1853, Archévêché, 4, E, II, 1; *Vie*, 2:553; *O.C.*, 18:78; *L'Univers*, 10 March 1853.
[133]*O.C.*, 18:84.
[134]*Ibid.*, pp. 70-71.
[135]*Ibid.*, pp. 79-80, 82-83; *Vie*, 554-555.
[136]*Vie*, pp. 558-559; *O.C.*, 18:95-96; text in *ibid.*, 31:376-377.
[137]Bibliothèque de Saint-Sulpice, *Classiques*, 2:1831; Archévêché, 4, E, II, 1.
[138]Louis to Eugène, 4 March 1853, *O.C.*, 18:71-73.
[139]Veuillot to editors of *L'Univers*, 4 March 1853, *ibid.*, pp. 74-76; *L'Ami de la Religion*, 15 March 1853.
[140]*Ibid.*, pp. 76-79.
[141]*Vie*, 2:557.
[142]Rayneval to Drouyn de Lhuys, 10 March 1853, AE, CP 1000 (Rome), p. 111.
[143]Same to same, 14 March 1853, J. Maurain, *Saint-Siège et La France*, p. 178.
[144]Same to same, 20 March 1853, AE, CP 1000 (Rome), p. 132.
[145]Louis to Eugène, 18 March 1853, *O.C.*, 18:88-90.
[146]Same to same, 4 March 1853, *ibid.*, p. 72.
[147]*Vie*, 2:559.
[148]Veuillot to Pius IX, 22 March 1853, *ibid.*, 2:559. This short note is not in Veuillot's *Œuvres complètes.*
[149]Same to Eugène, 14 March 1853, *O.C.*, 18:82.
[150]Same to same, 27 March 1853, *ibid.*, pp. 95-97; *ibid.*, 31:376-377.
[151]Same to same, 31 March 1853, *ibid.*, 18:97-98.
[152]Rayneval to Drouyn de Lhuys, 24 March 1853, AE, CP 1000 (Rome), p. 136.
[153]Sibour to Dupanloup, 28 March 1853, Bibliothèque Saint-Sulpice, *Classiques*, 2:1799-1800.
[154]Louis to Eugène, 18 March 1853, *O.C.*, 18:82.
[155]*Vie*, 2:557-569.
[156]Drouyn de Lhuys, 5 April 1853, AE, CP 1000 (Rome), p. 163.
[157]Sibour to Dupanloup, 3 April 1853, Bibliothèque Saint-Sulpice, *Classiques*, 2:1811.
[158]Ordinance of Sibour, 8 April 1853, *ibid.*, p. 1831; Archévêché, 4, E, II, 1.
[159]*O.C.*, 18, see note on page 103.
[160]Louis to Eugène, 3 April 1853, BN NAF, 24220.
[161]J. Maurain, *Saint-Siège et la France*, p. 211.
[162]Veuillot to Msgr. Mabille, 6 April 1853, BN NAF, 24631, p. 141.
[163]Drouyn de Lhuys to Rayneval, 5 April 1853. AE, CP 1000 (Rome), p. 163.
[164]Louis to Eugène, 8 April 1853, *O.C.*, 18:110-111.
[165]*Ibid.*, note, p. 11.
[166]Louis to Eugène, 14 April 1853, *ibid.*, p. 117.
[167]Same to same 27 March 1853, *ibid.*, p. 96; *Vie*, 2:569.
[168]Same to same, 17 April 1853, *ibid.*, p. 121.
[169]Same to Sibour, 16 April 1853, *ibid.*, p. 120.
[170]Same to Eugène, 3 April 1853, *ibid.*, p. 104.
[171]Same to Salinis, 27 April 1853, *ibid.*, pp. 124-126, see note, p. 125.

[172]Rayneval to Drouyn de Lhuys, 20 April 1853, AE, CP 1000 (Rome), p. 178.
[173]Veuillot to Baronne de Mosfart, 6 May 1853, *O.C.*, 18:127.
[174]Same to Bernier, May 1853, *ibid.*, pp. 135-136.
[175]Fioramonti to Veuillot, 28 Aug. 1853, BN NAF, 24633, p. 302.
[176]Veuillot to Parisis, 22 March 1854, *O.C.*, 18:189.
[177]Same to Élise, 2 Sept. 1854, *ibid.*, p. 233.
[178]*Vie*, 3:13-15.
[179]12 June 1853, BN NAF, 24620, p. 49.
[180]12 Aug. 1853, *ibid.*, p. 50.
[181]Veuillot to Abbé Pimont, 8 May 1853, *O.C.*, 18:132.
[182]Same to Blanc de Saint-Bonnet, 28 July 1853, *ibid.*, p. 146.
[183]*O.C.*, 31:392-410.
[184]*Ibid.*, pp. 440-459.
[185]*Ibid.*, p. 505.
[186]Veuillot to Msgr. Angebault, 16 Aug. 1853, *O.C.*, 18:149-151.
[187]*L'Univers*, 7 Aug. 1853.
[188]*O.C.*, 31:493.
[189]Lecanuet, Montalembert, 3:91-93.
[190]*O.C.*, 31:497.
[191]May, 1853, APP, E A/15.
[192]*Vie*, 3:17.
[193]*O.C.*, 31:526-527.
[194]*Ibid.*, pp. 537-539.
[195]*Vie*, 3:17.
[196]Veuillot to Auguste Bouchet, 12 Dec. 1853, *O.C.*, 18:169. Curiously, his editorial of 6 Dec. 1853 spoke of *Le Siècle* as having 35,000 subscribers.
[197]*L'Univers*, 6 Jan. 1854.
[198]*Ibid.*, 8 Jan. 1854.
[199]*Ibid.*, 14 Jan. 1854.
[200]Msgr. Blum, Bishop of Limbourg, to Veuillot, 23 April 1854, BN NAF, 24226, p. 116.
[201]*L'Univers*, 16 Jan. 1854.
[202]Maurain, *La politique ecclésiastique*, p. 92.
[203]Veuillot to La Tour, 7 Nov. 1853, *O.C.*, 18:164.
[204]3 March 1854, *O.C.*, 32:34.
[205]5 March 1854, *ibid.*, p. 37.
[206]2 Oct. 1854, *ibid.*, p. 97.
[207]3 March 1855, *ibid.*, p. 173.
[208]2 June 1855, *ibid.*, p. 252.
[209]30 Dec. 1855, *ibid.*, pp. 405-407.
[210]*O.C.*, 6:213-404. The chapter on "Prête et Soldat" appeared in the editorial column of *L'Univers*, 12 Jan. 1855.
[211]*Ibid.*, 32:90, see note.
[212]*Ibid.*, 18:193, see note.
[213]*Ibid.*, 6:27.
[214]Louis to Élise, 7 June 1855, *ibid.*, 18:293.
[215]Same to Arthur Murcier, 9 Aug. 1854, *ibid.*, p. 214.
[216]*O.C.*, 6:viii-x.
[217]*Ibid.*, p. 6.
[218]*Ibid.*, 18:206.
[219]*Ibid.*, p. 203.

[220]Veuillot to Abbé Blanc, Curé de Domazan (Gard), 9 Dec. 1854, *ibid.*, pp. 251-252.
[221]*Vie*, 3:20.
[222]Veuillot to Abbé Bernier, 15 Dec. 1854, *ibid.*, 18:253; *ibid.*, 32:117-125.
[223]Falloux, *Mémoires d'un royaliste*, 2:255-263.
[224]*O.C.*, 18:103-114.
[225]La Tour to Veuillot, 11 Sept. 1854, BN NAF, 24226, p. 139.
[226]*O.C.*, 18:200.
[227]Sister M. Caroline Ann Gimpl, *The* Correspondant *and the Founding of the Third Republic* (Washington: Catholic University Press, 1959), pp. 13-14. See also Falloux, *Mémoires d'un royaliste*, 2:249-254, and Lecanuet, *Montalembert*, 3:114 ff.
[228]Lacordaire to Montalembert, 18 Nov. 1855, Charles de Montalembert, *Catholicisme et liberté; correspondance inéditée avec P. Lacordaire, Mgr. Mérode, et A. de Falloux* (Paris: Cerf, 1970), p. 81.
[229]Same to same, 17 Sept. 1854, *ibid.*, p. 50.
[230]Veuillot to Abbé Belorgey, 15 Dec. 1854, BN NAF, 24631, p. 149.
[231]Lecanuet, *Montalembert*, 3:96.
[232]Montalembert to Lacordaire, 13 Jan. 1855, *Catholicisme et liberté*, pp. 53-55.
[233]*Ibid.*, p. 77.
[234]Veuillot to Msgr. Gignoux, Bishop of Beauvais, 9 Dec. 1855, *O.C.*, 18:351.
[235]Spencer, *Politics of Belief*, p. 218.
[236]*O.C.*, 32:136-149.
[237]*Ibid.*, pp. 253-281.
[238]*Ibid.*, p. 255.
[239]*Vie*, 3:43.
[240]*O.C.*, 32:218-241.
[241]*Ibid.*, p. 241.
[242]Maurain, *La Politique ecclésiastique*, p. 171.
[243]*Vie*, 3:43.
[244]Veuillot to La Tour, 15 May 1855, BN NAF 24220, pp. 387-390.
[245]Same to Père d'Alzan, 25 May 1855, *ibid.*, p. 377.
[246]*Ibid.*
[247]Veuillot to Parisis, 23 Nov. 1856, *ibid.*, p. 447.
[248]*O.C.*, 18:214-216.
[249]Louis to Eugène, 8 Feb. 1855, *ibid.*, pp. 262-263.
[250]*O.C.*, 18:263.
[251]Some persons in this family seem to have spelled the name "Bussierre" and others "Bussières."
[252]*O.C.*, 18:295; *Vie*, 3:46-49.
[253]*O.C.*, 18:297.
[254]Veuillot to Ctesse de Montsaulnin, 1 July 1855, *ibid.*, p. 303.
[255]Same to Élise, 2 July 1855, BN NAF 24220, p. 402; *O.C.*, 18:306.
[256]BN NAF, 24220; *Vie*, 3:50-54.
[257]*O.C.*, 14:430-431.

CHAPTER VI

[1]For Cavour see especially Denis Mack Smith, *Victor Emanuel, Cavour and the Risorgimento* (London: Oxford Univ. Press, 1971) and Massimo Salvadori, *Cavour*

and the Unification of Italy (New York: Van Nostrand, 1961).
[2]*O.C.*, 32:489.
[3]*Ibid.*, pp. 489-493.
[4]*Ibid.*, p. 493.
[5]*Vie*, 3:33.
[6]29 Jan. 1856, *O.C.* 18:367.
[7]*Vie*, 3:80-81.
[8]Note of Veuillot, BN NAF, 24619, p. 298.
[9]Veuillot to Léon Lavedan, 2 Feb. 1856, *O.C.*, 18:372-373; AN, 305 AP 5, Dr. 7. This letter was printed in *L'Univers.*
[10]*O.C.*, 18:373.
[11]*Ibid.*, pp. 387-388; *Vie*, 3:83-85.
[12]19 Feb. 1856, BN NAF 24226, p. 673.
[13]11 Feb. 1856, *ibid.*, p. 428.
[14]*O.C.*, 18:391; *Vie*, 3:85-89; A. de Falloux, *Le parti catholique, ce qu'il a été, ce qu'il est devenu* (Paris: Bray, 1856).
[15]*O.C.*, 6:404-488.
[16]*Ibid.*, pp. 483-488.
[17]*Ibid.*, p. 413.
[18]*Vie*, 3:88.
[19]Montalembert, *Catholicisme et liberté,* p. 98; *Vie*, 3:135-138.
[20]*L'Univers jugé par lui-même,* p. 18.
[21]*Ibid.*, p. 17.
[22]*Ibid.*, p. 23.
[23]*Vie*, 3:98-101.
[24]BN NAF, 24239, pp. 450-452; *Vie*, 3: 136-137.
[25]29 July 1856, *O.C.*, 19:29.
[26]*Ibid.*, pp. 1, 101.
[27]*Ibid.*, p. 130.
[28]*Ibid.*, p. 41.
[29]*Ibid.*, p. 65.
[30]*Ibid.*, p. 64.
[31]*Ibid.*, p. 75.
[32]Article of J. Ernest-Charles in *L'Homme libre*, 25 Nov. 1913 in BN NAF 24626, p. 7.
[33]In BN NAF 24226 there is a total of 131 letters, so over half were from prelates. For 1857 it was 18 of 59, and 1858, 36 of 51.
[34]*Vie*, 3:93-95.
[35]Oct. 1856, BN NAF, 24631, p. 201[bis]. *O.C.*, 19:35.
[36]*O.C.*, 33:30-34; *Vie*, 3:103-106.
[37]Gousset to Parisis, 9 Aug. 1856, BN NAF, 24226, pp. 516-518.
[38]BN NAF, 24239 (6-9 Aug. 1856).
[39]Msgr. Jolly-Mellon to Veuillot, 16 Aug. 1856, BN NAF 24226, p. 538.
[40]Bonald to Veuillot, 18 Aug. 1856, *ibid.*, p. 445.
[41]Msgr. Jordany to same, 27 Aug. 1856, *ibid.*, p. 541.
[42]29 Aug. 1856, *ibid.*, p. 581.
[43]5 Sept., 14 Oct. 1856, *ibid.*, pp. 411, 413.
[44]6 Sept. 1856, BN NAF, 24633, p. 387.
[45]26 Sept. 1856, BN NAF 24631, p. 202.
[46]19 Aug. 1856, *O.C.*, 19:55.
[47]1 Sept. 1856, BN NAF, 24220, p. 437.

[48]16 Sept. 1856, *ibid.*, p. 422.
[49]Veuillot to Pie, 8 Sept. 1856, *O.C.*, 19:91; *Vie*, 3:115-116.
[50]*Vie*, 3:118-119.
[51]Abbé Planty to Veuillot, 21 Dec. 1856, BN NAF, 24633, pp. 404-406. Veuillot to Parisis, Dec. 1856, *ibid*, 24220, p. 451.
[52]*Vie*, 3:97-98, 134.
[53]*O.C.*, 33:1-71.
[54]*Vie*, 3:131-134.
[55]Veuillot to Parisis, 23 Nov. 1856, BN NAF, 24220, p. 447.
[56]*Vie*, 3:129.
[57]Veuillot to Segrétain, 19 Jan. 1857, *O.C.*, 19:146-147.
[58]Same to Msgr. Léon Sibour, 3 March 1857, BN NAF, 24220, p. 561.
[59]Bonnechose to Veuillot, 16 and 20 Jan. 1857; Msgr. Bondinet (Amiens) to same, same dates, BN NAF, 24227, pp. 8, 10, 12, 14.
[60]31 Jan. 1857, *ibid.*, pp. 116-117.
[61]*Vie*, 3:148.
[62]*Ibid.*, p. 140.
[63]*Ibid.*, p. 169.
[64]*Ibid.*, p. 189; *O.C.*, 33:89-93.
[65]27 Feb. 1857, *ibid.*, p. 19:161.
[66]*Ibid.*, 33:72-74.
[67]2 April 1857, *ibid.*, 19:175.
[68]*Ibid.*, p. 162.
[69]Père Laurent to Veuillot, 31 March 1857, BN NAF, 24633, p. 438.
[70]June 1857, *O.C.*, 19:197-198.
[71]*Ibid.*, p. 198.
[72]*Ibid.*
[73]Veuillot to Élise, 30 May 1857, *ibid.*, p. 185.
[74]*Vie*, 3:165-168.
[75]*O.C.*, 19:196.
[76]Veuillot to Abbé Delor, 3 June 1857, *ibid.*, p. 189.
[77]At least we know that Montalembert's interest was purchased, and that he still subscribed. *Ibid.*, p. 214.
[78]*Ibid.*, p. 188.
[79]*Ibid.*, 33:181-182.
[80]*Ibid.*, pp. 216-229.
[81]*Vie*, 3:175.
[82]*O.C.*, 33:348-371; *Vie*, 3:374-378.
[83]Veuillot to Parisis, 15 Feb. 1858, *O.C.*, 19:265-266.
[84]*Vie*, 3:190.
[85]15 Oct. 1856, *O.C.*, 19:119-122.
[86]*O.C.*, 33:154-160.
[87]*Ibid.*, 33:160, 19:207.
[88]La Tour to Veuillot, 23 June 1857, BN NAF, 24227, p. 50.
[89]*O.C.*, 19:207.
[90]*Ibid.*, 33:118-119.
[91]*Ibid.*, pp. 266-293.
[92]La Tour to Veuillot, 24 Dec. 1857, BN NAF, 24227, p. 59.
[93]Lacordaire to Montalembert, 30 Jan. 1858, Montalembert, *Catholicisme et liberté*, pp. 130-133.
[94]*Ibid*, p. 213.
[95]Montalembert to Veuillot, 29 March 1859, BN NAF, 24227, p. 272.

[96]Montalembert to Guizot, La Roche-en-Brény, 10 Sept. 1859, Montalembert, *Catholicisme et liberté*, p. 446.
[97]Lecanuet, *Montalembert*, 3:217.
[98]La Gorce, *Second Empire*, 2:212-249.
[99]*O.C.*, 33:322-324.
[100]*Ibid.*, pp. 324-329.
[101]*Ibid.*, pp. 329-336.
[102]*Ibid.*, pp. 337-371.
[103]Veuillot to Parisis, 8 Jan. 1858, 15 Feb. 1858, BN NAF 24220, pp. 606-609, 612-615; *O.C.*, 19:259-262; *Vie*, 3:202-209.
[104]*Vie*, 3:203.
[105]*O.C.*, 37:37-62.
[106]For a complete account of the interview see the above. *Vie*, 3:209-216; Veuillot to Parisis, 20 Feb. 1858, BN NAF, 24220, pp. 614-616.
[107]*O.C.*, 37:47.
[108]*Ibid.*
[109]Veuillot to Parisis, 15 Feb. 1858, BN NAF, 24220, pp. 612-613.
[110]Same to same, 20 Feb. 1858, *ibid.*, p. 615.
[111]*O.C.*, 33:406.
[112]*Ibid.*, pp. 379-390.
[113]*Ibid.*, pp. 526-528.
[114]For the general background of the war of 1859, see Lynn M. Case, *French Opinion on War and Diplomacy during the Second Empire* (Philadelphia: Univ. of Pennsylvania Press, 1954), pp. 51-68.
[115]Veuillot to Parisis, 22 Sept. 1858, BN NAF, 24220, p. 618.
[116]Same to Blanc de Saint-Bonnet, 13 Oct. 1858, *O.C.*, 19:369.
[117]Same to same, 2 Jan. 1858, *Ibid.*, p. 257.
[118]Same to Mme Eugène Veuillot, 25 Oct. 1858, *ibid.*, pp. 378-379.
[119]*Ibid.*, pp. 318-319; Louis to Eugène, 24 July 1858, BN NAF, 24220, p. 636.
[120]Louis to Eugène, 28 June 1858, *ibid.*, p. 316.
[121]*O.C.*, 33:535-568.
[122]Veuillot to Msgr. Landriot, 17 Aug. 1858, *ibid.*, 19:331-334.
[123]*Ibid.*, 33:522-526.
[124]Louis to Eugène, 20 Aug. 1858, *ibid.*, 19:335.
[125]Msgr. Guibert to Msgr. X, BN NAF, 24626, p. 7.
[126]26 Aug. 1858, *ibid.*, p. 7.
[127]*Ibid.*
[128]*O.C.*, 19:262-264.
[129]*Vie*, 3:216-224.
[130]Lacordaire to Salinis, 24 Dec. 1858, Montalembert, *Catholicisme et liberté*, p. 21.
[131]*Vie*, 3:218.
[132]*Ibid*,; *O.C.*, 19:382.
[133]*O.C.*, 34:75-135.
[134]*Ibid.*, pp. 81-82.
[135]*Ibid.*, 19:380; 34:34.
[136]*Vie*, 3:363.
[137]*O.C.*, 34:45-55.
[138]Central Consistory of Israelites of France to Ministry of Justice, Paris, 20 Nov. 1858, AN, BB[18]1587, Dr. 684.
[139]*O.C.*, 19:386.

[140]P. Spencer, *Politics of Belief*, p. 217.
[141]Louis to Eugène, February 1859, *O.C.*, 19:403.
[142]Louis to Élise, 20 June 1858, BN NAF, 24220, p. 626.
[143]Same to Arthur Murcier, 27 July 1859, *O.C.*, 20:59.
[144]*Ibid.*, pp. 210-212, 233-283.
[145]*Vie*, 3:238-245.
[146]Veuillot to Maguelonne, 27 Nov. 1858, BN NAF, 24631, 260-261.
[147]Same to same, no date, BN NAF, 24220, p. 651.
[148]*Vie*, 3:252.
[149]Montalembert, *Catholicisme et liberté*, p. 213.
[150]Louis to Eugène, 25 Jan. 1859, *O.C.*, 19:399-400. According to a note of Eugène, these were words Montalembert had used.
[151]*O.C.*, 19:402-404.
[152]*Ibid.*, 20:4.
[153]*Ibid.*, p. 5.
[154]*Ibid.*, pp. 11, 16.
[155]Veuillot to Bastide, 25 Feb. 1859, BN NAF, 24220, p. 649.
[156]*O.C.*, 33:413-440.
[157]*Ibid.*, pp. 427-428.
[158]*Ibid.*, 34:136-145.
[159]*Ibid.*, p. 186.
[160]*Ibid.*, pp. 195-196.
[161]*Ibid.*, p. 195. In *Vie*, 3:263 Eugène has the interview on 14 May 1859.
[162]Sibour to Veuillot, 23 Feb. 1859, BN NAF, 24227, p. 301.
[163]Same to same, 2 May 1859, *ibid.*, p. 303.
[164]Doney to Veuillot, no date, 1859, *ibid.*, p. 240.
[165]Fillion to same, 14 July 1859, *ibid.*, p. 246.
[166]Dreux-Brézé to same, 16 March 1859, *ibid.*, pp. 142-143.
[167]Msgr. Cousseau to same, 14 April 1859, *ibid.*, p. 234.
[168]Louis to Eugène, 24 Feb. 1859, *O.C.*, 20:4.
[169]*Ibid.*, 34:223-224.
[170]*Vie*, 3:268-269.
[171]Veuillot to Mme Cuverville, 7 May 1859, *O.C.*, 20:34.
[172]Same to Maguelonne, 5 June 1859, *ibid*, p. 44.
[173]*Ibid.*, 20:47-48; 34:225-226.
[174]*Ibid.*, 34:226-231.
[175]*Ibid.*, pp. 231-235.
[176]*Ibid.*, pp. 246-254.
[177]Veuillot to Maguelonne, no date, BN NAF 24220, p. 651.
[178]Report of A. de La Guéronnière to minister of interior, 10 July 1859, BN NAF, 24227, p. 313.
[179]*O.C.*, 34:253-254.
[180]Veuillot to Maguelonne, August 1859, BN NAF, 24220, pp. 653-655.
[181]Same to Ctesse de Ségur, 27 July 1859, *O.C.*, 20:57.
[182]Same to Segrétain, Sept. 1859, BN NAF, 24220, pp. 677-678.
[183]Same to Ctesse de Ségur, 25 Sept. 1859, *O.C.*, 20:85.
[184]Key editorials of the period are in *O.C.*, volume 34.
[185]Louis to Eugène, 20 Aug. 1859, *ibid.*, 20:73.
[186]*Ibid.*, 34:381-389.
[187]*Ibid.*, 389-390.
[188]*Ibid.*, pp. 374-378.

[189]*Ibid.*, p. 378.
[190]Report of Joegle, Paris, 12 Oct. 1859, AN 305 AP 5, Dr. 7.
[191]Veuillot to La Tour, 14 Nov. 1859, *O.C.*, 20:103.
[192]*Ibid.*, 34:426-427.
[193]Veuillot to Msgr. Gignoux, 24 Dec. 1859, *ibid.*, 20:125.
[194]L. M. Case, *French Opinion*, pp. 110-114.
[195]*O.C.*, 34:417-418.
[196]*Avertissement* dated 26 Dec. 1859, AN 305, AP 5, Dr. 7.
[197]*O.C.*, 34:443.
[198]Veuillot to Parisis, 12 Oct. 1859, BN NAF, 24631, p. 297.
[199]Veuillot to Maguelonne, 4 Dec. 1859, *ibid.*, 24220.
[200]La Tour to Veuillot, 30 Oct. 1859, *ibid*, 24227, p. 266.
[201]Veuillot to Parisis, 14 Oct. 1859, *ibid.*, 24631, p. 299.
[202]Same to Maguelonne, 15 Jan. 1860, *O.C.*, 20:129.
[203]Same to Abbé Delor, 7 Feb. 1860, *ibid.*, pp. 139-140.
[204]*Ibid.*, 34:32; *Vie*, 3:307.
[205]Decree of suppression, 29 Jan. 1860, AN, F^{18} 423. A collection of *avertissements* to *L'Univers* are to be found here.
[206]Editors of *L'Univers* to the pope [2 Feb. 1860], *O.C.*, 34:445.
[207]*Vie*, 3:313.
[208]*O.C.*, 34:446.
[209]*Ibid.*, pp. 447-448.
[210]*Vie*, 3:317.
[211]Veuillot to Msgr. Gignoux, 6 Feb. 1860, *O.C.*, 20:136-137.
[212]Same to Msgr. Laurent (Bishop of Chersonèse), 6 Feb. 1860, *ibid*, pp. 138-139.
[213]R. Aubert, *Pontificat de Pie IX*, p. 310; G. Bazin, *Vie de Msgr. Maret*, II, 356 (citing a religious journal of Nîmes).
[214]Montalembert to Mérode, 28 Nov. 1863, Montalembert, *Catholicisme et liberté*, p. 288.

CHAPTER VII

[1]*Vie*, 3:317-346. Eugène was careful to reproduce some of the reactions still hostile to his brother. Indeed, his biography (referred to here as *Vie*) is very useful for studying the press as a whole, and, like the collection of condolences at the death of Louis, reveals that Eugène, as well as Louis, was a collector of papers.
[2]AN, 305, AP 5, Dr. 7; *O.C.*, 20:146.
[3]*Vie*, 3:347; *O.C.*, 20:136, 150.
[4]Veuillot to Parisis, 4 Feb. 1860, BN NAF, 24220, p. 738.
[5]Same to Du Lac, 2 March 1860, *O.C.*, 20:156-158.
[6]Veuillot to Maguelonne, 8 May 1860, *ibid.*, p. 191.
[7]Same to Élise, 20 March 1860, *ibid.*, pp. 170-171.
[8]Same to Mme de Pitray, 16 April 1860, *ibid.*, p. 182.
[9]Report of "Fin," 1 Nov. and 17 Nov. 1860, AN, 305, AP 5, Dr. 7.
[10]Louis to Élise, 12 Feb. 1860, *O.C.*, 20:144.
[11]Extracts of Veuillot's papers, Feb.-March 1860, AN, 305, AP 5, Dr. 7.
[12]Montalembert to Mérode, 11 Feb. 1860, Montalembert, *Catholicisme et liberté*, pp. 232-233.
[13]*O.C.*, 20:147, 154.

[14]*Ibid.*, 147-149.
[15]26 Feb. 1860, BN NAF, 24220, p. 740.
[16]Veuillot to Du Lac, 2 March 1860, *ibid.*, pp. 156-158.
[17]Two reports of 3 March 1860, AN, 305, AP 5, Dr. 7.
[18]Report of 3 Feb. 1860, *ibid.*
[19]Veuillot to Du Lac, 2 March 1860, *O.C.*, 20:156-158.
[20]Same to Élise, 20 March 1860, *ibid.*, p. 168.
[21]*Ibid.*, p. 144.
[22]Extract of a police report (Lagrange), 8 May 1860, AN, AB XIX, 524, Dr. 8.
[23]Louis to Élise, 20 Feb. 1860, BN NAF 24220, p. 764.
[24]3 March 1860, AN, AB XIX, 524, Dr. 8.
[25]Reports of 3 March, 21 April, and 12 May 1860, AN, 305 AP 5, Dr. 7.
[26]*O.C.*, 20:164.
[27]Louis to Elise, 8 March 1860, *ibid.*
[28]Same to same, 20 March 1860, *ibid.*, p. 160.
[29]Same to Eugène, 3 March 1860, *ibid.*, p. 158.
[30]Report of "Fin," 20 March 1860, AN, 305 AP 5, Dr. 7.
[31]Louis to Élise, 18 June 1860, *O.C.*, 20:209.
[32]Same to Maguelonne, 8 May 1860, *ibid.*, pp. 189-191.
[33]Same to same, April 1860, *ibid.*, p. 188.
[34]AN, 305 AP 5, Dr. 7.
[35]Veuillot to Segrétain, 17 March 1860, BN NAF, 24220, p. 742.
[36]Same to Élise, 26 March 1860, *ibid.*, p. 776.
[37]*O.C.*, 20:178.
[38]*Vie*, 3:359-376. Eugène gives a careful account. A report of "L", dated 1 April 1860 but transmitted later, indicates that there was suspicion that excommunication of the emperor was the goal of his trip to Rome. AN, 305 AP 5, Dr. 7.
[39]Report signed "Bernard," transmitted 4 April 1860, *ibid.*
[40]*Vie*, 3:369-370.
[41]Veuillot to Du Lac, 18 April 1860, BE NAF, 24220, p. 710.
[42]Report of 9 May 1860, AN, 305, AP 5, Dr. 7.
[43]Report of "Fin," 9 Sept. 1860, *ibid.*
[44]Report of 17 Nov. 1860, *ibid.*
[45]Lecanuet, *Montalembert*, 3:215.
[46]*Vie*, 3:378.
[47]*Ibid.*, p. 377.
[48]P. La Gorce, *Second Empire*, 3:187-188.
[49]Report of "L", 5 June 1860, AN, 305 AP 5, Dr. 7.
[50]Undated record, *ibid.*
[51]Veuillot to Maguelonne, 12 July 1860, BN NAF, 24220, p. 720.
[52]Report of inspector of police, Mellander, 11 August 1860, AN, 305 AP 5, Dr. 7.
[53]Veuillot to Du Lac, 20 July 1860, BN NAF, 24631, p. 313.
[54]*Vie*, 3:406.
[55]20 April 1860, *ibid.*, p. 383. This letter is not in his published correspondence.
[56]For Lamoricière see Émile Keller, *Le Général de La Moricière, sa vie militaire, politique et religieuse*, 2 vols. (Paris: J. Dumaine, 1874).
[57]Veuillot to Du Lac, 22 July 1860, *O.C.*, 20:247-248. For a view of papal defenses see Gustave Gautherot, *Un demi-siècle de défense nationale et religieuse: Émile Keller, 1828-1909* (Paris: Plon, 1922), pp. 115-122.
[58]Veuillot to Maguelonne, 5 May 1860, *O.C.*, 20:190.

[59]Same to Msgr. Berteaud, 28 Sept. 1860, *ibid.*, p. 289.
[60]Same to Maguelonne, end of Sept. 1860, *ibid.*, p. 291. The piece is also published in *O.C.*, 34:459-467. See *Vie*, 3:383 and *O.C.*, 20:295.
[61]Same to Aubineau, 6 Oct. 1860, *O.C.*, 20:294.
[62]*Ibid.*, 8:433.
[63]*Ibid.*, 20:358-359.
[64]In his intimate papers, BN NAF, 24620, are many undated fragments. Most of these bear on religion, one way or another.
[65]*Vie*, 3:381.
[66]BN NAF, 24620, p. 226.
[67]*Ibid.*, p. 211.
[68]*Ibid.*, p. 201.
[69]Veuillot to Guitaut, 28 Dec. 1860, *O.C.*, 20:336-338: same to La Tour, 3 Jan. 1861, *ibid.*, pp. 348-350.
[70]*Ibid.*, p. 349; Veuillot to Persigny, 12 Jan. 1861, BN NAF, 24221, pp. 44-45.
[71]It appears in *O.C.*, 10:215-269.
[72]*Ibid.*, p. 215.
[73]*Ibid.*, p. 254.
[74]*Ibid.*, p. ix.
[75]Report of "L", 12 Dec. 1860, AN, 305 AP 5, Dr. 7.
[76]Report of "Fin", 7 March 1861, *ibid.*
[77]Clipping of Veuillot, BN NAF, 24622, pp. 13-26.
[78]Veuillot to Du Lac, 2 March 1860, *O.C.*, 20:156-158.
[79]Phillips, *Church in France, 1848-1907*, pp. 20-21.
[80]Veuillot to Guéranger, 2 June 1861, *O.C.*, 21:16. He had used very similar words to Maguelonne somewhat earlier; 23 March 1861, BN NAF, 24221, p. 17.
[81]Solesmes, [July] 1861, *O.C.*, 21:44-45.
[82]Veuillot to Arthur Murcier, 8 Sept. 1861, BN NAF, 24221, p. 31.
[83]Same to Maguelonne, 23 March 1861, *ibid.*, p. 16.
[84]*Vie*, 3:424.
[85]*Ibid.*, pp. 426-428.
[86]*Ibid.*, p. 430.
[87]*O.C.*, 9:14.
[88]*Ibid.*, p. 27.
[89]*Ibid.*, pp. 54-55.
[90]*Ibid.*, pp. 315-319.
[91]*Ibid.*, pp. 64-65.
[92]Report dated 6 Aug. 1861, AN, 305 AP 5, Dr. 7.
[93]BN NAF, 24221, p. 143.
[94]Guéranger to Veuillot, 15 Jan. 1862, *ibid.*, 24228, p. 49.
[95]Veuillot to Mme Adèle Genton, 18 March 1861, *ibid.*, 24221, pp. 12-13.
[96]*O.C.*, 10:v-vi, xiv-xv.
[97]These pieces were entitled *Les Jeux de Pouliguen, Journal des Vacances et Fantasies, 1860-1861-1862. Ibid.*, pp. 550-617.
[98]Veuillot to Mme Bacon de Seigneux, 18 Dec. 1861, BN NAF, 24221, pp. 6-7.
[99]*O.C.*, 10:270-290.
[100]*Ibid.*, p. 290.
[101]Veuillot to Abbé Louis Klingenhoffen, 9 May 1861, *O.C.*, 21:11-12.
[102]Same to Guibert, May 1861, Archévêché, 1, D, IX, 3.
[103]Same to same, 3 July 1863, *ibid.*

[104]Same to Maguelonne, 29 Sept. 1861, BN NAF, 24221, p. 26.
[105]Report of 20 May 1861, AN, 305, AP 5, Dr. 7.
[106]Pie to Veuillot, 18 June 1862, BN NAF, 24225, p. 585.
[107]Reports dated 28 April, 19 May, 5 June 1862, AN, 305 AP 5, Dr. 7.
[108]Dansette, *Religious History of Modern France*, p. 303.
[109]Louis to Eugène, 14 May 1862, *O.C.*, 21:188-190.
[110]Dansette, *Religious History of Modern France*, p. 303.
[111]Louis to Eugene, 14 May 1862; same to Élise, same date, *O.C.*, 21:188-192.
[112]Same to Mathilde, 11 June 1862, *ibid.*, p. 205.
[113]*Ibid.*, p. 198.
[114]*Ibid.*, p. 199.
[115]Undated, BN NAF, 24620, p. 132.
[116]Davignon, *Le Roman de Louis Veuillot*, p. 119.
[117]Undated note; BN NAF, 24620, p. 113.
[118]*Ibid.*, pp. 134-135.
[119]*Ibid.*, p. 140.
[120]*Vie*, 3:461-465.
[121]*Ibid.*, p. 125.
[122]Louis to Eugène, 28 Feb. 1862, BN NAF, 24221, p. 168; Same to B. Jouvin, rédacteur of *Le Figaro*, 27 July 1862, *O.C.*, 21:230-231.
[123]*Vie*, 3:462.
[124]*O.C.*, 33:230-236; Veuillot to Msgr. Roess, 1 Feb. 1862, BN NAF, 24221, p. 147-148.
[125]*Vie*, 3:462-463.
[126]Veuillot to Arthur Murcier, 16 Aug. 1862, *O.C.*, 21:251-252.
[127]*Ibid.*, pp. 254, 262, 280.
[128]Veuillot to Abbé Taillandier, 23 Oct. 1864, BN NAF, 24221, p. 292.
[129]Davignon, *Le Roman de Louis Veuillot*, p. 10 says she was 32, but also that she died in 1900 in her seventy-fifth year. Her own observations about herself in her correspondence, and the way she could hold her own in exchanges with Veuillot, would seem to indicate 37 as perhaps a more likely age.
[130]*Ibid.*, p. 11.
[131]*Ibid.*, pp. 45, 187.
[132]*Ibid.*, pp. 11-12.
[133]*Ibid.*, p. 138.
[134]E. Gauthier, *Le vrai Louis Veuillot*, pp. 219-248.
[135]Davignon, *Roman de Louis Veuillot,*, p. 79.
[136]Veuillot to Arthur Murcier, 1 Sept. 1862, BN NAF, 24221, p. 139.
[137]Same to Charlotte de Grammont, 28 June 1863, *O.C.*, 21:358-359.
[138]E. Gauthier, *Le vrai Louis Veuillot*, p. 239.
[139]*Vie*, 3:338-449; *O.C.*, 11:xiv-xv.
[140]*Ibid.*, p. 451.
[141]*Ibid.*, p. 450.
[142]*O.C.*, 11:409.
[143]Lecanuet, *Montalembert*, 3:332.
[144]*Ibid.*, 229-242.
[145]*Ibid.*, pp. 332-333.
[146]Louis to Élise, 28 Aug. 1863, BN NAF, 24221, p. 260.
[147]Same to Mermillod, 10 Oct. 1863, *O.C.*, 22:12.
[148]*Vie*, 3:445-448.
[149]For an excellent summary of the general reaction to the book, see Dora Bierer

[Weiner], "Renan and His Interpreters: A Study in Intellectual Warfare," *Journal of Modern History*, 25 (Dec. 1953):375-389.
[150]*La Vie de Notre Seigneur Jésus-Christ* is the first and main part of the first volume of his *Œuvres Complètes.*
[151]*O.C.*, 1:xli.
[152]Giovanni Papini, *Life of Christ*, trans. Dorothy Canfield Fisher (New York: Harcourt, Brace, 1923).
[153]Pius IX to Veuillot, 9 July 1864, *Vie*, 3:477-478.
[154]Cardinal Sacconi to same, 2 July 1864, BN NAF, 24228, pp. 268-269.
[155]Msgr. Gauthier to same, 27 July 1864, *ibid.*, 24634, p. 101.
[156]Gueranger to same, same date, *ibid.*, p. 102.
[157]La Tour to same, 3 June 1863, BN NAF, 24228, p. 122.
[158]Same to same, 28 July 1864, BN NAF, 24229, p. 229.
[159]Veuillot to Mme Testas, 27 July 1864, BN NAF, 24231, pp. 495-496.
[160]Same to same, 4 Nov. 1864, *ibid.*, p. 525.
[161]Same to Maguelonne, early Dec. 1862, BN NAF, 24221, p. 121.
[162]Same to Charlotte de Grammont, no date, 1864, *ibid.*, 24224, pp. 44-45.
[163]Same to Parisis, 17 Sept. 1863, *ibid.*, 24221, p. 215.
[164]Same to Pie, 17 Sept. 1863, *ibid.*, p. 221.
[165]Same to Élise, 1 Sept. 1864, *ibid.*, p. 312.
[166]*O.C.*, 22:364.
[167]Louis to Eugène, 4 Oct. 1862, *ibid.*, 21-273-274.
[168]Same to Élise, 10 July 1864, *ibid.*, 22:110.
[169]Roussel to Veuillot, 24 April 1864, BN NAF, 24228, 261-262.
[170]Parisis to Emperor, 9 May 1864, *ibid.*, pp. 252-254.
[171]Emperor to Parisis, 7 June 1864, *ibid.*, p. 254.
[172]Report dated 11 April 1865, AN, 305 AP 5, Dr. 7.
[173]Veuillot to Mme de Pitray, 23 Oct. 1864, *O.C.*, 22:180.
[174]Louis to Eugène, 10 Dec. 1864, *ibid.*, pp. 161-162.
[175]Same to same, 21 Sept. 1864, *ibid.*, pp. 161-162.
[176]Report dated 1 Dec. 1864, AN, 305 AP 5, Dr. 7.
[176]Report dated 1 Dec. 1864, AN, 305 AP 5, Dr. 7.
[177]*O.C.*, 22:189, 197, 207; *Vie*, 3:406-407.
[178]*O.C.*, 22:189.
[179]Veuillot to Aubineau, 15 Jan. 1865, *ibid.*, pp. 206-207.
[180]Same to Eugène, 27 Dec. 1864, *ibid.*, pp. 192-194.
[181]Same to Msgr. Berardi, 7 Feb. 1865, *ibid.*, pp. 217-218.
[182]*O.C.*, 22:189-230.
[183]Louis to Eugène, 14 Jan. 1865, *ibid.*, p. 202.
[184]Same to Mme Cuverville, 18 Feb. 1865, BN NAF, 24221, pp. 363-364.
[185]Same to Élise, 16 April 1865, *ibid.*, p. 393.
[186]Same to same 18 April 1865, *ibid.*, p. 396.
[187]In the definitive edition of his works, *O.C.*, 10, it covers pp. 315-361.
[188]*Ibid.*, p. 320.
[189]*Ibid.*, p. 361.
[190]Report of *contrôleur-général à Marseilles*, 29 April 1866, AN, 305 AP Dr. 7.
[191]*Vie*, 3:503.
[193]*O.C.*, 10:291-314.
[194]*Ibid.*, p. x. Veuillot to Mme Bacon de Seigneux, 27 June 1865, *ibid.*, 22:280.
[195]Veuillot to Charlotte de Grammont, 6 June 1865, *ibid.*, 22:274.
[196]*Ibid.*, 10:362-380.

[197]Report dated 28 May 1866, AN, 305 AP 5, Dr. 7.
[198]Report of 6 Nov. 1866, *ibid.*
[199]Reports dated 22 and 25 Nov. 1866, AN, BB[18], 1742, Dr. 606.
[200]*O.C.*, 11:30-31.
[201]*Ibid.*, p. 49.
[202]*Ibid.*, p. 253.
[203]*Ibid.*, pp. 105-116.
[204]*Ibid.*, 23:132-133.
[205]*Ibid.*, p. 167.
[206]Veuillot to Charlotte de Grammont, Sept. 1866, BN NAF, 24224, p. 151.
[207]Same to same, Dec. 1866, *ibid.*, pp. 152-155.
[208]Cardinal Manning to Veuillot, 11 Jan. 1867, *ibid.*, 24634, p. 231.
[209]*Ibid.*, p. 505.
[210]*Vie*, 3:544.
[211]Veuillot to Mermillod, 16 Dec. 1866, *O.C.*, 23:130-132.
[212]*Ibid.*, p. 131; Lecanuet, *Montalembert*, 3:416-418; *Vie*, 3:538-539.
[213]Veuillot to Charlotte de Grammont, Summer, 1866, *O.C.*, 23:25-26.
[214]*Ibid.*, pp. 26-30.
[215]*Ibid.*, p. vi.
[216]*Ibid.*, 10:155-193, 499-548.
[217]*Ibid.*, 23:174.
[218]Veuillot to Maisonneuve, 21 Jan. 1867, AN, AB, XIX, 3321, Dr. 3.
[219]Same to Quid'bœuf, 21 Jan. 1867, *O.C.*, 23:173-174.
[220]*Vie*, 3:547.
[221]17 Feb. 1867, BN NAF, 24632, p. 35; *O.C.*, 23:184.
[222]*O.C.*, 23:178.
[223]Veuillot to Mme Bacon de Seigneux, BN NAF, 24632, p. 179.
[224]*Ibid.*
[225]*Ibid.*, p. 186.
[226]Report dated 22 Feb. 1867, AN, 305 AP 5, Dr. 7.
[227]Report dated 25 Feb. 1867, *ibid.*
[228]Louis to Élise, 25 Feb. 1867, *ibid.*, pp. 189-190.
[229]Report dated 23 March 1867, AN, 305 AP 5, Dr. 7.
[230]Report dated 5 March 1867, *ibid.*
[231]Louis to Élise, 16 April 1865, BN NAF, 24221, p. 393.
[232]*O.C.*, 10:455-456.
[233]*Ibid.*, 23:183.
[234]Report dated 13 March 1867, AN, 305 AP 5, Dr. 7.
[235]Report dated 9 March 1867, *ibid.*
[236]The main part of this exchange is between 19 March and 25 March 1867, BN NAF, 24634, pp. 276-279.
[237]*O.C.*, 23:231.
[238]*Ibid.*, p. 216.
[239]Between 21 Feb. and 16 June 1867 he wrote Veuillot at least six letters, BN NAF, 24634, 201-213.
[240]*O.C.*, 10:448-451.
[241]*Vie*, 3:548.

CHAPTER VIII

[1]C. S. Phillips, *Church in France, 1848-1907*, pp. 130-133; J. Maurain, *Politique ecclésiastique*, p. 735-736.
[2]P. Spencer, *Politics of Belief*, pp. 192-193.
[3]Guibert to Veuillot, 20 Feb. 1867, BN NAF, 24634, pp. 219-220; 11 April 1867, pp. 221-222.
[4]Mermillod to Veuillot, 16 Feb. 1867, *ibid.*, pp. 234-235.
[5]Veuillot to Maguelonne, 17 April 1867, *ibid.*, 24221, p. 553.
[6]*Vie*, 3:561.
[7]Veuillot to Prosper Dugas, late Feb. 1868, *O.C.*, 23:367.
[8]Same to Charlotte de Grammont, 2 March 1868, *ibid.*, p. 367.
[9]Note in Dupanloup's file. Paris, 28 Feb. 1867, AN, AB, XIX, 524, Dr. 8.
[10]Dupanloup to Bishop of Geneva, [1867], *ibid.*
[11]Report of 10 May 1867, AN, BB[24], 71.
[12]*O.C.*, 35:49-51.
[13]*Ibid.*, p. 51.
[14]Veuillot to Lansade, 8 April 1867, *ibid.*, 23:240.
[15]*Ibid.*, 15:80-82.
[16]*Ibid.*, p. 93.
[17]*Ibid.*, p. 147.
[18]*Ibid.*, pp. 120-128.
[19]*Ibid.*, pp. 130-145.
[20]Veuillot to Mme Aupick, 23 Sept. 1867, *ibid.*, 23:508-509.
[21]*Ibid.*, 23:181.
[22]Veuillot to Mme de Ségur, 11 April 1867, *O.C.*, 23:243.
[23]Same to Charlotte de Grammont, 17 April 1867, *ibid.*, pp. 244-245.
[24]Same to same, 12 May 1867, *ibid.*, pp. 248-249.
[25]*O.C.*, 35:52-55.
[26]*Ibid.*, pp. 292-297; 23:249.
[27]*Ibid.*, 23:261.
[28]20 June 1867, *ibid.*, 23:252.
[29]Louis to Élise, 2 July 1867, *ibid.*, 264.
[30]Same to same, 23 June 1867, *ibid.*, p. 254.
[31]Same to same, 1 July 1867, *ibid.*, pp. 262-263.
[32]*Vie*, 3:563-564.
[33]*Ibid.*, p. 561.
[34]Veuillot to Charlotte de Grammont, 20 July 1867, *O.C.*, 23:272.
[35]Same to Élise, 23 July 1867, *ibid.*, p. 273.
[36]*Ibid.*, 35:211-213.
[37]*Ibid.*, pp. 151, 222. See P. La Gorce, *Second Empire*, 5:242-315.
[38]Veuillot to Père d'Alzon, 8 Nov. 1867, *O.C.*, 23:324.
[39]Same to Cte Guitaut, 5 Nov. 1867, *ibid.*, pp. 322-323.
[40]*Ibid.*, 35:223.
[41]*Ibid.*, p. 247.
[42]*Ibid.*, p. 266.
[43]David H, Pinkney, *Napoleon III and the Rebuilding of Paris* (Princeton: Princeton University Press, 1958) gives careful study of Haussmann's work.
[44]*O.C.*, 35:252-253.
[45]Émile Ollivier, *Journal*, 1:248.

[46]*O.C.*, 35:287-288.
[47]Émile Ollivier, *Journal*, 2:332.
[48]*O.C.*, 36:36-41.
[49]*Ibid.*, pp. 45-50.
[50]*Ibid.*, pp. 55-58.
[51]*Ibid.*, pp. 22-26.
[52]*Ibid.*, pp. 18-21.
[53]*Ibid.*, pp. 77-82, 84-86, 174-178.
[54]*Ibid.*, pp. 87-97; *O.C.*, 24:92.
[55]*Ibid.*, 24:2-3. For the Cercles see Sister Miriam Lynch, *The Organized Apostolate of Albert de Mun* (Washington: Catholic University Press, 1952), pp. 41-60.
[56]*O.C.*, 35:365-371; *Vie*, 3:568-571.
[57]Livry to Préfet. 28 March 1868, AN, 305 AP 5, Dr. 7.
[58]Louis to Élise, 7 Oct. 1868, BN NAF, 24222, p. 79.
[59]Same to Cte de Ségur, 22 Feb. 1869, *O.C.*, 24:107.
[60]Same to Élise, 9 Oct. 1868, BN NAF, 24222, p. 83.
[61]Same to Lafon, Jan. 1868, 6 March 1868, 6 May 1868, *O.C.*, 24:352-353, 376-378, 384-385.
[62]*Ibid.*, 36:58-65.
[63]*Ibid.*, pp. 148-149.
[64]15 Dec. 1868, BN NAF, 24229, pp. 8-10.
[65]Maurice de Bonald to Veuillot, 17 Dec. 1868, *ibid.*, pp. 11-13.
[66]Cte de Quatrebarbes to same, 21 Oct. 1868, *ibid.*, 24634, pp. 331-334.
[67]*O.C.*, 36:185-187.
[68]His principal articles are found in *ibid.*, pp. 221-267.
[69]*Ibid.*, p. 231.
[70]*Ibid.*, p. 242.
[71]*Ibid.*, p. 223, 254-257.
[72]*Ibid.*, p. 249.
[73]*Ibid.*, p. 245-267.
[74]BN NAF, 24221, p. 541.
[75]Montalembert to Falloux, 10 Jan. 1869, Montalembert. *Catholicisme et liberté*, p. 396.
[76]Same to same, *ibid.*, p. 394.
[77]Falloux to Montalembert, 9 Aug. 1868, *ibid.*, p. 381.
[78]Same to same, 18 Dec. 1868, *ibid.*, p. 393.
[79]E. Ollivier, *L'Église et l'état au concile du Vatican*, 2 vols. (Paris: Garnier, 1879), 1:304-306.
[80]*O.C.*, 35:438-503.
[81]*Ibid.*, 36:367.
[82]R. Bazin, *Maret*, 3:34-36.
[83]*O.C..*, 36:272-275.
[84]Veuillot to Msgr. Plantier, 7 Oct. 1869, *ibid.*, 24:209-210.
[85]Veuillot to Abbé Lamaron, 24 Nov. 1869, *O.C.*, 24:232-233.
[86]This theme has been emphasized by Philip Spencer in his *Politics of Belief in Nineteenth-Century France*, pp. 192-260.
[87]*Ibid.*, 36:268-269.
[88]*Ibid.*, p. 271.
[89]*Ibid.*, pp. 371-375.
[90]See note, *ibid.*, 24:226.

[91]*Ibid.*, 12:72-74.
[92]*Vie*, 4:48-49; AN, F^{19} 2553.
[93]Louis to Eugène, 4 Dec. 1869, *O.C.*, 24:236-237.
[94]*Ibid.*, 12:16.
[95]*Ibid.*, pp. 34-41.
[96]Lynn M. Case, "Anticipating the Death of Pius IX in 1861," *Catholic Historical Review*, 43(Oct. 1957):309-323.
[97]P. La Gorce, *Second Empire*, 6:2-32.
[98]*O.C.*, 12:54-58.
[99]*Ibid.*, p. 56.
[100]Veuillot to Mme Bacon de Seigneux, 13 Nov. 1869, BN NAF, 24632, pp. 79-80.
[101]R. Aubert, *Pontificat de Pie IX*, p. 324.
[102]*Vie*, 4:65-67; *O.C.*, 24:235.
[103]James Ward and Bertil Grezzi, "Pius IX's Voltaire: Louis Veuillot and Vatican I," *Thought* 45(Autumn, 1970):346-370, gives a lively picture of Veuillot at the council. The study, though based largely on Veuillot's *Œuvres completes*, is not very sympathetic.
[104]*Ibid.*, pp. 352-353; *O.C.*, 24:253, 257.
[105]*O.C.*, 24:242.
[106]*Ibid.*, p. 269. I have used the Ward-Grezzi translation of *gargotier*, p. 362.
[107]Louis to Eugène, 13 Dec. 1869, *O.C.* 24:239.
[108]Ward and Grezzi, "Pius IX's Voltaire," p. 359.
[109]The official account of the council was to have been written by Eugenio Cecconi, Canon of Florence, but the two volumes he eventually published in 1873 and 1879 dealt only with the antecedents of the council.
[110]Émile Ollivier's *L'Église et l'état au concile du Vatican* is the fullest analysis of the council from the point of view of the French government. Edward C. Butler, *The Vatican Council: The Story Told from inside in Bishop Ullathorne's Letters*, 2 vols.(London: Longmans, Green, 1930) is called the "best expose" by Roger Aubert.
[111]R. Aubert, *Pontificat de Pie IX*, p. 324.
[112]Ward-Grezzi, *op cit.*, pp. 355-356, have a good summary of this situation.
[113]Louis to Eugène, 4 Dec. 1869, *O.C.*, 24:236-237.
[114]Same to Mme de Pitray, early Dec. 1869, *ibid.*, p. 235.
[115]*Ibid.*, 12:75.
[116]L. Lacroix to Veuillot, Lavarcac, 26 Nov. 1869, BN NAF, 24229, p. 247.
[117]Abbé Poncet to Veuillot, 2 Dec. 1869, *ibid.*, p. 307.
[118]Abbé Charpentier, to Veuillot, Gentelles, 8 Dec. 1869, *ibid.*, p. 155.
[119]Abbé Starbach to same, 29 Nov. 1869, *ibid.*, p. 332.
[120]*O.C.*, 24:255.
[121]*Ibid.*, p. 237.
[122]Falloux to Montalembert, 18 Jan. 1870, Montalembert, *Catholicisme et liberté*, p. 426.
[123]*Vie*, 4:70.
[124]*Ibid.*, pp. 77-78; *O.C.*, 24:239.
[125]*Vie*, 4:72.
[126]*Ibid.*, pp. 79-87.
[127]*Ibid.*, p. 81; E. Ollivier, *L'Église et l'état*, 1:1-30; E. C. Butler, *The Vatican Council*, 1:157-185.
[128]Butler, *op. cit.*, 1:77, 172; 2:119-133.

[129]*O.C.*, 24:250, 235, 263-264.
[130]E. C. Butler, *The Vatican Council*, 1:168-177, 269-283.
[131]*O.C.*, 12:79-82.
[132]*Ibid.*, p. 78.
[133]*Ibid.*, p. 83.
[134]*Ibid.*, pp. 79-80.
[135]*Ibid.*, p. 81.
[136]*Ibid.*, p. 93.
[137]*Ibid.*, p. 90-92.
[138]*O.C.*, 24:240, 244.
[139]*Ibid.*, 12:*passim.*
[140]E. Ollivier, *L'Église et l'état,* 1:508; C. S. Phillips, *Church in France, 1848-1907*, p. 138.
[141]C. S. Phillips, *op. cit.*, p. 146.
[142]Banneville to Daru, 16 Feb. 1870, AE, CP 1045 (Rome), p. 302.
[143]Albeit brief, Phillips, *op. cit.*, gives an excellent summary, pp. 145-162. La Gorce, *Second Empire*, 6:33-77.
[144]*O.C.*, 12:108.
[145]*Ibid.*, pp. 123-125.
[146]*Ibid.*, pp. 129-130.
[147]*Ibid.*, 24:251.
[148]Banneville to Grammont, 1 June 1870, AE, CP 1047 (Rome), p. 4.
[149]*Vie*, 4:106-114.
[150]*Ibid.*, p. 110.
[151]*O.C.*, 24:272; *Vie*, 4:117-119; C. S. Phillips, *Church in France, 1848-1907*, p. 154.
[152]*O.C.*, p. 272.
[153]*L'Univers*, 17 March 1870.
[154]Veuillot to Arthur Murcier, 24 March 1870, *O.C.*, 24:273-274.
[155]*Ibid.*, 12:268.
[156]*Ibid.*, p. 271.
[157]*Ibid.*, p. 270.
[158]*L'Univers*, 7 April 1870.
[159]29 March 1870, *O.C.*, 24:277.
[160]*L'Univers*, 7 April 1870.
[161]*O.C.*, 12:271.
[162]*L'Univers*, 2 April 1870.
[163]*O.C.*, 12:363.
[164]*L'Univers*, 18 March 1870.
[165]R. Aubert, *Pontificat de Pie IX*, pp. 340-341; E. C. Butler, *The Vatican Council*, 2:29.
[166]*O.C.*, 12:331-340.
[167]*Ibid.*, 210-212.
[168]*Ibid.*, p. 363.
[169]*Ibid.*, p. 353.
[170]Banneville to Gramont, 18 May 1870, AE, CP 1046(Rome), p. 371.
[171]*O.C.*, 12:285-290.
[172]C. S. Phillips, *Church in France,* 1848-1907, p. 129.
[173]É. Ollivier, *L'Église et l'etat*, 2:91-95.
[174]*O.C.*, 12:366; *Vie*, 4:162-164.
[175]*O.C.*, 24:243, 290; *ibid.*, 12:425.

[176] *Vie*, 4:163.
[177] *Ibid.*, pp. 163-164.
[178] *O.C.*, 12:366-369.
[179] *Ibid.*, pp. 366, 369-370, 380-385.
[180] *Ibid.*, p. 370.
[181] *Ibid.*, p. 416.
[182] *Ibid.*, p. 417.
[183] *Ibid.*, pp. 425-426. The letter was published in *L'Univers* on 30 May 1870.
[184] *Vie*, 4:164.
[185] Abbé Gastelet (Auvilliers), 22 June 1870, BN NAF 24634, pp. 367-369.
[186] Banneville to Grammont, 1 June 1870, AE, CP 1047(Rome), p. 4.
[187] *O.C.*, 24:275.
[188] *L'Univers*, 14 Feb. 1870.
[189] Louis to Eugène, 19 June 1870, *O.C.*, 24:293.
[190] Same to same, 11 June 1870, *ibid.*, p. 292.
[191] *L'Univers*, 5 July 1870.
[192] *Ibid.*, 8 July 1870.
[193] *Ibid.*, 6 July 1870.
[194] *Ibid.*, 11 July 1870.
[195] Louis to Eugène, 13 July 1870, *O.C.*, 24:298-299.
[196] *Vie*, 4:170-171; E. Ollivier, *L'Église et l'état,* 2:335.
[197] C. S. Phillips, *Church in France, 1848-1907*, p. 161.
[198] *L'Univers*, 20 July 1870.
[199] *Ibid.*
[200] *O.C.*, 12:541-542.
[201] *Ibid.*, pp. 546-555.
[202] 26 July 1870, BN NAF, 24229, p. 413.

CHAPTER IX

[1] See La Gorce, *Second Empire*, 6:124-320.
[2] *Ibid.*, pp. 323-357.
[3] *L'Univers*, 31 July 1870.
[4] *Ibid.*, 22 July 1870.
[5] *Ibid.*, 24 July 1870.
[6] *Ibid.*, 1 Aug. 1870.
[7] *O.C.*, 13:19.
[8] *Ibid.*, p. 15.
[9] *Ibid.*, pp. 21-24, 36-41, 133-137.
[10] *Ibid.*, pp. 36-38.
[11] *Ibid.*, pp. 39-41.
[12] *Ibid.*, pp. 61-62.
[13] *Ibid.*, p. 20.
[14] *Ibid.*, p. 59.
[15] *Ibid.*, pp. 32-36.
[16] *Ibid.*, p. 45.
[17] *Vie*, 4:183-184.
[18] *O.C.*, 13:54-55.
[19] *Ibid.*, pp. 66-67.
[20] *Ibid.*, pp. 6-12.
[21] *Ibid.*, p. 97.

[22] *Ibid.*, 24:306.
[23] *Ibid.*, pp. 306-307; *Vie*, 4:184-185.
[24] *Ibid.*, pp. 307-308.
[25] *Ibid.*, pp. 303, 305, 309.
[26] *Vie*, 4:202-203.
[27] François Veuillot gives considerable detail about Rastoul's peregrinations. He says, however, that the first number appeared 19 September, which was impossible. Perhaps he meant that all was in order by 29 September. The first number of the Nantes edition in the Duke University Library is dated 30 September 1870.
[28] *Vie*, 4:216-219. François gives 15 January 1871 as the date, but it was 10 January 1871.
[29] G. Hanotaux, *Contemporary France*, 2:615.
[30] *L'Univers*, 5 Sept. 1870.
[31] *Ibid.*, 13 Sept. 1870.
[32] *Ibid.*, 15 Sept. 1870.
[33] *O.C.*, 13:69.
[34] *L'Univers*, 17 Sept., 10 Oct. 1870.
[35] *Ibid.*, 14 September 1870.
[36] *O.C.*, 13:117-119.
[37] *Ibid.*, p. 126.
[38] *Ibid.*, pp. 137-138.
[39] *Ibid.*, pp. 165-166.
[40] *Ibid.*, pp. 172-175.
[41] *L'Univers*, 9 Nov. 1870.
[42] *O.C.*, 13:138.
[43] *Ibid.*, p. 171.
[44] *Ibid.*, p. 218.
[45] *Ibid.*, 24:322. Eugène to Louis, 22 Feb. 1871, BN NAF, 24634, p. 376.
[46] *O.C.*, p. 314.
[47] *Ibid.*, 13:163-165.
[48] *Ibid.*, p. 94.
[49] Dec. 1870, BN NAF, 24620, pp. 67-99.
[50] *O.C.*, 13:300-314.
[51] BN NAF, 24620, p. 131.
[52] *O.C.*, 13:347.
[53] *Ibid.*, 358-360.
[54] *O.C.*, 24:316.
[55] G. Hanotaux, *Contemporary France*, 1:22-43.
[56] *O.C.*, 13:384-386.
[57] *Ibid.*, pp. 373-384.
[58] *Ibid.*
[59] *Ibid.*, p. 398.
[60] *Ibid.*, pp. 393-394.
[61] For the legitimists in 1871, see especially Robert R. Locke, *French Legitimists and the Politics of Moral Order in the Early Third Republic*, (Princeton: Princeton University Press, 1974), pp. 10-53.
[62] *O.C.*, pp. 405-407.
[63] E. Veuillot, *Hommages*, pp. 27-28.
[64] G. Hanotaux, *Contemporary France*, 1:30-72.
[65] Louis to Eugène, 20 Feb. 1871, *O.C.*, 24:317-319.

[66]*Vie*, 4:221-222.
[67]Charlotte de Grammont to Veuillot, 10 Feb. 1871, BN NAF, 24229, p. 589.
[68]Veuillot to Charlotte de Grammont, 27 or 28 Feb. 1871, *O.C.*, 24:320-322.
[69]Louis to Eugène, early March 1871, *ibid.*, pp. 323-324.
[70]Veuillot to Agnès and Luce Veuillot, 24 Feb. 1871, *ibid.*, pp. 319-320.
[71]*O.C.*, 13:413-418.
[72]*Ibid.*, p. 418.
[73]*Ibid.*, pp. 420-421.
[74]Keller to Veuillot, Ostend, 13 March 1871, BN NAF, 24229, p. 598.
[75]See Stewart Edwards, *The Paris Commune of 1871* (London: Eyre and Spottiswood, 1971) and Melvin Kranzberg, *The Siege of Paris, 1870-1871: A Political and Social History*, (Ithaca: Cornell University Press, 1950).
[76]*O.C.*, 13:424.
[77]*Ibid.*, p. 425.
[78]*Vie*, 4:230.
[79]23 March 1871, *O.C.*, 24:325.
[80]Around 25 March 1871, *ibid.*, p. 326.
[81]*Ibid.*, pp. 327-328.
[82]22 March 1871, BN NAF, 24229, p. 609.
[83]*O.C.*, 13:437-439.
[84]*Ibid.*, p. 440.
[85]*Ibid.*, pp. 430-435.
[86]*Ibid.*, pp. 441-442.
[87]*Ibid.*, pp. 450-456, 469-470.
[88]*Ibid*, 24:330.
[89]*Ibid.*, 14:455.
[90]*Ibid.*, 13:472-474; M. L. Brown, *Chambord*, p. 87.
[91]*O.C.*, 13:472; *Vie*, 4:274-275.
[92]Louis to Élise, 6 May 1871, *O.C.*, 24:331.
[93]*Vie*, 4:255-256.
[94]Louis to Eugène, end of May 1871, *O.C.*, 14:340-341.
[95]E. Lacanuet, *Les Dernières années du pontificat de Pie IX* (Paris: Alcan, 1931), pp. 120-121; G. Hanotaux, *Contemporary France*, 1:218. The word "murder" is used by the latter author.
[96]*O.C.*, 13:125-127, 479-481.
[97]*Ibid.*, p. 488.
[98]*Ibid.*, p. 496.
[99]*Ibid.*, p. 498.
[100]*O.C.*, 24:340.
[101]Veuillot to Roumainville, Paris, 7 June 1871, *ibid.*, p. 342.
[102]Veuillot to Mercurelli, 9 June 1871, BN NAF, 24632, pp. 133-134.
[103]*Vie*, 4:308.
[104]9 June 1871, BN NAF, 24632, p. 134.
[105]Veuillot to Nardi, 3 or 4 June 1871, *O.C.*, 24:351-352.
[106]*Vie*, 4:247.
[107]E. Lecanuet, *Dernières années*, pp. 49-51.
[108]*Vie*, 4:289.
[109]Abbé Eugène Terrien, *Mgr. Freppel, apologiste et défenseur des droits de l'église* (Paris: Maison de la Bonne Presse, 1927), and also *Mgr. Freppel, sa vie, ses ouvrages, ses œuvres, son influence et son temps, d'après des documents inconnus*, 2 vols.(Angers: chez l'auteur, 1931-1932). For Freppel's subsequent

career the Archives of the Paris Préfecture of Police, B a/1086, throw much light.

[111]Freppel to Veuillot, 19 June 1871, BN NAF, 24229, p. 584.

[112]Same to same, 4 July 1871, *ibid.*, p. 588.

[113]For a biography in English, see M. L. Brown, *The Comte de Chambord*. See also Arthur Loth, *L'Échec de la restauration monarchique en 1873* (Paris: Perrin, 1910).

[114]*L'Univers*, 3 June 1871.

[115]A. de Cazenove to Veuillot, 3 July 1871 BN NAF, 24229, pp. 562-563.

[116]La Tour to same, 6 July 1871, *ibid.*, pp. 612-613.

[117]Letter of 8 July 1871 quoted in *Vie*, 4:282.

[118]H. de Vanssay to Veuillot, 19 Sept. 1871, BN NAF, 24229, pp. 677-678.

[119]Belcastel to same, 12 Sept. 1871, *ibid.*, p. 545.

[120]2 July 1871, BN NAF, 24229, p. 567.

[121]*L'Univers*, 5 July 1871.

[122]*Vie*, 4:309-311.

[123]25 July 1871, *O.C.*, 24:356.

[124]*Ibid.*, p. 259.

[125]17 August 1871, BN NAF, 24222, p. 242.

[126]*L'Univers*, 30 August 1871.

[127]*Ibid.*, 14 Sept. 1871.

[128]*Vie*, 4:295.

[129]*O.C.*, 37:37-62.

[130]*Ibid.*, pp. 1-3, 14-16, 32-34.

[131]*Ibid.*, pp. 94-97.

[132]*Ibid.*, pp. 135-138.

[133]E. Michaud to Veuillot, 12 Feb. 1872, BN NAF, 24634, pp. 439-440.

[134]*O.C.*, 37:34-37.

[135]G. Hanotaux, *Contemporary France*, 1:567-568; E. Lecanuet, *Dernières Années*, pp. 130-168.

[136]Hanotaux, *op. cit.*, 1:566.

[137]*O.C.*, 37:72-74.

[138]Veuillot to Maguelonne, Paris, 17 Nev. 1871, BN NAF, 24222, p. 232.

[139]*O.C.*, 37:3-5.

[140]*Ibid.*, p. 150.

[141]*Ibid.*, pp. 149-168.

[142]*Ibid.*, pp. 158-161.

[143]*Ibid.*, pp. 205-207.

[144]*Ibid.*, pp. 215-222.

[145]*Ibid.*, p. 179.

[146]*Vie*, 4:326.

[147]*O.C.*, 37:179.

[148]24 April 1872, *ibid.*, 25:38-40.

[149]*Ibid.*, 37:183-184.

[150]*Ibid.*, 25:45.

[151]*Ibid.*, 37:179-192.

[152]*Ibid.*, 25:38.

[153]25 April 1872, *ibid.*, p. 42.

[154]BN NAF, 24634, p. 391.

[155]18 April 1872, *ibid.*, p. 380.

[156]19 and 29 April 1872, *ibid.*, pp. 52, 57.

[157]20 April 1872, *ibid.*, p. 388.
[158]Abbé Boullay to Veuillot, St. Calias, 22 April 1872, BN NAF, 24230, p. 35.
[159]Veuillot to Abbé Picard, 27 April 1872, *O.C.*, 25:52.
[160]Same to Charlotte de Grammont, April 1872, *ibid.*, p. 55.
[161]Same to Abbé Labarre, April 1872, *ibid.*, p. 57.
[162]*O.C.*, 37:185-189.
[163]Report of "22", 7 Aug. 1872, APP, B a/874.
[164]Veuillot to Prosper Dugas, 17 June 1872, *O.C.*, 25:75.
[165]26 April, 4 May 1872, BN NAF, 24230, pp. 123-126.
[166]*Ibid.; Vie*, 4:337.
[167]*Vie*, 4:330-334; BN NAF, 24230 contains a great many letters of comfort.
[168]BN NAF, 24222, p. 312.
[169]*Vie*, 4:347-348.
[170]Rome, 25 May 1872, BN NAF, 24220, p. 33.
[171]*Ibid.*, 24222, pp. 303-304.
[172]*Ibid.*, p. 314.
[173]25 June 1872, *ibid.*, 24230, p. 319.
[174]*Vie*, 4:487-494.
[175]*O.C.*, 37:284-287.
[176]*Ibid.*, pp. 252-255.
[177]*O.C.*, 25:80.
[178]Veuillot to Baron de Ferussac, 26 July 1872, *ibid.*, p. 86.
[179]*O.C.*, 37:317-324.
[180]*Ibid.*, 25:91.
[181]Orleans, 13 Aug. 1872, BN NAF, 24230.
[182]Veuillot to Mme Bacon de Seigneux, around 30 July 1872, *O.C.*, 25:87-89.
[183]18 Sept. 1872, BN NAF, 24230, p. 306.
[184]25 Sept. 1872, *ibid.*, p. 319.
[185]Veuillot to Freppel, 11 Nov. 1872, *O.C.*, 25:136.
[186]Same to Élise, 5 Sept. 1872, *ibid.*, p. 113.
[187]*Ibid.*, p. 116.
[188]27 Sept. 1872, *ibid.*, p. 131.
[189]*O.C.*, 37:354-367.
[190]*Ibid.*, pp. 299-314.
[191]*Ibid.*, pp. 443-446.
[192]*Ibid.*, pp. 368-390.
[193]*Ibid.*, pp. 143-145.
[194]*Ibid.; Vie*, 4:408-410.
[195]*O.C.*, 25:144-145.
[196]*Ibid.*, p. 138.
[197]*Ibid.*, pp. 150-151.
[198]Louis to Élise, 7 Jan. 1873, *ibid.*, p. 156.
[199]Same to same, 8 Jan. 1873, *ibid.*, p. 157.
[200]20 Jan. 1873, *ibid.*, pp. 167-168.
[201]3 Sept. 1873, *ibid.*, p. 239; *Vie*, 4:381-384.
[202]*O.C.*, 38:45-47.
[203]*Ibid.*, 25:173-174.
[204]Charlotte de Grammont to Veuillot, 31 Aug. 1871, BN NAF, 24229, p. 591.
[205]Bazaine to Veuillot, 10 July 1873, BN NAF, 24230, p. 392.
[206]*O.C.*, 25:262-263.
[207]*Ibid.*, 25:242, 245; 37:301-302, 382-385.

[208]Veuillot to Charlotte de Grammont, 19 March 1872, BN NAF, 24224, p. 217.
[209]Same to Adolphe Dechamps, 20 Jan. 1873, *ibid.*, 24632, p. 158.
[210]*O.C.*, 38:47-58.
[211]*Ibid.*, pp. 96-110.
[212]*L'Univers*, 13 Feb. 1873.
[213]*Ibid.*, 25 Feb. 1873; M. L. Brown, *Chambord*, pp. 99-100.
[214]15 March 1873, BN NAF, 24224, p. 241.
[215]*L'Univers*, 24, 26 March 1873.
[216]*Ibid.*, 1, 7, 10 April 1873.
[217]Veuillot to Belcastel, 4 July 1873, *O.C.*, 25:214; G. Hanotaux, *Contemporary France*, 2:80-83.
[218]*L'Univers*, 11 April 1873.
[219]Hanotaux, *op. cit.*, 2:606-611.
[220]*O.C.*, 38:133-143.
[221]*L'Univers*, 27 April 1873.
[222]*Ibid.*, 25 April 1873.
[223]*Ibid.*, 12 April 1873.
[224]*Ibid.*, 14 March 1873.
[225]*O.C.*, 38:186-195.
[226]See A. Loth, *L'Échec de la restauration monarchique*, pp. 173-208, and M. L. Brown, *Chambord*, pp. 102-138.
[227]*L'Univers*, 4 Aug. 1873.
[228]*Ibid.*, 6 Aug. 1873.
[229]*Ibid.*, 7 Aug. 1873.
[230]*Ibid.*, 20 Aug. 1873.
[231]*Ibid.*, 13 Sept. 1873.
[232]*Ibid.*, 29 Aug. 1873.
[233]*Ibid.*, 3 Sept. 1873.
[234]*Ibid.*, 30 Sept. 1873. Bismarck was told by his representative in Paris that every curé, in the opinion of Decazes, was "Veuillotist." *Die Grosse Politik der Europäischen Kabinette*, 40 vols.(Berlin, 1922-1929), 1:237.
[235]*L'Univers*, 5 Sept. 1873.
[236]*Ibid.*, 9 Sept. 1873.
[237]Alphonso of Borbon to Veuillot, 4 Oct. 1872, BN NAF, 24230, p. 37.
[238]*L'Univers* 3 Oct. 1873.
[239]*Ibid.*, 28 Aug. 1873.
[240]*Ibid.*, 2 Oct. 1873.
[241]*Ibid.*, 16 Oct. 1873.
[242]*Ibid.*, 10 Oct. 1873.
[243]G. Hanotaux, *Contemporary France*, 2:271; M. L. Brown, *Chambord*, p. 131; *O.C.*, 38:326-328, 331-334. Eugène Veuillot, *Hommages à Louis Veuillot*, (Paris: Palmé, 1884), pp. 27-28.
[244]Brown, *op. cit.*, pp. 130-131.
[245]*O.C.*, 38:326.
[246]*Ibid.*, pp. 350-356.
[247]Alexandre de Saint-Albin, *Histoire d'Henri V* (Paris: Palmé, 1874).
[248]13 Nov. 1873, BN NAF, 24230, p. 615.
[249]*O.C.*, 38:344-346, 347-350.
[250]APP, B a/874; *L'Univers* 25, 27, and 30 Nov. 1872.
[251]Report of "3"(Lombard), 30 Nov. 1872, APP, B a/874.
[252]Marvin L. Brown, Jr., "Catholic Legitimist Militancy in the Early Years of the Third French Republic," *The Catholic Historical Review*, 60(July 1974):233-254.

CHAPTER X

[1]Veuillot to Cte de Guitaut, 29 Nov. 1873, *O.C.*, 25:247-248.
[2]2 Dec. 1873, *ibid.*, pp. 248-249.
[3]*O.C.*, 25:252-270. These notes by Veuillot's secretary, Paul Lapeyre, are found in the BN NAF, 24620, filed in December.
[4]*Ibid.*, pp. 262-263; BN NAF, 24620, p. 84.
[5]*O.C.*, 38:328-330.
[6]Veuillot to Élise, 24 Dec. 1873, *ibid.*, 25:273-274.
[7]*Ibid.*, pp. 271-273; *Vie*, 4:495-497.
[8]Extract of a report "PM"(Fontaine), 16 Nov. 1873, APP, B a/874.
[9]*Le Temps*, 19 Dec. 1873 (article dated 15 Dec.), in *ibid.*
[10]*O.C.*, 38:367.
[11]*Ibid.*, pp. 367-369.
[12]*Le Français*, 8 Jan. 1874, AN, F^{19}, 2553.
[13]BN NAF, 24231, p. 271.
[14]Marvin L. Brown, Jr., "The Monarchical Principle in European Diplomacy after 1870," *The Historian* 15(Autumn, 1952):41-56.
[15]Gontaut-Biron to Decazes, Berlin, 14 Jan. 1874, AE, CP 12 (Allemagne), p. 94.
[16]Same to same, 17 Jan. 1874, *ibid.*, p. 94.
[17]*Vie*, 4:505.
[18]Belcastel to Broglie, 4 March 1874, BN NAF, 24231, p. 65.
[19]5 Feb. 1874, *O.C.*, 25:293-294.
[20]6 Feb. 1874, *ibid.*, pp. 295-296.
[21]AE, CP 12(Allemagne), p. 140.
[22]21 Jan. 1874, *ibid.*, p. 149.
[23]Despatch No. 8, 22 Jan. 1874, telegram, 26 Jan. 1874, *ibid.*, pp. 154, 178.
[24]Veuillot to Lansade, 6 Feb. 1874, *O.C.*, 25:298-299. For *Cara* see *ibid.*, 14:491-568.
[25]Same to Pius IX, 19 Jan. 1874, *ibid.*, p. 276.
[26]C. S. Phillips, *Church in France, 1848-1907*, p. 179.
[27]*Vie*, 4:514-515.
[28]Joseph Alemany to Veuillot, 30 Jan. 1874, BN NAF, 24231, pp. 18-21.
[29]Abbé Allemand to same, Valence, 15 Jan. 1874, *ibid.*, pp. 22-23.
[30]Veuillot to Cte de Mun, 15 Feb. 1874, *O.C.*, 25:306-307.
[31]31 Jan. 1874, BN NAF, 24632, pp. 166-167.
[32]Jan. 1874, *ibid.*, p. 174. What appears to be the same letter is dated 17 Feb. 1874, in *O.C.*., 25:311-312.
[33]End of January 1874, *O.C., ibid.*, p. 281.
[34]28 Feb. 1874, APP, B a/874.
[35]19 March 1874, *ibid.*
[36]Report of "18", 28 June 1874, *ibid.*
[37]*O.C.*, 38:394-395.
[38]*Ibid.*, p. 396.
[39]*Ibid.*, pp. 369-382.
[40]*Ibid.*, pp. 432-434.
[41]*Ibid.*, pp. 448-449.
[42]*Ibid.*, pp. 458-461.
[43]*Ibid.*, p. 397.
[44]*Ibid.*, pp. 413-415.

[45]*Ibid.*, pp. 427-428.
[46]*Ibid.*, pp. 484-486.
[47]*Vie*, 4:550.
[48]Clipping from *Gaulois*, dated 11 Sept. 1874, APP, B a/874.
[49]Veuillot to Msgr. Ladoue, 9 Sept. 1874, *O.C.*, 25:384.
[50]Same to Bazaine, 20 Aug. 1874, *ibid.*, p. 379.
[51]*Ibid.*, 38:491-500.
[52]Report of "32", 30 Sept. 1874, B a/874.
[53]*O.C.*, 25:471-479.
[54]Veuillot to Mme Bacon de Seigneux, 3 March 1874, *ibid.*, pp. 330-331. *Vie*, 4:530 cites the letter as of 8 March 1874.
[55]Report of 12 Dec. 1876, APP, B a/874.
[56]*O.C.*, 25:330-331.
[57]8 March 1874, *ibid.*, pp. 337-338.
[58]27-28 March 1874, *ibid.*, pp. 345-346.
[59]*Vie*, 4:571-572. Amusingly, the chapel was located on the Rue d'Enfer, where also was located a factory for religious medals, 31 May 1874, APP, B a/401.
[60]*O.C.*, 25:354.
[61]*Ibid.*, pp. 364-369; *Vie*, 4:534-535.
[62]26 March 1873, *O.C.*, 25:190-191.
[63]*Vie*, 4:570-571. A note in *O.C.*, 25:386 indicates 4 Dec. 1874.
[64]*O.C.*, 25:386-387, 389-391.
[65]*Ibid.*, p. 191.
[66]*Vie*, 4:567-568.
[67]G. Hanotaux, *Contemporary France*, 2:622.
[68]26 Nov. 1874, *O.C.*, 25:386.
[69]*Vie*, 4:617.
[70]*O.C.*, 26:65.
[71]*Ibid*, 39:15-42.
[72]*Ibid.*, pp. 36-55.
[73]Freppel to Villemessant, 1 April 1875, BN NAF, 24232, pp. 114-115.
[74]Abbé Cathaud to Veuillot, St. Paul-en-Chalançon, 17 March 1875, *ibid.*, p. 54.
[75]*Le Temps*, 16 Apr. 1875, in APP, B a/874. The press generally made it seem that Veuillot personally was being sued, but François indicated *L'Univers* was the object. *Vie*, 4:606.
[76]*Le National*, 25 Apr. 1875, *ibid.*
[77]Report of 7 May 1875, *ibid.*
[78]Report of 8 Nov. 1875, *ibid.; Vie*, 4:606.
[79]*O.C.*, 39:74-76.
[80]Michaud to Veuillot, 21 Apr. 1875, BN NAF, 24232, pp. 182-183.
[81]*O.C.*, 39:75.
[82]*Ibid.*, pp. 95-97.
[83]22 March 1875, BN NAF, 24232, p. 109.
[84]Report of 7 July 1875, APP, B a/874.
[85]Report of "678", 30 July 1875, *ibid.*
[86]Chef de Cabinet to M. Marseille, 9 Aug. 1875, *ibid.*
[87]8 Nov. 1875, *ibid.*
[88]Antonin Debidour, *L'Église catholique et l'état sous la troisième république*, 2 vols.(Paris: Alcan, 1906-1907), 1:419; Joseph Brugerette, *Le prêtre français et la société contemporaine*, 2 vols.(Paris: Lethielleux, 1933-1935), 2:737.
[89]Debidour, *op. cit.*, p. 435.

[90] *O.C.*, 39:97-103.
[91] *Ibid.*, pp. 98, 103.
[92] Hanotaux, *Contemporary France*, 2:554.
[93] *O.C.*, 39:140-147.
[94] Freppel to Veuillot, 16 Aug. 1875, BN NAF, 24232, p. 116.
[95] Same to same, 20 Nov. 1875, *ibid.*, p. 118.
[96] *Vie*, 4:589.
[97] *O.C.*, 39:103.
[98] Eugène Tavernier, *Louis Veuillot: L'Homme, le lutteur, l'écrivain* (Paris:Plon-Nourrit, 1913), p. 1.
[99] *O.C.*, 26:12.
[100] *Ibid.*, p. 40.
[101] *Ibid.*, p. 22-23.
[102] *Ibid.*, p. 60.
[103] *Ibid.*, p. 88.
[104] *Vie*, 4:632-635; BN NAF, 24232, pp. 515-518.
[105] 20 Feb. 1876, *O.C.*, 26:110-111.
[106] Louis to Eugène, 16 June 1876, *ibid.*, p. 140.
[107] *O.C.*, 39:332-335.
[108] 22 March, 14 July 1876, BN NAF, 24232, 347, 349.
[109] *O.C.*, 39:304-306.
[110] 10 March 1876, BN NAF, 24222, pp. 554-555; *O.C.*, 26:117.
[111] Maurice Vallet, *À propos d'un centenaire. Louis Veuillot (1813-1883). Sa vie, ses idées sociales, ses idées politiques, ses idées littéraires* (Paris: Société française d'imprimerie et de librairie, 1913), p. 110.
[112] *O.C.*, 29:365-366.
[113] Report of "678", 2 March 1876, APP, B a/874.
[114] *O.C.*, 39:370.
[115] 9 July 1876, *ibid.*, 26:145.
[116] Louis to Eugène, 19 June 1876, *ibid.*, p. 140.
[117] *Ibid.*, p. 145.
[118] *Ibid.*, 39:424-433.
[119] *Ibid.*, pp. 431, 432.
[120] 22 March 1876, BN NAF, 24232, p. 347.
[121] Letters of 26, 29 Sept., 20 Oct., 1 Dec. 1876, BN NAF, 24232, pp. 350, 352-355, 356, 358.
[122] *O.C.*, 39:433-443.
[123] *Ibid.*, 40:6-7.
[124] Paul Féval to Veuillot, 18 June 1877, BN NAF, 24233, p. 75.
[125] *O.C.*, 40:21-33.
[126] *Ibid.*, pp. 68-80.
[127] *Ibid.*, pp. 110-112.
[128] *Ibid.*, pp. 114-128.
[129] 14 Oct. 1877, *O.C.*, 26:198.
[130] Veuillot to Cte Henri d'Ideville, 10 Dec. 1877, *ibid.*, p. 200.
[131] Item dated 7 Apr. 1883 containing passport, APP E A/15.
[132] E. Tavernier, *Louis Veuillot*, p. 17.
[133] 27 Sept. 1875, *O.C.*, 26:68-70.
[134] 15 Jan. 1877, APP, E A/15.
[135] 18 Feb. 1877, *ibid.*, B a/874.
[136] 31 Dec. 1876, *ibid.*

[137]Report of 4 June 1877, *ibid.*
[138]*O.C.*, 40:199-201.
[139]*Ibid.*, pp. 207-209.
[140]8 Feb. 1874, BN NAF, 24233, p. 294.
[141]20 Aug. and 26 Dec. 1877, BN NAF, 24233. pp. 20, 167.
[142]*Vie*, 4:712-713.
[143]*L'Univers*, 2 March 1878.
[144]*O.C.*, 40:218-220.
[145]Veuillot to Msgr. Mermillod, 28 Feb. 1878, *ibid.*, p. 207; same to Henri Parrot, 25 March 1878, *ibid.*, pp. 207-208.
[146]Same to Freppel, 26 March 1878, *ibid.*, p. 209.
[147]*Vie*, p. 716.
[148]Élise to Eugène, 7 May 1878, quoted in *Vie*, 4:719-721.
[149]Same to same, 5 May 1878, quoted in *ibid.*, p. 720.
[150]*O.C.*, 40:274-275.
[151]*Ibid.*, pp. 275-278.
[152]*Ibid.*, pp. 277-278.
[153]Veuillot to Gabriel de Chaulnes, end of 1878, *O.C.*, 26:200.
[154]Report dated 11 June 1878, APP, B a/874.
[155]Report of 17 May 1878, *ibid.*
[156]Report of "P", 8 July 1878, *ibid.*
[157]*O.C.*, 40:255-260.
[158]*Ibid.*, p. 279.
[159]*Vie*, 4:747, *L'Univers*, 20 May 1880.
[160]*O.C.*, 26:224-225.
[161]*Vie*, 4:747.
[162]Abbé Corbini to Veuillot, 23 May 1879, *ibid.*, p. 749.
[163]*Ibid.*, pp. 750-754.
[164]Report of 5 March 1880, APP, B a/874.
[165]Report of 11 Sept. 1880, *ibid.*
[166]Report of 18 Feb. 1881, *ibid.*
[167]BN NAF, 24632, pp. 486-487.
[168]*Ibid.*, p. 480.
[169]E. Veuillot, *Hommages*, p. 525.
[170]*Ibid.*, p. 5.
[171]*Ibid.*, p. 24.
[172]Report of "P", 9 April 1883, APP, B a/874.
[173]Report of "Ernest", 9 April 1883, *ibid.*
[174]E. Veuillot, *Hommages*, pp. 15-19.
[175]Report dated 10 April 1883, APP, B a/874.
[176]BN NAF, 24622, pp. 209-220.
[177]23 April 1883, *Hommages*, pp. 27-28.
[178]11 April 1883, *ibid.*, pp. 28-29.
[179]*Ibid.*, p. 29.
[180]*Ibid.*, pp. 30-473.
[181]*Ibid.*, pp. 40-42.
[182]*Ibid.*, pp. 273-274.
[183]*Ibid.*, pp. 474-481.
[184]*Ibid.*, p. 512.
[185]*Ibid.*, pp. 508-509.
[186]*Ibid.*, pp. 543-544.

[187]*Ibid.*, pp. 554.
[188]*Ibid.*, p. 550.
[189]*Ibid.*, pp. 547-549.
[190]*Ibid.*, pp. 531-532.
[191]*Ibid.*, pp. 531-532.
[192]*Ibid.*, p. 543.
[193]*Ibid.*, p. 513-514.
[194]AN, 305 AP 5, Dr. 7.
[195]A. Latreille *et al, Histoire du catholicisme,* 3:432-433.
[196]E. Veuillot, *Hommages*, pp. 183-184.
[197]*Ibid.*, pp. 458-460.
[198]*Ibid.*, pp. 469-470.
[199]*Ibid.*, p. 467.
[200]BN NAF, 24628.
[201]*Nouvelliste*, 22 Feb. 1913, BN NAF, 24624, p. 9.
[202]*Gazette du Centre* (Limoges), 4 Sept. 1913, BN NAF, *ibid.*, p. 96.
[203]*Progrès de la Somme*, 16 Sept. 1913, *ibid.*, p. 112.
[204]*Ibid.*, 24625, p. 44.
[205]*Ibid.*, 11 Oct. 1913, p. 13.
[206]*Ibid.*, 25 Nov. 1913.
[207]*Ibid.*, 24619, 12 Nov. 1913, p. 28.
[208]*Ibid.*, p. 20.
[209]*Ibid.*, 13 Nov. 1913, p. 7.
[210]*Ibid.*, 26 Sept. 1913, pp. 3-4.
[211]*La Croix*, 26 Nov. 1913, *ibid.*, 24626, p. 14.
[212]Pius X to François Veuillot, 22 Oct. 1913, *ibid.*, 24627, p. 83.
[213]12 and 14 June 1913, *ibid.*, 24619, pp. 40-41.
[214]28 Aug. 1913, *ibid.*, pp. 32-33.
[215]*Ibid.*, 24628, pp. 151-152.
[216]*Ibid.*, 24619, pp. 5-6.
[217]*Ibid.*, 24629-24630.
[218]28 Nov. 1913, *ibid.*, 24626, p. 93.
[219]*Le Figaro*, 26 Nov. 1913, *ibid.*, p. 21.
[220]G. Hanotaux, *Contemporary France*, 2:622.

BIBLIOGRAPHY

Louis Veuillot is discussed in a very wide variety of studies of French history. In many ways a product of the modern age, he was also at war with this age. Accordingly the bulk of French and American historians of modern France treat him harshly. I do not pretend to exhaust the list of studies bearing on him, but only those that have influenced me one way or another. I have made some annotations. The acrimony directed at Veuillot, as well as some of the adoring treatment, is testimony to Veuillot's importance, as well as to the subjective approach of the various authors dealing with him.

Eugène Veuillot, supplemented by his son François for the period after the Vatican Council, tells an extremely full and well written account of his brother's life. These four large volumes were first published by V. Retaux, 1899-1913. Lethielleux issued a new edition in 1913, and the many references in this study are to the latter edition. This inside story is invaluable for any study of religion or the press in France in the nineteenth century. Eugène is careful and thorough, but the work was intended as a memorial to his brother and a continuing argument for their cause. Although one-sided, this biography is an inescapable frame of reference for any other study of Louis Veuillot.

Louis Veuillot never wrote his own memoirs, but his voluminous writings furnish a great deal about his life. His works have appeared in many editions, with V. Palmé, Poussielgue, E. Vitte, Gaume Frères et J. Duprey, J. Lecoffre, L. Vivès, R. Muffat, Waille, Plon, E. Duverger, L. Guérin, A. Mame, F. Levé, Libaros, O. Fulgence, and various other publishers bringing out his works. The definitive collection was put out by Lethielleux in the period between the wars. His major works (vols. 1-14), correspondence (vols. 15-26), and his *Mélanges,* essentially his major articles in *L'Univers* (vols. 27-39), appeared between 1924 and 1938, with a supplementary volume containing an index and some additional correspondence in 1940.

Fortunately, not only were Veuillot's letters preserved, practically in their entirety, in bound form in the *Nouvelles Acquisitions françaises* of the Bibliothèque nationale, letters addressed to him have also been preserved and indexed, together with other papers. These I have used in conjunction with his published correspondence. While I have compared the two sources on many occasions, some of my citations are from the originals and others from the *Œuvres complètes,* the latter being cited when my notes did not cover the former.

A complete file of *L'Univers* existed at the University of Louvain, but it was burned in 1940, and the file in the Bibliothèque nationale is not quite complete. Fortunately for me, Duke University has a practically complete file for the years Veuillot was with *L'Univers.* The dossiers in the Préfecture de Police of Paris, especially the main one for Veuillot himself (B a/874), have various values, including press clippings and special material, especially for his latter years. Many sections of the Archives nationales contain material on Veuillot. Among the more interesting are the papers of Léon Lavedan, which were given by this rival when he became *chef de bureau de la presse* in the 1870's. Also interesting are the Fonds Guizot, for the use of which I am indebted to Mme Anne Grüner. The Bibliothèque de la Compagnie de Saint-Sulpice contains considerable material on the question of the classics and some other letters of Veuillot. The correspondence of the Ministère des Affaires étrangères show the attention French diplomats devoted to Veuillot.

ARCHIVAL MATERIAL

BIBLIOTHÈQUE NATIONALE, NOUVELLES ACQUISTIONS FRANÇAISES
Première Série.

Tomes 24220-24224, *Lettres de Louis Veuillot.*
" 24225-24233, *Lettres adressés à Louis Veuillot.*
Tome 24234, *Lettres adresses à la famille Veuillot, 1850-1899.*
" 24235, *Correspondence des rédacteurs de L'Univers*, 1841-1882.
" 24236, *Copies de lettres du comte de Montalembert au comte Gustave de la Tour, 29 Oct. 1850- 11 août 1853.*
" 24237, *Fragments de manuscrits, épreuves corrigées.*
" 24238, *Épreuves corrigées avec pages manuscrites intercalées.*
" 24239, *Documents relatifs à L'Univers.*

Deuxième Série.

Tome 24617, *Articles et fragments d'articles publiés dans les Mélanges.*
" 24618-24619, *Études, essais, articles et fragments d'articles.*
" 24620, *Notes intimes, pensées, notes diverses.*
" 24621, *Lettres de personnalités au moment du centenaire de Louis Veuillot, 1913.*
" 24622, *Articles sur Louis Veuillot.*
" 24623, *Journaux et coupures de presse, 1870-1871.*
" 24624-24625, *Centenaire de Louis Veuillot: extraits de presse française.*
" 24626-24628, *Centenaire de Louis Veuillot: extraits de brochures et revues*
" *françaises.*
" 24629-24630, *Centenaire de Louis Veuillot: extraits de presse étrangère.*
" 24631, *Lettres de Louis Veuillot, 1834-1866.*
" 24632, " " " , 1867-1878.
" 24633, *Lettres adressés à Louis Veuillot, 1840-1862.*
" 24634, *Lettres adressés à Louis Veuillot, 1863-1877, et a sa famille.*
" 24635, *Varia.*

ARCHIVES NATIONALES
AB XIX, 524, Dr. 8.
AB XIX, 3321, Dr. 7.
BB^{18}, 1645, Dr. 6274
BB^{18}, 1742, Dr. 6006.
BB^{18}, 1747, Dr. 647.
BB^{18} 1587, Dr. 684.
BB^{18}, 1415, Dr. 7117.
BB^{24}, 71
BB^{30}, 383-384.

F^7 12477-12479, *Agissements cléricaux*
F^7 12431, *Agissements royalistes*
F7 12428, *Agissements bonapartistes*
F^{18} 423
F^{19} 1933
F^{19} 2553
F^{19} 5594

(Fonds d'archives privées deposes aux Archives Nationales)
42 AP 150, 154 (*Fonds Guizot*)
305 AP 5, Dr. 7 (*Papiers Lavedan)*

PRÉFECTURE DE POLICE (PARIS)

Dossiers B a/874 and E a/15 (Louis Veuillot)
Dossiers B a/401-402 (Menées légitimistes)
Dossier B a/870 (Charette)
Dossiers B a/871-872 (Chambord)
Dossier B a/956 (Belcastel)
" B a/986 (Lucien Brun)
" B a/1011 (Chesnelong)
" B a/1086 (Freppel)
" B a/1195 (Albert de Mun)
" B/a 1541 (Menées et intrigues religieuses)

ARCHIVES DE MINISTÈRE DES AFFAIRES ÉTRANGÈRES

CP (Rome) 1000, 1045-1047
CP (Allemagne) 12

BIBLIOTHÈQUE DE COMPAGNIE DE SAINT-SULPICE

Affaire de Classiques, I and II
Dossier Veuillot

ARCHÉVÊCHÉ DE PARIS
Affaires Ecclésiastiques, 1 D IX 3, and 4, E, II, 1

PRESS

In the various archives and in Veuillot's papers I have seen clippings from a very wide variety of journals. The ones which I have followed myself are:

L'Événement
Le Figaro
Le Gaulois
La Gazette de France
Le Journal Officiel
La République Française
Le Siècle
L'Union
L'Univers

PUBLISHED MATERIAL

Albalat, Antoine. *Louis François Veuillot. Pages choisies*. Paris: Lethielleux, 1910.

Arnaud, René. *The Second Republic and Napoléon III*. Translated by E. F. Buckley. London: William Heinemann, 1930.

Aubert, Robert. *Le Pontificat de Pie IX, 1846-1878*. Paris: Bloud et Gay, 1952. Vol. XXI of Fliche and Martin, *Histoire de l'église dupuis les origines jusqu'à nos jours*. Very important work.

Bascoul, Abbé Louis. *Étude sur Louis Veuillot*. Nimes: Gervais-Bedot, 1893.

———. *Louis Veuillot, sa jeunesse, ses premiers années à l'Univers*. Paris: A Savaète, 1903.

Baunard, Louis. *Histoire du Cardinal Pie, Évêque de Poitiers*. 2 vols. Poitiers: Oudin, 1886. Very one-sided, but valuable for information about a key supporter of Veuillot.

Bazin, Abbé G., *Vie de Mgr. Maret, Évêque de Sura*. 3 vols. Paris: Berche et Tralin, 1891.

Bellanger, Claude; Godechot, Jacques; Guiral, Pierre; and Terrou, Fernand. *Histoire générale de la presse française*. Part II, 1815-1871. Paris: P.U.F., 1969. The key study of the French press.

Besson, Louis. *Vie du Cardinal Bonnechose, Archévêque de Rouen*. 2 vols. Paris: Retaux-Bray, 1887.

Bierer (Weiner), Dora. "Renan and His Interpreters: A Study in Intellectual Warfare." *Journal of Modern History* 25(Dec., 1953):375-389.

Bontoux, Abbé G. *Louis Veuillot et les mauvais maîtres de son temps*. Paris: Perrin, 1914.

———. *Louis Veuillot et les mauvais maîtres des XVIe, XVIIe, et XVIIIe siècles*. Paris: Perrin, 1919.

Boutard, Charles. *Lamennais: sa vie et ses doctrines*. 3 vols. Paris: Perrin, 1905-1913.

Bouvard, Charles. *Louis Veuillot et son pays natal*. Pithiviers: Imprimerie Moderne, 1913.

Brown, Marvin L., Jr. *The Comte de Chambord: The Third Republic's Uncompromising King*. Durham: Duke University Press, 1967.

———. "Catholic-Legitimist Militancy in the Early Years of the Third French Republic." *The Catholic Historical Review* 60(July, 1974):233-254.

Brugerette, Joseph. *Le Prêtre français et la société contemporaine*. 3 vols. Paris: Lethielleux, 1933-1938.

Bury, John Bagnell. *History of the Papacy in the Nineteenth Century*. New York: MacMillan, 1964.

Butler, Edward Cuthbert. *The Vatican Council. The Story Told from Inside in Bishop Ullathorne's Letters*. 2 vols. London: Longmans, Green & Co., 1930. Aubert regards this as especially revealing.

Carroll, Eber Malcolm. *French Public Opinion and Foreign Affairs, 1870-1914*. Hamden(Conn.): Archon Books, 1964 (first published in 1931).

Case, Lynn M. "Anticipating the Death of Pius IX in 1861." *The Catholic Historical Review* 53 (Oct. 1957):309-323.

———. *French Opinion on War and Diplomacy during the Second Empire*. Philadelphia: University of Pennsylvania Press, 1954.

Cerceau, Abbé G. *L'Âme d'un grand chrétien : Esprit de foi de Louis Veuillot d'après sa correspondance. L'Homme intime.* Paris: Lethielleux, 1908.

. *L'Âme d'un grand catholique: Esprit de foi de Louis Veuillot, journaliste et polemististe d'après sa correspondance: L'Homme public.* 2 vols. Paris: Lethielleux, 1910.

Chapman, Guy. *The Third Republic of France: The First Phase, 1871-1894.* London: MacMillan, 1962.

Chastenet, Jacques. *Histoire de la Troisième République.* 7 vols. Paris: Hachette, 1952-1963. Vol. 1 covers 1870-1879.

Christophe, Lucien. *Louis Veuillot.* Paris: Wesmael-Charlier, 1967.

Collins, Ross William. *Catholicism and the Second French Republic, 1848-1852.* New York: Columbia University Press, 1923.

Cornu, Étienne. *Louis Veuillot: Étude morale et littéraire,* Paris, 1891.

Crosnier, Alexis. *Louis Veuillot, apologiste.* Paris: Beauchesne, 1913.

Dansette, Adrien. *Religious History of Modern France.* Translated by John Dingle. 2 vols. New York: Herder and Herder, 1961. The leading general guide available in English. Not very sympathetic.

Davignon, Henri (editor). *Le Roman de Louis Veuillot et Juliette de Robesart.* Paris: Lethielleux, 1936. The "romance" of Louis Veuillot "amoureux" is not what some might have hoped to find. These papers, which Veuillot would have preferred not to come to light, only mildly supplement his other correspondence. In general they reveal the same man who corresponded with Charlotte de Grammont.

Debidour, Antonin. *Histoire des rapports de l'église et de l'état de 1789 à 1870.* Paris: Alcan, 1898. Very penetrating and very hostile to the church.

. *L'Église catholique et l'état sous la troisième république*. 2 vols. Paris: Alcan, 1906-1909. Vol. 1 treats the years 1870-1889, and like his other study is hostile to the church.

Dedessuslamare, Pierre. *Veuillot.* Rouen: Albert Laine, 1927.

Delatte, Dom Paul. *Dom Guéranger, abbé de Solesmes.* Paris: Plon-Nourrit, 1909-1910.

Delmont, Théodore. *Le Centenaire de Louis Veuillot.* Lyon: Vitte, 1914.

Dimier, Louis. *Les Maîtres de la contre-révolution au XIXe siècle.* Paris: Librairie des Saints-Pères, 1907.

. *Veuillot.* Paris: Nouvelle Librairie Nationale, s.d.

Duroselle, Jean-Baptiste. *Les Débuts du catholicisme social en France (1822-1870).* Paris: P.U.F., 1951. A great thesis by a great scholar.

Duveau, Georges. *1848: The Making of A Revolution.* Translated by Anne Carter. New York: Pantheon Books, 1967.

Falloux, Alfred, Comte de. *Mémoires d'un royaliste.* 2 vols. Paris: Perrin, 1888. 3rd edition. Important memoirs of a key Catholic enemy of Veuillot.

. *Le Parti catholique, ce qu'il a été, ce qu'il est devenu.* Paris: A Bray, 1856. Important tract generated by the quarrel of Veuillot and Falloux.

Faÿ, Bernard. *L'École de l'imprécation, ou les prophètes catholiques du dernier siècle, 1850-1950.* Paris: E. Vitte, 1961.

Fernessole, Abbé Pierre. *Les Origines littéraires de Louis Veuillot, 1813-1843.* Paris: J. de Gigord, 1923. Exhaustive thesis.

. *Pour qu'on lise Louis Veuillot.* Paris: Lethielleux, 1928. Much insight.

Follioley, Abbé Leopold Humbert. *Montalembert et Mgr. Parisis d'après des documents inédits, 1843-1848.* Paris: Le Coffre, 1901.

Foulon, Msgr. Joseph Alfred. *Histoire de la vie et des œuvres de Mgr. Darboy.*

Paris: Poussielgue, 1889.

Gadille, Jacques. *La Pensée et l'action politiques des évêques en France au début de la IIIe République, 1870-1882.* 2 vols. Paris: Hachette, 1967. Important new work.

Gaume, Abbé Jean-Joseph. *Le Ver rongeur des sociétés modernes, ou le paganisme dans l'éducation.* Paris: Gaume Frères, 1851. Significant book by a firebrand priest whom Veuillot supported.

Gauthier, Emmanuel. *Le Génie satyrique de Louis Veuillot.* Lyon: E. Vitte, 1953. Penetrating and sympathetic, though based on published works entirely.

———. *Le Vrai Louis Veuillot, étude, psychologique et morale de l'écrivain d'après sa correspondance.* Paris: Alsatia, 1938. Very similar to later work.

Géradin, Amand. *Louis Veuillot, héraut du Jésus-Christ.* Paris: Lethielleux, 1948. Notable example of pro-Veuillot literature.

Gimpl, Sister M. Caroline Ann. *The Correspondant and the Founding of the Third Republic.* Washington: Catholic University Press, 1959.

Giraud, Victor. "Louis Veuillot d'après sa correspondance." *Revue des Deux Mondes*, 25 (8th per., Jan. 1935):458-470.

Goyau, Georges. *Histoire religieuse de la France.* Tome 6 of G. Hanotaux, *Histoire de la nation française.* Paris: Plon-Nourrit, 1922.

Guillemant, Charles. *Pierre Louis Parisis.* 3 vols. Paris: J. Gabulda, 1916-1924.

Guillemin, Henri. *Histoire des catholiques français au XIXe siècle (1815-1905).* Geneva: Edition du Milieu de Monde, 1947.

Guizot, François Pierre Guillaume. *Mémoires pour servir à l'histoire de mon temps.* 8 vols. Paris: Michel Lévy Frères, 1858-1867.

Gurian, Waldemar. "Louis Veuillot." *The Catholic Historical Review* 36 (Jan., 1951):385-414. An excellent survey by a master of the field.

———. "Lamennais." *Review of Politics* 9 (Apr., 1947):205-229.

———. *Die politischen und sozialen Ideen des französischen Katholismus, 1789-1914.* Munich-Gladbach: Volksvereins Verlag, 1929.

Hales, Edward Elton Young. *Pio Nono, A Study in European Politics and Religion in the Nineteenth Century.* New York: P. J. Kenedy, 1954.

Hanotaux, Gabriel. *Contemporary France.* 4 vols. Vols. 1 and 2 translated by J. C. Tarver and E. Sparvel-Bayley. Westminister: A Constable, 1903-1909.

Hatin, Louis Eugène. *Histoire politique et littéraire de la presse en France.* Paris: Poulet-Malassis et De Broise, 1859-1861. The guide for a century and still useful.

Hayward, Fernand. *Pie IX et son temps.* Paris: Plon, 1948.

Hazera, Msgr. *Louis Veuillot: Discours prononcé par Monseigneur Hazera, Évêque de Digne, 29 Novembre 1899 à l'inauguration du monument de Louis Veuillot dans la Basilique du Sacre-Cœur.* Paris: Retaux, 1900.

Huckaby, John K. "Roman Catholic Reaction to the Falloux Law." *French Historical Studies* 4(1965):203-213.

Jabouley, Michel-Ange. *A l'école de Louis Veuillot.* Paris: Mignard, 1943.

Johnson, Douglas. *Guizot.* London: Routledge and Kegan Paul, 1963.

Keller, Émile. *Le Général de Lamoricière; Sa vie militaire, politique et religieuse.* 2 vols. Paris: R. Haton, 1891.

Gautherot, Gustave. *Un demi-siècle de défense nationale et religieuse. Émile Keller, 1828-1909.* Paris: Plon, 1922.

Kranzberg, Melvin. *The Siege of Paris, 1870-1871: A political and Social History.* Ithaca: Cornell University Press, 1950.

La Gorce, Pierre François Gustave de. *Histoire du Second Empire.* 7 vols. Paris: E.

Plon-Nourrit, 1895-1905.

_____. *Histoire de la Seconde République Française.* 2 vols. Paris: E. Plon-Nourrit, 1898.

_____. *Louis Philippe (1830-1848).* Paris: Plon, 1931.

Lagrange, François. *Lettres choisies de Mgr. Dupanloup, Évêque, d'Orléans.* 2 vols. Paris: Poussielgue, 1888.

_____. *Mgr. Dupanloup.* 3 vols. Paris: Poussielgue, 1886.

Lamothe, Armand. *Louis Veuillot, 1813-1883.* Paris (private printing), 1893.

Lasserre, Maurice. *Essai sur les poésies de Louis Veuillot.* Paris: Lethielleux, 1957.

Latreille, André; Delaruelle, E.; Palanque, J. R., Rémond, René. *Histoire du catholicisme en France.* 3 vols. Paris: Spes, 1962.

Laurentie, François. *Louis Veuillot.* Paris: Le Coffre, 1898. Treatment by a journalist of the right.

Lecanuet, Père Edouard. *L'Église de France sous la Troisième République.* 2 vols. Vol. 1: *Les dernières années du pontificat de Pie IX, 1870-1878.* Vol. 2: *Le Pontificat de Léon XIII.* Paris: Poussielgue, 1910.

_____. *Montalembert d'après ses papiers et sa correspondence.* 3 vols. Paris: Poussielgue, 1895-1902.

Lecigne, C. *Louis Veuillot.* Paris: Lethielleux, 1913. Part of the adoring literature of 1913, but contains some very interesting points.

Ledré, Charles. *La Presse à l'assault de la monarchie, 1815-1848.* Paris: Colin, 1960. Valuable, though not much on *L'Univers.*

Leflon, Jean. *La Crise révolutionnaire.* Vol. 20 of the 21 vols. Augustin Fliche and Victor Martin, *Histoire de l'église depuis ses origines jusqu'à nos jours.* Paris: Bloud et Gay, 1949.

Leroy-Beaulieu, Anatole. "Études politiques et religieuses: Les mécomptes du liberalism." *Revue des Deux Mondes.* Vol. 69 (May 15, 1885), 421-450.

Lemaitre, Jules. *Les Contemporains: Études et Portraits littéraires.* 8 vols. Paris: Boivin, 1893.

Locke, Robert R. *French Legitimists and the Politics of Moral Order in the Early Third Republic.* Princeton: Princeton University Press, 1974.

Lucas-Dubreton. *The Restoration and the July Monarchy.* London: Heinemann, 1929.

Lynch, Sister Miriam. *The Organized Apostolate of Albert de Mun.* Washington: Catholic University Press, 1952.

MacDevitt, Mildred Mary. *Louis Veuillot d'après sa correspondance.* Paris: Lethielleux, 1935.

Marcilhacy, Christianne. *Le Diocèse d'Orléans sous l'espiscopat de Mgr. Dupanloup, 1849-1879.* Paris: Plon, 1962.

Maurain, Jean. *La Politique ecclésiastique du Second Empire de 1852 a 1869.* Paris: Alcan, 1930. A major work of great value.

_____. *Le Saint-Siège et la France de décembre 1851 à avril 1853.* Paris: Alcan, 1930. A valuable collection of documents.

May, Anita M. R. "The Falloux Law, the Catholic Press, and the Bishops: Crisis of Authority in the French." *French Historical Studies*, 8(1973), 77-94.

Maynard, Michel U. *Mgr. Dupanloup et M. Lagrange, son historien.* Paris: Société Générale de Librairie Catholique, 1884.

Michel, Henri. *La Loi Falloux.* Paris: Hachette, 1906.

Mirecourt (Jacquot), Eugène. *Louis Veuillot.* Paris: Havard, 1856. A scurrilous and inaccurate attack.

Montalembert, Charles Forbes René de Tryon, Comte de. *Catholicisme et liberté;*

correspondance inédité avec le Père Lacordaire, Mgr. de Mérode, et A. de Falloux. Paris: Cerf, 1970.

———. *L'Église libre dans l'état libre. Discours prononcés au Congrès catholique de Malines*. Paris: C. Counlol, 1863.

———. *Des Intérêts catholiques au XIXe siècle*. Paris: Le Coffre, 1852.

Moody, Joseph N. "The French Catholic Press of the 1840's on American Catholicism." *The Catholic Historical Review*, 60(July) 1974): 185-214. A significant study by an authority.

———, editor. *Church and Society; Catholic Social and Political Thought and Movements, 1789-1950*. New York: Arts Inc., 1953.

Morienval, Jean. *Louis Veuillot*. Paris: Lethielleux, 1941.

Mourret, Fernand. *Histoire générale de l'église*. 9 vols. Paris: Bloud et Gay, 1912-1923. Vol. 7, *L'Église contemporaine, 1823-1878*, and vol. 9, covering 1878-1903, are valuable for this period.

Mun, Albert de. *Ma vocation sociale. Souvenirs de la fondation de l'œuvre des cercles catholiques d'ouvriers, 1871-1875*. Paris: Lethielleux, 1908.

Narfon, Julien de. *Deux grands journalistes: Montalembert et Louis Veuillot*. Paris: Georges Crès, 1914.

Ollivier, Émile. *L'Église et l'état au Concile du Vatican*. 2 vols. Paris: Garnier, 1879. Valuable treatment of ultramontane-Gallican controversy by the protestant statesman.

———. *Journal*. 2 vols. Paris: Julliard, 1961.

Phillips, Charles Stanley. *The Church in France, 1789-1848: A Study in Revival*. New York: Russell and Russell, 1966 (first published in 1929).

———. *The Church in France, 1848-1907*. New York: Russell and Russell, 1967 (first published in 1936). Both of these volumes are stimulating and do an objective job of fitting Veuillot into the picture.

Pontal, Édouard. *Louis Veuillot et son frère, employés au ministère de l'intérieure*. Angers-Bordeaux: Imprimeries Siradeau, 1925.

Price, Roger. *The French Second Republic: A Social History*. Ithaca: Cornell University Press, 1972.

Reardon, Bernard. *Liberalism and Tradition. Aspects of Catholic Thought in Nineteenth Century France*. Cambridge: Cambridge University Press, 1975. An excellent work, but tends to disparage Veuillot's intellect.

Rénault, Jules. *Louis Veuillot*. Paris: Lethielleux, 1929.

Sainte-Beuve, Charles Augustin. *Causeries du lundi*. 15 vols. Paris: Garnier, 1890 (seventh edition).

Schérer, Edmond. *Études critiques sur la littérature contemporaine*. 10 vols. Paris: Michel-Lévy, 1863.

Ségur, Marquis de and Bellesort, André. *Deux conferences sur Louis Veuillot*. Paris, 1911.

Sevrin, Ernest *Mgr. Clausel de Montals, 1769-1857. Un évêque militant et gallican au XIXe siècles*. 2 vols. Paris: Vrin, 1955.

Sibot, Albert. *Louis Veuillot et Eugène Veuillot, notice biographique*. Pithiviers: Imprimerie Moderne, 1913.

Simpson, Frederick A. *The Rise of Louis Napoleon*. London: Frank Cass, 1968 (first published, 1909).

Spencer, Philip. *Politics of Belief in Nineteenth-Century France*. London: Faber and Faber, 1954.

Talvart, Hector. *Louis Veuillot et la monarchie*. Paris: Rupella, 1927.

Tavernier, Eugène. *Louis Veuillot, l'homme, le lutteur, l'écrivain*. Paris:

Plon-Nourrit, 1913.

Terrien, Abbé Eugène. *Mgr. Freppel, apologiste et défenseur des droits de l'église.* Paris: Maison de la Bonne Presse, 1927.

. *Mgr. Freppel, sa vie, ses ouvrages, ses œuvres, son influence et son temps, d'après des documents inconnus et inédits.* 2 vols. Angers: Chez l'auteur, 1931-1932.

Thureau-Dangin, Paul. *Histoire de la Monarchie de Juillet.* 7 vols. Paria: Plon-Nourrit, 1888-1892.

Vallet, Maurice. *A propos d'un centenaire: Louis Veuillot, 1813-1883. Sa vie, ses idées sociales, ses idées littéraires.* Paris: Société française d'imprimerie et de librairie, 1913.

Veuillot, Eugène. *Hommages a Louis Veuillot.* Paris: Société générale de librairie catholique, 1884.

Veuillot, François. *Louis Veuillot. Vie populaire.* Paris, 1914.

. *Louis Veuillot, sa vie, son âme, son œuvre.* Paris: Alsatia, 1937.

Villefranche, Jacques M. *Dix grands chrétiens du siècle.* Paris: Bloud et Barrai, 1892.

. *The Life and Times of Cardinal Wiseman.* 2 vols. London and New York: Longmans, Green, 1897.

Ward, Wilfred P. *William George Ward and the Catholic Revival.* London and New York, 1893.

Weill, Georges. *Histoire du catholicisme libéral en France, 1828-1908.* Paris: Alcan, 1909.

. *Le Journal; origines, évolution et rôle de la presse périodique.* Paris: La Renaissance du Livre, 1934.

UNPUBLISHED DISSERTATION

May, Anita M. R. "The Challenge of the French Catholic Press to Episcopal Authority, 1842-1860: A Crisis of Modernization." University of Pittsburgh, 1972. An unusually perceptive dissertation.

INDEX